Practical Business Math Procedures

Practical Business Math Procedures

Ninth Edition

JEFFREY SLATER
North Shore Community College
Danvers, Massachusetts

 **McGraw-Hill**
Irwin

Boston   Burr Ridge, IL   Dubuque, IA   New York   San Francisco   St. Louis
Bangkok   Bogotá   Caracas   Kuala Lumpur   Lisbon   London   Madrid   Mexico City
Milan   Montreal   New Delhi   Santiago   Seoul   Singapore   Sydney   Taipei   Toronto

 **McGraw-Hill Irwin**

Chapter opening photos: Chapter 1: Keith Brofsky/Getty Images. Chapter 2: PhotoLink/Getty Images. Chapter 3: The McGraw-Hill Companies, John Flournoy photographer. Chapter 4: Steve Cole/Photodisc Red/Getty Images. Chapter 5: Photodisc/Getty Images. Chapter 6: Image Source Pink/Getty Images. Chapter 7: Photodisc Red/Getty Images. Chapter 8: Teri Stratford. Chapter 9: Ryan McVay/Getty Images. Chapter 10: Tony Freeman/Photoedit. Chapter 11: Courtesy Bank of Internet USA. Chapter 12: Tony Freeman/Photoedit. Chapter 13: Don Farrall/Photodisc Green/Getty Images. Chapter 14: Digital Vision/Punchstock. Chapter 15: Photodisc/Getty Images. Chapter 16: Charles Osgood/MCT/Landov. Chapter 17: Harry Cabluck/AP Wide World. Chapter 18: RF/Corbis. Chapter 19: Stella/Getty Images. Chapter 20: Jim Craigmyle/Corbis. Chapter 21: Digital Vision/Getty Images. Chapter 22: Ryan McVay/Getty Images.

The Wall Street Journal articles republished by permission of The Wall Street Journal, Dow Jones & Company, Inc. All Rights Reserved Worldwide. Pepper . . . and Salt cartoon in Chapter 13, page 316, from The Wall Street Journal–Permission, Cartoon Features Syndicate.

Chapter 2, page 34: article reprinted by permission of the Associated Press.

Kiplinger's articles reprinted by permission of *Kiplinger's Personal Finance* magazine. Chapter 1: December 2006. Chapter 2: May 2006. Chapter 3: February 2007. Chapter 4: December 2006. Chapter 5: February 2007. Chapter 6: June 2005. Chapter 7: February 2007. Chapter 8: May 2006. Chapter 9: June 2006. Chapter 10: December 2006. Chapter 11: May 2006. Chapter 12: January 2006. Chapter 13: December 2006. Chapter 14: September 2006. Chapter 15: Kiplinger's *Buying and Selling a Home: Make the Right Choice in Any Market,* April, 2006. Chapter 16: March 2007. Chapter 17: September 2006. Chapter 18: April 2007. Chapter 19: February 2007. Chapter 20: September 2005. Chapter 21: May 2006. Chapter 22: March 2007.

PRACTICAL BUSINESS MATH PROCEDURES
Published by McGraw-Hill/Irwin, a business unit of The McGraw-Hill Companies, Inc., 1221 Avenue of the Americas, New York, NY, 10020. Copyright © 2008, 2006, 2003, 2000, 1997, 1994, 1991, 1987, 1983 by The McGraw-Hill Companies, Inc. All rights reserved. No part of this publication may be reproduced or distributed in any form or by any means, or stored in a database or retrieval system, without the prior written consent of The McGraw-Hill Companies, Inc., including, but not limited to, in any network or other electronic storage or transmission, or broadcast for distance learning.

Some ancillaries, including electronic and print components, may not be available to customers outside the United States.

This book is printed on acid-free paper.

1 2 3 4 5 6 7 8 9 0 DOW/DOW 0 9 8 7

ISBN   978-0-07-313767-4 (student edition)
MHID   0-07-313767-7 (student edition)
ISBN   978-0-07-327863-6 (teacher's edition)
MHID   0-07-327863-7 (teacher's edition)

Editorial director: *Stewart Mattson*
Executive editor: *Richard T. Hercher, Jr.*
Developmental editor: *Katie Jones*
Senior marketing manager: *Sankha Basu*
Senior project manager: *Susanne Riedell*
Senior production supervisor: *Debra R. Sylvester*
Design manager: *Kami Carter*
Senior photo research coordinator: *Jeremy Cheshareck*
Photo researcher: *Teri Stratford*
Lead media project manager: *Brian Nacik*
Media project manager: *Matthew Perry*
Cover design: *Kami Carter*
Interior design: *Kami Carter*
Typeface: *10/12 Times Roman*
Compositor: *Aptara*
Printer: *R. R. Donnelley*

Library of Congress Cataloging-in-Publication Data

Slater, Jeffrey, 1947-
    Practical business math procedures / Jeffrey Slater. -- 9th ed.
        p. cm.
    Includes index.
    ISBN-13: 978-0-07-313767-4 (student ed. : alk. paper)
    ISBN-10: 0-07-313767-7 (student ed. : alk. paper)
    ISBN-13: 978-0-07-327863-6 (teacher's ed. : alk. paper)
    ISBN-10: 0-07-327863-7 (teacher's ed. : alk. paper)
    1. Business mathematics--Problems, exercises, etc. I. Title.
HF5694.S57 2008
650.01'513--dc22
                            2007031147

www.mhhe.com

Dedication

Just for Matthew, Mia, Samuel, Gracie, Mabel, and Maggie
Love
PaPa Jeff

ROADMAP TO SUCCESS

How to use this book and the Total Slater Learning System.

Step 1: **Each chapter broken down into Learning Units. You should read one learning unit at a time.**

How do I know if I understand it?

- Try the practice quiz. All the worked out solutions are provided. If you still have questions, watch the author on your DVD (comes with your text) and work each problem out.
- Need more practice? Try the extra practice quiz provided. Check figures are at the end of the chapter. Your instructor has worked out solutions if needed.
- Go on to next Learning Unit in chapter.

Step 2: **Review the "Chapter Organizer" at the end of the chapter.**

How do I know if I understand it?

- Cover over the second or third column and see if you can explain the key points or the examples.

Step 3: **Do assigned problems at the end of the chapter (or Appendix A). These may include discussion questions, drill, word problems, challenge problems, video cases, as well as projects from the Business Math Scrapbook and Kiplinger's magazine.**

Can I check my homework?

- Appendix B has check figures for all the odd-numbered problems.

Step 4: **Take the Summary Practice Test.**

Can I check my progress?

- Appendix B has check figures for all problems.

What do I do if I do not match check figures?

- Review the video tutorial on the student DVD—the author works out each problem.

To aid you in studying the book, I have developed the following color code:

Blue: Movement, cancellations, steps to solve, arrows, blueprints

Gold: Formulas and steps

Green: Tables and forms

Red: Key items we are solving for

If you have difficulty with any text examples, pay special attention to the red and the blue. These will help remind you what you are looking for as well as what the procedures are.

FEATURES

Features students have told me have helped them the most.

Blueprint Aid Boxes

For the first eight chapters (not in Chapter 4), blueprint aid boxes are available to help you map out a plan to solve a word problem. I know that often the hardest thing to do in solving word problems is where to start. Use the blueprint as a model to get started.

Business Math Handbook

This reference guide contains all the tables found in the text. It makes homework, exams, etc. easier to deal with than flipping back and forth through the text. Also included is calculator reference guides with advice on how to use different calculators.

Chapter Organizer

At the end of each chapter is a quick reference guide called the Chapter Organizer and Study Guide. Key points, formulas, and examples are provided. A list of vocabulary terms is also included, as well as Check Figures for Extra Practice Quizzes. All have page references. (A complete glossary is found at the end of the text.) Think of the chapter organizer as your set of notes and use it as a reference when doing homework problems, and to review before exams.

DVD-ROM

The DVD packaged with the text includes practice quizzes, links to Web sites listed in the Business Math Internet Resource Guide, the Excel® templates, PowerPoint, videocases, and tutorial videos—which cover all the Learning Unit Practice Quizzes and Summary Practice Tests.

The Business Math Web site

Visit the site at www.mhhe.com/slater9e and find the Internet Resource Guide with hot links, tutorials, practice quizzes, and other study materials useful for the course.

Video Cases

There are seven video cases applying business math concepts to real companies such as Hotel Monaco, Louisville Slugger, American President Lines, Washburn Guitars, Online Banking, Buycostume.com, and Federal Signal Corporation. Video clips are included on the student DVD. Some background case information and assignment problems incorporating information on the companies are included at the end of Chapters 6, 7, 8, 9, 11, 16, and 21.

Compounding/Present Value Overlays

A set of color overlays are inserted in Chapter 13. These color graphics are intended to demonstrate for students the concepts of present value and future value and, even more important, the basic relationship between the two.

Business Math Scrapbook

At the end of each chapter you will find clippings from *The Wall Street Journal* and various other publications. These articles will give you a chance to use the theory provided in the chapter to apply to the real world. It allows you to put your math skills to work.

Group activity: Personal Finance, a Kiplinger Approach

In each chapter you can debate a business math issue based on a *Kiplinger's Personal Finance* magazine article that is presented. This is great for critical thinking, as well as improving your writing skills.

Spreadsheet Templates

Excel® templates are available for selected end-of-chapter problems. You can run these templates as is or enter your own data. The templates also include an interest table feature that enables you to input any percentage rate and any terms. The program will then generate table values for you.

Cumulative Reviews

At the end of Chapters 8 and 13 are word problems that test your retention of business math concepts and procedures. Check figures for *all* cumulative review problems are in Appendix B.

Acknowledgments

Academic Experts, Contributors

Anthony Aiken
Justin Barclay
Cheryl Bartlett
Ben Bean
George Bernard
Don Boyer
Gilbert Cohen
Laura Coliton
Judy Connell
Ronald Cooley
Kathleen Crall
Patrick Cunningham
John Davis
Tamra Davis
James DeMeuse

Doug Dorsey
Acie Earl
Rick Elder
Marsha Faircloth
Tony Franco
Bob Grenowski
Victor Hall
Frank Harber
James Hardman
Helen Harris
Ron Holm
William Hubert
Christy Isakson
Elizabeth Klooster
Libby Kurtz

Ken Koerber
Jennifer Lopez
Bruce MacLean
Lynda Mattes
Jon Matthews
Loretta McAdam
Jean McArthur
Sharon Meyer
Norma Montague
Christine Moreno
Fran Okoren
Roy Peterson
Cindy Phipps
Anthony Ponder
Joseph Reihling

Dana Richardson
Denver Riffe
David Risch
Joel Sacramento
Naim Saiti
Ellen Sawyer
Tim Samolis
Marguerite Savage
Warren Smock
Ray Sparks
William Tusang
Jennifer Wilbanks
Andrea Williams
Beryl Wright
Denise Wooten

Company/Applications

Chapter 1

Home Depot—*Problem solving*
Girl Scouts—*Reading, writing, and rounding numbers*
McDonald's—*Rounding*
Tootsie Roll—*Rounding all the way*
Toyota, Honda, Saturn—*Rounding*
Hershey—*Subtraction of whole numbers*

Chapter 2

M&M's/Mars—*Fractions and multiplication*
Wal-Mart—*Type of fractions*
TiVo—*Subraction of fractions*
M&M's/Mars—*Multiplying and dividing fractions*
Target, MinuteClinic, RediClinic—*Healthcare*
Exotic Car Share—*Fractional ownership*

Chapter 3

McDonald's—*Currency application*
M&M's/Mars—*Fractional decimal conversion*
Apple—*Decimal applications in foreign currency*
Cingular, T-Mobile—*Cost of phone calls*
Burberry, Tiffany—*Currency application*

Chapter 4

Bank of America—*Personal finance*
Continental, Amazon—*E-checks*
J.P. Morgan Chase—*Online banking*
eBay—*Online banking*
PayPal—*Online banking*
PNC Financial—*Online banking*
Visa, Mastercard—*Electronic bill paying*
Volkswagon—*Banking application*

Chapter 5

Calvin Klein, Burberry—*Unknown*
Stanley Consultants—*Workforce*
Snickers—*Solving for the Unknown*
Disney—*Solving for the Unknown*
American Quarter Coach—*Personal finance*
Yacht Smart—*Personal finance*

Chapter 6

Capital One Financial—*Cost of ATMs*
Ford—*Percents*
Dell, Apple, Gateway—*Percents*
HP, NEC, Sony, IBM—*Percents*
M&M's/Mars—*Percent, percent increase and decrease*
Kellogg—*Converting decimals to percents*
Wal-Mart—*Percent increase, decrease*

USA Today, The Wall Street Journal—*Portion, base, rate*
The New York Times, The Washington Post—*Portion, base, rate*
Chicago Tribune, Houston Chronicle—*Portion, base, rate*
UPS—*Portion, base, rate*

Chapter 7

Google, Overstock, AOL—*Online retailers*
Randall Scott Cycle, Condor Golf—*Discounts*
Lighting Galleries of Sarasota—*Discounts*
DHL, UPS—*Freight*
FedEx—*Freight*
Comcast, AT&T, Time Warner—*Personal finance*

Chapter 8

Disney, Payless Shoe Source—*Licensing*
Levi-Strauss, Target—*Markup*
H&M, GAP, French Connection, Wal-Mart—*Sourcing*
John Hancock—*Long-term care*
Bennigan's—*Markup*

Chapter 9

Delta Airlines—*Paycuts*
Fed Express—*Independent contractors*

Chapter 10

Federal Deposit Insurance Company—*Liability*

J.P. Morgan Chase, Citigroup—*Late Payment charges*

Bank of America—*Late payment charges*

Data Trac—*Cheaper loans*

Digital Equipment Corp.—*Cheaper loans*

Pentagon Federal Credit Union—*Cheaper loans*

Chapter 11

Bank of Internet, Citibank, E-Loan, Prosper.com—*Borrowing online*

Saks Inc.—*Notes*

Small Business Administration—*Line of credit*

U.S. Treasury—*Buying treasuries online*

Chapter 12

American Express, Bank of America—*Saving cash*

Bankrate.com—*Interest rates*

Chapter 13

Dunkin' Donuts—*Investing your savings*

State Lotteries—*Annuities*

D3 Financial Counselors—*Roth*

Chapter 14

Land Rover—*APR*

Boston Globe—*Monthly payments*

Chapter 15

Bank for International Settlements—*Home price appreciation*

Credit Suisse First Boston—*Monthly payments*

Lending Tree, Inc.—*Cost of refinancing*

Chapter 16

Coach, Inc.—*Net income*

Kodak—*Accounting errors*

H. J. Heinz Co.—*Profit/Sales*

L. G. Electronics, Phillips Electronics—*Impairment*

Samsung—*Impairment*

Wal-Mart, Target—*Profit margin*

Chapter 17

Land Rover—*Depreciation*

Kelley Blue Book—*Resale value*

BMW of North America—*Tax breaks*

Chapter 18

Wal-Mart—*Inventory identification*

ODW Logistics, Inc.—*Outsourcing*

Ryerson Tull—*LIFO, FIFO*

Global Sources Ltd.—*Just-in-time inventory*

Chapter 19

Hillerich & Bradsby Co.—*Bartering*

Deloitte & Touche USA—*Bartering*

Chapter 20

Mavlife Financial Co.—*Long-term care*

Home Depot, Lowes—*Renting a truck*

AccuQuote.com—*Cost of insurance*

Allstate, Amica Mutual—*Cost of insurance*

Progressive, Youdecide.com—*Cost of insurance*

Chapter 21

CCH Inc.—*Sale of stocks*

Home Depot—*Stock quotations*

Goodyear—*Bonds*

Putnam Investments—*Mutual funds*

Google—*PE ratio*

Viacom Inc., CBS Corporation—*Corporate strategy*

Chapter 22

American Institute of Certified Public Accountants—*Median*

Federal Reserve—*Retirement*

Wal-Mart, Sam's Club—*Live graphs, pie charts*

Apple, Microsoft—*Corporate reporting*

Target, Kmart, Costco—*Number reporting*

Exxon Mobil, General Motors, GE, Ford—*Number reporting*

Contents

Kiplinger's Personal Finance Magazine Subscription Form   xv

CHAPTER 1   Whole Numbers; How to Dissect and Solve Word Problems   1
- **LU 1–1**   Reading, Writing, and Rounding Whole Numbers   2
- **LU 1–2**   Adding and Subtracting Whole Numbers   8
- **LU 1–3**   Multiplying and Dividing Whole Numbers   12

CHAPTER 2   Fractions   33
- **LU 2–1**   Types of Fractions and Conversion Procedures   35
- **LU 2–2**   Adding and Subtracting Fractions   40
- **LU 2–3**   Multiplying and Dividing Fractions   46

CHAPTER 3   Decimals   64
- **LU 3–1**   Rounding Decimals; Fraction and Decimal Conversions   65
- **LU 3–2**   Adding, Subtracting, Multiplying, and Dividing Decimals   71

CHAPTER 4   Banking   88
- **LU 4–1**   The Checking Account   89
- **LU 4–2**   Bank Statement and Reconciliation Process; Trends in Online Banking   93

CHAPTER 5   Solving for the Unknown: A How-to Approach for Solving Equations   113
- **LU 5–1**   Solving Equations for the Unknown   114
- **LU 5–2**   Solving Word Problems for the Unknown   120

CHAPTER 6   Percents and Their Applications   137
- **LU 6–1**   Conversions   138
- **LU 6–2**   Application of Percents—Portion Formula   144
- **Video Case:** American President Lines   169

CHAPTER 7   Discounts: Trade and Cash   170
- **LU 7–1**   Trade Discounts—Single and Chain (Includes Discussion of Freight)   171
- **LU 7–2**   Cash Discounts, Credit Terms, and Partial Payments   179
- **Video Case:** Hillerich & Bradsby Company "Louisville Slugger"   202

CHAPTER 8   Markups and Markdowns; Perishables and Breakeven Analysis   203
- **LU 8–1**   Markups Based on Cost (100%)   205
- **LU 8–2**   Markups Based on Selling Price (100%)   210
- **LU 8–3**   Markdowns and Perishables   216
- **LU 8–4**   Breakeven Analysis   219
- **Video Case:** Hotel Monaco Chicago   233
- **Cumulative Review:** A Word Problem Approach—Chapters 6, 7, 8   234

CHAPTER 9   Payroll   235
- **LU 9–1**   Calculating Various Types of Employees' Gross Pay   236
- **LU 9–2**   Computing Payroll Deductions for Employees' Pay; Employers' Responsibilities   240
- **Video Case:** Washburn Guitars   257

CHAPTER 10 Simple Interest 258

    LU 10-1 Calculation of Simple Interest and Maturity Value 259

    LU 10-2 Finding Unknown in Simple Interest Formula 262

    LU 10-3 U.S. Rule—Making Partial Note Payments before Due Date 264

CHAPTER 11 Promissory Notes, Simple Discount Notes, and the Discount Process 278

    LU 11-1 Structure of Promissory Notes; the Simple Discount Note 279

    LU 11-2 Discounting an Interest-Bearing Note before Maturity 282

    Video Case: Online Banking 294

CHAPTER 12 Compound Interest and Present Value 295

    LU 12-1 Compound Interest (Future Value)—The Big Picture 296

    LU 12-2 Present Value—The Big Picture 303

CHAPTER 13 Annuities and Sinking Funds 316

    LU 13-1 Annuities: Ordinary Annuity and Annuity Due (Find Future Value) 317

    LU 13-2 Present Value of an Ordinary Annuity (Find Present Value) 323

    LU 13-3 Sinking Funds (Find Periodic Payments) 326

    Cumulative Review: A Word Problem Approach—Chapters 10, 11, 12, 13 339

CHAPTER 14 Installment Buying, Rule of 78, and Revolving Charge Credit Cards 341

    LU 14-1 Cost of Installment Buying 342

    LU 14-2 Paying Off Installment Loans before Due Date 347

    LU 14-3 Revolving Charge Credit Cards 350

CHAPTER 15 The Cost of Home Ownership 365

    LU 15-1 Types of Mortgages and the Monthly Mortgage Payment 367

    LU 15-2 Amortization Schedule—Breaking Down the Monthly Payment 370

CHAPTER 16 How to Read, Analyze, and Interpret Financial Reports 382

    LU 16-1 Balance Sheet—Report As of a Particular Date 383

    LU 16-2 Income Statement—Report for a Specific Period of Time 389

    LU 16-3 Trend and Ratio Analysis 394

    Video Case: Buycostumes.com 410

CHAPTER 17 Depreciation 412

    LU 17-1 Concept of Depreciation and the Straight-Line Method 413

    LU 17-2 Units-of-Production Method 415

    LU 17-3 Declining-Balance Method 417

    LU 17-4 Modified Accelerated Cost Recovery System (MACRS) with Introduction to ACRS 418

CHAPTER 18 Inventory and Overhead 429

    LU 18-1 Assigning Costs to Ending Inventory—Specific Identification; Weighted Average; FIFO; LIFO 431

    LU 18-2 Retail Method; Gross Profit Method; Inventory Turnover; Distribution of Overhead 436

CHAPTER 19   Sales, Excise, and Property Taxes   453
    LU 19–1 Sales and Excise Taxes   454
    LU 19–2 Property Tax   456

CHAPTER 20   Life, Fire, and Auto Insurance   466
    LU 20–1 Life Insurance   467
    LU 20–2 Fire Insurance   472
    LU 20–3 Auto Insurance   475

CHAPTER 21   Stocks, Bonds, and Mutual Funds   490
    LU 21–1 Stocks   491
    LU 21–2 Bonds   495
    LU 21–3 Mutual Funds   497
    Video Case: Federal Signal Corporation   509

CHAPTER 22   Business Statistics   510
    LU 22–1 Mean, Median, and Mode   511
    LU 22–2 Frequency Distributions and Graphs   514
    LU 22–3 Measures of Dispersion (Optional)   520

    APPENDIX A: Additional Homework by Learning Unit   A
    APPENDIX B: Check Figures   B
    APPENDIX C: Glossary   C
    APPENDIX D: Metric System   D

    Index   IN

Because Money Matters...

Subscribe to *Kiplinger's* at Special Student Rates!

Every month, more than three million Americans turn to *Kiplinger's Personal Finance* magazine for advice and information about how to manage their money. How to save it. Spend it. Invest it. Protect it. Insure it. And make more of it.

If it affects you and your money, then you'll find it in the pages of *Kiplinger's*. From our annual ranking of the nation's best mutual funds to our yearly rating of new automobiles, we provide you with a different kind of investment publication.

We make it easy for you to subscribe with the lowest rates available to students and educators. Just provide your name and address below. Make checks payable to *Kiplinger's Personal Finance*. Or, if you prefer we will bill you later.

_____
Student's Name

_____   _____
Address   Apt. #

_____   _____   _____
City   State   Zip

(___)_____
Phone

Term: One year for $12.00

After completing the form, please mail it to: *Kiplinger's Personal Finance,*
P.O. Box 3291, Harlan, Iowa 51593-2471.

CODE: J5MCGRAW

CHAPTER 1

Whole Numbers; How to Dissect and Solve Word Problems

Quick Fix

Insuring a Child in College

■ **The Problem:** You want to avoid paying $1,000 or more for college health insurance for your university-bound child.

■ **The Solution:** Most group and individual health insurance will cover dependents up to the age of 23 years old—in some cases 25—as long as they are enrolled full time at an accredited college or university.

To receive that extension, you or your employer has to send the insurer a form stating your child's college and semester course load. Insurers usually require a copy of a transcript or a receipt from a bursar's office, but some will accept just your signature. You have to repeat that process annually. Most big insurers have student-coverage forms available online.

If you have a health-maintenance organization and the college is out of state, make sure the plan's service area covers that region. Students not enrolled in university health plans may have to pay in advance to use the campus facilities, but most insurers will reimburse you. —*Paola Singer*

LEARNING UNIT OBJECTIVES

LU 1–1: Reading, Writing, and Rounding Whole Numbers

- Use place values to read and write numeric and verbal whole numbers *(p. 3)*.
- Round whole numbers to the indicated position *(pp. 4–5)*.
- Use blueprint aid for dissecting and solving a word problem *(p. 6)*.

LU 1–2: Adding and Subtracting Whole Numbers

- Add whole numbers; check and estimate addition computations *(p. 8)*.
- Subtract whole numbers; check and estimate subtraction computations *(pp. 9–10)*.

LU 1–3: Multiplying and Dividing Whole Numbers

- Multiply whole numbers; check and estimate multiplication computations *(pp. 12–13)*.
- Divide whole numbers; check and estimate division computations *(pp. 14–15)*.

People of all ages make personal business decisions based on the answers to number questions. Numbers also determine most of the business decisions of companies. For example, click on your computer, go to the website of a company such as Home Depot and note the importance of numbers in the company's business decision-making process.

The following *Wall Street Journal* clipping "Home Depot Plans Gas-Mart Format in Four-Store Test" announces plans to test convenience stores with gasoline stations located in parking lots of four of its Nashville, Tennessee, stores:

Home Depot Plans Gas-Mart Format In Four-Store Test

By Desiree J. Hanford
Dow Jones Newswires

Home Depot Inc. will test convenience stores located in the parking lots of four of its Nashville, Tenn., stores this year and could expand the pilot to other markets.

The Atlanta-based home-improvement retailer plans to test convenience stores with gasoline stations starting in December, spokeswoman Paula Smith said. The stores will have items typically found in convenience stores, such as milk and soda, and prepackaged items for breakfast, lunch and dinner, she said. Some of the locations will have car washes.

Wall Street Journal © 2005

Companies often follow a general problem-solving procedure to arrive at a change in company policy. Using Home Depot as an example, the following steps illustrate this procedure:

Step 1.	State the problem(s).	Growth strategy is to continue drive for top-line growth.
Step 2.	Decide on the best methods to solve the problem(s).	Add convenience stores to adjacent Home Depot stores (some with car washes).
Step 3.	Does the solution make sense?	Good use of unproductive space, and customers can save time shopping.
Step 4.	Evaluate the results.	Home Depot will evaluate the four-store test cases.

Your study of numbers begins with a review of basic computation skills that focuses on speed and accuracy. You may think, "But I can use my calculator." Even if your instructor allows you to use a calculator, you still must know the basic computation skills. You need these skills to know what to calculate, how to interpret your calculations, how to make estimates to recognize errors you made in using your calculator, and how to make calculations when you do not have a calculator. (The *Business Math Handbook* and the text website explain how to use calculators.)

The United States' numbering system is the **decimal system** or *base 10 system*. Your calculator gives the 10 single-digit numbers of the decimal system—0, 1, 2, 3, 4, 5, 6, 7, 8, and 9. The center of the decimal system is the **decimal point.** When you have a number with a decimal point, the numbers to the left of the decimal point are **whole numbers** and the numbers to the right of the decimal point are decimal numbers (discussed in Chapter 3). When you have a number *without* a decimal, the number is a whole number and the decimal is assumed to be after the number.

This chapter discusses reading, writing, and rounding whole numbers; adding and subtracting whole numbers; and multiplying and dividing whole numbers.

Learning Unit 1–1: Reading, Writing, and Rounding Whole Numbers

Girl Scout cookies are baked throughout the year. More than 200 million boxes of cookies are produced annually. This means that approximately 2 billion, 400 million cookies are produced. Numerically, we can write this as 2,400,000,000.

Now let's begin our study of whole numbers.

Mona Sullivan, Courtesy Girl Scouts USA

Reading and Writing Numeric and Verbal Whole Numbers

The decimal system is a *place-value system* based on the powers of 10. Any whole number can be written with the 10 digits of the decimal system because the position, or placement, of the digits in a number gives the value of the digits.

To determine the value of each digit in a number, we use a place-value chart (Figure 1.1) that divides numbers into named groups of three digits, with each group separated by a comma. To separate a number into groups, you begin with the last digit in the number and insert commas every three digits, moving from right to left. This divides the number into the named groups (units, thousands, millions, billions, trillions) shown in the place-value chart. Within each group, you have a ones, tens, and hundreds place. Keep in mind that the leftmost group may have fewer than three digits.

In Figure 1.1, the numeric number 1,605,743,891,412 illustrates place values. When you study the place-value chart, you can see that the value of each place in the chart is 10 times the value of the place to the right. We can illustrate this by analyzing the last four digits in the number 1,605,743,891,412 :

$$1,412 = (1 \times 1,000) + (4 \times 100) + (1 \times 10) + (2 \times 1)$$

So we can also say, for example, that in the number 745, the "7" means seven hundred (700); in the number 75, the "7" means 7 tens (70).

To read and write a numeric number in verbal form, you begin at the left and read each group of three digits as if it were alone, adding the group name at the end (except the last units group and groups of all zeros). Using the place-value chart in Figure 1.1, the number 1,605,743,891,412 is read as one trillion, six hundred five billion, seven hundred forty-three million, eight hundred ninety-one thousand, four hundred twelve. You do not read zeros. They fill vacant spaces as placeholders so that you can correctly state the number values. Also, the numbers twenty-one to ninety-nine must have a hyphen. And most important, when you read or write whole numbers in verbal form, do not use the word *and.* In the decimal system, *and* indicates the decimal, which we discuss in Chapter 3.

By reversing this process of changing a numeric number to a verbal number, you can use the place-value chart to change a verbal number to a numeric number. Remember that you must keep track of the place value of each digit. The place values of the digits in a number determine its total value.

Before we look at how to round whole numbers, we should look at how to convert a number indicating parts of a whole number to a whole number. We will use the Girl Scout cookies as an example.

FIGURE 1.1

Whole number place-value chart

Whole Number Groups

Trillions				Billions				Millions				Thousands				Units			
Hundred trillions	Ten trillions	Trillions	Comma	Hundred billions	Ten billions	Billions	Comma	Hundred millions	Ten millions	Millions	Comma	Hundred thousands	Ten thousands	Thousands	Comma	Hundreds	Tens	Ones (units)	Decimal Point
	1	,	6	0	5	,	7	4	3	,	8	9	1	,	4	1	2	.	

The 2,400,000,000 Girl Scout cookies could be written as 2.4 billion cookies. This amount is two billion plus four hundred million of an additional billion. The following steps explain how to convert these decimal numbers into a regular whole number:

CONVERTING PARTS OF A MILLION, BILLION, TRILLION, ETC., TO A REGULAR WHOLE NUMBER

Step 1. Drop the decimal point and insert a comma.

Step 2. Add zeros so the leftmost digit ends in the word name of the amount you want to convert. Be sure to add commas as needed.

EXAMPLE   Convert 2.4 billion to a regular whole number.

Step 1.   2.4 billion

        2,4   Change the decimal point to a comma.

Step 2.   2,400,000,000   Add zeros and commas so the whole number indicates billion.

Rounding Whole Numbers

Many of the whole numbers you read and hear are rounded numbers. Government statistics are usually rounded numbers. The financial reports of companies also use rounded numbers. All rounded numbers are *approximate* numbers. The more rounding you do, the more you approximate the number.

Rounded whole numbers are used for many reasons. With rounded whole numbers you can quickly estimate arithmetic results, check actual computations, report numbers that change quickly such as population numbers, and make numbers easier to read and remember.

Numbers can be rounded to any identified digit place value, including the first digit of a number (rounding all the way). To round whole numbers, use the following three steps:

ROUNDING WHOLE NUMBERS

Step 1. Identify the place value of the digit you want to round.

Step 2. If the digit to the right of the identified digit in Step 1 is 5 or more, increase the identified digit by 1 (round up). If the digit to the right is less than 5, do not change the identified digit.

Step 3. Change all digits to the right of the rounded identified digit to zeros.

EXAMPLE 1   Round 9,362 to the nearest hundred.

Step 1.   9,362   The digit 3 is in the hundreds place value.

Step 2.   The digit to the right of 3 is 5 or more (6). Thus, 3, the identified digit in Step 1, is now rounded to 4. You change the identified digit only if the digit to the right is 5 or more.

        9,462

Step 3.   9,400   Change digits 6 and 2 to zeros, since these digits are to the right of 4, the rounded number.

By rounding 9,362 to the nearest hundred, you can see that 9,362 is closer to 9,400 than to 9,300.

We can use the following *Wall Street Journal* clipping "Food for Thought" to illustrate rounding to the nearest hundred. For example, rounded to the nearest hundred, the 560 calories of Big Mac rounds to 600 calories, whereas the 290 calories of McDonald's Egg McMuffin rounds to 300 calories.

The McGraw-Hill Companies, John Flournoy photographer

Food for Thought

Nutrition information for some items on McDonald's menu:

	CALORIES	FAT(g)
Big Mac	560	30
Filet-O-Fish	400	18
Cheeseburger	310	12
Grilled Chicken Classic Sandwich	420	9
Medium French Fries	350	16
Chicken McNuggets (6)	250	15
Creamy Ranch Sauce (1.5 oz)	200	21

Cobb Salad w/Grilled Chicken	280	11
Newman's Own Cobb Dressing	120	9
Fruit & Walnut Salad	310	13
Egg McMuffin	290	11
Bacon, Egg & Cheese McGriddles	450	21
Fruit 'n Yogurt Parfait	160	2
Baked Apple Pie	250	11
Medium Coke	210	0

Source: the company

Wall Street Journal © 2005

Next, we show you how to round to the nearest thousand.

EXAMPLE 2   Round 67,951 to the nearest thousand.

Step 1.   6⎡7⎤,951   The digit 7 is in the thousands place value.

Step 2.   ⎣→ Digit to the right of 7 is 5 or more (9). Thus, 7, the identified digit in Step 1, is now rounded to 8.

68,951

Step 3.   68,000   Change digits 9, 5, and 1 to zeros, since these digits are to the right of 8, the rounded number.

By rounding 67,951 to the nearest thousand, you can see that 67,951 is closer to 68,000 than to 67,000.

Now let's look at **rounding all the way.** To round a number all the way, you round to the first digit of the number (the leftmost digit) and have only one nonzero digit remaining in the number.

EXAMPLE 3   Round 7,843 all the way.

Step 1.   7,843   Identified leftmost digit is 7.

Step 2.   ⎣→ Digit to the right of 7 is greater than 5, so 7 becomes 8.

8,843

Step 3.   8,000   Change all other digits to zeros.

Rounding 7,843 all the way gives 8,000.

Remember that rounding a digit to a specific place value depends on the degree of accuracy you want in your estimate. For example, 24,800 rounds all the way to 20,000 because the digit to the right of 2 is less than 5. This 20,000 is 4,800 less than the original 24,800. You would be more accurate if you rounded 24,800 to the place value of the identified digit 4, which is 25,000.

Before concluding this unit, let's look at how to dissect and solve a word problem.

How to Dissect and Solve a Word Problem

As a student, your author found solving word problems difficult. Not knowing where to begin after reading the word problem caused the difficulty. Today, students still struggle with word problems as they try to decide where to begin.

Solving word problems involves *organization* and *persistence.* Recall how persistent you were when you learned to ride a two-wheel bike. Do you remember the feeling of success you experienced when you rode the bike without help? Apply this persistence to word problems.

Do not be discouraged. Each person learns at a different speed. Your goal must be to FINISH THE RACE and experience the success of solving word problems with ease.

To be organized in solving word problems, you need a plan of action that tells you where to begin—a blueprint aid. Like a builder, you will refer to this blueprint aid constantly until you know the procedure. The blueprint aid for dissecting and solving a word problem follows. Note that the blueprint aid serves an important function—**it decreases your math anxiety.**

Blueprint Aid for Dissecting and Solving a Word Problem

The facts	Solving for?	Steps to take	Key points

Now let's study this blueprint aid. The first two columns require that you *read* the word problem slowly. Think of the third column as the basic information you must know or calculate before solving the word problem. Often this column contains formulas that provide the foundation for the step-by-step problem solution. The last column reinforces the key points you should remember.

It's time now to try your skill at using the blueprint aid for dissecting and solving a word problem.

The Word Problem On the 100th anniversary of Tootsie Roll Industries, the company reported sharply increased sales and profits. Sales reached one hundred ninety-four million dollars and a record profit of twenty-two million, five hundred fifty-six thousand dollars. The company president requested that you round the sales and profit figures all the way.

Study the following blueprint aid and note how we filled in the columns with the information in the word problem. You will find the organization of the blueprint aid most helpful. Be persistent! You *can* dissect and solve word problems! When you are finished with the word problem, make sure the answer seems reasonable.

Teri Stratford

The facts	Solving for?	Steps to take	Key points
Sales: One hundred ninety-four million dollars. *Profit:* Twenty-two million, five hundred fifty-six thousand dollars.	Sales and profit rounded all the way.	Express each verbal form in numeric form. Identify leftmost digit in each number.	Rounding all the way means only the leftmost digit will remain. All other digits become zeros.

Steps to solving problem

1. Convert verbal to numeric.
   One hundred ninety-four million dollars ⟶ $194,000,000
   Twenty-two million, five hundred fifty-six thousand dollars ⟶ $ 22,556,000

2. Identify leftmost digit of each number.

   $194,000,000 $22,556,000

3. Round.

   $200,000,000 $20,000,000

Note that in the final answer, $200,000,000 and $20,000,000 have only one nonzero digit.

Remember that you cannot round numbers expressed in verbal form. You must convert these numbers to numeric form.

Now you should see the importance of the information in the third column of the blueprint aid. When you complete your blueprint aids for word problems, do not be concerned if the order of the information in your boxes does not follow the order given in the text boxes. Often you can dissect a word problem in more than one way.

Your first Practice Quiz follows. Be sure to study the paragraph that introduces the Practice Quiz.

LU 1–1   PRACTICE QUIZ

Complete this **Practice Quiz** to see how you are doing

At the end of each learning unit, you can check your progress with a Practice Quiz. If you had difficulty understanding the unit, the Practice Quiz will help identify your area of weakness. Work the problems on scrap paper. Check your answers with the worked-out solutions that follow the quiz. Ask your instructor about specific assignments and the videos available on your DVD for each chapter Practice Quiz.

1. Write in verbal form:
    a. 7,948   b. 48,775   c. 814,410,335,414
2. Round the following numbers as indicated:

Nearest ten	Nearest hundred	Nearest thousand	Rounded all the way
a. 92	b. 745	c. 8,341	d. 4,752

3. Kellogg's reported its sales as five million, one hundred eighty-one thousand dollars. The company earned a profit of five hundred two thousand dollars. What would the sales and profit be if each number were rounded all the way? (*Hint:* You might want to draw the blueprint aid since we show it in the solution.)

✓ Solutions

1. a. Seven thousand, nine hundred forty-eight
    b. Forty-eight thousand, seven hundred seventy-five
    c. Eight hundred fourteen billion, four hundred ten million, three hundred thirty-five thousand, four hundred fourteen
2. a. 90   b. 700   c. 8,000   d. 5,000
3. Kellogg's sales and profit:

The facts	Solving for?	Steps to take	Key points
Sales: Five million, one hundred eighty-one thousand dollars. *Profit:* Five hundred two thousand dollars.	Sales and profit rounded all the way.	Express each verbal form in numeric form. Identify leftmost digit in each number.	Rounding all the way means only the leftmost digit will remain. All other digits become zeros.

Steps to solving problem

1. Convert verbal to numeric.
    Five million, one hundred eighty-one thousand ⟶ $5,181,000
    Five hundred two thousand ⟶ $ 502,000

2. Identify leftmost digit of each number.
    $5,181,000 $502,000

3. Round.
    $5,000,000 $500,000

Need more practice? Try this **Extra Practice Quiz** (check figures in Chapter Organizer, p. 19)

1. Write in verbal form:
   a. 8,682   b. 56,295   c. 732,310,444,888
2. Round the following numbers as indicated:

Nearest ten	Nearest hundred	Nearest thousand	Rounded all the way
a. 43	b. 654	c. 7,328	d. 5,980

3. Kellogg's reported its sales as three million, two hundred ninety-one thousand dollars. The company earned a profit of four hundred five thousand dollars. What would the sales and profit be if each number were rounded all the way?

Learning Unit 1–2: Adding and Subtracting Whole Numbers

Did you know that the cost of long-term care in nursing homes varies in different locations? The following *Wall Street Journal* clipping "Costly Long-Term Care" gives the daily top 10 rates and lowest 10 rates of long-care costs reported in various cities. For example, note the difference in daily long-term care costs between Alaska and Shreveport, Louisiana:

Alaska: $561
Sherveport: −   99
           $462

Costly Long-Term Care

The average daily rate for a private room in a nursing home is $192. The highest and lowest rates were reported in:

TOP 10

Alaska[1]	$561
Stamford, Conn.	331
New York	312
San Francisco	293
Boston	284
Hartford, Conn.	277
Worcester, Mass.	272
Washington, D.C.	260
Rochester, N.Y.	251
Bridgewater, N.J.	244

LOWEST 10

Shreveport, La.	$99
New Orleans	107
Kansas City. Mo.	129
Little Rock, Ark.	131
St. Louis	131
Birmingham, Ala.	133
Chicago	136
Charleston, S.C.	138
Salt Lake City	138
Wichita, Kan.[2]	142

[1]Statewide   [2]Tied with Jackson, Miss., and Billings, Mont.

Source: MetLife Mature Market Institute

Wall Street Journal © 2006

If you may have long-term nursing care in your future or in the future of someone in your family, be sure to research the cost (and conditions) of long-term care in various locations.

This unit teaches you how to manually add and subtract whole numbers. When you least expect it, you will catch yourself automatically using this skill.

Addition of Whole Numbers

To add whole numbers, you unite two or more numbers called **addends** to make one number called a **sum,** *total,* or *amount.* The numbers are arranged in a column according to their place values—units above units, tens above tens, and so on. Then, you add the columns of numbers from top to bottom. To check the result, you re-add the columns from bottom to top. This procedure is illustrated in the steps that follow.

ADDING WHOLE NUMBERS
Step 1. Align the numbers to be added in columns according to their place values, beginning with the units place at the right and moving to the left (Figure 1.1).
Step 2. Add the units column. Write the sum below the column. If the sum is more than 9, write the units digit and carry the tens digit.
Step 3. Moving to the left, repeat Step 2 until all place values are added.

EXAMPLE

Adding top bottom	2 1 1 1,362 5,913 8,924 + 6,594 **22,793**	Checking bottom to to top	**Alternate check** Add each column as a separate total and then combine. The end result is the same.

$$
\begin{array}{r}
1,362 \\
5,913 \\
8,924 \\
+\ 6,594 \\
\hline
13 \\
18 \\
2\ 6 \\
20 \\
\hline
22,793
\end{array}
$$

How to Quickly Estimate Addition by Rounding All the Way

In Learning Unit 1–1, you learned that rounding whole numbers all the way gives quick arithmetic estimates. Using the following *Wall Street Journal* clipping "Hottest Models," note how you can round each number all the way and the total will not be rounded all the way. Remember that rounding all the way does not replace actual computations, but it is helpful in making quick commonsense decisions.

Hottest Models

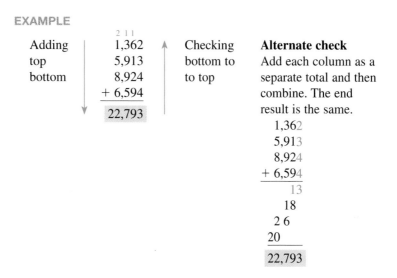

Model	Days on Lot	Average Price	Rounded all the way
Toyota Prius	5	$25,365	$ 30,000
Scion tC	9	$18,278	20,000
Scion xB	10	$15,834	20,000
BMW 7 Series	13	$80,507	80,000
Scion xA	14	$14,532	10,000
Lexus RX 400h	14	$50,131	50,000
Honda Odyssey	16	$31,001	30,000
Toyota Corolla	16	$16,290	20,000
Mazda MX-5	17	$25,380	30,000
Lexus RX 330	17	$39,467	40,000
Saturn VUE	17	$22,553	+ 20,000
			$350,000

Rounding all the way means each number has only one nonzero digit.

Note: The final answer could have more than one nonzero digit since the total is not rounded all the way.

Subtraction of Whole Numbers

Subtraction is the opposite of addition. Addition unites numbers; subtraction takes one number away from another number. In subtraction, the top (largest) number is the **minuend.** The number you subtract from the minuend is the **subtrahend,** which gives you the **difference** between the minuend and the subtrahend. The steps for subtracting whole numbers follow.

SUBTRACTING WHOLE NUMBERS
Step 1. Align the minuend and subtrahend according to their place values.
Step 2. Begin the subtraction with the units digits. Write the difference below the column. If the units digit in the minuend is smaller than the units digit in the subtrahend, borrow 1 from the tens digit in the minuend. One tens digit is 10 units.
Step 3. Moving to the left, repeat Step 2 until all place values in the subtrahend are subtracted.

EXAMPLE   The following *Wall Street Journal* clipping "Big Bills Ahead" illustrates the subtraction of whole numbers:

Big Bills Ahead

A look at average long-term-care costs in 2004

■ **Private Nursing Home**
Daily rate: $192
Highest rate: Alaska—$561
Lowest rate: Shreveport, La.—$99

■ **Assisted-Living Facility**
Monthly rate: $2,524
Highest rate: Stamford, Conn.—$4,327
Lowest rate: Miami—$1,340

■ **Home-Health Aide**
Hourly rate: $18
Highest rate: Hartford, Conn.—$28
Lowest rate: Jackson, Miss.—$13

Source: MetLife Inc.

What is the difference in cost between the Stamford, Connecticut, and the Miami, Florida, assisted-living facilities? As shown below, you can use subtraction to arrive at the $2,987 difference.

$$
\begin{array}{r}
\overset{\overset{12}{3\ \not2\ 12}}{\$4,327} \leftarrow \text{Minuend (larger number)} \\
-1,340 \leftarrow \text{Subtrahend} \\
\hline
\$2,987 \leftarrow \text{Difference}
\end{array}
$$

Check
$$
\begin{array}{r}
\$2,987 \\
+1,340 \\
\hline
\$4,327
\end{array}
$$

In subtraction, borrowing from the column at the left is often necessary. Remember that 1 ten = 10 units, 1 hundred = 10 tens, and 1 thousand = 10 hundreds.

Step 1.   In the above example, the 0 in the subtrahend of the rightmost column (ones or units column) can be subtracted from the 7 in the minuend to give a difference of 7. This means we do not have to borrow from the tens column at the left. However, in the tens column, we cannot subtract 4 in the subtrahend from 2 in the minuend, so we move left and borrow 1 from the hundreds column. Since 1 hundred = 10 tens, we have 10 + 2, or 12 tens in the minuend. Now we can subtract 4 tens in the subtrahend from 12 tens in the minuend to give us 8 tens in the difference.

Step 2.   Since we borrowed 1 hundred from our original 3 hundred, we now have 2 hundred in the minuend. The 3 hundred in the subtrahend will not subtract from the 2 hundred in the minuend, so again we must move left. We take 1 thousand from the 4 thousand in the thousands column. Since 1 thousand is 10 hundreds, we have 10 + 2, or 12 hundreds in the hundreds column. The 3 hundred in the subtrahend subtracted from the 12 hundred in the minuend gives us 9 hundred in the difference. The 1 thousand in the subtrahend subtracted from the 3 thousand in the minuend gives 2 thousand. Our total difference between the subtrahend $1,340 and the minuend $4,327 is $2,987 as proved in the check.

Checking subtraction requires adding the difference ($2,987) to the subtrahend ($1,340) to arrive at the minuend ($4,327). The Stamford, Connecticut, assisted-living facility costs $2,987 more than the Miami, Florida, assisted-living facility.

How to Dissect and Solve a Word Problem

Accurate subtraction is important in many business operations. In Chapter 4 we discuss the importance of keeping accurate subtraction in your checkbook balance. Now let's check your progress by dissecting and solving a word problem.

Teri Stratford

The Word Problem Hershey's produced 25 million Kisses in one day. The same day, the company shipped 4 million to Japan, 3 million to France, and 6 million throughout the United States. At the end of that day, what is the company's total inventory of Kisses? What is the inventory balance if you round the number all the way?

The facts	Solving for?	Steps to take	Key points
Produced: 25 million. *Shipped:* Japan, 4 million; France, 3 million; United States, 6 million.	Total Kisses left in inventory. Inventory balance rounded all the way.	Total Kisses produced − Total Kisses shipped = Total Kisses left in inventory.	Minuend − Subtrahend = Difference. Rounding all the way means rounding to last digit on the left.

Steps to solving problem

1. Calculate the total Kisses shipped.

$$\begin{array}{r} 4,000,000 \\ 3,000,000 \\ +\ 6,000,000 \\ \hline 13,000,000 \end{array}$$

2. Calculate the total Kisses left in inventory.

$$\begin{array}{r} 25,000,000 \\ -\ 13,000,000 \\ \hline 12,000,000 \end{array}$$

3. Rounding all the way.

Identified digit is 1. Digit to right of 1 is 2, which is less than 5. *Answer:* 10,000,000 .

The Practice Quiz that follows will tell you how you are progressing in your study of Chapter 1.

LU 1–2   PRACTICE QUIZ

Complete this **Practice Quiz** to see how you are doing

1. Add by totaling each separate column:

   8,974
   6,439
   + 16,941

2. Estimate by rounding all the way (do not round the total of estimate) and then do the actual computation:

   4,241
   8,794
   + 3,872

3. Subtract and check your answer:

   9,876
   − 4,967

4. Jackson Manufacturing Company projected its year 2003 furniture sales at $900,000. During 2003, Jackson earned $510,000 in sales from major clients and $369,100 in sales from the remainder of its clients. What is the amount by which Jackson over- or underestimated its sales? Use the blueprint aid, since the answer will show the completed blueprint aid.

✓ **Solutions**

1.
$$\begin{array}{r} 14 \\ 14 \\ 2\,2 \\ 20 \\ \hline 22,354 \end{array}$$

2.

Estimate	Actual
4,000	4,241
9,000	8,794
+ 4,000	+ 3,872
17,000	16,907

3.
$$\begin{array}{r} {\scriptstyle 8\ 18\,6\,16} \\ 9{,}876 \\ -\ 4{,}967 \\ \hline 4{,}909 \end{array}$$

Check
$$\begin{array}{r} 4,909 \\ +\ 4,967 \\ \hline 9,876 \end{array}$$

4. Jackson Manufacturing Company over- or underestimated sales:

The facts	Solving for?	Steps to take	Key points
Projected 2003 sales: $900,000. *Major clients:* $510,000. *Other clients:* $369,100.	How much were sales over- or underestimated?	Total projected sales – Total actual sales = Over- or underestimated sales.	Projected sales (minuend) – Actual sales (subtrahend) = Difference.

Steps to solving problem

1. Calculate total actual sales.

2. Calculate overestimated or underestimated sales.

$510,000
+ 369,100
$879,100

$900,000
– 879,100
$ 20,900 (overestimated)

LU 1–2a EXTRA PRACTICE QUIZ

Need more practice? Try this **Extra Practice Quiz** (check figures in Chapter Organizer, p. 19)

1. Add by totaling each separate column:
    9,853
    7,394
    +8,843

2. Estimate by rounding all the way (do not round the total of estimate) and then do the actual computation:
    3,482
    6,981
    +5,490

3. Subtract and check your answer:
    9,787
    −5,968

4. Jackson Manufacturing Company projected its year 2008 furniture sales at $878,000. During 2008, Jackson earned $492,900 in sales from major clients and $342,000 in sales from the remainder of its clients. What is the amount by which Jackson over- or underestimated its sales?

Learning Unit 1–3: Multiplying and Dividing Whole Numbers

At the beginning of Learning Unit 1–2, you learned how you would save $462 on the purchase of daily long-term care in a Shreveport, Louisiana, nursing home instead of in an Alaska nursing home.

If you stay in the Alaska and Shreveport nursing homes for 5 days, the Alaska nursing home would cost you $2,805, but the Shreveport nursing home would cost you $495, and you would save $2,310:

Alaska: $561 × 5 = $2,805
Shreveport: 99 × 5 = −   495
                          $2,310

If you divide $2,310 by 5, you will get the $462 difference in price between Alaska and Shreveport as shown at the beginning of Learning Unit 1–2.

This unit will sharpen your skills in two important arithmetic operations—multiplication and division. These two operations frequently result in knowledgeable business decisions.

Multiplication of Whole Numbers—Shortcut to Addition

From calculating your purchase of 5 days of long-term care in Shreveport, you know that multiplication is a *shortcut to addition:*

$$\$99 \times 5 = \$495 \qquad \text{or} \qquad \$99 + \$99 + \$99 + \$99 + \$99 = \$495$$

Before learning the steps used to multiply whole numbers with two or more digits, you must learn some multiplication terminology.

Note in the following example that the top number (number we want to multiply) is the **multiplicand.** The bottom number (number doing the multiplying) is the **multiplier.** The final number (answer) is the **product.** The numbers between the multiplier and the product are **partial products.** Also note how we positioned the partial product 2090. This number is the result of multiplying 418 by 50 (the 5 is in the tens position). On each line in the partial products, we placed the first digit directly below the digit we used in the multiplication process.

EXAMPLE

```
                    418  ←———————— Top number (multiplicand)
        Partial  ×   52  ←———————— Bottom number (multiplier)       2 × 418 =      836
        products    836                                            50 × 418 = + 20,900
                 20 90
                 ———————
                 21,736  ←———————— Product answer ——————————→       21,736
```

We can now give the following steps for multiplying whole numbers with two or more digits:

MULTIPLYING WHOLE NUMBERS WITH TWO OR MORE DIGITS
Step 1. Align the multiplicand (top number) and multiplier (bottom number) at the right. Usually, you should make the smaller number the multiplier.
Step 2. Begin by multiplying the right digit of the multiplier with the right digit of the multiplicand. Keep multiplying as you move left through the multiplicand. Your first partial product aligns at the right with the multiplicand and multiplier.
Step 3. Move left through the multiplier and continue multiplying the multiplicand. Your partial product right digit or first digit is placed directly below the digit in the multiplier that you used to multiply.
Step 4. Continue Steps 2 and 3 until you have completed your multiplication process. Then add the partial products to get the final product.

Checking and Estimating Multiplication

We can check the multiplication process by reversing the multiplicand and multiplier and then multiplying. Let's first estimate 52×418 by rounding all the way.

EXAMPLE
```
         50  ←       52
     ×  400  ←    × 418
     ———————      ——————
     20,000          416
                      52
                   20 8
                   ——————
                   21,736
```

By estimating before actually working the problem, we know our answer should be about 20,000. When we multiply 52 by 418, we get the same answer as when we multiply 418×52—and the answer is about 20,000. Remember, if we had not rounded all the way, our estimate would have been closer. If we had used a calculator, the rounded estimate would have helped us check the calculator's answer. Our commonsense estimate tells us our answer is near 20,000—not 200,000.

Before you study the division of whole numbers, you should know (1) the multiplication shortcut with numbers ending in zeros and (2) how to multiply a whole number by a power of 10.

MULTIPLICATION SHORTCUT WITH NUMBERS ENDING IN ZEROS
Step 1. When zeros are at the end of the multiplicand or the multiplier, or both, disregard the zeros and multiply.
Step 2. Count the number of zeros in the multiplicand and multiplier.
Step 3. Attach the number of zeros counted in Step 2 to your answer.

EXAMPLE

$$
\begin{array}{r}
65{,}000 \\
\times\ 420 \\
\hline
\end{array}
$$

$$
\begin{array}{r}
65 \\
\times\ 42 \\
\hline
1\ 30 \\
26\ 0 \\
\hline
27{,}300{,}000 \\
\end{array}
$$

3 zeros
+ 1 zero
4 zeros

No need to multiply rows of zeros

$$
\begin{array}{r}
65{,}000 \\
\times\qquad 420 \\
\hline
00\ 000 \\
1\ 300\ 00 \\
26\ 000\ 0 \\
\hline
27{,}300{,}000 \\
\end{array}
$$

MULTIPLYING A WHOLE NUMBER BY A POWER OF 10
Step 1. Count the number of zeros in the power of 10 (a whole number that begins with 1 and ends in one or more zeros such as 10, 100, 1,000, and so on).
Step 2. Attach that number of zeros to the right side of the other whole number to obtain the answer. Insert comma(s) as needed every three digits, moving from right to left.

EXAMPLE $99 \times 10\ \ \ = 990\ \ \ = \boxed{990}$ ←Add 1 zero

$99 \times 100\ \ \ = 9{,}900\ \ \ = \boxed{9{,}900}$ ←Add 2 zeros

$99 \times 1{,}000 = 99{,}000 = \boxed{99{,}000}$ ←Add 3 zeros

When a zero is in the center of the multiplier, you can do the following:

EXAMPLE

$$
\begin{array}{r}
658 \\
\times\ 403 \\
\hline
1\ 974 \\
263\ 2\square \\
\hline
265{,}174 \\
\end{array}
$$

$$
\begin{array}{r}
3 \times 658 =\qquad 1{,}974 \\
400 \times 658 = +\ 263{,}200 \\
\hline
265{,}174 \\
\end{array}
$$

Division of Whole Numbers

Division is the reverse of multiplication and a time-saving shortcut related to subtraction. For example, in the introduction to this learning unit, you determined that you would save $2,310 by staying for 5 days in a nursing home in Shreveport, Louisiana, versus Alaska. If you subtract $462—the difference between the cost of Alaska and Shreveport—5 times from the difference of $2,310, you would get to zero. You can also multiply $462 times 5 to get $2,310. Since division is the reverse of multiplication, you can say that $2,310 ÷ 5 = $462.

Division can be indicated by the common symbols ÷ and $\overline{)}$, or by the bar — in a fraction and the forward slant / between two numbers, which means the first number is divided by the second number. Division asks how many times one number (**divisor**) is contained in another number (**dividend**). The answer, or result, is the **quotient.** When the divisor (number used to divide) doesn't divide evenly into the dividend (number we are dividing), the result is a **partial quotient,** with the leftover amount the **remainder** (expressed as fractions in later chapters). The following example illustrates *even division* (this is also an example of *long division* because the divisor has more than one digit).

EXAMPLE

$$
\begin{array}{r}
18 \quad \longleftarrow \text{Quotient} \\
\text{Divisor} \longrightarrow 15\overline{)270} \quad \longleftarrow \text{Dividend} \\
\underline{15} \\
120 \\
\underline{120}
\end{array}
$$

This example divides 15 into 27 once with 12 remaining. The 0 in the dividend is brought down to 12. Dividing 120 by 15 equals 8 with no remainder; that is, even division. The following example illustrates *uneven division with a remainder* (this is also an example of *short division* because the divisor has only one digit).

EXAMPLE

$$
\begin{array}{r}
24\,\text{R1} \quad \longleftarrow \text{Remainder} \\
7\overline{)169} \\
\underline{14} \\
29 \\
\underline{28} \\
1
\end{array}
$$

Check

$$(7 \times 24) + 1 = 169$$

Divisor × Quotient + Remainder = Dividend

Note how doing the check gives you assurance that your calculation is correct. When the divisor has one digit (short division) as in this example, you can often calculate the division mentally as illustrated in the following examples:

EXAMPLES

$$
\begin{array}{r}
108 \\
8\overline{)864}
\end{array}
\qquad
\begin{array}{r}
16\,\text{R6} \\
7\overline{)118}
\end{array}
$$

Next, let's look at the value of estimating division.

Estimating Division

Before actually working a division problem, estimate the quotient by rounding. This estimate helps check the answer. The example that follows is rounded all the way. After you make an estimate, work the problem and check your answer by multiplication.

EXAMPLE

| | 36 R111 | **Estimate** | **Check** |

$$
\begin{array}{r}
36\,\text{R111} \\
138\overline{)5,079} \\
\underline{4\,14} \\
939 \\
\underline{828} \\
111
\end{array}
\qquad
\begin{array}{r}
50 \\
100\overline{)5,000}
\end{array}
\qquad
\begin{array}{r}
138 \\
\times \quad 36 \\
\hline
828 \\
4\,14 \\
\hline
4,968 \\
+ \quad 111 \quad \longleftarrow \text{Add remainder} \\
\hline
5,079
\end{array}
$$

Now let's turn our attention to division shortcuts with zeros.

Division Shortcuts with Zeros

The steps that follow show a shortcut that you can use when you divide numbers with zeros.

DIVISION SHORTCUT WITH NUMBERS ENDING IN ZEROS
Step 1. When the dividend and divisor have ending zeros, count the number of ending zeros in the divisor.
Step 2. Drop the same number of zeros in the dividend as in the divisor, counting from right to left.

Note the following examples of division shortcut with numbers ending in zeros. Since two of the symbols used for division are ÷ and $\overline{)}$, our first examples show the zero shortcut method with the ÷ symbol.

EXAMPLES

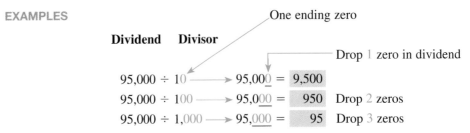

Dividend   Divisor

One ending zero

Drop 1 zero in dividend

$95,000 \div 10 \longrightarrow 95,00\underline{0} = \boxed{9,500}$

$95,000 \div 100 \longrightarrow 95,0\underline{00} = \boxed{950}$ Drop 2 zeros

$95,000 \div 1,000 \longrightarrow 95,\underline{000} = \boxed{95}$ Drop 3 zeros

In a long division problem with the $\overline{)}$ symbol, you again count the number of ending zeros in the divisor. Then drop the same number of ending zeros in the dividend and divide as usual.

EXAMPLE $6,5\underline{00})\overline{88,0\underline{00}}$ ← Drop 2 zeros

$65)\overline{880}$ ←

$$
\begin{array}{r}
13\ \text{R}35 \\
65)\overline{880} \\
\underline{65} \\
230 \\
\underline{195} \\
35
\end{array}
$$

You are now ready to practice what you learned by dissecting and solving a word problem.

How to Dissect and Solve a Word Problem

The blueprint aid that follows will be your guide to dissecting and solving the following word problem.

The Word Problem Dunkin' Donuts sells to four different companies a total of $3,500 worth of doughnuts per week. What is the total annual sales to these companies? What is the yearly sales per company? (Assume each company buys the same amount.) Check your answer to show how multiplication and division are related.

The facts	Solving for?	Steps to take	Key points
Sales per week: $3,500. *Companies:* 4.	Total annual sales to all four companies. Yearly sales per company.	Sales per week × Weeks in year (52) = Total annual sales. Total annual sales ÷ Total companies = Yearly sales per company.	Division is the reverse of multiplication.

Steps to solving problem

1. Calculate total annual sales. $3,500 × 52 weeks = $182,000

2. Calculate yearly sales per company, $182,000 ÷ 4 = $45,500

Check

$45,500 × 4 = $182,000

It's time again to check your progress with a Practice Quiz.

LU 1–3   PRACTICE QUIZ

1. Estimate the actual problem by rounding all the way, work the actual problem, and check:

Actual   **Estimate**   **Check**
3,894
× 18

2. Multiply by shortcut method:

77,000
× 1,800

3. Multiply by shortcut method:

95 × 10,000

4. Divide by rounding all the way, complete the actual calculation, and check, showing remainder as a whole number.

26)5,325

5. Divide by shortcut method:

4,000)96,000

6. Assume General Motors produces 960 Chevrolets each workday (Monday through Friday). If the cost to produce each car is $6,500, what is General Motors' total cost for the year? Check your answer.

✓ **Solutions**

1.

Estimate	**Actual**	**Check**
4,000	3,894	8 × 3,894 = 31,152
× 20	× 18	10 × 3,894 = + 38,940
80,000	31 152	70,092
	38 94	
	70,092	

2. 77 × 18 = 1,386 + 5 zeros = 138,600,000

3. 95 + 4 zeros = 950,000

4.

Rounding	**Actual**	**Check**
166 R20	204 R21	26 × 204 = 5,304
30)5,000	26)5,325	+ 21
3 0	5 2	5,325
2 00	125	
1 80	104	
200	21	
180		
20		

5. Drop 3 zeros = 4)96 → 24

6. General Motors' total cost per year:

The facts	Solving for?	Steps to take	Key points
Cars produced each workday: 960. *Workweek:* 5 days. *Cost per car:* $6,500.	Total cost per year.	Cars produced per week × 52 = Total cars produced per year. Total cars produced per year × Total cost per car = Total cost per year.	Whenever possible, use multiplication and division shortcuts with zeros. Multiplication can be checked by division.

Steps to solving problem

1. Calculate total cars produced per week.   5 × 960 = 4,800 cars produced per week

2. Calculate total cars produced per year.   4,800 cars × 52 weeks = 249,600 total cars produced per year

3. Calculate total cost per year.   249,600 cars × $6,500 = $1,622,400,000 (multiply 2,496 × 65 and add zeros)

Check

$1,622,400,000 ÷ 249,600 = $6,500 (drop 2 zeros before dividing)

Need more practice? Try this **Extra Practice Quiz** (check figures in Chapter Organizer, p. 19)

1. Estimate the actual problem by rounding all the way, work the actual problem, and check:

Actual	Estimate	Check

   $$\begin{array}{r} 4,938 \\ \times \quad 19 \\ \hline \end{array}$$

2. Multiply by shortcut method:

   $$\begin{array}{r} 86,000 \\ \times 1,900 \\ \hline \end{array}$$

3. Multiply by shortcut method:

   $86 \times 10,000$

4. Divide by rounding all the way, complete the actual calculation, and check, showing remainder as a whole number.

   $26\overline{)6,394}$

5. Divide by the shortcut method:

   $3,000\overline{)99,000}$

6. Assume General Motors produces 850 Chevrolets each workday (Monday through Friday). If the cost to produce each car is $7,000, what is General Motors's total cost for the year? Check your answer.

CHAPTER ORGANIZER AND STUDY GUIDE WITH CHECK FIGURES FOR EXTRA PRACTICE QUIZZES

Topic	Key point, procedure, formula	Example(s) to illustrate situation
Reading and writing numeric and verbal whole numbers, p. 3	Placement of digits in a number gives the value of the digits (Figure 1.1). Commas separate every three digits, moving from right to left. Begin at left to read and write number in verbal form. Do not read zeros or use *and*. Hyphenate numbers twenty-one to ninety-nine. Reverse procedure to change verbal number to numeric.	462 → Four hundred sixty-two 6,741 → Six thousand, seven hundred forty-one
Rounding whole numbers, p. 4	1. Identify place value of the digit to be rounded. 2. If digit to the right is 5 or more, round up; if less than 5, do not change. 3. Change all digits to the right of rounded identified digit to zeros.	643 to nearest ten 4 in tens place value. 3 is not 5 or more Thus, 643 rounds to 640 .
Rounding all the way, p. 5	Round to first digit of number. One nonzero digit remains. In estimating, you round each number of the problem to one nonzero digit. The final answer is not rounded.	468,451 ⟶ 500,000 The 5 is the only nonzero digit remaining.
Adding whole numbers, p. 8	1. Align numbers at the right. 2. Add units column. If sum more than 9, carry tens digit. 3. Moving left, repeat Step 2 until all place values are added. Add from top to bottom. Check by adding bottom to top or adding each column separately and combining.	$$\begin{array}{r} \overset{1}{6}5 \\ +\ 47 \\ \hline 112 \end{array} \quad \begin{array}{r} 12 \\ +\ 10 \\ \hline 112 \end{array}$$ Checking sum of each digit

(continues)

CHAPTER ORGANIZER AND STUDY GUIDE
WITH CHECK FIGURES FOR EXTRA PRACTICE QUIZZES (concluded)

Topic	Key point, procedure, formula	Example(s) to illustrate situation
Subtracting whole numbers, p. 9	1. Align minuend and subtrahend at the right. 2. Subtract units digits. If necessary, borrow 1 from tens digit in minuend. 3. Moving left, repeat Step 2 until all place values are subtracted. Minuend less subtrahend equals difference.	**Check** $\begin{array}{r} {}^{5\,18}\!\!\!685 \\ -492 \\ \hline 193 \end{array}$ $\begin{array}{r} 193 \\ +492 \\ \hline 685 \end{array}$
Multiplying whole numbers, p. 12	1. Align multiplicand and multiplier at the right. 2. Begin at the right and keep multiplying as you move to the left. First partial product aligns at the right with multiplicand and multiplier. 3. Move left through multiplier and continue multiplying multiplicand. Partial product right digit or first digit is placed directly below digit in multiplier. 4. Continue Steps 2 and 3 until multiplication is complete. Add partial products to get final product. **Shortcuts:** (a) When multiplicand or multiplier, or both, end in zeros, disregard zeros and multiply; attach same number of zeros to answer. If zero in center of multiplier, no need to show row of zeros. (b) If multiplying by power of 10, attach same number of zeros to whole number multiplied.	$\begin{array}{r} 223 \\ \times\ 32 \\ \hline 446 \\ 6\ 69 \\ \hline 7{,}136 \end{array}$ a. $\begin{array}{r} 48{,}000 \\ \times\ \ \ \ 40 \end{array}$ $\begin{array}{r} 48 \\ 4 \end{array}$ 3 zeros $+1$ zero $\boxed{1{,}920{,}000}$ ◄ 4 zeros $\begin{array}{r} 524 \\ \times\ 206 \\ \hline 3\ 144 \\ 104\ 8 \\ \hline \boxed{107{,}944} \end{array}$ b. $14 \times\ \ \ \ 10 = \boxed{140}$ (attach 1 zero) $14 \times 1{,}000 = \boxed{14{,}000}$ (attach 3 zeros)
Dividing whole numbers, p. 14	1. When divisor is divided into the dividend, the remainder is less than divisor. 2. Drop zeros from dividend right to left by number of zeros found in the divisor. Even division has no remainder; uneven division has a remainder; divisor with one digit is short division; and divisor with more than one digit is long division.	1. $\begin{array}{r} \boxed{5\ R6} \\ 14\overline{)76} \\ 70 \\ \hline 6 \end{array}$ 2. $5{,}000 \div 100\ \ \ = 50 \div 1 = \boxed{50}$ $5{,}000 \div 1{,}000 = 5 \div 1 = \boxed{5}$
KEY TERMS	addends, *p. 8* decimal point, *p. 2* decimal system, *p. 2* difference, *p. 9* dividend, *p. 14* divisor, *p. 14*	minuend, *p. 9* multiplicand, *p. 13* multiplier, *p. 13* partial products, *p. 13* partial quotient, *p. 14* product, *p. 13* quotient, *p. 14* remainder, *p. 14* rounding all the way, *p. 5* subtrahend, *p. 9* sum, *p. 8* whole number, *p. 2*
CHECK FIGURE FOR EXTRA PRACTICE QUIZZES WITH PAGE REFERENCES	LU 1–1a (p. 8) 1. A. Eight thousand, six hundred eighty-two; B. Fifty-six thousand, two hundred ninety-five; C. Seven hundred thirty two billion, three hundred ten million, four hundred forty-four thousand, eight hundred eighty-eight 2. A. 40; B. 700; C. 7,000; D. 6,000 3. 3,000,000; 400,000	LU 1–2a (p. 12) 1. 26,090 2. 15,000; 15,953 3. 3,819 4. 43,100 (over) LU 1–3a (p. 18) 1. 100,000; 93,822 2. 163,400,000 3. 860,000 4. 255 R19 5. 33 6. $1,547,000,000

Critical Thinking Discussion Questions

1. List the four steps of the decision-making process. Do you think all companies should be required to follow these steps? Give an example.

2. Explain the three steps used to round whole numbers. Pick a whole number and explain why it should not be rounded.

3. How do you check subtraction? If you were to attend a movie, explain how you might use the subtraction check method.

4. Explain how you can check multiplication. If you visit a local supermarket, how could you show multiplication as a shortcut to addition?

5. Explain how division is the reverse of multiplication. Using the supermarket example, explain how division is a timesaving shortcut related to subtraction.

Name _____ Date _____

DRILL PROBLEMS

Add the following:

1–1. $\begin{array}{r} 88 \\ +\ 16 \\ \hline \end{array}$	**1–2.** $\begin{array}{r} 855 \\ +\ 699 \\ \hline \end{array}$	**1–3.** $\begin{array}{r} 79 \\ +\ 79 \\ \hline \end{array}$	**1–4.** $\begin{array}{r} 66 \\ +\ 92 \\ \hline \end{array}$

1–5. $\begin{array}{r} 6,251 \\ +\ 7,329 \\ \hline \end{array}$	**1–6.** $\begin{array}{r} 59,481 \\ 51,411 \\ +\ 70,821 \\ \hline \end{array}$	**1–7.** $\begin{array}{r} 78,159 \\ 15,850 \\ +\ 19,681 \\ \hline \end{array}$

Subtract the following:

1–8. $\begin{array}{r} 68 \\ -\ 19 \\ \hline \end{array}$	**1–9.** $\begin{array}{r} 80 \\ -\ 42 \\ \hline \end{array}$	**1–10.** $\begin{array}{r} 287 \\ -\ 199 \\ \hline \end{array}$

1–11. $\begin{array}{r} 9,000 \\ -\ 5,400 \\ \hline \end{array}$	**1–12.** $\begin{array}{r} 9,800 \\ -\ 8,900 \\ \hline \end{array}$	**1–13.** $\begin{array}{r} 1,622 \\ -\ 548 \\ \hline \end{array}$

Multiply the following:

1–14. $\begin{array}{r} 66 \\ \times\ 9 \\ \hline \end{array}$	**1–15.** $\begin{array}{r} 510 \\ \times\ 61 \\ \hline \end{array}$	**1–16.** $\begin{array}{r} 900 \\ \times\ 300 \\ \hline \end{array}$

1–17. $\begin{array}{r} 677 \\ \times\ 503 \\ \hline \end{array}$	**1–18.** $\begin{array}{r} 309 \\ \times\ 850 \\ \hline \end{array}$	**1–19.** $\begin{array}{r} 450 \\ \times\ 280 \\ \hline \end{array}$

Divide the following by short division:

1–20. $6\overline{)1,200}$ **1–21.** $9\overline{)810}$ **1–22.** $4\overline{)164}$

Divide the following by long division. Show work and remainder.

1–23. $6\overline{)520}$ **1–24.** $62\overline{)8,915}$

Add the following without rearranging:

1–25. $99 + 210$ **1–26.** $1,055 + 88$

1–27. $666 + 950$ **1–28.** $1,011 + 17$

1–29. Add the following and check by totaling each column individually without carrying numbers:

              Check

    8,539
    6,842
  + 9,495

Estimate the following by rounding all the way and then do actual addition:

	Actual	Estimate			Actual	Estimate
1–30.	7,700			**1–31.**	6,980	
	9,286				3,190	
	+ 3,900				+ 7,819	

Subtract the following without rearranging:

1–32. $190 - 66$

1–33. $950 - 870$

1–34. Subtract the following and check answer:

    591,001
  − 375,956

Multiply the following horizontally:

1–35. 16×9 **1–36.** 84×8 **1–37.** 27×8 **1–38.** 17×6

Divide the following and check by multiplication:

1–39. $45\overline{)876}$ **Check**   **1–40.** $46\overline{)1,950}$ **Check**

Complete the following:

1–41.	9,200		**1–42.**	3,000,000
	− 1,510			− 769,459
	− 700			− 68,541

1–43. Estimate the following problem by rounding all the way and then do the actual multiplication:

    Actual   **Estimate**
      870
    × 81

Divide the following by the shortcut method:

1–44. $1,000\overline{)850,000}$ **1–45.** $100\overline{)70,000}$

1–46. Estimate actual problem by rounding all the way and do actual division:

Actual   **Estimate**

$695)\overline{8,950}$

WORD PROBLEMS

1–47. The January 8, 2007 issue of *Retailing Today*, reported on price cuts implemented by Wal-Mart ahead of the holiday season. A Panasonic 42-inch HD plasma TV was reduced to one-thousand, two hundred ninety-four dollars from one-thousand, seven hundred ninety-four dollars. A Polaroid 37-inch LDC HDTV priced at nine hundred ninety-seven dollars was reduced from one-thousand, two hundred ninety-seven dollars. **(a)** In numerical form, how much was saved by purchasing a HD plasma TV? **(b)** How much was saved by purchasing the LCD HDTV? **(c)** Prior to price reduction, how much more was the HDTV compared to the LCD HDTV?

1–48. On February 3, 2007, *The Boston Globe* reported on ticket reseller Admit One Ticket Agency's ticket price for games the Red Sox played against the New York Yankees and Baltimore Orioles. Admit One paid $135,550, in 2005, for 14 loge box seat season tickets with a face value of $90,720. The average price per ticket was $120. The transaction netted the company 1,134 tickets to 81 games. Admit One Ticket resold 1,084 of the tickets for a total of $231,976. **(a)** How much did Admit One pay over the face value for the tickets? **(b)** What was the average price for the resold tickets? **(c)** What was the difference between the average price paid and average reselling price?

1–49. The *Buffalo News* on January 25, 2007, reported season-ticket prices for the Buffalo Bills 15-yard line on the lower bowl. Tickets will rise from $480 for a 10-game package to $600. Fans sitting in the best seats in the upper deck will pay an increase from $440 to $540. Don Manning plans to purchase 2 season tickets for either lower bowl or upper deck. **(a)** How much more will 2 tickets cost for lower bowl? **(b)** How much more will 2 tickets cost for upper deck? **(c)** What will be his total cost for a 10-game package for lower bowl? **(d)** What will be his total cost for a 10-game package for upper deck?

1–50. The *Billboard* reported that ticket prices for the Old Friends concert tour of Paul Simon and Art Garfunkel are $251 (VIP), $126, $86, and $51. For a family of four, estimate the cost of the $86 tickets by rounding all the way and then do the actual multiplication:

1–51. *USA Today* reports that Walt Disney World Resort and United Vacations got together to create a special deal. The air-inclusive package features accommodations for three nights at Disney's All-Star Resort, hotel taxes, and a four-day unlimited Magic Pass. Prices are $609 per person traveling from Washington, DC, and $764 per person traveling from Los Angeles. (a) What would be the cost for a family of four leaving from Washington, DC? (b) What would be the cost for a family of four leaving from Los Angeles? (c) How much more will it cost the family from Los Angeles?

1–52. NTB Tires bought 910 tires from its manufacturer for $36 per tire. What is the total cost of NTB's purchase? If the store can sell all the tires at $65 each, what will be the store's gross profit, or the difference between its sales and costs (Sales − Costs = Gross profit)?

1–53. What was the total average number of visits for these Internet Web sites?

Web site	Average daily unique visitor
1. Orbitz.com	1,527,000
2. Mypoints.com	1,356,000
3. Americangreetings.com	745,000
4. Bizrate.com	503,000
5. Half.com	397,000

1–54. Lee Wong bought 5,000 shares of GE stock. She held the stock for 6 months. Then Lee sold 190 shares on Monday, 450 shares on Tuesday and again on Thursday, and 900 shares on Friday. How many shares does Lee still own? The average share of the stock Lee owns is worth $48 per share. What is the total value of Lee's stock?

1–55. *USA Today* reported that the Center for Science in the Public Interest—a consumer group based in Washington, DC—released a study listing calories of various ice cream treats sold by six of the largest ice cream companies. The worst treat tested by the group was 1,270 total calories. People need roughly 2,200 to 2,500 calories per day. Using a daily average, how many additional calories should a person consume after eating the ice cream?

1–56. At Rose State College, Alison Wells received the following grades in her online accounting class: 90, 65, 85, 80, 75, and 90. Alison's instructor, Professor Clark, said he would drop the lowest grade. What is Alison's average?

1–57. Lee Wills, professor of business, has 18 students in Accounting I, 26 in Accounting II, 22 in Introduction to Computers, 23 in Business Law, and 29 in Introduction to Business. What is the total number of students in Professor Wills's classes? If 12 students withdraw, how many total students will Professor Wills have?

1–58. Ron Alf, owner of Alf's Moving Company, bought a new truck. On Ron's first trip, he drove 1,200 miles and used 80 gallons of gas. How many miles per gallon did Ron get from his new truck? On Ron's second trip, he drove 840 miles and used 60 gallons. What is the difference in miles per gallon between Ron's first trip and his second trip?

1–59. Office Depot reduced its $450 Kodak digital camera by $59. What is the new selling price of the digital camera? If Office Depot sold 1,400 cameras at the new price, what were the store's digital camera dollar sales?

1–60. Barnes and Noble.com has 289 business math texts in inventory. During one month, the online bookstore ordered and received 1,855 texts; it also sold 1,222 on the Web. What is the bookstore's inventory at the end of the month? If each text costs $59, what is the end-of-month inventory cost?

1–61. Cabot Company produced 2,115,000 cans of paint in August. Cabot sold 2,011,000 of these cans. If each can cost $18, what were Cabot's ending inventory of paint cans and its total ending inventory cost?

1–62. Long College has 30 faculty members in the business department, 22 in psychology, 14 in English, and 169 in all other departments. What is the total number of faculty at Long College? If each faculty member advises 30 students, how many students attend Long College?

1–63. Hometown Buffet had 90 customers on Sunday, 70 on Monday, 65 on Tuesday, and a total of 310 on Wednesday to Saturday. How many customers did Hometown Buffet serve during the week? If each customer spends $9, what were the total sales for the week?

If Hometown Buffet had the same sales each week, what were the sales for the year?

1–64. Longview Agency projected its year 2006 sales at $995,000. During 2006, the agency earned $525,960 sales from its major clients and $286,950 sales from the remainder of its clients. How much did the agency overestimate its sales?

1–65. Jim Floyd works at US Airways and earned $61,000 last year before tax deductions. From Jim's total earnings, his company subtracted $1,462 for federal income taxes, $3,782 for Social Security, and $884 for Medicare taxes. What was Jim's actual, or net, pay for the year?

1–66. Macy's received the following invoice amounts from suppliers. How much does the company owe?

Per item	
22 paintings	$210
39 rockers	75
40 desk lamps	65
120 coffee tables	155

1–67. Roger Company produces beach balls and operates three shifts. Roger produces 5,000 balls per shift on shifts 1 and 2. On shift 3, the company can produce 6 times as many balls as on shift 1. Assume a 5-day workweek. How many beach balls does Roger produce per week and per year?

1–68. *The New York Times* reported on the changes in the prices of Disneyland tickets. Disneyland lowered the age limit for adult tickets from 12 years old to 10 years old. This raised the cost of admission from $31 to $41. If 125 children attending the park each day are in this age bracket, how much additional revenue will Disneyland receive each day?

1–69. Moe Brink has a $900 balance in his checkbook. During the week, Moe wrote the following checks: rent, $350; telephone, $44; food, $160; and entertaining, $60. Moe also made a $1,200 deposit. What is Moe's new checkbook balance?

1–70. Sports Authority, an athletic sports shop, bought and sold the following merchandise:

	Cost	Selling price
Tennis rackets	$ 2,900	$ 3,999
Tennis balls	70	210
Bowling balls	1,050	2,950
Sneakers	+ 8,105	+ 14,888

What was the total cost of the merchandise bought by Sports Authority? If the shop sold all its merchandise, what were the sales and the resulting gross profit (Sales − Costs = Gross profit)?

1–71. Matty Kaminsky, the bookkeeper for Maggie's Real Estate, and his manager are concerned about the company's telephone bills. Last year the company's average monthly phone bill was $34. Matty's manager asked him for an average of this year's phone bills. Matty's records show the following:

January	$ 34	July	$ 28
February	60	August	23
March	20	September	29
April	25	October	25
May	30	November	22
June	59	December	41

What is the average of this year's phone bills? Did Matty and his manager have a justifiable concern?

1–72. The Associated Press reported that bankruptcy filings were up for the first three months of the year. Filings reached 366,841 in the January–March period, the highest ever for a first quarter, up from 312,335 a year earlier. How much was the increase in quarterly filings?

1–73. On Monday, True Value Hardware sold 15 paint brushes at $3 each, 6 wrenches at $5 each, 7 bags of grass seed at $3 each, 4 lawn mowers at $119 each, and 28 cans of paint at $8 each. What were True Value's total dollar sales on Monday?

1–74. While redecorating, Pete Allen went to Sears and bought 125 square yards of commercial carpet. The total cost of the carpet was $3,000. How much did Pete pay per square yard?

1–75. Washington Construction built 12 ranch houses for $115,000 each. From the sale of these houses, Washington received $1,980,000. How much gross profit (Sales − Costs = Gross profit) did Washington make on the houses?

The four partners of Washington Construction split all profits equally. How much will each partner receive?

CHALLENGE PROBLEMS

1–76. The *St. Paul Pioneer Press* reported that after implementing a new parking service called e-Park, the Minneapolis–St. Paul International Airport reduced the number of its parking garage cashiers. E-Park is expected to allow the airport to cut 35 parking cashiers from its force of 130. Cashiers make about $11 an hour plus benefits. For a 40-hour week, **(a)** what has been the yearly cost of salaries? and **(b)** what will be the savings in labor costs for a year?

1–77. Paula Sanchez is trying to determine her 2009 finances. Paula's actual 2008 finances were as follows:

Income:		Assets:	
Gross income	$69,000	Checking account	$ 1,950
Interest income	450	Savings account	8,950
Total	$69,450	Automobile	1,800
		Personal property	14,000
Expenses:		Total	$26,700
Living	$24,500	Liabilities:	
Insurance premium	350	Note to bank	4,500
Taxes	14,800	Net worth	$22,200 ($26,700 − $4,500)
Medical	585		
Investment	4,000		
Total	$44,235		

Net worth = Assets − Liabilities
    (own)   (owe)

Paula believes her gross income will double in 2009 but her interest income will decrease $150. She plans to reduce her 2009 living expenses by one-half. Paula's insurance company wrote a letter announcing that her insurance premiums would triple in 2009. Her accountant estimates her taxes will decrease $250 and her medical costs will increase $410. Paula also hopes to cut her investments expenses by one-fourth. Paula's accountant projects that her savings and checking accounts will each double in value. On January 2, 2009, Paula sold her automobile and began to use public transportation. Paula forecasts that her personal property will decrease by one-seventh. She has sent her bank a $375 check to reduce her bank note. Could you give Paula an updated list of her 2009 finances? If you round all the way each 2008 and 2009 asset and liability, what will be the difference in Paula's net worth?

SUMMARY PRACTICE TEST

1. Translate the following verbal forms to numbers and add. *(p. 3)*

   a. Four thousand, eight hundred thirty-nine

   b. Seven million, twelve

   c. Twelve thousand, three hundred ninety-two

2. Express the following number in verbal form. *(p. 3)*

   9,622,364

3. Round the following numbers. *(p. 4)*

Nearest ten	**Nearest hundred**	**Nearest thousand**	**Round all the way**
a. 68	b. 888	c. 8,325	d. 14,821

4. Estimate the following actual problem by rounding all the way, work the actual problem, and check by adding each column of digits separately. *(pp. 5, 8)*

   Actual   **Estimate**   **Check**
   ```
      1,886
      9,411
   +  6,395
   ```

5. Estimate the following actual problem by rounding all the way and then do the actual multiplication. *(pp. 5, 12)*

   Actual   **Estimate**
   ```
      8,843
   ×    906
   ```

6. Multiply the following by the shortcut method. *(p. 14)*

   829,412 × 1,000

7. Divide the following and check the answer by multiplication. *(p. 15)*

   Check

   39)$\overline{14,800}$

8. Divide the following by the shortcut method. *(p. 15)*

   6,000 ÷ 60

9. Ling Wong bought a $299 ipod that was reduced to $205. Ling gave the clerk 3 $100 bills. What change will Ling receive? *(p. 9)*

10. Sam Song plans to buy a $16,000 Ford Saturn with an interest charge of $4,000. Sam figures he can afford a monthly payment of $400. If Sam must pay 40 equal monthly payments, can he afford the Ford Saturn? *(p. 14)*

11. Lester Hal has the oil tank at his business filled 20 times per year. The tank has a capacity of 200 gallons. Assume **(a)** the price of oil fuel is $3 per gallon and **(b)** the tank is completely empty each time Lester has it filled. What is Lester's average monthly oil bill? Complete the following blueprint aid for dissecting and solving the word problem. *(pp. 6, 12, 15)*

The facts	Solving for?	Steps to take	Key points

Steps to solving problem

Saving the world with FRENCH FRIES

Interview by Jessica Anderson

PHOTOGRAPH BY REENA BAMMI

Justin Carven's business sells kits that let diesel cars run on vegetable oil.

A typical fuel tank holds 15 gallons. Where do people get that much vegetable oil? Most of our customers are using recycled cooking oil from restaurants.

So I can get all the fuel I need at the local fast-food joint? Restaurants can produce as much as 100 gallons of waste oil per week, which they're willing to give away. Plus, the converted vehicles have one tank for diesel and one for vegetable oil–so you have backup fuel.

How far will a tank take me? Vegetable oil is similar to diesel. Many diesel cars get 40 miles per gallon, so a tank should take you 600 miles.

Will my car smell like fries? It will smell like food cooking, but not what was cooked in that oil.

How much does the kit cost? It starts at $795 and includes a manual and all the parts to install it yourself. To have a professional install it will run $500 to $1,000.

Is using your kit a violation of the Clean Air Act? Any aftermarket automotive product must go through an evaluation process with the Environmental Protection Agency to be certified–we're in the process of doing that.

Could customers be fined in the meantime? The EPA has never fined anyone for using vegetable oil.

How many kits have you sold? We've sold about 3,000 conversion kits since I founded the business six years ago. Sales broke $1 million last year.

What are the benefits? Besides cheap fuel, there are incredible environmental benefits. You're putting less carbon dioxide into the atmosphere than plants take out.

Is this a step toward curing our "addiction to oil"? I believe so. It's still going to be an addiction; it's just going to be an addiction to something a bit healthier for us. [For more information, go to www.greasecar.com.] ◀

BUSINESS MATH ISSUE

Vegetable oil will not solve our oil problem.

1. List the key points of the article and information to support your position.
2. Write a group defense of your position using math calculations to support your view.

Slater's Business Math Scrapbook

with Internet Application

Putting Your Skills to Work

PROJECT A
Show the math using the shortcut method of multiplication to prove the million dollars.

Pipe Dream / *By Gwendolyn Bounds*

How Selling Pixels May Yield a Million Bucks

IT WAS JUST a few months ago that 21-year-old Alex Tew of Great Britain was stumped about how to pay for college. He'd filled a notebook with ideas before jotting down this simple, if rather audacious, query to himself: How Can I Become a Millionaire?

In the annals of entrepreneurship, what followed is an instructional tale of how a brainstorm, coupled with the Internet's powerful word-of-mouth culture, can set a trend in motion with lightning speed. Mr. Tew says his strategy was to find an idea simple to understand and cheap to set up, with a catchy name that would garner attention online, where he gained experience from having free-lanced as a Web designer for a few years.

Ultimately, his solution amounted to making money via Internet advertising—but with a twist. Instead of selling banner ads, text links or splashy videolike ads that fill a screen, Mr. Tew opted to hawk the simplest graphical denominator of a computer screen: the pixel. A pixel is a tiny dot of light and color, and each screen has tens of thousands of them.

Mr. Tew created a home page, www.milliondollarhomepage.com, where he divided the screen into 10,000 small squares of 100 pixels each. His plan: to sell the pixels for $1 a piece, with a minimum order of 100 pixels. In each space, buyers could put a graphical ad of their choosing that links

*Alex Tew sells tiny ad spaces on his Web page (inset) and has **generated $623,800** toward his $1 million goal.*

to their own site when clicked on. The end result is a cluttered collage of ads in various shapes and colors all amassed on a single digital billboard. (Mr. Tew doesn't charge his advertisers anything when a visitor clicks on the ads.)

Mr. Tew pledged to keep the site up for at least five years and to close the page when his goal of one million dollars was reached. "I had to think big," he says.

The notion seemed absurd. Who would want to advertise on an unknown site that had no target audience, no track record of attracting visitors or even the slightest brand recognition?

But as with many gimmicks, its newness gave it legs, as did Mr. Tew's shrewd marketing. He first roped his friends and family into buying pixels and placing ads to make the page seem legitimate. He then began touting his site, and himself, to bloggers, who wrote about his crazy idea and linked to the site, which directed traffic his way. The media in Britain picked up on his efforts, fueling more visitors.

Within two weeks of the site's Aug. 26 launch Mr. Tew says he sold $40,000 in ads. More important, the traffic numbers started gaining attention among the U.S. Internet community.

Wall Street Journal © 2005

 Internet Projects: See text Web site (www.mhhe.com/slater9e) and The Business Math Internet Resource Guide.

CHAPTER 2

Fractions

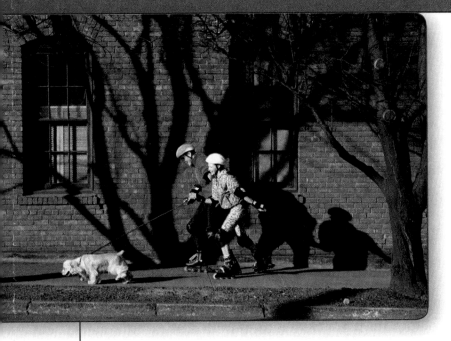

Lifestyle Changes Could Prevent Almost Half of Cancer Deaths

By KRISTEN GERENCHER

SAN FRANCISCO—As many as half of cancer deaths could be prevented if more people made lifestyle changes such as avoiding smoking and excessive sun exposure, eating nutritiously and getting regular exercise and recommended health screenings, according to a study from the American Cancer Society.

Whether due to socioeconomic or personal challenges, many people have trouble following common health precautions, said Vilma Cokkinides, co-author of the report and program director of risk-factor surveillance for the American Cancer Society in Atlanta.

"What's astonishing is how small the numbers are in terms of the population actually doing these things," Ms. Cokkinides said. "It's a disconnect....The awareness that theoretically half [of cancer deaths] could be prevented hasn't gotten in the mindset."

Smoking is the biggest sticking point because it increases the risk of many kinds of cancer, not just lung, and is expected to kill 170,000 this year. About a third of the 564,830 expected cancer deaths in 2006 will be related to poor diets, physical inactivity and obesity, which itself causes many chronic illnesses, the report said.

Americans have been receiving the antitobacco message for decades, but one in five adults still lights up. Despite calls for better nutrition and more physical activity to maintain a healthy weight, waistlines are growing dangerously wider. And few people do enough to protect their skin from the sun's harmful rays, leading to high rates of skin cancer.

People also fail to follow commonly recommended screenings based on age, family and medical history to catch cancer in its earliest, most treatable phases, the study said.

The ability to keep up with recommended screenings for colorectal, cervical and breast cancer—where evidence of effective treatment and reduced chance of death is greatest—is largely dependent on whether people have health insurance, Ms. Cokkinides said. "It's perhaps the single most important determinant."

LEARNING UNIT OBJECTIVES

LU 2–1: Types of Fractions and Conversion Procedures

- Recognize the three types of fractions *(pp. 35–36)*.
- Convert improper fractions to whole or mixed numbers and mixed numbers to improper fractions *(p. 36)*.
- Convert fractions to lowest and highest terms *(pp. 36–38)*.

LU 2–2: Adding and Subtracting Fractions

- Add like and unlike fractions *(pp. 40–41)*.
- Find the least common denominator (LCD) by inspection and prime numbers *(pp. 41–42)*.
- Subtract like and unlike fractions *(p. 43)*.
- Add and subtract mixed numbers with the same or different denominators *(pp. 42–45)*.

LU 2–3: Multiplying and Dividing Fractions

- Multiply and divide proper fractions and mixed numbers *(pp. 46–48)*.
- Use the cancellation method in the multiplication and division of fractions *(pp. 47–48)*.

The following two *Wall Street Journal* clippings "Product Piracy Rises in China, U.S. Says" and "Fruitcake Makers See a Way to Boost Sales: Slice the Serving Size" illustrate the use of fractions. For example, from the first clipping you learn that almost two-thirds ($\frac{2}{3}$) of all seizures of fake products come from China.

Product Piracy Rises In China, U.S. Says

Associated Press

SHANGHAI—Illegal copying of music, movies and other goods by Chinese product pirates is rising despite Beijing's promises to stamp it out, U.S. officials said.

Almost two-thirds of all seizures of fake products by U.S. Customs officials come from China, and despite stronger laws and pledges to crack down the problem has been getting worse, they said.

Fruitcake Makers See A Way to Boost Sales: Slice the Serving Size

By Jane Zhang

EVEN FRUITCAKE bakers count calories now: Four of them recently petitioned the Food and Drug Administration to cut the serving size for fruitcake by two-thirds.

Now let's look at Milk Chocolate M&M's® candies as another example of using fractions.

As you know, M&M's® candies come in different colors. Do you know how many of each color are in a bag of M&M's®? If you go to the M&M's website, you learn that a typical bag of M&M's® contains approximately 17 brown, 11 yellow, 11 red, and 5 each of orange, blue, and green M&M's®.[1]

The 1.69-ounce bag of M&M's® shown here contains 55 M&M's®. In this bag, you will find the following colors:

18 yellow	9 blue	6 brown
10 red	7 orange	5 green

55 pieces in the bag

The number of yellow candies in a bag might suggest that yellow is the favorite color of many people. Since this is a business math text, however, let's look at the 55 M&M's® in terms of fractional arithmetic.

Of the 55 M&M's® in the 1.69-ounce bag, 5 of these M&M's® are green, so we can say that 5 parts of 55 represent green candies. We could also say that 1 out of 11 M&M's® is green. Are you confused?

For many people, fractions are difficult. If you are one of these people, this chapter is for you. First you will review the types of fractions and the fraction conversion procedures. Then you will gain a clear understanding of the addition, subtraction, multiplication, and division of fractions.

[1]Off 1 due to rounding.

Learning Unit 2–1: Types of Fractions and Conversion Procedures

This chapter explains the parts of whole numbers called **fractions.** With fractions you can divide any object or unit—a whole—into a definite number of equal parts. For example, the bag of 55 M&M's® shown at the beginning of this chapter contains 6 brown candies. If you eat only the brown M&M's®, you have eaten 6 parts of 55, or 6 parts of the whole bag of M&M's®. We can express this in the following fraction:

6 is the **numerator,** or top of the fraction. The numerator describes the number of equal parts of the whole bag that you ate.

$$\frac{6}{55}$$

55 is the **denominator,** or bottom of the fraction. The denominator gives the total number of equal parts in the bag of M&M's®.

Before reviewing the arithmetic operations of fractions, you must recognize the three types of fractions described in this unit. You must also know how to convert fractions to a workable form.

Types of Fractions

Wal-Mart Buys Stake in Retailer In Latin America

By Ann Zimmerman

Wal-Mart Stores Inc., in another move to expand its international holdings, said it purchased a one-third stake in Central America's largest retailer.

Wal-Mart didn't disclose how much it paid for the stake in **Central American Retail Holding** Co., which it purchased from Dutch retailer **Royal Ahold** NV. The Bentonville, Ark., retailer said the deal includes an agreement to eventually buy additional interest in the company "toward achieving majority ownership."

This is Wal-Mart's first store expansion into Central America, although the retailer said it directly imports more than $350 million in goods—mostly apparel—from Guatemala, Honduras, El Salvador, Nicaragua and Costa Rica.

Wall Street Journal © 2005

When you read the *Wall Street Journal* clipping "Wal-Mart Buys Stake in Retailer in Latin America," you see that Wal-Mart is buying a one-third ($\frac{1}{3}$) stake in Central America's largest retailer. The fraction $\frac{1}{3}$ is a proper fraction.

PROPER FRACTIONS
A **proper fraction** has a value less than 1; its numerator is smaller than its denominator.

EXAMPLES $\dfrac{1}{2}, \dfrac{1}{10}, \dfrac{1}{12}, \dfrac{1}{3}, \dfrac{4}{7}, \dfrac{9}{10}, \dfrac{12}{13}, \dfrac{18}{55}$

IMPROPER FRACTIONS
An **improper fraction** has a value equal to or greater than 1; its numerator is equal to or greater than its denominator.

EXAMPLES $\dfrac{14}{14}, \dfrac{7}{6}, \dfrac{15}{14}, \dfrac{22}{19}$

MIXED NUMBERS
A **mixed number** is the sum of a whole number greater than zero and a proper fraction.

EXAMPLES $5\frac{1}{6}, 5\frac{9}{10}, 8\frac{7}{8}, 33\frac{5}{6}, 139\frac{9}{11}$

Conversion Procedures

In Chapter 1 we worked with two of the division symbols ($\div$ and $\overline{)}$). The horizontal line (or the diagonal) that separates the numerator and the denominator of a fraction also indicates division. The numerator, like the dividend, is the number we are dividing into. The denominator, like the divisor, is the number we use to divide. Then, referring to the 6 brown M&M's® in the bag of 55 M&M's® ($\frac{6}{55}$) shown at the beginning of this unit, we can say that we are dividing 55 into 6, or 6 is divided by 55. Also, in the fraction $\frac{3}{4}$, we can say that we are dividing 4 into 3, or 3 is divided by 4.

Working with the smaller numbers of simple fractions such as $\frac{3}{4}$ is easier, so we often convert fractions to their simplest terms. In this unit we show how to convert improper fractions to whole or mixed numbers, mixed numbers to improper fractions, and fractions to lowest and highest terms.

Converting Improper Fractions to Whole or Mixed Numbers

Business situations often make it necessary to change an improper fraction to a whole number or mixed number. You can use the following steps to make this conversion:

CONVERTING IMPROPER FRACTIONS TO WHOLE OR MIXED NUMBERS
Step 1. Divide the numerator of the improper fraction by the denominator.
Step 2. **a.** If you have no remainder, the quotient is a whole number.
b. If you have a remainder, the whole number part of the mixed number is the quotient. The remainder is placed over the old denominator as the proper fraction of the mixed number.

EXAMPLES

$$\frac{15}{15} = 1 \qquad \frac{16}{5} = 3\frac{1}{5} \qquad \begin{array}{r} 3\,R1 \\ 5\overline{)16} \\ \underline{15} \\ 1 \end{array}$$

Converting Mixed Numbers to Improper Fractions

By reversing the procedure of converting improper fractions to mixed numbers, we can change mixed numbers to improper fractions.

CONVERTING MIXED NUMBERS TO IMPROPER FRACTIONS
Step 1. Multiply the denominator of the fraction by the whole number.
Step 2. Add the product from Step 1 to the numerator of the old fraction.
Step 3. Place the total from Step 2 over the denominator of the old fraction to get the improper fraction.

EXAMPLE $6\frac{1}{8} = \frac{(8 \times 6) + 1}{8} = \frac{49}{8}$ — Note that the denominator stays the same.

Converting (Reducing) Fractions to Lowest Terms

When solving fraction problems, you always reduce the fractions to their lowest terms. This reduction does not change the value of the fraction. For example, in the bag of M&M's®, 5 out of 55 were green. The fraction for this is $\frac{5}{55}$. If you divide the top and bottom of the fraction by 5, you have reduced the fraction to $\frac{1}{11}$ without changing its value. Remember, we said in the chapter introduction that 1 out of 11 M&M's® in the bag of 55 M&M's® represents green candies. Now you know why this is true.

To reduce a fraction to its lowest terms, begin by inspecting the fraction, looking for the largest whole number that will divide into both the numerator and the denominator without leaving a remainder. This whole number is the **greatest common divisor,** which cannot be zero. When you find this largest whole number, you have reached the point where the fraction is reduced to its **lowest terms.** At this point, no number (except 1) can divide evenly into both parts of the fraction.

REDUCING FRACTIONS TO LOWEST TERMS BY INSPECTION

Step 1. By inspection, find the largest whole number (greatest common divisor) that will divide evenly into the numerator and denominator (does not change the fraction value).

Step 2. Now you have reduced the fraction to its lowest terms, since no number (except 1) can divide evenly into the numerator and denominator.

EXAMPLE $\dfrac{24}{30} = \dfrac{24 \div 6}{30 \div 6} = \dfrac{4}{5}$

Using inspection, you can see that the number 6 in the above example is the greatest common divisor. When you have large numbers, the greatest common divisor is not so obvious. For large numbers, you can use the following step approach to find the greatest common divisor:

STEP APPROACH FOR FINDING GREATEST COMMON DIVISOR

Step 1. Divide the smaller number (numerator) of the fraction into the larger number (denominator).

Step 2. Divide the remainder of Step 1 into the divisor of Step 1.

Step 3. Divide the remainder of Step 2 into the divisor of Step 2. Continue this division process until the remainder is a 0, which means the last divisor is the greatest common divisor.

EXAMPLE

$$\begin{array}{ccc} & \textbf{Step 1} & \textbf{Step 2} \\ \dfrac{24}{30} & \begin{array}{r} 1 \\ 24\overline{)30} \\ \underline{24} \\ 6 \end{array} & \begin{array}{r} 4 \\ 6\,\overline{)24} \\ \underline{24} \\ 0 \end{array} \end{array} \qquad \dfrac{24 \div 6}{30 \div 6} = \dfrac{4}{5}$$

Reducing a fraction by inspection is to some extent a trial-and-error method. Sometimes you are not sure what number you should divide into the top (numerator) and bottom (denominator) of the fraction. The following reference table on divisibility tests will be helpful. Note that to reduce a fraction to lowest terms might result in more than one division.

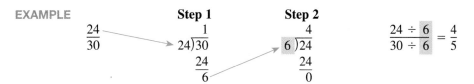

	2	3	4	5	6	10
Will divide evenly into number if	Last digit is 0, 2, 4, 6, 8.	Sum of the digits is divisible by 3.	Last two digits can be divided by 4.	Last digit is 0 or 5.	The number is even and 3 will divide into the sum of the digits.	The last digit is 0.
Examples	$\dfrac{12}{14} = \dfrac{6}{7}$	$\dfrac{36}{69} = \dfrac{12}{23}$ $3 + 6 = 9 \div 3 = 3$ $6 + 9 = 15 \div 3 = 5$	$\dfrac{140}{160} = \dfrac{1(40)}{1(60)}$ $= \dfrac{35}{40} = \dfrac{7}{8}$	$\dfrac{15}{20} = \dfrac{3}{4}$	$\dfrac{12}{18} = \dfrac{2}{3}$	$\dfrac{90}{100} = \dfrac{9}{10}$

Converting (Raising) Fractions to Higher Terms

Later, when you add and subtract fractions, you will see that sometimes fractions must be raised to **higher terms.** Recall that when you reduced fractions to their lowest terms, you looked for the largest whole number (greatest common divisor) that would divide evenly into both the numerator and the denominator. When you raise fractions to higher terms, you do the opposite and multiply the numerator and the denominator by the same whole number. For example, if you want to raise the fraction $\frac{1}{4}$, you can multiply the numerator and denominator by 2.

EXAMPLE $\quad \dfrac{1}{4} \times \dfrac{2}{2} = \dfrac{2}{8}$

The fractions $\frac{1}{4}$ and $\frac{2}{8}$ are **equivalent** in value. By converting $\frac{1}{4}$ to $\frac{2}{8}$, you only divided it into more parts.

Let's suppose that you have eaten $\frac{4}{7}$ of a pizza. You decide that instead of expressing the amount you have eaten in 7ths, you want to express it in 28ths. How would you do this?

To find the new numerator when you know the new denominator (28), use the steps that follow.

RAISING FRACTIONS TO HIGHER TERMS WHEN DENOMINATOR IS KNOWN
Step 1. Divide the *new* denominator by the *old* denominator to get the common number that raises the fraction to higher terms.
Step 2. Multiply the common number from Step 1 by the old numerator and place it as the new numerator over the new denominator.

EXAMPLE $\quad \dfrac{4}{7} = \dfrac{?}{28}$

Step 1. Divide 28 by 7 = 4.

Step 2. Multiply 4 by the numerator 4 = 16.

Result:

$$\dfrac{4}{7} = \dfrac{16}{28} \qquad \left(\textit{Note:} \text{ This is the same as multiplying } \dfrac{4}{7} \times \dfrac{4}{4}.\right)$$

Note that the $\frac{4}{7}$ and $\frac{16}{28}$ are equivalent in value, yet they are different fractions.

Now try the following Practice Quiz to check your understanding of this unit.

LU 2–1 | **PRACTICE QUIZ**

Complete this **Practice Quiz** to see how you are doing

1. Identify the type of fraction—proper, improper, or mixed:

   a. $\dfrac{4}{5}$ b. $\dfrac{6}{5}$ c. $19\dfrac{1}{5}$ d. $\dfrac{20}{20}$

2. Convert to a mixed number:

   $\dfrac{160}{9}$

3. Convert the mixed number to an improper fraction:

   $9\dfrac{5}{8}$

4. Find the greatest common divisor by the step approach and reduce to lowest terms:

   a. $\dfrac{24}{40}$ b. $\dfrac{91}{156}$

5. Convert to higher terms:

   a. $\dfrac{14}{20} = \dfrac{}{200}$ b. $\dfrac{8}{10} = \dfrac{}{60}$

✓ **Solutions**

1. **a.** Proper
b. Improper
c. Mixed
d. Improper

2.
$$17\tfrac{7}{9}$$
$$9\overline{)160}$$
$$\underline{9}$$
$$70$$
$$\underline{63}$$
$$7$$

3. $\dfrac{(9 \times 8) + 5}{8} = \dfrac{77}{8}$

4. **a.**
$$24\overline{)40} \qquad 16\overline{)24} \qquad 8\overline{)16}$$
$$\underline{24} \qquad\quad \underline{16} \qquad\quad \underline{16}$$
$$16 \qquad\quad 8 \qquad\quad\;\; 0$$

8 is greatest common divisor.

$$\frac{24 \div 8}{40 \div 8} = \frac{3}{5}$$

b.
$$91\overline{)156} \qquad 65\overline{)91} \qquad 26\overline{)65} \qquad 13\overline{)26}$$
$$\underline{91} \qquad\quad\; \underline{65} \qquad\quad \underline{52} \qquad\quad \underline{26}$$
$$65 \qquad\quad\; 26 \qquad\quad\; 13 \qquad\quad\;\; 0$$

13 is greatest common divisor.

$$\frac{91 \div 13}{156 \div 13} = \frac{7}{12}$$

5. **a.**
$$20\overline{)200}^{\;10} \qquad 10 \times 14 = 140 \qquad \frac{14}{20} = \frac{140}{200}$$

b.
$$10\overline{)60}^{\;6} \qquad 6 \times 8 = 48 \qquad \frac{8}{10} = \frac{48}{60}$$

LU 2–1a   EXTRA PRACTICE QUIZ

Need more practice? Try this **Extra Practice Quiz** (check figures in Chapter Organizer, p. 52)

1. Identify the type of fraction—proper, improper, or mixed:

a. $\dfrac{2}{5}$ **b.** $\dfrac{7}{6}$ **c.** $18\dfrac{1}{3}$ **d.** $\dfrac{40}{40}$

2. Convert to a mixed number (do not reduce):

$\dfrac{155}{7}$

3. Convert the mixed number to an improper fraction:

$8\dfrac{7}{9}$

4. Find the greatest common divisor by the step approach and reduce to lowest terms:

a. $\dfrac{42}{70}$ **b.** $\dfrac{96}{182}$

5. Convert to higher terms:

a. $\dfrac{16}{30} = \dfrac{}{300}$ **b.** $\dfrac{9}{20} = \dfrac{}{60}$

Learning Unit 2–2: Adding and Subtracting Fractions

TiVo Slashes Recorder Price In Half, to $50

Latest Cut Is Made to Fend Off Competition From Cable Giants; Comparing the Monthly Costs

——

By Nick Wingfield

——

FACED WITH growing competition from powerful rivals with cheaper products, TiVo Inc. sharply cut the prices on its digital video recorders.

The *Wall Street Journal* clipping "TiVo Slashes Recorder Price in Half, to $50" states that TiVo cut the price of its recorder in half $(\frac{1}{2})$. Since a whole is $\frac{2}{2}$ ($\frac{2}{2} = 1$), you can determine the new selling price of the recorder by subtracting the numerator of the fraction $\frac{1}{2}$ from the numerator of the fraction $\frac{2}{2}$. You can make this subtraction because you are working with *like fractions*—fractions with the same denominators. Then you can prove that you are correct by adding the numerators of the fractions $\frac{1}{2}$ and $\frac{1}{2}$.

In this unit you learn how to add and subtract fractions with the same denominators (**like fractions**) and fractions with different denominators (**unlike fractions**). We have also included how to add and subtract mixed numbers.

Addition of Fractions

When you add two or more quantities, they must have the same name or be of the same denomination. You cannot add 6 quarts and 3 pints unless you change the denomination of one or both quantities. You must either make the quarts into pints or the pints into quarts. The same principle also applies to fractions. That is, to add two or more fractions, they must have a **common denominator.**

Adding Like Fractions

In our TiVo clipping at the beginning of this unit we stated that because the fractions had the same denominator, or a common denominator, they were *like fractions*. Adding like fractions is similar to adding whole numbers.

ADDING LIKE FRACTIONS
Step 1. Add the numerators and place the total over the original denominator.
Step 2. If the total of your numerators is the same as your original denominator, convert your answer to a whole number; if the total is larger than your original denominator, convert your answer to a mixed number.

EXAMPLE $\dfrac{1}{7} + \dfrac{4}{7} = \boxed{\dfrac{5}{7}}$

The denominator, 7, shows the number of pieces into which some whole was divided. The two numerators, 1 and 4, tell how many of the pieces you have. So if you add 1 and 4, you get 5, or $\frac{5}{7}$.

Adding Unlike Fractions

Since you cannot add *unlike fractions* because their denominators are not the same, you must change the unlike fractions to *like fractions*—fractions with the same denominators. To do this, find a denominator that is common to all the fractions you want to add. Then look for the **least common denominator (LCD).**[2] The LCD is the smallest nonzero whole number into which all denominators will divide evenly. You can find the LCD by inspection or with prime numbers.

——

[2]Often referred to as the *lowest common denominator.*

Finding the Least Common Denominator (LCD) by Inspection The example that follows shows you how to use inspection to find an LCD (this will make all the denominators the same).

EXAMPLE $\dfrac{3}{7} + \dfrac{5}{21}$

Inspection of these two fractions shows that the smallest number into which denominators 7 and 21 divide evenly is 21. Thus, 21 is the LCD.

You may know that 21 is the LCD of $\frac{3}{7} + \frac{5}{21}$, but you cannot add these two fractions until you change the denominator of $\frac{3}{7}$ to 21. You do this by building (raising) the equivalent of $\frac{3}{7}$, as explained in Learning Unit 2–1. You can use the following steps to find the LCD by inspection:

Step 1. Divide the new denominator (21) by the old denominator (7): $21 \div 7 = 3$.

Step 2. Multiply the 3 in Step 1 by the old numerator (3): $3 \times 3 = 9$. The new numerator is 9.

Result:

$$\dfrac{3}{7} = \dfrac{9}{21}$$

Now that the denominators are the same, you add the numerators.

$$\dfrac{9}{21} + \dfrac{5}{21} = \dfrac{14}{21} = \dfrac{2}{3}$$

Note that $\frac{14}{21}$ is reduced to its lowest terms $\frac{2}{3}$. Always reduce your answer to its lowest terms.

You are now ready for the following general steps for adding proper fractions with different denominators. These steps also apply to the following discussion on finding LCD by prime numbers.

ADDING UNLIKE FRACTIONS
Step 1. Find the LCD.
Step 2. Change each fraction to a like fraction with the LCD.
Step 3. Add the numerators and place the total over the LCD.
Step 4. If necessary, reduce the answer to lowest terms.

Finding the Least Common Denominator (LCD) by Prime Numbers When you cannot determine the LCD by inspection, you can use the prime number method. First you must understand prime numbers.

PRIME NUMBERS
A **prime number** is a whole number greater than 1 that is only divisible by itself and 1. The number 1 is not a prime number.

EXAMPLES   2, 3, 5, 7, 11, 13, 17, 19, 23, 29, 31, 37, 41, 43

Note that the number 4 is not a prime number. Not only can you divide 4 by 1 and by 4, but you can also divide 4 by 2.

A whole number that is greater than 1 and is only divisible by itself and 1 has become a source of interest to some people. These people are curious as to what is the largest known prime number. The accompanying newspaper clipping answers this question. This number, of course, is the known number at the time of the writing of this clipping. Probably by the time you become impressed with this large prime number, someone will have discovered a larger prime number.

EXAMPLE $\dfrac{1}{3} + \dfrac{1}{8} + \dfrac{1}{9} + \dfrac{1}{12}$

6,320,430 Number of digits in the largest known prime number (divisible only by itself and 1), more than 2 million digits larger than the previous record holder

211,000 Number of PCs involved in finding the number

GREG L. KOHUTH–MICHIGAN STATE UNIVERSITY/AP

Time 2003

Step 1.   Copy the denominators and arrange them in a separate row.

3   8   9   12

Step 2.   Divide the denominators in Step 1 by prime numbers. Start with the smallest number that will divide into at least two of the denominators. Bring down any number that is not divisible. Keep in mind that the lowest prime number is 2.

$$2 \,/\!\!\underline{\begin{array}{cccc} 3 & 8 & 9 & 12 \end{array}}$$
$$\begin{array}{cccc} 3 & 4 & 9 & 6 \end{array}$$

Note: The 3 and 9 were brought down, since they were not divisible by 2.

Step 3.   Continue Step 2 until no prime number will divide evenly into at least two numbers.

Note: The 3 is used, since 2 can no longer divide evenly into at least two numbers.

$$2 \,/\!\!\underline{\begin{array}{cccc} 3 & 8 & 9 & 12 \end{array}}$$
$$2 \,/\!\!\underline{\begin{array}{cccc} 3 & 4 & 9 & 6 \end{array}}$$
$$3 \,/\!\!\underline{\begin{array}{cccc} 3 & 2 & 9 & 3 \end{array}}$$
$$\begin{array}{cccc} 1 & 2 & 3 & 1 \end{array}$$

Step 4.   To find the LCD, multiply all the numbers in the divisors (2, 2, 3) and in the last row (1, 2, 3, 1).

$$\boxed{2 \times 2 \times 3} \times \boxed{1 \times 2 \times 3 \times 1} = \boxed{72} \ \text{(LCD)}$$

Divisors   ×   Last row

Step 5.   Raise each fraction so that each denominator will be 72 and then add fractions.

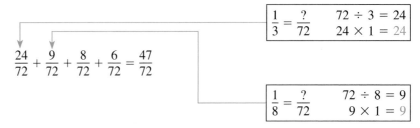

$$\boxed{\dfrac{1}{3} = \dfrac{?}{72} \qquad \begin{array}{l} 72 \div 3 = 24 \\ 24 \times 1 = 24 \end{array}}$$

$$\dfrac{24}{72} + \dfrac{9}{72} + \dfrac{8}{72} + \dfrac{6}{72} = \dfrac{47}{72}$$

$$\boxed{\dfrac{1}{8} = \dfrac{?}{72} \qquad \begin{array}{l} 72 \div 8 = 9 \\ 9 \times 1 = 9 \end{array}}$$

The above five steps used for finding LCD with prime numbers are summarized as follows:

FINDING LCD FOR TWO OR MORE FRACTIONS

Step 1.   Copy the denominators and arrange them in a separate row.

Step 2.   Divide the denominators by the smallest prime number that will divide evenly into at least two numbers.

Step 3.   Continue until no prime number divides evenly into at least two numbers.

Step 4.   Multiply all the numbers in divisors and last row to find the LCD.

Step 5.   Raise all fractions so each has a common denominator and then complete the computation.

Adding Mixed Numbers

The following steps will show you how to add mixed numbers:

ADDING MIXED NUMBERS

Step 1.   Add the fractions (remember that fractions need common denominators, as in the previous section).

Step 2.   Add the whole numbers.

Step 3.   Combine the totals of Steps 1 and 2. Be sure you do not have an improper fraction in your final answer. Convert the improper fraction to a whole or mixed number. Add the whole numbers resulting from the improper fraction conversion to the total whole numbers of Step 2. If necessary, reduce the answer to lowest terms.

Using prime numbers to find LCD of example

```
2 / 20   5   4
2 / 10   5   2
5 /  5   5   1
     1   1   1
```

$2 \times 2 \times 5 = 20$ LCD

EXAMPLE

$$4\frac{7}{20} \qquad 4\frac{7}{20}$$

$$6\frac{3}{5} \qquad 6\frac{12}{20}$$

$$+\,7\frac{1}{4} \qquad +\,7\frac{5}{20}$$

Step 1 → $\quad \dfrac{24}{20} = \quad 1\dfrac{4}{20}$

Step 2 $\quad +\;17$

Step 3 $\quad = 18\dfrac{4}{20} = 18\dfrac{1}{5}$

$$\frac{3}{5} = \frac{?}{20}$$

$$20 \div 5 = \quad 4$$

$$\times \; 3$$

$$\overline{\qquad 12}$$

Subtraction of Fractions

The subtraction of fractions is similar to the addition of fractions. This section explains how to subtract like and unlike fractions and how to subtract mixed numbers.

Subtracting Like Fractions

To subtract like fractions, use the steps that follow.

SUBTRACTING LIKE FRACTIONS
Step 1. Subtract the numerators and place the answer over the common denominator.
Step 2. If necessary, reduce the answer to lowest terms.

EXAMPLE $\quad \dfrac{9}{10} - \dfrac{1}{10} = \dfrac{8 \div 2}{10 \div 2} = \dfrac{4}{5}$

$\qquad\qquad\qquad\qquad\quad$ ↑ $\qquad$ ↑

$\qquad\qquad\qquad$ **Step 1** $\quad$ **Step 2**

Subtracting Unlike Fractions

Now let's learn the steps for subtracting unlike fractions.

SUBTRACTING UNLIKE FRACTIONS
Step 1. Find the LCD.
Step 2. Raise the fraction to its equivalent value.
Step 3. Subtract the numerators and place the answer over the LCD.
Step 4. If necessary, reduce the answer to lowest terms.

EXAMPLE

$$\begin{array}{cc} \dfrac{5}{8} & \dfrac{40}{64} \\[2ex] -\dfrac{2}{64} & -\dfrac{2}{64} \\[2ex] & \dfrac{38}{64} = \dfrac{19}{32} \end{array}$$

By inspection, we see that LCD is 64.
Thus $64 \div 8 = 8 \times 5 = 40$.

Subtracting Mixed Numbers

When you subtract whole numbers, sometimes borrowing is not necessary. At other times, you must borrow. The same is true of subtracting mixed numbers.

SUBTRACTING MIXED NUMBERS	
When Borrowing Is Not Necessary	*When Borrowing Is Necessary*
Step 1. Subtract fractions, making sure to find the LCD.	**Step 1.** Make sure the fractions have the LCD.
Step 2. Subtract whole numbers.	**Step 2.** Borrow from the whole number of the minuend (top number).
Step 3. Reduce the fraction(s) to lowest terms.	**Step 3.** Subtract the whole numbers and fractions.
	Step 4. Reduce the fraction(s) to lowest terms.

EXAMPLE   Where borrowing is not necessary: Find LCD of 2 and 8. LCD is 8.

$$6\frac{1}{2} \qquad\qquad\qquad 6\frac{4}{8}$$
$$-\frac{3}{8} \qquad\qquad\qquad -\frac{3}{8}$$
$$\qquad\qquad\qquad\qquad 6\frac{1}{8}$$

EXAMPLE   Where borrowing is necessary:

$$3\frac{1}{2} = \qquad 3\frac{2}{4} = \qquad 2\frac{6}{4}\ \left(\frac{4}{4} + \frac{2}{4}\right)$$
$$-1\frac{3}{4} = \qquad -1\frac{3}{4} = \qquad -1\frac{3}{4}$$
$$\text{LCD is } 4. \qquad\qquad\qquad\quad 1\frac{3}{4}$$

Since $\frac{3}{4}$ is larger than $\frac{2}{4}$, we must borrow 1 from the 3. This is the same as borrowing $\frac{4}{4}$. A fraction with the same numerator and denominator represents a whole. When we add $\frac{4}{4} + \frac{2}{4}$, we get $\frac{6}{4}$. Note how we subtracted the whole number and fractions, being sure to reduce the final answer if necessary.

How to Dissect and Solve a Word Problem

Let's now look at how to dissect and solve a word problem involving fractions.

The Word Problem The Albertsons grocery store has $550\frac{1}{4}$ total square feet of floor space. Albertsons' meat department occupies $115\frac{1}{2}$ square feet, and its deli department occupies $145\frac{7}{8}$ square feet. If the remainder of the floor space is for groceries, what square footage remains for groceries?

The facts	Solving for?	Steps to take	Key points
Total square footage: $550\frac{1}{4}$ sq. ft.	Total square footage for groceries.	Total floor space − Total meat and deli floor space = Total grocery floor space.	Denominators must be the same before adding or subtracting fractions.
Meat department: $115\frac{1}{2}$ sq. ft.			$\frac{8}{8} = 1$
Deli department: $145\frac{7}{8}$ sq. ft.			Never leave improper fraction as final answer.

Steps to solving problem

1. Calculate total square footage of the meat and deli departments.

Meat: $115\frac{1}{2} = \quad 115\frac{4}{8}$

Deli: $+\ 145\frac{7}{8} = +\ 145\frac{7}{8}$

$\qquad\qquad\qquad 260\frac{11}{8} = 261\frac{3}{8}$ sq. ft.

2. Calculate total grocery square footage.

$$550\frac{1}{4} = \quad 550\frac{2}{8} = \quad 549\frac{10}{8}$$
$$-261\frac{3}{8} = -261\frac{3}{8} = -261\frac{3}{8} \quad \left(\frac{2}{8}+\frac{8}{8}\right)$$
$$\boxed{288\frac{7}{8}} \text{ sq. ft.}$$

Check
$$261\frac{3}{8}$$
$$+288\frac{7}{8}$$
$$549\frac{10}{8} = 550\frac{2}{8} = 550\frac{1}{4} \text{ sq. ft.}$$

Note how the above blueprint aid helped to gather the facts and identify what we were looking for. To find the total square footage for groceries, we first had to sum the areas for meat and deli. Then we could subtract these areas from the total square footage. Also note that in Step 1 above, we didn't leave the answer as an improper fraction. In Step 2, we borrowed from the 550 so that we could complete the subtraction.

It's your turn to check your progress with a Practice Quiz.

LU 2–2 | **PRACTICE QUIZ**

Complete this **Practice Quiz** to see how you are doing

1. Find LCD by the division of prime numbers:

12, 9, 6, 4

2. Add and reduce to lowest terms if needed:

a. $\dfrac{3}{40} + \dfrac{2}{5}$

b. $2\dfrac{3}{4} + 6\dfrac{1}{20}$

3. Subtract and reduce to lowest terms if needed:

a. $\dfrac{6}{7} - \dfrac{1}{4}$

b. $8\dfrac{1}{4} - 3\dfrac{9}{28}$

c. $4 - 1\dfrac{3}{4}$

4. Computerland has $660\frac{1}{4}$ total square feet of floor space. Three departments occupy this floor space: hardware, $201\frac{1}{8}$ square feet; software, $242\frac{1}{4}$ square feet; and customer service, _____ square feet. What is the total square footage of the customer service area? You might want to try a blueprint aid, since the solution will show a completed blueprint aid.

✓ Solutions

1.
$$\begin{array}{c|cccc}
2 & 12 & 9 & 6 & 4 \\
2 & 6 & 9 & 3 & 2 \\
3 & 3 & 9 & 3 & 1 \\
& 1 & 3 & 1 & 1
\end{array}$$

$\text{LCD} = 2 \times 2 \times 3 \times 1 \times 3 \times 1 \times 1 = \boxed{36}$

2. a. $\dfrac{3}{40} + \dfrac{2}{5} = \dfrac{3}{40} + \dfrac{16}{40} = \boxed{\dfrac{19}{40}}$ $\quad \left(\begin{array}{c} \dfrac{2}{5} = \dfrac{?}{40} \\ 40 \div 5 = 8 \times 2 = 16 \end{array}\right)$

b.
$$2\dfrac{3}{4} \qquad 2\dfrac{15}{20}$$
$$+6\dfrac{1}{20} \qquad +6\dfrac{1}{20}$$
$$8\dfrac{16}{20} = \boxed{8\dfrac{4}{5}}$$

$\dfrac{3}{4} = \dfrac{?}{20}$

$20 \div 4 = 5 \times 3 = 15$

3. a.
$$\dfrac{6}{7} = \dfrac{24}{28}$$
$$-\dfrac{1}{4} = -\dfrac{7}{28}$$
$$\boxed{\dfrac{17}{28}}$$

b.
$$8\dfrac{1}{4} = 8\dfrac{7}{28} = 7\dfrac{35}{28} \qquad \left(\dfrac{28}{28}+\dfrac{7}{28}\right)$$
$$-3\dfrac{9}{28} = -3\dfrac{9}{28} = -3\dfrac{9}{28}$$
$$4\dfrac{26}{28} = \boxed{4\dfrac{13}{14}}$$

c.
$$3\dfrac{4}{4}$$
$$-1\dfrac{3}{4}$$
$$\boxed{2\dfrac{1}{4}}$$

Note how we showed the 4 as $3\dfrac{4}{4}$.

4. Computerland's total square footage for customer service:

The facts	Solving for?	Steps to take	Key points
Total square footage: $660\frac{1}{4}$ sq. ft. *Hardware:* $201\frac{1}{8}$ sq. ft. *Software:* $242\frac{1}{4}$ sq. ft.	Total square footage for customer service.	Total floor space − Total hardware and software floor space = Total customer service floor space.	Denominators must be the same before adding or subtracting fractions.

Steps to solving problem

1. Calculate the total square footage of hardware and software.

$$201\frac{1}{8} = \quad 201\frac{1}{8} \text{ (hardware)}$$
$$+\ 242\frac{1}{4} = +\ 242\frac{2}{8} \text{ (software)}$$
$$\overline{\qquad\qquad 443\frac{3}{8}}$$

2. Calculate the total square footage for customer service.

$$660\frac{1}{4} = \quad 660\frac{2}{8} = \ 659\frac{10}{8} \text{ (total square footage)}$$
$$-\ 443\frac{3}{8} = -\ 443\frac{3}{8} = -\ 443\frac{3}{8} \text{ (hardware plus software)}$$
$$\overline{\qquad\qquad 216\frac{7}{8} \text{ sq. ft. (customer service)}}$$

LU 2–2a   EXTRA PRACTICE QUIZ

Need more practice? Try this **Extra Practice Quiz** (check figures in Chapter Organizer, p. 52)

1. Find the LCD by the division of prime numbers:
10, 15, 9, 4

2. Add and reduce to lowest terms if needed:

   a. $\dfrac{2}{25} + \dfrac{3}{5}$ **b.** $3\dfrac{3}{8} + 6\dfrac{1}{32}$

3. Subtract and reduce to lowest terms if needed:

   a. $\dfrac{5}{6} - \dfrac{1}{3}$ **b.** $9\dfrac{1}{8} - 3\dfrac{7}{32}$ **c.** $6 - 1\dfrac{2}{5}$

4. Computerland has $985\frac{1}{4}$ total square feet of floor space. Three departments occupy this floor space: hardware, $209\frac{1}{8}$ square feet; software, $382\frac{1}{4}$ square feet; and customer service, _____ square feet. What is the total square footage of the customer service area?

Learning Unit 2–3: Multiplying and Dividing Fractions

The following recipe for Coconutty "M&M's"® Brownies makes 16 brownies. What would you need if you wanted to triple the recipe and make 48 brownies?

Coconutty "M&M's"® Brownies

   6 squares (1 ounce each) semi-sweet chocolate
   ½ cup (1 stick) butter
   ¾ cup granulated sugar
   2 large eggs
   1 tablespoon vegetable oil
   1 teaspoon vanilla extract
1¼ cups all-purpose flour
   3 tablespoons unsweetened cocoa powder
   1 teaspoon baking powder
   ½ teaspoon salt
1½ cups "M&M's"® Chocolate Mini Baking Bits, divided
   Coconut Topping (recipe follows)

Preheat oven to 350°F. Grease 8 × 8 × 2-inch pan; set aside. In small saucepan combine chocolate, butter, and sugar over low heat; stir constantly until smooth. Remove from heat; let cool. In bowl beat eggs, oil, and vanilla; stir in chocolate mixture until blended. Stir in flour, cocoa powder, baking powder, and salt. Stir in 1 cup "M&M's"® Chocolate Mini Baking Bits. Spread batter in prepared pan. Bake 35 to 40 minutes or until toothpick inserted in center comes out clean. Cool. Prepare a coconut topping. Spread over brownies; sprinkle with $\frac{1}{2}$ cup "M&M's"® Chocolate Mini Baking Bits.

In this unit you learn how to multiply and divide **fractions.**

Multiplication of Fractions

Multiplying fractions is easier than adding and subtracting fractions because you do not have to find a common denominator. This section explains the multiplication of proper fractions and the multiplication of mixed numbers.

MULTIPLYING PROPER FRACTIONS[3]
Step 1. Multiply the numerators and the denominators.
Step 2. Reduce the answer to lowest terms or use the cancellation method.

First let's look at an example that results in an answer that we do not have to reduce.

EXAMPLE $\dfrac{1}{7} \times \dfrac{5}{8} = \boxed{\dfrac{5}{56}}$

In the next example, note how we reduce the answer to lowest terms.

EXAMPLE $\dfrac{5}{1} \times \dfrac{1}{6} \times \dfrac{4}{7} = \dfrac{20}{42} = \boxed{\dfrac{10}{21}}$ Keep in mind $\dfrac{5}{1}$ is equal to 5.

We can reduce $\frac{20}{42}$ by the step approach as follows:

$$
\begin{array}{ccc}
2 & & 10 \\
20\overline{)42} & & 2\overline{)20} \\
\underline{40} & & \underline{20} \\
2 & & 0
\end{array}
$$

We could also have found the greatest common divisor by inspection.

$$\dfrac{20 \div 2}{42 \div 2} = \boxed{\dfrac{10}{21}}$$

As an alternative to reducing fractions to lowest terms, we can use the **cancellation** technique. Let's work the previous example using this technique.

EXAMPLE $\dfrac{5}{1} \times \dfrac{1}{\cancel{6}_{3}} \times \dfrac{\cancel{4}^{2}}{7} = \boxed{\dfrac{10}{21}}$ 2 divides evenly into 4 twice and into 6 three times.

Note that when we cancel numbers, we are reducing the answer before multiplying. We know that multiplying or dividing both numerator and denominator by the same number gives an equivalent fraction. So we can divide both numerator and denominator by any number that divides them both evenly. It doesn't matter which we divide first. Note that this division reduces $\frac{10}{21}$ to its lowest terms.

Multiplying Mixed Numbers

The following steps explain how to multiply mixed numbers:

MULTIPLYING MIXED NUMBERS
Step 1. Convert the mixed numbers to improper fractions.
Step 2. Multiply the numerators and denominators.
Step 3. Reduce the answer to lowest terms or use the cancellation method.

[3]You would follow the same procedure to multiply improper fractions.

EXAMPLE $$2\frac{1}{3} \times 1\frac{1}{2} = \frac{7}{\overset{1}{\cancel{3}}} \times \frac{\overset{1}{\cancel{3}}}{2} = \frac{7}{2} = \boxed{3\frac{1}{2}}$$

Step 1   Step 2   Step 3

Division of Fractions

When you studied whole numbers in Chapter 1, you saw how multiplication can be checked by division. The multiplication of fractions can also be checked by division, as you will see in this section on dividing proper fractions and mixed numbers.

Dividing Proper Fractions

The division of proper fractions introduces a new term—the **reciprocal.** To use reciprocals, we must first recognize which fraction in the problem is the divisor—the fraction that we divide by. Let's assume the problem we are to solve is $\frac{1}{8} \div \frac{2}{3}$. We read this problem as "$\frac{1}{8}$ divided by $\frac{2}{3}$." The divisor is the fraction after the division sign (or the second fraction). The steps that follow show how the divisor becomes a reciprocal.

DIVIDING PROPER FRACTIONS
Step 1. Invert (turn upside down) the divisor (the second fraction). The inverted number is the *reciprocal.*
Step 2. Multiply the fractions.
Step 3. Reduce the answer to lowest terms or use the cancellation method.

Do you know why the inverted fraction number is a reciprocal? Reciprocals are two numbers that when multiplied give a product of 1. For example, 2 (which is the same as $\frac{2}{1}$) and $\frac{1}{2}$ are reciprocals because multiplying them gives 1.

EXAMPLE $\dfrac{1}{8} \div \dfrac{2}{3}$ $\dfrac{1}{8} \times \dfrac{3}{2} = \boxed{\dfrac{3}{16}}$

Dividing Mixed Numbers

Now you are ready to divide mixed numbers by using improper fractions.

DIVIDING MIXED NUMBERS
Step 1. Convert all mixed numbers to improper fractions.
Step 2. Invert the divisor (take its reciprocal) and multiply. If your final answer is an improper fraction, reduce it to lowest terms. You can do this by finding the greatest common divisor or by using the cancellation technique.

EXAMPLE $8\dfrac{3}{4} \div 2\dfrac{5}{6}$

Step 1. $\dfrac{35}{4} \div \dfrac{17}{6}$

Step 2. $\dfrac{35}{\underset{2}{\cancel{4}}} \times \dfrac{\overset{3}{\cancel{6}}}{17} = \dfrac{105}{34} = 3\dfrac{3}{34}$ Here we used the cancellation technique.

How to Dissect and Solve a Word Problem

The Word Problem   Jamie Slater ordered $5\frac{1}{2}$ cords of oak. The cost of each cord is $150. He also ordered $2\frac{1}{4}$ cords of maple at $120 per cord. Jamie's neighbor, Al, said that he would share the wood and pay him $\frac{1}{5}$ of the total cost. How much did Jamie receive from Al?

Note how we filled in the blueprint aid columns. We first had to find the total cost of all the wood before we could find Al's share—$\frac{1}{5}$ of the total cost.

The facts	Solving for?	Steps to take	Key points
Cords ordered: $5\frac{1}{2}$ at \$150 per cord; $2\frac{1}{4}$ at \$120 per cord. *Al's cost share:* $\frac{1}{5}$ the total cost.	What will Al pay Jamie?	Total cost of wood $\times$ $\frac{1}{5}$ = Al's cost.	Convert mixed numbers to improper fractions when multiplying. Cancellation is an alternative to reducing fractions.

Steps to solving problem

1. Calculate the cost of oak.

$$5\frac{1}{2} \times \$150 = \frac{11}{\cancel{2}_1} \times \$\cancel{150}^{\$75} = \$825$$

2. Calculate the cost of maple.

$$2\frac{1}{4} \times \$120 = \frac{9}{\cancel{4}_1} \times \$\cancel{120}^{\$30} = +270$$

$$\overline{\$1,095} \text{ (total cost of wood)}$$

3. What Al pays.

$$\frac{1}{\cancel{5}_1} \times \$\cancel{1,095}^{\$219} = \boxed{\$219}$$

You should now be ready to test your knowledge of the final unit in the chapter.

LU 2–3 PRACTICE QUIZ

Complete this **Practice Quiz** to see how you are doing

1. Multiply (use cancellation technique):

   a. $\dfrac{4}{8} \times \dfrac{4}{6}$ **b.** $35 \times \dfrac{4}{7}$

2. Multiply (do not use canceling; reduce by finding the greatest common divisor):

   $\dfrac{14}{15} \times \dfrac{7}{10}$

3. Complete the following. Reduce to lowest terms as needed.

   a. $\dfrac{1}{9} \div \dfrac{5}{6}$ **b.** $\dfrac{51}{5} \div \dfrac{5}{9}$

4. Jill Estes bought a mobile home that was $8\frac{1}{8}$ times as expensive as the home her brother bought. Jill's brother paid \$16,000 for his mobile home. What is the cost of Jill's new home?

✓ Solutions

1. **a.** $\dfrac{\cancel{4}}{\cancel{8}} \times \dfrac{\cancel{4}}{\cancel{6}} = \dfrac{1}{3}$ **b.** $\cancel{35}^{5} \times \dfrac{4}{\cancel{7}_1} = \boxed{20}$

2. $\dfrac{14}{15} \times \dfrac{7}{10} = \dfrac{98 \div 2}{150 \div 2} = \boxed{\dfrac{49}{75}}$

$$
\begin{array}{cccccc}
1 & 1 & 1 & 7 & 1 & 2 \\
98\overline{)150} & 52\overline{)98} & 46\overline{)52} & 6\overline{)46} & 4\overline{)6} & 2\overline{)4} \\
\underline{98} & \underline{52} & \underline{46} & \underline{42} & \underline{4} & \underline{4} \\
52 & 46 & 6 & 4 & 2 & 0
\end{array}
$$

3. **a.** $\dfrac{1}{9} \times \dfrac{6}{5} = \dfrac{6 \div 3}{45 \div 3} = \boxed{\dfrac{2}{15}}$ **b.** $\dfrac{51}{5} \times \dfrac{9}{5} = \dfrac{459}{25} = \boxed{18\dfrac{9}{25}}$

4. Total cost of Jill's new home:

The facts	Solving for?	Steps to take	Key points
Jill's mobile home: $8\frac{1}{8}$ as expensive as her brother's. *Brother paid:* \$16,000.	Total cost of Jill's new home.	$8\frac{1}{8} \times$ Total cost of Jill's brother's mobile home = Total cost of Jill's new home.	Canceling is an alternative to reducing.

Steps to solving problem

1. Convert $8\frac{1}{8}$ to a mixed number. $\frac{65}{8}$

2. Calculate the total cost of Jill's home. $\frac{65}{\underset{1}{8}} \times \overset{\$2,000}{\cancel{\$16,000}} = \boxed{\$130,000}$

LU 2–3a | EXTRA PRACTICE QUIZ

Need more practice? Try this **Extra Practice Quiz** (check figures in Chapter Organizer, p. 52)

1. Multiply (use cancellation technique):

   a. $\frac{6}{8} \times \frac{3}{6}$ b. $42 \times \frac{1}{7}$

2. Multiply (do not use canceling; reduce by finding the greatest common divisor):

   $\frac{13}{117} \times \frac{9}{5}$

3. Complete the following. Reduce to lowest terms as needed.

   a. $\frac{1}{8} \div \frac{4}{5}$ b. $\frac{61}{6} \div \frac{6}{7}$

4. Jill Estes bought a mobile home that was $10\frac{1}{8}$ times as expensive as the home her brother brought. Jill's brother paid \$10,000 for his mobile home. What is the cost of Jill's new home?

CHAPTER ORGANIZER AND STUDY GUIDE
WITH CHECK FIGURES FOR EXTRA PRACTICE QUIZZES

Topic	Key point, procedure, formula	Example(s) to illustrate situation
Types of fractions, p. 35	*Proper:* Value less than 1; numerator smaller than denominator. *Improper:* Value equal to or greater than 1; numerator equal to or greater than denominator. *Mixed:* Sum of whole number greater than zero and a proper fraction.	$\frac{3}{5}, \frac{7}{9}, \frac{8}{15}$ $\frac{14}{14}, \frac{19}{18}$ $6\frac{3}{8}, 9\frac{8}{9}$
Fraction conversions, p. 36	*Improper to whole or mixed:* Divide numerator by denominator; place remainder over *old* denominator. *Mixed to improper:* $\frac{\text{Whole number} \times \text{Denominator} + \text{Numerator}}{\text{Old denominator}}$	$\frac{17}{4} = 4\frac{1}{4}$ $4\frac{1}{8} = \frac{32+1}{8} = \boxed{\frac{33}{8}}$
Reducing fractions to lowest terms, p. 37	1. Divide numerator and denominator by largest possible divisor (does not change fraction value). 2. When reduced to lowest terms, no number (except 1) will divide evenly into both numerator and denominator.	$\frac{18 \div 2}{46 \div 2} = \boxed{\frac{9}{23}}$
Step approach for finding greatest common denominator, p. 37	1. Divide smaller number of fraction into larger number. 2. Divide remainder into divisor of Step 1. Continue this process until no remainder results. 3. The last divisor used is the greatest common divisor.	$15 \longrightarrow 15\overline{)65} \quad 5\overline{)15}$ $65 \quad\quad \frac{60}{5} \quad\quad \frac{15}{0}$ $\boxed{5}$ is greatest common divisor.
Raising fractions to higher terms, p. 38	Multiply numerator and denominator by same number. Does not change fraction value.	$\frac{15}{41} = \frac{?}{410}$ $410 \div 41 = 10 \times 15 = \boxed{150}$

(continues)

CHAPTER ORGANIZER AND STUDY GUIDE
WITH CHECK FIGURES FOR EXTRA PRACTICE QUIZZES (Continued)

Topic	Key point, procedure, formula	Example(s) to illustrate situation
Adding and subtracting like and unlike fractions, p. 40	When denominators are the same (like fractions), add (or subtract) numerators, place total over original denominator, and reduce to lowest terms. When denominators are different (unlike fractions), change them to like fractions by finding LCD using inspection or prime numbers. Then add (or subtract) the numerators, place total over LCD, and reduce to lowest terms.	$\frac{4}{9} + \frac{1}{9} = \boxed{\frac{5}{9}}$ $\frac{4}{9} - \frac{1}{9} = \frac{3}{9} = \boxed{\frac{1}{3}}$ $\frac{4}{5} + \frac{2}{7} = \frac{28}{35} + \frac{10}{35} = \frac{38}{35} = \boxed{1\frac{3}{35}}$
Prime numbers, p. 41	Whole numbers larger than 1 that are only divisible by itself and 1.	2, 3, 5, 7, 11
LCD by prime numbers, p. 42	1. Copy denominators and arrange them in a separate row. 2. Divide denominators by smallest prime number that will divide evenly into at least two numbers. 3. Continue until no prime number divides evenly into at least two numbers. 4. Multiply all the numbers in the divisors and last row to find LCD. 5. Raise fractions so each has a common denominator and complete computation.	$\frac{1}{3} + \frac{1}{6} + \frac{1}{8} + \frac{1}{12} + \frac{1}{9}$ $\begin{array}{r|ccccc} 2 & 3 & 6 & 8 & 12 & 9 \\ 2 & 3 & 3 & 4 & 6 & 9 \\ 3 & 3 & 3 & 2 & 3 & 9 \\ \hline & 1 & 1 & 2 & 1 & 3 \end{array}$ $2 \times 2 \times 3 \times 1 \times 1 \times 2 \times 1 \times 3 = \boxed{72}$
Adding mixed numbers, p. 42	1. Add fractions. 2. Add whole numbers. 3. Combine totals of Steps 1 and 2. If denominators are different, a common denominator must be found. Answer cannot be left as improper fraction.	$1\frac{4}{7} + 1\frac{3}{7}$ Step 1: $\frac{4}{7} + \frac{3}{7} = \frac{7}{7}$ Step 2: $1 + 1 = 2$ Step 3: $2\frac{7}{7} = \boxed{3}$
Subtracting mixed numbers, p. 44	1. Subtract fractions. 2. If necessary, borrow from whole numbers. 3. Subtract whole numbers and fractions if borrowing was necessary. 4. Reduce fractions to lowest terms. If denominators are different, a common denominator must be found.	$12\frac{2}{5} - 7\frac{3}{5}$ $11\frac{7}{5} - 7\frac{3}{5}$ $= 4\frac{4}{5}$ Due to borrowing $\frac{5}{5}$ from number 12 $\frac{5}{5} + \frac{2}{5} = \frac{7}{5}$ The whole number is now 11.
Multiplying proper fractions, p. 47	1. Multiply numerators and denominators. 2. Reduce answer to lowest terms or use cancellation method.	$\frac{4}{7} \times \frac{7}{9} = \boxed{\frac{4}{9}}$
Multiplying mixed numbers, p. 47	1. Convert mixed numbers to improper fractions. 2. Multiply numerators and denominators. 3. Reduce answer to lowest terms or use cancellation method.	$1\frac{1}{8} \times 2\frac{5}{8}$ $\frac{9}{8} \times \frac{21}{8} = \frac{189}{64} = \boxed{2\frac{61}{64}}$
Dividing proper fractions, p. 48	1. Invert divisor. 2. Multiply. 3. Reduce answer to lowest terms or use cancellation method.	$\frac{1}{4} \div \frac{1}{8} = \frac{1}{4} \times \frac{8}{1} = \boxed{2}$

(continues)

CHAPTER ORGANIZER AND STUDY GUIDE
WITH CHECK FIGURES FOR EXTRA PRACTICE QUIZZES (Concluded)

Topic	Key point, procedure, formula	Example(s) to illustrate situation
Dividing mixed numbers, p. 48	1. Convert mixed numbers to improper fractions. 2. Invert divisor and multiply. If final answer is an improper fraction, reduce to lowest terms by finding greatest common divisor or using the cancellation method.	$1\frac{1}{2} \div 1\frac{5}{8} = \frac{3}{2} \div \frac{13}{8}$ $= \frac{3}{2} \times \frac{\overset{4}{8}}{13}$ $= \frac{12}{13}$

KEY TERMS	Cancellation, *p. 47*
	Common denominator, *p. 40*
	Denominator, *p. 40*
	Equivalent, *p. 38*
	Fraction, *p. 35*
	Greatest common
	  divisor, *p. 37*
		Higher terms, *p. 38*
		Improper fraction, *p. 35*
		Least common denominator
		  (LCD), *p. 40*
		Like fractions, *p. 40*
		Lowest terms, *p. 37*
		Mixed numbers, *p. 36* Numerator, *p. 35*
		Prime numbers, *p. 41*
		Proper fractions, *p. 35*
		Reciprocal, *p. 48*
		Unlike fractions, *p. 40*

CHECK FIGURE FOR EXTRA PRACTICE QUIZZES WITH PAGE REFERENCES	LU 2–1a (p. 39) 1. a. P b. I c. M d. I 2. $22\frac{1}{7}$ 3. $\frac{79}{9}$ 4. a. 14; $\frac{3}{5}$ b.2; $\frac{48}{91}$ 5. a. 160; b. 27	LU 2–2a (p. 46) 1. 180 2. a. $\frac{17}{25}$ b. $9\frac{13}{32}$ 3. a. $\frac{1}{2}$ b. $5\frac{29}{32}$ c. $4\frac{3}{5}$ 4. $393\frac{7}{8}$ ft.	LU 2–3a (p. 50) 1. a. $\frac{3}{8}$ b. 6 2. 117; $\frac{1}{5}$ 3. a. $\frac{5}{32}$ b. $11\frac{31}{36}$ 4. $101,250

Note: For how to dissect and solve a word problem, see page 44.

Critical Thinking Discussion Questions

1. What are the steps to convert improper fractions to whole or mixed numbers? Give an example of how you could use this conversion procedure when you eat at Pizza Hut.

2. What are the steps to convert mixed numbers to improper fractions? Show how you could use this conversion procedure when you order doughnuts at Dunkin' Donuts.

3. What is the greatest common divisor? How could you use the greatest common divisor to write an advertisement showing that 35 out of 60 people prefer MCI to AT&T?

4. Explain the step approach for finding the greatest common divisor. How could you use the MCI–AT&T example in question 3 to illustrate the step approach?

5. Explain the steps of adding or subtracting unlike fractions. Using a ruler, measure the heights of two different-size cans of food and show how to calculate the difference in height.

6. What is a prime number? Using the two cans in question 5, show how you could use prime numbers to calculate the LCD.

7. Explain the steps for multiplying proper fractions and mixed numbers. Assume you went to Staples (a stationery superstore). Give an example showing the multiplying of proper fractions and mixed numbers.

Name _____ Date _____

DRILL PROBLEMS

Identify the following types of fractions:

2–1. $\dfrac{11}{10}$

2–2. $12\dfrac{1}{8}$

2–3. $\dfrac{2}{9}$

Convert the following to mixed numbers:

2–4. $\dfrac{79}{8}$

2–5. $\dfrac{921}{15}$

Convert the following to improper fractions:

2–6. $8\dfrac{7}{8}$

2–7. $19\dfrac{2}{3}$

Reduce the following to the lowest terms. Show how to calculate the greatest common divisor by the step approach.

2–8. $\dfrac{16}{38}$

2–9. $\dfrac{44}{52}$

Convert the following to higher terms:

2–10. $\dfrac{9}{10} = \dfrac{}{70}$

Determine the LCD of the following (a) by inspection and (b) by division of prime numbers:

2–11. $\dfrac{3}{4}, \dfrac{7}{12}, \dfrac{5}{6}, \dfrac{1}{5}$ **Check**

    Inspection

2–12. $\dfrac{5}{6}, \dfrac{7}{18}, \dfrac{5}{9}, \dfrac{2}{72}$ **Check**

    Inspection

2–13. $\dfrac{1}{4}, \dfrac{3}{32}, \dfrac{5}{48}, \dfrac{1}{8}$ **Check**

    Inspection

Add the following and reduce to lowest terms:

2–14. $\dfrac{3}{9} + \dfrac{3}{9}$

2–15. $\dfrac{3}{7} + \dfrac{4}{21}$

2–16. $6\dfrac{1}{8} + 4\dfrac{3}{8}$

2–17. $6\dfrac{3}{8} + 9\dfrac{1}{24}$

2–18. $9\dfrac{9}{10} + 6\dfrac{7}{10}$

Subtract the following and reduce to lowest terms:

2–19. $\dfrac{11}{12} - \dfrac{1}{12}$

2–20. $14\dfrac{3}{8} - 10\dfrac{5}{8}$

2–21. $12\dfrac{1}{9} - 4\dfrac{2}{3}$

Multiply the following and reduce to lowest terms. Do not use the cancellation technique for these problems.

2–22. $17 \times \dfrac{4}{2}$

2–23. $\dfrac{5}{6} \times \dfrac{3}{8}$

2–24. $8\dfrac{7}{8} \times 64$

Multiply the following. Use the cancellation technique.

2–25. $\dfrac{4}{10} \times \dfrac{30}{60} \times \dfrac{6}{10}$

2–26. $3\dfrac{3}{4} \times \dfrac{8}{9} \times 4\dfrac{9}{12}$

Divide the following and reduce to lowest terms. Use the cancellation technique as needed.

2–27. $\dfrac{12}{9} \div 4$

2–28. $18 \div \dfrac{1}{5}$

2–29. $4\dfrac{2}{3} \div 12$

2–30. $3\dfrac{5}{6} \div 3\dfrac{1}{2}$

WORD PROBLEMS

2–31. *The Baltimore Sun* on January 10, 2007, ran a story about Cal Ripken being inducted in the Baseball Hall of Fame with $98\frac{1}{2}$ percent of the votes cast. Ripken was named on 537 of the 545 ballots submitted by the Baseball Writers' Association of America, the largest number of votes ever received. In order to be named to the Hall, a former player must receive at least $\frac{3}{4}$ of the votes cast. **(a)** What are the minimum votes needed to be inducted? **(b)** How many votes did Ripken receive over the total needed?

2–32. The February 2007 issue of *Taunton's Fine Woodworking* has measurements for constructing a country hutch. The measurements for the upper portion, in inches, were: $9\frac{3}{4}$, $12\frac{9}{16}$, $10\frac{3}{8}$, and $16\frac{7}{16}$. The total height of the hutch is $82\frac{3}{8}$ inches. **(a)** What is the height of the upper portion? **(b)** What is the height of the lower portion?

2–33. Jet Blue pays Paul Lose $140 per day to work in the maintenance department at the airport. Paul became ill on Monday and went home after $\frac{1}{4}$ of a day. What did he earn on Monday? Assume no work, no pay.

2–34. Britney Summers visited Curves and lost $2\frac{1}{4}$ pounds in week 1, $1\frac{3}{4}$ pounds in week 2, and $\frac{5}{8}$ pound in week 3. What is the total weight loss for Britney?

2–35. Joy Wigens, who works at Putnam Investments, received a check for $1,600. She deposited $\frac{1}{4}$ of the check in her Citibank account. How much money does Joy have left after the deposit?

2–36. Pete Hall worked the following hours as a manager for News.com: $12\frac{1}{4}$, $5\frac{1}{4}$, $8\frac{1}{2}$, and $7\frac{1}{4}$. How many total hours did Pete work?

2–37. *Woodsmith* magazine tells how to build a country wall shelf. The two side panels are $\frac{3}{4} \times 7\frac{1}{2} \times 31\frac{5}{8}$ inches long. **(a)** What is the total length of board you will need? **(b)** If you have a board $74\frac{1}{3}$ inches long, how much of the board will remain after cutting?

2–38. Lester bought a piece of property in Vail, Colorado. The sides of the land measure $115\frac{1}{2}$ feet, $66\frac{1}{4}$ feet, $106\frac{1}{8}$ feet, and $110\frac{1}{4}$ feet. Lester wants to know the perimeter (sum of all sides) of his property. Can you calculate the perimeter for Lester?

2–39. The February 2007 issue of *Woodsmith* provided measurements to construct a storage center. The measurements were, in inches, $31\frac{1}{2}$, $11\frac{1}{2}$, $5\frac{1}{2}$, $4\frac{3}{4}$, $31\frac{3}{8}$, and $43\frac{1}{2}$. The Home Depot has boards in 7 foot lengths. **(a)** What is the total length needed? **(b)** After cutting, how much of the board will be left over?

2–40. From Lowes, Pete Wong ordered $\frac{6}{7}$ of a ton of crushed rock to make a patio. If Pete used only $\frac{3}{4}$ of the rock, how much crushed rock remains unused?

2–41. At a Wal-Mart store, a Coke dispenser held $19\frac{1}{4}$ gallons of soda. During working hours, $12\frac{3}{4}$ gallons were dispensed. How many gallons of Coke remain?

2–42. Matt Kaminsky bought a home from Century 21 in San Antonio, Texas, that is $8\frac{1}{2}$ times as expensive as the home his parents bought. Matt's parents paid $20,000 for their home. What is the cost of Matt's new home?

2–43. Ajax Company charges $150 per cord of wood. If Bill Ryan orders $3\frac{1}{2}$ cords, what will his total cost be?

2–44. Learning.com bought 90 pizzas at Pizza Hut for their holiday party. Each guest ate $\frac{1}{6}$ of a pizza and there was no pizza left over. How many guests did Learning.com have for the party?

2–45. Marc, Steven, and Daniel entered into a Subway sandwich shop partnership. Marc owns $\frac{1}{9}$ of the shop and Steven owns $\frac{1}{4}$. What part does Daniel own?

2–46. Lionel Sullivan works for Burger King. He is paid time and one-half for Sundays. If Lionel works on Sunday for 6 hours at a regular pay of $8 per hour, what does he earn on Sunday?

2–47. Hertz pays Al Davis, an employee, $125 per day. Al decides to donate $\frac{1}{5}$ of a day's pay to his church. How much will Al donate?

2–48. A trip to the White Mountains of New Hampshire from Boston will take you $2\frac{3}{4}$ hours. Assume you have traveled $\frac{1}{11}$ of the way. How much longer will the trip take?

2–49. Andy, who loves to cook, makes apple cobbler for his family. The recipe (serves 6) calls for $1\frac{1}{2}$ pounds of apples, $\frac{1}{4}$ cups of flour, $\frac{1}{4}$ cup of margarine, $2\frac{3}{8}$ cups of sugar, and 2 teaspoons of cinnamon. Since guests are coming, Andy wants to make a cobbler that will serve 15 (or increase the recipe $2\frac{1}{2}$ times). How much of each ingredient should Andy use?

2–50. Mobil allocates $1{,}692\frac{3}{4}$ gallons of gas per month to Jerry's Service Station. The first week, Jerry sold $275\frac{1}{2}$ gallons; second week, $280\frac{1}{4}$ gallons; and third week, $189\frac{1}{8}$ gallons. If Jerry sells $582\frac{1}{2}$ gallons in the fourth week, how close is Jerry to selling his allocation?

2–51. A marketing class at North Shore Community College conducted a viewer preference survey. The survey showed that $\frac{5}{6}$ of the people surveyed preferred DVDs to videotapes. Assume 2,400 responded to the survey. How many favored using traditional tapes?

2–52. The price of a new Ford Explorer has increased to $1\frac{1}{4}$ times its earlier price. If the original price of the Ford Explorer was $28,000, what is the new price?

2–53. Chris Rong felled a tree that was 299 feet long. Chris decided to cut the tree into pieces $3\frac{1}{4}$ feet long. How many pieces can Chris cut from this tree?

2–54. Tempco Corporation has a machine that produces $12\frac{1}{2}$ baseball gloves each hour. In the last 2 days, the machine has run for a total of 22 hours. How many baseball gloves has Tempco produced?

2–55. McGraw-Hill/Irwin publishers stores some of its inventory in a warehouse that has 14,500 square feet of space. Each book requires $2\frac{1}{2}$ square feet of space. How many books can McGraw-Hill/Irwin keep in this warehouse?

2–56. Alicia, an employee of Dunkin' Donuts, receives $23\frac{1}{4}$ days per year of vacation time. So far this year she has taken $3\frac{1}{8}$ days in January, $5\frac{1}{2}$ days in May, $6\frac{1}{4}$ days in July, and $4\frac{1}{4}$ days in September. How many more days of vacation does Alicia have left?

2–57. Amazon.com offered a new portable color TV for $250 with a rebate of $\frac{1}{5}$ off the regular price. What is the final cost of the TV after the rebate?

2–58. Shelly Van Doren hired a contractor to refinish her kitchen. The contractor said the job would take $49\frac{1}{2}$ hours. To date, the contractor has worked the following hours:

Monday	$4\frac{1}{4}$
Tuesday	$9\frac{1}{8}$
Wednesday	$4\frac{1}{4}$
Thursday	$3\frac{1}{2}$
Friday	$10\frac{5}{8}$

How much longer should the job take to be completed?

ADDITIONAL SET OF WORD PROBLEMS

2–59. An issue of *Taunton's Fine Woodworking* included plans for a hall stand. The total height of the stand is $81\frac{1}{2}$ inches. If the base is $36\frac{5}{16}$ inches, how tall is the upper portion of the stand?

2–60. Albertsons grocery planned a big sale on apples and received 750 crates from the wholesale market. Albertsons will bag these apples in plastic. Each plastic bag holds $\frac{1}{9}$ of a crate. If Albertsons has no loss to perishables, how many bags of apples can be prepared?

2–61. Frank Puleo bought 6,625 acres of land in ski country. He plans to subdivide the land into parcels of $13\frac{1}{4}$ acres each. Each parcel will sell for $125,000. How many parcels of land will Frank develop? If Frank sells all the parcels, what will be his total sales?

If Frank sells $\frac{3}{5}$ of the parcels in the first year, what will be his total sales for the year?

2–62. A local Papa Gino's conducted a food survey. The survey showed that $\frac{1}{9}$ of the people surveyed preferred eating pasta to hamburger. If 5,400 responded to the survey, how many actually favored hamburger?

2–63. Tamara, Jose, and Milton entered into a partnership that sells men's clothing on the Web. Tamara owns $\frac{3}{8}$ of the company, and Jose owns $\frac{1}{4}$. What part does Milton own?

2–64. *Quilters Newsletter Magazine* gave instructions on making a quilt. The quilt required $4\frac{1}{2}$ yards of white-on-white print, 2 yards blue check, $\frac{1}{2}$ yard blue-and-white stripe, $2\frac{3}{4}$ yards blue scraps, $\frac{3}{4}$ yard yellow scraps, and $4\frac{7}{8}$ yards lining. How many total yards are needed?

2–65. A trailer carrying supplies for a Krispy Kreme from Virginia to New York will take $3\frac{1}{4}$ hours. If the truck traveled $\frac{1}{5}$ of the way, how much longer will the trip take?

2–66. Land Rover has increased the price of a FreeLander by $\frac{1}{5}$ from the original price. The original price of the FreeLander was $30,000. What is the new price?

2–67. Norman Moen, an employee at Subway, prepared a 90-foot submarine sandwich for a party. Norman decided to cut the submarine into sandwiches of $1\frac{1}{2}$ feet. How many sandwiches can Norman cut from this submarine?

CHALLENGE PROBLEMS

2–68. *Woodsmith* magazine gave instructions on how to build a pine cupboard. Lumber will be needed for 2 shelves $10\frac{1}{4}$ inches long, 2 base sides $12\frac{1}{2}$ inches long, and 2 door stiles $29\frac{1}{8}$ inches long. Your lumber comes in six-foot lengths. **(a)** How many feet of lumber will you need? **(b)** If you want $\frac{1}{2}$ a board left over, is this possible with two boards?

2–69. Jack MacLean has entered into a real estate development partnership with Bill Lyons and June Reese. Bill owns $\frac{1}{4}$ of the partnership, while June has a $\frac{1}{5}$ interest. The partners will divide all profits on the basis of their fractional ownership.

The partnership bought 900 acres of land and plans to subdivide each lot into $2\frac{1}{4}$ acres. Homes in the area have been selling for $240,000. By time of completion, Jack estimates the price of each home will increase by $\frac{1}{3}$ of the current value. The partners sent a survey to 12,000 potential customers to see whether they should heat the homes with oil or gas. One-fourth of the customers responded by indicating a 5-to-1 preference for oil. From the results of the survey, Jack now plans to install a 270-gallon oil tank at each home. He estimates that each home will need 5 fills per year. Current price of home heating fuel is $1 per gallon. The partnership estimates its profit per home will be $\frac{1}{8}$ the selling price of each home.

From the above, please calculate the following:

a. Number of homes to be built.

b. Selling price of each home.

c. Number of people responding to survey.

d. Number of people desiring oil.

d. Average monthly cost to run oil heat per house.

e. Amount of profit Jack will receive from the sale of homes.

 SUMMARY PRACTICE TEST

Identify the following types of fractions. *(p. 35)*

1. $5\frac{1}{8}$

2. $\frac{2}{7}$

3. $\frac{20}{19}$

4. Convert the following to a mixed number. *(p. 36)*

$$\frac{163}{9}$$

5. Convert the following to an improper fraction. *(p. 36)*

$$8\frac{1}{8}$$

6. Calculate the greatest common divisor of the following by the step approach and reduce to lowest terms. *(p. 37)*

$$\frac{63}{90}$$

7. Convert the following to higher terms. *(p. 38)*

$$\frac{16}{94} = \frac{?}{376}$$

8. Find the LCD of the following by using prime numbers. Show your work. *(p. 41)*

$$\frac{1}{8} + \frac{1}{3} + \frac{1}{2} + \frac{1}{12}$$

9. Subtract the following. *(p. 43)*

$$15\frac{4}{5}$$
$$-8\frac{19}{20}$$

Complete the following using the cancellation technique. *(p. 47)*

10. $\frac{3}{4} \times \frac{2}{4} \times \frac{6}{9}$

11. $7\frac{1}{9} \times \frac{6}{7}$

12. $\frac{3}{7} \div 6$

13. A trip to Washington from Boston will take you $5\frac{3}{4}$ hours. If you have traveled $\frac{1}{3}$ of the way, how much longer will the trip take? *(p. 49)*

14. Quizno produces 640 rolls per hour. If the oven runs $12\frac{1}{4}$ hours, how many rolls will the machine produce? *(p. 49)*

15. A taste-testing survey of Zing Farms showed that $\frac{2}{3}$ of the people surveyed preferred the taste of veggie burgers to regular burgers. If 90,000 people were in the survey, how many favored veggie burgers? How many chose regular burgers? *(p. 48)*

16. Jim Janes, an employee of Enterprise Co., worked $9\frac{1}{4}$ hours on Monday, $4\frac{1}{2}$ hours on Tuesday, $9\frac{1}{4}$ hours on Wednesday, $7\frac{1}{2}$ hours on Thursday, and 9 hours on Friday. How many total hours did Jim work during the week? *(p. 41)*

17. JCPenney offered a $\frac{1}{3}$ rebate on its $39 hair dryer. Joan bought a J.C. Penney hair dryer. What did Joan pay after the rebate? *(p. 48)*

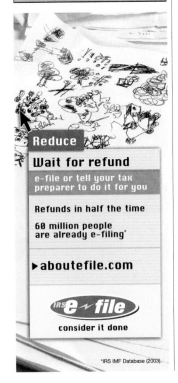
HEALTH | Retail kiosks offer routine services at a fraction of physician prices. *By Thomas M. Anderson*

CHECKUPS on the run

YOUR CHILD wakes up with an earache—and you take him to Target. You suspect your nagging cough may signal bronchitis, so you have it checked—at Wal-Mart. You don't need an appointment for either visit, the cost is a fraction of what you would have paid if you had cooled your heels in your doctor's office all morning, and your insurance might even cover it.

Walk-in clinics are coming soon to a retailer, pharmacy or grocery store near you. Minneapolis-based MinuteClinic, the country's largest chain of retail clinics, expects to have 250 facilities in 20 states by year-end.

Customers appreciate the convenience of one-stop shopping. Stores get a boost in sales of drugs and other health-related products. And patients and insurers save money as routine care, which accounts for one-fourth of U.S. health spending, moves out of doctor's offices and into settings with lower overhead.

At express medical clinics, one nurse practitioner usually runs the whole operation, from reception to diagnosis to prescription. A visit takes about 15 minutes per patient.

Retail clinics put a clear price tag on your health care. RediClinic, with kiosks in three Wal-Marts, charges a flat fee of $45 for all its basic services. A sore-throat checkup with a strep test costs $62 at a Minneapolis MinuteClinic, compared with $109 at a doc-

● MinuteClinic posts prices for services, which are often covered by insurance.

tor's office, $125 at an urgent-care center and $406 at an emergency room, according to the Minnesota Council of Health Plans.

Clinics generally accept cash and major credit cards. You can be reimbursed with money you've contributed to an employer-sponsored flexible-spending account or to a health savings account, and now some health insurers are picking up the tab.

MinuteClinic, for example, has signed agreements with Aetna, Cigna and United-Healthcare. If you're covered by one of those insurers, you'll pay your plan's co-payment rather than the full cost of the clinic visit. Some employers, including Best Buy, Black & Decker and Carlson Cos., offer lower co-payments to encourage employees to use MinuteClinics.

Retail clinics generally won't treat children younger than 18 months old. If you're on multiple medications or are older than 65, it's better to visit an urgent-care center or your doctor's office. If you have chest pain, head straight for the emergency room.

Have questions about using a clinic? "Call your family doctor," advises Larry Fields, president of the American Academy of Family Physicians. "It's free."

PROJECT A

What is the total cost of a Bentley boat? Prove your answer using fractions.

Luxury yachts, cars and RVs are among the goods available for fractional ownership.

All 1/8 of This Could Be Yours

Fractional Ownership Moves Beyond Jets to Include Yachts, Bentleys, Even Deluxe RVs

By RON LIEBER

TRAVELING THE INTERSTATE like a rock star seemed like a swell idea to Tom Roegner until he began to do the math.

The motor coach itself would cost more than a quarter million dollars, insurance and storage fees were expensive, and the depreciation would be immediate and dramatic. So the retired banker from Palos Heights, Ill. did what bankers before him have been doing with jets for years: he bought himself a chunk of the vehicle instead.

Fractional ownership, where buyers purchase a share of an expensive asset and pay the seller fees to handle the scheduling and maintenance, is a fixture of the private jet industry and a growing force in the market for vacation properties. Now, this model of ownership is creeping into other asset classes, too.

Increasingly it is becoming possible to buy a piece of a yacht, a fancy sports car, or even a luxury recreational vehicle—and share the use of it with other owners. **Exotic Car Share,** based in the Chicago suburb of Palatine, Ill., is in the middle of parceling out pieces of a new Bentley Conti-

usual boats and cars: an explosives-detection device that eight owners could share. Price: $2,475 each.

Despite the recent activity, there is still only a handful of companies offering fractional ownership outside aviation and real estate. But buyers and sellers say the economic logic behind shares in jets and vacation properties applies to other luxury discretionary goods, too.

Fractional ownership has been around in one form or another for quite a while, starting of course with the long-running practice of groups of friends going in on boats and condos. In the 1990s, the business of selling shares of small jets and managing them grew rapidly; it gained further respect in 1998 when Warren Buffett's **Berkshire Hathaway** bought the aircraft-sharing company NetJets.

Internet Projects: See text Web site (www.mhhe.com/slater9e) and The Business Math Internet Resource Guide.

CHAPTER 3

Decimals

LEARNING UNIT OBJECTIVES

LU 3–1: Rounding Decimals; Fraction and Decimal Conversions

- Explain the place values of whole numbers and decimals; round decimals (pp. 65–67).
- Convert decimal fractions to decimals, proper fractions to decimals, mixed numbers to decimals, and pure and mixed decimals to decimal fractions (pp. 67–70).

LU 3–2: Adding, Subtracting, Multiplying, and Dividing Decimals

- Add, subtract, multiply, and divide decimals (pp. 71–73).
- Complete decimal applications in foreign currency (p. 73).
- Multiply and divide decimals by shortcut methods (p. 74).

What It Costs to Buy Health Insurance

What a healthy 30-year-old would pay monthly for the most affordable private insurance policy available in the 10 most- and least-expensive major cities.

■ The 10 Cheapest Cities		■ The 10 Most Costly Cities	
Long Beach, Cailf.	$54.00	New York	$334.09
Sacramento, Calif.	56.00	Boston	267.57
Fresno, Calif.	56.00	Miami	151.20
San Diego	57.00	Dallas	146.42
Columbus, Ohio	57.91	Houston	146.28
San Jose, Calif.	58.00	Seattle	143.00
San Francisco	58.00	San Juan, P.R.	133.00
Oakland, Calif.	58.00	Washington, D.C.	132.00
Mesa, Ariz.	58.74	Fort Worth, Texas	129.53
Tucson, Ariz.	58.77	New Orleans	126.11

Source: eHealthInsurance.com

Wall Street Journal © 2005

Are you looking to buy health insurance? As you can see from the *Wall Street Journal* clipping "What It Costs to Buy Health Insurance," health insurance is $280.09 cheaper in Long Beach, California, than in New York:

New York: $334.09
Long Beach: −   54.00
                 $280.09

If you plan to move to another city, you might consider the cost of health insurance in that city. Also, remember that health insurance is a cost that continues to increase.

Chapter 2 introduced the 1.69-ounce bag of M&M's® shown in Table 3.1. In Table 3.1 (p. 66), the six colors in the 1.69-ounce bag of M&M's® are given in fractions and their values expressed in decimal equivalents that are rounded to the nearest hundredths.

This chapter is divided into two learning units. The first unit discusses rounding decimals, converting fractions to decimals, and converting decimals to fractions. The second unit shows you how to add, subtract, multiply, and divide decimals, along with some shortcuts for multiplying and dividing decimals. Added to this unit is a global application of decimals dealing with foreign exchange rates.

The increase in the United States of the cost of a stamp from $.39 to $.41 is indicated by decimals. If you think $.41 is high, compare this with Norway ($.87), Italy ($.73), Japan ($.57), and the United Kingdom ($.53). One of the most common uses of decimals occurs when we spend dollars and cents, which is a *decimal number*.

A **decimal** is a decimal number with digits to the right of a *decimal point*, indicating that decimals, like fractions, are parts of a whole that are less than one. Thus, we can interchange the terms *decimals* and *decimal numbers*. Remembering this will avoid confusion between the terms *decimal, decimal number,* and *decimal point*.

Learning Unit 3–1: Rounding Decimals; Fraction and Decimal Conversions

Remember to read the decimal point as *and*.

In Chapter 1 we stated that the **decimal point** is the center of the decimal numbering system. So far we have studied the whole numbers to the left of the decimal point and the parts of whole numbers called fractions. We also learned that the position of the digits in a whole number gives the place values of the digits (Figure 1.1, p. 3). Now we will study the position (place values) of the digits to the right of the decimal point (Figure 3.1, p. 66). Note that the words to the right of the decimal point end in *ths*.

You should understand why the decimal point is the center of the decimal system. If you move a digit to the left of the decimal point by place (ones, tens, and so on), *you increase its value 10 times for each place (power of 10)*. If you move a digit to the right of the decimal point by place (tenths, hundredths, and so on), *you decrease its value 10 times for each place.*

| TABLE | 3.1 |

Analyzing a bag of M&M's®

Sharon Hoogstraten

Color*	Fraction	Decimal
Yellow	$\frac{18}{55}$	.33
Red	$\frac{10}{55}$	.18
Blue	$\frac{9}{55}$	.16
Orange	$\frac{7}{55}$	.13
Brown	$\frac{6}{55}$	.11
Green	$\frac{5}{55}$	.09
Total	$\frac{55}{55} = 1$	1.00

*The color ratios currently given are a sample used for educational purposes. They do not represent the manufacturer's color ratios.

EXAMPLES $.06 \longrightarrow$ The 6 is in the hundred*ths* place value.

$1.527 \longrightarrow$ The 5 is in the ten*ths* place value.

$2.8394 \longrightarrow$ The 4 is in the ten thousand*ths* place value.

$.33 \longrightarrow$ The thirty-three hundred*ths* represents the yellow M&M's® in our M&M's® bag of 55 M&M's®.

1.69 oz. $\longrightarrow$ The one ounce and sixty-nine hundred*ths* of another ounce is the weight of our bag of M&M's®.

Do you recall from Chapter 1 how you used a place-value chart to read or write whole numbers in verbal form? To read or write decimal numbers, you read or write the decimal number as if it were a whole number. Then you use the name of the decimal place of the last digit as given in Figure 3.1. For example, you would read or write the decimal .0796 as seven hundred ninety-six ten thousandths (the last digit, 6, is in the ten thousandths place).

To read a decimal with four or fewer whole numbers, you can also refer to Figure 3.1. For larger whole numbers, refer to the whole-number place-value chart in Chapter 1 (Figure 1.1, p. 3). For example, from Figure 3.1 you would read the number 126.2864 as one hundred twenty-six and two thousand eight hundred sixty-four ten thousandths. Remember that the *and* is the decimal point.

Now let's round decimals. Rounding decimals is similar to the rounding of whole numbers that you learned in Chapter 1.

| FIGURE | 3.1 |

Decimal place-value chart

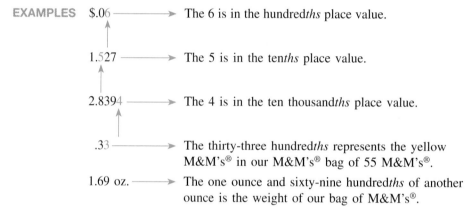

Whole Number Groups					Decimal Place Values				
Thousands	Hundreds	Tens	Ones (units)	Decimal point (and)	Tenths	Hundredths	Thousandths	Ten thousandths	Hundred thousandths
1,000	100	10	1	and	$\frac{1}{10}$	$\frac{1}{100}$	$\frac{1}{1,000}$	$\frac{1}{10,000}$	$\frac{1}{100,000}$

Rounding Decimals

From Table 3.1, you know that the 1.69-ounce bag of M&M's® introduced in Chapter 2 contained $\frac{18}{55}$, or .33, yellow M&M's®. The .33 was rounded to the nearest hundredth. **Rounding decimals** involves the following steps:

ROUNDING DECIMALS TO A SPECIFIED PLACE VALUE
Step 1. Identify the place value of the digit you want to round.
Step 2. If the digit to the right of the identified digit in Step 1 is 5 or more, increase the identified digit by 1. If the digit to the right is less than 5, do not change the identified digit.
Step 3. Drop all digits to the right of the identified digit.

Let's practice rounding by using the $\frac{18}{55}$ yellow M&M's® that we rounded to .33 in Table 3.1. Before we rounded $\frac{18}{55}$ to .33, the number we rounded was .32727. This is an example of a **repeating decimal** since the 27 repeats itself.

EXAMPLE   Round .3272727 to nearest hundredth.

Step 1.   .3272727   The identified digit is 2, which is in the hundredths place (two places to the right of the decimal point).

Step 2.   The digit to the right of 2 is more than 5 (7). Thus, 2, the identified digit in Step 1, is changed to 3.

.3372727

Step 3.   .33   Drop all other digits to right of the identified digit 3.

We could also round the .3272727 M&M's® to the nearest tenth or thousandth as follows:

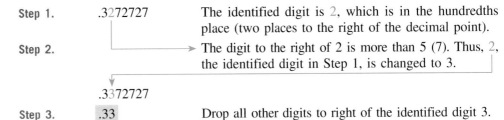

	Tenth	**or**	**Thousandth**
.3272727 ⟶	.3	.3272727 ⟶	.327

OTHER EXAMPLES

Round to nearest dollar:	$166.39	⟶	$166
Round to nearest cent:	$1,196.885	⟶	$1,196.89
Round to nearest hundredth:	$38.563	⟶	$38.56
Round to nearest thousandth:	$1,432.9981	⟶	$1,432.998

The rules for rounding can differ with the situation in which rounding is used. For example, have you ever bought one item from a supermarket produce department that was marked "3 for $1" and noticed what the cashier charged you? One item marked "3 for $1" would not cost you $33\frac{1}{3}$ cents rounded to 33 cents. You will pay 34 cents. Many retail stores round to the next cent even if the digit following the identified digit is less than $\frac{1}{2}$ of a penny. In this text we round on the concept of 5 or more.

Fraction and Decimal Conversions

In business operations we must frequently convert fractions to decimal numbers and decimal numbers to fractions. This section begins by discussing three types of fraction-to-decimal conversions. Then we discuss converting pure and mixed decimals to decimal fractions.

Converting Decimal Fractions to Decimals

From Figure 3.1 you can see that a **decimal fraction** (expressed in the digits to the right of the decimal point) is a fraction with a denominator that has a power of 10, such as $\frac{1}{10}$, $\frac{17}{100}$, and $\frac{23}{1,000}$. To convert a decimal fraction to a decimal, follow these steps:

CONVERTING DECIMAL FRACTIONS TO DECIMALS
Step 1. Count the number of zeros in the denominator.
Step 2. Place the numerator of the decimal fraction to the right of the decimal point the same number of places as you have zeros in the denominator. (The number of zeros in the denominator gives the number of digits your decimal has to the right of the decimal point.) Do not go over the total number of denominator zeros.

Now let's change $\frac{3}{10}$ and its higher multiples of 10 to decimals.

EXAMPLES

Verbal form	Decimal fraction	Decimal[1]	Number of decimal places to right of decimal point
a. Three tenths	$\frac{3}{10}$	.3	1
b. Three hundredths	$\frac{3}{100}$	.03	2
c. Three thousandths	$\frac{3}{1,000}$	.003	3
d. Three ten thousandths	$\frac{3}{10,000}$	.0003	4

Note how we show the different values of the decimal fractions above in decimals. The zeros after the decimal point and before the number 3 indicate these values. If you add zeros after the number 3, you do not change the value. Thus, the numbers .3 , .30 , and .300 have the same value. So 3 tenths of a pizza, 30 hundredths of a pizza, and 300 thousandths of a pizza are the same total amount of pizza. The first pizza is sliced into 10 pieces. The second pizza is sliced into 100 pieces. The third pizza is sliced into 1,000 pieces. Also, we don't need to place a zero to the left of the decimal point.

Converting Proper Fractions to Decimals

Recall from Chapter 2 that proper fractions are fractions with a value less than 1. That is, the numerator of the fraction is smaller than its denominator. How can we convert these proper fractions to decimals? Since proper fractions are a form of division, it is possible to convert proper fractions to decimals by carrying out the division.

CONVERTING PROPER FRACTIONS TO DECIMALS
Step 1. Divide the numerator of the fraction by its denominator. (If necessary, add a decimal point and zeros to the number in the numerator.)
Step 2. Round as necessary.

EXAMPLES

$$\frac{3}{4} = 4\overline{)3.00} \quad\quad \frac{3}{8} = 8\overline{)3.000} \quad\quad \frac{1}{3} = 3\overline{)1.000}$$

$$
\begin{array}{r} .75 \\ 4\overline{)3.00} \\ \underline{2\,8} \\ 20 \\ \underline{20} \end{array}
\qquad
\begin{array}{r} .375 \\ 8\overline{)3.000} \\ \underline{2\,4} \\ 60 \\ \underline{56} \\ 40 \\ \underline{40} \end{array}
\qquad
\begin{array}{r} .33\overline{3} \\ 3\overline{)1.000} \\ \underline{9} \\ 10 \\ \underline{9} \\ 10 \\ \underline{9} \\ 1 \end{array}
$$

[1]From .3 to .0003, the values get smaller and smaller, but if you go from .3 to .3000, the values remain the same.

Note that in the last example $\frac{1}{3}$, the 3 in the quotient keeps repeating itself (never ends). The short bar over the last 3 means that the number endlessly repeats.

Converting Mixed Numbers to Decimals

A mixed number, you will recall from Chapter 2, is the sum of a whole number greater than zero and a proper fraction. To convert mixed numbers to decimals, use the following steps:

CONVERTING MIXED NUMBERS TO DECIMALS
Step 1. Convert the fractional part of the mixed number to a decimal (as illustrated in the previous section).
Step 2. Add the converted fractional part to the whole number.

EXAMPLE

$$8\frac{2}{5} = \textbf{(Step 1)} \quad 5\overline{)2.0} \quad \begin{array}{r} .4 \\ \underline{2\ 0} \end{array} \qquad \textbf{(Step 2)} = \begin{array}{r} 8.00 \\ +\ .40 \\ \hline 8.40 \end{array}$$

Now that we have converted fractions to decimals, let's convert decimals to fractions.

Converting Pure and Mixed Decimals to Decimal Fractions

A **pure decimal** has no whole number(s) to the left of the decimal point (.43, .458, and so on). A **mixed decimal** is a combination of a whole number and a decimal. An example of a mixed decimal follows.

EXAMPLE   737.592 = Seven hundred thirty-seven and five hundred ninety-two thousandths

Note the following conversion steps for converting pure and mixed decimals to decimal fractions:

CONVERTING PURE AND MIXED DECIMALS TO DECIMAL FRACTIONS
Step 1. Place the digits to the right of the decimal point in the numerator of the fraction. Omit the decimal point. (For a decimal fraction with a fractional part, see examples **c** and **d** below.)
Step 2. Put a 1 in the denominator of the fraction.
Step 3. Count the number of digits to the right of the decimal point. Add the same number of zeros to the denominator of the fraction. For mixed decimals, add the fraction to the whole number.

If desired, you can reduce the fractions in Step 3.

EXAMPLES		Step 1	Step 2	Places	Step 3
a.	.3	$\frac{3}{}$	$\frac{3}{1}$	1	$\frac{3}{10}$
b.	.24	$\frac{24}{}$	$\frac{24}{1}$	2	$\frac{24}{100}$
c.	.24$\frac{1}{2}$	$\frac{245}{}$	$\frac{245}{1}$	3	$\frac{245}{1,000}$

Before completing Step 1 in example **c**, we must remove the fractional part, convert it to a decimal ($\frac{1}{2} = .5$), and multiply it by .01 ($.5 \times .01 = .005$). We use .01 because the 4 of .24 is in the hundredths place. Then we add $.005 + .24 = .245$ (three places to right of the decimal) and complete Steps 1, 2, and 3.

d.	.07$\frac{1}{4}$	$\frac{725}{}$	$\frac{725}{1}$	4	$\frac{725}{10,000}$

In example **d**, be sure to convert $\frac{1}{4}$ to .25 and multiply by .01. This gives .0025. Then add .0025 to .07, which is .0725 (four places), and complete Steps 1, 2, and 3.

$$\textbf{e.}\quad 17.45 \qquad \underline{45} \qquad \frac{45}{1} \qquad 2 \qquad \frac{45}{100} = 17\frac{45}{100}$$

Example **e** is a mixed decimal. Since we substitute *and* for the decimal point, we read this mixed decimal as seventeen and forty-five hundredths. Note that after we converted the .45 of the mixed decimals to a fraction, we added it to the whole number 17.

The Practice Quiz that follows will help you check your understanding of this unit.

LU 3–1   PRACTICE QUIZ

Complete this **Practice Quiz** to see how you are doing

DVD

Write the following as a decimal number.

1. Four hundred eight thousandths

Name the place position of the identified digit:

2. 6.8241   **3.** 9.3942

Round each decimal to place indicated:

	Tenth	**Thousandth**
4. .62768	**a.**	**b.**
5. .68341	**a.**	**b.**

Convert the following to decimals:

6. $\dfrac{9}{10,000}$ **7.** $\dfrac{14}{100,000}$

Convert the following to decimal fractions (do not reduce):

8. .819   **9.** 16.93   **10.** $.05\frac{1}{4}$

Convert the following fractions to decimals and round answer to nearest hundredth:

11. $\dfrac{1}{6}$ **12.** $\dfrac{3}{8}$ **13.** $12\frac{1}{8}$

✓ **Solutions**

1. .408 (3 places to right of decimal)

2. Hundredths   **3.** Thousandths

4. a. .6 (identified digit 6—digit to right less than 5)   **b.** .628 (identified digit 7—digit to right greater than 5)

5. a. .7 (identified digit 6—digit to right greater than 5)   **b.** .683 (identified digit 3—digit to right less than 5)

6. .0009 (4 places)   **7.** .00014 (5 places)

8. $\dfrac{819}{1,000}$ $\left(\dfrac{819}{1+3 \text{ zeros}}\right)$ **9.** $16\dfrac{93}{100}$

10. $\dfrac{525}{10,000}$ $\left(\dfrac{525}{1+4 \text{ zeros}} \dfrac{1}{4} \times .01 = .0025 + .05 = .0525\right)$

11. .16666 = .17   **12.** .375 = .38   **13.** 12.125 = 12.13

LU 3–1a   EXTRA PRACTICE QUIZ

Need more practice? Try this **Extra Practice Quiz** (check figures in Chapter Organizer, p. 78)

Write the following as a decimal number:

1. Three hundred nine thousandths

Name the place position of the identified digit:

2. 7.9324   **3.** 8.3682

Round each decimal to place indicated:

	Tenth	Thousandth
4. .84361	**a.**	**b.**
5. .87938	**a.**	**b.**

Convert the following to decimals:

6. $\dfrac{8}{10,000}$

7. $\dfrac{16}{100,000}$

Convert the following to decimal fractions (do not reduce):

8. .938   **9.** 17.95   **10.** $.03\frac{1}{4}$

Convert the following fractions to decimals and round answer to nearest hundredth:

11. $\dfrac{1}{8}$ **12.** $\dfrac{4}{7}$ **13.** $13\frac{1}{9}$

Learning Unit 3–2: Adding, Subtracting, Multiplying, and Dividing Decimals

People who are contemplating a career move to another city or state usually want to know the cost of living in that city or state. Also, you will hear retirees saying they are moving to another city or state because the cost of living is cheaper in this city or state. The following *Wall Street Journal* clipping "City by City" gives you some interesting statistics on the costs of various items in selected locations:

City by City

How the cost of living compares for selected locations (all amounts in U.S. dollars)

CITY	CUP OF COFFEE, WITH SERVICE	FAST-FOOD HAMBURGER MEAL	DRY CLEANING, MEN'S BLAZER	TOOTHPASTE, FLUORIDE, 4.2 OUNCES	2 MOVIE TICKETS, INT'L. RELEASE
Tokyo	$4.76	$5.99	$10.48	$2.02	$32.66
London	3.11	7.62	13.30	3.07	28.41
New York	3.30	5.75	8.80	3.12	20.00
Sydney	2.42	4.45	8.28	2.73	20.71
Chicago	2.10	4.99	9.99	3.23	18.00
San Francisco	3.52	5.29	6.50	2.48	19.50
Boston	2.90	4.39	5.25	2.05	18.00
Atlanta	1.71	3.70	5.95	2.24	16.00
Toronto	2.11	4.62	7.37	1.66	18.05
Rio de Janeiro	0.94	2.99	6.32	1.38	9.90

Source: Mercer Human Resource Consulting, 2004 Cost of Living Survey

If you frequent coffee restaurants, you might want to check the cost of a cup of coffee with service in various locations. The "City by City" clipping helps you do this. For example, a cup of coffee with service costs $1.71 in Atlanta, while a cup of coffee with service costs $4.76 in Tokyo. The coffee with service in Atlanta saves you $3.05 per cup. If you drink 1 cup of coffee per day for a year in Atlanta, you would save $1,113.25.

Tokyo: $4.76
Atlanta: − 1.71
              $3.05 × 365 days = $1,113.25

This learning unit shows you how to add, subtract, multiply, and divide decimals. You also make calculations involving decimals, including decimals used in foreign currency.

Addition and Subtraction of Decimals

Since you know how to add and subtract whole numbers, to add and subtract decimal numbers you have only to learn about the placement of the decimals. The following steps will help you:

ADDING AND SUBTRACTING DECIMALS
Step 1. Vertically write the numbers so that the decimal points align. You can place additional zeros to the right of the decimal point if needed without changing the value of the number.
Step 2. Add or subtract the digits starting with the right column and moving to the left.
Step 3. Align the decimal point in the answer with the above decimal points.

EXAMPLES Add $4 + 7.3 + 36.139 + .0007 + 8.22$.

Whole number to the right of the last digit is assumed to have a decimal.

$$
\begin{array}{r}
4.0000 \\
7.3000 \\
36.1390 \\
.0007 \\
8.2200 \\
\hline
55.6597
\end{array}
$$

Extra zeros have been added to make calculation easier.

Subtract $45.3 - 15.273$.

$$
\begin{array}{r}
^{2\ 9\ 10}\\
45.3\cancel{0}\cancel{0} \\
-15.273 \\
\hline
30.027
\end{array}
$$

Subtract $7 - 6.9$.

$$
\begin{array}{r}
^{6\ 10}\\
7.\cancel{0} \\
-6.9 \\
\hline
.1
\end{array}
$$

Multiplication of Decimals

The multiplication of decimal numbers is similar to the multiplication of whole numbers except for the additional step of placing the decimal in the answer (product). The steps that follow simplify this procedure.

MULTIPLYING DECIMALS
Step 1. Multiply the numbers as whole numbers ignoring the decimal points.
Step 2. Count and total the number of decimal places in the multiplier and multiplicand.
Step 3. Starting at the right in the product, count to the left the number of decimal places totaled in Step 2. Place the decimal point so that the product has the same number of decimal places as totaled in Step 2. If the total number of places is greater than the places in the product, insert zeros in front of the product.

EXAMPLES

Step 1
Step 2
$$
\begin{array}{r}
8.52 \quad (2\ \text{decimal places}) \\
\times\ 6.7 \quad (1\ \text{decimal place}) \\
\hline
5\ 964 \\
51\ 12 \\
\hline
57.084
\end{array}
$$
Step 3

$$
\begin{array}{r}
2.36 \quad (2\ \text{places}) \\
\times\ .016 \quad (3\ \text{places}) \\
\hline
1416 \\
236 \\
\hline
.03776
\end{array}
$$
Need to add zero

Division of Decimals

If the divisor in your decimal division problem is a whole number, first place the decimal point in the quotient directly above the decimal point in the dividend. Then divide as usual. If the divisor has a decimal point, complete the steps that follow.

DIVIDING DECIMALS
Step 1. Make the divisor a whole number by moving the decimal point to the right.
Step 2. Move the decimal point in the dividend to the right the same number of places that you moved the decimal point in the divisor (Step 1). If there are not enough places, add zeros to the right of the dividend.
Step 3. Place the decimal point in the quotient above the new decimal point in the dividend. Divide as usual.

EXAMPLE

Step 3

Step 1

Step 2

Stop a moment and study the above example. Note that the quotient does not change when we multiply the divisor and the dividend by the same number. This is why we can move the decimal point in division problems and always divide by a whole number.

Bargain Hunting

The dollar's fall creates deals for British shoppers in the U.S.

■ Apple iPod
(20GB: 5,000 songs)
New York City: **$299**

Wall Street Journal © 2004

Decimal Applications in Foreign Currency

The *Wall Street Journal* clipping "Bargain Hunting" showed the cost of an Apple iPod in New York City at $299. Using the updated currency table that follows, what would be the cost of the iPod in pounds? Check your answer.

Key Currency Cross Rates   Late New York Trading Wednesday, October 25, 2006

	Dollar	Euro	Pound	SFranc	Peso	Yen	CdnDlr
Canada	1.1256	1.4194	2.1145	0.8906	.10471	.00946	...
Japan	119.02	150.08	223.58	94.168	11.071	...	105.737
Mexico	10.7504	13.5562	20.195	8.5057	...	.09032	9.5506
Switzerland	1.2639	1.5938	2.3742	...	.11757	.01062	1.1229
U.K.	.53230	.6713	...	.4212	.04952	.00447	.47293
Euro	.79300	...	1.4897	.62744	.07377	.00666	.70452
U.S.	...	1.2610	1.8785	.79120	.09302	.00840	.88840

Source: Reuters

Wall Street Journal © 2006

EXAMPLE

$$\$299 \times .53230 = \boxed{159.1577} \text{ pounds}$$

Check   159.1577 pounds × 1.8785 = $298.98 (cost of iPod in New York City)

Multiplication and Division Shortcuts for Decimals

The shortcut steps that follow show how to solve multiplication and division problems quickly involving multiples of 10 (10,100, 1,000, 10,000, etc.).

SHORTCUTS FOR MULTIPLES OF 10
Multiplication
Step 1. Count the zeros in the multiplier.
Step 2. Move the decimal point in the multiplicand the same number of places to the right as you have zeros in the multiplier.
Division
Step 1. Count the zeros in the divisor.
Step 2. Move the decimal point in the dividend the same number of places to the left as you have zeros in the divisor.

In multiplication, the answers are *larger* than the original number.

Ric Francis/AP Wide World

EXAMPLE   If Toyota spends $60,000 for magazine advertising, what is the total value if it spends this same amount for 10 years? What would be the total cost?

$60,000 \times 10 = \boxed{\$600,000}$ (1 place to the right)

OTHER EXAMPLES $6.89 \times 10 = \boxed{68.9}$ (1 place to the right)

$6.89 \times 100 = \boxed{689.}$ (2 places to the right)

$6.89 \times 1,000 = \boxed{6,890.}$ (3 places to the right)

In division, the answers are *smaller* than the original number.

EXAMPLES $6.89 \div 10 = \boxed{.689}$ (1 place to the left)

$6.89 \div 100 = \boxed{.0689}$ (2 places to the left)

$6.89 \div 1,000 = \boxed{.00689}$ (3 places to the left)

$6.89 \div 10,000 = \boxed{.000689}$ (4 places to the left)

Next, let's dissect and solve a word problem.

How to Dissect and Solve a Word Problem

The Word Problem May O'Mally went to Sears to buy wall-to-wall carpet. She needs 101.3 square yards for downstairs, 16.3 square yards for the upstairs bedrooms, and 6.2 square yards for the halls. The carpet cost $14.55 per square yard. The padding cost $3.25 per square yard. Sears quoted an installation charge of $6.25 per square yard. What was May O'Mally's total cost?

By completing the following blueprint aid, we will slowly dissect this word problem. Note that before solving the problem, we gather the facts, identify what we are solving for, and list the steps that must be completed before finding the final answer, along with any key points we should remember. Let's go to it!

The facts	Solving for?	Steps to take	Key points
Carpet needed: 101.3 sq. yd.; 16.3 sq. yd.; 6.2 sq. yd. *Costs:* Carpet, $14.55 per sq. yd.; padding, $3.25 per sq. yd.; installation, $6.25 per sq. yd.	Total cost of carpet	Total square yards × Cost per square yard = Total cost.	Align decimals. Round answer to nearest cent.

Steps to solving problem

1. Calculate the total number of square yards.

101.3
16.3
6.2
───
123.8 square yards

2. Calculate the total cost per square yard.

$14.55
3.25
6.25
───
$24.05

3. Calculate the total cost of carpet.

123.8 × $24.05 = $2,977.39

It's time to check your progress.

LU 3–2   PRACTICE QUIZ

Complete this **Practice Quiz**
to see how you are doing

1. Rearrange vertically and add:
   14, .642, 9.34, 15.87321

2. Rearrange and subtract:
   28.1549 − .885

3. Multiply and round the answer to the nearest tenth:
   28.53 × 17.4

4. Divide and round to the nearest hundredth:
   2,182 ÷ 2.83

Complete by the shortcut method:

5. 14.28 × 100   6. 9,680 ÷ 1,000   7. 9,812 ÷ 10,000

8. Could you help Mel decide which product is the "better buy"?
   Dog food A: $9.01 for 64 ounces   **Dog food B:** $7.95 for 50 ounces

Round to the nearest cent as needed.

9. At Avis Rent-A-Car, the cost per day to rent a medium-size car is $39.99 plus 29 cents per mile. What will it cost to rent this car for 2 days if you drive 602.3 miles? Since the solution shows a completed blueprint, you might use a blueprint also.

10. A trip to Mexico cost 6,000 pesos. What would this be in U.S. dollars? Check your answer.

✓ **Solutions**

1. 14.00000
   .64200
   9.34000
   15.87321
   ────────
   39.85521

2.   7 10 14 14
   28.1549
   − .8850
   ───────
   27.2699

3.   28.53
     × 17.4
     ──────
     11 412
     199 71
     285 3
     ──────
     496.422 = 496.4

4.   771.024 = 771.02
   2.83)218200.000
         1981
         ────
         2010
         1981
         ────
          290
          283
          ───
          7 00
          5 66
          ────
          1 340
          1 132

5. 14.28 = 1,428   6. 9.680 = 9.680   7. .9812 = .9812

8. A: $9.01 ÷ 64 = $.14   B: $7.95 ÷ 50 = $.16   Buy A.

9. Avis Rent-A-Car total rental charge:

The facts	Solving for?	Steps to take	Key points
Cost per day, $39.99. 29 cents per mile. Drove 602.3 miles. 2-day rental.	Total rental charge.	Total cost for 2 days' rental + Total cost of driving = Total rental charge.	In multiplication, count the number of decimal places. Starting from right to left in the product, insert decimal in appropriate place. Round to nearest cent.

Steps to solving problem

1. Calculate total costs for 2 days' rental. $39.99 × 2 = $79.98

2. Calculate the total cost of driving. $.29 × 602.3 = $174.667 = $174.67

3. Calculate the total rental charge.

$ 79.98
+ 174.67
$254.65

10. 6,000 × $.09302 = $558.12

   Check $558.12 × 10.7504 = 6.000.01 pesos due to rounding

LU 3–2a EXTRA PRACTICE QUIZ

Need more practice? Try this **Extra Practice Quiz** (check figures in Chapter Organizer, p. 78)

1. Rearrange vertically and add:
16, .831, 9.85, 17.8321

2. Rearrange and subtract:
29.5832 − .998

3. Multiply and round the answer to the nearest tenth:
29.64 × 18.2

4. Divide and round to the nearest hundredth:
3,824 ÷ 4.94

Complete by the shortcut method:

5. 17.48 × 100   **6.** 8,432 ÷ 1,000   **7.** 9,643 ÷ 10,000

8. Could you help Mel decide which product is the "better buy"?
   Dog food A: $8.88 for 64 ounces   **Dog food B:** $7.25 for 50 ounces

Round to the nearest cent as needed:

9. At Avis Rent-A-Car, the cost per day to rent a medium-size car is $29.99 plus 22 cents per mile. What will it cost to rent this car for 2 days if you drive 709.8 miles?

10. A trip to Mexico costs 7,000 pesos. What would this be in U.S. dollars? Check your answer.

CHAPTER ORGANIZER AND STUDY GUIDE
WITH CHECK FIGURES FOR EXTRA PRACTICE QUIZZES

Topic	Key point, procedure, formula	Example(s) to illustrate situation
Identifying place value, p. 66	$10, 1, \frac{1}{10}, \frac{1}{100}, \frac{1}{1,000}$, etc.	.439 in thousandths place value
Rounding decimals, p. 67	1. Identify place value of digit you want to round. 2. If digit to right of identified digit in Step 1 is 5 or more, increase identified digit by 1; if less than 5, do not change identified digit. 3. Drop all digits to right of identified digit.	.875 rounded to nearest tenth = .9 Identified digit

(continues)

CHAPTER ORGANIZER AND STUDY GUIDE
WITH CHECK FIGURES FOR EXTRA PRACTICE QUIZZES (continued)

Topic	Key point, procedure, formula	Example(s) to illustrate situation
Converting decimal fractions to decimals, p. 68	1. Decimal fraction has a denominator with multiples of 10. Count number of zeros in denominator. 2. Zeros show how many places are in the decimal.	$\dfrac{8}{1,000} = .008$ $\dfrac{6}{10,000} = .0006$
Converting proper fractions to decimals, p. 68	1. Divide numerator of fraction by its denominator. 2. Round as necessary.	$\dfrac{1}{3}$ (to nearest tenth) $= .3$
Converting mixed numbers to decimals, p. 69	1. Convert fractional part of the mixed number to a decimal. 2. Add converted fractional part to whole number.	$6\dfrac{1}{4}$ $\dfrac{1}{4} = .25 + 6 = 6.25$
Converting pure and mixed decimals to decimal fractions, p. 69	1. Place digits to right of decimal point in numerator of fraction. 2. Put 1 in denominator. 3. Add zeros to denominator, depending on decimal places of original number. For mixed decimals, add fraction to whole number.	.984 (3 places) 1. $\dfrac{984}{}$ 2. $\dfrac{984}{1}$ 3. $\dfrac{984}{1,000}$
Adding and subtracting decimals, p. 71	1. Vertically write and align numbers on decimal points. 2. Add or subtract digits, starting with right column and moving to the left. 3. Align decimal point in answer with above decimal points.	Add $1.3 + 2 + .4$ 1.3 2.0 .4 3.7 Subtract $5 - 3.9$ $\overset{4\ 10}{\cancel{5}.0}$ -3.9 1.1
Multiplying decimals, p. 72	1. Multiply numbers, ignoring decimal points. 2. Count and total number of decimal places in multiplier and multiplicand. 3. Starting at right in the product, count to the left the number of decimal places totaled in Step 2. Insert decimal point. If number of places greater than space in answer, add zeros.	2.48 (2 places) $\times .018$ (3 places) 1 984 2 48 .04464
Dividing a decimal by a whole number, p. 73	1. Place decimal point in quotient directly above the decimal point in dividend. 2. Divide as usual.	$\begin{array}{r} 1.1 \\ 42\overline{)46.2} \\ \underline{42} \\ 42 \\ \underline{42} \end{array}$
Dividing if the divisor is a decimal, p. 73	1. Make divisor a whole number by moving decimal point to the right. 2. Move decimal point in dividend to the right the same number of places as in Step 1. 3. Place decimal point in quotient above decimal point in dividend. Divide as usual.	$\begin{array}{r} 14.2 \\ 2.9\overline{)41.39} \\ \underline{29} \\ 123 \\ \underline{116} \\ 79 \\ \underline{58} \\ 21 \end{array}$

(continues)

CHAPTER ORGANIZER AND STUDY GUIDE
WITH CHECK FIGURES FOR EXTRA PRACTICE QUIZZES (concluded)

Topic	Key point, procedure, formula	Example(s) to illustrate situation
Shortcuts on multiplication and division of decimals, p. 74	When multiplying by 10, 100, 1,000, and so on, move decimal point in multiplicand the same number of places to the right as you have zeros in multiplier. For division, move decimal point to the left.	$4.85 \times 100 = 485$ $4.85 \div 100 = .0485$
KEY TERMS	Decimal, *p. 65* Mixed decimal, *p. 69* Rounding decimals, *p. 67* Decimal fraction, *p. 67* Pure decimal, *p. 69* Decimal point, *p. 65* Repeating decimal, *p. 67*	

CHECK FIGURES FOR EXTRA PRACTICE QUIZZES WITH PAGE REFERENCES

LU 3–1a (p. 70)		LU 3–2a (p. 76)	
1. .309	8. $\dfrac{938}{1,000}$	1. 44.5131	6. 8.432
2. Hundredths		2. 28.5852	7. .9643
3. Ten-thousandths	9. $17\dfrac{95}{100}$	3. 539.4	8. Buy A $.14
4. A. .8		4. 774.09	9. $216.14
B. .844	10. $\dfrac{325}{10,000}$	5. 1,748	10. $651.14
5. A. .9	11. .13		
B. .879	12. .57		
6. .0008	13. 13.11		
7. .00016			

Note: For how to dissect and solve a word problem, see page 74.

Critical Thinking Discussion Questions

1. What are the steps for rounding decimals? Federal income tax forms allow the taxpayer to round each amount to the nearest dollar. Do you agree with this?

2. Explain how to convert fractions to decimals. If 1 out of 20 people buys a Land Rover, how could you write an advertisement in decimals?

3. Explain why .07, .70, and .700 are not equal. Assume you take a family trip to Disney World that covers 500 miles. Show that $\frac{8}{10}$ of the trip, or .8 of the trip, represents 400 miles.

4. Explain the steps in the addition or subtraction of decimals. Visit a car dealership and find the difference between two sticker prices. Be sure to check each sticker price for accuracy. Should you always pay the sticker price?

Name _____ Date _____

DRILL PROBLEMS

Identify the place value for the following

3–1. 8.56932
↑

3–2. 293.9438
↑

Round the following as indicated:

	Tenth	**Hundredth**	**Thousandth**
3–3. .7582			
3–4. 4.9832			
3–5. 5.8312			
3–6. 6.8415			
3–7. 6.5555			
3–8. 75.9913			

Round the following to the nearest cent:

3–9. $4,822.775

3–10. $4,892.046

Convert the following types of decimal fractions to decimals (round to nearest hundredth as needed):

3–11. $\dfrac{9}{100}$

3–12. $\dfrac{3}{10}$

3–13. $\dfrac{91}{1,000}$

3–14. $\dfrac{910}{1,000}$

3–15. $\dfrac{64}{100}$

3–16. $\dfrac{979}{1,000}$

3–17. $14\dfrac{91}{100}$

Convert the following decimals to fractions. Do not reduce to lowest terms.

3–18. .3

3–19. .62

3–20. .006

3–21. .0125

3–22. .609

3–23. .825

3–24. .9999

3–25. .7065

Convert the following to mixed numbers. Do not reduce to the lowest terms.

3–26. 7.4

3–27. 28.48

3–28. 6.025

Write the decimal equivalent of the following:

3–29. Four thousandths

3–30. Three hundred three and two hundredths

3–31. Eighty-five ten thousandths

3–32. Seven hundred seventy-five thousandths

Rearrange the following and add:

3–33. .115, 10.8318, 4.7, 802.4811

3–34. .005, 2,002.181, 795.41, 14.0, .184

Rearrange the following and subtract:

3–35. 9.2 − 5.8

3–36. 7 − 2.0815

3–37. 3.4 − 1.08

Estimate by rounding all the way and multiply the following (do not round final answer):

3–38. 6.24 × 3.9

Estimate

3–40. 675 × 1.92

Estimate

3–39. .413 × 3.07

Estimate

3–41. 4.9 × .825

Estimate

Divide the following and round to the nearest hundredth:

3–42. .8931 ÷ 3

3–44. .0065 ÷ .07

3–46. 8.95 ÷ 1.18

3–43. 29.432 ÷ .0012

3–45. 7,742.1 ÷ 48

3–47. 2,600 ÷ .381

Convert the following to decimals and round to the nearest hundredth:

3–48. $\frac{1}{8}$

3–49. $\frac{1}{25}$

3–50. $\frac{5}{6}$

3–51. $\frac{5}{8}$

Complete these multiplications and divisions by the shortcut method (do not do any written calculations):

3–52. 96.7 ÷ 10

3–55. .86 ÷ 100

3–58. 750 × 10

3–61. 7.9132 × 1,000

3–53. 258.5 ÷ 100

3–56. 9.015 × 100

3–59. 3,950 ÷ 1,000

3–54. 8.51 × 1,000

3–57. 48.6 × 10

3–60. 8.45 ÷ 10

WORD PROBLEMS

As needed, round answers to the nearest cent.

3–62. A Ford Explorer costs $ 30,000. What would be the cost in pounds in London? Use the currency table and check your answer.

3–63. Ken Griffey, Jr. got 7 hits out of 12 at bats. What was his batting average to the nearest thousandths place?

3–64. An article in *The Boston Globe* dated January 11, 2007 reported ticket prices for Rod Stewart's February 3rd concert at the TD Banknorth Garden at $125 per ticket. In addition to the price of a ticket, there is a $14.80 convenience charge, a $2.50 facility fee, and a $2.50 electronic delivery fee. Richard Evans purchased 4 tickets to the concert. What was Richard's total cost for the tickets?

3–65. At Wal-Mart, Alice Rose purchased 19.10 yards of ribbon. Each yard costs 89 cents. What was the total cost of the ribbon?

3–66. Douglas Noel went to Home Depot and bought 4 doors at $42.99 each and 6 bags of fertilizer at $8.99 per bag. What was the total cost to Douglas? If Douglas had $300 in his pocket, what does he have left to spend?

3–67. The stock of Intel has a high of $30.25 today. It closed at $28.85. How much did the stock drop from its high?

3–68. Ed Weld is traveling by car to a comic convention in San Diego. His company will reimburse him $.39 per mile. If Ed travels 906.5 miles, how much will Ed receive from his company?

3–69. Mark Ogara rented a truck from Avis Rent-A-Car for the weekend (2 days). The base rental price was $29.95 per day plus $14\frac{1}{2}$ cents per mile. Mark drove 410.85 miles. How much does Mark owe?

3–70. The *Houston Chronicle* on January 13, 2007 reported on Texans' ticket prices to be charged Texas football fans for the 2007 season. The average ticket price will be $60.63, an increase of $2.88 from last year. Before the 2006 season, 22 teams increased ticket prices. The average ticket price was $62.38 with the New England Patriots having the highest average ticket at $90.90 per game. **(a)** What was the price of ticket to a Texan game last year? **(b)** How much below the average is the Texans' ticket. **(c)** How much above the average are the Patriots tickets? **(d)** What is the average price between Texans' tickets and the Patriots' tickets? Round to the nearest hundredth.

3–71. Pete Allan bought a scooter on the Web for $99.99. He saw the same scooter in the mall for $108.96. How much did Pete save by buying on the Web?

3–72. Russell is preparing the daily bank deposit for his coffee shop. Before the deposit, the coffee shop had a checking account balance of $3,185.66. The deposit contains the following checks:

| No. 1 | $ 99.50 | No. 3 | $8.75 |
| No. 2 | 110.35 | No. 4 | 6.83 |

Russell included $820.55 in currency with the deposit. What is the coffee shop's new balance, assuming Russell writes no new checks?

3–73. The *Chattanooga Times/Free Press* ran a story on US Airways offering lower fares for Chattanooga, Tennessee–New York City flights. US Airways Express is offering a $190 round-trip fare for those who buy tickets in the next couple of weeks. Ticket prices had been running between $230 and $330 round-trip. Mark VanLoh, Airport Authority president, said the new fare is lower than the $219 ticket price offered by Southwest Airlines. How much would a family of four save using US Airways versus Southwest Airlines?

3–74. Randi went to Lowes to buy wall-to-wall carpeting. She needs 110.8 square yards for downstairs, 31.8 square yards for the halls, and 161.9 square yards for the bedrooms upstairs. Randi chose a shag carpet that costs $14.99 per square yard. She ordered foam padding at $3.10 per square yard. The carpet installers quoted Randi a labor charge of $3.75 per square yard. What will the total job cost Randi?

3–75. Art Norton bought 4 new Aquatred tires at Goodyear for $89.99 per tire. Goodyear charged $3.05 per tire for mounting, $2.95 per tire for valve stems, and $3.80 per tire for balancing. If Art paid no sales tax, what was his total cost for the 4 tires?

3–76. Shelly is shopping for laundry detergent, mustard, and canned tuna. She is trying to decide which of two products is the better buy. Using the following information, can you help Shelly?

Laundry detergent A	Mustard A	Canned tuna A
$2.00 for 37 ounces	$.88 for 6 ounces	$1.09 for 6 ounces

Laundry detergent B	Mustard B	Canned tuna B
$2.37 for 38 ounces	$1.61 for $12\frac{1}{2}$ ounces	$1.29 for $8\frac{3}{4}$ ounces

3–77. Roger bought season tickets for weekend games to professional basketball games. The cost was $945.60. The season package included 36 home games. What is the average price of the tickets per game? Round to the nearest cent. Marcelo, Roger's friend, offered to buy 4 of the tickets from Roger. What is the total amount Roger should receive?

3–78. A nurse was to give each of her patients a 1.32-unit dosage of a prescribed drug. The total remaining units of the drug at the hospital pharmacy were 53.12. The nurse has 38 patients. Will there be enough dosages for all her patients?

3–79. Audrey Long went to Japan and bought an animation cel of Mickey Mouse. The price was 25,000 yen. What is the price in U.S. dollars? Check your answer.

ADDITIONAL SET OF WORD PROBLEMS

3–80. On Monday, the stock of IBM closed at $88.95. At the end of trading on Tuesday, IBM closed at $94.65. How much did the price of stock increase from Monday to Tuesday?

3–81. Tie Yang bought season tickets to the Boston Pops for $698.55. The season package included 38 performances. What is the average price of the tickets per performance? Round to nearest cent. Sam, Tie's friend, offered to buy 4 of the tickets from Tie. What is the total amount Tie should receive?

3–82. Morris Katz bought 4 new tires at Goodyear for $95.49 per tire. Goodyear also charged Morris $2.50 per tire for mounting, $2.40 per tire for valve stems, and $3.95 per tire for balancing. Assume no tax. What was Morris's total cost for the 4 tires?

3–83. The *Denver Post* reported that Xcel Energy is revising customer charges for monthly residential electric bills and gas bills. Electric bills will increase $3.32. Gas bills will decrease $1.74 a month. **(a)** What is the resulting new monthly increase for the entire bill? **(b)** If Xcel serves 2,350 homes, how much additional revenue would Excel receive each month?

3–84. Steven is traveling to a computer convention by car. His company will reimburse him $.29 per mile. If Steven travels 890.5 miles, how much will he receive from his company?

3–85. Gracie went to Home Depot to buy wall-to-wall carpeting for her house. She needs 104.8 square yards for downstairs, 17.4 square yards for halls, and 165.8 square yards for the upstairs bedrooms. Gracie chose a shag carpet that costs $13.95 per square yard. She ordered foam padding at $2.75 per square yard. The installers quoted Gracie a labor cost of $5.75 per square yard in installation. What will the total job cost Gracie?

3–86. On February 1, 2007 *The Kansas City Star,* reported the Dow Jones Industrial Average rose 98.38 points from the previous day, and closed at 12,621.69. The blue-chip index set a trading high, at 12,657.02 and just missed the record of 12,621.77 points. **(a)** What were closing points on January 31, 2007? **(b)** This closing on February 1 was how many points from the record? **(c)** What were the average points from January 31, 2007's lowest to February 1, 2007's highest? Round to the nearest hundredth.

> ## CHALLENGE PROBLEMS

3–87. The *Miami Herald* ran a story on Carnival Cruise's profit per share. For the third quarter, Carnival earned $734.3 million with 815.9 million shares of stock outstanding. Last year, earnings were $500.8 million, or 85 cents a share. **(a)** How much were the earnings per shareholder for the third quarter? Round to the nearest cent. **(b)** How many shareholders did Carnival Cruise have last year? Round to the nearest hundred thousands. Check your answers.

3–88. Jill and Frank decided to take a long weekend in New York. City Hotel has a special getaway weekend for $79.95. The price is per person per night, based on double occupancy. The hotel has a minimum two-night stay. For this price, Jill and Frank will receive $50 credit toward their dinners at City's Skylight Restaurant. Also included in the package is a $3.99 credit per person toward breakfast for two each morning.

Since Jill and Frank do not own a car, they plan to rent a car. The car rental agency charges $19.95 a day with an additional charge of $.22 a mile and $1.19 per gallon of gas used. The gas tank holds 24 gallons.

From the following facts, calculate the total expenses of Jill and Frank (round all answers to nearest hundredth or cent as appropriate). Assume no taxes.

Car rental (2 days):		Dinner cost at Skylight	$182.12
Beginning odometer reading	4,820	Breakfast for two:	
Ending odometer reading	4,940	Morning No. 1	24.17
Beginning gas tank: $\frac{3}{4}$ full.		Morning No. 2	26.88
Gas tank on return: $\frac{1}{2}$ full.			
Tank holds 24 gallons.			

 SUMMARY PRACTICE TEST

1. Add the following by translating the verbal form to the decimal equivalent. *(p. 71)*

Three hundred thirty-eight and seven hundred five thousandths
Nineteen and fifty-nine hundredths
Five and four thousandths
Seventy-five hundredths
Four hundred three and eight tenths

Convert the following decimal fractions to decimals. *(p. 68)*

2. $\dfrac{7}{10}$ **3.** $\dfrac{7}{100}$ **4.** $\dfrac{7}{1,000}$

Convert the following to proper fractions or mixed numbers. Do not reduce to the lowest terms. *(p. 68)*

5. .9   **6.** 6.97   **7.** .685

Convert the following fractions to decimals (or mixed decimals) and round to the nearest hundredth as needed. *(p. 68)*

8. $\dfrac{2}{7}$ **9.** $\dfrac{1}{8}$ **10.** $4\dfrac{4}{7}$ **11.** $\dfrac{1}{13}$

12. Rearrange the following decimals and add. *(p. 71)*

5.93,   11.862,   284.0382,   88.44

13. Subtract the following and round to the nearest tenth. *(p. 71)*

13.111 − 3.872

14. Multiply the following and round to the nearest hundredth. *(p. 72)*

7.4821 × 15.861

15. Divide the following and round to the nearest hundredth. *(p. 73)*

203,942 ÷ 5.88

Complete the following by the shortcut method. *(p. 74)*

16. 62.94 × 1,000

17. 8,322,249.821 × 100

18. The average pay of employees is $795.88 per week. Lee earns $820.44 per week. How much is Lee's pay over the average? *(p. 71)*

19. Lowes reimburses Ron $.49 per mile. Ron submitted a travel log for a total of 1,910.81 miles. How much will Lowes reimburse Ron? Round to the nearest cent. *(p. 72)*

20. Lee Chin bought 2 new car tires from Michelin for $182.11 per tire. Michelin also charged Lee $3.99 per tire for mounting, $2.50 per tire for valve stems, and $4.10 per tire for balancing. What is Lee's final bill? *(p. 72)*

21. Could you help Judy decide which of the following products is cheaper per ounce? *(p. 73)*

Canned fruit A

$.37 for 3 ounces

Canned fruit B

$.58 for $3\frac{3}{4}$ ounces

22. Paula Smith bought an iPod for 350 euros. What is this price in U.S. dollars? *(p. 73)*

23. Google stock traded at a high of $438.22 and closed at $410.12. How much did the stock fall from its high? *(p. 71)*

JULIETTE BORDA

TRAVEL SLEUTH | You don't have to break the bank to phone home from the Alps. *By Sean O'Neill*

Call **U.S.** for less

During a recent trip to Germany and Austria, I called the States five times, using pay phones and charging my Visa card. I returned home to find a $105 bill for a 20-minute call and a $192 bill for all my other calls, which each lasted fewer than ten minutes. What might I have done differently? —**RAY TAYLOR**, Bend, Ore.

Ouch. Your credit card is one of many that charge sky-high rates for placing international phone calls. For your next trip, try this: If you own a cell phone, ask your wireless carrier if you can use it overseas for a low rate. Cingular (the nation's largest provider) and T-Mobile have adopted GSM technology, the standard for much of the world. If you own a relatively new phone and use one of these providers, you can usually place calls from overseas. Check first

with your provider, and ask to buy a temporary plan that will allow you to call home cheaply while traveling abroad. Cingular, for instance, lets many of its customers call home from several European countries at rates of about $1 a minute, plus a fee of about $6 for each month of travel.

Or buy a prepaid phone card that lets you call for rates of about 10 cents to 15 cents per minute. We like the $20 cards from Nobel (www.nobel .com) and $10 cards from OneSuite (www.onesuite.com). You can use any phone overseas, but note that a hotel phone may come with a high fee.

REBOOK FOR LESS

To get the lowest fares, I usually need to book air tickets well in advance. But my next trip will be to celebrate the birth of my granddaughter, and I can't know for sure the date I'll be

flying cross-country to New York City. How can I book a cheap ticket today that will let me change my flight dates later without paying hefty fees? —**CHARLES KUTTNER**, Portland, Ore.

Congratulations on becoming a grandparent. If you can make an educated guess about when you're most likely to travel, you'll save by booking early on a discount airline. In the best case, you'll have a cheap ticket and you'll arrive at the right time. In the worst case, you'll need to rebook, your new flight date will come with a higher round-trip fare—which is typical—and you'll have to pay the difference plus a rebooking fee.

But here's why booking with a discounter is a good idea, even if a discounter and a major airline offer similar advance ticket prices: You'll face lower 11th-hour fares *and* the rebooking fee will be smaller. Major carriers typically charge $100 to rebook, while top discounters charge less. Rebooking fees for ATA are $50 and for JetBlue, $30. Southwest doesn't charge a fee.

Given that you know the due date of your granddaughter, we suggest you book your trip from Portland to New York City now (more than a month ahead). You'll pay $403 before taxes and fees of $50 on JetBlue. In the past year on this route, fares booked just days before departure weren't much higher than $400 before taxes, says FareCompare.com, a site that gives you the lowest average fares available on most routes. We estimate you'll save between $75 and $300 by rebooking on JetBlue instead of a major airline.

What if no discounter serves your route? If you have to go with a major airline and you need to rebook, ask the agent to waive the rebooking fee when you call to change flight dates. Agents often have discretion to waive fees—but you'll always pay the difference between the old and new fare.

Have a money-related travel question? Write us at travelsleuth@kiplinger.com.

BUSINESS MATH ISSUE

Prepaid phone cards do not really save you money.

1. List the key points of the article and information to support your position.
2. Write a group defense of your position using math calculations to support your view.

Slater's Business Math Scrapbook

with Internet Application
Putting Your Skills to Work

PROJECT A
Calculate market total.

Revenue Search

In Latest Deal, Google Steps Further Into World of Old Media

Internet Giant Expands Role
As an Advertising Broker;
Automating Radio Sales

Next Target May Be Television

By KEVIN J. DELANEY

Google Inc. has brought in billions of dollars in revenue by brokering advertisements that appear on Web sites. Now it is taking its ad machine beyond the Internet in an ambitious quest to place ads in traditional media such as newspapers and radio.

The move could open enormous new markets to the search company. But it could also test the limits of Google's automated ad-placement technology that brought it more than $3 billion in online ad revenue in 2004.

Wall Street Journal © 2006

Following the Money
Estimated U.S. spending on advertising for 2005, in billions:

TV	$55.4
Newspapers	$50.2
Direct Mail	$44.5
Magazines	$23.9
Radio	$20.6
Internet	$10.0
Outdoor	$5.7
Cinema	$0.4
Other	$45.8

Source: ZenithOptimedia

	U.K. retail price (converted into dollars)	U.S. retail price
Burberry short raincoat	£465.00 ($914.14)	$695.00
iPod Nano special edition (8GB)	£169.00 ($332.24)	$249.00
Tiffany Lace bracelet	£6,775.00 ($13,318.97)	$9,800.00
Dior J'Adore 50ml	£39.50 ($77.65)	$58.00
Nintendo Wii	£179.99 ($353.84)	$249.99

PROJECT B
Show how to calculate
A. $914.14
B. $332.24
C. $13,318.97
D. $353.84

Internet Projects: See text Web site (www.mhhe.com/slater9e) and The Business Math Internet Resource Guide.

CHAPTER 4

Banking

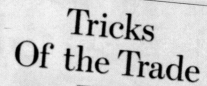

LEARNING UNIT OBJECTIVES

LU 4–1: The Checking Account

- Define and state the purpose of signature cards, checks, deposit slips, check stubs, check registers, and endorsements (pp. 89–91).
- Correctly prepare deposit slips and write checks (pp. 91–92).

LU 4–2: Bank Statement and Reconciliation Process; Trends in Online Banking

- Define and state the purpose of the bank statement (pp. 93–94).
- Complete a check register and a bank reconciliation (pp. 96–98).
- Explain the trends in online banking (pp. 98–100).

Tricks Of the Trade

Money Adviser Pays Bills

Allison Shipley, an adviser to high-net-worth clients at Pricewater-houseCoopers' Private Company Services practice, once spent long hours in front of the computer reconciling the family checkbook. But Ms. Shipley freed herself from that with a simple strategy: She puts as many bills as possible on automatic bill paying using a single credit card. This way she not only saves time from writing checks (now just two a month), but she accrues credit-card reward points for a trip to Europe. For bills not covered by her card, Ms. Shipley has funds directly withdrawn from her checking account and sent to the companies, including her credit card. She spends a minute or two a day watching the running balances online to make sure they match the accounts' activity. She says she gets enough information about her family's spending from monthly statements. She prints online confirmations of bills paid and keeps them in separate files like car payments and electric bills.—*Sarah Tilton*

Wall Street Journal © 2005

Mark Lennihan/AP Wide World

Bank of America To Pay $2.5 Billion For China Foothold

Bank of America Corp., moving to make one of the largest single foreign investments to date in China's fast-changing banking sector, said it has reached a deal to buy a stake in **China Construction Bank** for $2.5 billion.

Wall Street Journal © 2005

Too often people think their bank is their best friend. You should remember that your bank is a business. The banking industry is very competitive. Note in the *Wall Street Journal* clipping "Bank of America to Pay $2.5 Billion for China Foothold" how quickly the banking sectors are changing all over the world to be more competitive.

An important fixture in today's banking is the **automatic teller machine (ATM).** The ability to get instant cash is a convenience many bank customers enjoy. However, more than half of the ATM customers do not like to deposit checks because they are afraid the checks will not be correctly deposited to their account. Bank of America, Bank One, and Wells Fargo are testing new ATMs that accept a check, scan the check, and print a receipt with a photographic image of the check. When these machines are widely available, they will eliminate the fear of depositing checks.

The effect of using an ATM card is the same as using a **debit card**—both transactions result in money being immediately deducted from your checking account balance. As a result, debit cards have been called enhanced ATM cards or *check cards*. Often banks charge fees for these card transactions. The frequent complaints of bank customers have made many banks offer their ATMs as a free service, especially if customers use an ATM in the same network as their bank. Some banks charge fees for using another bank's ATM.

Remember that the use of debit cards involves planning. As *check cards,* you must be aware of your bank balance every time you use a debit card. Also, if you use a credit card instead of a debit card, you can only be held responsible for $50 of illegal charges; and during the time the credit card company investigates the illegal charges, they are removed from your account. However, with a debit card, this legal limit only applies if you report your card lost or stolen within two business days.

We should add that debit cards are profitable for banks. When shopping, if you use a debit card that does not require a personal identification number, the store pays a fee to the bank that issued the card—usually from 1.4 to 2 cents on the dollar.

This chapter begins with a discussion of the checking account. You will follow Molly Kate as she opens a checking account for Gracie's Natural Superstore and performs her banking transactions. Pay special attention to the procedure used by Gracie's to reconcile its checking account and bank statement. This information will help you reconcile your checkbook records with the bank's record of your account. The chapter concludes by discussing how the trends in online banking may affect your banking procedures.

Learning Unit 4-1: The Checking Account

A **check** or **draft** is a written order instructing a bank, credit union, or savings and loan institution to pay a designated amount of your money on deposit to a person or an organization. Checking accounts are offered to individuals and businesses. Businesses may be charged $.39 per check received for a business transaction. Note that the business checking account usually receives more services than the personal checking account.

Most small businesses depend on a checking account for efficient record keeping. In this learning unit you will follow the checking account procedures of a newly organized small business. You can use many of these procedures in your personal check writing. You will also learn about e-checks—a new trend.

Opening the Checking Account

Molly Kate, treasurer of Gracie's Natural Superstore, went to Ipswich Bank to open a business checking account. The bank manager gave Molly a **signature card.** The signature card contained space for the company's name and address, references, type of account, and the signature(s) of the person(s) authorized to sign checks. If necessary, the bank will use the signature card to verify that Molly signed the checks. Some companies authorize more than one person to sign checks or require more than one signature on a check.

| FIGURE | 4.1 | Deposit slip

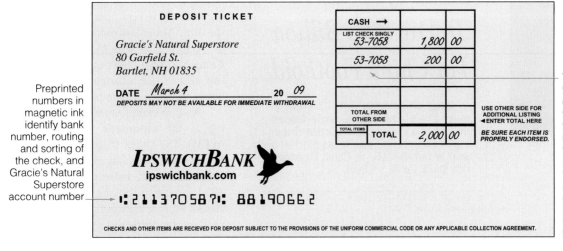

Molly then lists on a **deposit slip** (or deposit ticket) the checks and/or cash she is depositing in her company's business account. The bank gave Molly a temporary checkbook to use until the company's printed checks arrived. Molly also will receive *preprinted* checking account deposit slips like the one shown in Figure 4.1. Since the deposit slips are in duplicate, Molly can keep a record of her deposit. Note that the increased use of making deposits at ATM machines has made it more convenient for people to make their deposits.

Writing business checks is similar to writing personal checks. Before writing any checks, however, you must understand the structure of a check and know how to write a check. Carefully study Figure 4.2. Note that the verbal amount written in the check should

| FIGURE | 4.2 | The structure of a check

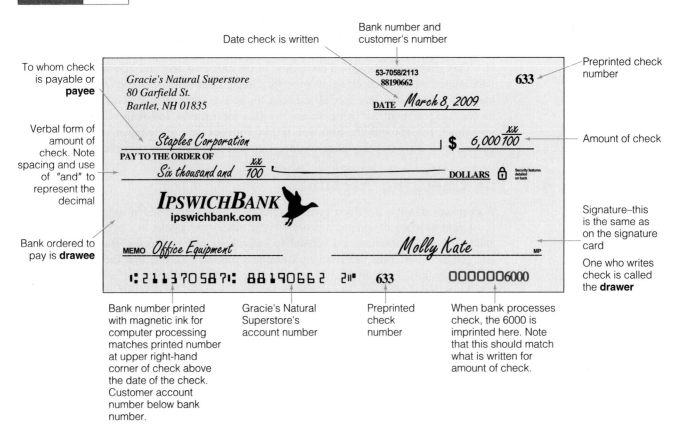

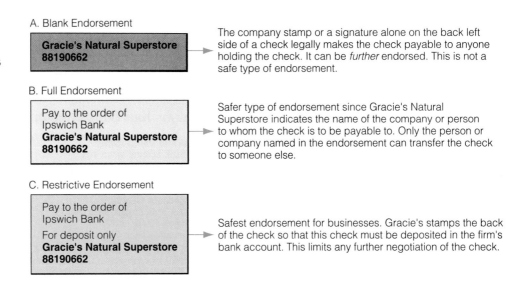

FIGURE 4.3

Types of common endorsements

A. Blank Endorsement

> Gracie's Natural Superstore
> 88190662

The company stamp or a signature alone on the back left side of a check legally makes the check payable to anyone holding the check. It can be *further* endorsed. This is not a safe type of endorsement.

B. Full Endorsement

> Pay to the order of
> Ipswich Bank
> **Gracie's Natural Superstore**
> **88190662**

Safer type of endorsement since Gracie's Natural Superstore indicates the name of the company or person to whom the check is to be payable to. Only the person or company named in the endorsement can transfer the check to someone else.

C. Restrictive Endorsement

> Pay to the order of
> Ipswich Bank
> For deposit only
> **Gracie's Natural Superstore**
> **88190662**

Safest endorsement for businesses. Gracie's stamps the back of the check so that this check must be deposited in the firm's bank account. This limits any further negotiation of the check.

match the figure amount. If these two amounts are different, by law the bank uses the verbal amount. Also, note the bank imprint on the bottom right section of the check. When processing the check, the bank imprints the check's amount. This makes it easy to detect bank errors.

Using the Checking Account

Once the check is written, the writer must keep a record of the check. Knowing the amount of your written checks and the amount in the bank should help you avoid writing a bad check. Business checkbooks usually include attached **check stubs** to keep track of written checks. The sample check stub in the margin shows the information that the check writer will want to record. Some companies use a **check register** to keep their check records instead of check stubs. Figure 4.6 (p. 96) shows a check register with a ✔ column that is often used in balancing the checkbook with the bank statement (Learning Unit 4–2).

Gracie's Natural Superstore has had a busy week, and Molly must deposit its checks in the company's checking account. However, before she can do this, Molly must **endorse,** or sign, the back left side of the checks. Figure 4.3 explains the three types of check endorsements: **blank endorsement, full endorsement,** and **restrictive endorsement.** These endorsements transfer Gracie's ownership to the bank, which collects the money from the person or company issuing the check. Federal Reserve regulation limits all endorsements to the top $1\frac{1}{2}$ inches of the trailing edge on the back left side of the check.

After the bank receives Molly's deposit slip, shown in Figure 4.1 (p. 90), it increases (or credits) Gracie's account by $2,000. Often Molly leaves the deposit in a locked bag in a night depository. Then the bank credits (increases) Gracie's account when it processes the deposit on the next working day.

E-Checks—A New Trend

Before concluding this unit, let's look at a new trend using e-checks. In the *Wall Street Journal* clipping "Taking Rain Check on 'E-Checks,'" p. 92, we see that retailers are now trying to get your bank account number and "routing" number at the bottom of your checks so bills can be paid directly from your bank account when your bills are due.

Check Stub

It should be completed before the check is written.

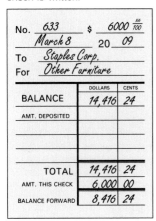

No. *633*	$ *6000 $\frac{00}{100}$*	
March 8	20 *09*	
To	*Staples Corp.*	
For	*Other Furniture*	
	DOLLARS	CENTS
BALANCE	*14,416*	*24*
AMT. DEPOSITED		
TOTAL	*14,416*	*24*
AMT. THIS CHECK	*6,000*	*00*
BALANCE FORWARD	*8,416*	*24*

Taking Rain Check on 'E-Checks'

More Retailers Ask for Your Bank-Account Info—Here's Why

RETAILERS NOW WANT to siphon money straight out of your bank account when you reach the checkout counter—a move that saves them money, but may cost you in other ways.

This process—known variously as e-check, ACH (which stands for automated clearing house) and direct debit—has been around for a number of years. It's common among utilities and others that send out monthly bills: They ask for your bank-account number and the "routing" number at the bottom of your checks, then withdraw what you owe when your bill's due.

Now, other retailers are getting into the game. Last month, **Amazon.com** Inc. began inviting customers to "pay directly from your bank account" as a payment option. Also in October, Stop&Shop, a unit of **Ahold** NV, started testing a system in 12 grocery stores that links customers' loyalty cards to their checking accounts. **Continental Airlines** has allowed e-check payments on its Web site for just over a year.

Check Mate

Some retailers now let customers give them bank-account information and have money withdrawn for purchases.

■ **Pluses:** It costs retailers less money; you don't need plastic to shop

■ **Minuses:** Can't earn rewards for using credit card or borrow against it to fund a shopping spree

Cash, e-check, or credit? Send your preferences to ron.lieber@wsj.com.

Let's check your understanding of the first unit in this chapter.

LU 4–1 **PRACTICE QUIZ**

Complete this **Practice Quiz** to see how you are doing

Complete the following check and check stub for Long Company. Note the $9,500.60 balance brought forward on check stub No. 113. You must make a $690.60 deposit on May 3. Sign the check for Roland Small.

Date	Check no.	Amount	Payable to	For
June 5, 2009	113	$83.76	Angel Corporation	Rent

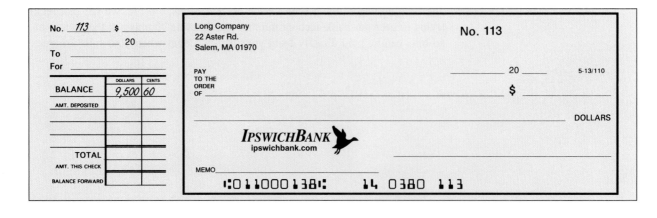

✓ Solution with page reference to check your progress

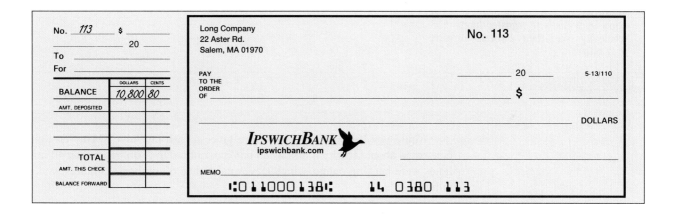

No. _113_	$ _83.76_			Long Company 22 Aster Rd. Salem, MA 01970		No. 113	
June 5 20 _09_							
To _Angel Corp._				PAY	_June 5_ 20 _09_		5-13/110
For _Rent_				TO THE ORDER OF _Angel Corporation_	$ _83 76/100_		
	DOLLARS	CENTS					
BALANCE	9,500	60		_Eighty-three and 76/100_			DOLLARS
AMT. DEPOSITED	690	60					
				IPSWICHBANK ipswichbank.com	_Roland Small_		
TOTAL	10,191	20					
AMT. THIS CHECK	83	76		MEMO _Rent_			
BALANCE FORWARD	10,107	44		⑈011000138⑈ 14 0380 113			

LU 4–1a EXTRA PRACTICE QUIZ

Need more practice? Try this **Extra Practice Quiz** (check figures in Chapter Organizer, p. 101)

Complete the following check and stub for Long Company. Note the $10,800.80 balance brought forward on check stub No. 113. You must make an $812.88 deposit on May 3. Sign the check for Roland Small.

Date	Check No.	Amount	Payable to	For
July 8, 2009	113	$79.88	Lowe Corp	Advertising

No. _113_	$ _____			Long Company 22 Aster Rd. Salem, MA 01970		No. 113	
_____ 20 _____							
To _____				PAY	_____ 20 ____		5-13/110
For _____				TO THE ORDER OF _____	$ _____		
	DOLLARS	CENTS					
BALANCE	10,800	80					DOLLARS
AMT. DEPOSITED							
				IPSWICHBANK ipswichbank.com			
TOTAL							
AMT. THIS CHECK				MEMO_____			
BALANCE FORWARD				⑈011000138⑈ 14 0380 113			

Learning Unit 4–2: Bank Statement and Reconciliation Process; Trends in Online Banking

This learning unit is divided into two sections: (1) bank statement and reconciliation process, and (2) trends in online banking. The bank statement discussion will teach you why it was important for Gracie's Natural Superstore to reconcile its checkbook balance with the balance reported on its bank balance. Note that you can also use this reconciliation process in reconciling your personal checking account and avoiding the expensive error of an overdrawn account.

To introduce you to the "Trends in Online Banking" section, we have included the following *Wall Street Journal* clipping "Financial Institutions Give Cash to Induce Customers to Use Web-Based Services," p. 94. As you probably know, financial institutions favor online banking because it is less expensive for them.

Financial Institutions Give Cash to Induce Customers To Use Web-Based Services

By Jennifer Saranow

Financial institutions, eager to get more consumers to pay their bills online, are offering a new incentive: cash.

Citigroup Inc.'s Citibank introduced a promotion in October offering as much as $200 to new online bill-paying customers, depending on the number of bills they pay electronically. The promotion runs until the end of the year.

FAMILY FINANCE

At **Wells Fargo** & Co., customers in certain markets who are new to the service can get $10 if they pay at least one bill online by January. **E*Trade Financial** Corp. is paying $25 to customers who pay at least two bills online and hold specific types of accounts. Last month, **J.P. Morgan Chase** & Co. ran a sweepstakes where customers in select markets received a chance to win a grand prize of $5,000 if they paid bills electronically. Online bill-pay services allow individuals to transfer funds electronically from their accounts directly to a biller.

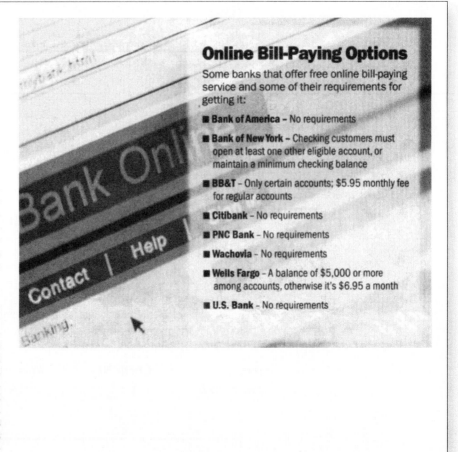

Online Bill-Paying Options

Some banks that offer free online bill-paying service and some of their requirements for getting it:

- **Bank of America** – No requirements
- **Bank of New York** – Checking customers must open at least one other eligible account, or maintain a minimum checking balance
- **BB&T** – Only certain accounts; $5.95 monthly fee for regular accounts
- **Citibank** – No requirements
- **PNC Bank** – No requirements
- **Wachovia** – No requirements
- **Wells Fargo** – A balance of $5,000 or more among accounts, otherwise it's $6.95 a month
- **U.S. Bank** – No requirements

Would you bank online if you were given a cash incentive? Many customers are still concerned about security issues when banking online. In 2006, more than 40 million households were banking online, which leaves more than 60 million customers who do not bank online.

Bank Statement and Reconciliation Process

Each month, Ipswich Bank sends Gracie's Natural Superstore a **bank statement** (Figure 4.4, p. 95). We are interested in the following:

1. Beginning bank balance.
2. Total of all the account increases. Each time the bank increases the account amount, it *credits* the account.
3. Total of all account decreases. Each time the bank decreases the account amount, it *debits* the account.
4. Final ending balance.

Due to differences in timing, the bank balance on the bank statement frequently does not match the customer's checkbook balance. Also, the bank statement can show transactions that have not been entered in the customer's checkbook. Figure 4.5, p. 95, tells you what to look for when comparing a checkbook balance with a bank balance.

FIGURE   **4.4**

Bank statement

Ipswich Bank
1 Pleasant St.
Bartlett, NH 01835

Account Statement

Gracie's Natural Superstore
80 Garfield St.
Bartlett, NH 01835

Checking Account: 881900662

Checking Account Summary as of 3/31/09

Beginning Balance	Total Deposits	Total Withdrawals	Service Charge	Ending Balance
$13,112.24	$8,705.28	$9,926.00	$28.50	$11,863.02

Checking Accounts Transactions

Deposits	Date	Amount
Deposit	3/05	2,000.00
Deposit	3/05	224.00
Deposit	3/09	389.20
EFT leasing: Bakery dept.	3/18	1,808.06
EFT leasing: Meat dept.	3/27	4,228.00
Interest	3/31	56.02

Charges	Date	Amount
Service charge: Check printing	3/31	28.50
EFT: Health insurance	3/21	722.00
NSF	3/21	104.00

Checks				Daily Balance			
Number	Date	Amount		Date	Balance	Date	Balance
301	3/07	200.00		2/28	13,112.24	3/18	10,529.50
633	3/13	6,000.00		3/05	15,232.24	3/21	9,807.50
634	3/13	300.00		3/07	14,832.24	3/28	14,035.50
635	3/11	200.00		3/09	15,221.44	3/31	11,863.02
636	3/18	200.00		3/11	15,021.44		
637	3/31	2,200.00		3/13	8,721.44		

FIGURE   **4.5**

Reconciling checkbook with bank statement

Checkbook balance		Bank balance
+ EFT (electronic funds transfer)	− NSF check	+ Deposits in transit
+ Interest earned	− Online fees	− Outstanding checks
+ Notes collected	− Automatic payments*	± Bank errors
+ Direct deposits	− Overdrafts[†]	
− ATM withdrawals	− Service charges	
− Automatic withdrawals	− Stop payments[‡]	
	± Book errors[§]	

*Preauthorized payments for utility bills, mortgage payments, insurance, etc.
[†]**Overdrafts** occur when the customer has no overdraft protection and a check bounces back to the company or person who received the check because the customer has written a check without enough money in the bank to pay for it.
[‡]A stop payment is issued when the writer of check does not want the receiver to cash the check.
[§]If a $60 check is recorded at $50, the checkbook balance must be decreased by $10.

Gracie's Natural Superstore is planning to offer to its employees the option of depositing their checks directly into each employee's checking account. This is accomplished through the **electronic funds transfer (EFT)**—a computerized operation that electronically transfers funds among parties without the use of paper checks. Gracie's, who sublets space in the store, receives rental payments by EFT. Gracie's also has the bank pay the store's health insurance premiums by EFT.

To reconcile the difference between the amount on the bank statement and in the checkbook, the customer should complete a **bank reconciliation.** Today, many companies and home computer owners are using software such as Quicken and QuickBooks to complete their bank reconciliation. However, you should understand the following steps for manually reconciling a bank statement.

RECONCILING A BANK STATEMENT
Step 1. Identify the outstanding checks (checks written but not yet processed by the bank). You can use the ✓ column in the check register (Figure 4.6) to check the canceled checks listed in the bank statement against the checks you wrote in the check register. The unchecked checks are the outstanding checks.
Step 2. Identify the deposits in transit (deposits made but not yet processed by the bank), using the same method in Step 1.
Step 3. Analyze the bank statement for transactions not recorded in the check stubs or check registers (like EFT).
Step 4. Check for recording errors in checks written, in deposits made, or in subtraction and addition.
Step 5. Compare the adjusted balances of the checkbook and the bank statement. If the balances are not the same, repeat Steps 1–4.

Molly uses a check register (Figure 4.6) to keep a record of Gracie's checks and deposits. By looking at Gracie's check register, you can see how to complete Steps 1 and 2 above. The explanation that follows for the first four bank statement reconciliation steps will help you understand the procedure.

FIGURE 4.6

Gracie's Natural Superstore check register

		RECORD ALL CHARGES OR CREDITS THAT AFFECT YOUR ACCOUNT						BALANCE	
NUMBER	DATE 2007	DESCRIPTION OF TRANSACTION	PAYMENT/DEBIT (−)	✓	FEE (IF ANY) (−)	DEPOSIT/CREDIT (+)		$ 12,912	24
	3/04	Deposit	$		$	$ 2,000 00		+ 2,000	00
								14,912	24
	3/04	Deposit				224 00		+ 224	00
								15,136	24
633	3/08	Staples Company	6,000 00	✓				− 6,000	00
								9,136	24
634	3/09	Health Foods Inc.	1,020 00	✓				− 1,020	00
								8,116	24
	3/09	Deposit				389 20		+ 389	20
								8,505	44
635	3/10	Liberty Insurance	200 00	✓				− 200	00
								8,305	44
636	3/18	Ryan Press	200 00	✓				− 200	00
								8,105	44
637	3/29	Logan Advertising	2,200 00	✓				− 2,200	00
								5,905	44
	3/30	Deposit				3,383 26		+ 3,383	26
								9,288	70
638	3/31	Sears Roebuck	572 00					− 572	00
								8,716	70
639	3/31	Flynn Company	638 94					− 638	94
								8,077	76
640	3/31	Lynn's Farm	166 00					− 166	00
								7,911	76
641	3/31	Ron's Wholesale	406 28					− 406	28
								7,505	48
642	3/31	Grocery Natural, Inc.	917 06					− 917	06
								86,588	42
		REMEMBER TO RECORD AUTOMATIC PAYMENTS/DEPOSITS ON DATE AUTHORIZED.							

Step 1. Identify Outstanding Checks

Outstanding checks are checks that Gracie's Natural Superstore has written but Ipswich Bank has not yet recorded for payment when it sends out the bank statement. Gracie's treasurer identifies the following checks written on 3/31 as outstanding:

No. 638	$572.00
No. 639	638.94
No. 640	166.00
No. 641	406.28
No. 642	917.06

Step 2. Identify Deposits in Transit

Deposits in transit are deposits that did not reach Ipswich Bank by the time the bank prepared the bank statement. The March 30 deposit of $3,383.26 did not reach Ipswich Bank by the bank statement date. You can see this by comparing the company's bank statement with its check register.

Step 3. Analyze Bank Statement for Transactions Not Recorded in Check Stubs or Check Register

The bank statement of Gracie's Natural Superstore (Figure 4.4, p. 95) begins with the deposits, or increases, made to Gracie's bank account. Increases to accounts are known as credits. These are the result of a **credit memo (CM).** Gracie's received the following increases or credits in March:

1. *EFT leasing:* $1,808.06 and $4,228.00.	Each month the bakery and meat departments pay for space they lease in the store.
2. *Interest credited:* $56.02.	Gracie's has a checking account that pays interest; the account has earned $56.02.

When Gracie's has charges against her bank account, the bank decreases, or debits, Gracie's account for these charges. Banks usually inform customers of a debit transaction by a **debit memo (DM).** The following items will result in debits to Gracie's account:

1. *Service charge:* $28.50	The bank charged $28.50 for printing Gracie's checks.
2. *EFT payment:* $722.	The bank made a health insurance payment for Gracie's.
3. *NSF check:* $104.	One of Gracie's customers wrote Gracie's a check for $104. Gracie's deposited the check, but the check bounced for **nonsufficient funds (NSF).** Thus, Gracie's has $104 less than it figured.

Step 4. Check for Recording Errors

The treasurer of Gracie's Natural Superstore, Molly Kate, recorded check No. 634 for the wrong amount—$1,020 (see the check register). The bank statement showed that check No. 634 cleared for $300. To reconcile Gracie's checkbook balance with the bank balance, Gracie's must add $720 to its checkbook balance. Neglecting to record a deposit also results in an error in the company's checkbook balance. As you can see, reconciling the bank's balance with a checkbook balance is a necessary part of business and personal finance.

Step 5. Completing the Bank Reconciliation

Now we can complete the bank reconciliation on the back side of the bank statement as shown in Figure 4.7 (p. 98). This form is usually on the back of a bank statement. If necessary, however, the person reconciling the bank statement can construct a bank reconciliation form similar to Figure 4.8 (p. 98).

FIGURE   4.7

Reconciliation process

CHECKS OUTSTANDING (NOT YET CHARGED TO ACCOUNT)		
NUMBER OR DATE	DOLLARS	CENTS
638	$572	00
639	638	94
640	166	00
641	406	28
642	917	06
TOTAL	$2,700	28

CHECKING ACCOUNT RECONCILEMENT

Enter the new balance shown on the other side of this statement. $ 11,863.02

ADD
Deposits not shown   3,383.26

ADD
Advances and Transfers to Checking not shown.

SUBTOTAL   15,246.28

DEDUCT
Checks outstanding   2,700.28

SUBTOTAL   12,546.00

DEDUCT
Transfers from Checking not shown
This amount should agree with the balance in your checkbook register. $ 12,546.00

Checkbook balance $6,588.42

+ EFT leasing $6,036.06
+ Interest   56.02
+ Checkbook error   720.00   6,812.08
− Service charge $ 28.50
− EFT: health insurance   722.00
− NSF   104.00   854.50

Ending checkbook balance $12,546.00

FIGURE   4.8

Bank reconciliation

GRACIE'S NATURAL SUPERSTORE Bank Reconciliation as of March 31, 2009				
Checkbook balance			Bank balance	
Gracie's checkbook balance	$6,588.42	Bank balance		$11,863.02
Add:		Add:		
EFT leasing: Bakery dept. $1,808.06		Deposit in transit, 3/30		3,383.26
EFT leasing: Meat dept. 4,228.00				$15,246.28
Interest 56.02				
Error: Overstated check No. 634 720.00	$ 6,812.08			
	$13,400.50			
Deduct:		Deduct:		
Service charge $ 28.50		Outstanding checks:		
NSF check 104.00		No. 638	$572.00	
EFT health insurance payment 722.00	854.50	No. 639	638.94	
		No. 640	166.00	
		No. 641	406.28	
		No. 642	917.06	2,700.28
Reconciled balance	$12,546.00	Reconciled balance		$12,546.00

Trends in Online Banking

In the introduction to this learning unit, you learned that financial institutions are offering cash incentives to induce customers to use web-based services. We also said that many customers are still concerned about security issues when banking online.

To combat fraud online, the following *Wall Street Journal* clipping "'Virtual Debit Card' Aims to Combat Online Fraud," discusses a new checking account with a "virtual debit card." As you can see from the clipping, this "eSpend" card is in addition to the regular debit card. With the eSpend card, you can get a daily limit for purchases online, over the phone, or by mail order.

'Virtual Debit Card' Aims to Combat Online Fraud

By Jennifer Saranow

Consumers typically have been wary of using bank cards online. One bank's solution is to get rid of the cards.

In an effort to ease customers' concerns about fraud and identity theft when shopping online, PNC Bank has launched a new checking account with a "virtual debit card." In addition to a regular debit card that can be used at automated teller machines and in stores, the "Digital Checking" account comes with an "eSpend" card. The card is basically a piece of paper with an account number, expiration date and verification code for making purchases online, over the phone and by mail order. Customers can set a daily limit for their eSpend card (say $1,000) and once that amount is spent, additional purchases won't be approved.

PNC Bank, a unit of **PNC Financial Services Group** Inc., Pittsburgh, hopes the eSpend card will attract people who want to make purchases online with their debit card but are uncomfortable doing so for fear of making their bank account vulnerable to fraud.

If an unauthorized person obtains a customer's eSpend number, only the specified daily limit could be taken out of a customer's bank account. If this occurs, PNC says customers aren't liable for the charges. Purchases made with the eSpend card show up separately on bank statements. The account, which is aimed at online-banking customers, also comes with identity-theft reimbursement insurance, a debit card rewards program and no fee for using non-PNC ATMs. The account has a monthly $11 service fee unless customers opt for direct deposit of paychecks or government checks such as Social Security, and pay at least three bills online.

Wall Street Journal © 2005

Today, with the increased use of computers, the trends in online banking are changing. In this section, you will learn about three of the changes. Changes are occurring in the use of the Internet—there is an increase in Internet banking. Customers are also seeing that new bank legislation has resulted in an increase in the speed of check clearing. Finally, the role of middlemen in the Internet is changing.

Increased Use of Internet

As time passes, people are realizing the convenience of using online banking in the Internet. An enormous amount of time is saved when people can avoid most of their trips to the bank by using the Internet. Also, Internet banking does not keep bank hours.

The most popular reason to use Internet banking is the ability to quickly pay your bills. The Internet method of bill paying has several advantages. You do not have to write checks, save the envelopes that come with bills, check to see if you have stamps to put on the envelopes, or be concerned that payments for bills will not reach their destination in time to make a deadline.

Online banking also has other advantages. You can transfer money between your accounts, and you can check your transactions and balances.

The broad objective of banks is to make your online banking experience the same as your physical bank experience. This objective, of course, cannot be completely fulfilled. If you want to make deposits or withdraw funds, you must do this by wire, mail, ATM, or a physical appearance at your bank. On some online bank websites, however, you can apply for loans and get information on other bank financing.

New Bank Legislation

Although banks are doing everything they can to get people to avoid writing checks, many people do not want to give up their check writing. In a recent Kansas City Bank presentation, it was emphasized that today more checks than ever are processed. To reduce the costs of paper checks, some banks no longer return canceled checks. Instead, these banks use a **safekeeping** procedure involving holding the checks for a period of time, keeping microfilm copies of checks for at least a year, and returning a check or a photocopy for a small fee.

In 2003, a new piece of legislation known as Check 21 was signed into law. This legislation means that canceled checks can now be transferred electronically to customers rather than bundling them up and sending them through the mail. The electronic transfer of their canceled checks gives customers time to study all their canceled checks without the concern for safekeeping.

Role of Middlemen on the Internet

Have you ever made a purchase on eBay? eBay is a popular website for many people who use the company to buy and sell items at auction and also to buy and sell items outright.

After you make a purchase on eBay, you have the option to pay by check, credit card, or use PayPal. Many people use PayPal because they believe it is safer than their check or credit card. Here, you can see a partial Web screen of eBay with PayPal.

PayPal acts like a third person operating between eBay and the seller. Since PayPal performs a service, it charges customers a fee. Obviously, banks and credit unions object to letting PayPal dominate the field and handle these transactions for a fee. As a result, PayPal recently agreed to be purchased by eBay. In the next five years, banks hope to eliminate middlemen like PayPal. At that time you might be able to e-mail cash to Internet-enabled ATM machines or use a cell phone to send your money.

The Practice Quiz that follows will test your knowledge of the bank reconciliation process.

LU 4–2   PRACTICE QUIZ

Complete this **Practice Quiz** to see how you are doing

Rosa Garcia received her February 3, 2009, bank statement showing a balance of $212.80. Rosa's checkbook has a balance of $929.15. The bank statement showed that Rosa had an ATM fee of $12.00 and a deposited check returned fee of $20.00. Rosa earned interest of $1.05. She had three outstanding checks: No. 300, $18.20; No. 302, $38.40; and No. 303, $68.12. A deposit for $810.12 was not on her bank statement. Prepare Rosa Garcia's bank reconciliation.

ROSA GARCIA Bank Reconciliation as of February 3, 2009					
Checkbook balance			**Bank balance**		
Rosa's checkbook balance		$929.15	Bank balance		$ 212.80
Add:			Add:		
Interest		1.05	Deposit in transit		810.12
		$930.20			$1,022.92
Deduct:			Deduct:		
Deposited check returned fee	$20.00		Outstanding checks:		
ATM	12.00	32.00	No. 300	$18.20	
			No. 302	38.40	
			No. 303	68.12	124.72
Reconciled balance		$898.20	Reconciled balance		$ 898.20

LU 4–2a   EXTRA PRACTICE QUIZ

Need more practice? Try this **Extra Practice Quiz** (check figures in Chapter Organizer, p. 101)

Earl Miller received his March 8, 2009, bank statement, which had a $300.10 balance. Earl's checkbook has a $1,200.10 balance. The bank statement showed a $15.00 ATM fee and a $30.00 deposited check returned fee. Earl earned $24.06 interest. He had three outstanding checks: No. 300, $22.88; No. 302, $15.90; and No. 303, $282.66. A deposit for $1,200.50 was not on his bank statement. Prepare Earl's bank reconciliation.

CHAPTER ORGANIZER AND STUDY GUIDE
WITH CHECK FIGURES FOR EXTRA PRACTICE QUIZZES

Topic	Key point, procedure, formula	Example(s) to illustrate situation
Types of endorsements, p. 91	*Blank:* Not safe; can be further endorsed.	Jones Co. 21-333-9
	Full: Only person or company named in endorsement can transfer check to someone else.	Pay to the order of Regan Bank Jones Co. 21-333-9
	Restrictive: Check must be deposited. Limits any further negotiation of the check.	Pay to the order of Regan Bank. For deposit only. Jones Co. 21-333-9

Bank reconciliation, p. 94	**Checkbook balance**
	+ EFT (electronic funds transfer)
	+ Interest earned
	+ Notes collected
	+ Direct deposits
	− ATM withdrawals
	− NSF check
	− Online fees
	− Automatic withdrawals
	− Overdrafts
	− Service charges
	− Stop payments
	± Book errors*
	CM—adds to balance
	DM—deducts from balance
	
	Bank balance
	+ Deposits in transit
	− Outstanding checks
	± Bank errors
	
	*If a $60 check is recorded as $50, we must decrease checkbook balance by $10.
		Checkbook balance
		Balance $800
		  − NSF 40
		          $760
		   − Service charge 4
		         $756
		
		Bank balance
		Balance $ 632
		 + Deposits in transit 416
		        $1,048
		 − Outstanding checks 292
		       $ 756

KEY TERMS			
	Automatic teller machine (ATM), *p. 89* Bank reconciliation, *p. 96* Bank statement, *p. 95* Blank endorsement, *p. 91* Check, *p. 89* Check register, *p. 96* Check stub, *p. 91* Credit memo (CM), *p. 97* Debit card, *p. 89*	Debit memo (DM), *p. 97* Deposit slip, *p. 90* Deposits in transit, *p. 97* Draft, *p. 89* Drawee, *p. 90* Drawer, *p. 90* Electronic funds transfer (EFT), *p. 95* Endorse, *p. 91* Full endorsement, *p. 91*	Nonsufficient funds (NSF), *p. 97* Outstanding checks, *p. 97* Overdrafts, *p. 95* Payee, *p. 90* Restrictive endorsement, *p. 91* Safekeeping, *p. 100* Signature card, *p. 89*

CHECK FIGURES FOR EXTRA PRACTICE QUIZZES WITH PAGE REFERENCES	LU 4–1a (p. 93) Ending Balance Forward $11,533.80	LU 4–2a (p. 100) Reconciled Balance $1,179.16

Critical Thinking Discussion Questions

1. Explain the structure of a check. The trend in bank statements is not to return the canceled checks. Do you think this is fair?

2. List the three types of endorsements. Endorsements are limited to the top $1\frac{1}{2}$ inches of the trailing edge on the back left side of your check. Why do you think the Federal Reserve made this regulation?

3. List the steps in reconciling a bank statement. Today, many banks charge a monthly fee for certain types of checking accounts. Do you think all checking accounts should be free? Please explain.

4. What are some of the trends in online banking? Will we become a cashless society in which all transactions are made with some type of credit card?

Classroom Notes

Name _____ Date _____

DRILL PROBLEMS

4–1. Fill out the check register that follows with this information:
2009

July	7	Check No. 482	Google	$133.50
	15	Check No. 483	Microsoft	55.10
	19	Deposit		700.00
	20	Check No. 484	Sprint	451.88
	24	Check No. 485	Krispy Kreme	319.24
	29	Deposit		400.30

		RECORD ALL CHARGES OR CREDITS THAT AFFECT YOUR ACCOUNT					BALANCE	
NUMBER	DATE 2009	DESCRIPTION OF TRANSACTION	PAYMENT/DEBIT (−)	√	FEE (IF ANY) (−)	DEPOSIT/CREDIT (+)	$	4,500 75
			$		$	$		

4–2. November 1, 2009, Payroll.com, an Internet company, has a $10,481.88 checkbook balance. Record the following transactions for Payroll.com by completing the two checks and check stubs provided. Sign the checks Garth Scholten, controller.

a. November 8, 2009, deposited $688.10

b. November 8, check No. 190 payable to Wal-Mart Corporation for office supplies—$766.88

c. November 15, check No. 191 payable to Compaq Corporation for computer equipment—$3,815.99.

No. _____	$ _____		PAYROLL.COM 1 LEDGER RD. ST. PAUL, MN 55113	No. 190
_____ 20 _____				
To _____				
For _____			PAY TO THE ORDER OF _____	_____ 20 _____ 5-13/110
	DOLLARS	CENTS		$ _____
BALANCE				
AMT. DEPOSITED			_____	DOLLARS
			IPSWICH BANK	
			ipswichbank.com	
TOTAL				
AMT. THIS CHECK			MEMO _____	
BALANCE FORWARD			⑈011000138⑈ 25 11103 190	

```
No. _____  $ _____          PAYROLL.COM                              No. 191
_____  20 _____         1 LEDGER RD.
To _____             ST. PAUL, MN 55113
For _____             PAY
              ┌────────┬──────┐   TO THE                      _____ 20 ____   5-13/110
              │ DOLLARS│ CENTS│   ORDER
 BALANCE      │        │      │   OF _____ $ _____
 AMT. DEPOSITED│        │      │
              │        │      │   _____ DOLLARS
              │        │      │
              │        │      │   IPSWICHBANK ✒
 TOTAL        │        │      │   ipswichbank.com      _____
 AMT. THIS CHECK│        │      │
 BALANCE FORWARD│        │      │   MEMO_____
              └────────┴──────┘    ⑆011000138⑆   25 11103 191
```

4–3. Using the check register in Problem 4–1 and the following bank statement, prepare a bank reconciliation for Lee.com.

BANK STATEMENT			
Date	Checks	Deposits	Balance
7/1 balance			$4,500.75
7/18	$133.50		4,367.25
7/19		$ 700.00	5,067.25
7/26	319.24		4,748.01
7/30	15.00 SC		4,733.01

WORD PROBLEMS

4–4. Bank fees are squeezing customers according to an article in *The Record* (Hackensack, NJ) dated April 20, 2006. Banks are having a hard time making money lending, so many are charging more and higher fees. Meanwhile, interest paid on interest-bearing checking accounts remains low. Kayla Siska received her bank statement from the Commerce Bank which increased its overdraft fee from $33 to $35. To avoid future overdraft fees and bounced-checks (NSF) fees, Kayla wants to make sure her checkbook is in balance. The following checks have not cleared the bank: No. 634, $58.30; No. 635, $108.75; and No. 637, $112.68. Her checkbook balance shows $695.23. She received $1.75 in interest. She also was charged a $35.00 overdraft fee. The bank shows a balance of $320.10. A $621.61 deposit was not recorded. Prepare Kayla's bank reconciliation.

4–5. In the February 2007 issue of *Consumer Reports Money Adviser* an article appeared, stating ATM surcharges and bounced-check fees have reached record highs. The report found the average bounced-check (NSF) fee was $27.40 up from $27.04 last spring. ATM fees rose 10 cents, to $1.64 since last fall's survey. Norman Rand uses his ATM several times a month. Norman received his June 2007 bank statement showing a balance of $835.38, the statement did not show a $178.79 deposit he had made. His checkbook balance shows $838.40. Check No. 234 for $88.70 and check No. 236 for $124.75 were outstanding. He had an ATM surcharge of $11.48 and had a bounced-check fee of $27.40. He received $1.20 in interest. Prepare Norman's bank reconciliation.

4–6. A local bank began charging $2.50 each month for returning canceled checks. The bank also has an $8.00 "maintenance" fee if a checking account slips below $750. Donna Sands likes to have copies of her canceled checks for preparing her income tax. She has received her bank statement with a balance of $535.85. Donna received $2.68 in interest and has been charged for the canceled checks and the maintenance fee. The following checks were outstanding: No. 94, $121.16; No. 96, $106.30; No. 98, $210.12; and No. 99, $64.84. A deposit of $765.69 was not recorded on Donna's bank statement. Her checkbook shows a balance of $806.94. Prepare Donna's bank reconciliation.

4–7. *USA Today* reported on April 18, 2006 that checking account charges are getting nastier. Even as more banks introduce checking accounts with no monthly service fees, they're raising other charges and making it harder for customers to avoid them. The average cost of bouncing a check is at a near-record $27.04. ATM fees for non-customers have risen to a record average of $1.60 per withdrawal. Ben Luna received his bank statement with a $27.04 fee for a bounced-check (NSF). He has an $815.75 monthly mortgage payment paid through his bank. There was also a $3.00 teller fee and a check printing fee of $3.50. His ATM card fee was $6.40. There was also a $530.50 deposit in transit. The bank shows a balance of $119.17. The bank paid Ben $1.23 in interest. Ben's checkbook shows a balance of $1,395.28. Check No. 234 for $80.30 and check No. 235 for $28.55 were outstanding. Prepare Ben's bank reconciliation.

4–8. John D. Hawks, Jr., controller of the currency, delivered an address titled "Banks—Fees! Fees! Fees!" He points out that consumers who were unable to meet minimum balance requirements paid an average of $217 a year, or $18 a month, to maintain a checking account. Kameron Gibson has a hard time maintaining the minimum balance. He was having difficulty balancing his checkbook because he did not notice this fee on his bank statement. His bank statement showed a balance of $717.72. Kameron's checkbook had a balance of $209.50. Check No. 104 for $110.07 and check No. 105 for $15.55 were outstanding. A $620.50 deposit was not on the statement. He has his payroll check electronically deposited to his checking account—the payroll check was for $1,025.10. There was also a $4 teller fee and an $18 service charge. Prepare Kameron Gibson's bank reconciliation.

4–9. Banks are finding more ways to charge fees, such as a $25 overdraft fee. Sue McVickers has an account in Fayetteville; she has received her bank statement with this $25 charge. Also, she was charged a $6.50 service fee; however, the good news is she earned $5.15 interest. Her bank statement's balance was $315.65, but it did not show the $1,215.15 deposit she had made. Sue's checkbook balance shows $604.30. The following checks have not cleared: No. 250, $603.15; No. 253, $218.90; and No. 254, $130.80. Prepare Sue's bank reconciliation.

4–10. Carol Stokke receives her April 6 bank statement showing a balance of $859.75; her checkbook balance is $954.25. The bank statement shows an ATM charge of $25.00, NSF fee of $27.00, earned interest of $2.75, and Carol's $630.15 refund check, which was processed by the IRS and deposited to her account. Carol has two checks that have not cleared—No. 115 for $521.15 and No. 116 for $205.50. There is also a deposit in transit for $1,402.05. Prepare Carol's bank reconciliation.

4–11. Lowell Bank reported the following checking account fees: $2 to see a real-live teller, $20 to process a bounced check, and $1 to $3 if you need an original check to prove you paid a bill or made a charitable contribution. This past month you had to transact business through a teller 6 times—a total $12 cost to you. Your bank statement shows a $305.33 balance; your checkbook shows a $1,009.76 balance. You received $1.10 in interest. An $801.15 deposit was not recorded on your statement. The following checks were outstanding: No. 413, $28.30; No. 414, $18.60; and No. 418, $60.72. Prepare your bank reconciliation.

4–12. Carolyn Crosswell, who banks in New Jersey, wants to balance her checkbook, which shows a balance of $985.20. The bank shows a balance of $1,430.33. The following transactions occurred: $135.20 automatic withdrawal to the gas company, $6.50 ATM fee, $8.00 service fee, and $1,030.05 direct deposit from the IRS. Carolyn used her debit card 5 times and was charged 45 cents for each transaction; she was also charged $3.50 for check printing. A $931.08 deposit was not shown on her bank statement. The following checks were outstanding: No. 235, $158.20; No. 237, $184.13; No. 238, $118.12; and No. 239, $38.83. Carolyn received $2.33 interest. Prepare Carolyn's bank reconciliation.

4–13. Melissa Jackson, bookkeeper for Kinko Company, cannot prepare a bank reconciliation. From the following facts, can you help her complete the June 30, 2009, reconciliation? The bank statement showed a $2,955.82 balance. Melissa's checkbook showed a $3,301.82 balance.

Melissa placed a $510.19 deposit in the bank's night depository on June 30. The deposit did not appear on the bank statement. The bank included two DMs and one CM with the returned checks: $690.65 DM for NSF check, $8.50 DM for service charges, and $400.00 CM (less $10 collection fee) for collecting a $400.00 non-interest-bearing note. Check No. 811 for $110.94 and check No. 912 for $82.50, both written and recorded on June 28, were not with the returned checks. The bookkeeper had correctly written check No. 884, $1,000, for a new cash register, but she recorded the check as $1,069. The May bank reconciliation showed check No. 748 for $210.90 and check No. 710 for $195.80 outstanding on April 30. The June bank statement included check No. 710 but not check No. 748.

SUMMARY PRACTICE TEST

1. Walgreens has a $12,925.55 beginning checkbook balance. Record the following transactions in the check stubs provided. *(p. 91)*

   a. November 4, 2009, check No. 180 payable to Johnson and Johnson Corporation, $1,700.88 for drugs.

   b. $5,250 deposit—November 24.

   c. November 24, 2009, check No. 181 payable to Gillette Corporation, $825.55 merchandise.

No. _____ $ _____			No. _____ $ _____		
_____ 20 _____			_____ 20 _____		
To _____			To _____		
For _____			For _____		
	DOLLARS	CENTS		DOLLARS	CENTS
BALANCE			BALANCE		
AMT. DEPOSITED			AMT. DEPOSITED		
TOTAL			TOTAL		
AMT. THIS CHECK			AMT. THIS CHECK		
BALANCE FORWARD			BALANCE FORWARD		

2. On April 1, 2009, Lester Company received a bank statement that showed a $8,950 balance. Lester showed an $8,000 checking account balance. The bank did not return check No. 115 for $750 or check No. 118 for $370. A $900 deposit made on March 31 was in transit. The bank charged Lester $20 for printing and $250 for NSF checks. The bank also collected a $1,400 note for Lester. Lester forgot to record a $400 withdrawal at the ATM. Prepare a bank reconciliation. *(p. 95)*

3. Felix Babic banks at Role Federal Bank. Today he received his March 31, 2009, bank statement showing a $762.80 balance. Felix's checkbook shows a balance of $799.80. The following checks have not cleared the bank: No. 140, $130.55; No. 149, $66.80; and No. 161, $102.90. Felix made a $820.15 deposit that is not shown on the bank statement. He has his $617.30 monthly mortgage payment paid through the bank. His $1,100.20 IRS refund check was mailed to his bank. Prepare Felix Babic's bank reconciliation. *(p. 95)*

4. On June 30, 2009, Wally Company's bank statement showed a $7,500.10 bank balance. Wally has a beginning checkbook balance of $9,800.00. The bank statement also showed that it collected a $1,200.50 note for the company. A $4,500.10 June 30 deposit was in transit. Check No. 119 for $650.20 and check No. 130 for $381.50 are outstanding. Wally's bank charges $.40 cents per check. This month, 80 checks were processed. Prepare a reconciled statement. *(p. 95)*

Personal Finance

CREDIT | Online banking is convenient but not foolproof. *By Joan Goldwasser*

Electronic bill-paying SNAFUS

WHEN EMILY and Greg Martinez moved from Philadelphia to Los Angeles earlier this year, they thought that transferring their online bank account would be a snap. They were wrong. Because they didn't notify Sprint in time, their monthly cellphone bill was paid twice— once from their Philadelphia account and again from their new Los Angeles bank account.

● Because of an online glitch, Emily Martinez ended up overpaying her cell-phone bill.

Other online bill-payers have had bills that narrowly escaped being paid late, or weren't paid at all. One couple failed to notify Checkfree, their bill-paying service, that their mortgage lender had changed addresses. Their mortgage check was forwarded and ended up arriving on time. However, a young teacher wasn't so fortunate. He assumed that his car payments would be automatically debited from his checking account. But he neglected to sign the necessary documents, and after several missed payments, he had to scramble to fix the problem—after his car had been repossessed in the middle of the night.

If you're among the two-thirds of U.S. consumers who no longer worry about writing checks or running out of stamps thanks to automatic bill-paying services, you still need to monitor your bills. After you sign up with a vendor or your bank, review your account statements on a regular basis, advises Mike Herd of Nacha, the electronic-payments association. And make sure that your payee mailing addresses are up-to-date.

When you sign up for automatic bill-paying with an individual vendor or with your bank, you can generally decide whether you want the funds debited from your checking account or charged to a credit card. You can change the amount, or even cancel the payment, sometimes as late as the day before your bill is due.

If you have a problem with unauthorized payments—which happens to about 25 out of every 100,000 transactions, according to Nacha—be sure to notify your bank or credit-card company immediately. Nacha rules require the financial institution to reimburse your account if a transaction is unauthorized. Neither Visa nor MasterCard holds consumers liable for unintended charges to their accounts.

In a rare instance, automatic bill-paying can be too efficient. Take the case of the Canadian man who died in his Winnipeg apartment but wasn't discovered for nearly two years. No one noticed because all of his monthly bills had been paid on time.

DAN CHAVKIN

BUSINESS MATH ISSUE

In ten years everyone will pay bills online.

1. List the key points of the article and information to support your position.
2. Write a group defense of your position using math calculations to support your view.

Slater's Business Math Scrapbook

with Internet Application
Putting Your Skills to Work

Volkswagen is among the car companies and retailers that are expanding into traditional banking areas.

Now Open: The Bank of VW

Auto Makers, Retailers Offer Checking Accounts and CDs; A $1,600 Rebate on Next Car

By JENNIFER SARANOW

THE NEXT TIME you are in the market for a Volkswagen, you may wind up with a certificate of deposit instead of a convertible.

From car makers to department stores, an increasing number of companies are getting into the consumer-banking business. While many long have offered limited financial products such as credit cards and auto loans, they now are increasingly expanding into more traditional banking areas, ranging from checking accounts to CDs.

This month, **Volkswagen of America Inc.'s** Volkswagen Bank USA plans to open an Internet bank, offering CDs and savings accounts to its Volkswagen and Audi customers online. By the first quarter of next year, the two-year-old affiliate—which currently offers only home-equity lines of credit, credit cards and auto financing—plans to roll out checking accounts.

Meanwhile, **Toyota Motor** Corp.'s Toyota Financial Services unit is developing a host of banking products, including money-market accounts, CDs and savings accounts.

Both **General Motors** Corp. and **BMW AG** already have U.S. banks offering personal banking products. **Nordstrom Inc.'s** Nordstrom Federal Savings Bank has offered a checking account, among other banking products, since 2001.

The moves come as retail banking is booming in the U.S. After the dot-com bubble burst, many consumers looking for safe investments put their money in banks. "The U.S. retail-banking industry has been terrifically profitable and very successful over the last half a dozen years. That is why you see retailers trying to get into retail banking," says Jim Eckenrode, vice president of banking and payments research at TowerGroup.

Internet Projects: See text Web site (www.mhhe.com/slater9e) and The Business Math Internet Resource Guide.

CHAPTER 5

Solving for the Unknown: A How-to Approach for Solving Equations

Why Suiting Up Will Cost More This Year

A menswear shake-up is changing the price equation for some popular suits; $50 extra for 'sweat guards'

By RAY A. SMITH

SOME SUIT BUYERS are going to have to tighten their belts this year—and it has nothing to do with a new fashion statement.

There's a shakeup in the suit business and it's prompting a big shift in the prices that have long distinguished a good suit from a cheap one. At the low end, the $200-$300 suit has gotten a major quality upgrade and is now bidding to compete with suits in the $500-$700 range. Meanwhile, some of the companies making those midrange suits are also trying to trade up, by offering features you might find in the made-to-measure segment, traditionally the province of higher-end names. For shoppers, the most obvious result of this jockeying: The standard suit from many established makers—everyone from Hart Schaffner Marx to Calvin Klein to Burberry—will cost between $50 and $100 more this fall.

Those suit makers say they have added touches that justify the higher prices. They include underarm guards that promise to prevent embarrassing sweat stains and an extra panel of fabric sewn into the chest area to make the suit feel less boxy. Some of the improvements are largely cosmetic, while others are more substantive—such as upgrading to super 120s wool, a finer, softer fabric that is starting to show up in some $700 suits but is more common in pricier menswear.

Higher prices aren't the only thing turning up on suits this fall. Shoppers will see lots of glen plaids and navy suits with pinstripes
Please Turn to Page P5, Column 1

LEARNING UNIT OBJECTIVES

LU 5–1: Solving Equations for the Unknown

- Explain the basic procedures used to solve equations for the unknown (*pp. 114–116*).
- List the five rules and the mechanical steps used to solve for the unknown in seven situations; know how to check the answers (*pp. 117–119*).

LU 5–2: Solving Word Problems for the Unknown

- List the steps for solving word problems (*p. 121*).
- Complete blueprint aids to solve word problems; check the solutions (*pp. 121–123*).

When you shop at Home Depot, have you noticed that Home Depot employs many older employees? Often you are greeted by an older employee. Older, experienced employees frequently are ready to answer customers' questions.

Traditionally, many employers have avoided hiring older people. Now this has changed. The following *Wall Street Journal* clipping "Gray Is Good: Employers Make Efforts to Retain Older, Experienced Workers" gives interesting facts about the hiring of older, experienced employees. Some companies are seeking employees 55 and over. Home Depot and Stanley Consultants are two examples. At Stanley Consultants about $\frac{1}{4}$ of the 1,100 employees are over 50. This means that 275 employees are over 50:

$$\frac{1}{4} \times 1,100 = 275$$

Gray Is Good: Employers Make Efforts To Retain Older, Experienced Workers

AT AGE 69, John Sayles retired as principal planner for **Stanley Consultants**, a civil-engineering firm. Or he thought he did.

A few months later, his employer tracked him down on a family vacation in Colorado and told him his skills were needed in Iraq. "I was dumfounded" but pleased to be asked, says Mr. Sayles. He spent the next two months working in the presidential palace in Baghdad, as part of a team of government contractors rebuilding the infrastructure. Mr. Sayles, who lives in the company's hometown of Muscatine, Iowa, is now 71, and still works part-time.

Traditionally, many employers have viewed older workers as inflexible, less productive than their younger colleagues, and more expensive because of higher salaries and health-care costs. When hard times force layoffs, older workers are often the first to get the ax. But now, many employers are at least giving lip service to retaining older workers. And a few are taking concrete steps to actually do so—seeking out older workers and retirees with needed skills, rooting out age bias, and setting up complex flexible work arrangements tailored to their needs.

For employers, the writing on the wall is hard to miss. Workers 55 and over are growing four times faster than the work force as a whole.

Some companies are recognizing that older workers are repositories of hard-to-replace knowledge critical to their businesses, says Eric Lesser, an associate partner in Cambridge, Mass., with IBM Business Consulting Services. As workers retire, companies worry about losing relationships with suppliers and distributors, as well as the ability to maintain aging equipment, such as plants, machinery or other gear built to past standards, he says.

In addition, as the work force ages, so do the customers, who often prefer to deal with older workers. At **Home Depot**, older employees serve as a powerful draw to baby-boomer shoppers by mirroring their knowledge and perspective, says Dennis Donovan, executive vice president, human resources, for the 2,000-store retailer. Similarly, **Westpac Banking** Corp., a big Australian financial-services concern, recruited 950 over-45 workers as financial planners, among other roles. Older clients, a spokeswoman says, prefer advisers with experience.

At Stanley Consultants, an 1,100-employee firm where more than one-fourth of employees are over 50, older workers are encouraged to continue part-time.

Wall Street Journal © 2005

Learning Unit 5–1 explains how to solve for unknowns in equations. In Learning Unit 5–2 you learn how to solve for unknowns in word problems. When you complete these learning units, you will not have to memorize as many formulas to solve business and personal math applications. Also, with the increasing use of computer software, a basic working knowledge of solving for the unknown has become necessary.

Learning Unit 5–1: Solving Equations for the Unknown

The Rose Smith letter at the top of the following page is based on a true story. Note how Rose states that the blueprint aids, the lesson on repetition, and the chapter organizers were important factors in the successful completion of her business math course.

Rose Smith
15 Locust Street
Lynn, MA 01915

Dear Professor Slater,

Thank you for helping me get through your Business Math class. When I first started, my math anxiety level was real high. I felt I had no head for numbers. When you told us we would be covering the chapter on solving equations, I'll never forget how I started to shake. I started to panic. I felt I could never solve a word problem. I thought I was having an algebra attack.

Now that it's over (90 on the chapter on unknowns), I'd like to tell you what worked for me so you might pass this on to other students. It was your blueprint aids. Drawing boxes helped me to think things out. They were a tool that helped me more clearly understand how to dissect each word problem. They didn't solve the problem for me, but gave me the direction I needed. Repetition was the key to my success. At first I got them all wrong but after the third time, things started to click. I felt more confident. Your chapter organizers at the end of the chapter were great. Thanks for your patience – your repetition breeds success – now students are asking me to help them solve a word problem. Can you believe it!

Best,

Rose

Rose Smith

Many of you are familiar with the terms *variables* and *constants.* If you are planning to prepare for your retirement by saving only what you can afford each year, your saving is a *variable;* if you plan to save the same amount each year, your saving is a *constant.* Now you can also say that you cannot buy clothes by size because of the many variables involved. This unit explains the importance of mathematical variables and constants when solving equations.

Basic Equation-Solving Procedures

Do you wait for the after-Christmas sales to make your purchases? What happens when retailers have fewer inventories to sell after Christmas because they had a good Christmas season and discounted merchandise deeply before Christmas? This means it will be harder for customers to find bargains. The best bargains will be found in computers and clothes.

Navigating the New World Of Post-Christmas Sales

Strong season, gift cards change the equation;

Wall Street Journal © 2005

From the *Wall Street Journal* heading "Navigating the New World of Post-Christmas Sales," you can see that stores had a strong Christmas season. To have merchandise to sell, retailers offered large discounts to gift-card recipients with the hope that retailers could sell the gift-card recipients new, full-priced items. The heading also stated that gift cards change the equation. But no explanation is given on how the equation is changed or what the equation was before the change. The definition of an equation given in the next paragraph may suggest to you what is meant by "the equation."

Do you know the difference between a mathematical expression, equation, and formula? A mathematical **expression** is a meaningful combination of numbers and letters called *terms*. Operational signs (such as + or −) within the expression connect the terms to show a relationship between them. For example, 6 + 2 or 6A − 4A are mathematical expressions. An **equation** is a mathematical statement with an equal sign showing that a mathematical expression on the left equals the mathematical expression on the right. An equation has an equal sign; an expression does not have an equal sign. A **formula** is an equation that expresses in symbols a general fact, rule, or principle. Formulas are shortcuts for expressing a word concept. For example, in Chapter 10 you will learn that the formula for simple interest is Interest (I) = Principal (P) × Rate (R) × Time (T). This means that when you see $I = P \times R \times T$, you recognize the simple interest formula. Now let's study basic equations.

As a mathematical statement of equality, equations show that two numbers or groups of numbers are equal. For example, 6 + 4 = 10 shows the equality of an equation. Equations also use letters as symbols that represent one or more numbers. These symbols, usually a letter of the alphabet, are **variables** that stand for a number. We can use a variable even though we may not know what it represents. For example, A + 2 = 6. The variable A represents the number or **unknown** (4 in this example) for which we are solving. We distinguish variables from numbers, which have a fixed value. Numbers such as 3 or −7 are **constants** or **knowns,** whereas A and 3A (this means 3 times the variable A) are variables. So we can now say that variables and constants are *terms of mathematical expressions.*

Usually in solving for the unknown, we place variable(s) on the left side of the equation and constants on the right. The following rules for variables and constants are important.

VARIABLES AND CONSTANTS RULES

1. If no number is in front of a letter, it is a 1: $B = 1B$; $C = 1C$.
2. If no sign is in front of a letter or number, it is a +: $C = +C$; $4 = +4$.

You should be aware that in solving equations, the meaning of the symbols +, −, ×, and ÷ has not changed. However, some variations occur. For example, you can also write $A \times B$ (A times B) as $A \cdot B$, $A(B)$, or AB. Also, A divided by B is the same as A/B. Remember that to solve an equation, you must find a number that can replace the unknown in the equation and make it a true statement. Now let's take a moment to look at how we can change verbal statements into variables.

Assume Dick Hersh, an employee of Nike, is 50 years old. Let's assign Dick Hersh's changing age to the symbol A. The symbol A is a variable.

Verbal statement	Variable A (age)
Dick's age 8 years ago	A − 8
Dick's age 8 years from today	A + 8
Four times Dick's age	4A
One-fifth Dick's age	A/5

To visualize how equations work, think of the old-fashioned balancing scale shown in Figure 5.1. The pole of the scale is the equals sign. The two sides of the equation are the two pans of the scale. In the left pan or left side of the equation, we have A + 8; in the right pan or right side of the equation, we have 58. To solve for the unknown (Dick's present age), we isolate or place the unknown (variable) on the left side and the numbers on the right. We will do this soon. For now, remember that to keep an equation (or scale) in balance, we must perform mathematical operations (addition, subtraction, multiplication, and division) to *both* sides of the equation.

SOLVING FOR THE UNKNOWN RULE

Whatever you do to one side of an equation, you must do to the other side.

FIGURE   5.1

Equality in equations

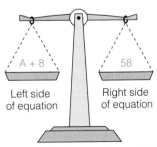

Left side   Right side
of equation   of equation

Dick's age in 8 years will equal 58.

How to Solve for Unknowns in Equations

This section presents seven drill situations and the rules that will guide you in solving for unknowns in these situations. We begin with two basic rules—the opposite process rule and the equation equality rule.

OPPOSITE PROCESS RULE

If an equation indicates a process such as addition, subtraction, multiplication, or division, solve for the unknown or variable by using the opposite process. For example, if the equation process is addition, solve for the unknown by using subtraction.

EQUATION EQUALITY RULE

You can add the same quantity or number to both sides of the equation and subtract the same quantity or number from both sides of the equation without affecting the equality of the equation. You can also divide or multiply both sides of the equation by the same quantity or number *(except zero)* without affecting the equality of the equation.

To check your answer(s), substitute your answer(s) for the letter(s) in the equation. The sum of the left side should equal the sum of the right side.

Drill Situation 1: Subtracting Same Number from Both Sides of Equation

Example	**Mechanical steps**	**Explanation**
$A + 8 = 58$	$A + 8 = 58$	8 is subtracted from *both*
Dick's age A plus 8	$\underline{-8 \quad -8}$	sides of equation to isolate
equals 58.	$A \quad = \boxed{50}$	variable A on the left.

Check

$50 + 8 = 58$

$58 = 58$

Note: Since the equation process used *addition,* we use the opposite process rule and solve for variable A with *subtraction.* We also use the equation equality rule when we subtract the same quantity from both sides of the equation.

Drill Situation 2: Adding Same Number to Both Sides of Equation

Example	**Mechanical steps**	**Explanation**
$B - 50 = 80$	$B - 50 = 80$	50 is added to *both* sides to
Some number B less 50	$\underline{+50 \quad +50}$	isolate variable B on the left.
equals 80.	$B \quad = \boxed{130}$	

Check

$130 - 50 = 80$

$80 = 80$

Note: Since the equation process used *subtraction,* we use the opposite process rule and solve for variable B with *addition.* We also use the equation equality rule when we add the same quantity to both sides of the equation.

Drill Situation 3: Dividing Both Sides of Equation by Same Number

Example	**Mechanical steps**	**Explanation**
$7G = 35$	$7G = 35$	By dividing both sides by
Some number G times	$\dfrac{7G}{7} = \dfrac{35}{7}$	7, G equals 5.
7 equals 35.	$G = \boxed{5}$	

Check

$7(5) = 35$

$35 = 35$

Note: Since the equation process used *multiplication,* we use the opposite process rule and solve for variable G with *division.* We also use the equation equality rule when we divide both sides of the equation by the same quantity.

Drill Situation 4: Multiplying Both Sides of Equation by Same Number

Example	**Mechanical steps**	**Explanation**
$\dfrac{V}{5} = 70$	$\dfrac{V}{5} = 70$	By multiplying both sides by 5, V is equal to 350.
Some number V divided by 5 equals 70.	$5\left(\dfrac{V}{5}\right) = 70(5)$ $V = \boxed{350}$	**Check** $\dfrac{350}{5} = 70$ $70 = 70$

Note: Since the equation process used *division,* we use the opposite process rule and solve for variable V with *multiplication.* We also use the equation equality rule when we multiply both sides of the equation by the same quantity.

Drill Situation 5: Equation That Uses Subtraction and Multiplication to Solve Unknown

> ### MULTIPLE PROCESSES RULE
>
> When solving for an unknown that involves more than one process, do the addition and subtraction before the multiplication and division.

Example	**Mechanical steps**	**Explanation**
$\dfrac{H}{4} + 2 = 5$	$\dfrac{H}{4} + 2 = 5$	1. Move constant to right side by subtracting 2 from both sides.
When we divide unknown H by 4 and add the result to 2, the answer is 5.	$\begin{aligned} \dfrac{H}{4} + 2 &= 5 \\ -2 \quad &-2 \\ \dfrac{H}{4} &= 3 \end{aligned}$	2. To isolate H, which is divided by 4, we do the opposite process and multiply 4 times *both* sides of the equation.
	$4\left(\dfrac{H}{4}\right) = 4(3)$ $H = \boxed{12}$	**Check** $\dfrac{12}{4} + 2 = 5$ $3 + 2 = 5$ $5 = 5$

Drill Situation 6: Using Parentheses in Solving for Unknown

> ### PARENTHESES RULE
>
> When equations contain parentheses (which indicate grouping together), you solve for the unknown by first multiplying each item inside the parentheses by the number or letter just outside the parentheses. Then you continue to solve for the unknown with the opposite process used in the equation. Do the additions and subtractions first; then the multiplications and divisions.

Example	**Mechanical steps**	**Explanation**
$5(P - 4) = 20$	$5(P - 4) = 20$	1. Parentheses tell us that everything inside parentheses is multiplied by 5. Multiply 5 by P and 5 by -4.
The unknown P less 4, multiplied by 5 equals 20.	$5P - 20 = 20$ $$\underline{+20 \quad +20}$$ $$\frac{\cancel{5}P}{\cancel{5}} = \frac{40}{5}$$ $$P = \boxed{8}$$	2. Add 20 to both sides to isolate $5P$ on left. 3. To remove 5 in front of P, divide both sides by 5 to result in P equals 8.

Check
$$5(8 - 4) = 20$$
$$5(4) = 20$$
$$20 = 20$$

Drill Situation 7: Combining Like Unknowns

LIKE UNKNOWNS RULE
To solve equations with like unknowns, you first combine the unknowns and then solve with the opposite process used in the equation.

Example	**Mechanical steps**	**Explanation**
$4A + A = 20$	$4A + A = 20$ $$\frac{\cancel{5}A}{\cancel{5}} = \frac{20}{5}$$ $$\boxed{A} = 4$$	To solve this equation: $4A + 1A = 5A$. Thus, $5A = 20$. To solve for A, divide both sides by 5, leaving A equals 4.

Before you go to Learning Unit 5–2, let's check your understanding of this unit.

LU 5–1   PRACTICE QUIZ

Complete this **Practice Quiz** to see how you are doing

1. Write equations for the following (use the letter Q as the variable). Do not solve for the unknown.
   a. Nine less than one-half a number is fourteen.
   b. Eight times the sum of a number and thirty-one is fifty.
   c. Ten decreased by twice a number is two.
   d. Eight times a number less two equals twenty-one.
   e. The sum of four times a number and two is fifteen.
   f. If twice a number is decreased by eight, the difference is four.

2. Solve the following:
   a. $B + 24 = 60$ b. $D + 3D = 240$ c. $12B = 144$
   d. $\dfrac{B}{6} = 50$ e. $\dfrac{B}{4} + 4 = 16$ f. $3(B - 8) = 18$

✓ Solutions

1. a. $\dfrac{1}{2}Q - 9 = 14$ b. $8(Q + 31) = 50$ c. $10 - 2Q = 2$
   d. $8Q - 2 = 21$ e. $4Q + 2 = 15$ f. $2Q - 8 = 4$

2. a. $B + 24 = -60$
   $$\underline{ -24 \quad -24}$$
   $$B = \boxed{36}$$
   b. $$\frac{\cancel{4}D}{\cancel{4}} = \frac{240}{4}$$
   $$D = \boxed{60}$$
   c. $$\frac{\cancel{12}B}{\cancel{12}} = \frac{144}{12}$$
   $$B = \boxed{12}$$

d. $6\left(\dfrac{B}{6}\right) = 50(6)$

$\qquad B = \boxed{300}$

e. $\dfrac{B}{4} + 4 = 16$

$\qquad \underline{-4 \quad -4}$

$\qquad \dfrac{B}{4} = 12$

$\qquad 4\left(\dfrac{B}{4}\right) = 12(4)$

$\qquad B = \boxed{48}$

f. $3(B - 8) = 18$

$\quad 3B - 24 = 18$

$\quad \underline{+24 \quad +24}$

$\quad \dfrac{3B}{3} = \dfrac{42}{3}$

$\qquad B = \boxed{14}$

LU 5–1a   EXTRA PRACTICE QUIZ

Need more practice? Try this
Extra Practice Quiz (check
figures in Chapter Organizer,
p. 127)

1. Write equations for the following (use the letter Q as the variable). Do not solve for the unknown.
    a. Eight less than one-half a number is sixteen.
    b. Twelve times the sum of a number and forty-one is 1,200.
    c. Seven decreased by twice a number is one.
    d. Four times a number less two equals twenty-four.
    e. The sum of three times a number and three is nineteen.
    f. If twice a number is decreased by six, the difference is five.

2. Solve the following:
    a. $B + 14 = 70$
    b. $D + 4D = 250$
    c. $11B = 121$
    d. $\dfrac{B}{8} = 90$
    e. $\dfrac{B}{2} + 2 = 16$
    f. $3(B - 6) = 18$

Learning Unit 5–2: Solving Word Problems for the Unknown

When you buy a candy bar such as a Snickers, you should turn the candy bar over and carefully read the ingredients and calories contained on the back of the candy bar wrapper.

For example, on the back of the Snickers wrapper you will read that there are "170 calories per piece." You could misread this to mean that the entire Snickers bar has 170 calories. However, look closer and you will see that the Snickers bar is divided into three pieces, so if you eat the entire bar, instead of consuming 170 calories, you will consume 510 calories. Making errors like this could result in a weight gain that you cannot explain.

$$\dfrac{1}{3}S = 170 \text{ calories}$$

$$3\left(\dfrac{1}{3}S\right) = 170 \times 3$$

$$S = \boxed{510} \text{ calories per bar}$$

In this unit, we use blueprint aids in six different situations to help you solve for unknowns. Be patient and *persistent*. Remember that the more problems you work, the easier the process becomes. Do not panic! Repetition is the key. Study the five steps that follow. They will help you solve for unknowns in word problems.

SOLVING WORD PROBLEMS FOR UNKNOWNS
Step 1. Carefully read the entire problem. You may have to read it several times.
Step 2. Ask yourself: "What is the problem looking for?"
Step 3. When you are sure what the problem is asking, let a variable represent the unknown. If the problem has more than one unknown, represent the second unknown in terms of the same variable. For example, if the problem has two unknowns, Y is one unknown. The second unknown is $4Y$—4 times the first unknown.
Step 4. Visualize the relationship between unknowns and variables. Then set up an equation to solve for unknown(s).
Step 5. Check your result to see if it is accurate.

Word Problem Situation 1: Number Problems From the *Wall Street Journal* clipping "The Flagging Division," you can determine that Disney Stores reduced its product offerings by 1,600. Disney now has 1,800 product offerings. What was the original number of product offerings?

Bill Aron/PhotoEdit

The Flagging Division ...

A snapshot of the Disney Stores

- **NUMBER OF STORES:** 740
- **STORE VISITORS:** 250 million annually
- **LOCATIONS:** 11 countries including Britain, Australia and Japan
- **PRODUCTS:** Toys, costumes, apparel, jewelry, accessories, videos and games, among others
- **PRODUCT PLANS:** Each store will have 1,800 product offerings, down from 3,400 in the past. Focus on adults will be narrowed to sleepwear and parenting products.

Reprinted by permission of The WallStreet Journal, © 2000 Dow Jones & Company, Inc. All Rights Reserved Worldwide.

Blueprint aid

Unknown(s)	Variable(s)	Relationship*
Original number of product offerings	P	$P - 1,600 =$ New offerings New offerings $= 1,800$

*This column will help you visualize the equation before setting up the actual equation.

Mechanical steps

$$
\begin{array}{rr}
P - 1,600 = & 1,800 \\
+ 1,600 & + 1,600 \\
\hline
P \quad = & 3,400
\end{array}
$$

Explanation

The original offerings less $1,600 = 1,800$. Note that we added 1,600 to both sides to isolate P on the left. Remember, $1P = P$.

Check

$$3,400 - 1,600 = 1,800$$
$$1,800 = 1,800$$

Word Problem Situation 2: Finding the Whole When Part Is Known A local Burger King budgets $\frac{1}{8}$ of its monthly profits on salaries. Salaries for the month were $12,000. What were Burger King's monthly profits?

Blueprint aid

Unknown(s)	Variable(s)	Relationship
Monthly profits	P	$\frac{1}{8}P$ Salaries = $12,000

Mechanical steps

$$\frac{1}{8}P = \$12,000$$

$$8\left(\frac{P}{8}\right) = \$12,000(8)$$

$$P = \boxed{\$96,000}$$

Explanation

$\frac{1}{8}P$ represents Burger King's monthly salaries. Since the equation used division, we solve for P by multiplying both sides by 8.

Check

$$\frac{1}{8}(\$96,000) = \$12,000$$
$$\$12,000 = \$12,000$$

Word Problem Situation 3: Difference Problems ICM Company sold 4 times as many computers as Ring Company. The difference in their sales is 27. How many computers of each company were sold?

Blueprint aid

Unknown(s)	Variable(s)	Relationship
ICM	$4C$	$4C$
Ring	C	$-C$ 27

Note: If problem has two unknowns, assign the variable to smaller item or one who sells less. Then assign the other unknown using the same variable. *Use the same letter.*

Mechanical steps

$$4C - C = 27$$
$$\frac{3C}{3} = \frac{27}{3}$$
$$C = \boxed{9}$$

Ring = $\boxed{9}$ computers

ICM = 4(9)

$\quad$ = $\boxed{36}$ computers

Explanation

The variables replace the names ICM and Ring. We assigned Ring the variable C, since it sold fewer computers. We assigned ICM $4C$, since it sold 4 times as many computers.

Check

$\quad$ 36 computers
$\quad \underline{-9}$
$\quad$ 27 computers

Word Problem Situation 4: Calculating Unit Sales Together Barry Sullivan and Mitch Ryan sold a total of 300 homes for Regis Realty. Barry sold 9 times as many homes as Mitch. How many did each sell?

Blueprint aid

Unknown(s)	Variable(s)	Relationship
Homes sold:		
B. Sullivan	$9H$	$9H$
M. Ryan	H^*	$+ H$ 300 homes

*Assign H to Ryan since he sold less.

Mechanical steps

$$9H + H = 300$$
$$\frac{10H}{10} = \frac{300}{10}$$
$$H = \boxed{30}$$

Ryan: $\boxed{30}$ homes

Sullivan: 9(30) = $\boxed{270}$ homes

Explanation

We assigned Mitch H, since he sold fewer homes. We assigned Barry $9H$, since he sold 9 times as many homes. Together Barry and Mitch sold 300 homes.

Check

30 + 270 = 300

Word Problem Situation 5: Calculating Unit and Dollar Sales (Cost per Unit) When Total Units Are Not Given Andy sold watches ($9) and alarm clocks ($5) at a flea market. Total sales were $287. People bought 4 times as many watches as alarm clocks. How many of each did Andy sell? What were the total dollar sales of each?

Blueprint aid

Unknown(s)	Variable(s)	Price	Relationship
Unit sales:			
Watches	4C	$9	36C
Clocks	C	5	+ 5C
			$287 total sales

Mechanical steps

$$36C + 5C = 287$$
$$\frac{41C}{41} = \frac{287}{41}$$
$$C = \boxed{7}$$

$\boxed{7}$ clocks

$4(7) = \boxed{28}$ watches

Explanation

Number of watches times $9 sales price plus number of alarm clocks times $5 equals $287 total sales.

Check

$$7(\$5) + 28(\$9) = \$287$$
$$\$35 + \$252 = \$287$$
$$\$287 = \$287$$

Word Problem Situation 6: Calculating Unit and Dollar Sales (Cost per Unit) When Total Units Are Given Andy sold watches ($9) and alarm clocks ($5) at a flea market. Total sales for 35 watches and alarm clocks were $287. How many of each did Andy sell? What were the total dollar sales of each?

Blueprint aid

Unknown(s)	Variable(s)	Price	Relationship
Unit sales:			
Watches	W*	$9	9W
Clocks	35 − W	5	+ 5(35 − W)
			$287 total sales

*The more expensive item is assigned to the variable first only for this situation to make the mechanical steps easier to complete.

Mechanical steps

$$9W + 5(35 - W) = 287$$
$$9W + 175 - 5W = 287$$
$$4W + 175 = 287$$
$$\underline{-175 \qquad -175}$$
$$\frac{4W}{4} = \frac{112}{4}$$
$$W = \boxed{28}$$

Watches = $\boxed{28}$

Clocks = 35 − 28 = $\boxed{7}$

Explanation

Number of watches (W) times price per watch plus number of alarm clocks times price per alarm clock equals $287. Total units given was 35.

Check

$$28(\$9) + 7(\$5) = \$287$$
$$\$252 + \$35 = \$287$$
$$\$287 = \$287$$

Why did we use 35 − W? Assume we had 35 pizzas (some cheese, others meatball). If I said that I ate all the meatball pizzas (5), how many cheese pizzas are left? Thirty? Right, you subtract 5 from 35. Think of 35 − W as meaning one number.

Note in Word Problem Situations 5 and 6 that the situation is the same. In Word Problem Situation 5, we were not given total units sold (but we were told which sold better). In Word Problem Situation 6, we were given total units sold, but we did not know which sold better.

Now try these six types of word problems in the Practice Quiz. Be sure to complete blueprint aids and the mechanical steps for solving the unknown(s).

LU 5–2 PRACTICE QUIZ

Complete this **Practice Quiz** to see how you are doing

Situations

1. An L. L. Bean sweater was reduced $30. The sale price was $90. What was the original price?
2. Kelly Doyle budgets $\frac{1}{8}$ of her yearly salary for entertainment. Kelly's total entertainment bill for the year is $6,500. What is Kelly's yearly salary?
3. Micro Knowledge sells 5 times as many computers as Morse Electronics. The difference in sales between the two stores is 20 computers. How many computers did each store sell?
4. Susie and Cara sell stoves at Elliott's Appliances. Together they sold 180 stoves in January. Susie sold 5 times as many stoves as Cara. How many stoves did each sell?
5. Pasquale's Pizza sells meatball pizzas ($6) and cheese pizzas ($5). In March, Pasquale's total sales were $1,600. People bought 2 times as many cheese pizzas as meatball pizzas. How many of each did Pasquale sell? What were the total dollar sales of each?

6. Pasquale's Pizza sells meatball pizzas ($6) and cheese pizzas ($5). In March, Pasquale's sold 300 pizzas for $1,600. How many of each did Pasquale's sell? What was the dollar sales price of each?

✓ Solutions

1.

Unknown(s)	Variable(s)	Relationship
Original price	P^*	$P - \$30 =$ Sale price Sale price $= \$90$

*$P =$ Orignal price.

Mechanical steps

$$P - \$30 = \quad \$90$$
$$\underline{+\ 30 \quad\quad +\ 30}$$
$$P \quad\quad\ = \boxed{\$120}$$

2.

Unknown(s)	Variable(s)	Relationship
Yearly salary	S^*	$\frac{1}{8}S$ Entertainment $= \$6,500$

*$S =$ Salary.

Mechanical steps

$$\frac{1}{8}S = \$6,500$$
$$8\left(\frac{S}{8}\right) = \$6,500(8)$$
$$S = \boxed{\$52,000}$$

3.

Unknown(s)	Variable(s)	Relationship
Micro	$5C^*$	$5C$
Morse	C	$\dfrac{-\ C}{\text{20 computers}}$

*$C =$ Computers.

Mechanical steps

$$5C - C = 20$$
$$\frac{4C}{4} = \frac{20}{4}$$
$$C = \boxed{5} \text{ (Morse)}$$
$$5C = \boxed{25} \text{ (Micro)}$$

4.

Unknown(s)	Variable(s)	Relationship
Stoves sold:		
Susie	$5S^*$	$5S$
Cara	S	$\dfrac{+\ S}{\text{180 stoves}}$

*$S =$ Stoves.

Mechanical steps

$$5S + S = 20$$
$$\frac{6S}{6} = \frac{180}{6}$$
$$S = \boxed{30} \text{ (Cara)}$$
$$5S = \boxed{150} \text{ (Susie)}$$

5.

Unknown(s)	Variable(s)	Price	Relationship
Meatball	M	$6	$6M$
Cheese	$2M$	5	$\dfrac{+\ 10M}{\text{\$1,600 total sales}}$

Mechanical steps

$$6M + 10M = 1,600$$
$$\frac{16M}{16} = \frac{1,600}{16}$$
$$M = \boxed{100} \text{ (meatball)}$$
$$2M = \boxed{200} \text{ (cheese)}$$

Check

$$(100 \times \$6) + (200 \times \$5) = \$1,600$$
$$\$600 + \$1,000 = \$1,600$$
$$\$1,600 = \$1,600$$

6.

Unknown(s)	Variable(s)	Price	Relationship
Unit sales:			
Meatball	M^*	$6	$6M$
Cheese	$300 - M$	5	$\dfrac{+\ 5(300 - M)}{\text{\$1,600 total sales}}$

*We assign the variable to the most expensive to make the mechanical steps easier to complete.

Mechanical steps

$$\begin{aligned} 6M + 5(300 - M) &= 1,600 \\ 6M + 1,500 - 5M &= 1,600 \\ M + 1,500 &= 1,600 \\ \underline{-\ 1,500 \quad\quad} &\ \underline{-\ 1,500} \\ M &= \boxed{100} \end{aligned}$$

Meatball $= \boxed{100}$

Cheese $= 300 - 100 = \boxed{200}$

Check

$$100(\$6) + 200(\$5) = \$600 + \$1,000$$
$$= \$1,600$$

LU 5–2a EXTRA PRACTICE QUIZ

Need more practice? Try this **Extra Practice Quiz** (check figures in Chapter Organizer, p. 127)

Situations

1. An L. L. Bean sweater was reduced $50. The sale price was $140. What was the original price?

2. Kelly Doyle budgets $\frac{1}{7}$ of her yearly salary for entertainment. Kelly's total entertainment bill for the year is $7,000. What is Kelly's yearly salary?

3. Micro Knowledge sells 8 times as many computers as Morse Electronics. The difference in sales between the two stores is 49 computers. How many computers did each store sell?

4. Susie and Cara sell stoves at Elliott's Appliances. Together they sold 360 stoves in January. Susie sold 2 times as many stoves as Cara. How many stoves did each sell?

5. Pasquale's Pizza sells meatball pizzas ($7) and cheese pizzas ($6). In March, Pasquale's total sales were $1,800. People bought 3 times as many cheese pizzas as meatball pizzas. How many of each did Pasquale sell? What were the total dollar sales of each?

6. Pasquale's Pizza sells meatball pizzas ($7) and cheese pizzas ($6). In March, Pasquale sold 288 pizzas for $1,800. What was the dollar sales price of each?

CHAPTER ORGANIZER AND STUDY GUIDE
WITH CHECK FIGURES FOR EXTRA PRACTICE QUIZZES

Solving for unknowns from basic equations	Mechanical steps to solve unknowns	Key point(s)
Situation 1: Subtracting same number from both sides of equation, p. 117	$D + 10 = 12$ $\quad\; -10 \quad -10$ $D \quad\;\; = \quad 2$	Subtract 10 from both sides of equation to isolate variable D on the left. Since equation used addition, we solve by using opposite process—subtraction.
Situation 2: Adding same number to both sides of equation, p. 117	$L - 24 = 40$ $\quad\; +24 \quad +24$ $L \quad\;\; = \quad 64$	Add 24 to both sides to isolate unknown L on left. We solve by using opposite process of subtraction—addition.
Situation 3: Dividing both sides of equation by same number, p. 117	$6B = 24$ $\dfrac{6B}{6} = \dfrac{24}{6}$ $B = 4$	To isolate B by itself on the left, divide both sides of the equation by 6. Thus, the 6 on the left cancels—leaving B equal to 4. Since equation used multiplication, we solve unknown by using opposite process—division.
Situation 4: Multiplying both sides of equation by same number, p. 118	$\dfrac{R}{3} = 15$ $3\left(\dfrac{R}{3}\right) = 15(3)$ $R = 45$	To remove denominator, multiply both sides of the equation by 3—the 3 on the left side cancels, leaving R equal to 45. Since equation used division, we solve unknown by using opposite process—multiplication.
Situation 5: Equation that uses subtraction and multiplication to solve for unknown, p. 118	$\dfrac{B}{3} + 6 = 13$ $\quad\quad -6 \quad -6$ $\dfrac{B}{3} \quad = \quad 7$ $3\left(\dfrac{B}{3}\right) = 7(3)$ $B = 21$	1. Move constant 6 to right side by subtracting 6 from both sides. 2. Isolate B by itself on left by multiplying both sides by 3.

(continues)

CHAPTER ORGANIZER AND STUDY GUIDE
WITH CHECK FIGURES FOR EXTRA PRACTICE QUIZZES (continued)

Solving for unknowns from basic equations	Mechanical steps to solve unknowns	Key point(s)
Situation 6: Using parentheses in solving for unknown, p. 118	$6(A - 5) = 12$ $6A - 30 = 12$ $ + 30 \quad + 30$ $\dfrac{6A}{6} = \dfrac{42}{6}$ $A = \boxed{7}$	Parentheses indicate multiplication. Multiply 6 times A and 6 times -5. Result is $6A - 30$ on left side of the equation. Now add 30 to both sides to isolate $6A$ on left. To remove 6 in front of A, divide both sides by 6, to result in A equal to 7. Note that when deleting parentheses, we did not have to multiply the right side.
Situation 7: Combining like unknowns, p. 119	$6A + 2A = 64$ $\dfrac{8A}{8} = \dfrac{64}{8}$ $A = \boxed{8}$	$6A + 2A$ combine to $8A$. To solve for A, we divide both sides by 8.

Solving for unknowns from word problems	Blueprint aid	Mechanical steps to solve unknown with check
Situation 1: Number problems, p. 121 U.S. Air reduced its airfare to California by $60. The sale price was $95. What was the original price?	<table><tr><th>Unknown(s)</th><th>Variable(s)</th><th>Relationship</th></tr><tr><td>Original price</td><td>P</td><td>$P - \$60 =$ Sale price Sale price $= \$95$</td></tr></table>	$P - \$60 = \$\ 95$ $\underline{ + 60 \quad + 60}$ $P = \boxed{\$155}$ **Check** $\$155 - \$60 = \$95$ $\$95 = \$95$
Situation 2: Finding the whole when part is known, p. 122 K. McCarthy spends ⅛ of her budget for school. What is the total budget if school costs $5,000?	<table><tr><th>Unknown(s)</th><th>Variable(s)</th><th>Relationship</th></tr><tr><td>Total budget</td><td>B</td><td>$\frac{1}{8}B$ School $= \$5,000$</td></tr></table>	$\dfrac{1}{8}B = \$5,000$ $8\left(\dfrac{B}{8}\right) = \$5,000(8)$ $B = \boxed{\$40,000}$ **Check** $\dfrac{1}{8}(\$40,000) = \$5,000$ $\$5,000 = \$5,000$
Situation 3: Difference problems, p. 122 Moe sold 8 times as many suitcases as Bill. The difference in their sales is 280 suitcases. How many suitcases did each sell?	<table><tr><th>Unknown(s)</th><th>Variable(s)</th><th>Relationship</th></tr><tr><td>Suitcases sold: Moe Bill</td><td> $8S$ S</td><td> $8S$ $\underline{- S}$ 280 suitcases</td></tr></table>	$8S - S = 280$ (Bill) $\dfrac{7S}{7} = \dfrac{280}{7}$ $S = \boxed{40}$ (Bill) $8(40) = \boxed{320}$ (Moe) **Check** $320 - 40 = 280$ $280 = 280$
Situation 4: Calculating unit sales, p. 122 Moe sold 8 times as many suitcases as Bill. Together they sold a total of 360. How many did each sell?	<table><tr><th>Unknown(s)</th><th>Variable(s)</th><th>Relationship</th></tr><tr><td>Suitcases sold: Moe Bill</td><td> $8S$ S</td><td> $8S$ $\underline{+ S}$ 360 suitcases</td></tr></table>	$8S + S = 360$ $\dfrac{9S}{9} = \dfrac{360}{9}$ $S = \boxed{40}$ (Bill) $8(40) = \boxed{320}$ (Moe) **Check** $320 + 40 = 360$ $360 = 360$

(continues)

CHAPTER ORGANIZER AND STUDY GUIDE
WITH CHECK FIGURES FOR EXTRA PRACTICE QUIZZES (concluded)

Solving for unknowns from word problems	Blueprint aid	Mechanical steps to solve unknown with check
Situation 5: Calculating unit and dollar sales (cost per unit) when *total units not given*, **p. 123** Blue Furniture Company ordered sleepers ($300) and nonsleepers ($200) that cost $8,000. Blue expects sleepers to outsell nonsleepers 2 to 1. How many units of each were ordered? What were dollar costs of each?	<table><tr><td>Unknown(s)</td><td>Variable(s)</td><td>Price</td><td>Relationship</td></tr><tr><td>Sleepers Nonsleepers</td><td>2N N</td><td>$300 200</td><td>600N +200N $8,000 total cost</td></tr></table>	$600N + 200N = 8,000$ $\dfrac{800N}{800} = \dfrac{8,000}{800}$ $N = \boxed{10}$ (nonsleepers) $2N = \boxed{20}$ (sleepers) **Check** $10 \times \$200 = \$2,000$ $20 \times \$300 = \underline{6,000}$ $ = \$8,000$
Situation 6: Calculating unit and dollar sales (cost per unit) when *total units given*, **p. 123** Blue Furniture Company ordered 30 sofas (sleepers and nonsleepers) that cost $8,000. The wholesale unit cost was $300 for the sleepers and $200 for the nonsleepers. How many units of each were ordered? What were dollar costs of each?	<table><tr><td>Unknown(s)</td><td>Variable(s)</td><td>Price</td><td>Relationship</td></tr><tr><td>*Unit costs* Sleepers Nonsleepers</td><td> S 30 − S</td><td> $300 200</td><td> 300S +200(30 − S) $ 8,000 total cost</td></tr></table> *Note:* When the total units are given, the higher-priced item (sleepers) is assigned to the variable first. This makes the mechanical steps easier to complete.	$300S + 200(30 - S) \;=\; 8,000$ $300S + 6,000 - 200S = 8,000$ $100S + 6,000 \;=\; 8,000$ $ - 6,000 \qquad\quad -6,000$ $\dfrac{100S}{100} \;=\; \dfrac{2,000}{100}$ $S = \boxed{20}$ Nonsleepers $= 30 - 20$ $= \boxed{10}$ **Check** $20(\$300) + 10(\$200) = \$8,000$ $\$6,000 + \$2,000 = \$8,000$ $\$8,000 = \$8,000$
KEY TERMS	Constants, *p. 116* Formula, *p. 116* Variables, *p. 116* Equation, *p. 116* Knowns, *p. 116* Expression, *p. 116* Unknown, *p. 116*	

CHECK FIGURES FOR EXTRA PRACTICE QUIZZES WITH PAGE REFERENCES	LU 5–1a (p. 120)
	1. A. $Q/2 - 8 = 16$ B. $12(Q + 41) = 1,200$
	  C. $7 - 2Q = 1$ D. $4Q - 2 = 24$
	  E. $3Q + 3 = 19$ F. $2Q - 6 = 5$
	2. A. 56 B. 50 C. 11
	  D. 720 E. 28 F. 12
		LU 5–2a (p. 125)
		1. $P = \$190$
		2. $S = \$49,000$
		3. Morse 7; Micro 56
		4. Cara 120; Susie 240
		5. Meatball 72; cheese 216; Meatball = $504; cheese = $1,296
		6. Meatball $504; cheese $1,296

Critical Thinking Discussion Questions

1. Explain the difference between a variable and a constant. What would you consider your monthly car payment—a variable or a constant?

2. How does the opposite process rule help solve for the variable in an equation? If a Mercedes costs 3 times as much as a Saab, how could the opposite process rule be used? The selling price of the Mercedes is $60,000.

3. What is the difference between Word Problem Situations 5 and 6 in Learning Unit 5–2? Show why the more expensive item in Word Problem Situation 6 is assigned to the variable first.

Classroom Notes

Name _____ Date _____

DRILL PROBLEMS (First of Three Sets)

Solve the unknown from the following equations:

5–1. $D + 19 = 100$ **5–2.** $E + 90 = 200$ **5–3.** $Q + 100 = 400$ **5–4.** $Q - 60 = 850$

5–5. $5Y = 75$ **5–6.** $\dfrac{P}{6} = 92$ **5–7.** $8Y = 96$ **5–8.** $\dfrac{N}{16} = 5$

5–9. $4(P - 9) = 64$ **5–10.** $3(P - 3) = 27$

WORD PROBLEMS (First of Three Sets)

5–11. On February 14, 2007, *The Fresno Bee* reported Yosemite Fitness Center recently opened its second indoor climbing gym. The new gym, which is 6,975 square feet, is 3 times larger than the former gym. What was the size of the old gym?

5–12. In 1955 only 435 Kaiser-Darrins were built, because Kaiser-Frazer bailed out of the car business. Only 435 of these fantastic cars were ever built, they sold for $3,668 according to an article in the *Chicago Sun-Times* March 5, 2007 edition. The Kaiser-Darrin ended up being the most prized of Henry J. Kaiser's cars. It's valued today at $62,125 if in excellent condition, which is $1\frac{3}{4}$ times as much as a car in very nice condition—if you can find an owner willing to part with one for any price. What would be the value of the car in very nice condition?

5–13. Joe Sullivan and Hugh Kee sell cars for a Ford dealer. Over the past year, they sold 300 cars. Joe sells 5 times as many cars as Hugh. How many cars did each sell?

5–14. Nanda Yueh and Lane Zuriff sell homes for ERA Realty. Over the past 6 months they sold 120 homes. Nanda sold 3 times as many homes as Lane. How many homes did each sell?

5–15. Dots sells T-shirts ($2) and shorts ($4). In April, total sales were $600. People bought 4 times as many T-shirts as shorts. How many T-shirts and shorts did Dots sell? Check your answer.

5–16. Dots sells 250 T-shirts ($2) and shorts ($4). In April, total sales were $600. How many T-shirts and shorts did Dots sell? Check your answer. *Hint:* Let S = Shorts.

DRILL PROBLEMS (Second of Three Sets)

5–17. $8D = 640$

5–18. $7(A - 5) = 63$

5–19. $\dfrac{N}{9} = 7$

5–20. $18(C - 3) = 162$

5–21. $9Y - 10 = 53$

5–22. $7B + 5 = 26$

WORD PROBLEMS (Second of Three Sets)

5–23. On a flight from New York to Portland, Delta reduced its Internet price by $170.00. The sale price was $315.99. What was the original price?

5–24. Jill, an employee at Old Navy, budgets $\frac{1}{5}$ of her yearly salary for clothing. Jill's total clothing bill for the year is $8,000. What is her yearly salary?

5–25. Bill's Roast Beef sells 5 times as many sandwiches as Pete's Deli. The difference between their sales is 360 sandwiches. How many sandwiches did each sell?

5–26. Some job seekers who have difficulty finding new employment are described as discouraged workers. The September 6, 2003, issue of *The New York Times* reported that job losses were mounting. In August 2003, the count of discouraged workers rose to 503,000, $2\frac{1}{2}$ times as many as in August 2002. How many discouraged workers were there in August 2002?

5–27. Computer City sells batteries ($3) and small boxes of pens ($5). In August, total sales were $960. Customers bought 5 times as many batteries as boxes of pens. How many of each did Computer City sell? Check your answer.

5–28. Staples sells cartons of pens ($10) and rubber bands ($4). Leona ordered a total of 24 cartons for $210. How many cartons of each did Leona order? Check your answer. *Hint:* Let P = Pens.

DRILL PROBLEMS (Third of Three Sets)

5–29. $A + 90 - 15 = \quad 210$

5–30. $5Y + 15(Y + 1) = \quad 35$

5–31. $3M + 20 = \quad 2M + 80$

5–32. $20(C - 50) = 19{,}000$

WORD PROBLEMS (Third of Three Sets)

5–33. The *St. Louis Post-Dispatch,* on October 25, 2006 reported on ticket scalpers. Cardinals World Series tickets were selling at 15 times more than the highest ticket at face value—others were about 8 times the lowest face value. Pete Moran paid $400 for the lowest ticket at face value. Dennis Spivey paid $9\frac{3}{8}$ times the amount paid by Pete.

How much did Dennis pay for his ticket?

5–34. At General Electric, shift 1 produced 4 times as much as shift 2. General Electric's total production for July was 5,500 jet engines. What was the output for each shift?

5–35. Ivy Corporation gave 84 people a bonus. If Ivy had given 2 more people bonuses, Ivy would have rewarded $\frac{2}{3}$ of the workforce. How large is Ivy's workforce?

5–36. Jim Murray and Phyllis Lowe received a total of $50,000 from a deceased relative's estate. They decided to put $10,000 in a trust for their nephew and divide the remainder. Phyllis received $\frac{3}{4}$ of the remainder; Jim received $\frac{1}{4}$. How much did Jim and Phyllis receive?

5–37. The first shift of GME Corporation produced $1\frac{1}{2}$ times as many lanterns as the second shift. GME produced 5,600 lanterns in November. How many lanterns did GME produce on each shift?

5–38. Wal-Mart sells thermometers ($2) and hot-water bottles ($6). In December, Wal-Mart's total sales were $1,200. Customers bought 7 times as many thermometers as hot-water bottles. How many of each did Wal-Mart sell? Check your answer.

5–39. Ace Hardware sells cartons of wrenches ($100) and hammers ($300). Howard ordered 40 cartons of wrenches and hammers for $8,400. How many cartons of each are in the order? Check your answer.

5–40. The *Omaha World-Herald* reported the number of homeless people counted during an August census. In homeless shelters, 572 men were counted. This number was $2\frac{3}{4}$ times the number of children and $2\frac{1}{2}$ times the number of women. **(a)** How many children were homeless? **(b)** How many women were homeless? **(c)** What was the total number of homeless? Round answers to the nearest whole number.

5–41. Bessy has 6 times as much money as Bob, but when each earns $6, Bessy will have 3 times as much money as Bob. How much does each have before and after earning the $6?

 SUMMARY PRACTICE TEST

1. Delta reduced its round-trip ticket price from Portland to Boston by $140. The sale price was $401.90. What was the original price? *(p. 121)*

2. David Role is an employee of Google. He budgets $\frac{1}{7}$ of his salary for clothing. If Dave's total clothing for the year is $12,000, what is his yearly salary? *(p. 122)*

3. A local Best Buy sells 8 times as many iPods as Sears. The difference between their sales is 490 iPods. How many iPods did each sell? *(p. 122)*

4. Working at Staples, Jill Reese and Abby Lee sold a total of 1,200 calculators. Jill sold 5 times as many calculators as Abby. How many did each sell? *(p. 122)*

5. Target sells sets of pots ($30) and dishes ($20) at the local store. On the July 4 weekend, Target's total sales were $2,600. People bought 6 times as many pots as dishes. How many of each did Target sell? Check your answer. *(p. 123)*

6. A local Dominos sold a total of 1,600 small pizzas ($9) and pasta dinners ($13) during the Super Bowl. How many of each did Dominos sell if total sales were $15,600? Check your answer. *(p. 123)*

Personal Finance

RETIRE A MILLIONAIRE Time is on your side (and so is Uncle Sam)

The road to $1 million starts early, but if you're a late bloomer, help is at hand. The table below shows how much you need to save each month to accumulate $1 million by age 65, along with strategies for achieving that goal. At age 25, you're starting from scratch. At ages 35, 45 and 55, we assume you already have money in savings, on which you're earning 8% annually. If you're setting your goal lower or higher than $1 million, go to **kiplinger.com/ links/whatyouneed** to see how much you need to save if you're aiming to stockpile $500,000 or $2 million.

IF YOU'RE 25

IF YOU'RE 35

IF YOU'RE 45

IF YOU'RE 55

	IF YOU'RE 25	IF YOU'RE 35	IF YOU'RE 45	IF YOU'RE 55
YOU'VE SAVED	$0	$0	$0	$0
WHAT YOU NEED TO SAVE PER MONTH	$286	$671	$1,698	$5,466
YOU'VE SAVED		$50,000	$50,000	$50,000
WHAT YOU NEED TO SAVE PER MONTH		$304	$1,298	$4,859
YOU'VE SAVED			$100,000	$100,000
WHAT YOU NEED TO SAVE PER MONTH			$861	$4,253
YOU'VE SAVED				$200,000
WHAT YOU NEED TO SAVE PER MONTH				$3,040

GET HELP FROM UNCLE SAM You may qualify for a retirement-savings tax credit of 10% to 50% of the amount you contribute to an IRA, 401(k) or other retirement account. The credit can reduce your tax bill by up to $1,000. To qualify, your income must be $25,000 or less if you're single, $37,500 or less if you're a head of household or $50,000 or less if you're married.

GET HELP FROM YOUR BOSS If your employer offers a matching contribution, contribute at least enough to your 401(k) to capture the full match. Otherwise, you're walking away from free money. Try to save 15% of your gross income for retirement, including your employer match.

PLAY CATCH-UP Aim to contribute the maximum $15,500 to your 401(k) this year or $4,000 to your traditional or Roth IRA. Once you turn 50, you can contribute an additional $5,000 in catch-up contributions to your 401(k) and an extra $1,000 to your IRA.

STAY ON THE JOB Working a few years longer can boost your savings.

SOURCE: Nuveen Investments

IS YOUR RETIREMENT SAVING ON COURSE? | Go to kiplinger.com/tools

BUSINESS MATH ISSUE

Saving at a young age is not realistic.

1. List the key points of the article and information to support your position.
2. Write a group defense of your position using math calculations to support your view.

Slater's Business Math Scrapbook

with Internet Application

Putting Your Skills to Work

PROJECT A

Calculate the total price tag for each item (do not include maintenance fee).

Owning Part of a Yacht or a Bentley

Sharing a Fancy Car or Boat

Several companies offer fractional ownership in recreational vehicles, fancy cars and large boats. A sampling:

Silverton Marine

COMPANY	THE GOODS	PRICE TAG	DETAILS
A. American QuarterCoach 800-789-4885 (ext. 712)	2005 Prevost, 45 feet, sleeps up to four people, location to be determined	$184,500 for a one-eighth share; $7,020 per year in maintenance	Owner gets five weeks of use per year; coach is sold after three years and owners split the proceeds.
B. Exotic Car Share 847-358-7522	2004 Bentley Continental GT, garaged in Palatine, Ill., outside of Chicago	$30,000 for a one-fifth share; $10,000 per year for maintenance	Exotic guarantees at least $18,500 back when it sells the Bentley after three years.
C. Great Lakes BoatShare 586-419-6798	2003 Silverton Motor Yacht 453, 48 feet, sleeps six to eight, will likely be docked in St. Clair Shores, Mich.	$102,363 for a one-sixth share; $7,243 per year for maintenance	Owner gets four weekends, and 15 weekdays between early May and the end of October. Boat is sold after three years.
D. YachtSmart of North America 866-869-2248	2004 Azimut, 85 feet, sleeps eight (not including crew), owners determine where yacht travels	$500,000 for a one-eighth share; $49,500 per year for maintenance	Four weeks of use per year (maintenance and transit eat up 20 weeks). Boat is sold after five years.

Wall Street Journal © 2005

Internet Projects: See text Web site (www.mhhe.com/slater9e) and The Business Math Internet Resource Guide.

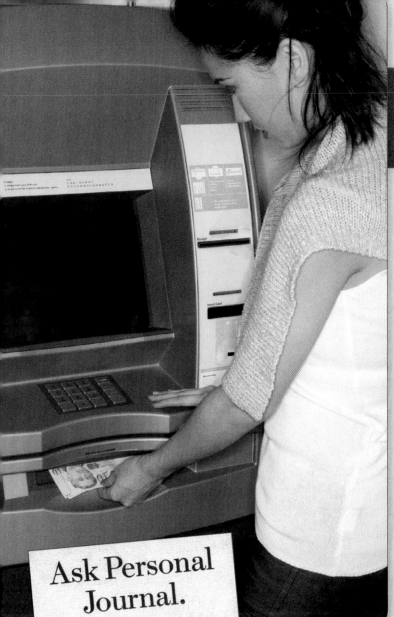

CHAPTER 6

Percents and Their Applications

LEARNING UNIT OBJECTIVES

LU 6–1: Conversions
- Convert decimals to percents (including rounding percents), percents to decimals, and fractions to percents *(pp. 139–141)*.
- Convert percents to fractions *(p. 142)*.

LU 6–2: Application of Percents—Portion Formula
- List and define the key elements of the portion formula *(pp. 144–145)*.
- Solve for one unknown of the portion formula when the other two key elements are given *(pp. 145–148)*.
- Calculate the rate of percent decreases and increases *(pp. 148–151)*.

Buying Potential

China has the second-highest number of Internet users after the U.S. ...

Internet users,
in millions

203.1

103.0

U.S.   China

China's Internet users,
by sex and age

Women — 40.4

59.6% — Men

Over 30 — 29.1

70.9% — Under 30

...But Chinese consumers show reluctance to make online purchases:

■ **0.1%** of survey respondents say they use the Internet primarily to make purchases.

■ **6.7%** of users say that online purchasing is among the services that they most frequently use.*

*Respondents could pick multiple choices.

Sources: China Internet Network Information Center, July 2005 survey of 18,136 responses; Nielsen/NetRatings (U.S. Internet users)

Ford to Cut 4,000 U.S. Salaried Jobs In Retooling Effort

By JEFFREY McCRACKEN

Ford Motor Co. has told employees it will eliminate 4,000 salaried jobs—or about 10% of its North American white-collar work force—in the first quarter of 2006.

The job cuts are the first concrete steps in a larger restructuring plan the struggling auto maker has been promising for months and now plans to announce early next year. Positions will be trimmed from within the company, as well from agencies and outside contractors to Ford.

The cuts were announced Friday afternoon in an email sent out by Ford's new North America president Mark Fields, who is overseeing the restructuring plan and its North American aspects.

Did you know that 60% of Internet users in China are men and that Ford plans to cut 10% of its workforce of salaried jobs? These facts are from the two *Wall Street Journal* clippings "Buying Potential" and "Ford to Cut 4,000 U.S. Salaried Jobs in Retooling Effort." Note in these *Wall Street Journal* clippings how companies frequently use percents to express various decreases and increases between two or more numbers, or to determine a decrease or increase.

To understand percents, you should first understand the conversion relationship between decimals, percents, and fractions as explained in Learning Unit 6–1. Then, in Learning Unit 6–2, you will be ready to apply percents to personal and business events.

Learning Unit 6–1: Conversions

When we described parts of a whole in previous chapters, we used fractions and decimals. Percents also describe parts of a whole. The word *percent* means per 100. The percent symbol (%) indicates hundredths (division by 100). **Percents** are the result of expressing numbers as part of 100. Thus, Ford's 10% cut in its workforce of salaried jobs represents 10 out of 100.

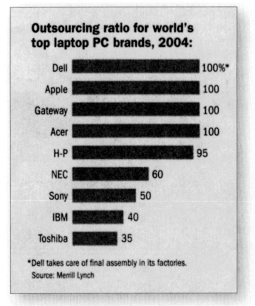

Outsourcing ratio for world's top laptop PC brands, 2004:

Dell   100%*
Apple   100
Gateway   100
Acer   100
H-P   95
NEC   60
Sony   50
IBM   40
Toshiba   35

*Dell takes care of final assembly in its factories.
Source: Merrill Lynch

Percents can provide some revealing information. The *Wall Street Journal* clipping "Outsourcing Ratio for World's Top Laptop PC Brands, 2004" shows that Dell, Apple, Gateway, and Acer outsource 100% of their top laptop PC brands.

TABLE	6.1

Analyzing a bag of M&M's®

		10%	5.5
		10%	5.5
		10%	5.5
		30%	14.5
		20%	11
		20%	11

What Colors Come In Your Bag?

Information adapted from http://us.mms.com/ us/about/products/milkchocolate/

Color	Fraction	Decimal (hundredth)	Percent (hundredth)
Yellow	$\frac{18}{55}$	.33	32.73%
Red	$\frac{10}{55}$	.18	18.18
Blue	$\frac{9}{55}$	.16	16.36
Orange	$\frac{7}{55}$	.13	12.73
Brown	$\frac{6}{55}$	.11	10.91
Green	$\frac{5}{55}$	.09	9.09
Total	$\frac{55}{55} = 1$	1.00	100.00%

Let's return to the M&M's® example from earlier chapters. In Table 6.1, we use our bag of 55 M&M's® to show how fractions, decimals, and percents can refer to the same parts of a whole. For example, the bag of 55 M&M's® contains 18 yellow M&M's®. As you can see in Table 6.1, the 18 candies in the bag of 55 can be expressed as a fraction ($\frac{18}{55}$), decimal (.33), and percent (32.73%). If you visit the M&M's® website, you will see that the standard is 11 yellow M&M's®. The clipping "What Colors Come in Your Bag?" shows an M&M's® Milk Chocolate Candies Color Chart.

In this unit we discuss converting decimals to percents (including rounding percents), percents to decimals, fractions to percents, and percents to fractions. You will see when you study converting fractions to percents why you should first learn how to convert decimals to percents.

Converting Decimals to Percents

The following Wall Street Journal clipping "Getting in the Door: More Online" shows that 2% or 2 out of 100 vendors are able to get a foot in the door of Wal-Mart. If the clipping had stated the 2% as a decimal (.02), could you give its equivalent in percent? The decimal .02 in decimal fraction is $\frac{2}{100}$. As you know, percents are the result of expressing numbers as part of 100, so $2\% = \frac{2}{100}$. You can now conclude that $.02 = \frac{2}{100} = 2\%$.

GETTING IN THE DOOR: *More Online*

Of the 10,000 suppliers who applied to become Wal-Mart vendors last year, only about 2% were accepted. For small businesses looking to get a foot in the door of the world's largest retailer, there are some ways to improve your chances.

Readers who would like to learn more can go to the Online Journal, at **WSJ.com/Free**, to hear an interview with the Journal's Gwendolyn Bounds as she offers tips gleaned from her reporting for this article. In the interview, Ms. Bounds discusses the importance of thinking locally and getting the price right, among other topics.

Wall Street Journal © 2005

The steps for converting decimals to percents are as follows:

CONVERTING DECIMALS TO PERCENTS

Step 1.	Move the decimal point two places to the right. You are multiplying by 100. If necessary, add zeros. This rule is also used for whole numbers and mixed decimals.
Step 2.	Add a percent symbol at the end of the number.

EXAMPLES

$$.66 = .66. = \boxed{66\%} \qquad\qquad .8 = .80. = \boxed{80\%} \qquad\qquad 8 = 8.00. = \boxed{800\%}$$

Add 1 zero to make two places.   Add 2 zeros to make two places.

$$.425 = .42.5 = \boxed{42.5\%} \qquad .007 = .00.7 = \boxed{.7\%} \qquad 2.51 = 2.51. = \boxed{251\%}$$

Caution: One percent means 1 out of every 100. Since .7% is less than 1%, it means $\frac{7}{10}$ of 1%—a very small amount. Less than 1% is less than .01. To show a number less than 1%, you must use more than two decimal places and add 2 zeros. Example: .7% = .007.

Rounding Percents

When necessary, percents should be rounded. Rounding percents is similar to rounding whole numbers. Use the following steps to round percents:

ROUNDING PERCENTS
Step 1. When you convert from a fraction or decimal, be sure your answer is in percent before rounding.
Step 2. Identify the specific digit. If the digit to the right of the identified digit is 5 or greater, round up the identified digit.
Step 3. Delete digits to right of the identified digit.

For example, Table 6.1 (p. 139) shows that the 18 yellow M&M's® rounded to the nearest hundredth percent is 32.73% of the bag of 55 M&M's®. Let's look at how we arrived at this figure.

When using a calculator, you press 18 ÷ 55 % . This allows you to go right to percent, avoiding the decimal step.

Step 1. $\dfrac{18}{55} = .3272727 = 32.72727\%$ Note that the number is in percent! Identify the hundredth percent digit.

Step 2.   32.73727%   Digit to the right of the identified digit is greater than 5, so the identified digit is increased by 1.

Step 3. $\boxed{32.73\%}$ Delete digits to the right of the identified digit.

Converting Percents to Decimals

Note that in the following Barron's clipping "Kellogg by the Numbers," 54.5% of Kellogg's revenue came from cereal sales.

Kellogg By the Numbers

While cereal dominates Kellogg's product line-up, snack foods are a growing business. Overseas, the company has exposure to rapidly expanding markets in Asia and Latin America, and better distribution than its peers.

'04 Revenue
By Product

Frozen & Specialty*
12%
34.5% Snacks
54.5% Cereal

'05 Revenue
By Region

5% Asia Pacific
Latin America 8%
20% Europe
67% North America

Note: 2005 data through first three quarters; Asia Pacific includes Australia.

Battle Creek Enquirer/Scott Erskine/ AP Wide World

In the paragraph and steps that follow, you will learn how to convert percents to decimals. The example below the steps using 2% comes from the clipping "Getting in the Door" (p. 139). As previously indicated, the example using 54.5% comes from the clipping "Kellogg by the Numbers."

To convert percents to decimals, you reverse the process used to convert decimals to percents. In our earlier discussion on converting decimals to percents (p. 139), we asked if the 2% in the "Getting in the Door" clipping had been in decimals and not percent, could you convert the decimals to the 2%? Once again, the definition of percent states that 2% = 2/100. The fraction 2/100 can be written in decimal form as .02. You can conclude that 2% = 2/100 = .02. Now you can see this procedure in the following conversion steps:

CONVERTING PERCENTS TO DECIMALS
Step 1. Drop the percent symbol.
Step 2. Move the decimal point two places to the left. You are dividing by 100. If necessary, add zeros.

EXAMPLES

Note that when a percent is less than 1%, the decimal conversion has at least two leading zeros before the number .0095.

$$.95\% = .00.95 = \boxed{.0095} \qquad 2\% = .02. = \boxed{.02} \qquad 66\% = .66. = \boxed{.66}$$

Add 2 zeros to make two places. 　　　Add 1 zero to make two places.

$$54.5\% = .54.5 = \boxed{.545} \qquad 824.4\% = 8.24.4 = \boxed{8.244}$$

Now we must explain how to change fractional percents such as $\frac{1}{5}\%$ to a decimal. Remember that fractional percents are values less than 1%. For example, $\frac{1}{5}\%$ is $\frac{1}{5}$ of 1%. Fractional percents can appear singly or in combination with whole numbers. To convert them to decimals, use the following steps:

CONVERTING FRACTIONAL PERCENTS TO DECIMALS
Step 1. Convert a single fractional percent to its decimal equivalent by dividing the numerator by the denominator. If necessary, round the answer.
Step 2. If a fractional percent is combined with a whole number (mixed fractional percent), convert the fractional percent first. Then combine the whole number and the fractional percent.
Step 3. Drop the percent symbol; move the decimal point two places to the left (this divides the number by 100).

EXAMPLES

$$\frac{1}{5}\% = .20\% = .00.20 = \boxed{.0020}$$

$$\frac{1}{4}\% = .25\% = .00.25 = \boxed{.0025}$$

$$7\frac{3}{4}\% = 7.75\% = .07.75 = \boxed{.0775}$$

$$6\frac{1}{2}\% = 6.5\% = .06.5 = \boxed{.065}$$

Think of $7\frac{3}{4}\%$ as

$$7\% = \qquad .07$$
$$+\frac{3}{4}\% = \quad +.0075$$
$$\overline{\qquad\qquad\qquad}$$
$$7\frac{3}{4}\% = \qquad .0775$$

Converting Fractions to Percents

When fractions have denominators of 100, the numerator becomes the percent. Other fractions must be first converted to decimals; then the decimals are converted to percents.

CONVERTING FRACTIONS TO PERCENTS
Step 1. Divide the numerator by the denominator to convert the fraction to a decimal.
Step 2. Move the decimal point two places to the right; add the percent symbol.

EXAMPLES

$$\frac{3}{4} = .75 = .75. = \boxed{75\%} \qquad \frac{1}{5} = .20 = .20. = \boxed{20\%} \qquad \frac{1}{20} = .05 = .05. = \boxed{5\%}$$

Converting Percents to Fractions

Using the definition of percent, you can write any percent as a fraction whose denominator is 100. Thus, when we convert a percent to a fraction, we drop the percent symbol and write the number over 100, which is the same as multiplying the number by $\frac{1}{100}$. This method of multiplying by $\frac{1}{100}$ is also used for fractional percents.

CONVERTING A WHOLE PERCENT (OR A FRACTIONAL PERCENT) TO A FRACTION
Step 1. Drop the percent symbol.
Step 2. Multiply the number by $\frac{1}{100}$.
Step 3. Reduce to lowest terms.

EXAMPLES

$$76\% = 76 \times \frac{1}{100} = \frac{76}{100} = \boxed{\frac{19}{25}} \qquad \frac{1}{8}\% = \frac{1}{8} \times \frac{1}{100} = \boxed{\frac{1}{800}}$$

$$156\% = 156 \times \frac{1}{100} = \frac{156}{100} = 1\frac{56}{100} = \boxed{1\frac{14}{25}}$$

Sometimes a percent contains a whole number and a fraction such as $12\frac{1}{2}\%$ or 22.5%. Extra steps are needed to write a mixed or decimal percent as a simplified fraction.

CONVERTING A MIXED OR DECIMAL PERCENT TO A FRACTION
Step 1. Drop the percent symbol.
Step 2. Change the mixed percent to an improper fraction.
Step 3. Multiply the number by $\frac{1}{100}$.
Step 4. Reduce to lowest terms.
Note: If you have a mixed or decimal percent, change the decimal portion to fractional equivalent and continue with Steps 1 to 4.

EXAMPLES $12\frac{1}{2}\% = \frac{25}{2} \times \frac{1}{100} = \frac{25}{200} = \boxed{\frac{1}{8}}$

$$12.5\% = 12\frac{1}{2}\% = \frac{25}{2} \times \frac{1}{100} = \frac{25}{200} = \boxed{\frac{1}{8}}$$

$$22.5\% = 22\frac{1}{2}\% = \frac{45}{2} \times \frac{1}{100} = \frac{45}{200} = \boxed{\frac{9}{40}}$$

It's time to check your understanding of Learning Unit 6–1.

LU 6-1 PRACTICE QUIZ

Convert to percents (round to the nearest tenth percent as needed):

1. .6666 _____   2. .832 _____
3. .004 _____   4. 8.94444 _____

Convert to decimals (remember, decimals representing less than 1% will have at least 2 leading zeros before the number):

5. $\frac{1}{4}\%$ _____   6. $6\frac{3}{4}\%$ _____
7. 87% _____   8. 810.9% _____

Convert to percents (round to the nearest hundredth percent):

9. $\frac{1}{7}$ _____   10. $\frac{2}{9}$ _____

Convert to fractions (remember, if it is a mixed number, first convert to an improper fraction):

11. 19% _____   12. $71\frac{1}{2}\%$ _____   13. 130% _____

14. $\frac{1}{2}\%$ _____   15. 19.9% _____

✓ **Solutions**

1. .66.66 = $\boxed{66.7\%}$
2. .83.2 = $\boxed{83.2\%}$
3. .00.4 = $.4\%$
4. 8.94.444 = $\boxed{894.4\%}$
5. $\frac{1}{4}\% = .25\% = \boxed{.0025}$
6. $6\frac{3}{4}\% = 6.75\% = \boxed{.0675}$
7. 87% = .87. = $\boxed{.87}$
8. 810.9% = 8.10.9 = $\boxed{8.109}$
9. $\frac{1}{7} = .14.285 = \boxed{14.29\%}$
10. $\frac{2}{9} = .22.2\bar{2} = \boxed{22.22\%}$
11. $19\% = 19 \times \frac{1}{100} = \boxed{\frac{19}{100}}$
12. $71\frac{1}{2}\% = \frac{143}{2} \times \frac{1}{100} = \boxed{\frac{143}{200}}$
13. $130\% = 130 \times \frac{1}{100} = \frac{130}{100} = 1\frac{30}{100} = 1\boxed{\frac{3}{10}}$
14. $\frac{1}{2}\% = \frac{1}{2} \times \frac{1}{100} = \boxed{\frac{1}{200}}$
15. $19\frac{9}{10}\% = \frac{199}{10} \times \frac{1}{100} = \boxed{\frac{199}{1,000}}$

LU 6-1a EXTRA PRACTICE QUIZ

Convert to percents (round to the nearest tenth percent as needed):

1. .4444   2. .782
3. .006   4. 7.93333

Convert to decimals (remember, decimals representing less than 1% will have at least 2 leading zeros before the number):

5. $\frac{1}{5}\%$ 6. $7\frac{4}{5}\%$
7. 92%   8. 765.8%

Convert to percents (round to the nearest hundredth percent):

9. $\frac{1}{3}$ 10. $\frac{3}{7}$

Convert to fractions (remember, if it is a mixed number, first convert to an improper fraction):

11. 17%   **12.** $82\frac{1}{4}\%$ **13.** 150%

14. $\frac{1}{4}\%$ **15.** 17.8%

Learning Unit 6–2: Application of Percents—Portion Formula

The bag of M&M's® we have been studying contains Milk Chocolate M&M's®. M&M/Mars also makes Peanut M&M's® and some other types of M&M's®. To study the application of percents to problems involving M&M's®, we make two key assumptions:

1. Total sales of Milk Chocolate M&M's®, Peanut M&M's®, and other M&M's® chocolate candies are $400,000.
2. Eighty percent of M&M's® sales are Milk Chocolate M&M's®. This leaves the Peanut and other M&M's® chocolate candies with 20% of sales (100% − 80%).

80% M&M's®	20% M&M's®	100%
Milk Chocolate +	Peanut and other =	Total sales
M&M's®	chocolate candies	($400,000)

Before we begin, you must understand the meaning of three terms—*base, rate,* and *portion.* These terms are the key elements in solving percent problems.

- **Base (B).** The **base** is the beginning whole quantity or value (100%) with which you will compare some other quantity or value. Often the problems give the base after the word *of.* For example, the whole (total) sales of M&M's®—Milk Chocolate M&M's, Peanut, and other M&M's® chocolate candies—are $400,000.

- **Rate (R).** The **rate** is a percent, decimal, or fraction that indicates the part of the base that you must calculate. The percent symbol often helps you identify the rate. For example, Milk Chocolate M&M's® currently account for 80% of sales. So the rate is 80%. Remember that 80% is also $\frac{4}{5}$, or .80.

- **Portion (P).** The **portion** is the amount or part that results from the base multiplied by the rate. For example, total sales of M&M's® are $400,000 (base); $400,000 times .80 (rate) equals $320,000 (portion), or the sales of Milk Chocolate M&M's®. *A key point to remember is that portion is a number and not a percent. In fact, the portion can be larger than the base if the rate is greater than 100%.*

Solving Percents with the Portion Formula

In problems involving portion, base, and rate, we give two of these elements. You must find the third element. Remember the following key formula:

$$\text{Portion } (P) = \text{Base } (B) \times \text{Rate } (R)$$

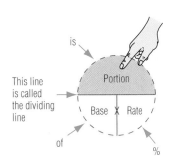

This line is called the dividing line

To help you solve for the portion, base, and rate, this unit shows pie charts. The shaded area in each pie chart indicates the element that you must solve for. For example, since we shaded *portion* in the pie chart at the left, you must solve for portion. To use the pie charts, put your finger on the shaded area (in this case portion). The formula that remains tells you what to do. So in the pie chart at the left, you solve the problem by multiplying base by the rate. Note the circle around the pie chart is broken since we want to emphasize that portion can be larger than base if rate is greater than 100%. The horizontal line in the pie chart is called the dividing line, and we will use it when we solve for base or rate.

The following example summarizes the concept of base, rate, and portion. Assume that you received a small bonus check of $100. This is a gross amount—your company did not withhold any taxes. You will have to pay 20% in taxes.

Base: 100%—whole. Usually given after the word *of*—but not always.	Rate: Usually expressed as a percent but could also be a decimal or fraction.	Portion: A number—not a percent and not the whole.
$100 bonus check	20% taxes	$20 taxes

First decide what you are looking for. You want to know how much you must pay in taxes—the portion. How do you get the portion? From the portion formula Portion (P) = Base (B) $\times$ Rate (R), you know that you must multiply the base ($100) by the rate (20%). When you do this, you get $100 $\times$ .20 = $20. So you must pay $20 in taxes.

Let's try our first word problem by taking a closer look at the M&M's® example to see how we arrived at the $320,000 sales of Milk Chocolate M&M's® given earlier. We will be using blueprint aids to help dissect and solve each word problem.

Solving for Portion

The Word Problem Sales of Milk Chocolate M&M's® are 80% of the total M&M's® sales. Total M&M's® sales are $400,000. What are the sales of Milk Chocolate M&M's®?

The facts	Solving for?	Steps to take	Key points
Milk Chocolate M&M's® sales: 80%. Total M&M's® sales: $400,000.	Sales of Milk Chocolate M&M's®.	Identify key elements. Base: $400,000. Rate: .80. Portion: ? Portion = Base $\times$ Rate.	Amount or part of beginning. Portion (?). Base ($400,000) $\times$ Rate (.80). Beginning whole quantity (often after "of"). Percent symbol or word (here we put into decimal). Portion and rate must relate to same piece of base.

Steps to solving problem

1. Set up the formula.

2. Calculate portion (sales of Milk Chocolate M&M's®).

Portion = Base $\times$ Rate

$P = \$400,000 \times .80$

$P = \$320,000$

In the first column of the blueprint aid, we gather the facts. In the second column, we state that we are looking for sales of Milk Chocolate M&M's®. In the third column, we identify each key element and the formula needed to solve the problem. Review the pie chart in the fourth column. Note that the portion and rate must relate to the same piece of the base. In this word problem, we can see from the solution below the blueprint aid that sales of Milk Chocolate M&M's® are $320,000. The $320,000 does indeed represent 80% of the base. Note here that the portion ($320,000) is less than the base of $400,000 since the rate is less than 100%.

Now let's work another word problem that solves for the portion.

The Word Problem Sales of Milk Chocolate M&M's® are 80% of the total M&M's® sales. Total M&M's® sales are $400,000. What are the sales of Peanut and other M&M's® chocolate candies?

The facts	Solving for?	Steps to take	Key points
Milk Chocolate M&M's® sales: 80%. *Total M&M's® sales:* $400,000.	Sales of Peanut and other M&M's® chocolate candies.	Identify key elements. *Base:* $400,000. *Rate:* .20 (100% − 80%). *Portion:* ? Portion = Base × Rate.	If 80% of sales are Milk Chocolate M&M's, then 20% are Peanut and other M&M's® chocolate candies. Portion (?) Base × Rate ($400,000) (.20) Portion and rate must relate to same piece of base.

Steps to solving problem

1. Set up the formula.

   Portion = Base × Rate

2. Calculate portion (sale of Peanut and other M&M's® chocolate candies).

   $P = \$400,000 \times .20$

   $P = \$80,000$

    In the previous blueprint aid, note that we must use a rate that agrees with the portion so the portion and rate refer to the same piece of the base. Thus, if 80% of sales are Milk Chocolate M&M's®, 20% must be Peanut and other M&M's® chocolate candies (100% − 80% = 20%). So we use a rate of .20.

    In Step 2, we multiplied $400,000 × .20 to get a portion of $80,000. This portion represents the part of the sales that were *not* Milk Chocolate M&M's®. Note that the rate of .20 and the portion of $80,000 relate to the same piece of the base—$80,000 is 20% of $400,000. Also note that the portion ($80,000) is less than the base ($400,000) since the rate is less than 100%.

    Take a moment to review the two blueprint aids in this section. Be sure you understand why the rate in the first blueprint aid was 80% and the rate in the second blueprint aid was 20%.

Solving for Rate

The Word Problem Sales of Milk Chocolate M&M's® are $320,000. Total M&M's® sales are $400,000. What is the percent of Milk Chocolate M&M's® sales compared to total M&M's® sales?

The facts	Solving for?	Steps to take	Key points
Milk Chocolate M&M's® sales: $320,000. *Total M&M's® sales:* $400,000.	Percent of Milk Chocolate M&M's® sales to total M&M's® sales.	Identify key elements. *Base:* $400,000. *Rate:* ? *Portion:* $320,000 Rate = $\dfrac{\text{Portion}}{\text{Base}}$	Since portion is less than base, the rate must be less than 100% Portion ($320,000) Base × Rate ($400,000) (?) Portion and rate must relate to the same piece of base.

Steps to solving problem

1. Set up the formula.

   Rate = $\dfrac{\text{Portion}}{\text{Base}}$

2. Calculate rate (percent of Milk Chocolate M&M's® sales).

   $R = \dfrac{\$320,000}{\$400,000}$

   $R = 80\%$

Note that in this word problem, the rate of 80% and the portion of $320,000 refer to the same piece of the base.

The Word Problem   Sales of Milk Chocolate M&M's® are $320,000. Total sales of Milk Chocolate M&M's, Peanut, and other M&M's® chocolate candies are $400,000. What percent of Peanut and other M&M's® chocolate candies are sold compared to total M&M's® sales?

The facts	Solving for?	Steps to take	Key points
Milk Chocolate M&M's® sales: $320,000. Total M&M's® sales: $400,000.	Percent of Peanut and other M&M's® chocolate candies sales compared to total M&M's® sales.	Identify key elements. Base: $400,000. Rate: ? Portion: $80,000 ($400,000 − $320,000). $Rate = \dfrac{Portion}{Base}$	Represents sales of Peanut and other M&M's® chocolate candies Portion ($80,000) Base × Rate ($400,000) (?) When portion becomes $80,000, the portion and rate now relate to same piece of base.

Steps to solving problem

1. Set up the formula.

$$Rate = \frac{Portion}{Base}$$

2. Calculate rate.

$$R = \frac{\$80,000}{\$400,000} \quad (\$400,000 - \$320,000)$$

$$R = \boxed{20\%}$$

The word problem asks for the rate of candy sales that are *not* Milk Chocolate M&M's. Thus, $400,000 of total candy sales less sales of Milk Chocolate M&M's® ($320,000) allows us to arrive at sales of Peanut and other M&M's® chocolate candies ($80,000). The $80,000 portion represents 20% of total candy sales. The $80,000 portion and 20% rate refer to the same piece of the $400,000 base. Compare this blueprint aid with the blueprint aid for the previous word problem. Ask yourself why in the previous word problem the rate was 80% and in this word problem the rate is 20%. In both word problems, the portion was less than the base since the rate was less than 100%.

Now we go on to calculate the base. Remember to read the word problem carefully so that you match the rate and portion to the same piece of the base.

Solving for Base

The Word Problem   Sales of Peanut and other M&M's® chocolate candies are 20% of total M&M's® sales. Sales of Milk Chocolate M&M's® are $320,000. What are the total sales of all M&M's®?

The facts	Solving for?	Steps to take	Key points
Peanut and other M&M's® chocolate candies sales: 20%. Milk Chocolate M&M's® sales: $320,000.	Total M&M's® sales.	Identify key elements. Base: ? Rate: .80 (100% − 20%) Portion: $320,000 $Base = \dfrac{Portion}{Rate}$	Portion ($320,000) Base × Rate (?) (.80) (100% − 20%) Portion ($320,000) and rate (.80) do relate to the same piece of base.

Steps to solving problem

1. Set up the formula.

$$\text{Base} = \frac{\text{Portion}}{\text{Rate}}$$

2. Calculate the base.

$$B = \frac{\$320,000}{.80} \quad \longleftarrow \$320,000 \text{ is 80\% of base}$$

$$B = \boxed{\$400,000}$$

Note that we could not use 20% for the rate. The $320,000 of Milk Chocolate M&M's® represents 80% (100% − 20%) of the total sales of M&M's®. We use 80% so that the portion and rate refer to same piece of the base. Remember that the portion ($320,000) is less than the base ($400,000) since the rate is less than 100%.

Calculating Percent Decreases and Increases

In the following *Wall Street Journal* clipping "Wal-Mart's Entry Likely to Reshape Warranty Game," we see a product's warranty as a percentage of the price of a 42-inch plasma TV. If you buy a 42-inch plasma TV, would you buy an extended warranty? Did you realize how much extended warranties can cost? Using this clipping, let's look at how to calculate percent decreases and increases.

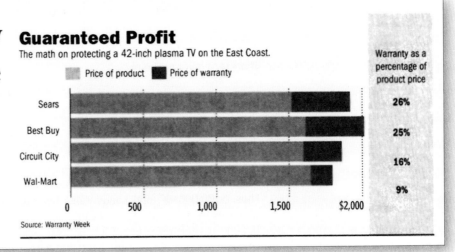

Wall Street Journal © 2005

Rate of Percent Decrease Using Sears

Assume: Sears drops its 42-inch plasma TV price to $900 from $1,500.

$$\text{Rate} = \frac{\text{Portion}}{\text{Base}} \quad \begin{array}{l} \longleftarrow \text{Difference between old and new TV price} \\ \longleftarrow \text{Old TV amount} \end{array}$$

$$R = \frac{\$600\,(\$1,500 - \$900)}{\$1,500}$$

$$R = \boxed{40\%}$$

Let's prove the 40% with a pie chart.

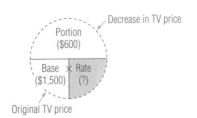

The formula for calculating Sears' **percent decrease** is as follows:

Percent decrease

$$\text{Percent of decrease } (R) = \frac{\text{Amount of decrease } (P)\ (\$600)}{\text{Original TV price } (B)\ (\$1,500)}$$
(40%)

Now let's look at how to calculate Best Buy's *percent increase* in plasma TVs using the portion formula for solving the rate.

Rate of Percent Increase Using Best Buy

Assume: Best Buy increases its 42-inch plasma TV price to $1,200 from $1,000.

$$\text{Rate} = \frac{\text{Portion}}{\text{Base}} \quad \begin{array}{l} \leftarrow \text{Difference between old and new TV price} \\ \leftarrow \text{Old TV amount} \end{array}$$

$$R = \frac{\$200\,(\$1,200 - \$1,000)}{\$1,000}$$

$$R = \boxed{20\%}$$

Let's prove the 20% with a pie chart.

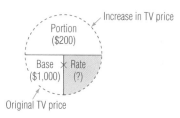

The formula for calculating Best Buy's **percent increase** is as follows:

Percent increase

$$\text{Percent of increase } (R) = \frac{\text{Amount of increase } (P)\ (\$200)}{\text{Original TV price } (B)\ (\$1,000)}$$
(20%)

In conclusion, the following steps can be used to calculate percent decreases and increases:

CALCULATING PERCENT DECREASES AND INCREASES
Step 1. Find the difference between amounts (such as advertising costs).
Step 2. Divide Step 1 by the original amount (the base): $R = P \div B$. Be sure to express your answer in percent.

Before concluding this chapter, we will show how to calculate a percent increase and decrease using M&M's® (Figure 6.1).

Additional Examples Using M&M's

The Word Problem Sheila Leary went to her local supermarket and bought the bag of M&M's® shown in Figure 6.1 (p. 149). The bag gave its weight as 18.40 ounces, which was 15% more than a regular 1-pound bag of M&M's®. Sheila, who is a careful shopper, wanted to check and see if she was actually getting a 15% increase. Let's help Sheila dissect and solve this problem.

The facts	Solving for?	Steps to take	Key points
New bag of M&M's®: 18.40 oz. *15% increase in weight.* *Original bag of M&M's®: 16 oz. (1 lb.)*	Checking percent increase of 15%.	Identify key elements. *Base: 16 oz.* *Rate: ?* *Portion: 2.40 oz.* $\left(\begin{array}{c} 18.40 \text{ oz.} \\ - 16.00 \\ \hline 2.40 \text{ oz.} \end{array}\right)$ Rate = $\dfrac{\text{Portion}}{\text{Base}}$	

Steps to solving problem

1. Set up the formula.

$$\text{Rate} = \frac{\text{Portion}}{\text{Base}}$$

2. Calculate the rate.

$$R = \frac{2.40 \text{ oz.}}{16.00 \text{ oz.}} \begin{array}{l} \leftarrow \text{Difference between base and new weight.} \\ \leftarrow \text{Old weight equals 100\%.} \end{array}$$

$$\boxed{R = 15\% \text{ increase}}$$

The new weight of the bag of M&M's® is really 115% of the old weight:

$$\begin{array}{rcl} 16.00 \text{ oz.} & = & 100\% \\ + \ 2.40 & = & + \ 15 \\ \hline 18.40 \text{ oz.} & = & 115\% \ = 1.15 \end{array}$$

We can check this by looking at the following pie chart:

Portion = Base × Rate

$$\boxed{18.40 \text{ oz.}} = 16 \text{ oz.} \times 1.15$$

Why is the portion greater than the base? Remember that the portion can be larger than the base only if the rate is greater than 100%. Note how the portion and rate relate to the same piece of the base—18.40 oz. is 115% of the base (16 oz.).

Let's see what could happen if M&M/Mars has an increase in its price of sugar. This is an additional example to reinforce the concept of percent decrease.

The Word Problem The increase in the price of sugar caused the M&M/Mars company to decrease the weight of each 1-pound bag of M&M's® to 12 ounces. What is the rate of percent decrease?

The facts	Solving for?	Steps to take	Key points
16-oz. bag of M&M's®: reduced to 12 oz.	Rate of percent decrease.	Identify key elements. *Base: 16 oz.* *Rate: ?* *Portion: 4 oz. (16 oz. − 12 oz.)* Rate = $\dfrac{\text{Portion}}{\text{Base}}$	

Steps to solving problem

1. Set up the formula.

$$\text{Rate} = \frac{\text{Portion}}{\text{Base}}$$

2. Calculate the rate.

$$R = \frac{4 \text{ oz.}}{16.00 \text{ oz.}}$$

$R = 25\%$ decrease

The new weight of the bag of M&M's® is 75% of the old weight:

$$
\begin{array}{rcr}
16 \text{ oz.} & = & 100\% \\
- \ 4 & & - \ 25 \\
\hline
12 \text{ oz.} & = & 75\% \\
\end{array}
$$

We can check this by looking at the following pie chart:

Portion = Base × Rate

12 oz. = 16 oz. × .75

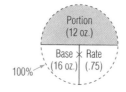

Note that the portion is smaller than the base because the rate is less than 100%. Also note how the portion and rate relate to the same piece of the base—12 ounces is 75% of the base (16 oz.).

After your study of Learning Unit 6-2, you should be ready for the Practice Quiz.

LU 6-2   PRACTICE QUIZ

Complete this **Practice Quiz** to see how you are doing

Solve for portion:

1. 38% of 900.   2. 60% of $9,000.

Solve for rate (round to nearest tenth percent as needed):

3. 430 is _____% of 5,000.   4. 200 is _____% of 700.

Solve for base (round to the nearest tenth as needed):

5. 55 is 40% of _____.   6. 900 is $4\frac{1}{2}\%$ of _____.

Solve the following (blueprint aids are shown in the solution; you might want to try some on scrap paper):

7. Five out of 25 students in Professor Ford's class received an A grade. What percent of the class *did not* receive the A grade?

8. Abby Biernet has yet to receive 60% of her lobster order. Abby received 80 lobsters to date. What was her original order?

9. In 2006, Dunkin' Donuts Company had $300,000 in doughnut sales. In 2007, sales were up 40%. What are Dunkin' Donuts sales for 2007?

10. The price of an Apple computer dropped from $1,600 to $1,200. What was the percent decrease?

11. In 1982, a ticket to the Boston Celtics cost $14. In 2007, a ticket cost $50. What is the percent increase to the nearest hundredth percent?

✓ **Solutions**

1. $342 = 900 \times .38$
   $(P) = (B) \times (R)$

2. $\$5,400 = \$9,000 \times .60$
   $(P) \ = \ (B) \ \times (R)$

3. $\dfrac{(P)430}{(B)5,000} = .086 = 8.6\% \ (R)$

4. $\dfrac{(P)200}{(B)700} = .2857 = 28.6\% \ (R)$

5. $\dfrac{(P)55}{(R).40} = 137.5 \ (B)$

6. $\dfrac{(P)900}{(R).045} = 20,000 \ (B)$

7. Percent of Professor Ford's class that did not receive an A grade:

The facts	Solving for?	Steps to take	Key points
5 As. 25 in class.	Percent that did not receive A.	Identify key elements. *Base:* 25 *Rate:* ? *Portion:* 20 (25 − 5). Rate = $\dfrac{\text{Portion}}{\text{Base}}$	 Portion (20) Base × Rate (25) (?) The whole Portion and rate must relate to same piece of base.

Steps to solving problem

1. Set up the formula.

$$\text{Rate} = \frac{\text{Portion}}{\text{Base}}$$

2. Calculate the rate.

$$R = \frac{20}{25}$$

$$\boxed{R = 80\%}$$

8. Abby Biernet's original order:

The facts	Solving for?	Steps to take	Key points
60% of the order not in. 80 lobsters received.	Total order of lobsters.	Identify key elements. *Base:* ? *Rate:* .40 (100% − 60%) *Portion:* 80. Base = $\dfrac{\text{Portion}}{\text{Rate}}$	 Portion (80) Base × Rate (?) (.40) 80 lobsters represent 40% of the order Portion and rate must relate to same piece of base.

Steps to solving problem

1. Set up the formula.

$$\text{Base} = \frac{\text{Portion}}{\text{Rate}}$$

2. Calculate the rate.

$$B = \frac{80}{.40} \leftarrow \text{80 lobsters is 40\% of base.}$$

$$\boxed{B = 200 \text{ lobsters}}$$

9. Dunkin' Donuts Company sales for 2007:

The facts	Solving for?	Steps to take	Key points
2006: $300,000 sales. *2007:* Sales up 40% from 2006.	Sales for 2007.	Identify key elements. *Base:* $300,000. *Rate:* 1.40. Old year 100% New year +40 ────── 140% *Portion:* ? Portion = Base × Rate.	2007 sales Portion (?) Base × Rate ($300,000) (1.40) 2006 sales When rate is greater than 100%, portion will be larger than base.

Steps to solving problem

1. Set up the formula.	Portion = Base × Rate
2. Calculate the portion.	$P = \$300,000 \times 1.40$
	$P = \$420,000$

10.   Percent decrease in Apple computer price:

The facts	Solving for?	Steps to take	Key points
Apple computer was $1,600; now, $1,200.	Percent decrease in price.	Identify key elements. *Base:* $1,600. *Rate:* ? *Portion:* $400 ($1,600 − $1,200). Rate = $\dfrac{\text{Portion}}{\text{Base}}$	Difference in price Portion ($400) Base ($1,600) × Rate (?) Original price

Steps to solving problem

1. Set up the formula.	Rate = $\dfrac{\text{Portion}}{\text{Base}}$
2. Calculate the rate.	$R = \dfrac{\$400}{\$1,600}$
	$R = 25\%$

11.   Percent increase in Boston Celtics ticket:

The facts	Solving for?	Steps to take	Key points
$14 ticket (old). $50 ticket (new).	Percent increase in price.	Identify key elements. *Base:* $14 *Rate:* ? *Portion:* $36 ($50 − $14) Rate = $\dfrac{\text{Portion}}{\text{Base}}$	Difference in price Portion ($36) Base ($14) × Rate (?) Original price When portion is greater than base, rate will be greater than 100%.

Steps to solving problem

1. Set up the formula.	Rate = $\dfrac{\text{Portion}}{\text{Base}}$
2. Calculate the rate.	$R = \dfrac{\$36}{\$14}$
	$R = 2.5714 = 257.14\%$

Need more practice? Try this **Extra Practice Quiz** (check figures in Chapter Organizer, p. 156)

Solve for portion:

1. 42% of 1,200

2. 7% of $8,000

Solve for rate (round to nearest tenth percent as needed):

3. 510 is _____ % of 6,000.

4. 400 is _____% of 900.

Solve for base (round to the nearest tenth as needed):

5. 30 is 60% of _____.

6. 1,200 is $3\frac{1}{2}$% of _____.

7. Ten out of 25 students in Professor Ford's class received an A grade. What percent of the class did not receive the A grade?

8. Abby Biernet has yet to receive 70% of her lobster order. Abby received 90 lobsters to date. What was her original order?

9. In 2006, Dunkin' Donuts Company had $400,000 in doughnut sales. In 2007, sales were up 35%. What are Dunkin' Donuts sales for 2007?

10. The price of an Apple computer dropped from $1,800 to $1,000. What was the percent decrease? (Round to the nearest hundredth percent.)

11. In 1982, a ticket to the Boston Celtics cost $14. In 2009, a ticket cost $75. What is the percent increase to the nearest hundredth percent?

CHAPTER ORGANIZER AND STUDY GUIDE
WITH CHECK FIGURES FOR EXTRA PRACTICE QUIZZES

Topic	Key point, procedure, formula	Example(s) to illustrate situation
Converting decimals to percents, p. 139	1. Move decimal point two places to right. If necessary, add zeros. This rule is also used for whole numbers and mixed decimals. 2. Add a percent symbol at end of number.	.81 = .81. = 81% .008 = .00.8 = .8% 4.15 = 4.15. = 415%
Rounding percents, p. 140	1. Answer must be in percent before rounding. 2. Identify specific digit. If digit to right is 5 or greater, round up. 3. Delete digits to right of identified digit.	Round to the nearest hundredth percent. $\frac{3}{7}$ = .4285714 = 42.85714% = 42.86%
Converting percents to decimals, p. 141	1. Drop percent symbol. 2. Move decimal point two places to left. If necessary, add zeros. For fractional percents: 1. Convert to decimal by dividing numerator by denominator. If necessary, round answer. 2. If a mixed fractional percent, convert fractional percent first. Then combine whole number and fractional percent. 3. Drop percent symbol, move decimal point two places to left.	.89% = .0089 95% = .95 195% = 1.95 $8\frac{3}{4}$% = 8.75% = .0875 $\frac{1}{4}$% = .25% = .0025 $\frac{1}{5}$% = .20% = .0020
Converting fractions to percents, p. 142	1. Divide numerator by denominator. 2. Move decimal point two places to right; add percent symbol.	$\frac{4}{5}$ = .80 = 80%

(continues)

CHAPTER ORGANIZER AND STUDY GUIDE
WITH CHECK FIGURES FOR EXTRA PRACTICE QUIZZES (continued)

Topic	Key point, procedure, formula	Example(s) to illustrate situation
Converting percents to fractions, p. 142	Whole percent (or fractional percent) to a fraction: 1. Drop percent symbol. 2. Multiply number by 3. Reduce to lowest terms. Mixed or decimal percent to a fraction: 1. Drop percent symbol. 2. Change mixed percent to an improper fraction. 3. Multiply number by 4. Reduce to lowest terms. If you have a mixed or decimal percent, change decimal portion to fractional equivalent and continue with Steps 1 to 4.	$64\% \rightarrow 64 \times \dfrac{1}{100} = \dfrac{64}{100} = \boxed{\dfrac{16}{25}}$ $\dfrac{1}{4}\% \rightarrow \dfrac{1}{4} \times \dfrac{1}{100} = \boxed{\dfrac{1}{400}}$ $119\% \rightarrow 119 \times \dfrac{1}{100} = \dfrac{119}{100} = \boxed{1\dfrac{19}{100}}$ $16\dfrac{1}{4}\% \rightarrow \dfrac{65}{4} \times \dfrac{1}{100} = \dfrac{65}{400} = \boxed{\dfrac{13}{80}}$ $16.25\% \rightarrow 16\dfrac{1}{4}\% = \dfrac{65}{4} \times \dfrac{1}{100}$ $= \dfrac{65}{100} = \boxed{\dfrac{13}{80}}$
Solving for portion, p. 145		10% of Mel's paycheck of $1,000 goes for food. What portion is deducted for food? $\boxed{\$100} = \$1,000 \times .10$ *Note:* If question was what amount does not go for food, the portion would have been: $\boxed{\$900} = \$1,000 \times .90$ (100% − 10% = 90%
Solving for rate, p. 146		Assume Mel spends $100 for food from his $1,000 paycheck. What percent of his paycheck is spent on food? $\dfrac{\$100}{\$1,000} = .10 = \boxed{10\%}$ *Note:* Portion is less than base since rate is less than 100%.
Solving for base, p. 147		Assume Mel spends $100 for food, which is 10% of his paycheck. What is Mel's total paycheck? $\dfrac{\$100}{.10} = \boxed{\$1,000}$
Calculating percent decreases and increases, p. 148		Stereo, $2,000 original price. Stereo, $2,500 new price. $\dfrac{\$500}{\$2,000} = .25 = \boxed{25\%}$ increase **Check** $\$2,000 \times 1.25 = \$2,500$ *Note:* Portion is greater than base since rate is greater than 100%.
KEY TERMS	Base, *p. 144* Percent decrease, *p. 149*	Percent increase, *p. 149* Portion, *p. 144* Percents, *p. 138* Rate, *p. 144*

(continues)

CHAPTER ORGANIZER AND STUDY GUIDE
WITH CHECK FIGURES FOR EXTRA PRACTICE QUIZZES (concluded)

Topic	Key point, procedure, formula	Example(s) to illustrate situation
CHECK FIGURES FOR EXTRA PRACTICE QUIZZES WITH PAGE REFERENCES	LU 6–1a (p. 143)	LU 6–2a (p. 154)

LU 6–1a (p. 143)

1. 44.4%   8. 7.658
2. 78.2%   9. 33.33%
3. .6%   10. 42.86%
4. 793.3%   11. $\frac{17}{100}$
5. .0020   12. $\frac{329}{400}$
6. .0780   13. $1\frac{1}{2}$
7. .92   14. $\frac{1}{400}$
                       15. $\frac{89}{500}$

LU 6–2a (p. 154)

1. 504   7. 60%
2. 560   8. 300
3. 8.5%   9. $540,000
4. 44.4%   10. 44.44%
5. 50   11. 435.71%
6. 34,285.7

Note: For how to dissect and solve a word problem, see page 145.

Critical Thinking Discussion Questions

1. In converting from a percent to a decimal, when will you have at least 2 leading zeros before the whole number? Explain this concept, assuming you have 100 bills of $1.

2. Explain the steps in rounding percents. Count the number of students who are sitting in the back half of the room as a percent of the total class. Round your answer to the nearest hundredth percent. Could you have rounded to the nearest whole percent without changing the accuracy of the answer?

3. Define portion, rate, and base. Create an example using Walt Disney World to show when the portion could be larger than the base. Why must the rate be greater than 100% for this to happen?

4. How do we solve for portion, rate, and base? Create an example using IBM computer sales to show that the portion and rate do relate to the same piece of the base.

5. Explain how to calculate percent decreases or increases. Many years ago, comic books cost 10 cents a copy. Visit a bookshop or newsstand. Select a new comic book and explain the price increase in percent compared to the 10-cent comic. How important is the rounding process in your final answer?

Name _____ Date _____

DRILL PROBLEMS

Convert the following decimals to percents:

6–1. .74   **6–2.** .824   **6–3.** .9

6–4. 8.00   **6–5.** 3.561   **6–6.** 6.006

Convert the following percents to decimals:

6–7. 8%   **6–8.** 14%   **6–9.** $64\frac{3}{10}\%$

6–10. 75.9%   **6–11.** 119%   **6–12.** 89%

Convert the following fractions to percents (round to the nearest tenth percent as needed):

6–13. $\dfrac{1}{12}$ **6–14.** $\dfrac{1}{400}$

6–15. $\dfrac{7}{8}$ **6–16.** $\dfrac{11}{12}$

Convert the following to fractions and reduce to the lowest terms:

6–17. 4%   **6–18.** $18\frac{1}{2}\%$

6–19. $31\frac{2}{3}\%$ **6–20.** $61\frac{1}{2}\%$

6–21. 6.75%   **6–22.** 182%

Solve for the portion (round to the nearest hundredth as needed):

6–23. 7% of 150   **6–24.** 125% of 4,320   **6–25.** 25% of 410

6–26. 119% of 128.9   **6–27.** 17.4% of 900   **6–28.** 11.2% of 85

                                     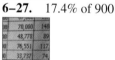

6–29. $12\frac{1}{2}\%$ of 919   **6–30.** 45% of 300

6–31. 18% of 90   **6–32.** 30% of 2,000

Solve for the base (round to the nearest hundredth as needed):

6–33. 170 is 120% of _____   **6–34.** 36 is .75% of _____

6–35. 50 is .5% of _____   **6–36.** 10,800 is 90% of _____

6–37. 800 is $4\frac{1}{2}\%$ of _____

Solve for rate (round to the nearest tenth percent as needed):

6–38. _____ of 80 is 50   **6–39.** _____ of 85 is 92

6–40. _____ of 250 is 65   **6–41.** 110 is _____ of 100

6–42. .09 is _____ of 2.25   **6–43.** 16 is _____ of 4

Solve the following problems. Be sure to show your work. Round to the nearest hundredth or hundredth percent as needed:

6–44. What is 180% of 310?

6–45. 66% of 90 is what?

6–46. 40% of what number is 20?

6–47. 770 is 70% of what number?

6–48. 4 is what percent of 90?

6–49. What percent of 150 is 60?

Complete the following table:

	Sales in millions		Amount of decrease	Percent change (to nearest
	2007	2008	or increase	hundredth percent as needed)
Product				
6–50. Digital cameras	$380	$410		
6–51. DVD players	$ 50	$ 47		

WORD PROBLEMS (First of Four Sets)

6–52. At a local Wendy's, a survey showed that out of 12,000 customers eating lunch, 3,000 ordered Diet Pepsi with their meal. What percent of customers ordered Diet Pepsi?

6–53. What percent of customers in Problem 6–52 did not order Diet Pepsi?

6–54. The *Rhinelander Daily News* March 4, 2007 issue, ran a story on rising gas prices. Last week, gas was selling for $1.99 a gallon and the world looked rosy. Not so now. The price of a gallon of regular unleaded nosed up to $2.24. What was the percent increase? Round to the nearest hundredth percent.

6–55. Wally Chin, the owner of an Exxon-Mobil station, bought a used Ford pickup truck, paying $2,000 as a down payment. He still owes 80% of the selling price. What was the selling price of the truck?

6–56. Maria Fay bought 4 Aquatread tires at a local Goodyear store. The salesperson told her that her mileage would increase by 6%. Before this purchase, Maria was getting 22 mpg. What should her mileage be with the new tires to nearest hundredth?

6–57. Jeff Rowe went to Best Buy and bought a Cannon digital camera. The purchase price was $400. Jeff made a down payment of 40%. How much was Jeff's down payment?

6–58. Assume that in the year 2009, 800,000 people attended the Christmas Eve celebration at Walt Disney World. In 2010, attendance for the Christmas Eve celebration is expected to increase by 35%. What is the total number of people expected at Walt Disney World for this event?

6–59. Pete Smith found in his attic a Woody Woodpecker watch in its original box. It had a price tag on it for $4.50. The watch was made in 1949. Pete brought the watch to an antiques dealer and sold it for $35. What was the percent of increase in price? Round to the nearest hundredth percent.

6–60. Fuel inventories were lower than last year according to the San Francisco Chronicle dated February 24, 2007. This year there are 31.7 million barrels of inventory, a 7.32 percent drop. **(a)** What was the amount of inventory last year to nearest tenth? **(b)** What was the amount of the decrease?

6–61. Christie's Auction sold a painting for $24,500. It charges all buyers a 15% premium of the final bid price. How much did the bidder pay Christie's?

WORD PROBLEMS (Second of Four Sets)

6–62. Out of 9,000 college students surveyed, 540 responded that they do not eat breakfast. What percent of the students do not eat breakfast?

6–63. What percent of college students in Problem 6–62 eat breakfast?

6–64. Alice Hall made a $3,000 down payment on a new Ford Explorer wagon. She still owes 90% of the selling price. What was the selling price of the wagon?

6–65. The *Kansas City Star* on February 16, 2007 reported on the lowering prices of natural gas. With lower natural gas prices and unseasonably warm weather early this winter the forecast is that gas-heating customers will pay $825 as compared to $1,019 last year. At Kansas Gas Service, last year, the price of 1,000 cubic feet of gas was $9.95; this has been reduced by 12.1608 percent. **(a)** What percent was the decrease for customer's bills? **(b)** What was the amount of decreased charge for 1,000 cubic feet of gas? Round to nearest cent. **(c)** What is the new price for 1,000 cubic feet? Round to the nearest hundredth percent.

6–66. Jim and Alice Lange, employees at Wal-Mart, have put themselves on a strict budget. Their goal at year's end is to buy a boat for $15,000 in cash. Their budget includes the following:

40% food and lodging   20% entertainment   10% educational

Jim earns $1,900 per month and Alice earns $2,400 per month. After one year, will Alice and Jim have enough cash to buy the boat?

6–67. The price of a Fossil watch dropped from $49.95 to $30.00. What was the percent decrease in price? Round to the nearest hundredth percent.

6–68. The Museum of Science in Boston estimated that 64% of all visitors came from within the state. On Saturday, 2,500 people attended the museum. How many attended the museum from out of state?

6–69. Staples pays George Nagovsky an annual salary of $36,000. Today, George's boss informs him that he will receive a $4,600 raise. What percent of George's old salary is the $4,600 raise? Round to the nearest tenth percent.

6–70. In 2009, Dairy Queen had $550,000 in sales. In 2010, Dairy Queen's sales were up 35%. What were Dairy Queen's sales in 2010?

6–71. Blue Valley College has 600 female students. This is 60% of the total student body. How many students attend Blue Valley College?

6–72. Dr. Grossman was reviewing his total accounts receivable. This month, credit customers paid $44,000, which represented 20% of all receivables (what customers owe) due. What was Dr. Grossman's total accounts receivable?

6–73. Massachusetts has a 5% sales tax. Timothy bought a Toro lawn mower and paid $20 sales tax. What was the cost of the lawn mower before the tax?

6–74. The price of an antique doll increased from $600 to $800. What was the percent of increase? Round to the nearest tenth percent.

6–75. Borders bookstore ordered 80 marketing books but received 60 books. What percent of the order was missing?

6–76. At a Christie's auction, the auctioneer estimated that 40% of the audience was from within the state. Eight hundred people attended the auction. How many out-of-state people attended?

6–77. Due to increased mailing costs, the new rate will cost publishers $50 million; this is 12.5% more than they paid the previous year. How much did it cost publishers last year? Round to the nearest hundreds.

6–78. In 2010, Jim Goodman, an employee at Walgreens, earned $45,900, an increase of 17.5% over the previous year. What were Jim's earnings in 2009? Round to the nearest cent.

6–79. If the number of mortgage applications declined by 7% to 1,625,415, what had been the previous year's number of applications?

6–80. In 2010, the price of a business math text rose to $100. This is 6% more than the 2009 price. What was the old selling price? Round to the nearest cent.

6–81. Web Consultants, Inc., pays Alice Rose an annual salary of $48,000. Today, Alice's boss informs her that she will receive a $6,400 raise. What percent of Alice's old salary is the $6,400 raise? Round to nearest tenth percent.

6–82. Earl Miller, a lawyer, charges Lee's Plumbing, his client, 25% of what he can collect for Lee from customers whose accounts are past due. The attorney also charges, in addition to the 25%, a flat fee of $50 per customer. This month, Earl collected $7,000 from 3 of Lee's past-due customers. What is the total fee due to Earl?

6–83. Petco ordered 100 dog calendars but received 60. What percent of the order was missing?

6–84. Blockbuster Video uses MasterCard. MasterCard charges $2\frac{1}{2}\%$ on net deposits (credit slips less returns). Blockbuster made a net deposit of $4,100 for charge sales. How much did MasterCard charge Blockbuster?

6–85. In 2009, Internet Access had $800,000 in sales. In 2010, Internet Access sales were up 45%. What are the sales for 2010?

WORD PROBLEMS (Fourth of Four Sets)

6–86. Saab Corporation raised the base price of its popular 900 series by $1,200 to $33,500. What was the percent increase? Round to the nearest tenth percent.

6–87. The sales tax rate is 8%. If Jim bought a new Buick and paid a sales tax of $1,920, what was the cost of the Buick before the tax?

6–88. Puthina Unge bought a new Compaq computer system on sale for $1,800. It was advertised as 30% off the regular price. What was the original price of the computer? Round to the nearest dollar.

6–89. John O'Sullivan has just completed his first year in business. His records show that he spent the following in advertising:

Newspaper $600   Radio $650   Yellow Pages $700   Local flyers $400

What percent of John's advertising was spent on the Yellow Pages? Round to the nearest hundredth percent.

6–90. The *Cincinnati Post* reported holiday spending predictions. Columbus-based Big Research LLC surveyed nearly 7,700 consumers. The survey found 22% of consumers planned to begin shopping in either September or October, and another 17% had started in August or earlier. **(a)** How many consumers planned to begin shopping in September or October? **(b)** How many consumers planned to begin in August or earlier?

6–91. Abby Kaminsky sold her ski house at Attitash Mountain in New Hampshire for $35,000. This sale represented a loss of 15% off the original price. What was the original price Abby paid for the ski house? Round your answer to the nearest dollar.

6–92. Out of 4,000 colleges surveyed, 60% reported that SAT scores were not used as a high consideration in viewing their applications. How many schools view the SAT as important in screening applicants?

6–93. If refinishing your basement at a cost of $45,404 would add $18,270 to the resale value of your home, what percent of your cost is recouped? Round to the nearest percent.

6–94. A major airline laid off 4,000 pilots and flight attendants. If this was a 12.5% reduction in the workforce, what was the size of the workforce after the layoffs?

6–95. Assume 450,000 people line up on the streets to see the Macy's Thanksgiving Parade in 2008. If attendance is expected to increase 30%, what will be the number of people lined up on the street to see the 2009 parade?

6–96. Continental Airlines stock climbed 4% from $18.04. Shares of AMR Corporation, American Airlines' parent company, closed up 7% at $12.55. AirTran Airways went from $17.27 to $17.96. Round answers to the nearest hundredth. **(a)** What is the new price of Continental Airlines stock? **(b)** What had been the price of AMR Corporation stock? **(c)** What percent did AirTran Airways increase? Round to the nearest percent.

6–97. A local Dunkin' Donuts shop reported that its sales have increased exactly 22% per year for the last 2 years. This year's sales were $82,500. What were Dunkin' Donuts sales 2 years ago? Round each year's sales to the nearest dollar.

 SUMMARY PRACTICE TEST

Convert the following decimals to percents. *(p. 139)*

1. .921   **2.** .4   **3.** 15.88   **4.** 8.00

Convert the following percents to decimals. *(p. 141)*

5. 42%   **6.** 7.98%   **7.** 400%   **8.** $\frac{1}{4}$%

Convert the following fractions to percents. Round to the nearest tenth percent. *(p. 142)*

9. $\frac{1}{6}$ **10.** $\frac{1}{3}$

Convert the following percents to fractions and reduce to the lowest terms as needed. *(p. 142)*

11. $19\frac{3}{8}$%   **12.** 6.2%

Solve the following problems for portion, base, or rate:

13. An Arby's franchise has a net income before taxes of $900,000. The company's treasurer estimates that 40% of the company's net income will go to federal and state taxes. How much will the Arby's franchise have left? *(p. 145)*

14. Domino's projects a year-end net income of $699,000. The net income represents 30% of its annual sales. What are Domino's projected annual sales? *(p. 147)*

15. Target ordered 400 iPods. When Target received the order, 100 iPods were missing. What percent of the order did Target receive? *(p. 146)*

16. Matthew Song, an employee at Putnam Investments, receives an annual salary of $120,000. Today his boss informed him that he would receive a $3,200 raise. What percent of his old salary is the $3,200 raise? Round to the nearest hundredth percent. *(p. 146)*

17. The price of a Delta airline ticket from Los Angeles to Boston increased to $440. This is a 15% increase. What was the old fare? Round to the nearest cent. *(p. 147)*

18. Scupper Grace earns a gross pay of $900 per week at Office Depot. Scupper's payroll deductions are 29%. What is Scupper's take-home pay? *(p. 145)*

19. Mia Wong is reviewing the total accounts receivable of Wong's department store. Credit customers paid $90,000 this month. This represents 60% of all receivables due. What is Mia's total accounts receivable? *(p. 147)*

HOME | Will remodeling pay off when you move? *By Patricia Mertz Esswein*

Live better and SELL HIGHER

REMODELING projects are enticing investments. You get to play the Iron Chef in a new, modern kitchen or pamper yourself in a spa-style bathroom, then recoup your money when you sell your house. In fact, anticipating that payback is often a driving force in convincing yourself—or your spouse—that a project is worth the money. But how much return can you count on? The latest report from *Remodeling* magazine says it's not uncommon to recover 80% or more.

Despite unrelenting new construction, the average U.S. home is 32 years old and in need of lifts, tucks and add-ons. So, home remodeling has become a national obsession. In 2004, Americans spent $186 billion on remodeling, according to Harvard University's Joint Center for Housing Studies.

The accompanying table shows the average price tag for a dozen popular projects, based on figures provided by HomeTech Information Systems, a company that develops software for estimating remodeling costs. The percentage of cost recouped at resale is based on estimates by members of the National Association of Realtors.

The numbers are national averages; the full report (which can be ordered for $37.50 at www.remodelingmaga zine.com) includes estimates by region and for 60 cities. The payback can vary dramatically by region.

Sal Alfano, editorial director of *Remodeling* magazine, notes that in extremely hot markets and those with a lot of new construction, resale values may slip below national averages. That's because buyers would just as soon purchase a new house with all the amenities than a remodeled house.
—*Research:* **KATY MARQUARDT**

PAYBACK The dollars and sense of a dozen popular projects

Check out the national average costs for 12 remodeling projects and estimates of how much that cost will be recouped. Payback can vary dramatically by region. The recovery for new siding, for example, ranges from 80% in the West to 105% in the East.

THE PROJECT	THE PRICE	% COST RECOUPED
Minor kitchen remodel	$15,273	93%
Major kitchen remodel, mid-range	$42,660	79%
Major kitchen remodel, upscale	$75,206	80%
Bathroom remodel, mid-range	$9,861	90%
Bathroom remodel, upscale	$25,273	86%
Bathroom addition, mid-range	$21,087	86%
Bathroom addition, upscale	$41,587	81%
Master suite, mid-range	$70,245	80%
Master suite, upscale	$134,364	78%
Window replacement, mid-range	$9,273	85%
Window replacement, upscale	$15,383	84%
Siding replacement	$6,946	93%

SOURCE: Hanley Wood, LLC

BUSINESS MATH ISSUE

In today's real estate market these % recouped numbers are unrealistic.

1. List the key points of the article and information to support your position.
2. Write a group defense of your position using math calculations to support your view.

Slater's Business Math Scrapbook

with Internet Application
Putting Your Skills to Work

PROJECT A
What was the original circulation figure of the *New York Daily News*? Round to nearest hundredth. Check your answer.

Newspapers

Issues
Average weekday circulation for the six months ended March 31 and change from the year-earlier period

NEWSPAPER	CIRCULATION*	% CHANGE
USA Today	2,272,815	0.1%
The Wall Street Journal	2,049,786	-1.0
New York Times	1,142,464	0.5
Los Angeles Times	851,832	-5.4
Washington Post	724,242	-3.7
New York Daily News	708,477	-3.7
New York Post	673,379	-0.7
Chicago Tribune	579,079	0.9
Houston Chronicle	513,387	-3.6
Arizona Republic	438,722	-2.1

*Preliminary figures, subject to audit; includes bulk sales
Source: Audit Bureau of Circulations

Wall Street Journal © 2006

UPS to Raise Rates by Nearly 5%

ATLANTA—**United Parcel Service Inc.** will raise its 2007 list rates for ground shipments, air express and international shipments originating in the U.S. by nearly 5% on average.

The increases, which take effect Jan. 1, exceed those UPS announced a year ago for 2006 and come on the heels of air-shipment rate rises announced earlier this month by rival **FedEx Corp.**, underscoring confidence that demand for delivery services will remain strong.

UPS said list rates for ground shipments will go up 4.9% on average. The increase for air express and international shipments is based on a 6.9% rise in the base rate, minus two percentage points in the current fuel surcharge because of the declining price of oil. Last year the company, the world's largest package carrier in terms of deliveries, raised ground-shipment rates by 3.9% and air and international service rates by 3.5%, excluding two percentage points related to fuel surcharges.

FedEx, the leader in air shipments, said on Nov. 3 that it would increase its net average shipping rate for FedEx Express, including U.S. domestic and U.S. export express package and freight shipments, by 3.5% as of Jan. 1, matching increases made for this year. FedEx is expected to match the ground rates at UPS.

Wall Street Journal © 2006

PROJECT B
Assume a package cost $42 to deliver by UPS in 2006. What would it cost assuming a new list rate increase of 4.9%?

Internet Projects: See text Web site (www.mhhe.com/slater9e) and The Business Math Internet Resource Guide.

American President Lines (APL) has automated its terminal so the average turnaround time for a trucker picking up a 40-foot container is only 17 minutes.

APL uses an automated wireless system to track containers parked across its recently remodeled 160-acre facility in Seattle.

The fast turnaround time gives customers who operate under the just-in-time mode the opportunity to make more trips. Independent truck drivers also benefit.

The international freight industry is plagued by red tape and inefficiency. APL has used its website to help clients like Excel Corporation, the country's second-largest beef packer and processor, speed up its billing time. Excel now wants to ask online for a place on a ship and for a call from APL when room will be available.

The shipping market is enormous, estimated anywhere from $100 billion to $1 trillion. Imports in the United States alone totaled 10 million containers, while exports totaled 6.5 million containers, together carrying $375 billion worth of goods. One of the most difficult transactions is to source goods from overseas and have them delivered with minimal paperwork all the way through to the end customer. Shipping lines must provide real-time information on the location of ships and goods.

Most significant are attempts to automate shipping transactions online. The industry's administrative inefficiencies, which account for 4% to 10% of international trade costs, are targeted. Industry insiders peg error rates on documents even higher, at 25% to 30%. It's no secret that start-ups must overcome the reluctance of hidebound shipping lines, which have deep-seated emotional fears of dot-coms coming between them and their customers.

In conclusion, American President Lines needs to get on board by staying online, or it might go down with the ship.

PROBLEM 1

The $170 billion in international trade volume per year given in the video is expected to increase by 50% in 5 years and expected to double over the next 25 years. **(a)** What is the expected total dollar amount in 5 years? **(b)** What is the expected total dollar amount in 25 years?

PROBLEM 2

The video stated that thousands of containers arrive each day. Each 40-foot container will hold, for example, 16,500 boxes of running shoes, 132,000 videotapes, or 25,000 blouses. At an average retail price of $49.50 for a pair of running shoes, $14.95 for a videotape, and $26.40 for a blouse, what would be the total retail value of the goods in these three containers (assume different goods in each container)?

PROBLEM 3

APL spent $600 million to build a 230-acre shipping terminal in California. The terminal can handle 4 wide-body container ships. Each ship can hold 4,800 20-foot containers, or 2,400 40-foot containers. **(a)** What was the cost per acre to build the facility? **(b)** How many 20-foot containers can the terminal handle at one time? **(c)** How many 40-foot containers can the terminal handle at one time?

PROBLEM 4

According to *Shanghai Daily,* the recent decline in China's export container prices (which fell by 1.4%) has not taken its toll on the general interest in this sector. China's foreign trade grew by 35%, reaching $387.1 billion. APL reported that it would increase its services from Asia to Europe to take advantage of China's growth in exports. What was the dollar amount of China's foreign trade last year?

PROBLEM 5

APL has expanded its domestic fleet to 5,100 53-foot containers; it is expanding its global fleet to 253,000 containers. The 5,100 containers represent what percent of APL's total fleet? Round to the nearest hundredth percent.

PROBLEM 6

The cost of owning a shipping vessel is very high. Operating costs for large vessels can run between $75,000 and $80,000 per day. Using an average cost per day, what would be the operating costs for one week?

PROBLEM 7

The Port of Los Angeles financed new terminal construction through operating revenues and bonds. They will collect about $30 million a year in rent from APL, who signed a 30-year lease on the property. What is APL's monthly payment?

PROBLEM 8

According to port officials, APL expanded cargo-handling capabilities at the Los Angeles facility that are expected to generate 10,500 jobs, with $335 million in wages and annual industry sales of $1 billion. What would be the average wage received? Round to the nearest dollar.

PROBLEM 9

APL has disclosed that it ordered over 34,000 containers from a Chinese container manufacturer. With 253,000 containers in its possession, what will be the percent increase in containers owned by APL? Round to the nearest hundredth percent.

CHAPTER 7

Discounts: Trade and Cash

LEARNING UNIT OBJECTIVES

LU 7-1: Trade Discounts—Single and Chain (Includes Discussion of Freight)

- Calculate single trade discounts with formulas and complements (pp. 171–172).

- Explain the freight terms *FOB shipping point* and *FOB destination (pp. 172–174)*.

- Find list price when net price and trade discount rate are known (p. 174).

- Calculate chain discounts with the net price equivalent rate and single equivalent discount rate (pp. 175–177).

LU 7-2: Cash Discounts, Credit Terms, and Partial Payments

- List and explain typical discount periods and credit periods that a business may offer (pp. 179–185).

- Calculate outstanding balance for partial payments (p. 186).

Online Retailers Are Watching You

Sites Take Shopper-Tracking To New Level to Customize Deals in Holiday Season

By Jessica E. Vascellaro

THIS HOLIDAY SHOPPING season, the price you pay online may depend on your gender and where you live. It may also hinge on what time of day you shop, the speed of your Internet connection, if you are an AOL user, or perhaps even your Google browsing habits.

It means a woman with a high-speed Internet connection in the South may get a flat-rate shipping offer from a retailer like Overstock.com, while a male counterpart in the West may see a promotion for live customer service

instead. Some who logged on to Ice.com through AOL may be teased with a first-time buyer discount while someone who accessed the site directly would be left perkless. And someone using the word "cheap" while searching for gift baskets using Google may be surprised with a free shipping deal at a gourmet-food retailer like DelightfulDeliveries.com.

Browser beware: While they are loath to reveal which attributes affect which promotions—both in response to concerns about privacy and intense competition among online retailers—Internet merchants are picking up on a shopper's digital trail and mining the wealth of information they collect about shoppers to tailor their promotional offers with ever-greater precision.

Wall Street Journal © 2006

A Deal Seeker's Cheat Sheet

Veteran online bargain hunters employ a variety of strategies to secure the best prices. A look at some of them:

STRATEGY	WHERE TO GO	COMMENTS
Look for promotional coupon codes	CouponMountain.com, WOW-Coupons.com, CouponCraze.com, slickdeals.net	These and similar coupon Web sites list promotional codes and offer print-out coupons for discounts at many online retailers and stores. A Google search for a retailer's name and "coupons" can often lead to savings.
"Stack" mail-in rebates	fatwallet.com, GottaDeal.com	Learn of multiple mail-in rebates—a shopping strategy known as "stacking"—by monitoring the forums of these two sites. Occasionally, the value of the rebates can exceed the cost of the product, earning money for the buyer.
Shop via sites that share their commissions	fatwallet.com, Ebates.com, mrrebates.com	These Web sites earn commissions from referring customers to hundreds of online retailers and split some of the money with their members. Membership is free, but you must click on the participating retailers through the sites to qualify. One downside: As with mail-in rebates, it can take months to receive the cash.
Sign up for email alerts	fatwallet.com, FareAlert.net	Fatwallet sends out an early-morning, daily email alert filled with new and expiring online bargains, plus "hot deals" discovered by its members. FareAlert.net sends out occasional email alerts for "extraordinary" travel deals, including airline price mistakes.

Wall Street Journal © 2005

Are you a good online bargain hunter? The *Wall Street Journal* clipping "A Deal Seeker's Cheat Sheet" shows a variety of strategies customers can use to get the best price online.

This chapter discusses two types of discounts taken by retailers—trade and cash. A **trade discount** is a reduction off the original selling price (list price) of an item and is not related to early payment. A **cash discount** is the result of an early payment based on the terms of the sale.

Learning Unit 7–1: Trade Discounts—Single and Chain (Includes Discussion of Freight)

New Deals

Some of the non-car "employee discount" offerings:

- About 30% off on some bicycles at **Randall Scott Cycle Co.**, in Pompano Beach, Fla. (Sells online.)

- Discounts of 10% to 30% on golf gear at **Condor Golf** in Phoenix. (Sells online.)

- Price cuts on lamps (a $100 piece selling for between $30 and $35) at **Lighting Galleries** of Sarasota, Fla.

Wall Street Journal © 2005

Today we see "employee discounts" offered to nonemployees. The *Wall Street Journal* clipping "New Deals" shows three examples of these nonemployee discounts offered by companies.

Where do companies like Randall Scott Cycle Co. get their merchandise? The merchandise sold by retailers is bought from manufacturers and wholesalers who sell only to retailers and not to customers. These manufacturers and wholesalers offer retailer discounts so retailers can resell the merchandise at a profit. The discounts are off the manufacturers' and wholesalers' **list price** (suggested retail price), and the amount of discount that retailers receive off the list price is the **trade discount amount.**

When you make a purchase, the retailer (seller) gives you a purchase **invoice.** Invoices are important business documents that help sellers keep track of sales transactions and buyers keep track of purchase transactions. North Shore Community College Bookstore is a retail seller of textbooks to students. The bookstore usually purchases its textbooks directly from publishers. Figure 7.1 (p. 172) shows a textbook invoice from McGraw-Hill/Irwin Publishing Company to the North Shore Community College Bookstore. Note that the trade discount amount is given in percent. This is the **trade discount rate,** which is a percent off the list price that retailers can deduct. The following formula

FIGURE **7.1**

Bookstore invoice showing a trade discount

Invoice No.: 5582

McGraw-Hill/Irwin Publishing Co.
1333 Burr Ridge Parkway
Burr Ridge, Illinois 60527

Date: July 8, 2008
Ship: Two-day UPS
Terms: 2/10, n/30

Sold to: North Shore Community College Bookstore
1 Ferncroft Road
Danvers, MA 01923

Description	Unit list price	Total amount
50 Financial Management—Block/Hirt	$95.66	$4,783.00
10 Introduction to Business—Nichols	89.50	895.00
Total List Price		$5,678.00
Less: Trade Discount 25%		−1,419.50
Net Price		$4,258.50
Plus: Prepaid Shipping Charge		125.00
Total Invoice Amount		$4,383.50

for calculating a trade discount amount gives the numbers from the Figure 7.1 invoice in parentheses:

TRADE DISCOUNT AMOUNT FORMULA
Trade discount amount = List price × Trade discount rate
($1,419.50)   ($5,678.00)   (25%)

The price that the retailer (bookstore) pays the manufacturer (publisher) or wholesaler is the **net price.** The following formula for calculating the net price gives the numbers from the Figure 7.1 invoice in parentheses:

NET PRICE FORMULA
Net price   =   List price   −   Trade discount amount
($4,258.50)   ($5,678.00)   ($1,419.50)

Frequently, manufacturers and wholesalers issue catalogs to retailers containing list prices of the seller's merchandise and the available trade discounts. To reduce printing costs when prices change, these sellers usually update the catalogs with new *discount sheets.* The discount sheet also gives the seller the flexibility of offering different trade discounts to different classes of retailers. For example, some retailers buy in quantity and service the products. They may receive a larger discount than the retailer who wants the manufacturer to service the products. Sellers may also give discounts to meet a competitor's price, to attract new retailers, and to reward the retailers who buy product-line products. Sometimes the ability of the retailer to negotiate with the seller determines the trade discount amount.

Retailers cannot take trade discounts on freight, returned goods, sales tax, and so on. Trade discounts may be single discounts or a chain of discounts. Before we discuss single trade discounts, let's study freight terms.

Freight Terms

Do you know how successful the shipping businesses of DHL, UPS, and FedEx are in China? The *Wall Street Journal* clipping "Faster, Faster . . ." shows that the shipping businesses of these three companies can be quite profitable.

Claro Cortes IV/Reuters/Landov

Faster, Faster...

Helping manufacturers in China save time and money by managing increasingly complex supply chains.

■ **DHL's** business in China increased by more than 50% in the first half of this year. It started express deliveries there in 1981 and operates through a joint-venture with China's biggest delivery company Sinotrans. DHL ranks first among the foreign-express companies in China with an estimated third of the market.

■ **UPS** first flew to China in 1988 and posted a 125% increase in volume of packages handled during the July-September period of this year. It has a joint-venture with Sinotrans in Beijing but pays the company a fee to deliver its packages everywhere else. UPS has an estimated market share of 15%.

■ **FedEx** reported a 52% rise in exports from China for the three months ended in August. It began deliveries in 1984 and runs a joint-venture with DTW, a smaller Chinese concern. FedEx has a market share that investment bank CSFB estimates at 20%.

Sources: the companies; Credit Suisse First Boston

Wall Street Journal © 2004

The most common **freight terms** are *FOB shipping point* and *FOB destination*. These terms determine how the freight will be paid. The key words in the terms are *shipping point* and *destination*.

FOB shipping point means free on board at shipping point; that is, the buyer pays the freight cost of getting the goods to the place of business.

For example, assume that IBM in San Diego bought goods from Argo Suppliers in Boston. Argo ships the goods FOB Boston by plane. IBM takes title to the goods when the aircraft in Boston receives the goods, so IBM pays the freight from Boston to San Diego. Frequently, the seller (Argo) prepays the freight and adds the amount to the buyer's (IBM) invoice. When paying the invoice, the buyer takes the cash discount off the net price and adds the freight cost. FOB shipping point can be illustrated as follows:

FOB shipping point (Boston)

FOB destination means the seller pays the freight cost until it reaches the buyer's place of business. If Argo ships its goods to IBM FOB destination or FOB San Diego, the title to the goods remains with Argo. Then it is Argo's responsibility to pay the freight from Boston to IBM's place of business in San Diego. FOB destination can be illustrated as follows:

FOB destination (San Diego)

The following *Wall Street Journal* clipping (p. 174) shows the results of a performance test of four companies: Federal Express, DHL, United Parcel Service, and the United States Postal Service. Note the costs and conveniences of these four online delivery services relating to pickup fees, fuel surcharge/own packaging, and website discounts. From the comments on the clipping, which of the four companies was most impressive?

SITE/TOTAL PRICE	PICK-UP FEE	FUEL SURCHARGE/OWN PACKAGING?	WEB SITE DISCOUNT	COMMENTS
dhl-usa.com $48.24	$0	$8.70/Yes	No	The most consistent site in several browsers, and the fewest printing headaches for shipping label and postage. Could have used more guidance on taxes and duties.
fedex.com $49.36	$4	$7.56/Yes	Yes, 10% savings on freight charges only when you register online.	The postage confirmation email we first received was not a firm commitment. We rescheduled online and got a real confirmation. An agent arrived that evening.
ups.com $49.22	No fee for international parcels	$5.47/Yes	Yes, retail site would have charged $54.56	Despite difficulties using PDF files to print invoices and download instructions, phone and email support was fast and efficient.
usps.com $23.51	$12.50 for pickup on demand service	No/No, needed clear envelope from post office	Yes, $1 cheaper than going to a post office.	Having to use USPS packaging makes a trip to the post office inevitable. Email customer support was good.

Wall Street Journal © 2005

Now you are ready for the discussion on single trade discounts.

Single Trade Discount

In the introduction to this unit, we showed how to use the trade discount amount formula and the net price formula to calculate the McGraw-Hill/Irwin Publishing Company textbook sale to the North Shore Community College Bookstore. Since McGraw-Hill/Irwin gave the bookstore only one trade discount, it is a **single trade discount.** In the following word problem, we use the formulas to solve another example of a single trade discount. Again, we will use a blueprint aid to help dissect and solve the word problem.

The Word Problem The list price of a Macintosh computer is $2,700. The manufacturer offers dealers a 40% trade discount. What are the trade discount amount and the net price?

The facts	Solving for?	Steps to take	Key points
List price: $2,700. *Trade discount rate:* 40%.	Trade discount amount. Net price.	Trade discount amount = List price × Trade discount rate. Net price = List price − Trade discount amount.	Trade discount amount — Portion (?) — Base ($2,700) × Rate (.40) — List price — Trade discount rate

Steps to solving problem

1. Calculate the trade discount amount. $2,700 × .40 = $1,080

2. Calculate the net price. $2,700 − $1,080 = **$1,620**

Now let's learn how to check the dealers' net price of $1,620 with an alternate procedure using a complement.

How to Calculate the Net Price Using Complement of Trade Discount Rate

The **complement** of a trade discount rate is the difference between the discount rate and 100%. The following steps show you how to use the complement of a trade discount rate:

CALCULATING NET PRICE USING COMPLEMENT OF TRADE DISCOUNT RATE
Step 1. To find the complement, subtract the single discount rate from 100%.
Step 2. Multiply the list price times the complement (from Step 1).

Think of a complement of any given percent (decimal) as the result of subtracting the percent from 100%.

Step 1.   100%
            – 40 ← Trade discount rate
            60% or .60

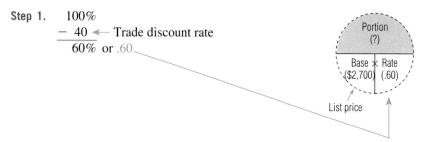

The complement means that we are spending 60 cents per dollar because we save 40 cents per dollar. Since we planned to spend $2,700, we multiply .60 by $2,700 to get a net price of $1,620.

Step 2. $1,620 = $2,700 × .60

Note how the portion ($1,620) and rate (.60) relate to the same piece of the base ($2,700). The portion ($1,620) is smaller than the base, since the rate is less than 100%.

Be aware that some people prefer to use the trade discount amount formula and the net price formula to find the net price. Other people prefer to use the complement of the trade discount rate to find the net price. The result is always the same.

Finding List Price When You Know Net Price and Trade Discount Rate

The following formula has many useful applications:

CALCULATING LIST PRICE WHEN NET PRICE AND TRADE DISCOUNT RATE ARE KNOWN
List price = $\dfrac{\text{Net price}}{\text{Complement of trade discount rate}}$

Next, let's see how to dissect and solve a word problem calculating list price.

The Word Problem   A Macintosh computer has a $1,620 net price and a 40% trade discount. What is its list price?

The facts	Solving for?	Steps to take	Key points
Net price: $1,620. *Trade discount rate:* 40%.	List price.	List price = $\dfrac{\text{Net price}}{\text{Complement of trade discount rate}}$	Net price → Portion ($1,620) Base (?) × Rate (.60) List price 100% – 40%

Steps to solving problem

1. Calculate the complement of the trade discount.

            100%
            – 40
            60% = .60

2. Calculate the list price.

            $\dfrac{\$1,620}{.60}$ = $2,700

Note that the portion ($1,620) and rate (.60) relate to the same piece of the base.

Let's return to the McGraw-Hill/Irwin invoice in Figure 7.1 (p. 172) and calculate the list price using the formula for finding list price when net price and trade discount rate are known. The net price of the textbooks is $4,258.50. The complement of the trade discount rate is 100% − 25% = 75% = .75. Dividing the net price $4,258.50 by the complement .75

equals $5,678.00, the list price shown in the McGraw-Hill/Irwin invoice. We can show this as follows:

$$\frac{\$4,258.50}{.75} = \$5,678.00, \text{ the list price}$$

Chain Discounts

Frequently, manufacturers want greater flexibility in setting trade discounts for different classes of customers, seasonal trends, promotional activities, and so on. To gain this flexibility, some sellers give **chain** or **series discounts**—trade discounts in a series of two or more successive discounts.

Sellers list chain discounts as a group, for example, 20/15/10. Let's look at how Mick Company arrives at the net price of office equipment with a 20/15/10 chain discount.

EXAMPLE   The list price of the office equipment is $15,000. The chain discount is 20/15/10. The long way to calculate the net price is as follows:

Step 1	**Step 2**	**Step 3**	**Step 4**
$15,000	$15,000	$12,000	$10,200
× .20	− 3,000	− 1,800	− 1,020
$ 3,000	$12,000	$10,200	$ 9,180 net price
	× .15	× .10	
	$ 1,800	$ 1,020	

Never add the 20/15/10 together.

Note how we multiply the percent (in decimal) times the new balance after we subtract the previous trade discount amount. For example, in Step 3, we change the last discount, 10%, to decimal form and multiply times $10,200. Remember that each percent is multiplied by a successively *smaller* base. You could write the 20/15/10 discount rate in any order and still arrive at the same net price. Thus, you would get the $9,180 net price if the discount were 10/15/20 or 15/20/10. However, sellers usually give the larger discounts first. *Never try to shorten this step process by adding the discounts.* Your net price will be incorrect because, when done properly, each percent is calculated on a different base.

Net Price Equivalent Rate

In the example above, you could also find the $9,180 net price with the **net price equivalent rate**—a shortcut method. Let's see how to use this rate to calculate net price.

CALCULATING NET PRICE USING NET PRICE EQUIVALENT RATE
Step 1. Subtract each chain discount rate from 100% (find the complement) and convert each percent to a decimal.
Step 2. Multiply the decimals. Do not round off decimals, since this number is the net price equivalent rate.
Step 3. Multiply the list price times the net price equivalent rate (Step 2).

The following word problem with its blueprint aid illustrates how to use the net price equivalent rate method.

The Word Problem The list price of office equipment is $15,000. The chain discount is 20/15/10. What is the net price?

The facts	Solving for?	Steps to take	Key points
List price: $15,000. *Chain discount:* 20/15/10	Net price.	Net price equivalent rate. Net price = List price × Net price equivalent rate.	Do not round net price equivalent rate.

Steps to solving problem

1. Calculate the complement of each rate and convert each percent to a decimal.	100% − 20 80% ↓ .8	100% − 15 85% ↓ .85	100% − 10 90% ↓ .9	

2. Calculate the net price equivalent rate. (Do not round.) $.8 \times .85 \times .9 = .612$ Net price equivalent rate
For each $1, you are spending about 61 cents.

3. Calculate the net price (actual cost to buyer). $\$15,000 \times .612 = \boxed{\$9,180}$

Next we see how to calculate the trade discount amount with a simpler method.

In the previous word problem, we could calculate the trade discount amount as follows:

$15,000 ←List price
− 9,180 ←Net price
$ 5,820 ←Trade discount amount

Single Equivalent Discount Rate

You can use another method to find the trade discount by using the **single equivalent discount rate.**

CALCULATING TRADE DISCOUNT AMOUNT USING SINGLE EQUIVALENT DISCOUNT RATE
Step 1. Subtract the net price equivalent rate from 1. This is the single equivalent discount rate.
Step 2. Multiply the list price times the single equivalent discount rate. This is the trade discount amount.

Let's now do the calculations.

Step 1.   1.000 ← If you are using a calculator, just press 1.
  − .612
    .388 ← This is the single equivalent discount rate.

Step 2. $\$15,000 \times .388 = \boxed{\$5,820}$ → This is the trade discount amount.

Remember that when we use the net price equivalent rate, the buyer of the office equipment pays $.612 on each $1 of list price. Now with the single equivalent discount rate, we can say that the buyer saves $.388 on each $1 of list price. The .388 is the single equivalent discount rate for the 20/15/10 chain discount. Note how we use the .388 single equivalent discount rate as if it were the only discount.

It's time to try the Practice Quiz.

LU 7–1 PRACTICE QUIZ

Complete this **Practice Quiz** to see how you are doing[1]

1. The list price of a dining room set with a 40% trade discount is $12,000. What are the trade discount amount and net price (use complement method for net price)?
2. The net price of a video system with a 30% trade discount is $1,400. What is the list price?
3. Lamps Outlet bought a shipment of lamps from a wholesaler. The total list price was $12,000 with a 5/10/25 chain discount. Calculate the net price and trade discount amount. (Use the net price equivalent rate and single equivalent discount rate in your calculation.)

[1]For all three problems we will show blueprint aids. You might want to draw them on scrap paper.

✓ Solutions

1. Dining room set trade discount amount and net price:

The facts	Solving for?	Steps to take	Key points
List price: $12,000. *Trade discount rate:* 40%.	Trade discount amount. Net price.	Trade discount amount = List price × Trade discount rate. Net price = List price × Complement of trade discount rate.	Trade discount amount Portion (?) Base × Rate ($12,000) (.40) List price Trade discount rate

Steps to solving problem

1. Calculate the trade discount. $12,000 × .40 = $4,800 Trade discount amount

2. Calculate the net price. $12,000 × .60 = $7,200 (100% − 40% = 60%)

2. Video system list price:

The facts	Solving for?	Steps to take	Key points
Net price: $1,400. *Trade discount rate:* 30%.	List price.	List price = $\dfrac{\text{Net price}}{\text{Complement of trade discount}}$	Net price Portion ($1,400) Base × Rate (?) (.70) List price 100% −30%

Steps to solving problem

1. Calculate the complement of trade discount.

$$\begin{array}{r} 100\% \\ -\ 30 \\ \hline 70\% \end{array} = .70$$

2. Calculate the list price. $\dfrac{\$1,400}{.70} = \$2,000$

3. Lamps Outlet's net price and trade discount amount:

The facts	Solving for?	Steps to take	Key points
List price: $12,000. *Chain discount:* 5/10/25.	Net price. Trade discount amount.	Net price = List price × Net price equivalent rate. Trade discount amount = List price × Single equivalent discount rate.	Do not round off net price equivalent rate or single equivalent discount rate.

Steps to solving problem

1. Calculate the complement of each chain discount.

$$\begin{array}{r} 100\% \\ -\ 5 \\ \hline 95\% \end{array} \qquad \begin{array}{r} 100\% \\ -\ 10 \\ \hline 90\% \end{array} \qquad \begin{array}{r} 100\% \\ -\ 25 \\ \hline 75\% \end{array}$$

2. Calculate the net price equivalent rate. $.95 \times .90 \times .75 = .64125$

3. Calculate the net price. $12,000 × .64125 = $7,695

4. Calculate the single equivalent discount rate.   1.00000
                                                        − .64125
                                                        ―――――
                                                          .35875

5. Calculate the trade discount amount. $12,000 × .35875 = $4,305

LU 7–1a   EXTRA PRACTICE QUIZ

Need more practice? Try this **Extra Practice Quiz** (check figures in Chapter Organizer, p. 190)

1. The list price of a dining room set with a 30% trade discount is $16,000. What are the trade discount amount and net price (use complement method for net price)?
2. The net price of a video system with a 20% trade discount is $400. What is the list price?
3. Lamps Outlet bought a shipment of lamps from a wholesaler. The total list price was $14,000 with a 4/8/20 chain discount. Calculate the net price and trade discount amount. (Use the net price equivalent rate and single equivalent discount rate in your calculation.)

Learning Unit 7–2: Cash Discounts, Credit Terms, and Partial Payments

Sean Clayton/The Image Works

To introduce this learning unit, we will use the New Hampshire Propane Company invoice that follows. The invoice shows that if you pay your bill early, you will receive a 19-cent discount. Every penny counts.

New Hampshire Propane Company

Date	Description	Qty.	Price	Total
	Previous Balance			**$0.00**
06/24/08	PROPANE	3.60	$3.40	$12.24

Invoice No.	
004433L	

Totals this invoice: $12.24

AMOUNT DUE: $12.24

Invoice Date	
6/26/08	

Prompt Pay Discount: $0.19

Net Amount Due if RECEIVED by 07/10/08: $12.05

Due Date	7/26/08

Now let's study cash discounts.

Cash Discounts

In the New Hampshire Propane Company invoice, we receive a cash discount of 19 cents. This amount is determined by the **terms of the sale,** which can include the credit period, cash discount, discount period, and freight terms.

Buyers can often benefit from buying on credit. The time period that sellers give buyers to pay their invoices is the **credit period.** Frequently, buyers can sell the goods bought during this credit period. Then, at the end of the credit period, buyers can pay sellers with the funds from the sales of the goods. When buyers can do this, they can use the consumer's money to pay the invoice instead of their money.

A cash discount is for prompt payment. A trade discount is not.

Sellers can also offer a cash discount, or reduction from the invoice price, if buyers pay the invoice within a specified time. This time period is the **discount period,** which is part of the total credit period. Sellers offer this cash discount because they can use the dollars to better advantage sooner than later. Buyers who are not short of cash like cash discounts because the goods will cost them less and, as a result, provide an opportunity for larger profits.

Remember that buyers do not take cash discounts on freight, returned goods, sales tax, and trade discounts. Buyers take cash discounts on the *net price* of the invoice. Before we discuss how to calculate cash discounts, let's look at some aids that will help you calculate credit **due dates** and **end of credit periods.**

Trade discounts should be taken before cash discounts.

Aids in Calculating Credit Due Dates

Sellers usually give credit for 30, 60, or 90 days. Not all months of the year have 30 days. So you must count the credit days from the date of the invoice. The trick is to remember the number of days in each month. You can choose one of the following three options to help you do this.

Years divisible by 4 are leap years. Leap years occur in 2008 and 2012.

Option 1: Days-in-a-Month Rule You may already know this rule. Remember that every 4 years is a leap year.

> Thirty days has September, April, June, and November; all the rest have 31 except February has 28, and 29 in leap years.

Option 2: Knuckle Months Some people like to use the knuckles on their hands to remember which months have 30 or 31 days. Note in the following diagram that each knuckle represents a month with 31 days. The short months are in between the knuckles.

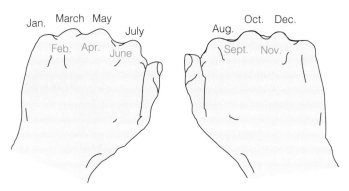

31 days: Jan., March, May, July, Aug., Oct., Dec.

Option 3: Days-in-a-Year Calendar The days-in-a-year calendar (excluding leap year) is another tool to help you calculate dates for discount and credit periods (Table 7.1). For example, let's use Table 7.1 to calculate 90 days from August 12.

EXAMPLE   By Table 7.1: August 12 = $\begin{array}{r} 224 \text{ days} \\ +\ 90 \\ \hline 314 \text{ days} \end{array}$

Search for day 314 in Table 7.1. You will find that day 314 is November 10. In this example, we stayed within the same year. Now let's try an example in which we overlap from year to year.

EXAMPLE   What date is 80 days after December 5?

Table 7.1 shows that December 5 is 339 days from the beginning of the year. Subtracting 339 from 365 (the end of the year) tells us that we have used up 26 days by the end of the year. This leaves 54 days in the new year. Go back in the table and

| TABLE | 7.1 | Exact days-in-a-year calendar (excluding leap year)* |

Day of month	31 Jan.	28 Feb.	31 Mar.	30 Apr.	31 May	30 June	31 July	31 Aug.	30 Sept.	31 Oct.	30 Nov.	31 Dec.
1	1	32	60	91	121	152	182	213	244	274	305	335
2	2	33	61	92	122	153	183	214	245	275	306	336
3	3	34	62	93	123	154	184	215	246	276	307	337
4	4	35	63	94	124	155	185	216	247	277	308	338
5	5	36	64	95	125	156	186	217	248	278	309	339
6	6	37	65	96	126	157	187	218	249	279	310	340
7	7	38	66	97	127	158	188	219	250	280	311	341
8	8	39	67	98	128	159	189	220	251	281	312	342
9	9	40	68	99	129	160	190	221	252	282	313	343
10	10	41	69	100	130	161	191	222	253	283	314	344
11	11	42	70	101	131	162	192	223	254	284	315	345
12	12	43	71	102	132	163	193	224	255	285	316	346
13	13	44	72	103	133	164	194	225	256	286	317	347
14	14	45	73	104	134	165	195	226	257	287	318	348
15	15	46	74	105	135	166	196	227	258	288	319	349
16	16	47	75	106	136	167	197	228	259	289	320	350
17	17	48	76	107	137	168	198	229	260	290	321	351
18	18	49	77	108	138	169	199	230	261	291	322	352
19	19	50	78	109	139	170	200	231	262	292	323	353
20	20	51	79	110	140	171	201	232	263	293	324	354
21	21	52	80	111	141	172	202	233	264	294	325	355
22	22	53	81	112	142	173	203	234	265	295	326	356
23	23	54	82	113	143	174	204	235	266	296	327	357
24	24	55	83	114	144	175	205	236	267	297	328	358
25	25	56	84	115	145	176	206	237	268	298	329	359
26	26	57	85	116	146	177	207	238	269	299	330	360
27	27	58	86	117	147	178	208	239	270	300	331	361
28	28	59	87	118	148	179	209	240	271	301	332	362
29	29	—	88	119	149	180	210	241	272	302	333	363
30	30	—	89	120	150	181	211	242	273	303	334	364
31	31	—	90	—	151	—	212	243	—	304	—	365

*Often referred to as a Julian calendar.

start with the beginning of the year and search for 54 (80 − 26) days. The 54th day is February 23.

By table

365 days in year
− 339 days until December 5
   26 days used in year

   80 days from December 5
   − 26 days used in year
   54 days in new year or
       February 23

Without use of table

December 31
− December   5
              26
+ 31 days in January
              57
+ 23 due date (February 23)
   80 total days

When you know how to calculate credit due dates, you can understand the common business terms sellers offer buyers involving discounts and credit periods. Remember that discount and credit terms vary from one seller to another.

Common Credit Terms Offered by Sellers

The common credit terms sellers offer buyers include *ordinary dating, receipt of goods (ROG),* and *end of month (EOM).* In this section we examine these credit terms. To determine the due dates, we used the exact days-in-a-year calendar (Table 7.1, p. 181).

Ordinary Dating

Today, businesses frequently use the **ordinary dating** method. It gives the buyer a cash discount period that begins with the invoice date. The credit terms of two common ordinary dating methods are 2/10, n/30 and 2/10, 1/15, n/30.

2/10, n/30 Ordinary Dating Method   The 2/10, n/30 is read as "two ten, net thirty." Buyers can take a 2% cash discount off the gross amount of the invoice if they pay the bill within 10 days from the invoice date. If buyers miss the discount period, the net amount—without a discount—is due between day 11 and day 30. *Freight, returned goods, sales tax, and trade discounts must be subtracted from the gross before calculating a cash discount.*

EXAMPLE $400 invoice dated July 5: terms 2/10, n/30; no freight; paid on July 11.

Step 1.   Calculate end of 2% discount period:

> July   5 date of invoice
> $\underline{+ \ 10}$ days
> July 15 end of 2% discount period

Step 2.   Calculate end of credit period:

> July 5 by Table 7.1
> 186 days
> $\underline{+ \ 30}$
> 216 days

> Search in Table 7.1 for 216 → August 4 → end of credit period

Step 3.   Calculate payment on July 11:

> .02 × $400 = $8 cash discount
> $400 − $8 = $392 paid

> *Note:* A 2% cash discount means that you save 2 cents on the dollar and pay 98 cents on the dollar. Thus, $.98 × $400 = $392.

The following time line illustrates the 2/10, n/30 ordinary dating method beginning and ending dates of the above example:

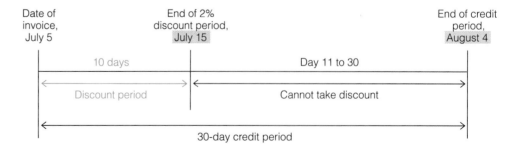

2/10, 1/15, n/30 Ordinary Dating Method   The 2/10, 1/15, n/30 is read "two ten, one fifteen, net thirty." The seller will give buyers a 2% (2 cents on the dollar) cash discount if they pay within 10 days of the invoice date. If buyers pay between day 11 and day 15 from the date of the invoice, they can save 1 cent on the dollar. If buyers do not pay on day 15, the net or full amount is due 30 days from the invoice date.

EXAMPLE $600 invoice dated May 8; $100 of freight included in invoice price; paid on May 22. Terms 2/10, 1/15, n/30.

Step 1. Calculate the end of the 2% discount period:

May   8 date of invoice
+ 10 days

May 18 end of 2% discount period

Step 2. Calculate end of 1% discount period:

May 18 end of 2% discount period
+   5 days

May 23 end of 1% discount period

Step 3. Calculate end of credit period:

May 8 by Table 7.1
128 days
+ 30
158 days

Search in Table 7.1 for 158 → June 7 → end of credit period

Step 4. Calculate payment on May 22 (14 days after date of invoice):

$600 invoice
− 100 freight
$500
× .01
$5.00

$500 − $5.00 + $100 freight = $595

> A 1% discount means we pay $.99 on the dollar or
> $500 × $.99 = $495 + $100 freight = $595.
>
> *Note:* Freight is added back since no cash discount is taken on freight.

The following time line illustrates the 2/10, 1/15, n/30 ordinary dating method beginning and ending dates of the above example:

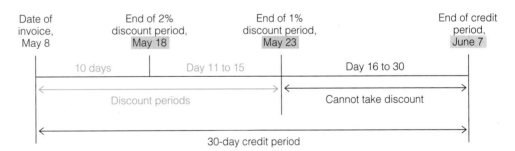

Date of invoice, May 8	End of 2% discount period, May 18	End of 1% discount period, May 23	End of credit period, June 7
10 days	Day 11 to 15	Day 16 to 30	
	Discount periods	Cannot take discount	
		30-day credit period	

Receipt of Goods (ROG)

3/10, n/30 ROG With the **receipt of goods (ROG),** the cash discount period begins when buyer receives goods, *not* the invoice date. Industry often uses the ROG terms when buyers cannot expect delivery until a long time after they place the order. Buyers can take a 3% discount within 10 days *after* receipt of goods. Full amount is due between day 11 and day 30 if cash discount period is missed.

EXAMPLE $900 invoice dated May 9; no freight or returned goods; the goods were received on July 8; terms 3/10, n/30 ROG; payment made on July 20.

Step 1.   Calculate the end of the 3% discount period:

July   8 date goods arrive
+ 10 days
July 18 end of 3% discount period

Step 2.   Calculate the end of the credit period:

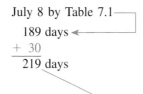

July 8 by Table 7.1
189 days
+ 30
219 days

Search in Table 7.1 for 219 → August 7 → end of credit period

Step 3.   Calculate payment on July 20:

Missed discount period and paid net or full amount of $900.

The following time line illustrates 3/10, n/30 ROG beginning and ending dates of the above example:

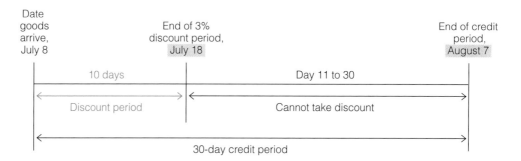

Date goods arrive, July 8	End of 3% discount period, July 18	End of credit period, August 7
	10 days	Day 11 to 30
Discount period		Cannot take discount
30-day credit period		

End of Month (EOM)[2]

In this section we look at terms involving **end of the month (EOM).** If an invoice is dated the *25th or earlier* of a month, we follow one set of rules. If an invoice is dated after the 25th of the month, a new set of rules is followed. Let's look at each situation.

Invoice Dated 25th or Earlier in Month, 1/10 EOM   If sellers date an invoice on the 25th or earlier in the month, buyers can take the cash discount if they pay the invoice by the first 10 days of the month following the sale (next month). If buyers miss the discount period, the full amount is due within 20 days after the end of the discount period.

EXAMPLE $600 invoice dated July 6; no freight or returns; terms 1/10 EOM; paid on August 8.

Step 1.   Calculate the end of the 1% discount period:

August 10   First 10 days of month following sale.

Step 2.   Calculate the end of the credit period:

August 10
+ 20 days
August 30 → Credit period is 20 days after discount period.

Step 3.   Calculate payment on August 8:

.99 × $600 = $594

---

[2]Sometimes the Latin term *proximo* is used. Other variations of EOM exist, but the key point is that the seller guarantees the buyer 15 days' credit. We assume a 30-day month.

The following timeline illustrates the beginning and ending dates of the EOM invoice of the above example:

*Even though the discount period begins with the next month following the sale, if buyers wish, they can pay before the discount period (date of invoice until the discount period).

Invoice Dated after 25th of Month, 2/10 EOM   When sellers sell goods *after* the 25th of the month, buyers gain an additional month. The cash discount period ends on the 10th day of the second month that follows the sale. Why? This occurs because the seller guarantees the 15 days' credit of the buyer. If a buyer bought goods on August 29, September 10 would be only 12 days. So the buyer gets the extra month.

EXAMPLE $800 invoice dated April 29; no freight or returned goods; terms 2/10 EOM; payment made on June 18.

Step 1.   Calculate the end of the 2% discount period:

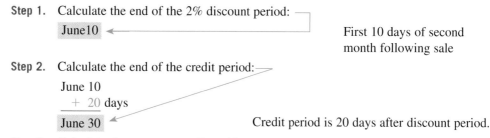

June 10   First 10 days of second
                                                                      month following sale

Step 2.   Calculate the end of the credit period:

June 10
+ 20 days
June 30   Credit period is 20 days after discount period.

Step 3.   Calculate the payment on June 18:

No discount; $800 paid.

The following time line illustrates the beginning and ending dates of the EOM invoice of the above example:

*Even though the discount period begins with the second month following the sale, if buyers wish, they can pay before the discount date (date of invoice until the discount period)

Solving a Word Problem with Trade and Cash Discount

Now that we have studied trade and cash discounts, let's look at a combination that involves both a trade and a cash discount.

The Word Problem   Hardy Company sent Regan Corporation an invoice for office equipment with a $10,000 list price. Hardy dated the invoice July 29 with terms of 2/10 EOM (end of month). Regan receives a 30% trade discount and paid the invoice on September 6. Since terms were FOB destination, Regan paid no freight charge. What was the cost of office equipment for Regan?

The facts	Solving for?	Steps to take	Key points
List price: $10,000. *Trade discount rate:* 30%. *Terms:* 2/10 EOM. *Invoice date:* 7/29. *Date paid:* 9/6.	Cost of office equipment.	Net price = List price × Complement of trade discount rate. After 25th of month for EOM. Discount period is 1st 10 days of second month that follows sale.	Trade discounts are deducted before cash discounts are taken. Cash discounts are not taken on freight or returns.

Steps to solving problem

1. Calculate the net price. $10,000 × .70 = $7,000   ⎡ 100%
                                                            ⎣ − 30% (trade discount)

2. Calculate the discount period.   Sale: 7/29 Month 1: Aug. Month 2: Sept 10 ⟶ Paid on Sept. 6—is entitled to 2% off.

3. Calculate the cost of office equipment. $7,000 × .98 = **$6,860**   If you save 2 cents on a dollar, you are spending 98 cents.
                                                            100%
                                                            − 2%

Partial Payments

Often buyers cannot pay the entire invoice before the end of the discount period. To calculate partial payments and outstanding balance, use the following steps:

CALCULATING PARTIAL PAYMENTS AND OUTSTANDING BALANCE
Step 1. Calculate the complement of a discount rate.
Step 2. Divide partial payments by the complement of a discount rate (Step 1). This gives the amount credited.
Step 3. Subtract Step 2 from the total owed. This is the outstanding balance.

EXAMPLE Molly McGrady owed $400. Molly's terms were 2/10, n/30. Within 10 days, Molly sent a check for $80. The actual credit the buyer gave Molly is as follows:

Step 1. $100\% - 2\% = 98\% \rightarrow .98$

Step 2. $\dfrac{\$80}{.98} = \$81.63$ $\dfrac{\$80}{1 - .02}$ ← Discount rate

Step 3. $400.00
              − 81.63   partial payment—although sent in $80
              $318.37   outstanding balance

Note: We do not multiply .02 × $80 because the seller did not base the original discount on $80. When Molly makes a payment within the 10-day discount period, 98 cents pays each $1 she owes. Before buyers take discounts on partial payments, they must have permission from the seller. Not all states allow partial payments.

You have completed another unit. Let's check your progress.

LU 7–2   PRACTICE QUIZ

Complete this **Practice Quiz** to see how you are doing

Complete the following table:

	Date of invoice	Date goods received	Terms	Last day* of discount period	End of credit period
1.	July 6		2/10, n/30		
2.	February 19	June 9	3/10, n/30 ROG		
3.	May 9		4/10, 1/30, n/60		
4.	May 12		2/10 EOM		
5.	May 29		2/10 EOM		

*If more than one discount, assume date of last discount.

6. Metro Corporation sent Vasko Corporation an invoice for equipment with an $8,000 list price. Metro dated the invoice May 26. Terms were 2/10 EOM. Vasko receives a 20% trade discount and paid the invoice on July 3. What was the cost of equipment for Vasko? (A blueprint aid will be in the solution to help dissect this problem.)

7. Complete amount to be credited and balance outstanding:

Amount of invoice: $600

Terms: 2/10, 1/15, n/30

Date of invoice: September 30

Paid October 3: $400

✓ Solutions

1. End of discount period: July 6 + 10 days =   July 16
End of credit period: By Table 7.1, July 6 =   187 days
+ 30 days
——————
217 → search ——→ Aug. 5

2. End of discount period: June 9 + 10 days = June 19
End of credit period: By Table7.1, June 9 =   160 days
+ 30 days
——————
190 → search ——→ July 9

3. End of discount period: By Table 7.1, May 9 =   129 days
+ 30 days
——————
159 → search ——→ June 8

End of credit period: By Table 7.1, May 9 =   129 days
+ 60 days
——————
189 → search ——→ July 8

4. End of discount period: June 10
End of credit period: June 10 + 20 = June 30

5. End of discount period: July 10
End of credit period: July 10 + 20 = July 30

6. Vasko Corporation's cost of equipment:

The facts	Solving for?	Steps to take	Key points
List price: $8,000. *Trade discount rate: 20%.* *Terms: 2/10 EOM.* *Invoice date: 5/26.* *Date paid: 7/3.*	Cost of equipment.	Net price = List price × Complement of trade discount rate. *EOM before 25th:* Discount period is 1st 10 days of month that follows sale.	Trade discounts are deducted before cash discounts are taken. Cash discounts are not taken on freight or returns.

Steps to solving problem

1. Calculate the net price. $8,000 × .80 = $6,400   ⌐ 100%
                                            └─ 20%

2. Calculate the discount period.   Until July 10

3. Calculate the cost of office equipment. $6,400 × .98 = $6,272

$$\left(\begin{array}{c}100\% \\ -\ 2\%\end{array}\right)$$

7. $\dfrac{\$400}{.98} = \$408.16$, amount credited.

   $\$600 - \$408.16 = \boxed{\$191.84,}$ balance outstanding.

LU 7–2a: EXTRA PRACTICE QUIZ

Need more practice? Try this **Extra Practice Quiz** (check figures in Chapter Organizer, p. 190)

Complete the following table:

	Date of invoice	Date goods received	Terms	Last day of discount period*	End of credit period
1.	July 8		2/10, n/30		
2.	February 24	June 12	3/10, n/30 ROG		
3.	May 12		4/10, 1/30, n/60		
4.	April 14		2/10 EOM		
5.	April 27		2/10 EOM		

*If more than one discount, assume date of last discount.

6. Metro Corporation sent Vasko Corporation an invoice for equipment with a $9,000 list price. Metro dated the invoice June 29. Terms were 2/10 EOM. Vasko receives a 30% trade discount and paid the discount on August 9. What was the cost of equipment for Vasko?

7. Complete amount to be credited and balance outstanding:

   Amount of invoice: $700
   Terms: 2/10, 1/15, n/30
   Date of invoice: September 28
   Paid October 3: $600

CHAPTER ORGANIZER AND STUDY GUIDE
WITH CHECK FIGURES FOR EXTRA PRACTICE QUIZZES

Topic	Key point, procedure, formula	Example(s) to illustrate situation
Trade discount amount, p. 171	$\text{Trade discount amount} = \text{List price} \times \text{Trade discount rate}$	$600 list price 30% trade discount rate Trade discount amount = $600 × .30 = $180
Calculating net price, p. 172	$\text{Net price} = \text{List price} - \text{Trade discount amount}$ or $\text{List price} \times \text{Complement of trade discount price}$	$600 list price 30% trade discount rate Net price = $600 × .70 = $420 $\begin{array}{r} 1.00 \\ -\ .30 \\ \hline .70 \end{array}$
Freight, p. 173	FOB shipping point—buyer pays freight. FOB destination—seller pays freight.	Moose Company of New York sells equipment to Agee Company of Oregon. Terms of shipping are FOB New York. Agee pays cost of freight since terms are FOB shipping point.
Calculating list price when net price and trade discount rate are known, p. 175	$\text{List price} = \dfrac{\text{Net price}}{\text{Complement of trade discount rate}}$	40% trade discount rate Net price, $120 $\dfrac{\$120}{.60} = \$200$ list price (1.00 − .40)

(continues)

CHAPTER ORGANIZER AND STUDY GUIDE
WITH CHECK FIGURES FOR EXTRA PRACTICE QUIZZES (continued)

Topic	Key point, procedure, formula	Example(s) to illustrate situation
Chain discounts, p. 176	Successively lower base.	5/10 on a $100 list item $\begin{array}{ll} \$100 & \$95 \\ \times\ .05 & \times\ .10 \\ \hline \$5.00 & \$9.50 \end{array}$ (running balance) $\begin{array}{l} \$95.00 \\ -\ 9.50 \\ \hline \$85.50 \end{array}$ net price
Net price equivalent rate, p. 176	$\dfrac{\text{Actual cost}}{\text{to buyer}} = \dfrac{\text{List}}{\text{price}} \times \dfrac{\text{Net price}}{\text{equivalent rate}}$ Take complement of each chain discount and multiply—do not round. $\dfrac{\text{Trade discount}}{\text{amount}} = \dfrac{\text{List}}{\text{price}} - \dfrac{\text{Actual cost}}{\text{to buyer}}$	Given: 5/10 on $1,000 list price Take complement: $.95 \times .90 = .855$ (net price equivalent) $\$1,000 \times .855 = \boxed{\$855}$ (actual cost or net price) $\begin{array}{l} \$1,000 \\ -\ 855 \\ \hline \$\ \ 145 \end{array}$ trade discount amount
Single equivalent discount rate, p. 177	$\dfrac{\text{Trade discount}}{\text{amount}} = \dfrac{\text{List}}{\text{price}} \times \dfrac{1-\text{Net price}}{\text{equivalent rate}}$	See preceding example for facts: $1 - .855 = .145$ $.145 \times \$1,000 = \boxed{\$145}$
Cash discounts, p. 179	Cash discounts, due to prompt payment, are not taken on freight, returns, etc.	Gross $1,000 (includes freight) Freight $25 Terms, 2/10, n/30 Returns $25 Purchased: Sept. 9; paid Sept. 15 Cash discount $= \$950 \times .02 = \boxed{\$19}$
Calculating due dates, p. 180	*Option 1:* Thirty days has September, April, June, and November; all the rest have 31 except February has 28, and 29 in leap years. *Option 2:* Knuckles—31-day month; in between knuckles are short months. *Option 3:* Days-in-a-year table.	Invoice $500 on March 5; terms 2/10, n/30 March 5 *End of discount* + 10 *period:* ────────▶ March 15 *End of credit* March 5 = 64 days *period by* + 30 *Table 7.1:* ────────▶ 94 days Search in Table 7.1 April 4
Common terms of sale **a. Ordinary dating, p. 182**	Discount period begins from date of invoice. Credit period ends 20 days from the end of the discount period unless otherwise stipulated; example, 2/10, n/60—the credit period ends 50 days from end of discount period.	Invoice $600 (freight of $100 included in price) dated March 8; payment on March 16; 3/10, n/30. March 8 *End of discount* + 10 *period:* ────────▶ March 18 *End of credit* March 8 = 67 days *period by* + 30 *Table 7.1:* ────────▶ 97 days Search in Table 7.1 April 7 *If paid on March 16:* $.97 \times \$500 = \$485$ $\begin{array}{l} +\ 100 \text{ freight} \\ \hline \$585 \end{array}$

(continues)

CHAPTER ORGANIZER AND STUDY GUIDE
WITH CHECK FIGURES FOR EXTRA PRACTICE QUIZZES (concluded)

Topic	Key point, procedure, formula	Example(s) to illustrate situation
b. Receipt of goods (ROG), p. 183	Discount period begins when goods are received. Credit period ends 20 days from end of discount period.	4/10, n/30, ROG. $600 invoice; no freight; dated August 5; goods received October 2, payment made October 20. October 2 End of discount + 10 period: ⟶ October 12 End of October 2 = 275 credit period + 30 by Table 7.1: ⟶ 305 Search in Table 7.1 November 1 *Payment on October 20:* No discount, pay $600
c. End of month (EOM), p. 184	On or before 25th of the month, discount period is 10 days after month following sale. After 25th of the month, an additional month is gained.	$1,000 invoice dated May 12; no freight or returns; terms 2/10 EOM. *End of discount period* ⟶ June 10 *End of credit period* ⟶ June 30
Partial payments, p. 186	$\text{Amount credited} = \dfrac{\text{Partial payment}}{1 - \text{Discount rate}}$	$200 invoice, terms 2/10, n/30, dated March 2, paid $100 on March 5. $\dfrac{\$100}{1-.02} = \dfrac{\$100}{.98} = \$102.04$
KEY TERMS	Cash discount, *p. 179* Chain discounts, *p. 176* Complement, *p. 174* Credit period, *p. 179* Discount period, *p. 179* Due dates, *p. 180* End of credit period, *p. 180* End of month (EOM), *p. 184* FOB destination, *p. 173*	FOB shipping point, *p. 173* Freight terms, *p. 173* Invoice, *p. 171* List price, *p. 171* Net price, *p. 172* Net price equivalent rate, *p. 176* Ordinary dating, *p. 182* Receipt of goods (ROG), *p. 183* Series discounts, *p. 176* Single equivalent discount rate, *p. 177* Single trade discount, *p. 174* Terms of the sale, *p. 179* Trade discount, *p. 171* Trade discount amount, *p. 171* Trade discount rate, *p. 171*
CHECK FIGURES FOR EXTRA PRACTICE QUIZZES WITH PAGE REFERENCES	LU 7–1a (p. 179) 1. $4,800 TD; $11,200 NP 2. $500 3. $9,891.84 NP; TD $4,108.16	LU 7–2a (p. 188) 1. July 18; Aug. 7 2. June 22; July 12 3. June 11; July 11 4. May 10; May 30 5. June 10; June 30 6. $6,174 7. a) $612.24 b) $87.76

Critical Thinking Discussion Questions

1. What is the net price? June Long bought a jacket from a catalog company. She took her trade discount off the original price plus freight. What is wrong with June's approach? Who would benefit from June's approach—the buyer or the seller?

2. How do you calculate the list price when the net price and trade discount rate are known? A publisher tells the bookstore its net price of a book along with a suggested trade discount of 20%. The bookstore uses a 25% discount rate. Is this ethical when textbook prices are rising?

3. Explain FOB shipping point and FOB destination. Think back to your last major purchase. Was it FOB shipping point or FOB destination? Did you get a trade or a cash discount?

4. What are the steps to calculate the net price equivalent rate? Why is the net price equivalent rate *not* rounded?

5. What are the steps to calculate the single equivalent discount rate? Is this rate off the list or net price? Explain why this calculation of a single equivalent discount rate may not always be needed.

6. What is the difference between a discount and credit period? Are all cash discounts taken before trade discounts? Agree or disagree? Why?

7. Explain the following credit terms of sale:
   a. 2/10, n/30.
   b. 3/10, n/30 ROG.
   c. 1/10 EOM (on or before 25th of month).
   d. 1/10 EOM (after 25th of month).

8. Explain how to calculate a partial payment. Whom does a partial payment favor—the buyer or the seller?

Classroom Notes

Name _____ Date _____

DRILL PROBLEMS

For all problems, round your final answer to the nearest cent. Do not round net price equivalent rates or single equivalent discount rates.

Complete the following:

Item	List price	Chain discount	Net price equivalent rate (in decimals)	Single equivalent discount rate (in decimals)	Trade discount	Net price
7–1. Apple iPod	$300	5/2				
7–2. Panasonic DVD player	$199	8/4/3				
7–3. IBM scanner	$269	7/3/1				

Complete the following:

Item	List price	Chain discount	Net price	Trade discount
7–4. Trotter treadmill	$3,000	9/4		
7–5. Maytag dishwasher	$450	8/5/6		
7–6. Hewlett-Packard scanner	$320	3/5/9		
7–7. Land Rover roofrack	$1,850	12/9/6		

7–8. Which of the following companies, A or B, gives a higher discount? Use the single equivalent discount rate to make your choice (convert your equivalent rate to the nearest hundredth percent).

Company A
8/10/15/3

Company B
10/6/16/5

Complete the following:

	Invoice	Dates when goods received	Terms	Last day* of discount period	Final day bill is due (end of credit period)
7–9.	June 18		1/10, n/30		
7–10.	Nov. 27		2/10 EOM		
7–11.	May 15	June 5	3/10, n/30, ROG		
7–12.	April 10		2/10, 1/30, n/60		
7–13.	June 12		3/10 EOM		
7–14.	Jan. 10	Feb. 3 (no leap year)	4/10, n/30, ROG		

*If more than one discount, assume date of last discount.

Complete the following by calculating the cash discount and net amount paid:

	Gross amount of invoice (freight charge already included)	Freight charge	Date of invoice	Terms of invoice	Date of payment	Cash discount	Net amount paid
7–15.	$7,000	$100	4/8	2/10, n/60	4/15		
7–16.	$600	None	8/1	3/10, 2/15, n/30	8/13		
7–17.	$200	None	11/13	1/10 EOM	12/3		
7–18.	$500	$100	11/29	1/10 EOM	1/4		

Complete the following:

	Amount of invoice	Terms	Invoice date	Actual partial payment made	Date of partial payment	Amount of payment to be credited	Balance outstanding
7–19.	$700	2/10, n/60	5/6	$400	5/15		

7–20. $600   4/10, n/60   7/5 $400   7/14

7–21. The list price of a Luminox watch is $475. Barry Katz receives a trade discount of 40%. Find the trade discount amount and the net price.

7–22. A model NASCAR race car lists for $79.99 with a trade discount of 40%. What is the net price of the car?

7–23. An article in *The* (Biloxi, MS) *Sun Herald* on August 4, 2006, discussed quantity discounts for schools and businesses. Publisher, Andrews McMeel's books are available at quantity discounts with bulk purchases for educational or business use. School district 510 purchased 50 books at $26.95 each with a quantity discount of 5%. **(a)** What was total list price for the books? **(b)** What was the total discount amount? **(c)** What was the total net price for the books? Round to the nearest cent.

7–24. Levin Furniture buys a living room set with a $4,000 list price and a 55% trade discount. Freight (FOB shipping point) of $50 is not part of the list price. What is the delivered price (including freight) of the living room set, assuming a cash discount of 2/10, n/30, ROG? The invoice had an April 8 date. Levin received the goods on April 19 and paid the invoice on April 25.

7–25. A manufacturer of skateboards offered a 5/2/1 chain discount to many customers. Bob's Sporting Goods ordered 20 skateboards for a total $625 list price. What was the net price of the skateboards? What was the trade discount amount?

7–26. Home Depot wants to buy a new line of shortwave radios. Manufacturer A offers a 21/13 chain discount. Manufacturer B offers a 26/8 chain discount. Both manufacturers have the same list price. What manufacturer should Home Depot buy from?

7–27. Maplewood Supply received a $5,250 invoice dated 4/15/06. The $5,250 included $250 freight. Terms were 4/10, 3/30, n/60. **(a)** If Maplewood pays the invoice on April 27, what will it pay? **(b)** If Maplewood pays the invoice on May 21, what will it pay?

7–28. Sport Authority ordered 50 pairs of tennis shoes from Nike Corporation. The shoes were priced at $85 for each pair with the following terms: 4/10, 2/30, n/60. The invoice was dated October 15. Sports Authority sent in a payment on October 28. What should have been the amount of the check?

7–29. Macy of New York sold Marriott of Chicago office equipment with a $6,000 list price. Sale terms were 3/10, n/30 FOB New York. Macy agreed to prepay the $30 freight. Marriott pays the invoice within the discount period. What does Marriott pay Macy?

7–30. Royal Furniture bought a sofa for $800. The sofa had a $1,400 list price. What was the trade discount rate Royal received? Round to the nearest hundredth percent.

7–31. Amazon.com paid a $6,000 net price for textbooks. The publisher offered a 30% trade discount. What was the publisher's list price? Round to the nearest cent.

7–32. Bally Manufacturing sent Intel Corporation an invoice for machinery with a $14,000 list price. Bally dated the invoice July 23 with 2/10 EOM terms. Intel receives a 40% trade discount. Intel pays the invoice on August 5. What does Intel pay Bally?

7–33. On August 1, Intel Corporation (Problem 7–32) returns $100 of the machinery due to defects. What does Intel pay Bally on August 5? Round to nearest cent.

7–34. Stacy's Dress Shop received a $1,050 invoice dated July 8 with 2/10, 1/15, n/60 terms. On July 22, Stacy's sent a $242 partial payment. What credit should Stacy's receive? What is Stacy's outstanding balance?

7–35. On March 11, Jangles Corporation received a $20,000 invoice dated March 8. Cash discount terms were 4/10, n/30. On March 15, Jangles sent an $8,000 partial payment. What credit should Jangles receive? What is Jangles' outstanding balance?

ADDITIONAL SET OF WORD PROBLEMS

7–36. In the February 2007 issue of *The Tax Adviser*, it was reported that trade discounts are not income. Westpac Pacific Food agreed to buy a minimum quantity of merchandise and receive a volume discount. Westpac Pacific Food received a 4 percent quantity discount. Total amount of an order placed by Westpac amounted to $20,500. What was the net price paid by Westpac?

7–37. Borders.com paid a $79.99 net price for each calculus textbook. The publisher offered a 20% trade discount. What was the publisher's list price?

7–38. Home Office.com buys a computer from Compaq Corporation. The computers have a $1,200 list price with a 30% trade discount. What is the trade discount amount? What is the net price of the computer? Freight charges are FOB destination.

7–39. Vail Ski Shop received a $1,201 invoice dated July 8 with 2/10, 1/15, n/60 terms. On July 22, Vail sent a $485 partial payment. What credit should Vail receive? What is Vail's outstanding balance?

7–40. True Value received an invoice dated 4/15/02. The invoice had a $5,500 balance that included $300 freight. Terms were 4/10, 3/30, n/60. True Value pays the invoice on April 29. What amount does True Value pay?

7–41. Staples purchased seven new computers for $850 each. It received a 15% discount because it purchased more than five and an additional 6% discount because it took immediate delivery. Terms of payment were 2/10, n/30. Staples pays the bill within the cash discount period. How much should the check be? Round to the nearest cent.

7–42. On May 14, Talbots of Boston sold Forrest of Los Angeles $7,000 of fine clothes. Terms were 2/10 EOM FOB Boston. Talbots agreed to prepay the $80 freight. If Forrest pays the invoice on June 8, what will Forrest pay? If Forrest pays on June 20, what will Forrest pay?

7–43. Sam's Ski Boards.com offers 5/4/1 chain discounts to many of its customers. The Ski Hut ordered 20 ski boards with a total list price of $1,200. What is the net price of the ski boards? What was the trade discount amount? Round to the nearest cent.

7–44. Majestic Manufacturing sold Jordans Furniture a living room set for an $8,500 list price with 35% trade discount. The $100 freight (FOB shipping point) was not part of the list price. Terms were 3/10, n/30 ROG. The invoice date was May 30. Jordans received the goods on July 18 and paid the invoice on July 20. What was the final price (include cost of freight) of the living room set?

7–45. Boeing Truck Company received an invoice showing 8 tires at $110 each, 12 tires at $160 each, and 15 tires at $180 each. Shipping terms are FOB shipping point. Freight is $400; trade discount is 10/5; and a cash discount of 2/10, n/30 is offered. Assuming Boeing paid within the discount period, what did Boeing pay?

7–46. The *Greeley Tribune* (Greeley, CO) on February 24, 2007 reported on discounts. Republican Representative Kevin Lundberg, of Berthoud, Colorado, said the law defined "cost" as the wholesale price of goods plus any overhead costs, but stores sell things below cost all the time. Jim Riesberg purchased slacks for $25.00, with an original price of $125. What was the percent discount Jim received?

7–47. Verizon offers to sell cellular phones listing for $99.99 with a chain discount of 15/10/5. Cellular Company offers to sell its cellular phones that list at $102.99 with a chain discount of 25/5. If Irene is to buy 6 phones, how much could she save if she buys from the lower-priced company?

7–48. Bryant Manufacture sells its furniture to wholesalers and retailers. It offers to wholesalers a chain discount of 15/10/5 and to retailers a chain discount of 15/10. If a sofa lists for $500, how much would the wholesaler and retailer pay?

CHALLENGE PROBLEMS

7–49. The original price of a 2003 Honda Insight to the dealer is $17,995, but the dealer will pay only $16,495. If the dealer pays Honda within 15 days, there is a 1% cash discount. **(a)** How much is the rebate? **(b)** What percent is the rebate? Round to nearest hundredth percent. **(c)** What is the amount of the cash discount if the dealer pays within 15 days? **(d)** What is the dealer's final price? **(e)** What is the dealer's total savings? Round answer to the nearest hundredth.

7–50. On March 30, Century Television received an invoice dated March 28 from ACME Manufacturing for 50 televisions at a cost of $125 each. Century received a 10/4/2 chain discount. Shipping terms were FOB shipping point. ACME prepaid the $70 freight. Terms were 2/10 EOM. When Century received the goods, 3 sets were defective. Century returned these sets to ACME. On April 8, Century sent a $150 partial payment. Century will pay the balance on May 6. What is Century's final payment on May 6? Assume no taxes.

 SUMMARY PRACTICE TEST (Round to the Nearest Cent as Needed)

Complete the following: *(p. 172)*

Item	List price	Single trade discount	Net price
1. Apple iPod	$350	5%	
2. Palm Pilot		10%	$190

Calculate the net price and trade discount (use net price equivalent rate and single equivalent discount rate) for the following: *(p. 176)*

Item	List price	Chain discount	Net price	Trade discount
3. Sony HD flat-screen TV	$899	5/4		

4. From the following, what is the last date for each discount period and credit period? *(p. 187)*

	Date of invoice	Terms	End of discount period	End of credit period
a.	Nov. 4	2/10, n/30		
b.	Oct. 3, 2009	3/10, n/30 ROG (Goods received March 10, 2010)		
c.	May 2	2/10 EOM		
d.	Nov. 28	2/10 EOM		

5. Best Buy buys an iPod from a wholesaler with a $300 list price and a 5% trade discount. What is the trade discount amount? What is the net price of the iPod? *(p. 182)*

70,000	148
48,778	89
76,551	117
33,737	74

6. Jordan's of Boston sold Lee Company of New York computer equipment with a $7,000 list price. Sale terms were 4/10, n/30 FOB Boston. Jordan's agreed to prepay the $400 freight. Lee pays the invoice within the discount period. What does Lee pay Jordan's? *(p. 174)*

7. Julie Ring wants to buy a new line of Tonka trucks for her shop. Manufacturer A offers a 14/8 chain discount. Manufacturer B offers a 15/7 chain discount. Both manufacturers have the same list price. Which manufacturer should Julie buy from? *(p. 177)*

8. Office.com received a $8,000 invoice dated April 10. Terms were 2/10, 1/15, n/60. On April 14, Office.com sent an $1,900 partial payment. What credit should Office.com receive? What is Office.com's outstanding balance? Round to the nearest cent. *(p. 186)*

610

5490

9. Logan Company received from Furniture.com an invoice dated September 29. Terms were 1/10 EOM. List price on the invoice was $8,000 (freight not included). Logan receives a 8/7 chain discount. Freight charges are Logan's responsibility, but Furniture.com agreed to prepay the $300 freight. Logan pays the invoice on November 7. What does Logan Company pay Furniture.com? *(p. 177)*

Personal Finance

TECH | Cable, phone and Internet packages

dangle attractive prices. *By Jeff Bertolucci*

Save a **BUNDLE** on telecom services

TYING UP your telecom services in a single package is the lure many local telephone and cable companies are casting in selected areas around the U.S. For about $100 a month, you can get cable or satellite TV, local and long-distance telephone service, plus high-speed Internet service. In addition to paying just one bill, you have just one company to call if you have a technical or billing issue. Then again, this one-stop-shop approach can backfire if your vendor's customer service stinks.

Many bundled deals (often marketed as "triple plays" or "triple packs") are limited-time offers ranging from three to 12 months. The Comcast Triple Play, for instance, includes Internet, phone and cable service for $99 per month for one year. After the year is up, will the hammer fall—and the price skyrocket? Not necessarily. You can expect Comcast's package to cost "about $130 per month," says company spokeswoman Jenni Moyer.

Patrick Matters, who lives in Indianapolis, signed up for Comcast's Triple Play about a year ago. He pays $100 to $110 per month ("a little more if my daughters buy a movie"), a savings of more than $50 over his previous a la carte plans. At $130 per month, he'd still be ahead.

The Triple Play is for new customers only. But current Comcast subscribers can also get discounts if they add new services. For example, a Comcast cable-TV customer can sign up for the company's phone service for $33 per month for one year. If you're already a sub-

● About $100 a month will buy you TV, phone and Internet service.

scriber, check your vendor's Web site for bundled discounts.

Some vendors are offering quadruple plays that add wireless phone service. AT&T's Quad Pack, for instance, bundles Internet, telephone, Dish Network satellite TV and Cingular Wireless service for $123 per month. Its Triple Pack—Internet, telephone and wireless—costs $95 per month.

Regional offers. Bundles vary depending on where you live. For example, in Qwest's 14-state region, the starting price for a package including Internet, phone and DirecTV is about $90 per

month. In southern California, bundles from Time Warner Cable with Internet, phone and cable start at about $100. And in areas of Massachusetts and other states where Verizon has wired homes with its FiOS high-speed fiber-optic service, subscribers can get Internet, telephone and nearly 200 digital cable TV and music channels for $105 per month. Verizon offers bundles with satellite TV in other markets.

Although price is a big draw, a bundle isn't worth it if it excludes services you want. The AT&T Quad Pack, for instance, allows only 100 minutes per month of direct-dial calls from your home. More long-distance minutes cost 9 cents each.

And there may be other drawbacks. If a single high-speed line brings all communications to your home, you could lose your phone, cable and Internet service at the same time if the line goes down. Some digital phone services that use the Internet for voice calls don't support faxing—a significant shortcoming for home-based businesses.

And bundles make it more difficult to change providers for a specific service—for instance, switching from cable to satellite TV. Of course, from a telecom company's perspective, that's the whole idea.

Still, the convenience and relatively low prices make bundled services appealing. And there should be plenty of competition as telephone and cable companies duke it out.

BUSINESS MATH ISSUE

If you get a bundled package you will always save.

1. List the key points of the article and information to support your position.
2. Write a group defense of your position using math calculations to support your view.

Slater's Business Math Scrapbook

with Internet Application
Putting Your Skills to Work

PROJECT A
Pick a product and how this article will change your buying habits.

Green Thumb / *Growing Your Money* ◈ *By Sarah McBride*

How Do You Get a Break in the Price Of Practically Anything? Easy, Just Ask

MOST PEOPLE don't think twice about bargaining when it comes to something big, like a new car or home. But getting a price cut on smaller things—cable bills, doctors' fees, electronics goods—can be surprisingly easy: Just ask.

That goes against the grain for millions of Americans. Maybe our ancestors haggled at the dry-goods store. But today's big-box supermarkets, laser price scanners and uniformed checkout personnel present a barrier.

The good news is, in many situations, it's getting easier to ask for, and get, a price break. Increasingly, retailers and others are empowering rank-and-file employees to give discounts. At hotels, for example, most desk clerks can give 10% to 25% off the advertised rate, whereas a few years ago that might have required a discussion with the manager, says Rick Doble, a discount-advice writer and accomplished haggler.

Don't just think retail. Doctors and hospitals have a surprising amount of leeway to bargain. Some patients have taken to negotiating fees in advance with doctors, but even after the bill comes in, it's not too late to ask for cuts. Sympathetic billing offices will often reduce the portion insurance didn't pay, or even waive it altogether. Another common approach: Interest-free installment plans, which are basically a free loan.

Mr. Doble himself goes to considerable lengths to save a buck, such as tracking down the manager of the grocery-store dairy aisle to get a break on about-to-expire milk and cheese. But getting a deal doesn't have to take a lot of time, or even require an appetite for dubious cheddar. Some guidance:

Pick your store, and your moment. Try small boutiques and family-owned businesses. Look for somebody who seems knowledgeable and comfortable in their job, not the high-school student who started last week. Go in when the store isn't busy—a harried staffer has less time or inclination to negotiate.

Ease into it. Chat with the salesperson, and ask a lot about prices, so they can see that is a concern. Ask if they take an American Automobile Association discount, or a local discount card, even if you know they don't. After a few leading questions, it's possible a shopkeeper will simply volunteer 10% off.

Offer to pay in cash. Credit-card companies take 2% to 3% of the price in fees out of the merchant's pocket. At some stores, nicely asking whether you get a break for paying in cash can quickly get you 5% or 10% off—more than the credit-card fees.

Make it easy for them to pull it off: Ask if it's possible for you to ride on the coattails of a "friends and family" discount, or employee discount.

Call your phone company, ISP and cable providers and say you're thinking about switching. Often, you'll immediately get transferred to the company's "retention" desk, where the staff is prepped with special offers designed to retain wavering customers.

Finally, assume there is a promotion going on. Mr. Doble, author of the book "Savvy Discounts," says he never checks into a hotel before asking, "Don't you have a special at this time of year?" Much of the time, the answer is "yes," he says. And after he has finished cutting a deal, he asks for an upgrade. And free breakfast.

Send comments to sarah.mcbride@wsj.com.

Discount Haggling

- Offer to pay cash; it saves shopkeepers on credit-card fees.
- Tell your phone or cable company you might switch; it can shake loose special deals.
- Doctors often have leeway to negotiate—it can't hurt to ask.

Internet Projects: See text Web site (www.mhhe.com/slater9e) and The Business Math Internet Resource Guide.

Video Case

HILLERICH & BRADSBY COMPANY "LOUISVILLE SLUGGER"

According to Bob Hill, author of *Crack of the Bat: The Louisville Slugger Story,* in 1884 the star outfielder Pete "The Gladiator" Browning of the Louisville Eclipses was in a batting slump. Bud Hillerich, son of J.F. Hillerich, made Browning a bat. After Browning got three hits with his new bat, his teammates began clamoring for the Hillerich bat.

In 1910, during the rebuilding process following a factory fire, Hillerich hired Frank Bradsby to oversee the company's sales policy. In 1916, Bradsby's salesman skills won him a partnership and the company's name was changed to Hillerich & Bradsby (H & B) Company. After 118 years, H & B remains the leading manufacturer of baseball bats. H & B makes customized bats for players according to their specifications for bat weight, length, and wood preference (white ash or maple). Players rarely use bats over 34.5 inches long and 33 ounces in weight. Maple bats are denser and heavier than ash. About 20% of the 200,000 big league bats produced by H & B are made of maple. Big league teams pay $41 for a white ash bat and $51 for a maple bat.

In the early 1970s, aluminum bats became very popular with amateur players. Aluminum bats are considered safer and more durable than wood bats. Aluminum bats are also more economical. Since batters can swing the aluminum bats faster, the ball travels farther. The decline in white ash availability led to the increased cost of wood bats and increased use of aluminum bats. While aluminum bats rarely break, a college team would go through more than 350 wood bats per season. Basic models of aluminum bats sell for around $100; high-tech metal bats sell for as much as $500.

Interest in bats was renewed after Sammy Sosa's bat broke, spraying cork in the infield. Players and fans wanted to know how bats differ and how batters benefited from different types of bats.

In 1971, aluminum bats were approved for Little League play; in 1975 they were approved for college play. As early as 1970, H & B contracted an outside aluminum company to manufacture H & B aluminum bats; however, H & B remained focused on Louisville Slugger wood bats. H & B felt aluminum bats would detract from the game of baseball.

After aluminum bats were introduced, the *Dayton Daily News* reported that Louisville Slugger wood bat sales shrank from seven million to 800,000. Now new sales are back up to one million. After being in a slump, it looks like H & B hit a "home run."

PROBLEM 1

The video stated that in 1974, when the NCAA legalized aluminum bats in college, production of wood bats dropped from 7,000,000 to 800,000. The average retail price of a wood bat is $46. (a) What was the percent decrease in production? Round to the nearest hundredth percent. (b) How much did revenue decrease?

PROBLEM 2

The video states that the Ontario, California, plant produces over 300 different models of aluminum baseball bats. The plant produces 5,500 bats each day. Assume the average price is $175 per bat. (a) What would be the revenue generated for a week's production (5-day week)? (b) How many bats would be produced annually? (c) What would be the total annual sales?

PROBLEM 3

The April 11, 2003, issue of the *Dayton Daily News* reported that the Massachusetts Interscholastic Athletic Association created a stir by switching from aluminum bats to wood, citing safety concerns. Of the state's 40 leagues, 62.5% have decided to use wood during the regular season. How many have decided to stay with aluminum bats?

PROBLEM 4

On April 14, 2003, *Forbes* reported that H & B receives nearly $\frac{3}{4}$ of its $110 million in annual revenue from baseball and softball bats. (a) What is the total amount received for baseball and softball bats? (b) How much revenue is received from other items?

PROBLEM 5

The average number of bats used by a Major Leaguer in a season is 90. There are 30 teams with a roster of 25 players. The cost of a bat is $41 to $51. (a) What is the percent increase? Round to the nearest tenth. (b) Using an average price, what is the total amount of dollars spent on baseball bats by Major Leaguers?

PROBLEM 6

On April 13, 2003, the *Chicago Sun-Times* reported aluminum bats typically cost $100 to $250 and have one-year warranties. Wood bats typically cost $35 to $90. Aluminum bats are cheaper in the long run because they don't break. A high school hitter can go through four wood bats in one season. (a) What is the most a high school hitter would pay for wood bats during the season? (b) What is the least amount paid for wood bats during the season? (c) What is the average percent savings using aluminum as compared to wood?

PROBLEM 7

On September 30, 2003, the *Chicago Sun-Times* reported that a 34-inch, 38-ounce Louisville Slugger commemorative bat honoring the Chicago Cubs 2003 National League Central Division Champions hit the market. The bats retail at $129.95 plus shipping. Personalized (recipient's name engraved) bats are sold by H & B for $54.00. (a) What is the percent change for the commemorative bat? Round to the nearest tenth. (b) If shipping costs for the commemorative bats are an additional 11.54%, what is the amount charged for shipping? Round to the nearest dollar. (c) What would be the total cost for the commemorative bat?

CHAPTER 8

Markups and Markdowns; Perishables and Breakeven Analysis

Disney Signs Direct Shoe Deal With Payless

By MERISSA MARR

Walt Disney Co. has forged an agreement for exclusive Disney-branded children's footwear to be made and sold by **Payless ShoeSource** Inc., the latest move by Disney to cut out licensees in favor of working directly with retailers.

Under Consumer Products Chairman Andy Mooney, Disney has been moving toward direct-to-retail deals, in which it collaborates closely with a retailer, which then gets an exclusive product. That is different from the traditional retail model in which the company signs deals with licensees, which in turn take the products to retailers.

The multiyear deal, set to be announced today, gives Disney more con-

trol over the design and sale of its shoes. The agreement, which will feature characters including Disney Princesses, Winnie the Pooh and the cast from Power Rangers, is both companies' first direct-to-retail program for character footwear.

Ranging between $12 and $22, the shoes will be available exclusively in Payless's almost 4,600 stores and on Payless.com. The footwear will start hitting Payless stores in the spring, with the full lines filling shelves over the summer.

"Traditional layers between the customers and brands have inflated pricing," says Matt Rubel, chief executive of Payless, who previously worked with Mr. Mooney at Nike Inc. Mr. Mooney

adds: "By going directly to the retailer, both the quality and price improves."

Payless, a leading retailer of kids shoes, has been shifting its strategy to sell more high-end footwear at moderate prices. Retailers in general are pushing for more exclusivity on branded and character products. "Our deal with Disney is the direction of the future," says Mr. Rubel.

As part of its direct-to-retail strategy, Disney has been opening offices in cities where major retailers have their headquarters, including Bentonville, Ark., where **Wal-Mart Stores** Inc. is located, and Paris, where **Carrefour** SA is based. Disney says it plans to bulk up those offices in the next few years.

LEARNING UNIT OBJECTIVES

LU 8–1: Markups[1] Based on Cost (100%)

- Calculate dollar markup and percent markup on cost (p. 205).
- Calculate selling price when you know the cost and percent markup on cost (p. 206).
- Calculate cost when dollar markup and percent markup on cost are known (p. 207).
- Calculate cost when you know the selling price and percent markup on cost (p. 208).

LU 8–2: Markups Based on Selling Price (100%)

- Calculate dollar markup and percent markup on selling price (p. 210).
- Calculate selling price when dollar markup and percent markup on selling price are known (p. 211).
- Calculate selling price when cost and percent markup on selling price are known (p. 211).
- Calculate cost when selling price and percent markup on selling price are known (p. 212).
- Convert from percent markup on cost to percent markup on selling price and vice versa (p. 213).

LU 8–3: Markdowns and Perishables

- Calculate markdowns; compare markdowns and markups (p. 216).
- Price perishable items to cover spoilage loss (p. 217).

LU 8–4: Breakeven Analysis

- Calculate contribution margin (p. 219).
- Calculate breakeven point (p. 219).

[1]Some texts use the term *markon* (selling price minus cost).

Levi Strauss Sells Low-Cost Jeans To Target in Bid to Increase Sales

By SALLY BEATTY

Levi Strauss & Co. has begun selling its new low-cost line of jeans to Target stores, in a gamble that the struggling jeansmaker can boost sales without alienating its core department-store customers.

The launch of the new Levi Strauss Signature brand in **Target** Corp.'s Target division stores should bolster revenue at a time when Levi sales have been sagging. But it also risks damaging the cachet of the Levi brand. The Signature line originally sold for about $23, while the company's main "red tab" label, sold at department stores, normally costs about $35. The company is betting that Signature, which debuted at **Wal-Mart Stores** Inc. in July, won't cut into sales of its "red tab" line, which continues to account for the bulk of Levi sales.

The McGraw-Hill Companies, Ken Cavanagh photographer

Are you one of the many shoppers who shop at Target? If you wear jeans, you may be interested in the *Wall Street Journal* clipping "Levi Strauss Sells Low-Cost Jeans to Target in Bid to Increase Sales." The clipping states that Levi Strauss & Co. has begun selling its Levi Strauss Signature™ brand jeans to Target. If you are familiar with products from Levi Strauss & Co. and shop at the mass-channel retail stores that carry Levi Strauss Signature™ brand jeans, such as Target and Wal-Mart, you will probably look at these lower-cost jeans. Levi Strauss & Co. wants to boost sales with their Levi Strauss Signature™ brand products by appealing to a new group of value-conscious consumers who don't buy their other branded products.

Before we study the two pricing methods available to Target (percent markup on cost and percent markup on selling price), we must know the following terms:

- **Selling price.** The price retailers charge consumers. The total selling price of all the goods sold by a retailer (like Target) represents the retailer's total sales.

- **Cost.** The price retailers pay to a manufacturer or supplier to bring the goods into the store.

- **Markup, margin, or gross profit.** These three terms refer to the difference between the cost of bringing the goods into the store and the selling price of the goods. As an example of high-margin sales, Sharper Image customers are buying more high-margin gadgets. This helps the company fuel a 15% rise in same-store sales.

- **Operating expenses or overhead.** The regular expenses of doing business such as wages, rent, utilities, insurance, and advertising.

- **Net profit or net incomes.** The profit remaining after subtracting the cost of bringing the goods into the store and the operating expenses from the sale of the goods (including any returns or adjustments). In Learning Unit 8–4 we will take a closer look at the point at which costs and expenses are covered. This is called the *breakeven* point.

From these definitions, we can conclude that **markup** represents the amount that retailers must add to the cost of the goods to cover their operating expenses and make a profit.[2]

Let's assume Target pays Levi Strauss & Co. $18 for a pair for jeans and sells them for $23.[3]

---

[2] In this chapter, we concentrate on the markup of retailers. Manufacturers and suppliers also use markup to determine selling price.

[3] Amounts used are hypothetical; prices and markups may vary.

Basic selling price formula

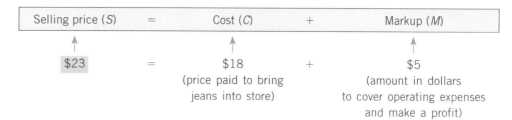

Selling price (S)	=	Cost (C)	+	Markup (M)
↑		↑		↑
$23	=	$18	+	$5
		(price paid to bring jeans into store)		(amount in dollars to cover operating expenses and make a profit)

Shirt Tale

Clothing sourcing for some retailers by supply region:

China   Other Asia   Europe   Others

H&M	33%	33%	33%
Gap	15	55 8	22
French Connection	15	40	45
Wal-Mart	10	40 30	20

Note: Figures may not add up to 100% due to rounding.
Source: Bain & Co.

Wall Street Journal © 2005

In the Levi Strauss example, the markup is a dollar amount, or a **dollar markup.** Markup is also expressed in percent. When expressing markup in percent, retailers can choose a percent based on *cost* (Learning Unit 8–1) or a percent based on *selling price* (Learning Unit 8–2).

When you study the *Wall Street Journal* clipping "Shirt Tale," you will see how the clothing sourcing for some retailers is divided by supply regions. These retailers include H&M, Gap, French Connection, and Wal-Mart. Do you shop at any of these retailers?

Learning Unit 8–1: Markups Based on Cost (100%)

In Chapter 6 you were introduced to the portion formula, which we used to solve percent problems. We also used the portion formula in Chapter 7 to solve problems involving trade and cash discounts. In this unit you will see how we use the basic selling price formula and the portion formula to solve percent markup situations based on cost. We will be using blueprint aids to show how to dissect and solve all word problems in this chapter.

Many manufacturers mark up goods on cost because manufacturers can get cost information more easily than sales information. Since retailers have the choice of using percent markup on cost or selling price, in this unit we assume Target has chosen percent markup on cost. In Learning Unit 8–2 we show how Target would determine markup if it decided to use percent markup on selling price.

Businesses that use **percent markup on cost** recognize that cost is 100%. This 100% represents the base of the portion formula. All situations in this unit use cost as 100%.

To calculate percent markup on cost, we will use the Levi Strauss Signature™ brand jeans sold at Target and begin with the basic selling price formula given in the chapter introduction. When we know the dollar markup, we can use the portion formula to find the percent markup on cost.

Markup expressed in dollars:

Selling price ($23) = Cost ($18) + Markup ($5)

Markup expressed as a percent markup on cost:

Cost	100.00%
+ Markup	+ 27.78
= Selling price	127.78%

➤ Cost is 100%—the base. Dollar markup is the portion, and percent markup on cost is the rate.

In Situation 1 (p. 206) we show why Target has a 27.78% markup based on cost by presenting the Levi Strauss Signature™ brand jeans as a word problem. We solve the problem with the blueprint aid used in earlier chapters. In the second column, however, you will see footnotes after two numbers. These refer to the steps we use below the blueprint aid to solve the problem. Throughout the chapter, the numbers that we are solving for are in red. Remember that cost is the base for this unit.

Situation 1: Calculating Dollar Markup and Percent Markup on Cost

Dollar markup is calculated with the basic selling price formula $S = C + M$. When you know the cost and selling price of goods, reverse the formula to $M = S - C$. Subtract the cost from the selling price, and you have the dollar markup.

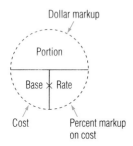

Dollar markup

Portion

Base × Rate

Cost   Percent markup
              on cost

The percent markup on cost is calculated with the portion formula. For Situation 1 the *portion* (P) is the dollar markup, which you know from the selling price formula. In this unit the *rate* (R) is always the percent markup on cost and the *base* (B) is always the cost (100%). To find the percent markup on cost (R), use the portion formula $R = \frac{P}{B}$ and divide the dollar markup (P) by the cost (B). Convert your answer to a percent and round if necessary.

Now we will look at the Target example to see how to calculate the 27.78% markup on cost.

The Word Problem Target buys Levi Strauss Signature™ brand jeans for $18 and plans to sell them for $23. What is Target's dollar markup? What is the percent markup on cost (round to the nearest hundredth percent)?

The facts	Solving for?	Steps to take	Key points
Signature™ jeans cost: $18. Signature™ jeans selling price: $23.	% $ C 100.00% $18 + M 27.78² 5¹ = S 127.78% $23 ¹Dollar markup. ²Percent markup on cost.	$\text{Dollar markup} = \frac{\text{Selling}}{\text{price}} - \text{Cost.}$ $\text{Percent markup on cost} = \frac{\text{Dollar markup}}{\text{Cost}}$	Dollar markup Portion ($5) Base × Rate ($18) (?) Cost

Steps to solving problem

1. Calculate the dollar markup.

$$\text{Dollar markup} = \text{Selling price} - \text{Cost}$$
$$\$5 = \$23 - \$18$$

2. Calculate the percent markup on cost.

$$\text{Percent markup on cost} = \frac{\text{Dollar markup}}{\text{Cost}}$$
$$= \frac{\$5}{\$18} = 27.78\%$$

To check the percent markup on cost, you can use the basic selling price formula $S = C + M$. Convert the percent markup on cost found with the portion formula to a decimal and multiply it by the cost. This gives the dollar markup. Then add the cost and the dollar markup to get the selling price of the goods.

You could also check the cost (B) by dividing the dollar markup (P) by the percent markup on cost (R).

Check

Selling price = Cost + Markup	or	$\text{Cost } (B) = \dfrac{\text{Dollar markup } (P)}{\text{Percent markup on cost } (R)}$

$$\$23 = \$18 + .2778(\$18)$$
$$\$23 = \$18 + \$5$$
$$\$23 = \$23$$

$$= \frac{\$5}{.2778} = \$18$$

Parentheses mean that you multiply the percent markup on cost in decimal by the cost.

Situation 2: Calculating Selling Price When You Know Cost and Percent Markup on Cost

When you know the cost and the percent markup on cost, you calculate the selling price with the basic selling formula $S = C + M$. Remember that when goods are marked up on cost, the cost is the base (100%). So you can say that the selling price is the cost plus the markup in dollars (percent markup on cost times cost).

Now let's look at Mel's Furniture where we calculate Mel's dollar markup and selling price.

The Word Problem Mel's Furniture bought a lamp that cost $100. To make Mel's desired profit, he needs a 65% markup on cost. What is Mel's dollar markup? What is his selling price?

The facts	Solving for?	Steps to take	Key points
Lamp cost: $100. *Markup on cost:* 65%.	% $ C 100% $100 + M 65 65[1] = S 165% $165[2] [1]Dollar markup. [2]Selling price.	Dollar markup: $S = C + M.$ or $S = \text{Cost} \times \left(1 + \dfrac{\text{Percent}}{\text{markup on cost}}\right)$	Selling price Portion (?) Base × Rate ($100) (1.65) 100% Cost +65%

Steps to solving problem

1. Calculate the dollar markup. $S = C + M$

$S = \$100 + .65(\$100)$ ← Parentheses mean you multiply the percent markup in decimal by the cost.

$S = \$100 + \boxed{\$65}$ ← Dollar markup

2. Calculate the selling price. $S = \boxed{\$165}$

You can check the selling price with the formula $P = B \times R$. You are solving for the portion (P)—the selling price. Rate (R) represents the 100% cost plus the 65% markup on cost. Since in this unit the markup is on cost, the base is the cost. Convert 165% to a decimal and multiply the cost by 1.65 to get the selling price of $165.

Check

Selling price = Cost × (1 + Percent markup on cost)	$= \$100 \times 1.65 = \boxed{\$165}$
(P) (B) (R)	

Situation 3: Calculating Cost When You Know Selling Price and Percent Markup on Cost

When you know the selling price and the percent markup on cost, you calculate the cost with the basic selling formula $S = C + M$. Since goods are marked up on cost, the percent markup on cost is added to the cost.

Let's see how this is done in the following Jill Sport example.

The Word Problem Jill Sport, owner of Sports, Inc., sells tennis rackets for $50. To make her desired profit, Jill needs a 40% markup on cost. What do the tennis rackets cost Jill? What is the dollar markup?

The facts	Solving for?	Steps to take	Key points
Selling price: $50. *Markup on cost:* 40%.	% $ C 100% $35.71[1] + M 40 14.29[2] = S 140% $50.00 [1]Cost. [2]Dollar markup.	$S = C + M.$ or $\text{Cost} = \dfrac{\text{Selling price}}{1 + \dfrac{\text{Percent}}{\text{markup on cost}}}$ $M = S - C.$	Selling price Portion ($50) Base × Rate (?) (1.40) 100% Cost +40%

Steps to solving problem

1. Calculate the cost. $S = C + M$

$\$50.00 = C + .40C$ ← This means 40% times cost. C is the same as $1C$. Adding $.40C$ to $1C$ gives the percent markup on cost of $1.40C$ in decimal.

$\dfrac{\$50.00}{1.40} = \dfrac{1.40C}{1.40}$

$\boxed{\$35.71} = C$

2. Calculate the dollar markup.

$$M = S - C$$
$$M = \$50.00 - \$35.71$$
$$M = \boxed{\$14.29}$$

You can check your cost answer with the portion formula $B = \frac{P}{R}$. Portion (P) is the selling price. Rate (R) represents the 100% cost plus the 40% markup on cost. Convert the percents to decimals and divide the portion by the rate to find the base, or cost.

Check

$$\text{Cost } (B) = \frac{\text{Selling price } (P)}{1 + \text{Percent markup on cost } (R)} \quad = \frac{\$50.00}{1.40} = \boxed{\$35.71}$$

Now try the following Practice Quiz to check your understanding of this unit.

LU 8–1 | PRACTICE QUIZ

Complete this **Practice Quiz** to see how you are doing

Solve the following situations (markups based on cost):

1. Irene Westing bought a desk for $400 from an office supply house. She plans to sell the desk for $600. What is Irene's dollar markup? What is her percent markup on cost? Check your answer.

2. Suki Komar bought dolls for her toy store that cost $12 each. To make her desired profit, Suki must mark up each doll 35% on cost. What is the dollar markup? What is the selling price of each doll? Check your answer.

3. Jay Lyman sells calculators. His competitor sells a new calculator line for $14 each. Jay needs a 40% markup on cost to make his desired profit, and he must meet price competition. At what cost can Jay afford to bring these calculators into the store? What is the dollar markup? Check your answer.

✓ Solutions

1. Irene's dollar markup and percent markup on cost:

The facts	Solving for?	Steps to take	Key points
Desk cost: $400. Desk selling price: $600.	$$\begin{array}{lcc} & \% & \$ \\ C & 100\% & \$400 \\ + M & 50^2 & 200^1 \\ = S & 150\% & \$600 \end{array}$$ ¹Dollar markup. ²Percent markup on cost.	$\dfrac{\text{Dollar}}{\text{markup}} = \dfrac{\text{Selling}}{\text{price}} - \text{Cost.}$ $\dfrac{\text{Percent}}{\text{markup}} = \dfrac{\text{Dollar markup}}{\text{Cost}}$ on cost	Dollar markup Portion ($200) Base × Rate ($400) (?) Cost

Steps to solving problem

1. Calculate the dollar markup.

$$\begin{array}{ccc} \text{Dollar markup} & = & \text{Selling price} - \text{Cost} \\ \boxed{\$200} & = & \$600 \quad - \$400 \end{array}$$

2. Calculate the percent markup on cost.

$$\text{Percent markup on cost} = \frac{\text{Dollar markup}}{\text{Cost}}$$
$$= \frac{\$200}{\$400} = \boxed{50\%}$$

Check

$$\text{Selling price} = \text{Cost} + \text{Markup} \qquad \textbf{or} \qquad \text{Cost } (B) = \frac{\text{Dollar markup } (P)}{\text{Percent markup on cost } (R)}$$
$$\$600 = \$400 + .50(\$400)$$
$$\$600 = \$400 + \$200 \qquad\qquad\qquad\qquad\qquad = \frac{\$200}{.50} = \$400$$
$$\$600 = \$600$$

2. Dollar markup and selling price of doll:

The facts	Solving for?	Steps to take	Key points
Doll cost: $12 each. *Markup on cost: 35%.*	% $ *C* 100% $12.00 + *M* 35 4.20[1] = *S* 135% $16.20[2] [1]Dollar markup. [2]Selling price.	Dollar markup: $S = C + M.$ or $S = \text{Cost} \times \left(1 + \begin{array}{c}\text{Percent}\\\text{markup}\\\text{on cost}\end{array}\right)$	Selling price Portion (?) Base × Rate ($12) (1.35) Cost 100% +35%

Steps to solving problem

1. Calculate the dollar markup.

$$S = C + M$$
$$S = \$12.00 + .35(\$12.00)$$
$$S = \$12.00 + \boxed{\$4.20} \leftarrow \text{Dollar markup}$$

2. Calculate the selling price.

$$S = \boxed{\$16.20}$$

Check

$$\underset{(P)}{\text{Selling price}} = \underset{(B)}{\text{Cost}} \times (1 + \underset{(R)}{\text{Percent markup on cost}}) = \$12.00 \times 1.35 = \boxed{\$16.20}$$

3. Cost and dollar markup:

The facts	Solving for?	Steps to take	Key points
Selling price: $14. *Markup on cost: 40%.*	% $ *C* 100% $10[1] + *M* 40 4[2] = *S* 140% $14 [1]Cost. [2]Dollar markup.	$S = C + M.$ or $\text{Cost} = \dfrac{\text{Selling price}}{\begin{array}{c}\text{Percent}\\1 + \text{markup}\\\text{on cost}\end{array}}$ $M = S - C.$	Selling price Portion ($14) Base × Rate (?) (1.40) Cost 100% +40%

Steps to solving problem

1. Calculate the cost.

$$S = C + M$$
$$\$14 = C + .40C$$
$$\frac{\$14}{1.40} = \frac{1.40C}{1.40}$$
$$\boxed{\$10} = C$$

2. Calculate the dollar markup.

$$M = S - C$$
$$M = \$14 - \$10$$
$$M = \boxed{\$4}$$

Check

$$\text{Cost } (B) = \frac{\text{Selling price } (P)}{1 + \text{Percent markup on cost } (R)} = \frac{\$14}{1.40} = \$10$$

LU 8-1a EXTRA PRACTICE QUIZ

Need more practice? Try this **Extra Practice Quiz** (check figures in Chapter Organizer, p. 222)

Solve the following situations (markups based on cost):

1. Irene Westing bought a desk for $800 from an office supply house. She plans to sell the desk for $1,200. What is Irene's dollar markup? What is her percent markup on cost? Check your answer.

2. Suki Komar bought dolls for her toy store that cost $14 each. To make her desired profit, Suki must mark up each doll 38% on cost. What is the dollar markup? What is the selling price of each doll? Check your answer.

3. Jay Lyman sells calculators. His competitor sells a new calculator line for $16 each. Jay needs a 42% markup on cost to make his desired profit, and he must meet price competition. At what cost can Jay afford to bring these calculators into the store? What is the dollar markup? Check your answer.

Learning Unit 8–2: Markups Based on Selling Price (100%)

Many retailers mark up their goods on the selling price since sales information is easier to get than cost information. These retailers use retail prices in their inventory and report their expenses as a percent of sales.

Businesses that mark up their goods on selling price recognize that selling price is 100%. We begin this unit by assuming Target has decided to use percent markup based on selling price. We repeat Target's selling price formula expressed in dollars.

Markup expressed in dollars:

Selling price ($23) = Cost ($18) + Markup ($5)

Markup expressed as **percent markup on selling price:**

Cost	78.26%
+ Markup	+ 21.74
= Selling price	100.00%

> Selling price is 100%—the base. Dollar markup is the portion, and percent markup on selling price is the rate.

In Situation 1 (below) we show why Target has a 21.74% markup based on selling price. In the last unit, markups were on *cost*. In this unit, markups are on *selling price*.

Situation 1: Calculating Dollar Markup and Percent Markup on Selling Price

The dollar markup is calculated with the selling price formula used in Situation 1, Learning Unit 8–1: $M = S - C$. To find the percent markup on selling price, use the portion formula $R = \frac{P}{B}$, where rate (the percent markup on selling price) is found by dividing the portion (dollar markup) by the base (selling price). Note that when solving for percent markup on cost in Situation 1, Learning Unit 8–1, you divided the dollar markup by the cost.

The Word Problem Target buys Levi Strauss Signature™ brand jeans for $18 and plans to sell them for $23. What is Target's dollar markup? What is its percent markup on selling price? (Round to nearest hundredth percent.)

The facts	Solving for?			Steps to take	Key points
Signature™ jeans cost: $18. Signature™ jeans selling price: $23.		%	$	$\dfrac{\text{Dollar}}{\text{markup}} = \dfrac{\text{Selling}}{\text{price}} - \text{Cost.}$	Dollar markup
	C	78.26%	$18		Portion ($5)
	+ M	21.74%[2]	5[1]	$\dfrac{\text{Percent}}{\text{markup on}} = \dfrac{\text{Dollar markup}}{\text{Selling}}$	
	= S	100.00%	$23	selling price price	Base × Rate ($23) (?)
	[1]Dollar markup.				
	[2]Percent markup on selling price.				Selling price

Steps to solving problem

1. Calculate the dollar markup.

Dollar markup = Selling price − Cost

$5 = $23 − $18

2. Calculate the percent markup on selling price.

$$\frac{\text{Percent markup}}{\text{on selling price}} = \frac{\text{Dollar markup}}{\text{Selling price}}$$

$$= \frac{\$5}{\$23} = 21.74\%$$

You can check the percent markup on selling price with the basic selling price formula $S = C + M$. You can also use the portion formula by dividing the dollar markup (P) by the percent markup on selling price (R).

Check

Selling price = Cost + Markup	**or**	Selling price (B) = $\dfrac{\text{Dollar markup } (P)}{\text{Percent markup on selling price } (R)}$

$23 = $18 + .2174($23)

$23 = $18 + $5

$23 = $23

$$= \frac{\$5}{.2174} = \$23$$

Parentheses mean you multiply the percent markup on selling price in decimal by the selling price.

Situation 2: Calculating Selling Price When You Know Cost and Percent Markup on Selling Price

When you know the cost and percent markup on selling price, you calculate the selling price with the basic selling formula $S = C + M$. Remember that when goods are marked up on selling price, the selling price is the base (100%). Since you do not know the selling price, the percent markup is based on the unknown selling price. To find the dollar markup after you find the selling price, use the selling price formula $M = S − C$.

The Word Problem Mel's Furniture bought a lamp that cost $100. To make Mel's desired profit, he needs a 65% markup on selling price. What are Mel's selling price and his dollar markup?

The facts	Solving for?			Steps to take	Key points
Lamp cost: $100. Markup on selling price: 65%.		%	$	$S = C + M.$ or $S = \dfrac{\text{Cost}}{1 - \dfrac{\text{Percent markup}}{\text{on selling price}}}$	
	C	35%	$100.00		
	$+ M$	65	185.71[2]		
	$= S$	100%	$285.71[1]		
	[1]Selling price. [2]Dollar markup.				

Steps to solving problem

1. Calculate the selling price.

$S = C + M$

$S = \$100.00 + .65S$

$$\left. \begin{array}{r} 1.00S \\ -.65S \\ = .35S \end{array} \right\}$$

$-.65S \qquad -.65S$

$$\frac{.35S}{.35} = \frac{\$100.00}{.35}$$

$S = \$285.71$

Do not multiply the .65 times $100.00. The 65% is based on selling price not cost.

2. Calculate the dollar markup.

$M = S − C$

$185.71 = $285.71 − $100.00

You can check your selling price with the portion formula $B = \frac{P}{R}$. To find the selling price (B), divide the cost (P) by the rate (100% − percent markup on selling price).

Check

Selling price (B) =	Cost (P)
	1 − Percent markup on selling price (R)

$$= \frac{\$100.00}{1 - .65} = \frac{\$100.00}{.35} = \boxed{\$285.71}$$

Situation 3: Calculating Cost When You Know Selling Price and Percent Markup on Selling Price

When you know the selling price and the percent markup on selling price, you calculate the cost with the basic formula $S = C + M$. To find the dollar markup, multiply the markup percent by the selling price. When you have the dollar markup, subtract it from the selling price to get the cost.

The Word Problem Jill Sport, owner of Sports, Inc., sells tennis rackets for $50. To make her desired profit, Jill needs a 40% markup on the selling price. What is the dollar markup? What do the tennis rackets cost Jill?

The facts	Solving for?	Steps to take	Key points
Selling price: $50. Markup on selling price: 40%.	% $ C 60% $30² + M 40 20¹ = S 100% $50 ¹Dollar markup. ²Cost.	$S = C + M$. or Cost = Selling price × $\left(1 - \dfrac{\text{Percent markup}}{\text{on selling price}}\right)$	Cost Portion (?) Base × Rate ($50) | (.60) Selling price 100% −40%

Steps to solving problem

1. Calculate the dollar markup.

$$S = C + M$$
$$\$50 = C + .40(\$50)$$

2. Calculate the cost.

$$\$50 = C + \boxed{\$20} \longleftarrow \text{Dollar markup}$$
$$\underline{-20 \qquad\quad -20}$$
$$\boxed{\$30} = C$$

To check your cost, use the portion formula Cost (P) = Selling price (B) × (100% selling price − Percent markup on selling price) (R).

Check

Cost = Selling price × $\left(1 - \dfrac{\text{Percent markup}}{\text{on selling price}}\right)$ (P) (B) (R)	= $50 × .60 = $30

$$(1.00 - .40)$$

In Table 8.1, we compare percent markup on cost with percent markup on retail (selling price). This table is a summary of the answers we calculated from the word problems in Learning Units 8–1 and 8–2. The word problems in the units were the same except in Learning Unit 8–1, we assumed markups were on cost, while in Learning Unit 8–2, markups were on selling price. Note that in Situation 1, the dollar markup is the same $5, but the percent markup is different.

Let's now look at how to convert from percent markup on cost to percent markup on selling price and vice versa. We will use Situation 1 from Table 8.1.

TABLE   8.1

Comparison of markup on cost versus markup on selling price

Markup based on cost— Learning Unit 8–1	Markup based on selling price— Learning Unit 8–2
Situation 1: Calculating dollar amount of markup and percent markup on cost. Signature™ jeans cost, $18. Signature™ jeans selling price, $23. $M = S - C$ $M = \$23 - \$18 =$ $5 markup (p. 206) $M \div C = \$5 \div \$18 = 27.78\%$	*Situation 1: Calculating dollar amount of markup and percent markup on selling price.* Signature™ jeans cost, $18. Signature™ jeans selling price, $23. $M = S - C$ $M = \$23 - \$18 =$ $5 markup (p. 211) $M \div S = \$5 \div \$23 = 21.74\%$
Situation 2: Calculating selling price on cost. Lamp cost, $100. 65% markup on cost $S = C \times (1 + \text{Percent markup on cost})$ $S = \$100 \times 1.65 =$ $165 (p. 207) $(100\% + 65\% = 165\% = 1.65)$	*Situation 2: Calculating selling price on selling price.* Lamp cost, $100. 65% markup on selling price $S = C \div (1 - \text{Percent markup on selling price})$ $S = \$100.00 \div .35$ $(100\% - 65\% = 35\% = .35)$ $S =$ $285.71 (p. 211)
Situation 3: Calculating cost on cost. Tennis racket selling price, $50. 40% markup on cost $C = S \div (1 + \text{Percent markup on cost})$ $C = \$50.00 \div 1.40$ $(100\% + 40\% = 140\% = 1.40)$ $C =$ $35.71 (p. 207)	*Situation 3: Calculating cost on selling price.* Tennis racket selling price, $50. 40% markup on selling price $C = S \times (1 - \text{Percent markup on selling price})$ $C = \$50 \times .60 =$ $30 (p. 212) $(100\% - 40\% = 60\% = .60)$

Formula for Converting Percent Markup on Cost to Percent Markup on Selling Price

To convert percent markup on cost to percent markup on selling price:

$$\dfrac{\text{Percent markup on cost}}{1 + \text{Percent markup on cost}}$$

$$\dfrac{.2778}{1 + .2778} = 21.74\% $$

Formula for Converting Percent Markup on Selling Price to Percent Markup on Cost

To convert percent markup on selling price to percent markup on cost:

$$\dfrac{\text{Percent markup on selling price}}{1 - \text{Percent markup on selling price}}$$

$$\dfrac{.2174}{1 - .2174} = 27.78\% $$

Key point: A 21.74% markup on selling price or a 27.78% markup on cost results in same dollar markup of $5.

Now let's test your knowledge of Learning Unit 8–2.

LU 8–2   PRACTICE QUIZ

Complete this **Practice Quiz** to see how you are doing

Solve the following situations (markups based on selling price). Note numbers 1, 2, and 3 are parallel problems to those in Practice Quiz 8–1.

1. Irene Westing bought a desk for $400 from an office supply house. She plans to sell the desk for $600. What is Irene's dollar markup? What is her percent markup on selling price (round to the nearest tenth percent)? Check your answer. Selling price will be slightly off due to rounding.

2. Suki Komar bought dolls for her toy store that cost $12 each. To make her desired profit, Suki must mark up each doll 35% on the selling price. What is the selling price of each doll? What is the dollar markup? Check your answer.

3. Jay Lyman sells calculators. His competitor sells a new calculator line for $14 each. Jay needs a 40% markup on the selling price to make his desired profit, and he must meet price competition. What is Jay's dollar markup? At what cost can Jay afford to bring these calculators into the store? Check your answer.

4. Dan Flow sells wrenches for $10 that cost $6. What is Dan's percent markup at cost? Round to the nearest tenth percent. What is Dan's percent markup on selling price? Check your answer.

✓ Solutions

1. Irene's dollar markup and percent markup on selling price:

The facts	Solving for?	Steps to take	Key points
Desk cost: $400. Desk selling price: $600.	% $ C 66.7% $400 + M 33.3² 200¹ = S 100% $600 ¹Dollar markup. ²Percent markup on selling price.	$\dfrac{\text{Dollar}}{\text{markup}} = \dfrac{\text{Selling}}{\text{price}} - \text{Cost}$ $\dfrac{\text{Percent}}{\substack{\text{markup on} \\ \text{selling price}}} = \dfrac{\text{Dollar markup}}{\text{Selling price}}$	

Steps to solving problem

1. Calculate the dollar markup.

$$\text{Dollar markup} = \text{Selling price} - \text{Cost}$$
$$\$200 = \$600 - \$400$$

2. Calculate the percent markup on selling price.

$$\dfrac{\text{Percent markup}}{\text{on selling price}} = \dfrac{\text{Dollar markup}}{\text{Selling price}}$$
$$= \dfrac{\$200}{\$600} = 33.3\%$$

Check

$\dfrac{\text{Selling}}{\text{price}} = \text{Cost} + \text{Markup}$ **or** $\dfrac{\text{Selling}}{\text{price }(B)} = \dfrac{\text{Dollar markup }(P)}{\text{Percent markup on selling price }(R)}$

$\$600 = \$400 + .333(\$600)$

$\$600 = \$400 + \$199.80$ $= \dfrac{\$200}{.333} = \$600.60*$

$\$600 = \$599.80*$ (not exactly $600 due to rounding)

*Off due to rounding.

2. Selling price of doll and dollar markup:

The facts	Solving for?	Steps to take	Key points
Doll cost: $12 each. Markup on selling price: 35%.	% $ C 65% $12.00 + M 35 6.46² = S 100% $18.46¹ ¹Selling price. ²Dollar markup.	$S = C + M.$ or $S = \dfrac{\text{Cost}}{1 - \substack{\text{Percent markup} \\ \text{on selling price}}}$	

Steps to solving problem

1. Calculate the selling price.

$$S = C + M$$
$$S = \$12.00 + .35S$$
$$\underline{-.35S \qquad\qquad -.35S}$$
$$\frac{.65S}{.65} = \frac{\$12.00}{.65}$$
$$S = \boxed{\$18.46}$$

2. Calculate the dollar markup.

$$M = S - C$$
$$\boxed{\$6.46} = \$18.46 - \$12.00$$

Check

$$\text{Selling price } (B) = \frac{\text{Cost } (P)}{1 - \text{Percent markup on selling price } (R)} = \frac{\$12.00}{.65} = \boxed{\$18.46}$$

3. Dollar markup and cost:

The facts	Solving for?		Steps to take	Key points
Selling price: $14. Markup on selling price: 40%.		%	$	$S = C + M.$ or $\text{Cost} = \text{Selling price} \times$ $\left(1 - \dfrac{\text{Percent markup}}{\text{on selling price}}\right)$	Cost Portion (?) Base × Rate ($14) (.60) Selling price 100% −40%
	C	60%	$ 8.40[2]		
	$+ M$	40	5.60[1]		
	$= S$	100%	$14.00		
	[1]Dollar markup. [2]Cost.				

Steps to solving problem

1. Calculate the dollar markup.

$$S = C + M$$
$$\$14.00 = C + .40(\$14.00)$$

2. Calculate the cost.

$$\$14.00 = C + \boxed{\$5.60} \leftarrow \text{Dollar markup}$$
$$\underline{-\,5.60 \qquad\qquad -\,5.60}$$
$$\boxed{\$8.40} = C$$

Check

$$\underset{(P)}{\text{Cost}} = \underset{(B)}{\text{Selling price}} \times \underset{(R)}{(1 - \text{Percent markup on selling price})} = \$14.00 \times .60 = \boxed{\$8.40}$$

$$(1.00 - .40)$$

4. $\quad$ Cost $= \dfrac{\$4}{\$6} = \boxed{66.7\%}$ $\qquad\qquad \dfrac{.40}{1 - .40} = \dfrac{.40}{.60} = \dfrac{2}{3} = 66.7\%$

$\quad\;\;$ Selling price $= \dfrac{\$4}{\$10} = \boxed{40\%}$ $\qquad \dfrac{.667}{1 + .667} = \dfrac{.667}{1.667} = 40\%$ (due to rounding)

LU 8–2a EXTRA PRACTICE QUIZ

Need more practice? Try this **Extra Practice Quiz** (check figures in Chapter Organizer, p. 222)

Solve the following situations (markups based on selling price).

1. Irene Westing bought a desk for $800 from an office supply house. She plans to sell the desk for $1,200. What is Irene's dollar markup? What is her percent markup on selling price (round to the nearest tenth percent)? Check your answer. Selling price will be slightly off due to rounding.

2. Suki Komar bought dolls for her toy store that cost $14 each. To make her desired profit, Suki must mark up each doll 38% on selling price. What is the selling price of each doll? What is the dollar markup? Check your answer.

3. Jay Lyman sells calculators. His competitor sells a new calculator line for $16 each. Jay needs a 42% markup on the selling price to make his desired profit, and he must meet price competition. What is Jay's dollar markup? At what cost can Jay afford to bring these calculators into the store? Check your answer.

4. Dan Flow sells wrenches for $12 that cost $7. What is Dan's percent markup at cost? Round to the nearest tenth percent. What is Dan's percent markup on selling price? Check your answer.

Learning Unit 8–3: Markdowns and Perishables

"Would you like to see the markup?"

Barron's © 2005

Have you ever wondered how your local retail store determines a typical markdown on clothing? The following *Wall Street Journal* clipping "Sale Rack Shuffle" explains the typical markdown money arrangement between a clothing vendor and a retailer. Evidently, the retailer does not always take the entire financial loss when a piece of clothing is marked down until it sells.

Sale Rack Shuffle

How a typical markdown-money arrangement between a clothing vendor and a retailer works:

1. Vendor makes dress at cost of **$50**

2. Sells to retailer at wholesale price of **$80**

3. Retailer marks up dress to **$200**

4. Dress gets marked down after 8 to 12 weeks (starting at 25% off) **$150**

5. The dress gets marked down again until it sells; the retailer and the vendor negotiate how to share the cost of the markdown.

Wall Street Journal © 2005

This learning unit focuses your attention on how to calculate markdowns. Then you will learn how a business prices perishable items that may spoil before customers buy them.

Markdowns

Markdowns are reductions from the original selling price caused by seasonal changes, special promotions, style changes, and so on. We calculate the markdown percent as follows:

$$\text{Markdown percent} = \frac{\text{Dollar markdown}}{\text{Selling price (original)}}$$

Let's look at the following Kmart example:

Dollar markdown

Portion ($7.20)

Base × Rate ($18)   (?)

Original selling price

EXAMPLE   Kmart marked down an $18 video to $10.80. Calculate the **dollar markdown** and the markdown percent.

$18.00 Original selling price
− 10.80 Sale price
$ 7.20 Markdown

$$\frac{\text{Dollar markdown, } \$7.20}{\text{Selling price (original), } \$18.00} = 40\%$$

Calculating a Series of Markdowns and Markups

Often the final selling price is the result of a series of markdowns (and possibly a markup in between markdowns). We calculate additional markdowns on the previous selling price. Note in the following example how we calculate markdown on selling price after we add a markup.

EXAMPLE   Jones Department Store paid its supplier $400 for a TV. On January 10, Jones marked the TV up 60% on selling price. As a special promotion, Jones marked the TV down 30% on February 8 and another 20% on February 28. No one purchased the TV, so Jones marked it up 10% on March 11. What was the selling price of the TV on March 11?

January 10: Selling price = Cost   + Markup

$$S = \$400 + .60S$$
$$-.60S \qquad\qquad -.60S$$
$$\frac{.40S}{.40} = \frac{\$400}{.40}$$
$$S = \$1,000$$

Check
$$S = \frac{\text{Cost}}{1 - \text{Percent markup on selling price}}$$

$$S = \frac{\$400}{1-.60} = \frac{\$400}{.40} = \$1,000$$

February 8 markdown:
$$\begin{array}{r}100\%\\ -\ 30\\ \hline 70\%\end{array}$$ → .70 × \$1,000 = \$700 selling price

February 28 additional markdown:
$$\begin{array}{r}100\%\\ -\ 20\\ \hline 80\%\end{array}$$ → .80 × \$700 = \$560

March 11 additional markup:
$$\begin{array}{r}100\%\\ +\ 10\\ \hline 110\%\end{array}$$ → 1.10 × \$560 = \$616

Pricing Perishable Items

The following formula can be used to determine the price of goods that have a short shelf life such as fruit, flowers, and pastry. (We limit this discussion to obviously **perishable** items.)

$$\text{Selling price of perishables} = \frac{\text{Total dollar sales}}{\text{Number of units produced} - \text{Spoilage}}$$

The Word Problem Audrey's Bake Shop baked 20 dozen bagels. Audrey expects 10% of the bagels to become stale and not salable. The bagels cost Audrey \$1.20 per dozen. Audrey wants a 60% markup on cost. What should Audrey charge for each dozen bagels so she will make her profit? Round to the nearest cent.

The facts	Solving for?	Steps to take	Key points
Bagels cost: \$1.20 per dozen. *Not salable:* 10%. *Baked:* 20 dozen. *Markup on cost:* 60%.	Price of a dozen bagels.	Total cost. Total dollar markup. Total selling price. Bagel loss. TS = TC + TM.	Markup is based on cost.

Steps to solving problem

1. Calculate the total cost.   TC = 20 dozen × \$1.20 = \$24.00

2. Calculate the total dollar markup.   TS = TC + TM

    TS = \$24.00 + .60(\$24.00)

    TS = \$24.00 + \$14.40 ◄— Total dollar markup

3. Calculate the total selling price.   TS = \$38.40 ◄— Total selling price

4. Calculate the bagel loss.   20 dozen × .10 = 2 dozen

5. Calculate the selling price for a dozen bagels. $\frac{\$38.40}{18}$ = \$2.13 per dozen $\begin{array}{r}20\\ -\ 2\end{array}$

It's time to try the Practice Quiz.

Complete this **Practice Quiz**
to see how you are doing

1. Sunshine Music Shop bought a stereo for $600 and marked it up 40% on selling price. To promote customer interest, Sunshine marked the stereo down 10% for one week. Since business was slow, Sunshine marked the stereo down an additional 5%. After a week, Sunshine marked the stereo up 2%. What is the new selling price of the stereo to the nearest cent? What is the markdown percent based on the original selling price to the nearest hundredth percent?

2. Alvin Rose owns a fruit and vegetable stand. He knows that he cannot sell all his produce at full price. Some of his produce will be markdowns, and he will throw out some produce. Alvin must put a high enough price on the produce to cover markdowns and rotted produce and still make his desired profit. Alvin bought 300 pounds of tomatoes at 14 cents per pound. He expects a 5% spoilage and marks up tomatoes 60% on cost. What price per pound should Alvin charge for the tomatoes?

✓ **Solutions**

1.
$$S = C + M$$

$$S = \$600 + .40S$$
$$- .40S \qquad - .40S$$

$$\frac{.60S}{.60} = \frac{\$600}{.60}$$

$$S = \$1,000$$

Check

$$S = \frac{\text{Cost}}{1 - \text{Percent markup on selling price}}$$

$$S = \frac{\$600}{1 - .40} = \frac{\$600}{.60} = \$1,000$$

First markdown: $.90 \times \$1,000 = \$900$ selling price

Second markdown: $.95 \times \$900 \ = \$855$ selling price

Markup: $1.02 \times \$855 \ = \boxed{\$872.10}$ final selling price

$$\$1,000 - \$872.10 = \frac{\$127.90}{\$1,000} = \boxed{12.79\%}$$

2. Price of tomatoes per pound.

The facts	Solving for?	Steps to take	Key points
300 lb. tomatoes at $.14 per pound. *Spoilage: 5%.* *Markup on cost: 60%.*	Price of tomatoes per pound.	Total cost. Total dollar markup. Total selling price. Spoilage amount. *TS = TC + TM.*	Markup is based on cost.

Steps to solving problem

1. Calculate the total cost.

   $TC = 300 \text{ lb.} \times \$.14 = \$42.00$

2. Calculate the total dollar markup.

   $TS = TC + TM$

   $TS = \$42.00 + .60(\$42.00)$

   $TS = \$42.00 + \$25.20 \leftarrow$ Total dollar markup

3. Calculate the total selling price.

   $TS = \$67.20 \leftarrow$ Total selling price

4. Calculate the tomato loss.

   300 pounds $\times$ .05 = 15 pounds spoilage

5. Calculate the selling price per pound of tomatoes.

   $\frac{\$67.20}{285} = \boxed{\$.24}$ per pound (rounded to nearest hundredth)

   (300 − 15)

Need more practice? Try this
Extra Practice Quiz (check
figures in Chapter Organizer,
p. 222)

1. Sunshine Music Shop bought a stereo for $800 and marked it up 30% on selling price. To promote customer interest, Sunshine marked the stereo down 10% for one week. Since business was slow, Sunshine marked the stereo down an additional 5%. After a week, Sunshine marked the stereo up 2%. What is the new selling price of the stereo to the nearest cent? What is the markdown percent based on the original selling price to the nearest hundredth percent?

2. Alvin Rose owns a fruit and vegetable stand. He knows that he cannot sell all his produce at full price. Some of his produce will be markdowns, and he will throw out some produce. Alvin must put a high enough price on the produce to cover markdowns and rotted produce and still make his desired profit. Alvin bought 500 pounds of tomatoes at 16 cents per pound. He expects a 10% spoilage and marks up tomatoes 55% on cost. What price per pound should Alvin charge for the tomatoes?

Learning Unit 8–4: Breakeven Analysis

So far in this chapter, cost is the price retailers pay to a manufacturer or supplier to bring the goods into the store. In this unit, we view costs from the perspective of manufacturers or suppliers who produce goods to sell in units, such as pens, calculators, lamps, and so on. These manufacturers or suppliers deal with two costs—fixed costs (FC) and variable costs (FC).

To understand how the owners of manufacturers or suppliers that produce goods per unit operate their businesses, we must understand fixed costs (FC), variable costs (VC), contribution margin (CM), and breakeven point (BE). Carefully study the following definitions of these terms:

- **Fixed costs (FC).** Costs that *do not change* with increases or decreases in sales; they include payments for insurance, a business license, rent, a lease, utilities, labor, and so on.

- **Variable costs (VC).** Costs that *do change* in response to changes in the volume of sales; they include payments for material, some labor, and so on.

- **Selling price (S).** In this unit we focus on manufacturers and suppliers who produce goods to sell in units.

- **Contribution margin (CM).** The difference between selling price (S) and variable costs (VC). This difference goes *first* to pay off total fixed costs (FC); when they are covered, *profits (or losses)* start to accumulate.

- **Breakeven point (BE).** The point at which the seller has covered all expenses and costs of a unit and has not made any profit or suffered any loss. Every unit sold after the breakeven point (BE) will bring some profit or cause a loss.

Learning Unit 8–4 is divided into two sections: calculating a contribution margin (CM) and calculating a breakeven point (BE). You will learn the importance of these two concepts and the formulas that you can use to calculate them. Study the example given for each concept to help you understand why the success of business owners depends on knowing how to use these two concepts.

Calculating a Contribution Margin (*CM*)

Before we calculate the breakeven point, we must first calculate the contribution margin. The formula is as follows:

$$\text{Contribution margin } (CM) = \text{Selling price } (S) - \text{Variable cost } (VC)$$

EXAMPLE   Assume Jones Company produces pens that have a selling price (S) of $2.00 and a variable cost (VC) of $.80. We calculate the contribution margin (CM) as follows:

$$\text{Contribution margin } (CM) = \$2.00 \ (S) - \$.80 \ (VC)$$
$$CM = \boxed{\$1.20}$$

This means that for each pen sold, $1.20 goes to cover fixed costs (FC) and results in a profit. It makes sense to cover fixed costs (FC) first because the nature of a FC is that it does not change with increases or decreases in sales.

Now we are ready to see how Jones Company will reach a breakeven point (BE).

Calculating a Breakeven Point (*BE*)

Sellers like Jones Company can calculate their profit or loss by using a concept called the **breakeven point (BE).** This important point results after sellers have paid all their expenses and costs. Study the following formula and the example:

$$\text{Breakeven point } (BE) = \frac{\text{Fixed costs } (FC)}{\text{Contribution margin } (CM)}$$

EXAMPLE   Jones Company produces pens. The company has a fixed cost (*FC*) of $60,000. Each pen sells for $2.00 with a variable cost (*VC*) of $.80 per pen.

Fixed cost (*FC*)	$60,000
Selling price (*S*) per pen	$2.00
Variable cost (*VC*) per pen	$.80

$$\text{Breakeven point } (BE) = \frac{\$60,000 \,(FC)}{\$2.00 \,(S) - \$.80 \,(VC)} = \frac{\$60,000 \,(FC)}{\$1.20 \,(CM)} = \boxed{50,000 \text{ units (pens)}}$$

At 50,000 units (pens), Jones Company is just covering its costs. Each unit after 50,000 brings in a profit of $1.20 (*CM*).

It is time to try the Practice Quiz.

LU 8–4 | PRACTICE QUIZ

Complete this **Practice Quiz** to see how you are doing

Blue Company produces holiday gift boxes. Given the following, calculate (1) the contribution margin (*CM*) and (2) the breakeven point (*BE*) for Blue Company.

Fixed cost (*FC*)	$45,000
Selling price (*S*) per gift box	$20
Variable cost (*VC*) per gift box	$8

✓ **Solutions**

1. Contribution margin (*CM*) = $20 (*S*) − $8 (*VC*) = $12

2. Breakeven point $(BE) = \dfrac{\$45,000(FC)}{\$20\,(S) - \$8\,(VC)} = \dfrac{\$45,000\,(FC)}{\$12\,(CM)} = \boxed{3,750 \text{ units (gift boxes)}}$

LU 8–4a | EXTRA PRACTICE QUIZ

Need more practice? Try this **Extra Practice Quiz** (check figures in Chapter Organizer, p. 222)

Angel Company produces car radios. Given the following, calculate (1) the contribution margin (*CM*) and (2) the breakeven point (*BE*) for Angel Company.

Fixed cost (*FC*)	$96,000
Selling price (*S*) per radio	$240
Variable cost (*VC*) per radio	$80

CHAPTER ORGANIZER AND STUDY GUIDE
WITH CHECK FIGURES FOR EXTRA PRACTICE QUIZZES

Topic	Key point, procedure, formula	Example(s) to illustrate situation
Markups based on cost: Cost is 100% (base), p. 205	Selling price (*S*) = Cost (*C*) + Markup (*M*)	$\boxed{\$400} = \$300 + \$100$ $S \quad = \quad C \quad + \quad M$
Percent markup on cost, p. 206	$\dfrac{\text{Dollar markup (portion)}}{\text{Cost (base)}} = \dfrac{\text{Percent markup}}{\text{on cost (rate)}}$	$\dfrac{\$100}{\$300} = \dfrac{1}{3} = 33\tfrac{1}{3}\%$
Cost, p. 206	$C = \dfrac{\text{Dollar markup}}{\text{Percent markup on cost}}$	$\dfrac{\$100}{.33} = \$303$ Off slightly due to rounding
Calculating selling price, p. 207	$S = C + M$ **Check** $S = \text{Cost} \times (1 + \text{Percent markup on cost})$	Cost, $6; percent markup on cost, 20% $S = \$6 + .20(\$6)$ **Check** $S = \$6 + \$1.20 \quad\downarrow$ $S = \boxed{\$7.20} \qquad \boxed{\$6 \times 1.20 = \$7.20}$

(continues)

CHAPTER ORGANIZER AND STUDY GUIDE
WITH CHECK FIGURES FOR EXTRA PRACTICE QUIZZES (continued)

Topic	Key point, procedure, formula	Example(s) to illustrate situation
Calculating cost, p. 207	$S = C + M$ **Check** $Cost = \dfrac{Selling\ price}{1 + Percent\ markup\ on\ cost}$	$S = \$100;\ M = 70\%$ of cost $S = C + M$ $\$100 = C + .70C$ $\left(\begin{array}{l}Remember,\\ C = 1.00C\end{array}\right)$ $\$100 = 1.7C$ $\dfrac{\$100}{1.7} = C$ **Check** $\$58.82 = C$ $\boxed{\dfrac{\$100}{1 + .70} = \$58.82}$
Markups based on selling price: selling price is 100% (Base), p. 210	Dollar markup = Selling price − Cost	$M = S - C$ $\$600 = \$1,000 - \$400$
Percent markup on selling price, p. 210	$\dfrac{Dollar\ markup\ (portion)}{Selling\ price\ (base)} = \dfrac{Percent\ markup}{selling\ price\ (rate)}$	$\dfrac{\$600}{\$1,000} = 60\%$
Selling price, p. 211	$S = \dfrac{Dollar\ markup}{Percent\ markup\ on\ selling\ price}$	$\dfrac{\$600}{.60} = \$1,000$
Calculating selling price, p. 211	$S = C + M$ **Check** $Selling\ price = \dfrac{Cost}{1 - \begin{array}{l}Percent\ markup\\ on\ selling\ price\end{array}}$	Cost, \$400; percent markup on S, 60% $S = C + M$ $S = \$400 + .60S$ $S - .60S = \$400 + .60S - .60S$ $\dfrac{.40S}{.40} = \dfrac{\$400}{.40}$ $S = \$1,000$ **Check** → $\boxed{\dfrac{\$400}{1 - .60} = \dfrac{\$400}{.40} = \$1,000}$
Calculating cost, p. 212	$S = C + M$ **Check** $Cost = \begin{array}{l}Selling\\ price\end{array} \times \left(1 - \begin{array}{l}Percent\ markup\\ on\ selling\ price\end{array}\right)$	$\$1,000 = C + 60\%(\$1,000)$ $\$1,000 = C + \$600$ $\$400 = C$ **Check** → $\boxed{\begin{array}{l}\$1,000 \times (1 - .60)\\ \$1,000 \times .40 = \$400\end{array}}$
Conversion of markup percent, p. 213	Percent markup on cost to Percent markup on selling price $\boxed{\dfrac{Percent\ markup\ on\ cost}{1 + Percent\ markup\ on\ cost}}$ Percent markup on selling price to Percent markup on cost $\boxed{\dfrac{Percent\ markup\ on\ selling\ price}{1 - Percent\ markup\ on\ selling\ price}}$	*Round to nearest percent:* 54% markup on cost → 35% markup on selling price $\dfrac{.54}{1 + .54} = \dfrac{.54}{1.54} = 35\%$ 35% markup on selling price → 54% markup on cost $\dfrac{.35}{1 - .35} = \dfrac{.35}{.65} = 54\%$
Markdowns, p. 216	$Markdown\ percent = \dfrac{Dollar\ markdown}{Selling\ price\ (original)}$	\$40 selling price 10% markdown $\$40 \times .10 = \$4$ markdown $\dfrac{\$4}{\$40} = 10\%$

(continues)

CHAPTER ORGANIZER AND STUDY GUIDE
WITH CHECK FIGURES FOR EXTRA PRACTICE QUIZZES (concluded)

Topic	Key point, procedure, formula	Example(s) to illustrate situation
Pricing perishables, p. 217	1. Calculate total cost and total selling price. 2. Calculate selling price per unit by dividing total sales in Step 1 by units expected to be sold after taking perishables into account.	50 pastries cost 20 cents each; 10 will spoil before being sold. Markup is 60% on cost. 1. $TC = 50 \times \$.20 = \$10$ $TS = TC + TM$ $TS = \$10 + .60(\$10)$ $TS = \$10 + \$6$ $TS = \boxed{\$16}$ 2. $\dfrac{\$16}{40 \text{ pastries}} = \boxed{\$.40}$ per pastry
Breakeven point (*BE*), p. 219	$$BE = \frac{\text{Fixed cost } (FC)}{\text{Contribution margin } (CM)}$$ $$(\text{Selling price, } S - \text{Variable cost, } VC)$$	Fixed cost (*FC*) $60,000 Selling price (*S*) $90 Variable cost (*VC*) $30 $$BE = \frac{\$60,000}{\$90 - \$30} = \frac{\$60,000}{\$60} = 1{,}000 \text{ units}$$
KEY TERMS	Breakeven point, *p. 219* Contribution margin, *p. 219* Cost, *p. 204* Dollar markdown, *p. 216* Dollar markup, *p. 205* Fixed cost, *p. 219* Gross profit, *p. 204*	Margin, *p. 204* Markdowns, *p. 216* Markup, *p. 204* Net profit (net income), *p. 204* Operating expenses (overhead), *p. 204* Percent markup on cost, *p. 205* Percent markup on selling price, *p. 210* Perishables, *p. 217* Selling price, *p. 204* Variable cost, *p. 219*
CHECK FIGURES FOR EXTRA PRACTICE QUIZZES WITH PAGE REFERENCES	LU 8–1a (p. 210) 1. $400; 50% 2. $5.32; $19.32 3. $11.27; $4.73 LU 8–2a (p. 215) 1. $400; 33.3% 2. $22.58; $8.58 3. $6.72; $9.28 4. 71.4%; 41.7%	LU 8–3a (p. 218) 1. $996.68; 12.79% 2. .28 LU 8–4a (p. 220) 1. $160; $600

Critical Thinking Discussion Questions

1. Assuming markups are based on cost, explain how the portion formula could be used to calculate cost, selling price, dollar markup, and percent markup on cost. Pick a company and explain why it would mark goods up on cost rather than on selling price.

2. Assuming markups are based on selling price, explain how the portion formula could be used to calculate cost, selling price, dollar markup, and percent markup on selling price. Pick a company and explain why it would mark up goods on selling price rather than on cost.

3. What is the formula to convert percent markup on selling price to percent markup on cost? How could you explain that a 40% markup on selling price, which is a 66.7% markup on cost, would result in the same dollar markup?

4. Explain how to calculate markdowns. Do you think stores should run one-day-only markdown sales? Would it be better to offer the best price "all the time"?

5. Explain the five steps in calculating a selling price for perishable items. Recall a situation where you saw a store that did *not* follow the five steps. How did it sell its items?

6. Explain how Wal-Mart uses breakeven analysis. Give an example.

Name _____ Date _____

DRILL PROBLEMS

Assume markups in Problems 8–1 to 8–6 are based on cost. Find the dollar markup and selling price for the following problems. Round answers to the nearest cent.

Item	Cost	Markup percent	Dollar markup	Selling price
8–1. Apple iPod	$300	40%		
8–2. Luminox Navy Seal watch	$300	30%		

Solve for cost (round to the nearest cent):

8–3. Selling price of office furniture at Staples, $6,000

Percent markup on cost, 40%

Actual cost?

8–4. Selling price of lumber at Home Depot, $4,000

Percent markup on cost, 30%

Actual cost?

Complete the following:

	Cost	Selling price	Dollar markup	Percent markup on cost*
8–5.	$15.10	$22.00	?	?
8–6.	?	?	$4.70	102.17%

*Round to the nearest hundredth percent.

Assume markups in Problems 8–7 to 8–12 are based on selling price. Find the dollar markup and cost (round answers to the nearest cent):

Item	Selling price	Markup percent	Dollar markup	Cost
8–7. Panasonic plasma TV	$450	40%		
8–8. IBM scanner	$80	30%		

Solve for the selling price (round to the nearest cent):

8–9. Selling price of a complete set of pots and pans at Wal-Mart?

40% markup on selling price

Cost, actual, $66.50

8–10. Selling price of a dining room set at Macy's?

55% markup on selling price

Cost, actual, $800

Complete the following:

	Cost	Selling price	Dollar markup	Percent markup on selling price (round to nearest tenth percent)
8–11.	$14.80	$49.00	?	?
8–12.	?	?	$4	20%

By conversion of the markup formula, solve the following (round to the nearest whole percent as needed):

	Percent markup on cost	Percent markup on selling price
8–13.	12.4%	?
8–14.	?	13%

Complete the following:

8–15. Calculate the final selling price to the nearest cent and markdown percent to the nearest hundredth percent:

Original selling price	First markdown	Second markdown	Markup	Final markdown
$5,000	20%	10%	12%	5%

	Item	Total quantity bought	Unit cost	Total cost	Percent markup on cost	Total selling price	Percent that will spoil	Selling price per brownie
8–16.	Brownies	20	$.79	?	60%	?	10%	?

Complete the following:

	Breakeven point	Fixed cost	Contribution margin	Selling price per unit	Variable cost per unit
8–17.		$65,000		$5.00	$1.00
8–18.		$90,000		$9.00	$4.00

WORD PROBLEMS

8–19. Matthew Kaminsky bought an old Walter Lantz Woody Woodpecker oil painting for $10,000. He plans to resell it on eBay for $15,000. What are the dollar markup and percent markup on cost? Check the cost figure.

8–20. Chin Yov, store manager for Best Buy, does not know how to price a GE freezer that cost the store $600. Chin knows his boss wants a 45% markup on cost. Help Chin price the freezer.

8–21. Cecil Green sells golf hats. He knows that most people will not pay more than $20 for a golf hat. Cecil needs a 40% markup on cost. What should Cecil pay for his golf hats? Round to the nearest cent.

8–22. Macy's was selling Calvin Klein jean shirts that were originally priced at $58.00 for $8.70. **(a)** What was the amount of the markdown? **(b)** Based on the selling price, what is the percent markdown?

8–23. The *Miami Herald*, on January 31, 2007, ran a story on Super Bowl ticket prices. Ticket reseller Stubhub.com reported the average Super Bowl seat was selling for $4,445 with a face value of $700. **(a)** What is the percent markup based on cost? **(b)** What is the percent markup based on selling price? Round to the nearest hundredth percent.

8–24. The February 3, 2007 issue of *Billboard* reported on hefty markups by leading music merchants. Canadian Indies say they generally sell all products to independent distributors at between $8.00 and $9.50 per unit, which is then supplied to retailers at between $13.50 and $14.50. **(a)** What is the percent markup on cost for the lower price? **(b)** What is the percent markup on cost for the higher price? Round to the nearest hundredth percent.

8–25. Misu Sheet, owner of the Bedspread Shop, knows his customers will pay no more than $120 for a comforter. Misu wants a 30% markup on selling price. What is the most that Misu can pay for a comforter?

8–26. Assume Misu Sheet (Problem 8–25) wants a 30% markup on cost instead of on selling price. What is Misu's cost? Round to the nearest cent.

8–27. Misu Sheet (Problem 8–25) wants to advertise the comforter as "percent markup on cost." What is the equivalent rate of percent markup on cost compared to the 30% markup on selling price? Check your answer. Is this a wise marketing decision? Round to the nearest hundredth percent.

8–28. DeWitt Company sells a kitchen set for $475. To promote July 4, DeWitt ran the following advertisement:

Beginning each hour up to 4 hours we will mark down the kitchen set 10%. At the end of each hour, we will mark up the set 1%.

Assume Ingrid Swenson buys the set 1 hour 50 minutes into the sale. What will Ingrid pay? Round each calculation to the nearest cent. What is the markdown percent? Round to the nearest hundredth percent.

8–29. Angie's Bake Shop makes birthday chocolate chip cookies that cost $2 each. Angie expects that 10% of the cookies will crack and be discarded. Angie wants a 60% markup on cost and produces 100 cookies. What should Angie price each cookie? Round to the nearest cent.

8–30. Assume that Angie (Problem 8–29) can sell the cracked cookies for $1.10 each. What should Angie price each cookie?

8–31. Jane Corporation produces model toy cars. Each sells for $29.99. Its variable cost per unit is $14.25. What is the breakeven point for Jane Corporation assuming it has a fixed cost of $314,800?

ADDITIONAL SET OF WORD PROBLEMS

8–32. PFS Fitness bought a treadmill for $700. PFS has a 70% markup on selling price. What is the selling price of the treadmill (to the nearest dollar)?

8–33. Sachi Wong, store manager for Hawk Appliance, does not know how to price a GE dishwasher that cost the store $399. Sachi knows her boss wants a 40% markup on cost. Can you help Sachi price the dishwasher?

8–34. Working off an 18% margin, with markups based on cost, the Food Co-op Club boasts that they have 5,000 members and a 200% increase in sales. The markup is 36% based on cost. What would be their percent markup if selling price were the base? Round to the nearest hundredth percent.

8–35. At a local Bed and Bath Superstore, the manager, Jill Roe, knows her customers will pay no more than $300 for a bedspread. Jill wants a 35% markup on selling price. What is the most that Jill can pay for a bedspread?

8–36. *U.S. News & World Report* October 9, 2006, reported RV dealer markups can top 40 percent. Jim Abbott purchased a $60,000 RV with a 40 percent markup on selling price. **(a)** What was the amount of the dealer's markup? **(b)** What was the dealers original cost?

8–37. Circuit City sells a hand-held personal planner for $199.99. Circuit City marked up the personal planner 35% on the selling price. What is the cost of the hand-held personal planner?

8–38. Arley's Bakery makes fat-free cookies that cost $1.50 each. Arley expects 15% of the cookies to fall apart and be discarded. Arley wants a 45% markup on cost and produces 200 cookies. What should Arley price each cookie? Round to the nearest cent.

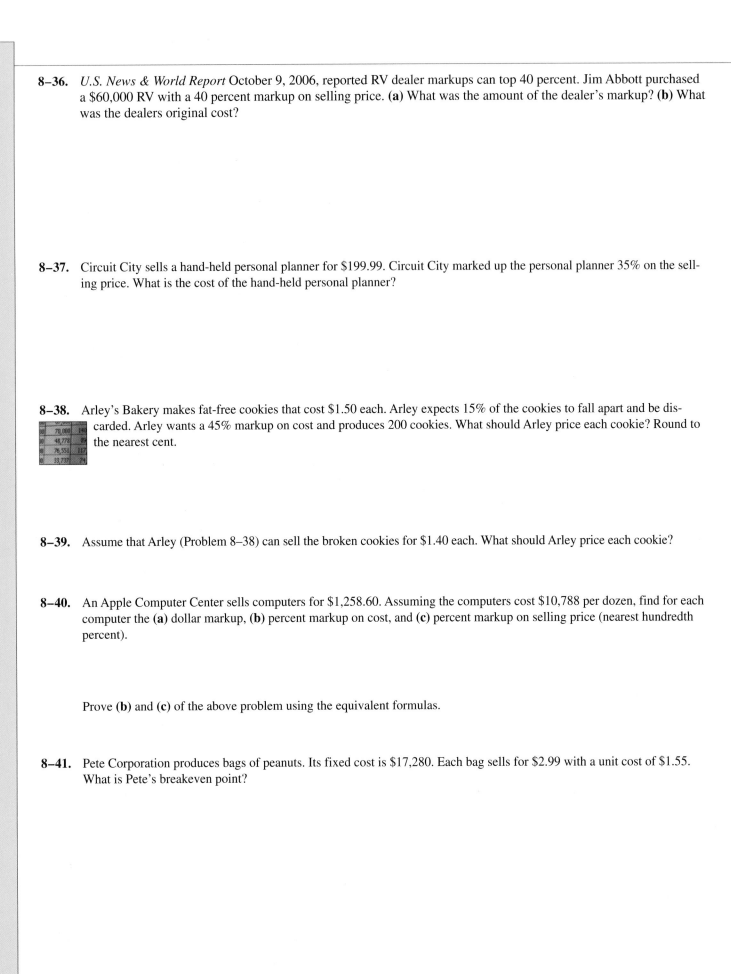

8–39. Assume that Arley (Problem 8–38) can sell the broken cookies for $1.40 each. What should Arley price each cookie?

8–40. An Apple Computer Center sells computers for $1,258.60. Assuming the computers cost $10,788 per dozen, find for each computer the **(a)** dollar markup, **(b)** percent markup on cost, and **(c)** percent markup on selling price (nearest hundredth percent).

Prove **(b)** and **(c)** of the above problem using the equivalent formulas.

8–41. Pete Corporation produces bags of peanuts. Its fixed cost is $17,280. Each bag sells for $2.99 with a unit cost of $1.55. What is Pete's breakeven point?

8–42. Virtual dealer, Dirt Cheap, says it marks up its jewelry a mere 8%. That is why Peter Bertling could buy a two-carat pair of diamond earrings for $5,000—49% of what he would pay at a conventional retailer. **(a)** Based on selling price, what is Dirt Cheap's cost? **(b)** What is Dirt Cheap's markup amount? **(c)** What was the selling price of the conventional retailer? **(d)** How much did Peter save? Round to the nearest hundredth.

8–43. On July 8, 2009, Leon's Kitchen Hut bought a set of pots with a $120 list price from Lambert Manufacturing. Leon's receives a 25% trade discount. Terms of the sale were 2/10, n/30. On July 14, Leon's sent a check to Lambert for the pots. Leon's expenses are 20% of the selling price. Leon's must also make a profit of 15% of the selling price. A competitor marked down the same set of pots 30%. Assume Leon's reduces its selling price by 30%.

    a. What is the sale price at Kitchen Hut?

    b. What was the operating profit or loss?

 SUMMARY PRACTICE TEST

1. Sunset Co. marks up merchandise 40% on cost. A DVD player costs Sunset $90. What is Sunset's selling price? Round to the nearest cent. *(p. 206)*

2. JCPenney sells jeans for $49.50 that cost $38.00. What is the percent markup on cost? Round to the nearest hundredth percent. Check the cost. *(p. 206)*

3. Best Buy sells a flat-screen high-definition TV for $700. Best Buy marks up the TV 45% on cost. What is the cost and dollar markup of the TV? *(p. 207)*

4. Sports Authority marks up New Balance sneakers $30 and sells them for $109. Markup is on cost. What are the cost and percent markup to the nearest hundredth percent? *(p. 206)*

5. The Shoe Outlet bought boots for $60 and marks up the boots 55% on the selling price. What is the selling price of the boots? Round to the nearest cent. *(p. 211)*

6. Office Max sells a desk for $450 and marks up the desk 35% on the selling price. What did the desk cost Office Max? Round to the nearest cent. *(p. 212)*

7. Zales sells diamonds for $1,100 that cost $800. What is Zales's percent markup on selling price? Round to the nearest hundredth percent. Check the selling price. *(p. 211)*

8. Earl Miller, a customer of J. Crew, will pay $400 for a new jacket. J. Crew has a 60% markup on selling price. What is the most that J. Crew can pay for this jacket? *(p. 212)*

9. Home Liquidators mark up its merchandise 35% on cost. What is the company's equivalent markup on selling price? Round to the nearest tenth percent. *(p. 213)*

10. The Muffin Shop makes no-fat blueberry muffins that cost $.70 each. The Muffin Shop knows that 15% of the muffins will spoil. If The Muffin Shop wants 40% markup on cost and produces 800 muffins, what should The Muffin Shop price each muffin? Round to the nearest cent. *(p. 217)*

11. Angel Corporation produces calculators selling for $25.99. Its unit cost is $18.95. Assuming a fixed cost of $80,960, what is the breakeven point in units? *(p. 219)*

INSURANCE | Yes, you can afford coverage that pays nursing-home costs. *By Kimberly Lankford*

A fresh look at
LONG TERM care

COULD YOU afford to withdraw $250,000 from your retirement savings to pay for one year in a nursing home? Based on current charges, that's the projected cost in 25 years, when today's 55-year-old is likely to need care. And with nursing-home stays averaging about 2.5 years, your total bill could top $600,000—which could quickly drain your retirement accounts, leaving you and your spouse with little savings and your heirs without an inheritance.

Buying long-term-care insurance is the best way to protect your retirement savings from astronomical bills. And a new law, which makes it more difficult to qualify for medicaid coverage of nursing-home costs, gives long-term-care policies a boost (see "Medicaid Gets Tough," on page 86).

Long-term-care coverage doesn't come cheap. Prices for new policies have jumped by 20% to 40% over the past few years. It can now cost a 55-year-old nearly $5,000 per year for a lifetime policy with a $200 daily benefit (the average nursing-home cost nationwide), 5% compound inflation protection and a 60-day waiting period before benefits begin. That's nearly $7,000 for a married couple, even with a spousal discount. But with some smart planning, you can buy all the coverage you need for a fraction of that amount.

A shorter benefit period. For starters, you probably don't need a policy that pays lifetime benefits. Milliman, an actuarial consulting firm, recently stud-

Glen and Joan Berwick stretched their premium dollars by buying six-year shared-care policies.

ied more than 1.6 million long-term-care policies and found that only about 8% of 70-year-old claimants are likely to need care for longer than five years—leaving 92% with claims of five years or fewer. Dawn Helwig, the study's co-author, points out that the average claim period is even shorter, because most people don't activate their policies until they are in their eighties.

Shortening the benefit period can

cut your premiums significantly. A John Hancock policy with a $200 daily benefit and a five-year benefit period would cost a 55-year-old $2,900 per year—about $2,000 less than lifetime coverage, or $3,000 less per couple annually. For example, Glen and Joan Berwick of South Glastonbury, Conn., each bought a six-year policy with a $150 daily benefit from John Hancock four years ago, when Glen was 63 and Joan was 59, saving them thousands of dollars.

One caveat: Of the 8% of nursing-home residents likely to need extended care, many will have chronic conditions, such as Alzheimer's. If you have a family history of a chronic disease, you're better off with a policy with a ten-year benefit period, which would still cost a 55-year-old $1,000 less a year than a lifetime-benefits policy.

Shared care. The best deal of all may be a shared-care policy, which gives you and your spouse a pool of benefits. If you each buy, say, a five-year shared-care policy, you actually get ten years to split between you. Most long-term-care insurers offer such policies, which generally cost about 10% more than separate policies with the same benefit period.

MIKI DUISTERHOF

For Dining Chains, Lucrative Drinks Could Make for Very Happy Hours

By Joseph T. Hallinan

CASH-STRAPPED CONSUMERS are eating out less often, leading Bennigan's, Applebee's and other so-called casual-dining chains to lean harder on some of their most profitable menu items: alcoholic drinks.

Beer, wine and liquor-based concoctions often have profit margins more than double those of food—making them just the ticket for a restaurant's sagging bottom line. And the timing is right: Americans' alcohol consumption, after dropping for nearly two decades, is on the rise again—due in large measure to recent effective marketing campaigns by wine and spirits makers.

In an effort to attract sales clerks, hotel workers and other late-shift service-industry workers looking for a place to go after work, **Applebee's International** Inc., of Overland Park, Kan., the nation's leading casual-dining chain, has knocked $1 off the price of a 16-ounce glass of draft beer after 9 p.m., and some Applebee's restaurants have begun offering half-price appetizers at that time. The chain also has introduced a new line of smoothies and fruit drinks, as well as specialty drinks like the "Dos 'Rita Rocks," a Margarita made with two premium tequilas, Red Apple Sangria and the Mucho Mary, a Bloody Mary drink.

Metromedia Restaurant Group's Bennigan's Grill & Tavern unit last month rolled out a menu of inexpensive "bar bites," in an effort to target 25- to 45-year-old working professionals and singles. Bennigan's goal is to boost alcohol sales to 25% of its total sales, up from the current 20%.

"It works for me," said Jeff Rykal, a 41-year-old telecommunications director, just after 5:30 p.m. on a recent Monday at a Chicago Bennigan's.

He was munching on a $4 basket of small cheeseburgers—"Burger Bites"—and fries, and washing it down with a $2.50 Budweiser.

With him, Mark Linman, 41, was working on his own Burger Bites and a bottle of Miller Genuine Draft. The men said it was their first trip to Bennigan's.

Bennigan's new bar menu, supported by TV and print ads, is part of a larger makeover of the chain's bar operations. Earlier this year, the company foresaw a softening in the economy, says Clay Dover, Bennigan's vice president of marketing, "and we wanted to react accordingly."

Across the casual-dining sector—where dinner tabs typically run between $10 and $30 per dinner—servings of alcoholic drinks for the first six months of 2006 were up 3% over a year ago, according to NPD Group, a Port Washington, N.Y., market research firm.

"Even though traffic may be down or moderating slightly, at these casual-dining restaurants their alcoholic beverage sales are up," says Tex McCarthy, president of national accounts and sales development in North America for **Diageo** PLC, the world's largest spirits maker by volume. He said this trend is true not only for spirits, but for beer and wine as well. Diageo sells all three.

Restaurants love to sell alcohol for good reason: It takes less time and fewer people to prepare a drink than it does to prepare a meal. That leads to tasty profit margins of about 35% for alcoholic beverages, compared with 15% for food, according to Technomic, a Chicago restaurant-consulting firm.

Profit Punch

Alcoholic beverages, including beer, wine and spirits, bring in more money for restaurants than food. Revenue breakdown:

Beverages		Food	
25%	Product cost	35%	
40%	Other direct costs	50%	
35%	Net profit margin	15%	

Source: Technomic

Margaritas and other alcoholic drinks help keep restaurants afloat.

Internet Projects: See text Web site (www.mhhe.com/slater9e) and The Business Math Internet Resource Guide.

232

Video Case

You may not have heard of the Kimpton Group, but you have probably heard the name of at least one of their 40 stylish boutique hotels that combine affordability with personality. The company believes it is cheaper to renovate old downtown buildings into charming hotels featuring popular restaurants than build new chain hotels. Developing a classy boutique property costs $150,000 per room compared to $350,000 a room for a new chain hotel. Investors also see a more rapid return.

The late Bill Kimpton, a former Lehman Bros. investment banker, created the boutique hotel concept and founded the Kimpton Hotel & Restaurant Group, a San Francisco–based chain, in 1981. Today the Kimpton Group runs 40 luxury hotels and 36 restaurants in the United States and Canada. Rates run from $100 to $200 per night, the average being $140, which is usually about 25% to 30% less than comparative nearby hotels. The average occupancy is 62%.

The Kimpton Group is known for its innovative ideas. All seven hotels offer the "Guppy Love" goldfish service. Steve Pinetti, senior vice president–sales and marketing, came up with the goldfish idea. He suggested providing complimentary goldfish to guests. Among the other concepts that Kimpton claims to have originated are pet-friendly hotels, custom-made "tall" beds, and complimentary wine hours for guests. U.S. hotel operators look to Kimpton for inspiration and credit it with inventing boutique hotels.

When a new hotel is planned, Kimpton invites people from theaters, galleries, and department stores in the area to offer ideas that might suit the particular location. Kimpton's philosophy is that travelers want something different and exciting in a hotel, and the element of excitement should not be underestimated no matter what the age group or location. Goldfish seem to be hooking customers for Kimpton.

PROBLEM 1

As shown in the video, Hotel Monaco's clients are 65% business travelers, of which 35% are with groups. Hotel Monaco has 192 rooms with the occupancy rate running about 62%. **(a)** On a given evening, how many guests would be business travelers? **(b)** How many would be group business travelers? Round to the nearest whole number.

PROBLEM 2

On May 16, 2003, the *Chicago Sun Times* reported Chicago downtown hotels were averaging occupancy of 50.5% for the first two months of 2003, with rates averaging $121. Regionwide, occupancy was 47.9%, up almost 4 percentage points from the same period a year ago, but average room rates inched down to $92 from $93 last year. Hotel Monaco has 192 rooms, averaging $199 per room. **(a)** What is the percent change in Hotel Monaco's average rate compared to the industry average rate? **(b)** What is the percent change in regionwide rates? Round to the nearest hundredths. **(c)** What would be the revenue generated by Hotel Monaco for one evening? Round to the nearest dollar.

PROBLEM 3

Hotel Monaco's occupancy rate topped 62% in 2001 and 70% in 2000. The average rate is $199 per evening. What would be the dollar change in total revenue for one week (7 days) based on 192 rooms? Round final answer to the nearest dollar.

PROBLEM 4

The average daily hotel room rate totaled $104.32 at year-end 2002, $113.12 at year-end 2001, and $116.42 at year-end 2000. **(a)** With 2000 as the base year, what were the percent changes each year? **(b)** Using 2002 as the base year, what were the percent changes each year? Round to the nearest hundredth.

PROBLEM 5

On April 9, 2002, *USA Today* reported total nationwide revenue for boutique hotels dropped 13% to $1.6 billion in 2001 from the previous year. Revenue per available room— another measure of the hotel industry's financial health—fell 16% in 2001 for boutique hotels, compared with 6% for all hotels. **(a)** What had been the total revenue in 2000? Round to the nearest tenth. **(b)** Based on an average room rate of $199, what was the dollar change for boutique hotels? **(c)** With the same average rate, what was the dollar change for hotels? Round to the nearest whole dollar.

PROBLEM 6

Thomas LaTour, CEO of the Kimpton Group, stated it is more profitable to develop boutique hotels than large chain hotels because it is cheaper to renovate an old downtown building than build new chain hotels. To develop a classy boutique property costs $150,000 per room compared to $350,000 per room for a new chain hotel. **(a)** What is the percent increase in the cost of a new chain hotel? Round to the nearest hundredth. **(b)** What would be the total cost of a 192-room boutique? **(c)** What would be the total cost of a 192-room new chain hotel?

PROBLEM 7

Revenue in 2001 for the private Kimpton Group fell 15% to $350 million. CEO Thomas LaTour predicted sales growth of 5% for 2002. Room occupancy rates, which sank to 45% after September 11, have risen to 66% during the month of April. **(a)** What had been the total revenue in 2002? Round to the nearest million. **(b)** What is the amount of sales growth projected for 2002? **(c)** With 192 rooms, what is the change in room occupancy? Round to the nearest whole number.

A Word Problem Approach—Chapters 6, 7, 8

1. Assume Kellogg's produced 715,000 boxes of Corn Flakes this year. This was 110% of the annual production last year. What was last year's annual production? (p. 150)

2. A new Sony camcorder has a list price of $420. The trade discount is 10/20 with terms of 2/10, n/30. If a retailer pays the invoice within the discount period, what is the amount the retailer must pay? (p. 175)

3. JCPenney sells loafers with a markup of $40. If the markup is 30% on cost, what did the loafers cost JCPenney? Round to the nearest dollar. (p. 207)

4. Aster Computers received from Ring Manufacturers an invoice dated August 28 with terms 2/10 EOM. The list price of the invoice is $3,000 (freight not included). Ring offers Aster a 9/8/2 trade chain discount. Terms of freight are FOB shipping point, but Ring prepays the $150 freight. Assume Aster pays the invoice on October 9. How much will Ring receive? (p. 175)

5. Runners World marks up its Nike jogging shoes 25% on selling price. The Nike shoe sells for $65. How much did the store pay for them? (p. 212)

6. Ivan Rone sells antique sleds. He knows that the most he can get for a sled is $350. Ivan needs a 35% markup on cost. Since Ivan is going to an antiques show, he wants to know the maximum he can offer a dealer for an antique sled. (p. 207)

7. Bonnie's Bakery bakes 60 loaves of bread for $1.10 each. Bonnie's estimates that 10% of the bread will spoil. Assume a 60% markup on cost. What is the selling price of each loaf? If Bonnie's can sell the old bread for one-half the cost, what is the selling price of each loaf? (p. 217)

Payroll

LEARNING UNIT OBJECTIVES

LU 9–1: Calculating Various Types of Employees' Gross Pay

- Define, compare, and contrast weekly, biweekly, semimonthly, and monthly pay periods *(p. 236)*.
- Calculate gross pay with overtime on the basis of time *(p. 237)*.
- Calculate gross pay for piecework, differential pay schedule, straight commission with draw, variable commission scale, and salary plus commission *(pp. 238–240)*.

LU 9–2: Computing Payroll Deductions for Employees' Pay; Employers' Responsibilities

- Prepare and explain the parts of a payroll register *(p. 241–244)*.
- Explain and calculate federal and state unemployment taxes *(p. 244)*.

Delta, Pilots Agree on Interim Pay Cuts

By Evan Perez

Averting a potentially crippling impasse, **Delta Air Lines** Inc. and its pilots union reached an agreement on interim pay cuts and a timetable for the two sides to negotiate a long-term deal on concessions the company says are necessary to complete its bankruptcy restructuring.

The Air Line Pilots Association agreed to accept a 14% wage cut and other cost cuts that would be equal to an additional 1% wage cut, and said it would submit the tentative agreement to its members for ratification by Dec. 28. Delta had sought a 19% wage reduction as part of a package of cuts totaling $325 million annually.

The agreement, reached yesterday, avoids for now a showdown over Delta's threat to abrogate the collective bargaining agreement with its 6,100 pilots. Bankruptcy-court hearings on Delta's request

to impose terms on the union were set to continue today, and a deadline loomed Friday, when Delta had said it could reject the union's contract. The union had threatened a possible strike in retaliation. Both the company and union leaders believed the company couldn't survive a labor shutdown.

Based on Delta's valuation of its earlier demand, the agreement on a 14% wage cut should save the company $143 million annually. That is higher than the union's initial offer of a 9% pay cut. The union estimated that initial offer would save Delta $90 million, not including other work-rule changes. In court filings, Delta says its average pilot salary is just under $170,000, though the union says that figure is misleadingly high.

The Atlanta company began seeking union concessions well before it filed for Chapter 11 reorganization Sept. 14, but the two sides have been at a standoff

ever since. Bankruptcy Court Judge Prudence Carter Beatty has pushed the two sides to come to an agreement in recent weeks to make it unnecessary for her to rule on Delta's motion to cancel the pilot contract.

The union and the company said they would continue negotiating to reach a permanent agreement by March 1.

In a letter to union members, Lee Moak, a Delta captain who chairs its leadership committee, said the interim agreement "buys us time. We were facing possible rejection of the contract in a matter of days."

Under the tentative deal, the company agreed to end a program to rehire recently retired pilots on a contract basis to fly some of its routes. Active pilots disliked the program because the retired pilots held higher-paid slots that they otherwise could move into.

Tom Uhlman/AP Wide World

The *Wall Street Journal* clipping "Delta, Pilots Agree on Interim Pay Cuts" shows how pilots have agreed to a 14% pay cut. Note that the average pilot salary is $170,000. A 14% pay cut means a loss of $23,800.

This chapter discusses (1) the type of pay people work for, (2) how employers calculate paychecks and deductions, and (3) what employers must report and pay in taxes.

Learning Unit 9–1: Calculating Various Types of Employees' Gross Pay

Logan Company manufactures dolls of all shapes and sizes. These dolls are sold worldwide. We study Logan Company in this unit because of the variety of methods Logan uses to pay its employees.

Companies usually pay employees **weekly, biweekly, semimonthly,** or **monthly.** How often employers pay employees can affect how employees manage their money. Some employees prefer a weekly paycheck that spreads the inflow of money. Employees who have monthly bills may find the twice-a-month or monthly paycheck more convenient. All employees would like more money to manage.

Let's assume you earn $50,000 per year. The following table shows what you would earn each pay period. Remember that 13 weeks equals one quarter. Four quarters or 52 weeks equals a year.

Salary paid	Period (based on a year)	Earnings for period (dollars)
Weekly	52 times (once a week)	$ 961.54 ($50,000 ÷ 52)
Biweekly	26 times (every two weeks)	$1,923.08 ($50,000 ÷ 26)
Semimonthly	24 times (twice a month)	$2,083.33 ($50,000 ÷ 24)
Monthly	12 times (once a month)	$4,166.67 ($50,000 ÷ 12)

Now let's look at some pay schedule situations and examples of how Logan Company calculates its payroll for employees of different pay status.

Situation 1: Hourly Rate of Pay; Calculation of Overtime

The **Fair Labor Standards Act** sets minimum wage standards and overtime regulations for employees of companies covered by this federal law. The law provides that employees working for an hourly rate receive time-and-a-half pay for hours worked in excess of their regular 40-hour week. The current hourly minimum wage is $5.85, rising to $6.55 in summer of 2008 and then $7.25 in summer of 2009. Many managerial people, however, are exempt from the time-and-a-half pay for all hours in excess of a 40-hour week.

Ryan McVay/Getty Images

As Tech Matures, Workers File A Spate of Salary Complaints

Fewer Dreams of Riches Mean More Suits for Overtime And Other Mundane Pay

Electronic Arts Rethinks Perks

By Pui-Wing Tam And Nick Wingfield

A hallmark of the boom years in high-tech was its work ethic: killer hours, often at modest salaries, without complaint. It was a small price for the excitement and the shot at a bonanza someday.

But as high-tech riches have faded, a different attitude toward employers is popping up: Pay me overtime, or I'll sue.

Wall Street Journal © 2005

In addition to many managerial people being exempt from time-and-a-half pay for more than 40 hours, other workers may also be exempt. Note in the *Wall Street Journal* clipping "As Tech Matures, Workers File a Spate of Salary Complaints" that many employees in the tech sector plan to sue if they do not get overtime pay.

Now we return to our Logan Company example. Logan Company is calculating the weekly pay of Ramon Valdez who works in its manufacturing division. For the first 40 hours Ramon works, Logan calculates his **gross pay** (earnings before **deductions**) as follows:

> Gross pay = Hours employee worked × Rate per hour

Ramon works more than 40 hours in a week. For every hour over his 40 hours, Ramon must be paid an **overtime** pay of at least 1.5 times his regular pay rate. The following formula is used to determine Ramon's overtime:

> Hourly overtime pay rate = Regular hourly pay rate × 1.5

Logan Company must include Ramon's overtime pay with his regular pay. To determine Ramon's gross pay, Logan uses the following formula:

> Gross pay = Earnings for 40 hours + Earnings at time-and-a-half rate (1.5)

We are now ready to calculate Ramon's gross pay from the following data:

EXAMPLE

Employee	M	T	W	Th	F	S	Total hours	Rate per hour
Ramon Valdez	13	$8\frac{1}{2}$	10	8	$11\frac{1}{4}$	$10\frac{3}{4}$	$61\frac{1}{2}$	$9

$61\frac{1}{2}$ total hours
-40 regular hours
$\overline{21\frac{1}{2}}$ hours overtime[1]   Time-and-a-half pay: $9 × 1.5 = $13.50

Gross pay = (40 hours × $9) + ($21\frac{1}{2}$ hours × $13.50)

   = $360   + $290.25

   = $650.25

Note that the $13.50 overtime rate came out even. However, throughout the text, *if an overtime rate is greater than two decimal places, do not round it. Round only the final answer. This gives greater accuracy.*

Situation 2: Straight Piece Rate Pay

Some companies, especially manufacturers, pay workers according to how much they produce. Logan Company pays Ryan Foss for the number of dolls he produces in a week. This gives Ryan an incentive to make more money by producing more dolls. Ryan receives $.96 per doll, less any defective units. The following formula determines Ryan's gross pay:

> Gross pay = Number of units produced × Rate per unit

Companies may also pay a guaranteed hourly wage and use a piece rate as a bonus. However, Logan uses straight piece rate as wages for some of its employees.

EXAMPLE   During the last week of April, Ryan Foss produced 900 dolls. Using the above formula, Logan Company paid Ryan $864.

Gross pay = 900 dolls × $.96

   = $864

Situation 3: Differential Pay Schedule

Some of Logan's employees can earn more than the $.96 straight piece rate for every doll they produce. Logan Company has set up a **differential pay schedule** for these employees. The company determines the rate these employees make by the amount of units the employees produce at different levels of production.

EXAMPLE   Logan Company pays Abby Rogers on the basis of the following schedule:

	Units produced	Amount per unit
First 50 →	1–50	$ .50
Next 100 →	51–150	.62
Next 50 →	151–200	.75
	Over 200	1.25

Last week Abby produced 300 dolls. What is Abby's gross pay?
Logan calculated Abby's gross pay as follows:

(50 × $.50) + (100 × $.62) + (50 × $.75) + (100 × $1.25)

   $25   + $62   + $37.50   + $125   = $249.50

---

[1]Some companies pay overtime for time over 8 hours in one day; Logan Company pays overtime for time over 40 hours per week.

Now we will study some of the other types of employee commission payment plans.

Situation 4: Straight Commission with Draw

Companies frequently use **straight commission** to determine the pay of salespersons. This commission is usually a certain percentage of the amount the salesperson sells. An example of one group of companies ceasing to pay commissions is the rental-car companies.

Companies such as Logan Company allow some of its salespersons to draw against their commission at the beginning of each month. A **draw** is an advance on the salesperson's commission. Logan subtracts this advance later from the employee's commission earned based on sales. When the commission does not equal the draw, the salesperson owes Logan the difference between the draw and the commission.

Commission

Portion

Base × Rate

Net sales   Commission
rate

EXAMPLE   Logan Company pays Jackie Okamoto a straight commission of 15% on her net sales (net sales are total sales less sales returns). In May, Jackie had net sales of $56,000. Logan gave Jackie a $600 draw in May. What is Jackie's gross pay?

Logan calculated Jackie's commission minus her draw as follows:

$$\$56,000 \times .15 = \begin{array}{r} \$8,400 \\ - \quad 600 \\ \hline \$7,800 \end{array}$$

Logan Company pays some people in the sales department on a variable commission scale. Let's look at this, assuming the employee had no draw.

Situation 5: Variable Commission Scale

A company with a **variable commission scale** uses different commission rates for different levels of net sales.

EXAMPLE   Last month, Jane Ring's net sales were $160,000. What is Jane's gross pay based on the following schedule?

Up to $35,000	4%
Excess of $35,000 to $45,000	6%
Over $45,000	8%

$$\text{Gross pay} = (\$35,000 \times .04) + (\$10,000 \times .06) + (\$115,000 \times .08)$$
$$= \quad \$1,400 \quad + \quad \$600 \quad + \quad \$9,200$$
$$= \boxed{\$11,200}$$

Situation 6: Salary Plus Commission

Logan Company pays Joe Roy a $3,000 monthly salary plus a 4% commission for sales over $20,000. Last month Joe's net sales were $50,000. Logan calculated Joe's gross monthly pay as follows:

$$\text{Gross pay} = \text{Salary} + (\text{Commission} \times \text{Sales over } \$20,000)$$
$$= \$3,000 + \quad (.04 \times \$30,000)$$
$$= \$3,000 + \quad\quad \$1,200$$
$$= \boxed{\$4,200}$$

Before you take the Practice Quiz, you should know that many managers today receive **overrides.** These managers receive a commission based on the net sales of the people they supervise.

LU 9–1 PRACTICE QUIZ

Complete this **Practice Quiz**
to see how you are doing

1. Jill Foster worked 52 hours in one week for Delta Airlines. Jill earns $10 per hour. What is Jill's gross pay, assuming overtime is at time-and-a-half?

2. Matt Long had $180,000 in sales for the month. Matt's commission rate is 9%, and he had a $3,500 draw. What was Matt's end-of-month commission?

3. Bob Meyers receives a $1,000 monthly salary. He also receives a variable commission on net sales based on the following schedule (commission doesn't begin until Bob earns $8,000 in net sales):

$8,000–$12,000	1%	Excess of $20,000 to $40,000	5%
Excess of $12,000 to $20,000	3%	More than $40,000	8%

   Assume Bob earns $40,000 net sales for the month. What is his gross pay?

✓ **Solutions**

1. 40 hours × $10.00 = $400.00
    12 hours × $15.00 = $\underline{180.00}$ ($10.00 × 1.5 = $15.00)
                         $\boxed{\$580.00}$

2. $180,000 × .09 = $16,200
                       $\underline{-\ 3,500}$
                       $\boxed{\$12,700}$

3. Gross pay = $1,000 + ($4,000 × .01) + ($8,000 × .03) + ($20,000 × .05)
             = $1,000 + $40   + $240   + $1,000
             = $\boxed{\$2,280}$

LU 9–1a EXTRA PRACTICE QUIZ

Need more practice? Try this
Extra Practice Quiz (check
figures in Chapter Organizer,
p. 247)

1. Jill Foster worked 54 hours in one week for Delta Airlines. Jill earns $12 per hour. What is Jill's gross pay, assuming overtime is at time-and-a-half?

2. Matt Long had $210,000 in sales for the month. Matt's commission rate is 8%, and he had a $4,000 draw. What was Matt's end-of-month commission?

3. Bob Myers receives a $1,200 monthly salary. He also receives a variable commission on net sales based on the following schedule (commission doesn't begin until Bob earns $9,000 in net sales).

$9,000–$12,000	1%	Excess of $20,000 to $40,000	5%
Excess of $12,000 to $20,000	3%	More than $40,000	8%

   Assume Bob earns $60,000 net sales for the month. What is his gross pay?

Learning Unit 9–2: Computing Payroll Deductions for Employees' Pay; Employers' Responsibilities

Did you know that Wal-Mart is the largest employer in twenty-one states? Can you imagine the accounting involved to pay all these employees?

This unit begins by dissecting a paycheck. Then we give you an insight into the tax responsibilities of employers.

Computing Payroll Deductions for Employees

Companies often record employee payroll information in a multicolumn form called a **payroll register.** The increased use of computers in business has made computerized registers a timesaver for many companies.

Glo Company uses a multicolumn payroll register. On page 241 is Glo's partial payroll register showing the payroll information for Alice Rey during week 44. Let's check each column to see if Alice's take-home pay of $1,324.36 is correct. Note how the circled letters in the register correspond to the explanations that follow.

GLO COMPANY
Payroll Register
Week #44

Employee name	Allow. & marital status	Cum. earn.	Sal. per week	Earnings			Cum. earn.	FICA Taxable Earnings		Deductions					
										FICA				Health	Net
				Reg.	Ovt.	Gross		S.S.	Med.	S.S.	Med.	FIT	SIT	ins.	pay
Rey, Alice	M-2	96,750	2,250	2,250	—	2,250	99,000	750	2,250	46.50	32.63	355.96	135	100	1,579.91
	Ⓐ	Ⓑ	Ⓒ			Ⓓ	Ⓔ	Ⓕ	Ⓖ	Ⓗ	Ⓘ	Ⓙ	Ⓚ	Ⓛ	Ⓜ

Payroll Register Explanations

Ⓐ—Allowance and marital status
Ⓑ,Ⓒ,Ⓓ—Cumulative earnings before payroll, salaries, earnings
Ⓔ—Cumulative earnings after payroll

When Alice was hired, she completed the **W-4 (Employee's Withholding Allowance Certificate)** form shown in Figure 9.1 stating that she is married and claims an allowance (exemption) of 2. Glo Company will need this information to calculate the federal income tax Ⓙ.

Before this pay period, Alice has earned $96,750 (43 weeks × $2,250 salary per week). Since Alice receives no overtime, her $2,250 salary per week represents her gross pay (pay before any deductions).

After this pay period, Alice has earned $99,000 ($96,750 + $2,250).

The **Federal Insurance Contribution Act (FICA)** funds the **Social Security** program. The program includes Old Age and Disability, Medicare, Survivor Benefits, and so on. The FICA tax requires separate reporting for Social Security and **Medicare.** We will use the following rates for Glo Company:

	Rate	Base
Social Security	6.20%	$97,500
Medicare	1.45	No base

These rates mean that Alice Rey will pay Social Security taxes on the first $97,500 she earns this year. After earning $97,500, Alice's wages will be exempt from Social Security. Note that Alice will be paying Medicare taxes on all wages since Medicare has no base cutoff.

Ⓕ,Ⓖ—Taxable earnings for Social Security and Medicare

To help keep Glo's record straight, the *taxable earnings column only shows what wages will be taxed. This amount is not the tax.* For example, in week 44, only $750 of Alice's salary will be taxable for Social Security.

$97,500 Social Security base
− 96,750 Ⓑ
$ 750

Employee's W-4 form

Form **W-4**	**Employee's Withholding Allowance Certificate**	OMB No. 1545-0010
Department of the Treasury Internal Revenue Service	▶ For Privacy Act and Paperwork Reduction Act Notice, see reverse.	20XX

1 Type or print your first name and middle initial	Last name	2 Your social security number
Alice	Rey	021 36 9494

Home address (number and street or rural route)	3 ☐ Single ☒ Married ☐ Married, but withhold at higher Single rate.
2 Roundy Road	Note: *If married, but legally separated, or spouse is a nonresident alien, check the Single box.*

City or town, state, and ZIP code	4 If your last name differs from that on your social security card, check
Marblehead, MA 01945	here and call 1-800-772-1213 for a new card . . . . . ▶ ☐

5 Total number of allowances you are claiming (from line G above or from the worksheets on page 2 if they apply) . **5** 2
6 Additional amount, if any, you want withheld from each paycheck . . . . **6** $
7 I claim exemption from withholding for 1995 and I certify that I meet **BOTH** of the following conditions for exemption:
 • Last year I had a right to a refund of **ALL** Federal income tax withheld because I had **NO** tax liability; **AND**
 • This year I expect a refund of **ALL** Federal income tax withheld because I expect to have **NO** tax liability.
 If you meet both conditions, enter "EXEMPT" here . . . . ▶ **7**
Under penalties of perjury, I certify that I am entitled to the number of withholding allowances claimed on this certificate or entitled to claim exempt status.

Employee's signature ▶ *Alice Rey*   Date ▶ 1/1   , 20 XX

8 Employer's name and address (Employer: Complete 8 and 10 only if sending to the IRS)	9 Office code (optional)	10 Employer identification number

Cat. No. 10220Q

Percentage method income tax
withholding table

Payroll Period	One Withholding Allowance
Weekly	$ 65.38
Biweekly	130.77
Semimonthly	141.67
Monthly	283.33
Quarterly	850.00
Semiannually	1,700.00
Annually	3,400.00
Daily or miscellaneous (each day of the payroll period)	13.08

Dept. of the Treasury, Internal Revenue Service Publication 15, Jan. 2007.

Ⓗ—Social Security

To calculate Alice's Social Security tax, we multiply $750 Ⓕ by 6.2%:

$$\$750 \times .062 = \boxed{\$46.50}$$

Ⓘ—Medicare

Since Medicare has no base, Alice's entire weekly salary is taxed 1.45%, which is multiplied by $2,250.

$$\$2,250 \times .0145 = \boxed{\$32.63}$$

Ⓙ—FIT

Using the W-4 form Alice completed, Glo deducts **federal income tax withholding (FIT).** The more allowances an employee claims, the less money Glo deducts from the employee's paycheck. Glo uses the percentage method to calculate FIT.[2]

The Percentage Method[3]

Today, since many companies do not want to store the tax tables, they use computers for their payroll. These companies use the **percentage method.** For this method we use Table 9.1 and Table 9.2 from Circular E to calculate Alice's FIT.

Step 1.   In Table 9.1, locate the weekly withholding for one allowance. Multiply this number by 2.

$$\$65.38 \times 2 = \$130.76$$

Step 2.   Subtract $130.76 in Step 1 from Alice's total pay.

$$
\begin{array}{r}
\$2,250.00 \\
-\quad 130.76 \\
\hline
\$2,119.24
\end{array}
$$

Step 3.   In Table 9.2, locate the married person's weekly pay table. The $2,119.24 falls between $1,360 and $2,573. The tax is $166.15 plus 25% of the excess over $1,360.00.

$$
\begin{array}{r}
\$2,119.24 \\
-\ 1,360.00 \\
\hline
\$\ \ 759.24
\end{array}
$$

$$\text{Tax}\quad \$166.15 + .25\,(\$759.24)$$

$$\$166.15 + \$189.81 = \boxed{\$355.96}$$

Ⓚ—SIT

We assume a 6% **state income tax (SIT).**

$$\$2,250 \times .06 = \$135.00$$

Ⓛ—Health insurance
Ⓜ—Net pay

Alice contributes $100 per week for health insurance.
Alice's **net pay** is her gross pay less all deductions.

$$
\begin{array}{rl}
\$2,250.00 & \text{gross} \\
-\quad\quad 46.50 & \text{Social Security} \\
-\quad\quad 32.63 & \text{Medicare} \\
-\quad\quad 355.96 & \text{FIT} \\
-\quad\quad 135.00 & \text{SIT} \\
-\quad\quad 100.00 & \text{health insurance} \\
\hline
= \boxed{\$1,579.91} & \text{net pay}
\end{array}
$$

[2]The *Business Math Handbook* has a sample of the wage bracket method.
[3]An alternative method is called the wage bracket method that is shown in the *Business Math Handbook.*

TABLE 9.2   Percentage method income tax withholding taxes

TABLE 1—WEEKLY Payroll Period

(a) SINGLE person (including head of household)—

If the amount of wages (after subtracting withholding allowances) is: The amount of income tax to withhold is:

Not over $51 . . . . . $0

Over—	But not over—		of excess over—
$51	—$195 . .	10%	—$51
$195	—$645 . .	$14.40 plus 15%	—$195
$645	—$1,482 . .	$81.90 plus 25%	—$645
$1,482	—$3,131 . .	$291.15 plus 28%	—$1,482
$3,131	—$6,763 . .	$752.87 plus 33%	—$3,131
$6,763	. . . . . .	$1,951.43 plus 35%	—$6,763

(b) MARRIED person—

If the amount of wages (after subtracting withholding allowances) is: The amount of income tax to withhold is:

Not over $154 . . . . . $0

Over—	But not over—		of excess over—
$154	—$449 . .	10%	—$154
$449	—$1,360 . .	$29.50 plus 15%	—$449
$1,360	—$2,573 . .	$166.15 plus 25%	—$1,360
$2,573	—$3,907 . .	$469.40 plus 28%	—$2,573
$3,907	—$6,865 . .	$842.92 plus 33%	—$3,907
$6,865	. . . . . .	$1,819.06 plus 35%	—$6,865

TABLE 2—BIWEEKLY Payroll Period

(a) SINGLE person (including head of household)—

If the amount of wages (after subtracting withholding allowances) is: The amount of income tax to withhold is:

Not over $102 . . . . . $0

Over—	But not over—		of excess over—
$102	—$389 . .	10%	—$102
$389	—$1,289 . .	$28.70 plus 15%	—$389
$1,289	—$2,964 . .	$163.70 plus 25%	—$1,289
$2,964	—$6,262 . .	$582.45 plus 28%	—$2,964
$6,262	—$13,525 . .	$1,505.89 plus 33%	—$6,262
$13,525	. . . . . .	$3,902.68 plus 35%	—$13,525

(b) MARRIED person—

If the amount of wages (after subtracting withholding allowances) is: The amount of income tax to withhold is:

Not over $308 . . . . . $0

Over—	But not over—		of excess over—
$308	—$898 . .	10%	—$308
$898	—$2,719 . .	$59.00 plus 15%	—$898
$2,719	—$5,146 . .	$332.15 plus 25%	—$2,719
$5,146	—$7,813 . .	$938.90 plus 28%	—$5,146
$7,813	—$13,731 . .	$1,685.66 plus 33%	—$7,813
$13,731	. . . . . .	$3,638.60 plus 35%	—$13,731

TABLE 3—SEMIMONTHLY Payroll Period

(a) SINGLE person (including head of household)—

If the amount of wages (after subtracting withholding allowances) is: The amount of income tax to withhold is:

Not over $110 . . . . . $0

Over—	But not over—		of excess over—
$110	—$422 . .	10%	—$110
$422	—$1,397 . .	$31.20 plus 15%	—$422
$1,397	—$3,211 . .	$177.45 plus 25%	—$1,397
$3,211	—$6,783 . .	$630.95 plus 28%	—$3,211
$6,783	—$14,652 . .	$1,631.11 plus 33%	—$6,783
$14,652	. . . . . .	$4,227.88 plus 35%	—$14,652

(b) MARRIED person—

If the amount of wages (after subtracting withholding allowances) is: The amount of income tax to withhold is:

Not over $333 . . . . . $0

Over—	But not over—		of excess over—
$333	—$973 . .	10%	—$333
$973	—$2,946 . .	$64.00 plus 15%	—$973
$2,946	—$5,575 . .	$359.95 plus 25%	—$2,946
$5,575	—$8,465 . .	$1,017.20 plus 28%	—$5,575
$8,465	—$14,875 . .	$1,826.40 plus 33%	—$8,465
$14,875	. . . . . .	$3,941.70 plus 35%	—$14,875

TABLE 4—MONTHLY Payroll Period

(a) SINGLE person (including head of household)—

If the amount of wages (after subtracting withholding allowances) is: The amount of income tax to withhold is:

Not over $221 . . . . . $0

Over—	But not over—		of excess over—
$221	—$843 . .	10%	—$221
$843	—$2,793 . .	$62.20 plus 15%	—$843
$2,793	—$6,423 . .	$354.70 plus 25%	—$2,793
$6,423	—$13,567 . .	$1,262.20 plus 28%	—$6,423
$13,567	—$29,304 . .	$3,262.52 plus 33%	—$13,567
$29,304	. . . . . .	$8,455.73 plus 35%	—$29,304

(b) MARRIED person—

If the amount of wages (after subtracting withholding allowances) is: The amount of income tax to withhold is:

Not over $667 . . . . . $0

Over—	But not over—		of excess over—
$667	—$1,946 . .	10%	—$667
$1,946	—$5,892 . .	$127.90 plus 15%	—$1,946
$5,892	—$11,150 . .	$719.80 plus 25%	—$5,892
$11,150	—$16,929 . .	$2,034.30 plus 28%	—$11,150
$16,929	—$29,750 . .	$3,652.42 plus 33%	—$16,929
$29,750	. . . . . .	$7,883.35 plus 35%	—$29,750

Dept. of the Treasury, Internal Revenue Service Publication 15, Jan. 2007.

Employers' Responsibilities

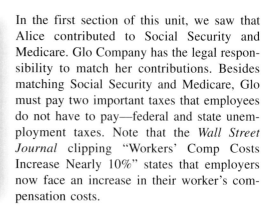

Workers' Comp Costs Increase Nearly 10%

WASHINGTON—Employers' costs for workers' compensation have risen nearly 10%, even though the number of people covered under such programs has declined, largely as a result of higher insurance premiums, according to a new study.

Wall Street Journal © 2005

In the first section of this unit, we saw that Alice contributed to Social Security and Medicare. Glo Company has the legal responsibility to match her contributions. Besides matching Social Security and Medicare, Glo must pay two important taxes that employees do not have to pay—federal and state unemployment taxes. Note that the *Wall Street Journal* clipping "Workers' Comp Costs Increase Nearly 10%" states that employers now face an increase in their worker's compensation costs.

RF/Corbis

Federal Unemployment Tax Act (FUTA)

The federal government participates in a joint federal-state unemployment program to help unemployed workers. At this writing, employers pay the government a 6.2% **FUTA** tax on the first $7,000 paid to employees as wages during the calendar year. Any wages in excess of $7,000 per worker are exempt wages and are not taxed for FUTA. If the total cumulative amount the employer owes the government is less than $100, the employer can pay the liability yearly (end of January in the following calendar year). If the tax is greater than $100, the employer must pay it within a month after the quarter ends.

Companies involved in a state unemployment tax fund can usually take a 5.4% credit against their FUTA tax. *In reality, then, companies are paying .8% (.008) to the federal unemployment program.* In all our calculations, FUTA is .008.

EXAMPLE Assume a company had total wages of $19,000 in a calendar year. No employee earned more than $7,000 during the calendar year. The FUTA tax is .8% (6.2% minus the company's 5.4% credit for state unemployment tax). How much does the company pay in FUTA tax?

The company calculates its FUTA tax as follows:

> 6.2% FUTA tax
> − 5.4% credit for SUTA tax
> = .8% tax for FUTA

.008 × $19,000 = $152 FUTA tax due to federal government

State Unemployment Tax Act (SUTA)

The current **SUTA** tax in many states is 5.4% on the first $7,000 the employer pays an employee. Some states offer a merit rating system that results in a lower SUTA rate for companies with a stable employment period. The federal government still allows 5.4% credit on FUTA tax to companies entitled to the lower SUTA rate. Usually states also charge companies with a poor employment record a higher SUTA rate. However, these companies cannot take any more than the 5.4% credit against the 6.2% federal unemployment rate.

EXAMPLE Assume a company has total wages of $20,000 and $4,000 of the wages are exempt from SUTA. What are the company's SUTA and FUTA taxes if the company's SUTA rate is 5.8% due to a poor employment record?

The exempt wages (over $7,000 earnings per worker) are not taxed for SUTA or FUTA. So the company owes the following SUTA and FUTA taxes:

> $20,000
> − 4,000 (exempt wages)
> $16,000 × .058 = $928 SUTA

Federal FUTA tax would then be:

> $16,000 × .008 = $128

You can check your progress with the following Practice Quiz.

LU 9–2 PRACTICE QUIZ

1. Calculate Social Security taxes, Medicare taxes, and FIT for Joy Royce. Joy's company pays her a monthly salary of $9,500. She is single and claims 1 deduction. Before this payroll, Joy's cumulative earnings were $94,000. (Social Security maximum is 6.2% on $97,500, and Medicare is 1.45%.) Calculate FIT by the percentage method.

2. Jim Brewer, owner of Arrow Company, has three employees who earn $300, $700, and $900 a week. Assume a state SUTA rate of 5.1%. What will Jim pay for state and federal unemployment taxes for the first quarter?

✓ **Solutions**

1. **Social Security**   **Medicare**

    $97,500 $9,500 × .0145 = $137.75
    − 94,000
    ─────────
    $ 3,500 × .062 = $217.00

    FIT
    Percentage method: $9,500.00
    $283.33 × 1 =   −   283.33 (Table 9.1)
                         ──────────
                         $9,216.67

                                        $6,423 to $13,567 → $1,262.20 plus 28% of excess over $6,423
                                                                                        (Table 9.2)

        $9,216.67
        − 6,423.00
        ──────────
        $2,793.67 × .28 = $ 782.23*
                          + 1,262.20
                          ──────────
                          $2,044.43

    *Due to rounding.

2. 13 weeks × $300 = $ 3,900
    13 weeks × $700 =   9,100 ($9,100 − $7,000) → $2,100 ⎫ Exempt wages
    13 weeks × $900 = 11,700 ($11,700 − $7,000) →   4,700 ⎬ (not taxed for
                      ───────   ─────── ⎭ FUTA or SUTA)
                      $24,700 $6,800

    $24,700 − $6,800 = $17,900 taxable wages   *Note:* FUTA remains at .008
    SUTA = .051 × $17,900 = $912.90   whether SUTA rate is higher
    FUTA = .008 × $17,900 = $143.20   or lower than standard.

LU 9–2a EXTRA PRACTICE QUIZ

1. Calculate Social Security taxes, Medicare taxes, and FIT for Joy Royce. Joy's company pays her a monthly salary of $10,000. She is single and claims 1 deduction. Before this payroll, Joy's cumulative earnings were $97,000. (Social Security maximum is 6.2% on $97,500, and Medicare is 1.45%.) Calculate FIT by the percentage method.

2. Jim Brewer, owner of Arrow Company, has three employees who earn $200, $800, and $950 a week. Assume a state SUTA rate of 5.1%. What will Jim pay for state and federal unemployment taxes for the first quarter?

CHAPTER ORGANIZER AND STUDY GUIDE
WITH CHECK FIGURES FOR EXTRA PRACTICE QUIZZES

Topic	Key point, procedure, formula	Example(s) to illustrate situation
Gross pay, p. 237	$$\text{Hours employee} \atop \text{worked} \times {\text{Rate per} \atop \text{hour}}$$	$6.50 per hour at 36 hours Gross pay = 36 × $6.50 = $234
Overtime, p. 237	$$\text{Gross} \atop \text{earnings} = {\text{Regular} \atop \text{pay}} + {\text{Earnings at} \atop \text{overtime rate}}$$ (pay) $(1\frac{1}{2})$	$6 per hour; 42 hours Gross pay = (40 × $6) + (2 × $9) = $240 + $18 = $258
Straight piece rate, p. 238	$$\text{Gross} \atop \text{pay} = {\text{Number of units} \atop \text{produced}} \times {\text{Rate per} \atop \text{unit}}$$	1,185 units; rate per unit, $.89 Gross pay = 1,185 × $.89 = $1,054.65
Differential pay schedule, p. 238	Rate on each item is related to the number of items produced.	1–500 at $.84; 501–1,000 at $.96; 900 units produced. $$\text{Gross} \atop \text{pay} = (500 \times \$.84) + (400 \times \$.96)$$ = $420 + $384 = $804
Straight commission, p. 239	Total sales × Commission rate Any draw would be subtracted from earnings.	$155,000 sales; 6% commission $155,000 × .06 = $9,300

Variable commission scale, p. 239	Sales at different levels pay different rates of commission.	Up to $5,000, 5%; $5,001 to $10,000, 8%; over $10,000, 10%
		 Sold: $6,500
		 Solution:
		    ($5,000 × .05) + ($1,500 × .08)
		       = $250 + $120 = $370

Salary plus commission, p. 239	$$\text{Regular wages} \atop \text{(fixed)} + {\text{Commissions} \atop \text{earned}}$$	Base $400 per week + 2% on sales over $14,000 Actual sales: $16,000 $400 (base) + (.02 × $2,000) = $440
Payroll register, p. 241	Multicolumn form to record payroll. Married and paid weekly. (Table 9.2) Claims 1 allowance. FICA rates from chapter.	(see table below)
FICA, p. 241 **Social Security** **Medicare**	6.2% on $97,500 (S.S.) 1.45% (Med.)	If John earns $99,000, what did he contribute for the year to Social Security and Medicare? S.S.: $97,500 × .062 = $6,045.00 Med.: $99,000 × .0145 = $1,435.50

FIT calculation (percentage method), p. 242	*Facts:*
	   Al Doe: Married
	   Claims: 2
	   Paid weekly: $1,600
		$1,600.00
		 − 130.76 ($65.38 × 2) Table 9.1
		 $1,469.24
		 By Table 9.2
		   $1,469.24
		   − 1,360.00
		   $ 109.24
		 $166.15 + .25($109.24)
		 $166.15 + $27.31 = $193.46

Payroll register table:

	Deductions			Net
Earnings	FICA			pay
Gross	S.S.	Med.	FIT	
1,100	68.20	15.95	117.34	898.51

(continues)

CHAPTER ORGANIZER AND STUDY GUIDE
WITH CHECK FIGURES FOR EXTRA PRACTICE QUIZZES (concluded)

Topic	Key point, procedure, formula	Example(s) to illustrate situation
State and federal unemployment, p. 244	Employer pays these taxes. Rates are 6.2% on $7,000 for federal and 5.4% for state on $7,000. 6.2% − 5.4% = .8% federal rate after credit. If state unemployment rate is higher than 5.4%, no additional credit is taken. If state unemployment rate is less than 5.4%, the full 5.4% credit can be taken for federal unemployment.	Cumulative pay before payroll, $6,400; this week's pay, $800. What are state and federal unemployment taxes for employer, assuming a 5.2% state unemployment rate? State → .052 × $600 = $31.20 Federal → .008 × $600 = $4.80 ($6,400 + $600 = $7,000 maximum)

KEY TERMS	Biweekly, *p. 236*
	Deductions, *p. 237*
	Differential pay
	  schedule, *p. 238*
	Draw, *p. 239*
	Employee's Withholding
	  Allowance Certificate
	  (W-4), *p. 241*
	Fair Labor Standards
	  Act, *p. 237*
	Federal income tax
	  withholding (FIT), *p. 242* — Federal Insurance
	  Contribution Act
	  (FICA), *p. 241*
	Federal Unemployment
	  Tax Act (FUTA), *p. 244*
	Gross pay, *p. 237*
	Medicare, *p. 241*
	Monthly, *p. 236*
	Net pay, *p. 242*
	Overrides, *p. 239*
	Overtime, *p. 237*
	Payroll register, *p. 240* — Percentage method, *p. 242*
	Semimonthly, *p. 236*
	Social Security, *p. 241*
	State income tax
	  (SIT), *p. 242*
	State Unemployment Tax Act
	  (SUTA), *p. 244*
	Straight commission, *p. 239*
	Variable commission
	  scale, *p. 239*
	W-4, *p. 241*
	Weekly, *p. 236*	

CHECK FIGURES FOR EXTRA PRACTICE QUIZZES WITH PAGE REFERENCES	LU 9–1a (p. 240) 1. $732 2. $12,800 3. $4,070	LU 9–2a (p. 245) 1. $31; 145; $2,184.43 2. $846.60; $132.80

Critical Thinking Discussion Questions

1. Explain the difference between biweekly and semimonthly. Explain what problems may develop if a retail store hires someone on straight commission to sell cosmetics.

2. Explain what each column of a payroll register records (p. 241) and how each number is calculated. Social Security tax is based on a specific rate and base; Medicare tax is based on a rate but no base. Do you think this is fair to all taxpayers?

3. What taxes are the responsibility of the employer? How can an employer benefit from a merit-rating system for state unemployment?

Classroom Notes

Name _____ Date _____

DRILL PROBLEMS

Complete the following table:

	Employee	M	T	W	Th	F	Hours	Rate per hour	Gross pay
9–1.	Tom Bradey	11	7	8	7	6		$7.50	
9–2.	Kristina Shaw	5	9	10	8	8		$8.10	

Complete the following table (assume the overtime for each employee is a time-and-a-half rate after 40 hours):

	Employee	M	T	W	Th	F	Sa	Total regular hours	Total overtime hours	Regular rate	Overtime rate	Gross earnings
9–3.	Blue	12	9	9	9	9	3			$8.00		
9–4.	Tagney	14	8	9	9	5	1			$7.60		

Calculate gross earnings:

	Worker	Number of units produced	Rate per unit	Gross earnings
9–5.	Lang	510	$2.10	
9–6.	Swan	846	$ .58	

Calculate the gross earnings for each apple picker based on the following differential pay scale:

1–1,000: $.03 each   1,001–1,600: $.05 each   Over 1,600: $.07 each

	Apple picker	Number of apples picked	Gross earnings
9–7.	Ryan	1,600	
9–8.	Rice	1,925	

	Employee	Total sales	Commission rate	Draw	End-of-month commission received
9–9.	Reese	$300,000	7%	$8,000	

Ron Company has the following commission schedule:

Commission rate	Sales
2%	Up to $80,000
3.5%	Excess of $80,000 to $100,000
4%	More than $100,000

Calculate the gross earnings of Ron Company's two employees:

	Employee	Total sales	Gross earnings
9–10.	Bill Moore	$ 70,000	
9–11.	Ron Ear	$155,000	

Complete the following table, given that A Publishing Company pays its salespeople a weekly salary plus a 2% commission on all net sales over $5,000 (no commission on returned goods):

	Employee	Gross sales	Return	Net sales	Given quota	Commission sales	Commission rates	Total commission	Regular wage	Total wage
9–12.	Ring	$ 8,000	$ 25		$5,000		2%		$250	
9–13.	Porter	$12,000	$100		$5,000		2%		$250	

Calculate the Social Security and Medicare deductions for the following employees (assume a tax rate of 6.2% on $97,500 for Social Security and 1.45% for Medicare):

	Employee	Cumulative earnings before this pay period	Pay amount this period	Social Security	Medicare
9–14.	Lee	$96,500	$2,000		
9–15.	Chin	$90,000	$8,000		
9–16.	Davis	$500,000	$4,000		

Complete the following payroll register. Calculate FIT by the percentage method for this weekly period; Social Security and Medicare are the same rates as in the previous problems. No one will reach the maximum for FICA.

	Employee	Marital status	Allowances claimed	Gross pay	FIT	FICA S.S.	FICA Med.	Net pay
9–17.	Jim Day	M	2	$1,400				
9–18.	Ursula Lang	M	4	$1,900				

9–19. Given the following, calculate the state (assume 5.3%) and federal unemployment taxes that the employer must pay for each of the first two quarters. The federal unemployment tax is .8% on the first $7,000.

PAYROLL SUMMARY		
	Quarter 1	Quarter 2
Bill Adams	$4,000	$ 8,000
Rich Haines	8,000	14,000
Alice Smooth	3,200	3,800

WORD PROBLEMS

9–20. On February 7, 2007 the *San Jose Mercury News* reported on Bay Area workers average pay. Bay Area workers pocketed 23 percent more pay last year than workers in Los Angeles with $26.10 compared to $21.21 an hour. Jim Moody, a Bay Area worker, worked $10\frac{1}{4}$, $8\frac{1}{2}$, $9\frac{3}{4}$, $8\frac{3}{4}$ and $9\frac{1}{4}$ hours last week. Jim is paid an overtime pay of 1.5 times his regular pay. What is Jim's total gross pay for the week? Round to the nearest cent.

9–21. *The Telegraph* (Nashau, NH) on December 6, 2006, described the living wage needed in New Hampshire. Jessica Bullard is a single parent with one child and claims 2. She needs to make $17.71 an hour to get by in Hillsborough County. However Jessica Bullard only earns $13.00 an hour. Jessica works 40 hours a week. Social Security tax is 6.2 percent and Medicare is 1.45 percent (a) What is her gross pay per week? (b) How much is deducted for Social Security Tax? (c) How much is deducted for Medicare? (d) How much is withheld for FIT, assuming she claims 2? (e) What is her net pay? Round to the nearest cent.

9–22. The Social Security Administration increased the taxable wage base from $94,200 to $97,500. The 6.2% tax rate is unchanged. Joe Burns earned over $100,000 each of the past two years. **(a)** What is the percent increase in the base? Round to the nearest hundredth percent. **(b)** What is Joe's increase in Social Security tax for the new year?

9–23. Dennis Toby is a salesclerk at Northwest Department Store. Dennis receives $8 per hour plus a commission of 3% on all sales. Assume Dennis works 30 hours and has sales of $1,900. What is his gross pay?

9–24. Owing to a bill signed by Governor Arnold Schwarzenegger that increased the minimum wage from $6.75 to $8.00 an hour, by 2008, *The Business Press* (San Bernardino, CA) on September 18, 2006 reports firms are weighing leaving the state. Donna Carter, single, works 37 hours per week with one withholding exemption. Using the same percentage withholding for wages paid in 2007, (a) what is the amount of FIT withheld for 2007? (b) What would be the amount of FIT withheld for 2008? Round to the nearest cent.

9–25. Robin Hartman earns $600 per week plus 3% of sales over $6,500. Robin's sales are $14,000. How much does Robin earn?

9–26. Pat Maninen earns a gross salary of $2,100 each week. What are Pat's first week's deductions for Social Security and Medicare? Will any of Pat's wages be exempt from Social Security and Medicare for the calendar year? Assume a rate of 6.2% on $97,500 for Social Security and 1.45% for Medicare.

9–27. Richard Gaziano is a manager for Health Care, Inc. Health Care deducts Social Security, Medicare, and FIT (by percentage method) from his earnings. Assume the same Social Security and Medicare rates as in Problem 9–26. Before this payroll, Richard is $1,000 below the maximum level for Social Security earnings. Richard is married, is paid weekly, and claims 2 exemptions. What is Richard's net pay for the week if he earns $1,300?

9–28. Len Mast earned $2,200 for the last two weeks. He is married, is paid biweekly, and claims 3 exemptions. What is Len's income tax? Use the percentage method.

9–29. Westway Company pays Suzie Chan $2,200 per week. By the end of week 50, how much did Westway deduct for Suzie's Social Security and Medicare for the year? Assume Social Security is 6.2% on $97,500 and 1.45% for Medicare. What state and federal unemployment taxes does Westway pay on Suzie's yearly salary? The state unemployment rate is 5.1%. FUTA is .8%.

9–30. Morris Leste, owner of Carlson Company, has three employees who earn $400, $500, and $700 per week. What are the total state and federal unemployment taxes that Morris owes for the first 11 weeks of the year and for week 30? Assume a state rate of 5.6% and a federal rate of .8%.

CHALLENGE PROBLEMS

9–31. The Victorville, California, *Daily Press* stated that the San Bernardino County Fair hires about 150 people during fair time. Their wages range from $6.75 to $8.00. California has a state income tax of 9%. Sandy Denny earns $8.00 per hour; George Barney earns $6.75 per hour. They both worked 35 hours this week. Both are married; however, Sandy claims 2 exemptions and George claims 1 exemption. Assume a rate of 6.2% on $97,500 for Social Security and 1.45% for Medicare. **(a)** What is Sandy's net pay after FIT, Social Security tax, state income tax, and Medicare have been taken out? **(b)** What is George's net pay after the same deductions? **(c)** How much more is Sandy's net pay versus George's net pay? Round to the nearest cent.

9–32. Bill Rose is a salesperson for Boxes, Inc. He believes his $1,460.47 monthly paycheck is in error. Bill earns a $1,400 salary per month plus a 9.5% commission on sales over $1,500. Last month, Bill had $8,250 in sales. Bill believes his traveling expenses are 16% of his weekly gross earnings before commissions. Monthly deductions include Social Security, $126.56; Medicare, $29.60; FIT, $239.29; union dues, $25.00; and health insurance, $16.99. Calculate the following: **(a)** Bill's monthly take-home pay, and indicate the amount his check was under- or overstated, and **(b)** Bill's weekly traveling expenses. Round your final answer to the nearest dollar.

SUMMARY PRACTICE TEST

1. Calculate Sam's gross pay (he is entitled to time-and-a-half). *(p. 237)*

M	T	W	Th	F	Total hours	Rate per hour	Gross pay
$9\frac{1}{4}$	$9\frac{1}{4}$	$10\frac{1}{2}$	$8\frac{1}{2}$	$11\frac{1}{2}$		\$8.00	

2. Mia Kaminsky sells shoes for Macy's. Macy's pays Mia \$12 per hour plus a 5% commission on all sales. Assume Mia works 37 hours for the week and has \$7,000 in sales. What is Mia's gross pay? *(p. 237)*

3. Lee Company pays its employees on a graduated commission scale: 6% on the first \$40,000 sales, 7% on sales from \$40,001 to \$80,000, and 13% on sales of more than \$80,000. May West, an employee of Lee, has \$230,000 in sales. What commission did May earn? *(p. 239)*

4. Matty Kim, an accountant for Vernitron, earned \$90,000 from January to June. In July, Matty earned \$20,000. Assume a tax rate of 6.2% for Social Security on \$97,500 and 1.45% on Medicare. How much are the July taxes for Social Security and Medicare? *(p. 241)*

5. Grace Kelley earns \$2,000 per week. She is married and claims 2 exemptions. What is Grace's income tax? Use the percentage method. *(p. 242)*

6. Jean Michaud pays his two employees \$900 and \$1,200 per week. Assume a state unemployment tax rate of 5.7% and a federal unemployment tax rate of .8%. What state and federal unemployment taxes will Jean pay at the end of quarter 1 and quarter 2? *(p. 244)*

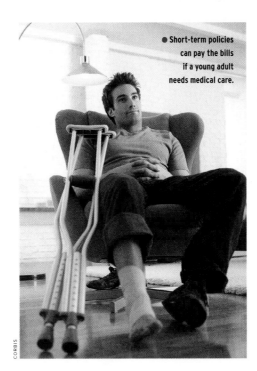

● Short-term policies can pay the bills if a young adult needs medical care.

CORBIS

INSURANCE | Earning a diploma often means losing medical coverage.

HEALTHY choices

Although finding a job may be the top priority for most new college graduates, parents are often more concerned about continuing their children's health coverage. Insurers typically drop kids from their parents' health plan once they grab that diploma (or by the time they turn 25).

Sandy D'Annunzio, a nurse in Sterling Heights, Mich., bought short-term health-insurance policies from Golden Rule (www .goldenrule.com) for her two daughters, Jennifer and Kelly. D'Annunzio pays about $57 a month for each policy, both of which have a $1,000 deductible and 20% co-insurance (meaning the insurer picks up 80% of a claim after the deductible is met). "If one of them broke a leg, it could cost 70 times as much," says D'Annunzio.

Most short-term policies last six months to a year, after which you may reapply, as long as you remain healthy. But they don't typically cover preventive care or preexisting conditions, so they're really just a temporary fix.

For longer coverage, consider an individual policy with a high deductible. For a policy with a $1,500 deductible and 20% co-insurance, a young female nonsmoker would pay $124 per month in Chicago. That's more expensive than short-term insurance, but it covers many of the medical expenses that short-term policies exclude.

If graduation is still a few months away, buying student health insurance may be a cheaper way to go. But don't delay. Assurant Health, a major provider of such plans, requires that coverage begin at least 31 days *before* a student graduates.

Like short-term health insurance, student health coverage has a long list of exclusions. But in most cases, it is less expensive than a short-term policy and is renewable. For example, a 22-year-old female nonsmoker in Chicago would pay $66 a month for a student health policy with a $1,000 deductible and 20% co-insurance through eHealthInsurance.com. A similar short-term policy would cost $104 a month.

If your child has a medical condition, such as asthma or depression, buying individual health insurance can be tough. In that case, take advantage of COBRA; the law allows your adult child to remain on your policy for up to 36 months. COBRA coverage isn't cheap because you have to pay both the employer share and the employee share of your group premium, but it can serve as a safety net while you look into other options. A number of states are taking steps to extend coverage for young adults.
—THOMAS M. ANDERSON

BUSINESS MATH ISSUE

If you're young you really don't need health insurance.

1. List the key points of the article and information to support your position.
2. Write a group defense of your position using math calculations to support your view.

Slater's Business Math Scrapbook

with Internet Application

Putting Your Skills to Work

PROJECT A

Do you think FedEx employees should be independent contractors?

FedEx Introduces Concessions To Drivers Amid Labor Discord

By COREY DADE

FedEx Corp., facing mounting regulatory and labor challenges to the use of independent contractors to drive delivery trucks in its FedEx Ground unit, is quietly rolling out concessions to more than 15,000 drivers.

The move comes as the Memphis, Tenn., company was dealt the latest in a series of setbacks on the issue Friday. The National Labor Relations Board announced that 32 drivers at two ground terminals in Wilmington, Mass., voted to join the International Brotherhood of Teamsters.

In part to quell complaints and head off further union efforts, FedEx, which is challenging the vote, recently began stationing 18 contractor "advocates," some pulled from the ranks of contract drivers, across North America. The company says they are responsible for helping drivers increase their shipment volumes, solve problems they might have with management, and other duties. The company also is creating an executive position in charge of contractor relations, reporting directly to the head of the ground unit. FedEx also has increased fuel subsidies to drivers who operate multiple trucks and is eliminating some fines on drivers resulting from customer claims of failed deliveries.

The Teamsters have targeted FedEx Ground, which specializes in lower-cost deliveries using a ground-based truck network, as one of its top priorities in a push to build membership. The union already represents nearly 250,000 drivers and others at **United Parcel Service** Inc. Sean O'Brien, president of the Teamsters Local 25 in Boston, said the FedEx vote was "historical and should also be inspirational to labor across the country."

The only major employee group represented by a union at FedEx is its pilots, and the company has argued strongly that its employees don't need or want union representation. Drivers in the company's FedEx Ground unit are classified not as employees but independent contractors who own and manage their own vehicles, routes and schedules. As contractors, they are also unable to organize themselves as a union and engage in collective bargaining with the company.

But several drivers, some with the backing of the Teamsters, recently have challenged their classification as independent contractors, saying FedEx doesn't actually allow them to set their own schedules or manage their business affairs. A California court determined that a group of drivers in that state were employees and ordered FedEx to pay the workers $5.3 million as part of an $18 million award. FedEx is appealing and oral arguments are scheduled to begin on Tuesday.

Wall Street Journal © 2006

PROJECT B

Why do you think Indian law forbids overtime?

A Stitch in Time

Orient Craft could boost capacity by 25% at its New Delhi factories, such as the one above, if workers did two extra hours of overtime a day, something not allowed under Indian law, says the company's chairman. At right, combined U.S. and EU clothing imports from India and China, from January through July, in billions

China	2004	$14.1
	2005	$22.0
India		$3.8
		$4.9

Sources: International Labor Organization; Global Trade Atlas

Wall Street Journal © 2006

Internet Projects: See text Web site (www.mhhe.com/slater9e) and The Business Math Internet Resource Guide.

Video Case

Washburn International, founded in 1883, makes 80 models of instruments, both custom and for the mass market. Washburn is a privately held company with over 100 employees and annual sales of $48 million. This compares to its annual sales of $300,000 when Rudy Schlacher took over in 1976. When he acquired the company, about 250 guitars were produced per month; now 15,000 are produced each month.

The Washburn tradition of craftsmanship and innovation has withstood the tests of economics, brand competition, and fashion. Since its birth in Chicago, the name Washburn has been branded into the world's finest stringed instruments. To maintain quality, Washburn must have an excellent pool of qualified employees who are passionate about craftsmanship.

Washburn consolidated its four divisions in an expansive new 130,000 square foot plant in Mundelein, Illinois. The catalyst for consolidating operations in Mundelein was a chronic labor shortage in Elkhart and Chicago. The Mundelein plant was the ideal home for all Washburn operations because it had the necessary space, was cost effective, and gave Washburn access to a labor pool.

To grow profitably, Washburn must also sell its other products. To keep Washburn's 16 domestic salespeople tuned in to the full line, the company offers an override incentive. It is essential that to produce quality guitars, Washburn must keep recruiting dedicated, well-qualified, and team-oriented employees and provide them with profitable incentives.

PROBLEM 1

$120,000 was paid to 16 of Washburn's salespeople in override commissions. **(a)** What was the average amount paid to each salesperson? **(b)** What amount of the average sales commission will go toward the salesperson's Social Security tax? **(c)** What amount will go toward Medicare?

PROBLEM 2

Washburn is seeking a Sales and Marketing Coordinator with a bachelor's degree or equivalent experience, knowledgeable in Microsoft Office. This position pays $25,000 to $35,000, depending on experience. Assume a person is paid weekly and earns $32,500. Using the percentage method, what would be the taxes withheld for a married person who claims 3 exemptions?

PROBLEM 3

Guitarists hoping for a little country music magic in their playing can now buy an instrument carved out of oak pews from the former home of the Grand Ole Opry. Only 243 of the Ryman Limited Edition Acoustic Guitars are being made, each costing $6,250. Among the first customers were singers Vince Gill, Amy Grant, and Loretta Lynn, Ms. Lynn purchased two guitars. What would be the total revenue received by Washburn if all the guitars are sold?

PROBLEM 4

Under Washburn's old pay system, phone reps received a commission of 1.5% only on instruments they sold. Now the phone reps are paid an extra .75% commission on field sales made in their territory; the outside salespeople still get a commission up to 8%, freeing them to focus on introducing new products and holding in-store clinics. Assume sales were $65,500: **(a)** How much would phone reps receive? **(b)** How much would the outside salespeople receive?

PROBLEM 5

Washburn introduced the Limited Edition EA27 Gregg Allman Signature Series Festival guitar—only 500 guitars were produced with a selling price of $1,449.90. If Washburn's markup is 35% on selling price, what was Washburn's total cost for the 500 guitars?

PROBLEM 6

Retailers purchased $511 million worth of guitars from manufacturers—some 861,300 guitars—according to a study done by the National Association of Music Merchants. **(a)** What would be the average selling price of a guitar? **(b)** Based on the average selling price, if manufacturer's markup on cost is 40%, what would be the average cost?

PROBLEM 7

A Model NV 300 acoustic-electric guitar is being sold for a list price of $1,899.90, with a cash discount of 3/10, n/30. Sales tax is 7% and shipping is $30.40. How much is the final price if the cash discount period was met?

PROBLEM 8

A Model M3SWE mandolin has a list price of $1,299.90, with a chain discount of 5/3/2. **(a)** What would be the trade discount amount? **(b)** What would be the net price?

PROBLEM 9

A purchase was made of 2 Model J282DL six-string acoustic guitars at $799.90 each, with cases priced at $159.90, and 3 Model EA10 festival series acoustic-electric guitars at $729.90, with cases listed at $149.90. If sales tax is 6%, what is the total cost?

PROBLEM 10

Production of guitars has increased by what percent since Rudy Schlacher took over Washburn?

CHAPTER 10

Simple Interest

Ask Personal Journal.

Q: *Is a bank's insolvency all that the FDIC insures for and only up to $100,000? Do banks cover situations like fraud or identity theft?*
—LAUREL GONSALVES, NEW YORK

A: The Federal Deposit Insurance Corp. insures deposits only when banks fail and only up to $100,000. Customers tend to get about 72 to 73 cents for each dollar above that, the FDIC says. As for unauthorized transactions, your bank will generally refund the full amount if you notify it in a timely manner, says Nessa Feddis, senior federal counsel for the American Bankers Association. How soon you have to notify your bank and your liability (typically $50 to $500) depends on the transaction, since electronic and paper transactions fall under different laws. Your bank will typically investigate to make sure you didn't give authorization. If a relative or friend was responsible for a fraud, you may have trouble getting your money.
—*Jennifer Saranow*

Wall Street Journal © 2005

LEARNING UNIT OBJECTIVES

LU 10–1: Calculation of Simple Interest and Maturity Value

- Calculate simple interest and maturity value for months and years *(p. 259).*
- Calculate simple interest and maturity value by **(a)** exact interest and **(b)** ordinary interest *(pp. 260–261).*

LU 10–2: Finding Unknown in Simple Interest Formula

- Using the interest formula, calculate the unknown when the other two (principal, rate, or time) are given *(pp. 262–263).*

LU 10–3: U.S. Rule—Making Partial Note Payments before Due Date

- List the steps to complete the U.S. Rule *(pp. 264–265).*
- Complete the proper interest credits under the U.S. Rule *(pp. 264–265).*

Digital Vision/Getty Images

Major Issuers Boost Costs For Late Payments Past 30% Amid Rising Interest Rates

By JANE J. KIM

Being late on your credit-card payments has never been more expensive, as penalty rates among major credit-card issuers hit new highs.

Some major issuers, including **J.P. Morgan Chase** & Co., **Citigroup** Inc.'s Citibank and **Bank of America** Corp., are now charging maximum penalty rates that have edged past 30%. Although some banks charge a fixed penalty rate, other rates are typically tied to the prime rate—

the rate banks charge their best customers–plus a fixed percentage that varies by bank. Now, many of those variable rates are expected to climb even higher given the Federal Reserve's increase in the short-term interest rate to 3.5% this week, which pushes the prime rate to 6.5%.

Penalty rates, which become the new rate paid on any outstanding balances, typically kick in when cardholders are late on a payment or two, exceed their credit limit or bounce a check. Bank of America's penalty rate, for example, could apply if cardholders miss two consecutive payments or are past due two times within a six-month period, according to a company spokeswoman.

Wall Street Journal © 2005

Are you careless about making your credit payments on time? Do you realize that some penalty rates can increase when the Federal Reserve increases its short-term interest rate? The *Wall Street Journal* clipping "Major Issuers Boost Costs for Late Payment Past 30% Amid Rising Interest Rates" shows how expensive it can be if you do not pay your credit bills on time, if you bounce checks, or if you exceed your credit limit.

In this chapter, you will study simple interest. The principles discussed apply whether you are paying interest or receiving interest. Let's begin by learning how to calculate simple interest.

Learning Unit 10–1: Calculation of Simple Interest and Maturity Value

Jan Carley, a young attorney, rented an office in a professional building. Since Jan recently graduated from law school, she was short of cash. To purchase office furniture for her new office, Jan went to her bank and borrowed $30,000 for 6 months at an 8% annual interest rate.

The original amount Jan borrowed ($30,000) is the **principal** (face value) of the loan. Jan's price for using the $30,000 is the interest rate (8%) the bank charges on a yearly basis. Since Jan is borrowing the $30,000 for 6 months, Jan's loan will have a **maturity value** of $31,200—the principal plus the interest on the loan. Thus, Jan's price for using the furniture before she can pay for it is $1,200 interest, which is a percent of the principal for a specific time period. To make this calculation, we use the following formula:

$$\text{Maturity value } (MV) = \text{Principal } (P) + \text{Interest } (I)$$

$$\$31,200 \quad = \quad \$30,000 \quad + \quad \$1,200$$

Jan's furniture purchase introduces **simple interest**—the cost of a loan, usually for 1 year or less. Simple interest is only on the original principal or amount borrowed. Let's examine how the bank calculated Jan's $1,200 interest.

Simple Interest Formula

To calculate simple interest, we use the following **simple interest formula**:

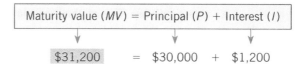

$$\text{Simple interest } (I) = \text{Principal } (P) \times \text{Rate } (R) \times \text{Time } (T)$$

In this formula, rate is expressed as a decimal, fraction, or percent; and time is expressed in years or a fraction of a year.

EXAMPLE Jan Carley borrowed $30,000 for office furniture. The loan was for 6 months at an annual interest rate of 8%. What are Jan's interest and maturity value?

Using the simple interest formula, the bank determined Jan's interest as follows:

In your calculator, multiply $30,000 times .08 times 6. Divide your answer by 12. You could also use the % key—multiply $30,000 times 8% times 6 and then divide your answer by 12.

Step 1. Calculate the interest.

$$I = \$30,000 \times .08 \times \frac{6}{12}$$
$$\quad (P) \qquad (R) \quad (T)$$
$$= \$1,200$$

Step 2. Calculate the maturity value.

$$MV = \$30,000 + \$1,200$$
$$\qquad (P) \qquad\quad (I)$$
$$= \boxed{\$31,200}$$

Now let's use the same example and assume Jan borrowed $30,000 for 1 year. The bank would calculate Jan's interest and maturity value as follows:

Step 1. Calculate the interest.

$$I = \$30,000 \times .08 \times 1 \text{ year}$$
$$\quad (P) \qquad (R) \qquad (T)$$
$$= \$2,400$$

Step 2. Calculate the maturity value.

$$MV = \$30,000 + \$2,400$$
$$\qquad (P) \qquad\quad (I)$$
$$= \boxed{\$32,400}$$

Let's use the same example again and assume Jan borrowed $30,000 for 18 months. Then Jan's interest and maturity value would be calculated as follows:

Step 1. Calculate the interest.

$$I = \$30,000 \times .08 \times \frac{18^1}{12}$$
$$\quad (P) \qquad (R) \quad (T)$$
$$= \$3,600$$

Step 2. Calculate the maturity value.

$$MV = \$30,000 + \$3,600$$
$$\qquad (P) \qquad\quad (I)$$
$$= \boxed{\$33,600}$$

Next we'll turn our attention to two common methods we can use to calculate simple interest when a loan specifies its beginning and ending dates.

Two Methods for Calculating Simple Interest and Maturity Value

Method 1: Exact Interest (365 Days) The Federal Reserve banks and the federal government use the **exact interest** method. The *exact interest* is calculated by using a 365-day year. For **time,** we count the exact number of days in the month that the borrower has the loan. The day the loan is made is not counted, but the day the money is returned is counted as a full day. This method calculates interest by using the following fraction to represent time in the formula:

From the *Business Math Handbook*

July 6	187th day
March 4	− 63rd day
	124 days
	(exact time of loan)
March	31
	− 4
	27
April	30
May	31
June	30
July	+ 6
	124 days

$$\text{Time} = \frac{\text{Exact number of days}}{365} \longleftarrow \text{Exact interest}$$

For this calculation, we use the exact days-in-a-year calendar from the *Business Math Handbook.* You learned how to use this calendar in Chapter 7, p. 181.

EXAMPLE On March 4, Peg Carry borrowed $40,000 at 8% interest. Interest and principal are due on July 6. What is the interest cost and the maturity value?

Step 1. Calculate the interest.

$$I = P \times R \times T$$
$$= \$40,000 \times .08 \times \frac{124}{365}$$
$$= \$1,087.12 \text{ (rounded to nearest cent)}$$

¹This is the same as 1.5 years.

Step 2. Calculate the maturity value.

$$MV = P + I$$
$$= \$40,000 + \$1,087.12$$
$$= \boxed{\$41,087.12}$$

Method 2: Ordinary Interest (360 Days) In the **ordinary interest** method, time in the formula $I = P \times R \times T$ is equal to the following:

$$\text{Time} = \frac{\text{Exact number of days}}{360} \longleftarrow \text{Ordinary interest}$$

Since banks commonly use the ordinary interest method, it is known as the **Banker's Rule.** Banks charge a slightly higher rate of interest because they use 360 days instead of 365 in the denominator. By using 360 instead of 365, the calculation is supposedly simplified. Consumer groups, however, are questioning why banks can use 360 days, since this benefits the bank and not the customer. The use of computers and calculators no longer makes the simplified calculation necessary. For example, after a court case in Oregon, banks began calculating interest on 365 days except in mortgages.

Now let's replay the Peg Carry example we used to illustrate Method 1 to see the difference in bank interest when we use Method 2.

EXAMPLE On March 4, Peg Carry borrowed $40,000 at 8% interest. Interest and principal are due on July 6. What are the interest cost and the maturity value?

Step 1. Calculate the interest.

$$I = \$40,000 \times .08 \times \frac{124}{360}$$
$$= \$1,102.22$$

Step 2. Calculate the maturity value.

$$MV = P + I$$
$$= \$40,000 + \$1,102.22$$
$$= \boxed{\$41,102.22}$$

Note: By using Method 2, the bank increases its interest by $15.10.

$$\begin{array}{l} \$1,102.22 \longleftarrow \text{Method 2} \\ \underline{-\ 1,087.12} \\ \$\quad 15.10 \longleftarrow \text{Method 1} \end{array}$$

Now you should be ready for your first Practice Quiz in this chapter.

LU 10–1 PRACTICE QUIZ

Complete this **Practice Quiz** to see how you are doing

Calculate simple interest (round to the nearest cent):

1. $14,000 at 4% for 9 months   **2.** $25,000 at 7% for 5 years

3. $40,000 at $10\frac{1}{2}$% for 19 months

4. On May 4, Dawn Kristal borrowed $15,000 at 8%. Dawn must pay the principal and interest on August 10. What are Dawn's simple interest and maturity value if you use the exact interest method?

5. What are Dawn Kristal's (Problem 4) simple interest and maturity value if you use the ordinary interest method?

✓ **Solutions**

1. $\$14,000 \times .04 \times \dfrac{9}{12} = \boxed{\$420}$

2. $\$25,000 \times .07 \times 5 = \boxed{\$8,750}$

3. $\$40,000 \times .105 \times \dfrac{19}{12} = \boxed{\$6,650}$

4. August 10 ⟶   222 $15,000 × .08 × $\dfrac{98}{365}$ = $322.19

      May 4   ⟶   − 124

                         98   *MV* = $15,000 + $322.19 = $15,322.19

5. $15,000 × .08 × $\dfrac{98}{360}$ = $326.67   *MV* = $15,000 + $326.67 = $15,326.67

LU 10–1a   **EXTRA PRACTICE QUIZ**

Need more practice? Try this **Extra Practice Quiz** (check figures in Chapter Organizer, p. 267)

Calculate simple interest (round to the nearest cent):

1. $16,000 at 3% for 8 months
2. $15,000 at 6% for 6 years
3. $50,000 at 7% for 18 months
4. On May 6, Dawn Kristal borrowed $20,000 at 7%. Dawn must pay the principal and interest on August 14. What are Dawn's simple interest and maturity value if you use the exact interest method?
5. What are Dawn Kristal's (Problem 4) simple interest and maturity value if you use the ordinary interest method?

Learning Unit 10–2: Finding Unknown in Simple Interest Formula

This unit begins with the formula used to calculate the principal of a loan. Then it explains how to find the *principal*, *rate*, and *time* of a simple interest loan. In all the calculations, we use 360 days and round only final answers.

Finding the Principal

EXAMPLE   Tim Jarvis paid the bank $19.48 interest at 9.5% for 90 days. How much did Tim borrow using ordinary interest method?

The following formula is used to calculate the principal of a loan:

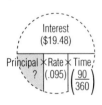

$$\text{Principal} = \frac{\text{Interest}}{\text{Rate} \times \text{Time}}$$

Note how we illustrated this in the margin. The shaded area is what we are solving for. When solving for principal, rate, or time, you are dividing. Interest will be in the numerator, and the denominator will be the other two elements multiplied by each other.

Step 1. Set up the formula.
$$P = \frac{\$19.48}{.095 \times \dfrac{90}{360}}$$

Step 2. When using a calculator, press
.095   ×   90   ÷   360   M+ .

Step 2. Multiply the denominator.
.095 times 90 divided by 360 (do not round)

$$P = \frac{\$19.48}{.02375}$$

Step 3. When using a calculator, press
19.48   ÷   MR   = .

Step 3. Divide the numerator by the result of Step 2. $P = \$820.21$

Step 4. Check your answer. $19.48 = $820.21 × .095 × $\dfrac{90}{360}$

                                    (*I*)   (*P*)   (*R*)   (*T*)

Finding the Rate

EXAMPLE   Tim Jarvis borrowed $820.21 from a bank. Tim's interest is $19.48 for 90 days. What rate of interest did Tim pay using ordinary interest method?

The following formula is used to calculate the rate of interest:

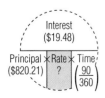

$$\text{Rate} = \frac{\text{Interest}}{\text{Principal} \times \text{Time}}$$

Step 1. Set up the formula. $R = \dfrac{\$19.48}{\$820.21 \times \dfrac{90}{360}}$

Step 2. Multiply the denominator. Do not round the answer. $R = \dfrac{\$19.48}{\$205.0525}$

Step 3. Divide the numerator by the result of Step 2. $\boxed{R = 9.5\%}$

Step 4. Check your answer. $\$19.48 = \$820.21 \times .095 \times \dfrac{90}{360}$

$\qquad\qquad\qquad\quad (I) \qquad\quad (P) \qquad (R) \qquad (T)$

Finding the Time

EXAMPLE Tim Jarvis borrowed \$820.21 from a bank. Tim's interest is \$19.48 at 9.5%. How much time does Tim have to repay the loan using ordinary interest method?

The following formula is used to calculate time:

$$\text{Time (in years)} = \frac{\text{Interest}}{\text{Principal} \times \text{Rate}}$$

Interest
($19.48)

Principal × Rate × Time
($820.21) (.095)   ?

Step 2. When using a calculator, press

820.21 × .095 M+ .

Step 3. When using a calculator, press

19.48 ÷ MR = .

Step 1. Set up the formula. $T = \dfrac{\$19.48}{\$820.21 \times .095}$

Step 2. Multiply the denominator. Do not round the answer. $T = \dfrac{\$19.48}{\$77.91995}$

Step 3. Divide the numerator by the result of Step 2. $T = .25 \text{ years}$

Step 4. Convert years to days (assume 360 days). $.25 \times 360 = \boxed{90 \text{ days}}$

Step 5. Check your answer. $\$19.48 = \$820.21 \times .095 \times \dfrac{90}{360}$

$\qquad\qquad\qquad\quad (I) \qquad\quad (P) \qquad (R) \qquad (T)$

Before we go on to Learning Unit 10–3, let's check your understanding of this unit.

LU 10–2 PRACTICE QUIZ

Complete this **Practice Quiz** to see how you are doing

Complete the following (assume 360 days):

	Principal	Interest rate	Time (days)	Simple interest
1.	?	5%	90 days	\$8,000
2.	\$7,000	?	220 days	350
3.	\$1,000	8%	?	300

✓ **Solutions**

1. $\dfrac{\$8,000}{.05 \times \dfrac{90}{360}} = \dfrac{\$8,000}{.0125} = \boxed{\$640,000}$ $\qquad P = \dfrac{I}{R \times T}$

2. $\dfrac{\$350}{\$7,000 \times \dfrac{220}{360}} = \dfrac{\$350}{\$4,277.7777} = \boxed{8.18\%}$ $\qquad R = \dfrac{I}{P \times T}$

(do not round)

3. $\dfrac{\$300}{\$1,000 \times .08} = \dfrac{\$300}{\$80} = 3.75 \times 360 = \boxed{1,350 \text{ days}}$ $\qquad T = \dfrac{I}{P \times R}$

Need more practice? Try this
Extra Practice Quiz (check
figures in Chapter Organizer,
p. 267)

Complete the following (assume 360 days):

	Principal	Interest rate	Time (days)	Simple interest
1.	?	4%	90 days	$9,000
2.	$6,000	?	180 days	280
3.	$900	6%	?	190

Learning Unit 10–3: U.S. Rule—Making Partial Note Payments before Due Date

Often a person may want to pay off a debt in more than one payment before the maturity date. The **U.S. Rule** allows the borrower to receive proper interest credits. This rule states that any partial loan payment first covers any interest that has built up. The remainder of the partial payment reduces the loan principal. Courts or legal proceedings generally use the U.S. Rule. The Supreme Court originated the U.S. Rule in the case of *Story* v. *Livingston*.

EXAMPLE   Joe Mill owes $5,000 on an 11%, 90-day note. On day 50, Joe pays $600 on the note. On day 80, Joe makes an $800 additional payment. Assume a 360-day year. What is Joe's adjusted balance after day 50 and after day 80? What is the ending balance due?
To calculate $600 payment on day 50:

Step 1. Calculate interest on principal from date of loan to date of first principal payment. Round to nearest cent.

$$I = P \times R \times T$$
$$I = \$5,000 \times .11 \times \frac{50}{360}$$
$$I = \$76.39$$

Step 2. Apply partial payment to interest due. Subtract remainder of payment from principal. This is the **adjusted balance** (principal).

$600.00 payment
−   76.39 interest
$523.61

$5,000.00   principal
−   523.61
$4,476.39 adjusted balance— principal

To calculate $800 payment on day 80:

Step 3. Calculate interest on adjusted balance that starts from previous payment date and goes to new payment date. Then apply Step 2.

Compute interest on $4,476.39 for 30 days (80 − 50)

$$I = \$4,476.39 \times .11 \times \frac{30}{360}$$
$$I = \$41.03$$

$800.00 payment
−   41.03 interest
$758.97

$4,476.39
−   758.97
$3,717.42 adjusted balance

Step 4. At maturity, calculate interest from last partial payment. *Add* this interest to adjusted balance.

Ten days are left on note since last payment.

$$I = \$3,717.42 \times .11 \times \frac{10}{360}$$
$$I = \$11.36$$

Balance owed = **$3,728.78** $\left(\begin{array}{c} \$3,717.42 \\ + \quad 11.36 \end{array}\right)$

Note that when Joe makes two partial payments, Joe's total interest is $128.78 ($76.39 + $41.03 + $11.36). If Joe had repaid the entire loan after 90 days, his interest payment would have been $137.50—a total savings of $8.72.

Let's check your understanding of the last unit in this chapter.

LU 10–3 | PRACTICE QUIZ

Complete this **Practice Quiz** to see how you are doing

Polly Flin borrowed $5,000 for 60 days at 8%. On day 10, Polly made a $600 partial payment. On day 40, Polly made a $1,900 partial payment. What is Polly's ending balance due under the U.S. Rule (assume a 360-day year)?

✓ Solutions

$$\$5,000 \times .08 \times \frac{10}{360} = \$11.11$$

$$
\begin{array}{r}
\$600.00 \\
-\ \ 11.11 \\
\hline
\$588.89
\end{array}
\qquad
\begin{array}{r}
\$5,000.00 \\
-\ \ 588.89 \\
\hline
\$4,411.11
\end{array}
$$

$$\$4,411.11 \times .08 \times \frac{30}{360} = \$29.41$$

$$
\begin{array}{r}
\$1,900.00 \\
-\ \ 29.41 \\
\hline
\$1,870.59
\end{array}
\qquad
\begin{array}{r}
\$4,411.11 \\
-\ 1,870.59 \\
\hline
\$2,540.52
\end{array}
$$

$$\$2,540.52 \times .08 \times \frac{20}{360} = \$11.29$$

$$
\begin{array}{r}
\$\ \ 11.29 \\
+\ 2,540.52 \\
\hline
\boxed{\$2,551.81}
\end{array}
$$

LU 10–3a | EXTRA PRACTICE QUIZ

Need more practice? Try this **Extra Practice Quiz** (check figures in Chapter Organizer, p. 267)

Polly Flin borrowed $4,000 for 60 days at 4%. On day 15, Polly made a $700 partial payment. On day 40, Polly made a $2,000 partial payment. What is Polly's ending balance due under the U.S. Rule (assume a 360-day year)?

CHAPTER ORGANIZER AND STUDY GUIDE
WITH CHECK FIGURES FOR EXTRA PRACTICE QUIZZES

Topic	Key point, procedure, formula	Example(s) to illustrate situation
Simple interest for months, p. 259	Interest = Principal × Rate × Time (*I*) (*P*) (*R*) (*T*)	$2,000 at 9% for 17 months $I = \$2,000 \times .09 \times \frac{17}{12}$ $I = \boxed{\$255}$
Exact interest, p. 260	$T = \dfrac{\text{Exact number of days}}{365}$ $I = P \times R \times T$	$1,000 at 10% from January 5 to February 20 $I = \$1,000 \times .10 \times \frac{46}{365}$ Feb. 20: 51 days Jan. 5: − 5 ─── 46 days $I = \boxed{\$12.60}$
Ordinary interest (Bankers Rule), p. 261	$T = \dfrac{\text{Exact number of days}}{360}$ $I = P \times R \times T$ \boxed{Higher interest costs}	$I = \$1,000 \times .10 \times \frac{46}{360}$ (51 − 5) $I = \boxed{\$12.78}$
Finding unknown in simple interest formula (use 360 days), p. 262	$I = P \times R \times T$	Use this example for illustrations of simple interest formula parts: $1,000 loan at 9%, 60 days $I = \$1,000 \times .09 \times \frac{60}{360} = \boxed{\$15}$

CHAPTER ORGANIZER AND STUDY GUIDE
WITH CHECK FIGURES FOR EXTRA PRACTICE QUIZZES (continued)

Topic	Key point, procedure, formula	Example(s) to illustrate situation
Finding the principal, p. 262	$P = \dfrac{I}{R \times T}$	$P = \dfrac{\$15}{.09 \times \dfrac{60}{360}} = \dfrac{\$15}{.015} = \boxed{\$1,000}$
Finding the rate, p. 262	$R = \dfrac{I}{P \times T}$	$R = \dfrac{\$15}{\$1,000 \times \dfrac{60}{360}} = \dfrac{\$15}{166.66666} = .09$ $= \boxed{9\%}$ *Note:* We did not round the denominator.
Finding the time, p. 263	$T = \dfrac{I}{P \times R}$ (in years) Multiply answer by 360 days to convert answer to days for ordinary interest.	$T = \dfrac{\$15}{\$1,000 \times .09} = \dfrac{\$15}{\$90} = .1666666$ $.1666666 \times 360 = 59.99 = \boxed{60\ days}$

U.S. Rule (use 360 days), p. 264	Calculate interest on principal from date of loan to date of first partial payment.
	
	 Calculate adjusted balance by subtracting from principal the partial payment less interest cost. The process continues for future partial payments with the adjusted balance used to calculate cost of interest from last payment to present payment.
		12%, 120 days, $2,000
		 Partial payments:
		    On day 40; $250
		    On day 60; $200
		 First payment:
		 $I = \$2,000 \times .12 \times \dfrac{40}{360}$
		 $I = \$26.67$
		    $\$250.00$ payment
		 $-\ \ \ \ 26.67$ interest
		    $\overline{\$223.33}$
		        $\$2,000.00$ principal
		        $-\ \ \ \ 223.33$
		        $\overline{\$1,776.67}$ adjusted balance
		 Second payment:
		 $I = \$1,776.67 \times .12 \times \dfrac{20}{360}$
		 $I = \$11.84$
		    $\$200.00$ payment
		 $-\ \ \ \ 11.84$ interest
		    $\overline{\$188.16}$
		        $\$1,776.67$
		        $-\ \ \ \ 188.16$
		        $\overline{\$1,588.51}$ adjusted balance

	Balance owed equals last adjusted balance plus interest cost from last partial payment to final due date.	*60 days left:*
		 $\$1,588.51 \times .12 \times \dfrac{60}{360} = \$31.77$
		 $\$1,588.51 + \$31.77 = \boxed{\begin{array}{c}\$1,620.28 \\ \text{balance due}\end{array}}$
		
		 Total interest $=$ $\$26.67$
		                 11.84
		             $+\ \ \ 31.77$
		               $\overline{\$70.28}$

(continues)

CHAPTER ORGANIZER AND STUDY GUIDE
WITH CHECK FIGURES FOR EXTRA PRACTICE QUIZZES (concluded)

Topic	Key point, procedure, formula		Example(s) to illustrate situation
KEY TERMS	Adjusted balance, *p. 264* Banker's Rule, *p. 261* Exact interest, *p. 260* Interest, *p. 259*	Maturity value, *p. 259* Ordinary interest, *p. 261* Principal, *p. 259* Simple interest, *p. 259*	Simple interest formula, *p. 259* Time, *p. 263* U.S. Rule, *p. 267*

CHECK FIGURES FOR EXTRA PRACTICE QUIZZES WITH PAGE REFERENCES	LU 10–1a (p. 262)
	1. $320
	2. $5,400
	3. $5,250
	4. $20,383.56;
	   Interest = $383.56
	5. $20,388.89;
	   Interest = $388.89
		LU 10–2a (p. 264)
		1. $900,000
		2. 9.33%
		3. 1,267 days
			LU 10–3a (p. 265)
			$1,318.78

Critical Thinking Discussion Questions

1. What is the difference between exact interest and ordinary interest? With the increase of computers in banking, do you think that the ordinary interest method is a dinosaur in business today?

2. Explain how to use the portion formula to solve the unknowns in the simple interest formula. Why would rounding the answer of the denominator result in an inaccurate final answer?

3. Explain the U.S. Rule. Why in the last step of the U.S. Rule is the interest added, not subtracted?

Classroom Notes

Name _____ Date _____

DRILL PROBLEMS

Calculate the simple interest and maturity value for the following problems. Round to the nearest cent as needed.

	Principal	Interest rate	Time	Simple interest	Maturity value
10–1.	$16,000	4%	18 mo.		
10–2.	$19,000	6%	$1\frac{3}{4}$ yr.		
10–3.	$18,000	$7\frac{1}{4}\%$	9 mo.		

Complete the following, using ordinary interest:

	Principal	Interest rate	Date borrowed	Date repaid	Exact time	Interest	Maturity value
10–4.	$1,000	8%	Mar. 8	June 9			
10–5.	$585	9%	June 5	Dec. 15			
10–6.	$1,200	12%	July 7	Jan. 10			

Complete the following, using exact interest:

	Principal	Interest rate	Date borrowed	Date repaid	Exact time	Interest	Maturity value
10–7.	$1,000	8%	Mar. 8	June 9			
10–8.	$585	9%	June 5	Dec. 15			
10–9.	$1,200	12%	July 7	Jan. 10			

Solve for the missing item in the following (round to the nearest hundredth as needed):

	Principal	Interest rate	Time (months or years)	Simple interest
10–10.	$400	5%	?	$100
10–11.	?	7%	$1\frac{1}{2}$ years	$200
10–12.	$5,000	?	6 months	$300

10–13. Use the U.S. Rule to solve for total interest costs, balances, and final payments (use ordinary interest).

   Given   Principal: $10,000, 8%, 240 days
   Partial payments: On 100th day, $4,000
   On 180th day, $2,000

WORD PROBLEMS

10–14. *The Kansas City Star* on March 11, 2007 featured a story on emergency savings in the U.S. Money in a checking account will not generate much interest. So Peggy Cooper decides to place her $1,300 in a savings account with a $5\frac{1}{8}$ percent return. After 7 months, Peggy needs to withdraw her savings. (a) What is the amount of interest she earned? (b) How much will Peggy receive from the bank? Round to the nearest cent.

10–15. Kim Lee borrowed $10,000 to pay for her child's education at River Community College. Kim must repay the loan at the end of 11 months in one payment with $6\frac{1}{2}$% interest. How much interest must Kim pay? What is the maturity value?

10–16. On September 12, Jody Jansen went to Sunshine Bank to borrow $2,300 at 9% interest. Jody plans to repay the loan on January 27. Assume the loan is on ordinary interest. What interest will Jody owe on January 27? What is the total amount Jody must repay at maturity?

10–17. Kelly O'Brien met Jody Jansen (Problem 10–16) at Sunshine Bank and suggested she consider the loan on exact interest. Recalculate the loan for Jody under this assumption.

10–18. May 3, 2007, Leven Corp. negotiated a short-term loan of $685,000. The loan is due October 1, 2007, and carries a 6.86% interest rate. Use ordinary interest to calculate the interest. What is the total amount Leven would pay on the maturity date?

10–19. Gordon Rosel went to his bank to find out how long it will take for $1,200 to amount to $1,650 at 8% simple interest. Please solve Gordon's problem. Round time in years to the nearest tenth.

10–20. Bill Moore is buying a van. His April monthly interest at 12% was $125. What was Bill's principal balance at the beginning of April? Use 360 days.

10–21. On April 5, 2008, Janeen Camoct took out an $8\frac{1}{2}$% loan for $20,000. The loan is due March 9, 2009. Use ordinary interest to calculate the interest. What total amount will Janeen pay on March 9, 2009?

10–22. Sabrina Bowers took out the same loan as Janeen (Problem 10–21). Sabrina's terms, however, are exact interest. What is Sabrina's difference in interest? What will she pay on March 9, 2009?

10–23. Max Wholesaler borrowed $2,000 on a 10%, 120-day note. After 45 days, Max paid $700 on the note. Thirty days later, Max paid an additional $630. What is the final balance due? Use the U.S. Rule to determine the total interest and ending balance due. Use ordinary interest.

ADDITIONAL SET OF WORD PROBLEMS

10–24. Limits are needed on payday-lending businesses, according to an article in the February 14, 2007 issue of *The Columbian* (Vancouver, WA). Interest rates on payday loans are so outrageous that the payday-lending industry only has itself to blame for states moving to rein them in. A typical $100 loan is payable in two **weeks** at $115. What is the percent of interest paid on this loan? Do not round denominator before dividing.

10–25. Availability of state and federal disaster loans was the featured article in *The Enterprise Ledger* (AL) on March 14, 2007. Alabama Deputy Treasurer Anthony Leigh said the state program allows the state treasurer to place state funds in Alabama banks at 2 percent below the market interest rate. The bank then agrees to lend the funds to individuals or businesses for 2 percent below the normal charge, to help Alabama victims of disaster to secure emergency short term loans. Laura Harden qualifies for an emergency loan. She will need $3,500 for 5 months and the local bank has an interest rate of $4\frac{3}{4}$ percent. **(a)** What would have been the maturity value of a non-emergency loan? **(b)** What will be the maturity value of the emergency loan? Round to the nearest cent.

10–26. On September 14, Jennifer Rick went to Park Bank to borrow $2,500 at $11\frac{3}{4}\%$ interest. Jennifer plans to repay the loan on January 27. Assume the loan is on ordinary interest. What interest will Jennifer owe on January 27? What is the total amount Jennifer must repay at maturity?

10–27. Steven Linden met Jennifer Rick (Problem 10–26) at Park Bank and suggested she consider the loan on exact interest. Recalculate the loan for Jennifer under this assumption.

10–28. Lance Lopes went to his bank to find out how long it will take for $1,000 to amount to $1,700 at 12% simple interest. Can you solve Lance's problem? Round time in years to the nearest tenth.

10–29. Margie Pagano is buying a car. Her June monthly interest at $12\frac{1}{2}\%$ was $195. What was Margie's principal balance at the beginning of June? Use 360 days. Do not round the denominator before dividing.

10–30. Shawn Bixby borrowed $17,000 on a 120-day, 12% note. After 65 days, Shawn paid $2,000 on the note. On day 89, Shawn paid an additional $4,000. What is the final balance due? Determine total interest and ending balance due by the U.S. Rule. Use ordinary interest.

10–31. Carol Miller went to Europe and forgot to pay her $740 mortgage payment on her New Hampshire ski house. For her 59 days overdue on her payment, the bank charged her a penalty of $15. What was the rate of interest charged by the bank? Round to the nearest hundredth percent (assume 360 days).

10–32. Abe Wolf bought a new kitchen set at Sears. Abe paid off the loan after 60 days with an interest charge of $9. If Sears charges 10% interest, what did Abe pay for the kitchen set (assume 360 days)?

10–33. Joy Kirby made a $300 loan to Robinson Landscaping at 11%. Robinson paid back the loan with interest of $6.60. How long in days was the loan outstanding (assume 360 days)? Check your answer.

10–34. Molly Ellen, bookkeeper for Keystone Company, forgot to send in the payroll taxes due on April 15. She sent the payment November 8. The IRS sent her a penalty charge of 8% simple interest on the unpaid taxes of $4,100. Calculate the penalty. (Remember that the government uses exact interest.)

10–35. Oakwood Plowing Company purchased two new plows for the upcoming winter. In 200 days, Oakwood must make a single payment of $23,200 to pay for the plows. As of today, Oakwood has $22,500. If Oakwood puts the money in a bank today, what rate of interest will it need to pay off the plows in 200 days (assume 360 days)?

CHALLENGE PROBLEMS

10–36. The *Downers Grove Reporter* ran an ad for a used 1998 Harley-Davidson Sportster 883 for $6,750. Patrick Schmidt is interested in the motorcycle but does not have the money right now. Patrick contacted the owner on October 19, and he agreed to give Patrick a loan plus 5.5% exact interest. The loan must be paid back by December 22 of the same year. The First National Bank will lend the $6,750 at 5%. Patrick would have 3 months to pay off the loan. **(a)** What is the total amount Patrick will have to pay the owner of the motorcycle assuming exact interest? **(b)** What is the total amount Patrick will have to pay the bank? **(c)** Which option offers the most savings to Patrick? **(d)** How much will Patrick save?

10–37. Janet Foster bought a computer and printer at Computerland. The printer had a $600 list price with a $100 trade discount and 2/10, n/30 terms. The computer had a $1,600 list price with a 25% trade discount but no cash discount. On the computer, Computerland offered Janet the choice of (1) paying $50 per month for 17 months with the 18th payment paying the remainder of the balance or (2) paying 8% interest for 18 months in equal payments.

    a. Assume Janet could borrow the money for the printer at 8% to take advantage of the cash discount. How much would Janet save (assume 360 days)?

    b. On the computer, what is the difference in the final payment between choices 1 and 2?

1. Lorna Hall's real estate tax of $2,010.88 was due on December 14, 2009. Lorna lost her job and could not pay her tax bill until February 27, 2010. The penalty for late payment is $6\frac{1}{2}\%$ ordinary interest. *(p. 261)*

    a. What is the penalty Lorna must pay?

    b. What is the total amount Lorna must pay on February 27?

2. Ann Hopkins borrowed $60,000 for her child's education. She must repay the loan at the end of 8 years in one payment with $5\frac{1}{2}\%$ interest. What is the maturity value Ann must repay? *(p. 260)*

3. On May 6, Jim Ryan borrowed $14,000 from Lane Bank at $7\frac{1}{2}\%$ interest. Jim plans to repay the loan on March 11. Assume the loan is on ordinary interest. How much will Jim repay on March 11? *(p. 261)*

4. Gail Ross met Jim Ryan (Problem 3) at Lane Bank. After talking with Jim, Gail decided she would like to consider the same loan on exact interest. Can you recalculate the loan for Gail under this assumption? *(p. 260)*

5. Claire Russell is buying a car. Her November monthly interest was $210 at $7\frac{3}{4}\%$ interest. What is Claire's principal balance (to the nearest dollar) at the beginning of November? Use 360 days. Do not round the denominator in your calculation. *(p. 262)*

6. Comet Lee borrowed $16,000 on a 6%, 90-day note. After 20 days, Comet paid $2,000 on the note. On day 50, Comet paid $4,000 on the note. What are the total interest and ending balance due by the U.S. Rule? Use ordinary interest. *(p. 264)*

Personal Finance

Christina Pridgen, with Sara, 11, and Alex, 9.

SOLVED | Sometimes it doesn't make much sense to pay the money you owe.

My unpaid **DEBT** still haunts me

CHRISTINA Pridgen struggled with debt as she went through a divorce and began a new life for herself and her two kids. She admits she never paid $14,000 in joint credit-card debt incurred while she was married. Collectors have pretty much stopped bugging her, but she wonders: If she could find the resources to pay off the debt, would her credit rating be resurrected? "I had an excellent credit history," says Pridgen, 34, a nursing student who lives near Charlotte, N.C. "I'd like to start over."

Believe it or not, paying back the $14,000 would do little to repair Pridgen's credit history. And the black marks on her credit report will disappear in 18 months, anyway. Under federal law, a report of a bad debt must be removed seven and a half years after the first missed payment. If the creditors had sued and won a judgment against Pridgen, they'd have had at least ten years to collect. But that didn't happen—probably because of the relatively small amounts involved with each card issuer. The statute of limitations for such suits (three years in North Carolina, but as many as six elsewhere) has passed.

There's no limit on how long debt collectors can try to collect (see "Debt Police Who Go Too Far," Nov.). For now, Pridgen is best off using her limited resources to finish her education and care for her kids. She can always try to cut a deal to clear the debt—and her conscience—when she's out of school, working full-time.

Do you have a money problem we can solve? E-mail us at solved@kiplinger.com.

MIKE CARROLL

BUSINESS MATH ISSUE

Christina should never pay back the debt.

1. List the key points of the article and information to support your position.
2. Write a group defense of your position using math calculations to support your view.

Slater's Business Math Scrapbook

with Internet Application

Putting Your Skills to Work

PROJECT A
Visit a local credit union and check their rates versus a regular bank.

Green Thumb / *By Ron Lieber*

Where to Look for Cheaper Loans

Credit Unions Often Do Better Than Banks; the 'Flower' Trick

IT'S GETTING EASIER to join a credit union—and if you're not checking their rates, you may be costing yourself a lot of money by not doing so.

That may come as a surprise. Credit unions have their roots early in the 20th century, when they were created to serve the needs of people of modest means whom banks were ignoring. Over the years, however, they've expanded their reach. Today they claim 88 million members in the U.S., including plenty of people who could just as easily use any regular bank.

Why do they choose credit unions instead? In large part because the interest rates they pay depositors are often higher, and their loan rates are frequently lower, than those at regular banks. For instance, the average credit-union 48-month used-car loan is 6.08%; at banks it's 7.94%, according to Datatrac, a research firm that surveys thousands of financial institutions for the Credit Union National Association, or CUNA.

The credit unions can afford these deals partly because they don't have to pay most income taxes. This irks bankers to no end, given they have to compete with credit unions—and pay taxes. They're fighting back: In November, the American Bankers Association filed two federal lawsuits challenging the membership rules at two credit unions.

Traditionally, it was tougher for consumers to get these deals: You often had to work for a certain company or live in a certain place.

Not anymore. Today, many credit unions are basically clubs that anyone can join. That's thanks in part to a 1998 law that permitted federal credit unions to invite other groups in who don't have much in common with each other.

Getting Credit

Credit unions can offer savings on everything from credit cards to auto loans. Here's how to find one:

- Use the zip-code search at cuna.org
- Ask at work if your employment makes you eligible for membership
- Look for membership groups that bestow eligibility

Do you like flowers? Then you can join the Tower Hill Botanic Garden in Boylston, Mass.—and one of the fringe benefits is eligibility for the Digital Federal Credit Union, which is still going strong even though the Digital Equipment Corp. brand no longer is. "Everyone Can Join DCU," its Web site says. (The credit union was originally founded to serve employees.)

The Pentagon Federal Credit Union, which lends nationwide, is open to anyone who joins the National Military Family Association, an advocacy group that anyone is eligible for. "It's kind of like an affinity partnership," says NMFA's Cynthia Fox, who says that a couple thousand people join each month just to get access to PenFed.

Looking for a credit union near you with equally liberal eligibility rules? Hunt by zip code at www.creditunion.coop/cu_locator, CUNA's Web site, then check its membership regulations. Inquire where you work too, since many companies that don't have their own affiliated credit unions arrange membership eligibility elsewhere as a perk.

Big credit unions may offer better rates than smaller ones. Online banking and other technology may not be state of the art at all institutions. And you'll often find better mortgage rates elsewhere. But credit unions generally do better than their normal bank competitors on car loans, personal loans, credit cards and home-equity lending.

If something feels slightly sneaky about benefiting from a credit union that wasn't really set up with you in mind, consider this: The tax breaks they enjoy ultimately come out of your pocket.

No bankers' hours at ron.lieber@wsj.com

Internet Projects: See text Web site (www.mhhe.com/slater9e) and The Business Math Internet Resource Guide.

CHAPTER 11

Promissory Notes, Simple Discount Notes, and the Discount Process

Borrowing Online

Financial-services firms are offering lower-cost alternatives to consumers who take out loans online. Here are a few new options:

COMPANY	LOAN
Bank of Internet USA (bankofinternet.com/LoanCenter)	Began offering home-equity loans online in seven states earlier this year, with a national rollout expected later this year. Annual percentage rates range from 7.1% to 7.7%. No closing costs.
Citibank (Citibank.com/lending)*	Citibank Direct plans to offer loans with lower online-only rates. The bank is promoting home-equity lines of credit with variable rates of 5.99% for six months or 7.24% for the life of the loans.
E-Loan (eloan.com)	Offers a range of online loans, including home and auto loans. The company is planning to launch personal lines of credit, with rates ranging from 7.99% to 19.99%.
Prosper.com	Offers person-to-person loans. Rates for borrowers have been averaging 8% for those with the best credit to 24% for those with the lowest or no credit. Offers 3-year loans ranging from $1,000 to $25,000.

*Web site should be active shortly.

Source: the companies

Wall Street Journal © 2006

LEARNING UNIT OBJECTIVES

LU 11–1: Structure of Promissory Notes; the Simple Discount Note

- Differentiate between interest-bearing and noninterest-bearing notes (pp. 279–280).
- Calculate bank discount and proceeds for simple discount notes (p. 280).
- Calculate and compare the interest, maturity value, proceeds, and effective rate of a simple interest note with a simple discount note (p. 281).
- Explain and calculate the effective rate for a Treasury bill (p. 281).

LU 11–2: Discounting an Interest-Bearing Note before Maturity

- Calculate the maturity value, bank discount, and proceeds of discounting an interest-bearing note before maturity (pp. 282–283).
- Identify and complete the four steps of the discounting process (p. 283).

> # Saks Inc.'s Debt Rating Is Cut After Default Notice on Notes

Wall Street Journal © 2005

This *Wall Street Journal* heading states that Saks is having financial problems. Unlike credit cardholders who fail to meet their financial obligations, Saks has the option of tapping a $650 million credit line to help its financial situation.

This chapter begins with a discussion of the structure of promissory notes and simple discount notes. We also look at the application of discounting with Treasury bills. The chapter concludes with an explanation of how to calculate the discounting of promissory notes.

Learning Unit 11–1: Structure of Promissory Notes; the Simple Discount Note

Although businesses frequently sign promissory notes, customers also sign promissory notes. For example, some student loans may require the signing of promissory notes. Appliance stores often ask customers to sign a promissory note when they buy large appliances on credit. In this unit, promissory notes usually involve interest payments.

Structure of Promissory Notes

To borrow money, you must find a lender (a bank or a company selling goods on credit). You must also be willing to pay for the use of the money. In Chapter 10 you learned that interest is the cost of borrowing money for periods of time.

Money lenders usually require that borrowers sign a **promissory note.** This note states that the borrower will repay a certain sum at a fixed time in the future. The note often includes the charge for the use of the money, or the rate of interest. Figure 11.1 shows a sample promissory note with its terms identified and defined. Take a moment to look at each term.

In this section you will learn the difference between interest-bearing notes and noninterest-bearing notes.

Interest-Bearing versus Noninterest-Bearing Notes

A promissory note can be interest bearing or noninterest bearing. To be **interest bearing,** the note must state the rate of interest. Since the promissory note in Figure 11.1 states that its interest is 9%, it is an interest-bearing note. When the note matures, Regal Corporation "will pay back the original amount (**face value**) borrowed plus interest. The simple interest formula (also known as the interest formula) and the maturity value formula from Chapter 10 are used for this transaction."

> Interest = Face value (principal) × Rate × Time
> Maturity value = Face value (principal) + Interest

FIGURE	11.1

Interest-bearing promissory note

$10,000 a.   LAWTON, OKLAHOMA *October 2, 2007* c.

_____*Sixty days* b._____ AFTER DATE we _PROMISE TO PAY TO_

THE ORDER OF   *G.J. Equipment Company* d.

_____*Ten thousand and 00/100*--------------------DOLLARS.

PAYABLE AT   *Able National Bank*

VALUE RECEIVED WITH INTEREST AT _9%_ e.   REGAL CORPORATION f.

NO. _114_   DUE *December 1, 2007*   *J.M. Moore*
                                    g.   TREASURER

a. **Face value:** Amount of money borrowed—$10,000. The face value is also the principal of the note.
b. **Term:** Length of time that the money is borrowed—60 days.
c. **Date:** The date that the note is issued—October 2, 2007.
d. **Payee:** The company extending the credit—G.J. Equipment Company.
e. **Rate:** The annual rate for the cost of borrowing the money—9%.
f. **Maker:** The company issuing the note and borrowing the money—Regal Corporation.
g. **Maturity date:** The date the principal and interest rate are due—December 1, 2007.

TABLE 11.1

Comparison of simple interest note and simple discount note (Calculations from the Pete Runnels example)

Simple interest note (Chapter 10)	Simple discount note (Chapter 11)
1. A promissory note for a loan with a term of usually less than 1 year. *Example:* 60 days.	1. A promissory note for a loan with a term of usually less than 1 year. *Example:* 60 days.
2. Paid back by one payment at maturity. Face value equals actual amount (or principal) of loan (this is not maturity value).	2. Paid back by one payment at maturity. Face value equals maturity value (what will be repaid).
3. Interest computed on face value or what is actually borrowed. *Example:* $186.67.	3. Interest computed on maturity value or what will be repaid and not on actual amount borrowed. *Example:* $186.67.
4. Maturity value = Face value + Interest. *Example:* $14,186.67.	4. Maturity value = Face value. *Example:* $14,000.
5. Borrower receives the face value. *Example:* $14,000.	5. Borrower receives proceeds = Face value − Bank discount. *Example:* $13,813.33.
6. Effective rate (true rate is same as rate stated on note). *Example:* 8%.	6. Effective rate is higher since interest was deducted in advance. *Example:* 8.11%.
7. Used frequently instead of the simple discount note. *Example:* 8%.	7. Not used as much now because in 1969 congressional legislation required that the true rate of interest be revealed. Still used where legislation does not apply, such as personal loans.

If you sign a **noninterest-bearing** promissory note for $10,000, you pay back $10,000 at maturity. The maturity value of a noninterest-bearing note is the same as its face value. Usually, noninterest-bearing notes occur for short time periods under special conditions. For example, money borrowed from a relative could be secured by a noninterest-bearing promissory note.

Simple Discount Note

The total amount due at the end of the loan, or the **maturity value (MV),** is the sum of the face value (principal) and interest. Some banks deduct the loan interest in advance. When banks do this, the note is a **simple discount note.**

In the simple discount note, the **bank discount** is the interest that banks deduct in advance and the **bank discount rate** is the percent of interest. The amount that the borrower receives after the bank deducts its discount from the loan's maturity value is the note's **proceeds.** Sometimes we refer to simple discount notes as noninterest-bearing notes. Remember, however, that borrowers *do* pay interest on these notes.

In the example that follows, Pete Runnels has the choice of a note with a simple interest rate (Chapter 10) or a note with a simple discount rate (Chapter 11). Table 11.1 provides a summary of the calculations made in the example and gives the key points that you should remember. Now let's study the example, and then you can review Table 11.1.

EXAMPLE Pete Runnels has a choice of two different notes that both have a face value (principal) of $14,000 for 60 days. One note has a simple interest rate of 8%, while the other note has a simple discount rate of 8%. For each type of note, calculate **(a)** interest owed, **(b)** maturity value, **(c)** proceeds, and **(d)** effective rate.

Simple interest note—Chapter 10	Simple discount note—Chapter 11
Interest	**Interest**
a. I = Face value (principal) $\times R \times T$	**a.** I = Face value (principal) $\times R \times T$
$I = \$14,000 \times .08 \times \dfrac{60}{360}$	$I = \$14,000 \times .08 \times \dfrac{60}{360}$
$I = \$186.67$	$I = \$186.67$
Maturity value	**Maturity value**
b. MV = Face value + Interest	**b.** MV = Face value
$MV = \$14,000 + \$186.67$	$MV = \$14,000$
$MV = \$14,186.67$	
Proceeds	**Proceeds**
c. Proceeds = Face value	**c.** Proceeds = MV − Bank discount
= $14,000	= $14,000 − $186.67
	= $13,813.33

Simple interest note—Chapter 10	Simple discount note—Chapter 11
Effective rate	**Effective rate**
d. $\text{Rate} = \dfrac{\text{Interest}}{\text{Proceeds} \times \text{Time}}$	d. $\text{Rate} = \dfrac{\text{Interest}}{\text{Proceeds} \times \text{Time}}$
$= \dfrac{\$186.67}{\$14,000 \times \dfrac{60}{360}}$	$= \dfrac{\$186.67}{\$13,813.33 \times \dfrac{60}{360}}$
$= 8\%$	$= 8.11\%$

Note that the interest of $186.67 is the same for the simple interest note and the simple discount note. The maturity value of the simple discount note is the same as the face value. In the simple discount note, interest is deducted in advance, so the proceeds are less than the face value. Note that the effective rate for a simple discount note is higher than the stated rate, since the bank calculated the rate on the face of the note and not on what Pete received.

Application of Discounting—Treasury Bills

Treasury-Bill Sales Will Raise $6 Billion

WASHINGTON—The Treasury plans to raise about $6 billion of new cash next week with the sale of short-term bills.

Details of the offerings:

■ A sale on Monday to sell about $32 billion in three- and six-month bills is planned to raise about $997 million in new cash.

Maturing bills outstanding total $31 billion. The offering will be divided between $17 billion of 13-week bills and $15 billion of 26-week bills maturing on Feb. 15, 2007, and May 17, 2007, respectively.

The Cusip number for the three-month bills is 912795YT2. The Cusip number for the six-month bills is 912795ZG9.

Wall Street Journal © 2006

When the government needs money, it sells Treasury bills. A **Treasury bill** is a loan to the federal government for 28 days (4 weeks), 91 days (13 weeks), or 1 year. Note that the *Wall Street Journal* clipping Treasury—bill sales will raise $6 billion.

Treasury bills can be bought over the phone or on the government website. (See Business Math Scrapbook, page 293, for details.) The purchase price (or proceeds) of a Treasury bill is the value of the Treasury bill less the discount. For example, if you buy a $10,000, 13-week Treasury bill at 8%, you pay $9,800 since you have not yet earned your interest ($10,000 $\times$ .08 $\times \frac{13}{52}$ = $200). At maturity—13 weeks—the government pays you $10,000. You calculate your effective yield (8.16% rounded to the nearest hundredth percent) as follows:

$$(\$10,000 - \$200) \longrightarrow \dfrac{\$200}{\$9,800 \times \dfrac{13}{52}} = \boxed{8.16\%} \text{ effective rate}$$

Now it's time to try the Practice Quiz and check your progress.

LU 11-1 **PRACTICE QUIZ**

Complete this **Practice Quiz** to see how you are doing

1. Warren Ford borrowed $12,000 on a noninterest-bearing, simple discount, $9\frac{1}{2}\%$, 60-day note. Assume ordinary interest. What are **(a)** the maturity value, **(b)** the bank's discount, **(c)** Warren's proceeds, and **(d)** the effective rate to the nearest hundredth percent?

2. Jane Long buys a $10,000, 13-week Treasury bill at 6%. What is her effective rate? Round to the nearest hundredth percent.

✓ **Solutions**

1. **a.** Maturity value = Face value = $12,000

   b. Bank discount = MV × Bank discount rate × Time

   $$= \$12{,}000 \times .095 \times \frac{60}{360}$$

   $$= \$190$$

   c. Proceeds = MV − Bank discount

   $$= \$12{,}000 - \$190$$

   $$= \$11{,}810$$

   d. Effective rate = $\dfrac{\text{Interest}}{\text{Proceeds} \times \text{Time}}$

   $$= \frac{\$190}{\$11{,}810 \times \dfrac{60}{360}}$$

   $$= \$9.65\%$$

2. $\$10{,}000 \times .06 \times \dfrac{13}{52} = \$150$ interest $\dfrac{\$150}{\$9{,}850 \times \dfrac{13}{52}} = 6.09\%$

LU 11–1a EXTRA PRACTICE QUIZ

Need more practice? Try this **Extra Practice Quiz** (check figures in Chapter Organizer, p. 286)

1. Warren Ford borrowed $14,000 on a noninterest-bearing, simple discount, $4^1/2\%$, 60-day note. Assume ordinary interest. What are **(a)** the maturity value, **(b)** the bank's discount, **(c)** Warren's proceeds, and **(d)** the effective rate to the nearest hundredth percent?

2. Jane Long buys a $10,000 13-week Treasury bill at 4%. What is her effective rate? Round to the nearest hundredth percent.

Learning Unit 11–2: Discounting an Interest-Bearing Note before Maturity

Manufacturers frequently deliver merchandise to retail companies and do not request payment for several months. For example, Roger Company manufactures outdoor furniture that it delivers to Sears in March. Payment for the furniture is not due until September. Roger will have its money tied up in this furniture until September. So Roger requests that Sears sign promissory notes.

If Roger Company needs cash sooner than September, what can it do? Roger Company can take one of its promissory notes to the bank, assuming the company that signed the note is reliable. The bank will buy the note from Roger. Now Roger has discounted the note and has cash instead of waiting until September when Sears would have paid Roger.

Remember that when Roger Company discounts the promissory note to the bank, the company agrees to pay the note at maturity if the maker of the promissory note fails to pay the bank. The potential liability that may or may not result from discounting a note is called a **contingent liability.**

Think of **discounting a note** as a three-party arrangement. Roger Company realizes that the bank will charge for this service. The bank's charge is a **bank discount.** The actual amount Roger receives is the **proceeds** of the note. The four steps below and the formulas in the example that follows will help you understand this discounting process.

DISCOUNTING A NOTE
Step 1. Calculate the interest and maturity value.
Step 2. Calculate the discount period (time the bank holds note).
Step 3. Calculate the bank discount.
Step 4. Calculate the proceeds.

EXAMPLE Roger Company sold the following promissory note to the bank:

Date of note	Face value of note	Length of note	Interest rate	Bank discount rate	Date of discount
March 8	$2,000	185 days	10%	9%	August 9

What are Roger's (1) interest and maturity value (*MV*)? What are the (2) discount period and (3) bank discount? (4) What are the proceeds?

1. *Calculate Roger's interest and maturity value (MV):*

    $$MV = \text{Face value (principal)} + \text{Interest}$$

    $$\text{Interest} = \$2,000 \times .10 \times \frac{185}{360} \quad \text{Exact number of days over 360}$$

    $$= \$102.78$$

    $$MV = \$2,000 + \$102.78$$

    $$= \$2,102.78$$

Calculating days without table:

March	31
	− 8
	23
April	30
May	31
June	30
July	31
August	9
	154

185 days—length of note
−154 days Roger held note
  31 days bank waits

2. *Calculate* **discount period:**

    Determine the number of days that the bank will have to wait for the note to come due (discount period).

August 9	221 days	
March 8	− 67	
	154	days passed before note is discounted
	185	days
	− 154	
	31	days bank waits for note to come due

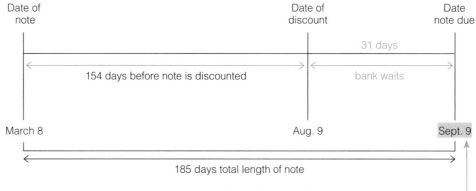

By table: March 8 =   67 days
                        + 185
                        252 search in table

3. *Calculate bank discount (bank charge):*

    $$\$2,102.78 \times .09 \times \frac{31}{360} = \$16.30$$

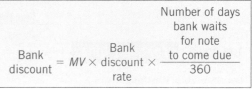

$$\text{Bank discount} = MV \times \text{Bank discount rate} \times \frac{\text{Number of days bank waits for note to come due}}{360}$$

Step 1

$\downarrow$

$$\text{Proceeds} = MV - \text{Bank discount (charge)}$$

$\uparrow$

Step 3

4. *Calculate proceeds:*

    $2,102.78
    −   16.30
    $2,086.48

    If Roger had waited until September 9, it would have received $2,102.78. Now, on August 9, Roger received $2,000 plus $86.48 interest.

Now let's assume Roger Company received a noninterest-bearing note. Then we follow the four steps for discounting a note except the maturity value is the amount of the loan. No interest accumulates on a noninterest-bearing note. Today, many banks use simple interest instead of discounting. Also, instead of discounting notes, many companies set up *lines of credit* so that additional financing is immediately available.

Finding Funding
Breaking down the basics of small-business borrowing

Loan Lineup

Among small businesses using credit, the percentage that tap these types of funding to finance their operations

- Personal credit card **46%**
- Business credit card **34**
- Line of credit **28**
- Vehicle loan **21**
- Owner loan* **14**
- Mortgage loan **13**
- Lease **11**
- Equipment loan **10**
- Other **10**

Getting Started

Here are selected resources where entrepreneurs can research small-business financing options

www.sba.gov/financing

The Small Business Administration's Web site provides a primer on the basics of financing, as well as calculators for estimating costs, lists of grant resources, a summary of loan requirements and information on the agency's own loan programs.

www.microenterpriseworks.org

The site of the Association for Enterprise Opportunity, a national member-based group dedicated to microenterprise development, provides a listing of microenterprise groups by state that can be tapped for financing guidance and funding itself.

www.smartonline.com

This for-profit company provides an array of financial calculators as well as Web-based services and templates on writing business and marketing plans, incorporating and applying for loans.

www.count-me-in.org

This site is aimed at helping women-run small businesses obtain business loans, consultation and education. An online microlender, Count Me In makes loans of $500 to $10,000 available to U.S. women who have difficulty finding funding elsewhere. The site also has a help resource center with checklists, educational videos, and an online library about credit and business planning.

*Loan from the owner to the business.   Sources: Small Business Administration, Office of Advocacy; WSJ research

Wall Street Journal © 2004

The *Wall Street Journal* clipping "Finding Funding" shows that 28% of small businesses surveyed use a line of credit to finance their operations.

The Practice Quiz that follows will test your understanding of this unit.

LU 11–2   PRACTICE QUIZ

Complete this **Practice Quiz** to see how you are doing

Date of note	Face value (principal) of note	Length of note	Interest rate	Bank discount rate	Date of discount
April 8	$35,000	160 days	11%	9%	June 8

From the above, calculate **(a)** interest and maturity value, **(b)** discount period, **(c)** bank discount, and **(d)** proceeds. Assume ordinary interest.

✔ Solutions

a. $I = \$35,000 \times .11 \times \dfrac{160}{360} =$ $\boxed{\$1,711.11}$

$MV = \$35,000 + \$1,711.11 =$ $\boxed{\$36,711.11}$

b.   Discount period $= 160 - 61 =$ $\boxed{99 \text{ days.}}$

April   30
      − 8
      22
May   + 31
      53
June   + 8
      61

Or by table:

June 8   159
April 8   − 98
        61

    c. Bank discount = $36,711.11 × .09 × $\frac{99}{360}$ = $908.60

    d. Proceeds = $36,711.11 − $908.60 = $35,802.51

LU 11–2a EXTRA PRACTICE QUIZ

Need more practice? Try this **Extra Practice Quiz** (check figures in Chapter Organizer, p. 286)

From the information below, calculate **(a)** interest and maturity value, **(b)** discount period, **(c)** bank discount, and **(d)** proceeds. Assume ordinary interest.

Date of note	Face value (principal) of note	Length of note	Interest rate	Bank discount rate	Date of discount
April 10	$40,000	170 days	5%	2%	June 10

CHAPTER ORGANIZER AND STUDY GUIDE
WITH CHECK FIGURES FOR EXTRA PRACTICE QUIZZES

Topic	Key point, procedure, formula	Example(s) to illustrate situation
Simple discount note, p. 280	Bank discount (interest) = MV × Bank discount rate × Time Interest based on amount paid back and not what received.	$6,000 × .09 × $\frac{60}{360}$ = $90 Borrower receives $5,910 (the proceeds) and pays back $6,000 at maturity after 60 days. A Treasury bill is a good example of a simple discount note.
Effective rate, p. 281	$\dfrac{\text{Interest}}{\text{Proceeds} \times \text{Time}}$ ↑ What borrower receives (Face value − Discount)	*Example:* $10,000 note, discount rate 12% for 60 days. $I = $10,000 × .12 × $\frac{60}{360}$ = $200 Effective rate: $\dfrac{\$200}{\$9,800 \times \frac{60}{360}} = \dfrac{\$200}{\$1,633.3333} = 12.24\%$ ↑ Amount borrower received

Discounting an interest-bearing note, p. 282	1. Calculate interest and maturity value.
	   I = Face value × Rate × Time
	   MV = Face value + Interest
	2. Calculate number of days bank will wait for note to come due (discount period).
	3. Calculate bank discount (bank charge).
	  MV × Bank discount rate × $\dfrac{\text{Number of days bank waits}}{360}$
	4. Calculate proceeds.
	  MV − Bank discount (charge)
		Example: $1,000 note, 6%, 60-day, dated November 1 and discounted on December 1 at 8%.
		
		1. I = $1,000 × .06 × $\frac{60}{360}$ = $10
		    MV = $1,000 + $10 = $1,010
		2. 30 days
		3. $1,010 × .08 × $\frac{30}{360}$ = $6.73
		4. $1,010 − $6.73 = $1,003.27

KEY TERMS	Bank discount, *pp. 280, 282* Bank discount rate, *p. 280* Contingent liability, *p. 282* Discounting a note, *p. 282* Discount period, *p. 283* Effective rate, *p. 281* Face value, *p. 279*	Interest-bearing note, *p. 279* Maker, *p. 279* Maturity date, *p. 279* Maturity value (*MV*), *p. 279* Noninterest-bearing note, *p. 280* Payee, *p. 279* Proceeds, *pp. 280, 283* Promissory note, *p. 279* Simple discount note, *p. 280* Treasury bill, *p. 281*

(continues)

CHAPTER ORGANIZER AND STUDY GUIDE
WITH CHECK FIGURES FOR EXTRA PRACTICE QUIZZES (concluded)

Topic	Key point, procedure, formula	Example(s) to illustrate situation
CHECK FIGURES FOR EXTRA PRACTICE QUIZZES WITH PAGE REFERENCES	LU 11–1a (p. 282) 1. A. $14,000 B. $105 C. $13,895 D. 4.53% 2. 4.04%	LU 11–2a (p. 285) 1. A. Int. = $944.44; $40,944.44 B. 109 days C. $247.94 D. $40,696.50

Critical Thinking Discussion Questions

1. What are the differences between a simple interest note and a simple discount note? Which type of note would have a higher effective rate of interest? Why?

2. What are the four steps of the discounting process? Could the proceeds of a discounted note be less than the face value of the note?

3. What is a line of credit? What could be a disadvantage of having a large credit line?

Name _____ Date _____

DRILL PROBLEMS

Complete the following table for these simple discount notes. Use the ordinary interest method.

	Amount due at maturity	Discount rate	Time	Bank discount	Proceeds
11–1.	$18,000	$4\frac{1}{4}\%$	300 days		
11–2.	$20,000	$6\frac{1}{4}\%$	180 days		

Calculate the discount period for the bank to wait to receive its money:

	Date of note	Length of note	Date note discounted	Discount period
11–3.	April 12	45 days	May 2	
11–4.	March 7	120 days	June 8	

Solve for maturity value, discount period, bank discount, and proceeds (assume for Problems 11–5 and 11–6 a bank discount rate of 9%).

	Face value (principal)	Rate of interest	Length of note	Maturity value	Date of note	Date note discounted	Discount period	Bank discount	Proceeds
11–5.	$50,000	11%	95 days		June 10	July 18			
11–6.	$25,000	9%	60 days		June 8	July 10			

11–7. Calculate the effective rate of interest (to the nearest hundredth percent) of the following Treasury bill.
Given: $10,000 Treasury bill, 4% for 13 weeks.

WORD PROBLEMS

Use ordinary interest as needed.

11–8. On March 19, 2006, *The Saint Paul Pioneer Press* reported on interest loans which include an additional, one time $20 fee. Wilbert McKee's bank deducts interest in advance and also deducts $20.00 fee in advance. Wilbert needs a loan for $500. The bank charges 5% interest. Wilbert will need the loan for 90 days. What is the effective rate for this loan? Round to the nearest hundredth percent. Do not round denominator in calculation.

11–9. Jack Tripper signed a $9,000 note at Fleet Bank. Fleet charges a $9\frac{1}{4}$% discount rate. If the loan is for 200 days, find **(a)** the proceeds and **(b)** the effective rate charged by the bank (to the nearest tenth percent).

11–10. On January 18, 2007, *BusinessWeek* reported yields on Treasury bills. Bruce Martin purchased a $10,000 13 week Treasury bill at $9,881.25. **(a)** What was the amount of interest? **(b)** What was the effective rate of interest? Round to the nearest hundredth percent.

11–11. On September 5, Sheffield Company discounted at Sunshine Bank a $9,000 (maturity value), 120-day note dated June 5. Sunshine's discount rate was 9%. What proceeds did Sheffield Company receive?

11–12. The Treasury Department auctioned $21 billion in three month bills in denominations of ten thousand dollars at a discount rate of 4.965%, according to the March 13, 2007 issue of the *Chicago Sun-Times*. What would be the effective rate of interest? Round your answer to the nearest hundredth percent.

11–13. Annika Scholten bought a $10,000, 13-week Treasury bill at 5%. What is her effective rate? Round to the nearest hundredth percent.

11–14. Ron Prentice bought goods from Shelly Katz. On May 8, Shelly gave Ron a time extension on his bill by accepting a $3,000, 8%, 180-day note. On August 16, Shelly discounted the note at Roseville Bank at 9%. What proceeds does Shelly Katz receive?

11–15. Rex Corporation accepted a $5,000, 8%, 120-day note dated August 8 from Regis Company in settlement of a past bill. On October 11, Rex discounted the note at Park Bank at 9%. What are the note's maturity value, discount period, and bank discount? What proceeds does Rex receive?

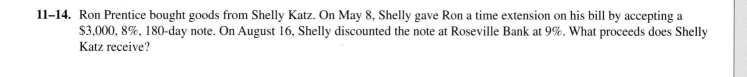

11–16. On May 12, Scott Rinse accepted an $8,000, 12%, 90-day note for a time extension of a bill for goods bought by Ron Prentice. On June 12, Scott discounted the note at Able Bank at 10%. What proceeds does Scott receive?

11–17. Hafers, an electrical supply company, sold $4,800 of equipment to Jim Coates Wiring, Inc. Coates signed a promissory note May 12 with 4.5% interest. The due date was August 10. Short of funds, Hafers contacted Charter One Bank on July 20; the bank agreed to take over the note at a 6.2% discount. What proceeds will Hafers receive?

11–18. *Market News Publishing* reported on the sale of a promissory note. ZTEST Electronics announced that it agreed to sell a promissory note (the "Note") in the principal amount of $318,019.95 owed to them by Parmatech Electronic Corporation. The note, negotiated on March 15, is a 360-day note with 8.5% interest per annum. Halfway through the life of the note, Alpha Bank offered to purchase the note at 8.75%. Baker Bank offered to purchase the note at 9.0%. **(a)** What proceeds will ZTEST receive from Alpha Bank? **(b)** What proceeds will ZTEST receive from Baker Bank? **(c)** How much more will ZTEST receive from Alpha Bank? Round to the nearest cent.

11–19. Tina Mier must pay a $2,000 furniture bill. A finance company will loan Tina $2,000 for 8 months at a 9% discount rate. The finance company told Tina that if she wants to receive exactly $2,000, she must borrow more than $2,000. The finance company gave Tina the following formula:

$$\text{What to ask for} = \frac{\text{Amount in cash to be received}}{1 - (\text{Discount} \times \text{Time of loan})}$$

Calculate Tina's loan request and the effective rate of interest to nearest hundredth percent.

 SUMMARY PRACTICE TEST

1. On December 12, Lowell Corporation accepted a $160,000, 120-day, noninterest-bearing note from Able.com. What is the maturity value of the note? *(p. 279)*

2. The face value of a simple discount note is $17,000. The discount is 4% for 160 days. Calculate the following. *(p. 280)*

   a. Amount of interest charged for each note.

   b. Amount borrower would receive.

   c. Amount payee would receive at maturity.

   d. Effective rate (to the nearest tenth percent).

3. On July 14, Gracie Paul accepted a $60,000, 6%, 160-day note from Mike Lang. On November 12, Gracie discounted the note at Lend Bank at 7%. What proceeds did Gracie receive? *(p. 282)*

4. Lee.com accepted a $70,000, $6\frac{3}{4}$%, 120-day note on July 26. Lee discounts the note on October 28 at LB Bank at 6%. What proceeds did Lee receive? *(p. 282)*

5. The owner of Lease.com signed a $60,000 note at Reese Bank. Reese charges a $7\frac{1}{4}$% discount rate. If the loan is for 210 days, find **(a)** the proceeds and **(b)** the effective rate charged by the bank (to the nearest tenth percent). *(p. 280)*

6. Sam Slater buys a $10,000, 13-week Treasury bill at $5\frac{1}{2}$%. What is the effective rate? Round to the nearest hundredth percent. *(p. 281)*

● Students who take out Stafford loans after July 1 will pay a fixed interest rate of 6.8%.

ML HARRIS/GETTY IMAGES

COLLEGE | To save on student-loan interest rates, consolidate your debt by July 1. *By Jane Bennett Clark*

Last chance to **LOCK** in

IT SEEMS LIKE only yesterday that student-loan rates were sinking faster than a December sun. Alas, the days of magically vanishing—or modestly rising—rates are about to end. Starting July 1, the Deficit Reduction Act of 2005 will set a fixed rate of 6.8% on new Stafford loans, about two percentage points above this past year's lowest rate. Similarly, PLUS loans for parent borrowers will be fixed at 8.5%, up from the current 6.1%.

But the fixed rates won't apply to outstanding Stafford and PLUS loans. On those loans, rates will continue to change each July 1 based on the 91-day Treasury-bill yield set the last Thursday in May. The T-bill rate is expected to rise, so it pays to consolidate your loans and lock in the lower rate.

Things get a little tricky if you con-solidated last spring to take advantage of bottom-cruising rates (as low as 2.87% for Stafford loans and 4.17% for PLUS loans) and have since taken out new loans. You can consolidate the new loans, but you'll want to keep the two consolidations separate, says Gary Carpenter, executive director of the National Institute of Certified College Planners (www.niccp.com). "If you roll an old consolidation into a new one, you get a blended rate—the lower rate is lost," says Carpenter. And you may have to shop for a lender; some balk at consolidating loans of less than $7,500.

Although financial-aid packages were calculated this spring, next fall's freshmen will pay the post-July, fixed rate on Staffords; likewise, PLUS loans for parents of incoming freshmen will carry the new fixed rate. However, parents of currently enrolled students

can apply for a PLUS now and consoli-date to lock in this year's rate, says Mark Brenner, of College Loan Corp. (www.collegeloan.com), which makes such loans. Ask your school's financial-aid office for details.

Other options. After July 1, parents choosing between a PLUS loan with an 8.5% fixed rate and a variable-rate home-equity line of credit should take a closer look at the latter, says Carpen-ter. The average rate for equity lines was recently 7.67%, and interest is deductible.

With rates fixed on Stafford loans, private loans, which are issued at variable rates, could someday end up costing less than Staffords. Sallie Mae (www.salliemae.com), the largest of the student-loan companies, offers private loans at the prime rate—lately 7.5%—with no fees for borrowers who have a good credit history.

Even if rates head south, borrowers "should exhaust federal loans first," says Sallie Mae spokeswoman Martha Holler. Unlike private loans, payments on those loans can be extended, de-ferred or forgiven in certain cases.

A mixed bag. As for the other provi-sions of the Deficit Reduction Act, they represent "a mixed bag" for under-graduates, says Brenner. For Stafford loans, the law boosts the maximum amount you can borrow in each of the first two years of college (the total amount remains the same), phases out origination fees and expands Pell Grants for math and science students. Married couples will no longer be able to consolidate loans taken out separate-ly into a single loan. And, as of July 1, students can no longer consolidate Staffords while they're still in school.

But Brenner says the changes "should in no way discourage American families from applying for the college of their choice." There's plenty of mon-ey for students who need it, he says, and federally sponsored loans remain "a hell of a deal."

BUSINESS MATH ISSUE

The Deficit Reduction Act of 2005 is too complicated for students needing loans.

1. List the key points of the article and information to support your position.
2. Write a group defense of your position using math calculations to support your view.

Slater's Business Math Scrapbook

with Internet Application

Putting Your Skills to Work

PROJECT A
Go to www.treasurydirect.gov and find out the latest rates for Treasury bills.

Investors Can More Easily Buy Treasurys Online

By ERIN E. ARVEDLUND

The federal government is making it easier to buy Treasury bonds online.

Beginning Monday, the Treasury Department will allow individual investors to purchase, manage and redeem Treasury bonds, bills and notes electronically by opening up an online account through its TreasuryDirect Web site (www.treasurydirect.gov). Previously, investors could buy or redeem only savings bonds in their online accounts. If they wanted to buy Treasury bonds, they had to open a paper-based account and, for the most part, pay by check for any transaction.

U.S. Treasurys are considered the safest investments for individuals, as they are backed by the full faith and credit of the U.S. government. What's more, any interest earned on Treasurys is exempt from state and local income taxes.

Once you open a TreasuryDirect account online, you are eligible to purchase and hold so-called marketable Treasury securities—which include bills, notes and bonds. Bills are short-term Treasurys sold at a discount to face value; notes are interest-bearing Treasurys with maturities of up to 10 years; and bonds are interest-bearing Treasurys with maturities of more than 10 years. "Marketable" means they can be bought and sold on secondary markets, though TreasuryDirect offers them only when issued.

Investors also can purchase Treasury Inflation Protected Securities, or TIPS, whose principal value increases with the rate of inflation. Previously, only Series I and EE U.S. Savings Bonds were available to online TreasuryDirect account holders since the Web site's inception in October 2002.

Currently, the three-month T-bill is yielding 3.54% and the 10-year bond is yielding 4.33%. The five-year real TIPS yield is 1.45% and the 20-year is 1.93%.

TIPS usually are purchased by investors seeking to outpace inflation, while regular bonds often are favored by those looking for a safe haven and to generate income. Treasurys also can be purchased through a broker, but investors usually will be charged a commission.

TreasuryDirect accounts are accessible by going to the Web site and clicking on "Open an Account." You need to provide your phone number, bank account, the bank's routing number, your Social Security number and driver's license or state identification number. All debits and credits for your Treasury purchases and redemptions will go directly into or out of your bank account.

Investors also can purchase bonds as gifts online. The minimum purchase for a savings bond is $25, and the minimum for Treasurys is $1,000 or a multiple of that amount, for all maturities. The accounts are free of any purchase charges or maintenance fees, but there is a sales charge of $45 per security.

> ## TIPS are usually purchased by investors seeking to outpace inflation.

Wall Street Journal © 2005

Internet Projects: See text Web site (www.mhhe.com/slater9e) and The Business Math Internet Resource Guide.

Video Case

Online banking is very cost effective for the banking industry. Many customers enjoy the convenience; others, however, have doubts. For these individuals, online banking is a different way of thinking.

Banks want customers flocking online because it costs less after initial startup fees. A teller transaction typically costs a bank on average $1 to $1.50, while Internet transactions cost less than 5 cents. Less cost means more profit.

The Gartner Group, a research firm, says that 27 million Americans—one in 10—now do at least some of their banking online, up from 9 million a year earlier. According to a new Gallup poll, online banking services soared by 60% in the year 2000. CyberDialogue, an Internet consulting firm, predicted online banking will rise to 50.9 million customers by 2005. Most sites allow customers to view account information, transfer money, and pay bills online; some sites offer investment account data and transactions. Other applications are coming, including the ability to view and print account statements and canceled checks.

Pundits wrote off most Web banking because of all the things customers couldn't do—close on a loan, sign for a mortgage, or withdraw cash. The startups are applying increasingly innovative strategies to clear these hurdles. Security was, and still is, an issue for many people. According to a recent study, 85% of information technology staffs at corporations and government agencies had detected a computer security breach in the past 12 months, and 64% acknowledged financial losses as a result. Measures are being taken to improve security.

In addition to the usual conveniences of online banking, online banks can pay higher rates on deposits than branch-based banks. However, problems do exist in online banking, such as you can rack up late fees for bill paying and not even know it.

When picking an online banking service, look for the following: (1) 128-bit encryption, the standard in the industry; (2) written guarantees to protect from losses in case of online fraud or bank error; (3) automatic lockout if you wrongly enter your password more than three or four times; and (4) evidence that the bank is FDIC insured.

PROBLEM 1

In 2000, the number of households accessing their accounts through a computer increased to 12.5 million, an 81.42% increase from a year earlier. These numbers support the push for online banking. What was the number of online users last year? Round to the nearest million.

PROBLEM 2

Jupiter Media Metrix, an online research firm, estimated that banking online will increase from 12.5 million to about 43.3 million in 2005. CyberDialogue, an Internet consulting firm, predicted that by the end of 2000, 24.6 million people would bank online and by 2005, the number would rise to 50.9 million. **(a)** What percent increase is Jupiter Media Metrix forecasting? **(b)** What percent increase is CyberDialogue forecasting? Round to the nearest hundredth percent.

PROBLEM 3

E*Trade Bank pays at least 3.1% on checking accounts with balances of $1,000 or more. The national average is 0.78% for interest-bearing checking. If you have $2,300 in your account and bank at E*Trade based on simple interest: **(a)** How much interest would you earn at the end of 30 days (ordinary interest)? **(b)** How much interest would you earn at a non-online bank?

PROBLEM 4

Online banking users—people who do basic banking tasks such as occasionally transferring money between accounts online—jumped to an estimated 20 million in December 2000 from 15.9 million in September 2000. What was the percent increase? Round to the nearest hundredth percent.

PROBLEM 5

On January 9, 2001, Bank of America Corporation announced that it had more than 3 million online banking customers. If 130,000 customers are added in a month, what is the percent increase? Round to the nearest hundredth percent.

PROBLEM 6

The E*Trade Bank is an Internet bank in Menlo Park, California, owned by Internet brokerage company E*Trade Group. On January 4, 2001, E*Trade Bank said it had added more than $1 billion in net new deposits in its fourth quarter of 2000, bringing its total deposits to more than $5.7 billion. E*Trade had a total of $1.1 billion in deposits at the end of 1998. What is the percent increase in net deposits in the year 2000 compared to 1998? Round to the nearest hundredth percent.

PROBLEM 7

The research firm The Gartner Group says that in 2001, 27 million Americans—one in 10—do at least some of their banking online, up from 9 million a year earlier. **(a)** How many were banking online last year? **(b)** What was the percent increase in online banking in 2001? Round to nearest hundredth percent.

PROBLEM 8

Industry experts expect that online banking and bill payment, like other forms of e-commerce, will continue to grow at a rapid pace. According to Killen & Associates, the number of bills paid online will rise to 11.7 billion by 2001, a 77% increase. What had been the amount of users in 2000? Round to the nearest tenth.

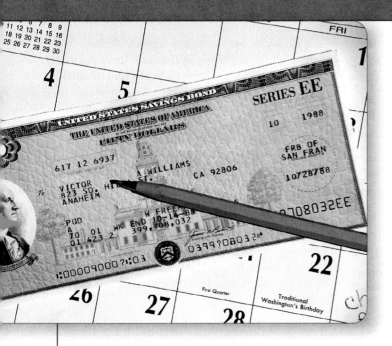

Compound Interest and Present Value

LEARNING UNIT OBJECTIVES

Note: **A complete set of plastic overlays showing the concepts of compound interest and present value is found in Chapter 13.**

LU 12–1: Compound Interest (Future Value)—The Big Picture

- Compare simple interest with compound interest (*pp. 296–298*).
- Calculate the compound amount and interest manually and by table lookup (*pp. 298–301*).
- Explain and compute the effective rate (APY) (*p. 301*).

LU 12–2: Present Value—The Big Picture

- Compare present value (PV) with compound interest (FV) (*p. 303*).
- Compute present value by table lookup (*pp. 304–306*).
- Check the present value answer by compounding (*p. 306*).

How Math Fattens Your Wallet

As the years roll by, this investment compounding can generate eye-popping performance. At a steady 8% annual return, you would earn a cumulative 47% after five years, 116% after 10 years, 585% after 25 years and 4,590% after 50 years. Impressed? It's amazing what you can amass with a little money and a lot of time.

Indeed, every so often, newspapers will carry stories about folks who die in their nineties and, to the shock of friends and neighbors, leave behind estates worth millions of dollars. The stories always have the same basic elements: These millionaires never earned a lot of money, they lived modestly, they drove used cars and they didn't have grand homes.

Often, the newspapers will speculate that these folks were brilliant investors. But the explanation is usually more prosaic.

Would you like to save a million dollars? We omitted the beginning of the *Wall Street Journal* clipping "How Math Fattens Your Wallet" because it explained the years involved in recouping losses when interest is only charged on the principal. The clipping contrasts this extended time by introducing compound interest, which means that interest is added to the principal and then additional interest is paid on both the old principal and its interest. This compounding can make it possible for you to save a million dollars.

In this chapter we look at the power of compounding—interest paid on earned interest. Let's begin by studying Learning Unit 12–1, which shows you how to calculate compound interest.

Wall Street Journal © 2005

Learning Unit 12–1: Compound Interest (Future Value)—The Big Picture

Check out the plastic overlays that appear within Chapter 13 to review these concepts.

So far we have discussed only simple interest, which is interest on the principal alone. Simple interest is either paid at the end of the loan period or deducted in advance. From the chapter introduction, you know that interest can also be compounded.

Compounding involves the calculation of interest periodically over the life of the loan (or investment). After each calculation, the interest is added to the principal. Future calculations are on the adjusted principal (old principal plus interest). **Compound interest,** then, is the interest on the principal plus the interest of prior periods. **Future value (FV),** or the **compound amount,** is the final amount of the loan or investment at the end of the last period. In the beginning of this unit, do not be concerned with how to calculate compounding but try to understand the meaning of compounding.

Figure 12.1 shows how $1 will grow if it is calculated for 4 years at 8% annually. This means that the interest is calculated on the balance once a year. In Figure 12.1, we start with $1, which is the **present value (PV).** After year 1, the dollar with interest is worth $1.08. At the end of year 2, the dollar is worth $1.17. By the end of year 4, the dollar is worth $1.36 . Note how we start with the present and look to see what the dollar will be worth in the future. *Compounding goes from present value to future value.*

FIGURE 12.1

Future value of $1 at 8% for four periods

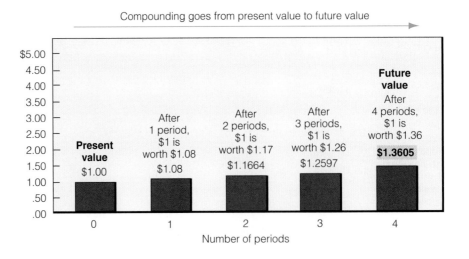

Before you learn how to calculate compound interest and compare it to simple interest, you must understand the terms that follow. These terms are also used in Chapter 13.

- **Compounded annually:** Interest calculated on the balance once a year.

- **Compounded semiannually:** Interest calculated on the balance every 6 months or every $\frac{1}{2}$ year.

- **Compounded quarterly:** Interest calculated on the balance every 3 months or every $\frac{1}{4}$ year.

- **Compounded monthly:** Interest calculated on the balance each month.

- **Compounded daily:** Interest calculated on the balance each day.

- **Number of periods:**[1] Number of years multiplied by the number of times the interest is compounded per year. For example, if you compound $1 for 4 years at 8% annually, semiannually, or quarterly, the following periods will result:

Annually:	4 years $\times$ 1 = 4 periods
Semiannually:	4 years $\times$ 2 = 8 periods
Quarterly:	4 years $\times$ 4 = 16 periods

- **Rate for each period:**[2] Annual interest rate divided by the number of times the interest is compounded per year. Compounding changes the interest rate for annual, semiannual, and quarterly periods as follows:

Annually:	8% $\div$ 1 = 8%
Semiannually:	8% $\div$ 2 = 4%
Quarterly:	8% $\div$ 4 = 2%

Note that both the number of periods (4) and the rate (8%) for the annual example did not change. You will see later that rate and periods (not years) will always change unless interest is compounded yearly.

Now you are ready to learn the difference between simple interest and compound interest.

Simple versus Compound Interest

Did you know that money invested at 6% will double in 12 years? The following *Wall Street Journal* clipping "Confused by Investing?" shows how to calculate the number of years it takes for your investment to double.

Confused by Investing?

If there's something about your investment portfolio that doesn't seem to add up, maybe you should check your math.

Lots of folks are perplexed by the mathematics of investing, so I thought a refresher course might help. Here's a look at some key concepts:

■ **10 Plus 10 is 21**

Imagine you invest $100, which earns 10% this year and 10% next. How much have you made? If you answered 21%, go to the head of the class.

Here's how the math works. This year's 10% gain turns your $100 into $110. Next year, you also earn 10%, but you start the year with $110. Result? You earn $11, boosting your wealth to $121.

Thus, your portfolio has earned a *cumulative* 21% return over two years, but the *annualized* return is just 10%. The fact that 21% is more than double 10% can be attributed to the effect of investment compounding, the way that you earn money each year not only on your original investment, but also on earnings from prior years that you've reinvested.

■ **The Rule of 72**

To get a feel for compounding, try the rule of 72. What's that? If you divide a particular annual return into 72, you'll find out how many years it will take to double your money. Thus, at 10% a year, an investment will double in value in a tad over seven years.

[1]Periods are often expressed with the letter *N* for number of periods.

[2]Rate is often expressed with the letter *i* for interest.

The following three situations of Bill Smith will clarify the difference between simple interest and compound interest.

Situation 1: Calculating Simple Interest and Maturity Value

EXAMPLE Bill Smith deposited $80 in a savings account for 4 years at an annual interest rate of 8%. What is Bill's simple interest?

To calculate simple interest, we use the following simple interest formula:

$$\text{Interest } (I) = \text{Principal } (P) \times \text{Rate } (R) \times \text{Time } (T)$$

$$\$25.60 \quad = \quad \$80 \quad \times \quad .08 \quad \times \quad 4$$

In 4 years Bill receives a total of $105.60 ($80.00 + $25.60)—principal plus simple interest.

Now let's look at the interest Bill would earn if the bank compounded Bill's interest on his savings.

Situation 2: Calculating Compound Amount and Interest without Tables[3]

You can use the following steps to calculate the compound amount and the interest manually:

CALCULATING COMPOUND AMOUNT AND INTEREST MANUALLY
Step 1. Calculate the simple interest and add it to the principal. Use this total to figure next year's interest.
Step 2. Repeat for the total number of periods.
Step 3. Compound amount − Principal = Compound interest.

EXAMPLE Bill Smith deposited $80 in a savings account for 4 years at an annual compounded rate of 8%. What are Bill's compound amount and interest?

The following shows how the compounded rate affects Bill's interest:

	Year 1	Year 2	Year 3	Year 4
	$80.00	$86.40	$ 93.31	$100.77
	× .08	× .08	× .08	× .08
Interest	$ 6.40	$ 6.91	$ 7.46	$ 8.06
Beginning balance	+ 80.00	+ 86.40	+ 93.31	+ 100.77
Amount at year-end	$86.40	$93.31	$100.77	$108.83

Note that the beginning year 2 interest is the result of the interest of year 1 added to the principal. At the end of each interest period, we add on the period's interest. This interest becomes part of the principal we use for the calculation of the next period's interest. We can determine Bill's compound interest as follows:[4]

Compound amount	$108.83	
Principal	− 80.00	*Note:* In Situation 1 the interest was $25.60.
Compound interest	$ 28.83	

We could have used the following simplified process to calculate the compound amount and interest:

---

[3]For simplicity of presentation, round each calculation to nearest cent before continuing the compounding process. The compound amount will be off by 1 cent.

[4]The formula for compounding is $A = P(1 + i)^N$, where A equals compound amount, P equals the principal, i equals interest per period, and N equals number of periods. The calculator sequence would be as follows for Bill Smith: 1 ⊞ .08 y^x 4 × 80 ⊟ 108.84. A Financial Calculator Guide booklet is available that shows how to operate HP 10BII and TI BA II Plus.

Year 1	Year 2	Year 3	Year 4
$80.00	$86.40	$ 93.31	$100.77
× 1.08	× 1.08	× 1.08	× 1.08
$86.40	$93.31	$100.77	$108.83 [5] ← Future value

When using this simplification, you do not have to add the new interest to the previous balance. Remember that compounding results in higher interest than simple interest. Compounding is the *sum* of principal and interest multiplied by the interest rate we use to calculate interest for the next period. So, 1.08 above is 108%, with 100% as the base and 8% as the interest.

Situation 3: Calculating Compound Amount by Table Lookup

To calculate the compound amount with a future value table, use the following steps:

CALCULATING COMPOUND AMOUNT BY TABLE LOOKUP
Step 1. Find the periods: Years multiplied by number of times interest is compounded in 1 year.
Step 2. Find the rate: Annual rate divided by number of times interest is compounded in 1 year.
Step 3. Go down the Period column of the table to the number of periods desired; look across the row to find the rate. At the intersection of the two columns is the table factor for the compound amount of $1.
Step 4. Multiply the table factor by the amount of the loan. This gives the compound amount.

In Situation 2, Bill deposited $80 into a savings account for 4 years at an interest rate of 8% compounded annually. Bill heard that he could calculate the compound amount and interest by using tables. In Situation 3, Bill learns how to do this. Again, Bill wants to know the value of $80 in 4 years at 8%. He begins by using Table 12.1 (p. 300).

Looking at Table 12.1, Bill goes down the Period column to period 4, then across the row to the 8% column. At the intersection, Bill sees the number 1.3605. The marginal notes show how Bill arrived at the periods and rate. The 1.3605 table number means that $1 compounded at this rate will increase in value in 4 years to about $1.36. Do you recognize the $1.36? Figure 12.1 showed how $1 grew to $1.36. Since Bill wants to know the value of $80, he multiplies the dollar amount by the table factor as follows:

$$\$80.00 \ \times \ 1.3605 \ = \ \$108.84$$

Principal × Table factor = Compound amount (future value)

Figure 12.2 (p. 300) illustrates this compounding procedure. We can say that compounding is a future value (FV) since we are looking into the future. Thus,

$$\$108.84 - \$80.00 = \$28.84 \text{ interest for 4 years at 8\%}$$
compounded annually on $80.00

Now let's look at two examples that illustrate compounding more than once a year.

EXAMPLE Find the interest on $6,000 at 10% compounded semiannually for 5 years. We calculate the interest as follows:

Periods = 2 × 5 years = 10

Rate = 10% ÷ 2 = 5%

10 periods, 5%, in Table 12.1 = 1.6289 (table factor)

$6,000 × 1.6289 = $9,773.40
− 6,000.00
$3,773.40
interest

Four Periods
No. of times
compounded × No. of years
in 1 year
1   ×   4

8% Rate
8% rate = $\dfrac{8\%}{1}$ → Annual rate
→ No. of times compounded in 1 year

---

[5]Off 1 cent due to rounding.

| TABLE | 12.1 | Future value of $1 at compound interest |

Period	1%	1½%	2%	3%	4%	5%	6%	7%	8%	9%	10%
1	1.0100	1.0150	1.0200	1.0300	1.0400	1.0500	1.0600	1.0700	1.0800	1.0900	1.1000
2	1.0201	1.0302	1.0404	1.0609	1.0816	1.1025	1.1236	1.1449	1.1664	1.1881	1.2100
3	1.0303	1.0457	1.0612	1.0927	1.1249	1.1576	1.1910	1.2250	1.2597	1.2950	1.3310
4	1.0406	1.0614	1.0824	1.1255	1.1699	1.2155	1.2625	1.3108	1.3605	1.4116	1.4641
5	1.0510	1.0773	1.1041	1.1593	1.2167	1.2763	1.3382	1.4026	1.4693	1.5386	1.6105
6	1.0615	1.0934	1.1262	1.1941	1.2653	1.3401	1.4185	1.5007	1.5869	1.6771	1.7716
7	1.0721	1.1098	1.1487	1.2299	1.3159	1.4071	1.5036	1.6058	1.7138	1.8280	1.9487
8	1.0829	1.1265	1.1717	1.2668	1.3686	1.4775	1.5938	1.7182	1.8509	1.9926	2.1436
9	1.0937	1.1434	1.1951	1.3048	1.4233	1.5513	1.6895	1.8385	1.9990	2.1719	2.3579
10	1.1046	1.1605	1.2190	1.3439	1.4802	1.6289	1.7908	1.9672	2.1589	2.3674	2.5937
11	1.1157	1.1780	1.2434	1.3842	1.5395	1.7103	1.8983	2.1049	2.3316	2.5804	2.8531
12	1.1268	1.1960	1.2682	1.4258	1.6010	1.7959	2.0122	2.2522	2.5182	2.8127	3.1384
13	1.1381	1.2135	1.2936	1.4685	1.6651	1.8856	2.1329	2.4098	2.7196	3.0658	3.4523
14	1.1495	1.2318	1.3195	1.5126	1.7317	1.9799	2.2609	2.5785	2.9372	3.3417	3.7975
15	1.1610	1.2502	1.3459	1.5580	1.8009	2.0789	2.3966	2.7590	3.1722	3.6425	4.1772
16	1.1726	1.2690	1.3728	1.6047	1.8730	2.1829	2.5404	2.9522	3.4259	3.9703	4.5950
17	1.1843	1.2880	1.4002	1.6528	1.9479	2.2920	2.6928	3.1588	3.7000	4.3276	5.0545
18	1.1961	1.3073	1.4282	1.7024	2.0258	2.4066	2.8543	3.3799	3.9960	4.7171	5.5599
19	1.2081	1.3270	1.4568	1.7535	2.1068	2.5270	3.0256	3.6165	4.3157	5.1417	6.1159
20	1.2202	1.3469	1.4859	1.8061	2.1911	2.6533	3.2071	3.8697	4.6610	5.6044	6.7275
21	1.2324	1.3671	1.5157	1.8603	2.2788	2.7860	3.3996	4.1406	5.0338	6.1088	7.4002
22	1.2447	1.3876	1.5460	1.9161	2.3699	2.9253	3.6035	4.4304	5.4365	6.6586	8.1403
23	1.2572	1.4084	1.5769	1.9736	2.4647	3.0715	3.8197	4.7405	5.8715	7.2579	8.9543
24	1.2697	1.4295	1.6084	2.0328	2.5633	3.2251	4.0489	5.0724	6.3412	7.9111	9.8497
25	1.2824	1.4510	1.6406	2.0938	2.6658	3.3864	4.2919	5.4274	6.8485	8.6231	10.8347
26	1.2953	1.4727	1.6734	2.1566	2.7725	3.5557	4.5494	5.8074	7.3964	9.3992	11.9182
27	1.3082	1.4948	1.7069	2.2213	2.8834	3.7335	4.8223	6.2139	7.9881	10.2451	13.1100
28	1.3213	1.5172	1.7410	2.2879	2.9987	3.9201	5.1117	6.6488	8.6271	11.1672	14.4210
29	1.3345	1.5400	1.7758	2.3566	3.1187	4.1161	5.4184	7.1143	9.3173	12.1722	15.8631
30	1.3478	1.5631	1.8114	2.4273	3.2434	4.3219	5.7435	7.6123	10.0627	13.2677	17.4494

Note: For more detailed tables, see your reference booklet, the *Business Math Handbook.*

EXAMPLE Pam Donahue deposits $8,000 in her savings account that pays 6% interest compounded quarterly. What will be the balance of her account at the end of 5 years?

Periods = 4 × 5 years = 20

Rate = 6% ÷ 4 = 1½%

| FIGURE | 12.2 |

Compounding (FV)

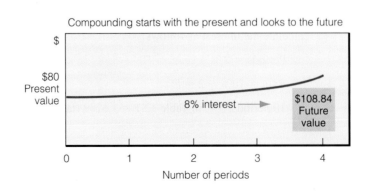

Compounding starts with the present and looks to the future

$
$80
Present value

8% interest →

$108.84
Future value

0   1   2   3   4

Number of periods

20 periods, $1\frac{1}{2}\%$, in Table 12.1 = 1.3469 (table factor)

$8,000 × 1.3469 = $10,775.20

Next, let's look at bank rates and how they affect interest.

Bank Rates—Nominal versus Effective Rates (Annual Percentage Yield, or APY)

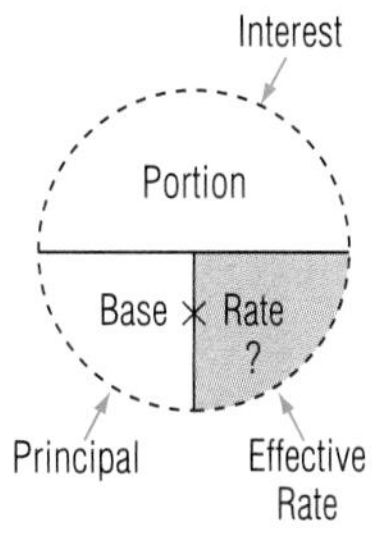

Banks often advertise their annual (nominal) interest rates and *not* their true or effective rate (annual percentage yield, or APY). This has made it difficult for investors and depositors to determine the actual rates of interest they were receiving. The Truth in Savings law forced savings institutions to reveal their actual rate of interest. The APY is defined in the Truth in Savings law as the percentage rate expressing the total amount of interest that would be received on a $100 deposit based on the annual rate and frequency of compounding for a 365-day period. As you can see from the advertisement on the left, banks now refer to the effective rate of interest as the annual percentage yield.

Let's study the rates of two banks to see which bank has the better return for the investor. Blue Bank pays 8% interest compounded quarterly on $8,000. Sun Bank offers 8% interest compounded semiannually on $8,000. The 8% rate is the **nominal rate,** or stated rate, on which the bank calculates the interest. To calculate the **effective rate (annual percentage yield, or APY),** however, we can use the following formula:

$$\text{Effective rate (APY)}^{6} = \frac{\text{Interest for 1 year}}{\text{Principal}}$$

Now let's calculate the effective rate (APY) for Blue Bank and Sun Bank.

Blue, 8% compounded quarterly	Sun, 8% compounded semiannually
Periods = 4 (4 × 1)	Periods = 2 (2 × 1)
Percent = $\frac{8\%}{4}$ = 2%	Percent = $\frac{8\%}{2}$ = 4%
Principal = $8,000	Principal = $8,000
Table 12.1 lookup: 4 periods, 2%	Table 12.1 lookup: 2 periods, 4%

1.0824
        × $8,000
Less $8,659.20
principal − 8,000.00
        $ 659.20
	1.0816
	       × $8,000
	    $8,652.80
	   − 8,000.00
	    $ 652.80

Effective rate (APY) = $\frac{\$659.20}{\$8,000}$ = .0824	$\frac{\$652.80}{\$8,000}$ = .0816
= 8.24%	= 8.16%

Figure 12.3 (p. 302) illustrates a comparison of nominal and effective rates (APY) of interest. This comparison should make you question any advertisement of interest rates before depositing your money.

Before concluding this unit, we briefly discuss compounding interest daily.

Compounding Interest Daily

Although many banks add interest to each account quarterly, some banks pay interest that is **compounded daily,** and other banks use *continuous compounding*. Remember that

---

[6]Round to the nearest hundredth percent as needed. In practice, the rate is often rounded to the nearest thousandth.

(Left margin notes:)

Interest

Portion

Base × Rate
?

Principal   Effective
Rate

Note the effective rates (APY) can be seen from Table 12.1 for $1:
1.0824 ← 4 periods, 2%
1.0816 ← 2 periods, 4%

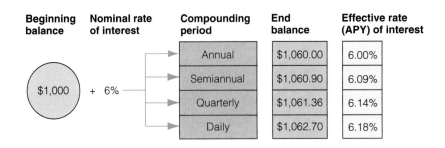

.

FIGURE	12.3

Nominal and effective rates
(APY) of interest compared

Compounding period	End balance	Effective rate (APY) of interest
Annual	$1,060.00	6.00%
Semiannual	$1,060.90	6.09%
Quarterly	$1,061.36	6.14%
Daily	$1,062.70	6.18%

$1,000 + 6%

Beginning balance — Nominal rate of interest

continuous compounding sounds great, but in fact, it yields only a fraction of a percent more interest over a year than daily compounding. Today, computers perform these calculations.

Table 12.2 is a partial table showing what $1 will grow to in the future by daily compounded interest, 360-day basis. For example, we can calculate interest compounded daily on $900 at 6% per year for 25 years as follows:

$900 × 4.4811 = **$4,032.99** daily compounding

Now it's time to check your progress with the following Practice Quiz.

LU 12–1	PRACTICE QUIZ

Complete this **Practice Quiz** to see how you are doing

1. Complete the following without a table (round each calculation to the nearest cent as needed):

Principal	Time	Rate of compound interest	Compounded	Number of periods to be compounded	Total amount	Total interest
$200	1 year	8%	Quarterly	**a.**	**b.**	**c.**

2. Solve the previous problem by using compound value (FV) in Table 12.1.
3. Lionel Rodgers deposits $6,000 in Victory Bank, which pays 3% interest compounded semiannually. How much will Lionel have in his account at the end of 8 years?
4. Find the effective rate (APY) for the year: principal, $7,000; interest rate, 12%; and compounded quarterly.
5. Calculate by Table 12.2 what $1,500 compounded daily for 5 years will grow to at 7%.

TABLE	12.2	Interest on a $1 deposit compounded daily—360-day basis

Number of years	6.00%	6.50%	7.00%	7.50%	8.00%	8.50%	9.00%	9.50%	10.00%
1	1.0618	1.0672	1.0725	1.0779	1.0833	1.0887	1.0942	1.0996	1.1052
2	1.1275	1.1388	1.1503	1.1618	1.1735	1.1853	1.1972	1.2092	1.2214
3	1.1972	1.2153	1.2337	1.2523	1.2712	1.2904	1.3099	1.3297	1.3498
4	1.2712	1.2969	1.3231	1.3498	1.3771	1.4049	1.4333	1.4622	1.4917
5	1.3498	1.3840	1.4190	1.4549	1.4917	1.5295	1.5682	1.6079	1.6486
6	1.4333	1.4769	1.5219	1.5682	1.6160	1.6652	1.7159	1.7681	1.8220
7	1.5219	1.5761	1.6322	1.6904	1.7506	1.8129	1.8775	1.9443	2.0136
8	1.6160	1.6819	1.7506	1.8220	1.8963	1.9737	2.0543	2.1381	2.2253
9	1.7159	1.7949	1.8775	1.9639	2.0543	2.1488	2.2477	2.3511	2.4593
10	1.8220	1.9154	2.0136	2.1168	2.2253	2.3394	2.4593	2.5854	2.7179
15	2.4594	2.6509	2.8574	3.0799	3.3197	3.5782	3.8568	4.1571	4.4808
20	3.3198	3.6689	4.0546	4.4810	4.9522	5.4728	6.0482	6.6842	7.3870
25	4.4811	5.0777	5.7536	6.5195	7.3874	8.3708	9.4851	10.7477	12.1782
30	6.0487	7.0275	8.1645	9.4855	11.0202	12.8032	14.8747	17.2813	20.0772

✓ **Solutions**

1. **a.** 4 (4 × 1)   **b.** $216.48   **c.** $16.48 ($216.48 − $200)
   $200 × 1.02 = $204 × 1.02 = $208.08 × 1.02 = $212.24 × 1.02 = $216.48
2. $200 × 1.0824 = $216.48 (4 periods, 2%)
3. 16 periods, $1\frac{1}{2}$%, $6,000 × 1.2690 = $7,614
4. 4 periods, 3%,
   $7,000 × 1.1255 = $7,878.50
    − 7,000.00 $\frac{$878.50}{$7,000.00}$ = 12.55%
    $ 878.50
5. $1,500 × 1.4190 = $2,128.50

Check out the plastic overlays that appear within Chapter 13 to review these concepts.

LU 12–1a   EXTRA PRACTICE QUIZ

Need more practice? Try this **Extra Practice Quiz** *(check figures in Chapter Organizer, p. 308)*

1. Complete the following without a table (round each calculation to the nearest cent as needed):

Principal	Time	Rate of compound interest	Compounded	Number of periods to be compounded	Total amount	Total interest
$500	1 year	8%	Quarterly	a.	b.	c.

2. Solve the previous problem by using compound value (FV). See Table 12.1.
3. Lionel Rodgers deposits $7,000 in Victory Bank, which pays 4% interest compounded semiannually. How much will Lionel have in his account at the end of 8 years?
4. Find the effective rate (APY) for the year: principal, $8,000; interest rate, 6%; and compounded quarterly. Round to the nearest hundredth percent.
5. Calculate by Table 12.2 what $1,800 compounded daily for 5 years will grow to at 6%.

Learning Unit 12–2: Present Value—The Big Picture

Figure 12.1 (p. 296) in Learning Unit 12–1 showed how by compounding, the *future value* of $1 became $1.36. This learning unit discusses *present value*. Before we look at specific calculations involving present value, let's look at the concept of present value.

Figure 12.4 shows that if we invested 74 cents today, compounding would cause the 74 cents to grow to $1 in the future. For example, let's assume you ask this question: "If I need $1 in 4 years in the future, how much must I put in the bank *today* (assume an 8% annual interest)?" To answer this question, you must know the present value of that $1 today. From Figure 12.4, you can see that the present value of $1 is .7350. Remember that the $1 is only worth 74 cents if you wait 4 periods to receive it. This is one reason why so many athletes get such big contracts—much of the money is paid in later years when it is not worth as much.

FIGURE   12.4

Present value of $1 at 8% for four periods

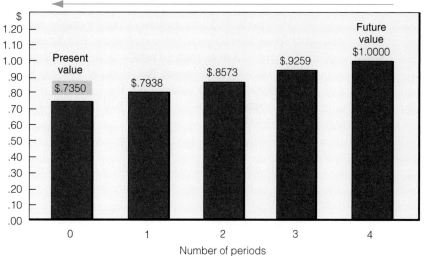

Present value goes from the future value to the present value

(Bar chart — "Number of periods" on x-axis from 0 to 4; dollar values on y-axis from $.00 to $1.20)
- Period 0: Present value $.7350
- Period 1: $.7938
- Period 2: $.8573
- Period 3: $.9259
- Period 4: Future value $1.0000

FIGURE	**12.5**

Present value

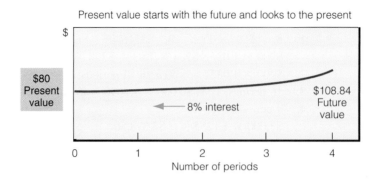

Present value starts with the future and looks to the present

$80 Present value

$108.84 Future value

← 8% interest

0   1   2   3   4

Number of periods

RF/Corbis

Relationship of Compounding (FV) to Present Value (PV)—The Bill Smith Example Continued

In Learning Unit 12–1, our consideration of compounding started in the *present* ($80) and looked to find the *future* amount of $108.84. Present value (PV) starts with the *future* and tries to calculate its worth in the *present* ($80). For example, in Figure 12.5, we assume Bill Smith knew that in 4 years he wanted to buy a bike that cost $108.84 (future). Bill's bank pays 8% interest compounded annually. How much money must Bill put in the bank *today* (present) to have $108.84 in 4 years? To work from the future to the present, we can use a present value (PV) table. In the next section you will learn how to use this table.

How to Use a Present Value (PV) Table[7]

To calculate present value with a present value table, use the following steps:

CALCULATING PRESENT VALUE BY TABLE LOOKUP
Step 1. Find the periods: Years multiplied by number of times interest is compounded in 1 year.
Step 2. Find the rate: Annual rate divided by numbers of times interest is compounded in 1 year.
Step 3. Go down the Period column of the table to the number of periods desired; look across the row to find the rate. At the intersection of the two columns is the table factor for the compound value of $1.
Step 4. Multiply the table factor times the future value. This gives the present value.

Periods

4 × 1 = 4
↑   ↑
No. of   No. of times
years   compounded
         in 1 year

Table 12.3 is a present value (PV) table that tells you what $1 is worth today at different interest rates. To continue our Bill Smith example, go down the Period column in Table 12.3 to 4. Then go across to the 8% column. At 8% for 4 periods, we see a table factor of .7350. This means that $1 in the future is worth approximately 74 cents today. If Bill invested 74 cents today at 8% for 4 periods, Bill would have $1.

Since Bill knows the bike will cost $108.84 in the future, he completes the following calculation:

$108.84 × .7350 = $80.00

This means that $108.84 in today's dollars is worth $80.00. Now let's check this.

---

[7]The formula for present value is $PV = \dfrac{A}{(1 + i)^N}$, where A equals future amount (compound amount), N equals number of compounding periods, and i equals interest rate per compounding period. The calculator sequence for Bill Smith would be as follows: 1 [+] .08 [y^x] 4 [=] [M+] 108.84 [÷] [MR] [=] 80.03.

| TABLE | 12.3 | Present value of $1 at end period |

Period	1%	1½%	2%	3%	4%	5%	6%	7%	8%	9%	10%
1	.9901	.9852	.9804	.9709	.9615	.9524	.9434	.9346	.9259	.9174	.9091
2	.9803	.9707	.9612	.9426	.9246	.9070	.8900	.8734	.8573	.8417	.8264
3	.9706	.9563	.9423	.9151	.8890	.8638	.8396	.8163	.7938	.7722	.7513
4	.9610	.9422	.9238	.8885	.8548	.8227	.7921	.7629	.7350	.7084	.6830
5	.9515	.9283	.9057	.8626	.8219	.7835	.7473	.7130	.6806	.6499	.6209
6	.9420	.9145	.8880	.8375	.7903	.7462	.7050	.6663	.6302	.5963	.5645
7	.9327	.9010	.8706	.8131	.7599	.7107	.6651	.6227	.5835	.5470	.5132
8	.9235	.8877	.8535	.7894	.7307	.6768	.6274	.5820	.5403	.5019	.4665
9	.9143	.8746	.8368	.7664	.7026	.6446	.5919	.5439	.5002	.4604	.4241
10	.9053	.8617	.8203	.7441	.6756	.6139	.5584	.5083	.4632	.4224	.3855
11	.8963	.8489	.8043	.7224	.6496	.5847	.5268	.4751	.4289	.3875	.3505
12	.8874	.8364	.7885	.7014	.6246	.5568	.4970	.4440	.3971	.3555	.3186
13	.8787	.8240	.7730	.6810	.6006	.5303	.4688	.4150	.3677	.3262	.2897
14	.8700	.8119	.7579	.6611	.5775	.5051	.4423	.3878	.3405	.2992	.2633
15	.8613	.7999	.7430	.6419	.5553	.4810	.4173	.3624	.3152	.2745	.2394
16	.8528	.7880	.7284	.6232	.5339	.4581	.3936	.3387	.2919	.2519	.2176
17	.8444	.7764	.7142	.6050	.5134	.4363	.3714	.3166	.2703	.2311	.1978
18	.8360	.7649	.7002	.5874	.4936	.4155	.3503	.2959	.2502	.2120	.1799
19	.8277	.7536	.6864	.5703	.4746	.3957	.3305	.2765	.2317	.1945	.1635
20	.8195	.7425	.6730	.5537	.4564	.3769	.3118	.2584	.2145	.1784	.1486
21	.8114	.7315	.6598	.5375	.4388	.3589	.2942	.2415	.1987	.1637	.1351
22	.8034	.7207	.6468	.5219	.4220	.3418	.2775	.2257	.1839	.1502	.1228
23	.7954	.7100	.6342	.5067	.4057	.3256	.2618	.2109	.1703	.1378	.1117
24	.7876	.6995	.6217	.4919	.3901	.3101	.2470	.1971	.1577	.1264	.1015
25	.7798	.6892	.6095	.4776	.3751	.2953	.2330	.1842	.1460	.1160	.0923
26	.7720	.6790	.5976	.4637	.3607	.2812	.2198	.1722	.1352	.1064	.0839
27	.7644	.6690	.5859	.4502	.3468	.2678	.2074	.1609	.1252	.0976	.0763
28	.7568	.6591	.5744	.4371	.3335	.2551	.1956	.1504	.1159	.0895	.0693
29	.7493	.6494	.5631	.4243	.3207	.2429	.1846	.1406	.1073	.0822	.0630
30	.7419	.6398	.5521	.4120	.3083	.2314	.1741	.1314	.0994	.0754	.0573
35	.7059	.5939	.5000	.3554	.2534	.1813	.1301	.0937	.0676	.0490	.0356
40	.6717	.5513	.4529	.3066	.2083	.1420	.0972	.0668	.0460	.0318	.0221

Note: For more detailed tables, see your booklet, the *Business Math Handbook.*

Comparing Compound Interest (FV) Table 12.1 with Present Value (PV) Table 12.3

We know from our calculations that Bill needs to invest $80 for 4 years at 8% compound interest annually to buy his bike. We can check this by going back to Table 12.1 and comparing it with Table 12.3. Let's do this now.

Compound value Table 12.1			Present value Table 12.3		
Table 12.1	Present value	Future value	Table 12.3	Future value	Present value
1.3605	× $80.00 =	$108.84	.7350	× $108.84 =	$80.00
(4 per., 8%)			(4 per., 8%)		
We know the present dollar amount and find what the dollar amount is worth in the future.			We know the future dollar amount and find what the dollar amount is worth in the present.		

FIGURE	12.6

Present value

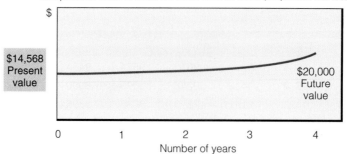

The present value is what we need **now** to have $20,000 in the future

$14,568 Present value

$20,000 Future value

Number of years

Note that the table factor for compounding is over 1 (1.3605) and the table factor for present value is less than 1 (.7350). The compound value table starts with the present and goes to the future. The present value table starts with the future and goes to the present.

Let's look at another example before trying the Practice Quiz.

EXAMPLE Rene Weaver needs $20,000 for college in 4 years. She can earn 8% compounded quarterly at her bank. How much must Rene deposit at the beginning of the year to have $20,000 in 4 years?

Remember that in this example the bank compounds the interest *quarterly*. Let's first determine the period and rate on a quarterly basis:

$$\text{Periods} = 4 \times 4 \text{ years} = 16 \text{ periods} \qquad \text{Rate} = \frac{8\%}{4} = 2\%$$

Now we go to Table 12.3 and find 16 under the Period column. We then move across to the 2% column and find the .7284 table factor.

$$\$20,000 \times .7284 = \boxed{\$14,568}$$

(future value)   (present value)

We illustrate this in Figure 12.6.

We can check the $14,568 present value by using the compound value Table 12.1:

16 periods, 2% column = 1.3728 × $14,568 = $19,998.95[8]

Let's test your understanding of this unit with the Practice Quiz.

LU 12–2	PRACTICE QUIZ

Complete this **Practice Quiz** to see how you are doing

Use the present value Table 12.3 to complete:

	Future amount desired	Length of time	Rate compounded	Table period	Rate used	PV factor	PV amount
1.	$ 7,000	6 years	6% semiannually	_____	_____	_____	_____
2.	$15,000	20 years	10% annually	_____	_____	_____	_____

3. Bill Blum needs $20,000 6 years from today to attend V.P.R. Tech. How much must Bill put in the bank today (12% quarterly) to reach his goal?
4. Bob Fry wants to buy his grandson a Ford Taurus in 4 years. The cost of a car will be $24,000. Assuming a bank rate of 8% compounded quarterly, how much must Bob put in the bank today?

✓ **Solutions**

1. 12 periods (6 years × 2)   3% (6% ÷ 2)   .7014 $4,909.80   ($7,000 × .7014)
2. 20 periods (20 years × 1)   10% (10% ÷ 1)   .1486 $2,229.00   ($15,000 × .1486)
3. 6 years × 4 = 24 periods $\dfrac{12\%}{4} = 3\%$ .4919 × $20,000 = $9,838
4. 4 × 4 years = 16 periods $\dfrac{8\%}{4} = 2\%$ .7284 × $24,000 = $17,481.60

[8]Not quite $20,000 due to rounding of table factors.

LU 12–2a EXTRA PRACTICE QUIZ

Need more practice? Try this **Extra Practice Quiz** (check figures in Chapter Organizer, p. 308)

Use the *Business Math Handbook* to complete:

	Future amount desired	Length of time	Rate compounded	Table period	Rate used	PV factor	PV amount
1.	$ 9,000	7 years	5% semiannually	___	___	___	___
2.	$20,000	20 years	4% annually	___	___	___	___

3. Bill Blum needs $40,000 6 years from today to attend V.P.R. Tech. How much must Bill put in the bank today (8% quarterly) to reach his goal?

4. Bob Fry wants to buy his grandson a Ford Taurus in 4 years. The cost of a car will be $28,000. Assuming a bank rate of 4% compounded quarterly, how much must Bob put in the bank today?

CHAPTER ORGANIZER AND STUDY GUIDE
WITH CHECK FIGURES FOR EXTRA PRACTICE QUIZZES

Topic	Key point, procedure, formula	Example(s) to illustrate situation
Calculating compound amount without tables (future value),* p. 298	Determine new amount by multiplying rate times new balance (that includes interest added on). Start in present and look to future. $$\frac{\text{Compound}}{\text{interest}} = \frac{\text{Compound}}{\text{amount}} - \text{Principal}$$ $\vdash$ Compounding $\longrightarrow$ PV $\qquad\qquad$ FV	$100 in savings account, compounded annually for 2 years at 8%: $100 $\qquad$ $108 × 1.08 $\qquad$ × 1.08 $108 $\qquad$ $116.64 (future value)
Calculating compound amount (future value) by table lookup, p. 299	$$\text{Periods} = \begin{array}{c}\text{Number of times}\\ \text{compounded}\\ \text{per year}\end{array} × \begin{array}{c}\text{Years of}\\ \text{loan}\end{array}$$ $$\text{Rate} = \frac{\text{Annual rate}}{\begin{array}{c}\text{Number of times compounded}\\ \text{per year}\end{array}}$$ Multiply table factor (intersection of period and rate) times amount of principal.	*Example:* $2,000 @ 12% 5 years compounded quarterly: Periods = 4 × 5 years = 20 Rate = $\frac{12\%}{4}$ = 3% 20 periods, 3% = 1.8061 (table factor) $2,000 × 1.8061 = $3,612.20 (future value)
Effective rate (APY), p. 301	$$\text{Effective rate (APY)} = \frac{\text{Interest for 1 year}}{\text{Principal}}$$ or Rate can be seen in Table 12.1 factor.	$1,000 at 10% compounded semiannually for 1 year. By Table 12.1: 2 periods, 5% 1.1025 means at end of year investor has earned 110.25% of original principal. Thus the interest is 10.25%. $1,000 × 1.1025 = $1,102.50 $\qquad\qquad\qquad$ − 1,000.00 $\qquad\qquad\qquad$ $ 102.50 $\frac{\$102.50}{\$1,000}$ = 10.25% effective rate (APY)

*A = *P*(1 + *i*)^*N*.

(continues)

CHAPTER ORGANIZER AND STUDY GUIDE
WITH CHECK FIGURES FOR EXTRA PRACTICE QUIZZES (concluded)

Topic	Key point, procedure, formula	Example(s) to illustrate situation
Calculating present value (PV) with table lookup*, p. 304	Start with future and calculate worth in the present. Periods and rate computed like in compound interest. ⊢—Present value —⊣ PV FV Find periods and rate. Multiply table factor (intersection of period and rate) times amount of loan.	*Example:* Want $3,612.20 after 5 years with rate of 12% compounded quarterly: Periods = 4 × 5 = 20; % = 3% By Table 12.3: 20 periods, 3% = .5537 $3,612.20 × .5537 = $2,000.08 Invested today will yield desired amount in future
KEY TERMS	Annual percentage yield (APY), *p. 301* Compound amount, *p. 296* Compounded annually, *p. 297* Compounded daily, *p. 297* Compounded monthly, *p. 297* Compounded quarterly, *p. 297* Compounded semiannually, *p. 297* Compounding, *p. 296* Compound interest, *p. 296* Effective rate, *p. 301* Future value (FV), *p. 296* Nominal rate, *p. 301* Number of periods, *p. 297* Present value (PV), *p. 296* Rate for each period, *p. 297*	
CHECK FIGURES FOR EXTRA PRACTICE QUIZZES WITH PAGE REFERENCES	LU 12–1a (p. 303) 1. 4 periods; Int. = $41.22; $541.21 2. $541.20 3. $9,609.60 4. 6.14% 5. $2,429.64	LU 12–2a (p. 307) 1. $6,369.30 2. $9,128 3. $24,868 4. $23,878.40

$*\dfrac{A}{(1 + i)^N}$ if table not used.

Critical Thinking Discussion Questions

1. Explain how periods and rates are calculated in compounding problems. Compare simple interest to compound interest.

2. What are the steps to calculate the compound amount by table? Why is the compound table factor greater than $1?

3. What is the effective rate (APY)? Why can the effective rate be seen directly from the table factor?

4. Explain the difference between compounding and present value. Why is the present value table factor less than $1?

Name _____ Date _____

DRILL PROBLEMS

Complete the following without using Table 12.1 (round to the nearest cent for each calculation) and then check by Table 12.1 (check will be off due to rounding).

	Principal	Time (years)	Rate of compound interest	Compounded	Periods	Rate	Total amount	Total interest
12–1.	$1,400	2	4%	Semiannually				

Complete the following using compound future value Table 12.1:

	Time	Principal	Rate	Compounded	Amount	Interest
12–2.	9 years	$10,000	3%	Annually		
12–3.	6 months	$10,000	8%	Quarterly		
12–4.	3 years	$2,000	12%	Semiannually		

Calculate the effective rate (APY) of interest for 1 year.

12–5. Principal: $15,500
Interest rate: 12%
Compounded quarterly
Effective rate (APY):

12–6. Using Table 12.2, calculate what $700 would grow to at $6\frac{1}{2}\%$ per year compounded daily for 7 years.

Complete the following using present value of Table 12.3 or *Business Math Handbook* Table.

	Amount desired at end of period	Length of time	Rate	Compounded	On PV Table 12.3 Period used	On PV Table 12.3 Rate used	PV factor used	PV of amount desired at end of period
12–7.	$4,500	7 years	2%	Semiannually				
12–8.	$8,900	4 years	6%	Monthly				
12–9.	$17,600	7 years	12%	Quarterly				
12–10.	$20,000	20 years	8%	Annually				

12–11. Check your answer in Problem 12–9 by the compound value Table 12.1. The answer will be off due to rounding.

WORD PROBLEMS

12–12. Savings plans and the cost of college attendance were discussed in the September 18, 2006 issue of *U.S. News & World Report*. Greg Lawrence anticipates he will need approximately $218,000 in 15 years to cover his 3 year old daughter's college bills for a 4 year degree. How much would he have to invest today, at an interest rate of 8 percent compounded semiannually?

12–13. Jennifer Toby, owner of a local Subway shop, loaned $25,000 to Mike Roy to help him open a Subway franchise. Mike plans to repay Jennifer at the end of 7 years with 4% interest compounded semiannually. How much will Jennifer receive at the end of 7 years?

12–14. Molly Slate deposited $35,000 at Quazi Bank at 6% interest compounded quarterly. What is the effective rate (APY) to the nearest hundredth percent?

12–15. Melvin Indecision has difficulty deciding whether to put his savings in Mystic Bank or Four Rivers Bank. Mystic offers 10% interest compounded semiannually. Four Rivers offers 8% interest compounded quarterly. Melvin has $10,000 to invest. He expects to withdraw the money at the end of 4 years. Which bank gives Melvin the better deal? Check your answer.

12–16. Brian Costa deposited $20,000 in a new savings account at 12% interest compounded semiannually. At the beginning of year 4, Brian deposits an additional $30,000 at 12% interest compounded semiannually. At the end of 6 years, what is the balance in Brian's account?

12–17. Lee Wills loaned Audrey Chin $16,000 to open a hair salon. After 6 years, Audrey will repay Lee with 8% interest compounded quarterly. How much will Lee receive at the end of 6 years?

12–18. *The Dallas Morning News* on June 12, 2006, reported on saving for retirement. Carl Hendrik is 56 years old and has worked for Texas Instruments Inc for 35 years. He has amassed a plump nest egg of $700,000. His bank compounds interest semiannually, at 6%. Carl plans to retire at 65, if he places his money in the bank, how much will his investment be worth at retirement?

12–19. John Roe, an employee of The Gap, loans $3,000 to another employee at the store. He will be repaid at the end of 4 years with interest at 6% compounded quarterly. How much will John be repaid?

12–20. On September 14, 2006 *USA Today* ran a story on funding for retirement. The average 65 year old woman can expect to live to nearly 87 according to the American Academy of Actuaries. Mary Tully is 40 years old. She expects to need at least $420,000 when she retires at age 65. How much money must she invest today, in an account paying 6% interest compounded annually, to have the amount of money she needs?

12–21. Security National Bank is quoting 1-year certificates of deposits with an interest rate of 5% compounded semiannually. Joe Saver purchased a $5,000 CD. What is the CD's effective rate (APY) to the nearest hundredth percent? Use tables in the *Business Math Handbook*.

12–22. Jim Jones, an owner of a Burger King restaurant, assumes that his restaurant will need a new roof in 7 years. He estimates the roof will cost him $9,000 at that time. What amount should Jim invest today at 6% compounded quarterly to be able to pay for the roof? Check your answer.

12–23. Tony Ring wants to attend Northeast College. He will need $60,000 4 years from today. Assume Tony's bank pays 12% interest compounded semiannually. What must Tony deposit today so he will have $60,000 in 4 years?

12–24. Could you check your answer (to the nearest dollar) in Problem 12–23 by using the compound value Table 12.1? The answer will be slightly off due to rounding.

12–25. Pete Air wants to buy a used Jeep in 5 years. He estimates the Jeep will cost $15,000. Assume Pete invests $10,000 now at 12% interest compounded semiannually. Will Pete have enough money to buy his Jeep at the end of 5 years?

12–26. Lance Jackson deposited $5,000 at Basil Bank at 9% interest compounded daily. What is Lance's investment at the end of 4 years?

12–27. Paul Havlik promised his grandson Jamie that he would give him $6,000 8 years from today for graduating from high school. Assume money is worth 6% interest compounded semiannually. What is the present value of this $6,000?

12–28. Earl Ezekiel wants to retire in San Diego when he is 65 years old. Earl is now 50. He believes he will need $300,000 to retire comfortably. To date, Earl has set aside no retirement money. Assume Earl gets 6% interest compounded semiannually. How much must Earl invest today to meet his $300,000 goal?

12–29. Lorna Evenson would like to buy a $19,000 car in 4 years. Lorna wants to put the money aside now. Lorna's bank offers 8% interest compounded semiannually. How much must Lorna invest today?

12–30. John Smith saw the following advertisement. Could you show him how $88.77 was calculated?

*As of January 31, 200X, and subject to change. Interest on the 9-month CD is credited on the maturity date and is not compounded. For example, a $2,000, 9-month CD on deposit for an interest rate of 6.00% (6.05% APY) will earn $88.77 at maturity. Withdrawals prior to maturity require the consent of the bank and are subject to a substantial penalty. There is $500 minimum deposit for IRA, SEP IRA, and Keogh CDs (except for 9-month CD for which the minimum deposit is $1,000). There is $1,000 minimum deposit for all personal CDs (except for 9-month CD for which the minimum deposit is $2,000). Offer not valid on jumbo CDs.

CHALLENGE PROBLEMS

12–31. Mary started her first job at 22. She began saving money immediately but stopped after five years. Mary invested $2,500 each year until age 27. She receives 10% interest compounded annually and plans to retire at 62. **(a)** What amount will Mary have when she reaches retirement age? Use the tables in the *Business Math Handbook*. **(b)** What is the total amount of interest she will have received?

12–32. You are the financial planner for Johnson Controls. Last year's profits were $700,000. The board of directors decided to forgo dividends to stockholders and retire high-interest outstanding bonds that were issued 5 years ago at a face value of $1,250,000. You have been asked to invest the profits in a bank. The board must know how much money you will need from the profits earned to retire the bonds in 10 years. Bank A pays 6% compounded quarterly, and Bank B pays $6\frac{1}{2}\%$ compounded annually. Which bank would you recommend, and how much of the company's profit should be placed in the bank? If you recommended that the remaining money not be distributed to stockholders but be placed in Bank B, how much would the remaining money be worth in 10 years? Use tables in the *Business Math Handbook*.* Round final answer to nearest dollar.

*Check glossary for unfamiliar terms.

SUMMARY PRACTICE TEST

1. Mia Kaminsky, owner of a Starbucks franchise, loaned $40,000 to Lee Reese to help him open a new flower shop online. Lee plans to repay Mia at the end of 5 years with 4% interest compounded semiannually. How much will Mia receive at the end of 5 years? *(p. 299)*

2. Joe Beary wants to attend Riverside College. Eight years from today he will need $50,000. If Joe's bank pays 6% interest compounded semiannually, what must Joe deposit today to have $50,000 in 8 years? *(p. 304)*

3. Shelley Katz deposited $30,000 in a savings account at 5% interest compounded semiannually. At the beginning of year 4, Shelley deposits an additional $80,000 at 5% interest compounded semiannually. At the end of 6 years, what is the balance in Shelley's account? *(p. 299)*

4. Earl Miller, owner of a Papa Gino's franchise, wants to buy a new delivery truck in 6 years. He estimates the truck will cost $30,000. If Earl invests $20,000 now at 5% interest compounded semiannually, will Earl have enough money to buy his delivery truck at the end of 6 years? *(pp. 299, 304)*

5. Minnie Rose deposited $16,000 in Street Bank at 6% interest compounded quarterly. What was the effective rate (APY)? Round to the nearest hundredth percent. *(p. 301)*

6. Lou Ling, owner of Lou's Lube, estimates that he will need $70,000 for new equipment in 7 years. Lou decided to put aside money today so it will be available in 7 years. Reel Bank offers Lou 6% interest compounded quarterly. How much must Lou invest to have $70,000 in 7 years? *(p. 304)*

7. Bernie Long wants to retire to California when she is 60 years of age. Bernie is now 40. She believes that she will need $900,000 to retire comfortably. To date, Bernie has set aside no retirement money. If Bernie gets 8% compounded semiannually, how much must Bernie invest today to meet her $900,000 goal? *(p. 304)*

8. Sam Slater deposited $19,000 in a savings account at 7% interest compounded daily. At the end of 6 years, what is the balance in Sam's account? *(p. 301)*

CREDIT | Some card issuers offer help to the shopping-addicted and the savings-impaired.

Keep the CHANGE

AS A NATION, we're big spenders, not savers. So it figures that banks would invent a way for us to do both at once. Buy something using one of the new cards from American Express, Bank of America and a handful of other issuers, and the banks will stash a cash rebate into a savings account. Shopping and traveling won't replace your IRA contributions, but if you use plastic for gas and groceries, the money can add up.

American Express's One card funnels 1% of all purchases into a savings account that now pays 3.5%. At that rate, if you charge $2,000 a month, you'll have $6,000 in 18 years—not enough for your child's college tuition, but maybe enough for books. Amex will waive the $35 annual fee the first year and seed your account with $25.

Bank of America effec-tively puts your pocket change into an electronic piggy bank. Sign up for its Keep the Change program and the bank rounds up all purchases on your debit card to the nearest dollar and moves the difference into a savings account. For three months, the bank matches your deposits 100%. After that, it matches 5% per year up to $250. That's no windfall. But look at it this way: A penny spent becomes a penny saved. —**JOAN GOLDWASSER**

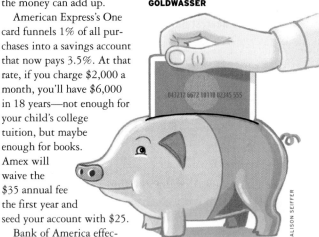

ALISON SEIFFER

BUSINESS MATH ISSUE

Keep the change is a gimmick that banks are using just to get new customers.

1. List the key points of the article and information to support your position.
2. Write a group defense of your position using math calculations to support your view.

Slater's Business Math Scrapbook

with Internet Application
Putting Your Skills to Work

PROJECT A
Go to Web and find out the latest rates for 6 months, 1 year, and 5-year CDs along with the current rates for markets.

Interest Rates Lofty

Tim Foley

Interest Over Rising Interest

Rates offered by banks on various deposits over the past year

Yields

5–Year CD	
3.90%	

1–Year CD	
3.29%	

6–Month CD	
2.84%	

Money–market account	
0.76%	

Note: Through Wed., Jan. 11
Source: Bankrate.com

J F M A M J J A S O N D J
2005   2006

Wall Street Journal © 2006

Internet Projects: See text Web site (www.mhhe.com/slater9e) and The Business Math Internet Resource Guide.

Chapter **13**

Annuities and Sinking Funds

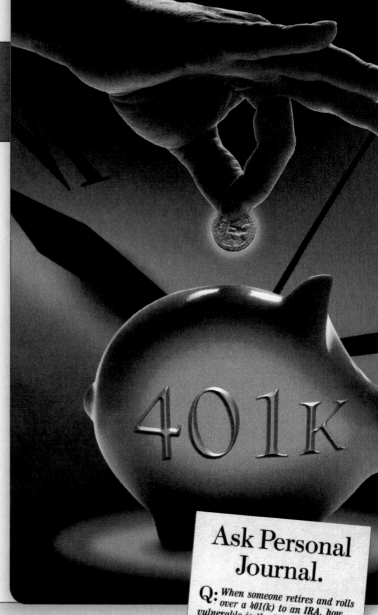

LEARNING UNIT OBJECTIVES

Note: A complete set of plastic overlays showing the concept of annuities is found at the end of the chapter (p. 336A).

LU 13–1: Annuities: Ordinary Annuity and Annuity Due (Find Future Value)

- Differentiate between contingent annuities and annuities certain (*p. 318*).
- Calculate the future value of an ordinary annuity and an annuity due manually and by table lookup (*pp. 319–323*).

LU 13–2: Present Value of an Ordinary Annuity (Find Present Value)

- Calculate the present value of an ordinary annuity by table lookup and manually check the calculation (*pp. 323–325*).
- Compare the calculation of the present value of one lump sum versus the present value of an ordinary annuity (*p. 325*).

LU 13–3: Sinking Funds (Find Periodic Payments)

- Calculate the payment made at the end of each period by table lookup (*pp. 326–327*).
- Check table lookup by using ordinary annuity table (*p. 327*).

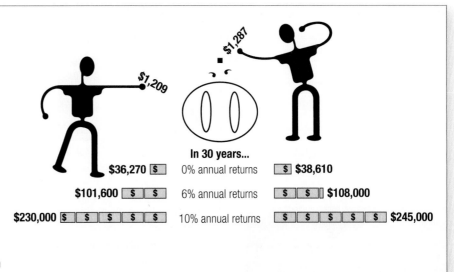

INVESTING YOUR SAVINGS
Assuming the price of coffee remains the same, we added up what you would save if you gave up coffee over 30 years and what you would save if you made coffee at home instead of buying it.

We then invested the savings. We compounded each amount weekly at annual rates: 0 percent, which means you did nothing with the money; at 6 percent, which is an average expected rate of return on a stock portfolio, and at 10 percent, an aggressive expected rate of return.

$1,209

$1,287

In 30 years...

$36,270 [$]   0% annual returns   [$] $38,610

$101,600 [$][$]   6% annual returns   [$][$] $108,000

$230,000 [$][$][$][$][$]   10% annual returns   [$][$][$][$][$] $245,000

Boston Sunday Globe © 2004

Lisa Poole/AP Wide World

A *Boston Globe* article entitled "Cost of Living: A Cup a Day" states at the beginning of the clipping that each month the *Globe* runs a feature on an everyday expense to see how much it costs an average person. Since many people are coffee drinkers, the Globe assumed that a person drank 3 cups a day of Dunkin' Donuts coffee at the cost of $1.65 a cup. For a five-day week, the person would spend $1,287 annually (52 weeks). If the person brewed the coffee at home, the cost of the beans per cup would be $0.10 a cup with an annual expense of $78, saving $1,209 over the Dunkin' Donuts coffee. If a person gave up drinking coffee, the person would save $1,287.

The clipping continued with the discussion on "Investing Your Savings" shown above. Note how much you would have in 30 years if you invested your money in 0%, 6%, and 10% annual returns. Using the magic of compounding, if you saved $1,287 a year, your money could grow to a quarter of a million dollars.

This chapter shows how to compute compound interest that results from a *stream* of payments, or an annuity. Chapter 12 showed how to calculate compound interest on a lump-sum payment deposited at the beginning of a particular time. Knowing how to calculate interest compounding on a lump sum will make the calculation of interest compounding on annuities easier to understand.

We begin the chapter by explaining the difference between calculating the future value of an ordinary annuity and an annuity due. Then you learn how to find the present value of an ordinary annuity. The chapter ends with a discussion of sinking funds.

Learning Unit 13–1: Annuities: Ordinary Annuity and Annuity Due (Find Future Value)

Many parents of small children are concerned about being able to afford to pay for their children's college educations. Some parents deposit a lump sum in a financial institution when the child is in diapers. The interest on this sum is compounded until the child is 18, when the parents withdraw the money for college expenses. Parents could also fund their children's educations with annuities by depositing a series of payments for a certain time. The concept of annuities is the first topic in this learning unit.

Concept of an Annuity—The Big Picture

All of us would probably like to win $1 million in a state lottery. What happens when you have the winning ticket? You take it to the lottery headquarters. When you turn in the ticket, do you immediately receive a check for $1 million? No. Lottery payoffs are not usually made in lump sums.

Lottery winners receive a series of payments over a period of time—usually years. This *stream* of payments is an **annuity.** By paying the winners an annuity, lotteries do not actually spend $1 million. The lottery deposits a sum of money in a financial institution.

Future value of an annuity
of $1 at 8%

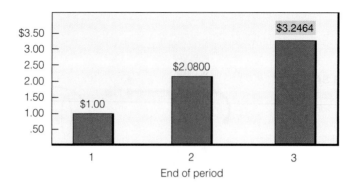

Sharon Hoogstraten

The continual growth of this sum through compound interest provides the lottery winner with a series of payments.

When we calculated the maturity value of a lump-sum payment in Chapter 12, the maturity value was the principal and its interest. Now we are looking not at lump-sum payments but at a series of payments (usually of equal amounts over regular **payment periods**) plus the interest that accumulates. So the **future value of an annuity** is the future *dollar amount* of a series of payments plus interest.[1] The **term of the annuity** is the time from the beginning of the first payment period to the end of the last payment period.

The concept of the future value of an annuity is illustrated in Figure 13.1. Do not be concerned about the calculations (we will do them soon). Let's first focus on the big picture of annuities. In Figure 13.1 we see the following:

At end of period 1: The $1 is still worth $1 because it was invested at the *end* of the period.

At end of period 2: An additional $1 is invested. The $2.00 is now worth $2.08. Note the $1 from period 1 earns interest but not the $1 invested at the end of period 2.

At end of period 3: An additional $1 is invested. The $3.00 is now worth $3.25. Remember that the last dollar invested earns no interest.

Before learning how to calculate annuities, you should understand the two classifications of annuities.

How Annuities Are Classified

Annuities have many uses in addition to lottery payoffs. Some of these uses are insurance companies' pension installments, Social Security payments, home mortgages, businesses paying off notes, bond interest, and savings for a vacation trip or college education.

Annuities are classified into two major groups: contingent annuities and annuities certain. **Contingent annuities** have no fixed number of payments but depend on an uncertain event (e.g., life insurance payments that cease when the insured dies). **Annuities certain** have a specific stated number of payments (e.g., mortgage payments on a home). Based on the time of the payment, we can divide each of these two major annuity groups into the following:

1. **Ordinary annuity**—regular deposits (payments) made at the *end* of the period. Periods could be months, quarters, years, and so on. An ordinary annuity could be salaries, stock dividends, and so on.

2. **Annuity due**—regular deposits (payments) made at the *beginning* of the period, such as rent or life insurance premiums.

The remainder of this unit shows you how to calculate and check ordinary annuities and annuities due. Remember that you are calculating the *dollar amount* of the annuity at the end of the annuity term or at the end of the last period.

---

[1]The term *amount of an annuity* has the same meaning as *future value of an annuity.*

Ordinary Annuities: Money Invested at End of Period (Find Future Value)

Before we explain how to use a table that simplifies calculating ordinary annuities, let's first determine how to calculate the future value of an ordinary annuity manually.

Calculating Future Value of Ordinary Annuities Manually

Remember that an ordinary annuity invests money at the *end* of each year (period). After we calculate ordinary annuities manually, you will see that the total value of the investment comes from the *stream* of yearly investments and the buildup of interest on the current balance.

Check out the plastic overlays that appear in Chapter 13, p. 336A, to review these concepts.

CALCULATING FUTURE VALUE OF AN ORDINARY ANNUITY MANUALLY
Step 1. For period 1, no interest calculation is necessary, since money is invested at the end of the period.
Step 2. For period 2, calculate interest on the balance and add the interest to the previous balance.
Step 3. Add the additional investment at the end of period 2 to the new balance.
Step 4. Repeat Steps 2 and 3 until the end of the desired period is reached.

EXAMPLE Find the value of an investment after 3 years for a $3,000 ordinary annuity at 8%. We calculate this manually as follows:

Step 1. → End of year 1:	$3,000.00	→	No interest, since this is put in at end of year 1. (Remember, payment is made at end of period.)
Year 2:	$3,000.00	→	Value of investment before investment at end of year 2.
Step 2. →	+ 240.00	→	Interest (.08 × $3,000) for year 2.
	$3,240.00	→	Value of investment at end of year 2 before second investment.
Step 3. → End of year 2:	+ 3,000.00	→	Second investment at end of year 2.
Year 3:	$6,240.00	→	Investment balance going into year 3.
	+ 499.20	→	Interest for year 3 (.08 × $6,240).
Step 4. →	$6,739.20	→	Value before investment at end of year 3.
→	+ 3,000.00	→	Investment at end of year 3.
End of year 3:	$9,739.20	→	Total value of investment after investment at end of year 3.

Note: We totally invested $9,000 over three different periods. It is now worth $9,739.20

Early years

```
       1                2                3
       |_____|_____|
$3,000 ──────────────────────────────────>
              $3,000 ───────────────────>
                        $3,000
```

When you deposit $3,000 at the end of each year at an annual rate of 8%, the total value of the annuity is $9,739.20 . What we called *maturity value* in compounding is now called the *future value of the annuity*. Remember that Interest = Principal × Rate × Time, with the principal changing because of the interest payments and the additional deposits. We can make this calculation easier by using Table 13.1 (p. 320).

TABLE	13.1	Ordinary annuity table: Compound sum of an annuity of $1

Period	2%	3%	4%	5%	6%	7%	8%	9%	10%	11%	12%	13%
1	1.0000	1.0000	1.0000	1.0000	1.0000	1.0000	1.0000	1.0000	1.0000	1.0000	1.0000	1.0000
2	2.0200	2.0300	2.0400	2.0500	2.0600	2.0700	2.0800	2.0900	2.1000	2.1100	2.1200	2.1300
3	3.0604	3.0909	3.1216	3.1525	3.1836	3.2149	3.2464	3.2781	3.3100	3.3421	3.3744	3.4069
4	4.1216	4.1836	4.2465	4.3101	4.3746	4.4399	4.5061	4.5731	4.6410	4.7097	4.7793	4.8498
5	5.2040	5.3091	5.4163	5.5256	5.6371	5.7507	5.8666	5.9847	6.1051	6.2278	6.3528	6.4803
6	6.3081	6.4684	6.6330	6.8019	6.9753	7.1533	7.3359	7.5233	7.7156	7.9129	8.1152	8.3227
7	7.4343	7.6625	7.8983	8.1420	8.3938	8.6540	8.9228	9.2004	9.4872	9.7833	10.0890	10.4047
8	8.5829	8.8923	9.2142	9.5491	9.8975	10.2598	10.6366	11.0285	11.4359	11.8594	12.2997	12.7573
9	9.7546	10.1591	10.5828	11.0265	11.4913	11.9780	12.4876	13.0210	13.5795	14.1640	14.7757	15.4157
10	10.9497	11.4639	12.0061	12.5779	13.1808	13.8164	14.4866	15.1929	15.9374	16.7220	17.5487	18.4197
11	12.1687	12.8078	13.4863	14.2068	14.9716	15.7836	16.6455	17.5603	18.5312	19.5614	20.6546	21.8143
12	13.4120	14.1920	15.0258	15.9171	16.8699	17.8884	18.9771	20.1407	21.3843	22.7132	24.1331	25.6502
13	14.6803	15.6178	16.6268	17.7129	18.8821	20.1406	21.4953	22.9534	24.5227	26.2116	28.0291	29.9847
14	15.9739	17.0863	18.2919	19.5986	21.0150	22.5505	24.2149	26.0192	27.9750	30.0949	32.3926	34.8827
15	17.2934	18.5989	20.0236	21.5785	23.2759	25.1290	27.1521	29.3609	31.7725	34.4054	37.2797	40.4174
16	18.6392	20.1569	21.8245	23.6574	25.6725	27.8880	30.3243	33.0034	35.9497	39.1899	42.7533	46.6717
17	20.0120	21.7616	23.6975	25.8403	28.2128	30.8402	33.7503	36.9737	40.5447	44.5008	48.8837	53.7390
18	21.4122	23.4144	25.6454	28.1323	30.9056	33.9990	37.4503	41.3014	45.5992	50.3959	55.7497	61.7251
19	22.8405	25.1169	27.6712	30.5389	33.7599	37.3789	41.4463	46.0185	51.1591	56.9395	63.4397	70.7494
20	24.2973	26.8704	29.7781	33.0659	36.7855	40.9954	45.7620	51.1602	57.2750	64.2028	72.0524	80.9468
25	32.0302	36.4593	41.6459	47.7270	54.8644	63.2489	73.1060	84.7010	98.3471	114.4133	133.3338	155.6194
30	40.5679	47.5754	56.0849	66.4386	79.0580	94.4606	113.2833	136.3077	164.4941	199.0209	241.3327	293.1989
40	60.4017	75.4012	95.0254	120.7993	154.7616	199.6346	259.0569	337.8831	442.5928	581.8260	767.0913	1013.7030
50	84.5790	112.7968	152.6669	209.3470	290.3351	406.5277	573.7711	815.0853	1163.9090	1668.7710	2400.0180	3459.5010

Note: This is only a sampling of tables available. The *Business Math Handbook* shows tables from ½% to 15%.

Calculating Future Value of Ordinary Annuities by Table Lookup

Use the following steps to calculate the future value of an ordinary annuity by table lookup.[2]

CALCULATING FUTURE VALUE OF AN ORDINARY ANNUITY BY TABLE LOOKUP
Step 1. Calculate the number of periods and rate per period.
Step 2. Look up the periods and rate in an ordinary annuity table. The intersection gives the table factor for the future value of $1.
Step 3. Multiply the payment each period by the table factor. This gives the future value of the annuity.

$$\frac{\text{Future value of}}{\text{ordinary annuity}} = \frac{\text{Annuity payment}}{\text{each period}} \times \frac{\text{Ordinary annuity}}{\text{table factor}}$$

EXAMPLE Find the value of an investment after 3 years for a $3,000 ordinary annuity at 8% (see p. 321).

---

[2]The formula for an ordinary annuity is $A = Pmt \times \left[\frac{(1 + i)^n - 1}{i}\right]$ where A equals future value of an ordinary annuity, Pmt equals annuity payment, i equals interest, and n equals number of periods. The calculator sequence for this example is: 1 $+$ .08 $=$ $\boxed{y^x}$ 3 $-$ 1 $\div$ .08 $\times$ 3,000 $=$ 9,739.20. A *Financial Calculator Guide* booklet is available that shows how to operate HP 10BII and TI BA II Plus.

Step 1. Periods = 3 years × 1 = 3   Rate = $\dfrac{8\%}{\text{Annually}} = 8\%$

Step 2. Go to Table 13.1, an ordinary annuity table. Look for 3 under the Period column. Go across to 8%. At the intersection is the table factor, 3.2464. (This was the example we showed in Figure 13.1.)

Step 3. Multiply $3,000 × 3.2464 = $9,739.20 (the same figure we calculated manually).

Annuities Due: Money Invested at Beginning of Period (Find Future Value)

In this section we look at what the difference in the total investment would be for an annuity due. As in the previous section, we will first make the calculation manually and then use the table lookup.

Calculating Future Value of Annuities Due Manually

Use the steps that follow to calculate the future value of an annuity due manually.

CALCULATING FUTURE VALUE OF AN ANNUITY DUE MANUALLY

Step 1. Calculate the interest on the balance for the period and add it to the previous balance.

Step 2. Add additional investment at the *beginning* of the period to the new balance.

Step 3. Repeat Steps 1 and 2 until the end of the desired period is reached.

Remember that in an annuity due, we deposit the money at the *beginning* of the year and gain more interest. Common sense should tell us that the *annuity due* will give a higher final value. We will use the same example that we used before.

EXAMPLE Find the value of an investment after 3 years for a $3,000 annuity due at 8%. We calculate this manually as follows:

Beginning year 1:	$3,000.00	→ First investment (will earn interest for 3 years).
Step 1. →	+ 240.00	→ Interest (.08 × $3,000).
	$3,240.00	→ Value of investment at end of year 1.
Step 2. → Year 2:	+ 3,000.00	→ Second investment (will earn interest for 2 years).
	$6,240.00	
Step 3. →	+ 499.20	→ Interest for year 2 (.08 × $6,240).
	$6,739.20	→ Value of investment at end of year 2.
Year 3:	+ 3,000.00	
	$9,739.20	→ Third investment (will earn interest for 1 year).
	+ 779.14	→ Interest (.08 × $9,739.20).
End of year 3:	$10,518.34	→ At the end of year 3, final value.

Beginning of years

Note: Our total investment of $9,000 is worth $10,518.34. For an ordinary annuity, our total investment was only worth $9,739.20.

Calculating Future Value of Annuities Due by Table Lookup

To calculate the future value of an annuity due with a table lookup, use the steps that follow.

CALCULATING FUTURE VALUE OF AN ANNUITY DUE BY TABLE LOOKUP[3]

Step 1. Calculate the number of periods and the rate per period. Add one extra period.

Step 2. Look up in an ordinary annuity table the periods and rate. The intersection gives the table *factor* for future value of $1.

Step 3. Multiply payment each period by the table factor.

Step 4. Subtract 1 payment from Step 3.

$$\text{Future value of an annuity due} = \left(\begin{array}{c} \text{Annuity} \\ \text{payment} \\ \text{each period} \end{array} \times \begin{array}{c} \text{Ordinary*} \\ \text{annuity} \\ \text{table factor} \end{array} \right) - 1 \text{ Payment}$$

*Add 1 period.

Let's check the $10,518.34 by table lookup.

Step 1. Periods = 3 years × 1 = 3
+ 1 extra
———
4

Rate = $\dfrac{8\%}{\text{Annually}} = 8\%$

Step 2. Table factor, 4.5061

Step 3. $3,000 × 4.5061 = $13,518.30

Step 4. − 3,000.00 ← Be sure to subtract 1 payment.
————
= $10,518.30 (off 4 cents due to rounding)

Note that the annuity due shows an ending value of $10,518.30, while the ending value of ordinary annuity was $9,739.20. We had a higher ending value with the annuity due because the investment took place at the beginning of each period.

Annuity payments do not have to be made yearly. They could be made semiannually, monthly, quarterly, and so on. Let's look at one more example with a different number of periods and rate.

Different Number of Periods and Rates

By using a different number of periods and rates, we will contrast an ordinary annuity with an annuity due in the following example:

EXAMPLE Using Table 13.1 (p. 320), find the value of a $3,000 investment after 3 years made quarterly at 8%.

In the annuity due calculation, be sure to add one period and subtract one payment from the total value.

	Ordinary annuity	**Annuity due**	
Step 1.	Periods = 3 years × 4 = 12	Periods = 3 years × 4 = 12	**Step 1**
	Rate = 8% ÷ 4 = 2%	Rate = 8% ÷ 4 = 2%	
Step 2.	Table 13.1:	Table 13.1:	**Step 2**
	12 periods, 2% = 13.4120	13 periods, 2% = 14.6803	
Step 3.	$3,000 × 13.4120 = $40,236	$3,000 × 14.6803 = $44,040.90	**Step 3**
		− 3,000.00	**Step 4**
		$41,040.90	

Again, note that with annuity due, the total value is greater since you invest the money at the beginning of each period.

Now check your progress with the Practice Quiz.

---

[3]The formula for an annuity due is $A = Pmt \times \frac{(1 + i)^n - 1}{i} \times (1 + i)$, where A equals future value of annuity due, *Pmt* equals annuity payment, *i* equals interest, and *n* equals number of periods. This formula is the same as that in footnote 2 except we multiply the future value of annuity by $1 + i$ since payments are made at the beginning of the period. The calculator sequence for this example is:
1 [+] .08 [=] [×] 9,739.20 [=] 10,518.34.

Complete this **Practice Quiz**
to see how you are doing

1. Using Table 13.1, **(a)** find the value of an investment after 4 years on an ordinary annuity of $4,000 made semiannually at 10%; and **(b)** recalculate, assuming an annuity due.
2. Wally Beaver won a lottery and will receive a check for $4,000 at the beginning of each 6 months for the next 5 years. If Wally deposits each check into an account that pays 6%, how much will he have at the end of the 5 years?

✓ **Solutions**

1. **a. Step 1.** Periods = 4 years × 2 = 8   **b.** Periods = 4 years × 2   **Step 1**

                                                        = 8 + 1 = 9

                             10% ÷ 2 = 5%   10% ÷ 2 = 5%

           Step 2. Factor = 9.5491   Factor = 11.0265   **Step 2**

           Step 3. $4,000 × 9.5491 $4,000 × 11.0265 = $44,106   **Step 3**

                      = $38,196.40   − 1 payment   − 4,000   **Step 4**

                                                        $40,106

2. **Step 1.** 5 years × 2 =   10 $\frac{6\%}{2} = 3\%$

                                + 1

                                11 periods

       Step 2. Table factor, 12.8078

       Step 3. $4,000 × 12.8078 = $51,231.20

       Step 4.   − 4,000.00

                                   $47,231.20

Need more practice? Try this
Extra Practice Quiz (check
figures in Chapter Organizer,
p. 329)

1. Using Table 13.1, **(a)** find the value of an investment after 4 years on an ordinary annuity of $5,000 made semiannually at 4%; and **(b)** recalculate, assuming an annuity due.
2. Wally Beaver won a lottery and will receive a check for $2,500 at the beginning of each 6 months for the next 6 years. If Wally deposits each check into an account that pays 6%, how much will he have at the end of the 6 years?

Learning Unit 13–2: Present Value of an Ordinary Annuity (Find Present Value)[4]

This unit begins by presenting the concept of present value of an ordinary annuity. Then you will learn how to use a table to calculate the present value of an ordinary annuity.

Concept of Present Value of an Ordinary Annuity— The Big Picture

Let's assume that we want to know how much money we need to invest *today* to receive a stream of payments for a given number of years in the future. This is called the **present value of an ordinary annuity.**

In Figure 13.2 (p. 324) you can see that if you wanted to withdraw $1 at the end of one period, you would have to invest 93 cents *today*. If at the end of each period for three periods, you wanted to withdraw $1, you would have to put $2.58 in the bank *today* at 8% interest. (Note that we go from the future back to the present.)

Now let's look at how we could use tables to calculate the present value of annuities and then check our answer.

Calculating Present Value of an Ordinary Annuity by Table Lookup

Use the steps on p. 324 to calculate by table lookup the present value of an ordinary annuity.[5]

---

[4]For simplicity we omit a discussion of present value of annuity due that would require subtracting a period and adding a 1.

[5]The formula for the present value of an ordinary annuity is $P = Pmt \times \frac{1 - 1 \div (1 + i)^n}{i}$, where P equals present value of annuity, Pmt equals annuity payment, i equals interest, and n equals number of periods. The calculator sequence would be as follows for the John Fitch example: 1 [+] .08 [yˣ] 3 [+−] [=] [M+] 1 [−] [MR] [÷] .08 [×] 8,000 [=] 21,000.

FIGURE **13.2**

Present value of an annuity of $1 at 8%

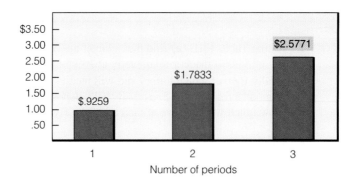

CALCULATING PRESENT VALUE OF AN ORDINARY ANNUITY BY TABLE LOOKUP

Step 1. Calculate the number of periods and rate per period.

Step 2. Look up the periods and rate in the present value of an annuity table. The intersection gives the table factor for the present value of $1.

Step 3. Multiply the withdrawal for each period by the table factor. This gives the present value of an ordinary annuity.

$$\text{Present value of ordinary annuity payment} = \text{Annuity payment} \times \text{Present value of ordinary annuity table}$$

TABLE **13.2**   Present value of an annuity of $1

Period	2%	3%	4%	5%	6%	7%	8%	9%	10%	11%	12%	13%
1	0.9804	0.9709	0.9615	0.9524	0.9434	0.9346	0.9259	0.9174	0.9091	0.9009	0.8929	0.8850
2	1.9416	1.9135	1.8861	1.8594	1.8334	1.8080	1.7833	1.7591	1.7355	1.7125	1.6901	1.6681
3	2.8839	2.8286	2.7751	2.7232	2.6730	2.6243	2.5771	2.5313	2.4869	2.4437	2.4018	2.3612
4	3.8077	3.7171	3.6299	3.5459	3.4651	3.3872	3.3121	3.2397	3.1699	3.1024	3.0373	2.9745
5	4.7134	4.5797	4.4518	4.3295	4.2124	4.1002	3.9927	3.8897	3.7908	3.6959	3.6048	3.5172
6	5.6014	5.4172	5.2421	5.0757	4.9173	4.7665	4.6229	4.4859	4.3553	4.2305	4.1114	3.9975
7	6.4720	6.2303	6.0021	5.7864	5.5824	5.3893	5.2064	5.0330	4.8684	4.7122	4.5638	4.4226
8	7.3255	7.0197	6.7327	6.4632	6.2098	5.9713	5.7466	5.5348	5.3349	5.1461	4.9676	4.7988
9	8.1622	7.7861	7.4353	7.1078	6.8017	6.5152	6.2469	5.9952	5.7590	5.5370	5.3282	5.1317
10	8.9826	8.5302	8.1109	7.7217	7.3601	7.0236	6.7101	6.4177	6.1446	5.8892	5.6502	5.4262
11	9.7868	9.2526	8.7605	8.3064	7.8869	7.4987	7.1390	6.8052	6.4951	6.2065	5.9377	5.6869
12	10.5753	9.9540	9.3851	8.8632	8.3838	7.9427	7.5361	7.1607	6.8137	6.4924	6.1944	5.9176
13	11.3483	10.6350	9.9856	9.3936	8.8527	8.3576	7.9038	7.4869	7.1034	6.7499	6.4235	6.1218
14	12.1062	11.2961	10.5631	9.8986	9.2950	8.7455	8.2442	7.7862	7.3667	6.9819	6.6282	6.3025
15	12.8492	11.9379	11.1184	10.3796	9.7122	9.1079	8.5595	8.0607	7.6061	7.1909	6.8109	6.4624
16	13.5777	12.5611	11.6523	10.8378	10.1059	9.4466	8.8514	8.3126	7.8237	7.3792	6.9740	6.6039
17	14.2918	13.1661	12.1657	11.2741	10.4773	9.7632	9.1216	8.5436	8.0216	7.5488	7.1196	6.7291
18	14.9920	13.7535	12.6593	11.6896	10.8276	10.0591	9.3719	8.7556	8.2014	7.7016	7.2497	6.8399
19	15.6784	14.3238	13.1339	12.0853	11.1581	10.3356	9.6036	8.9501	8.3649	7.8393	7.3658	6.9380
20	16.3514	14.8775	13.5903	12.4622	11.4699	10.5940	9.8181	9.1285	8.5136	7.9633	7.4694	7.0248
25	19.5234	17.4131	15.6221	14.0939	12.7834	11.6536	10.6748	9.8226	9.0770	8.4217	7.8431	7.3300
30	22.3964	19.6004	17.2920	15.3724	13.7648	12.4090	11.2578	10.2737	9.4269	8.6938	8.0552	7.4957
40	27.3554	23.1148	19.7928	17.1591	15.0463	13.3317	11.9246	10.7574	9.7790	8.9511	8.2438	7.6344
50	31.4236	25.7298	21.4822	18.2559	15.7619	13.8007	12.2335	10.9617	9.9148	9.0417	8.3045	7.6752

EXAMPLE John Fitch wants to receive an $8,000 annuity in 3 years. Interest on the annuity is 8% annually. John will make withdrawals at the end of each year. How much must John invest today to receive a stream of payments for 3 years? Use Table 13.2 (p. 324). Remember that interest could be earned semiannually, quarterly, and so on, as shown in the previous unit.

Step 1. 3 years $\times$ 1 = 3 periods $\dfrac{8\%}{\text{Annually}} = 8\%$

Step 2. Table factor, 2.5771   (we saw this in Figure 13.2)

Step 3. $8,000 $\times$ 2.5771 = $20,616.80

If John wants to withdraw $8,000 at the end of each period for 3 years, he will have to deposit $20,616.80 in the bank *today*.

$20,616.80
+   1,649.34 $\longrightarrow$ Interest at end of year 1 (.08 $\times$ $20,616.80)
$22,266.14
−   8,000.00 $\longrightarrow$ First payment to John
$14,266.14
+   1,141.29 $\longrightarrow$ Interest at end of year 2 (.08 $\times$ $14,266.14)
$15,407.43
−   8,000.00 $\longrightarrow$ Second payment to John
$ 7,407.43
+   592.59 $\longrightarrow$ Interest at end of year 3 (.08 $\times$ $7,407.43)
$ 8,000.02
−   8,000.00 $\longrightarrow$ After end of year 3 John receives his last $8,000
        .02[6]

Before we leave this unit, let's work out two examples that show the relationship of Chapter 13 to Chapter 12. Use the tables in your *Business Math Handbook*.

Lump Sum versus Annuities

EXAMPLE John Sands made deposits of $200 semiannually to Floor Bank, which pays 8% interest compounded semiannually. After 5 years, John makes no more deposits. What will be the balance in the account 6 years after the last deposit?

Step 1. Calculate amount of annuity: Table 13.1
            10 periods, 4% $200 $\times$ 12.0061 = $2,401.22

Step 2. Calculate how much the final value of the annuity will grow by the compound interest table.   Table 12.1
            12 periods, 4% $2,401.22 $\times$ 1.6010 = **$3,844.35**

For John, the stream of payments grows to $2,401.22. Then this *lump sum* grows for 6 years to $3,844.35. Now let's look at a present value example.

EXAMPLE Mel Rich decided to retire in 8 years to New Mexico. What amount should Mel invest today so he will be able to withdraw $40,000 at the end of each year for 25 years *after* he retires? Assume Mel can invest money at 5% interest (compounded annually).

Step 1. Calculate the present value of the annuity: Table 13.2
            25 periods, 5% $40,000 $\times$ 14.0939 = $563,756

Step 2. Find the present value of $563,756 since Mel will not retire for 8 years:

                              Table 12.3

            8 periods, 5% (PV table) $563,756 $\times$ .6768 = **$381,550.06**

If Mel deposits $381,550 in year 1, it will grow to $563,756 after 8 years.
    It's time to try the Practice Quiz and check your understanding of this unit.

[6]Off due to rounding.

LU 13–2 PRACTICE QUIZ

Complete this **Practice Quiz** to see how you are doing

(Use tables in *Business Math Handbook*)

1. What must you invest today to receive an $18,000 annuity for 5 years semiannually at a 10% annual rate? All withdrawals will be made at the end of each period.
2. Rase High School wants to set up a scholarship fund to provide five $2,000 scholarships for the next 10 years. If money can be invested at an annual rate of 9%, how much should the scholarship committee invest today?
3. Joe Wood decided to retire in 5 years in Arizona. What amount should Joe invest today so he can withdraw $60,000 at the end of each year for 30 years after he retires? Assume Joe can invest money at 6% compounded annually.

✓ Solutions

1. **Step 1.** Periods = 5 years × 2 = 10; Rate = 10% ÷ 2 = 5%
   Step 2. Factor, 7.7217
   Step 3. $18,000 × 7.7217 = $138,990.60
2. **Step 1.** Periods = 10; Rate = 9%
   Step 2. Factor, 6.4177
   Step 3. $10,000 × 6.4177 = $64,177
3. **Step 1.** Calculate present value of annuity: 30 periods, 6%.
   $60,000 × 13.7648 = $825,888
   Step 2. Find present value of $825,888 for 5 years: 5 periods, 6%.
   $825,888 × .7473 = $617,186.10

LU 13–2a EXTRA PRACTICE QUIZ

Need more practice? Try this **Extra Practice Quiz** (check figures in Chapter Organizer, p. 329)

1. What must you invest today to receive a $20,000 annuity for 5 years semiannually at a 5% annual rate? All withdrawals will be made at the end of each period.
2. Rase High School wants to set up a scholarship fund to provide five $3,000 scholarships for the next 10 years. If money can be invested at an annual rate of 4%, how much should the scholarship committee invest today?
3. Joe Wood decided to retire in 5 years in Arizona. What amount should Joe invest today so he can withdraw $80,000 at the end of each year for 30 years after he retires? Assume Joe can invest money at 3% compounded annually.

Learning Unit 13–3: Sinking Funds (Find Periodic Payments)

A **sinking fund** is a financial arrangement that sets aside regular periodic payments of a particular amount of money. Compound interest accumulates on these payments to a specific sum at a predetermined future date. Corporations use sinking funds to discharge bonded indebtedness, to replace worn-out equipment, to purchase plant expansion, and so on.

A sinking fund is a different type of an annuity. In a sinking fund, you determine the amount of periodic payments you need to achieve a given financial goal. In the annuity, you know the amount of each payment and must determine its future value. Let's work with the following formula:

> Sinking fund payment = Future value × Sinking fund table factor[7]

EXAMPLE To retire a bond issue, Moore Company needs $60,000 in 18 years from today. The interest rate is 10% compounded annually. What payment must Moore make at the end of each year? Use Table 13.3 (p. 327).

---

[7]Sinking fund table is the reciprocal of the ordinary annuity table.

	TABLE **13.3**

Sinking fund table based on $1

Period	2%	3%	4%	5%	6%	8%	10%
1	1.0000	1.0000	1.0000	1.0000	1.0000	1.0000	1.0000
2	0.4951	0.4926	0.4902	0.4878	0.4854	0.4808	0.4762
3	0.3268	0.3235	0.3203	0.3172	0.3141	0.3080	0.3021
4	0.2426	0.2390	0.2355	0.2320	0.2286	0.2219	0.2155
5	0.1922	0.1884	0.1846	0.1810	0.1774	0.1705	0.1638
6	0.1585	0.1546	0.1508	0.1470	0.1434	0.1363	0.1296
7	0.1345	0.1305	0.1266	0.1228	0.1191	0.1121	0.1054
8	0.1165	0.1125	0.1085	0.1047	0.1010	0.0940	0.0874
9	0.1025	0.0984	0.0945	0.0907	0.0870	0.0801	0.0736
10	0.0913	0.0872	0.0833	0.0795	0.0759	0.0690	0.0627
11	0.0822	0.0781	0.0741	0.0704	0.0668	0.0601	0.0540
12	0.0746	0.0705	0.0666	0.0628	0.0593	0.0527	0.0468
13	0.0681	0.0640	0.0601	0.0565	0.0530	0.0465	0.0408
14	0.0626	0.0585	0.0547	0.0510	0.0476	0.0413	0.0357
15	0.0578	0.0538	0.0499	0.0463	0.0430	0.0368	0.0315
16	0.0537	0.0496	0.0458	0.0423	0.0390	0.0330	0.0278
17	0.0500	0.0460	0.0422	0.0387	0.0354	0.0296	0.0247
18	0.0467	0.0427	0.0390	0.0355	0.0324	0.0267	0.0219
19	0.0438	0.0398	0.0361	0.0327	0.0296	0.0241	0.0195
20	0.0412	0.0372	0.0336	0.0302	0.0272	0.0219	0.0175
24	0.0329	0.0290	0.0256	0.0225	0.0197	0.0150	0.0113
28	0.0270	0.0233	0.0200	0.0171	0.0146	0.0105	0.0075
32	0.0226	0.0190	0.0159	0.0133	0.0110	0.0075	0.0050
36	0.0192	0.0158	0.0129	0.0104	0.0084	0.0053	0.0033
40	0.0166	0.0133	0.0105	0.0083	0.0065	0.0039	0.0023

We begin by looking down the Period column in Table 13.3 until we come to 18. Then we go across until we reach the 10% column. The table factor is .0219.

Now we multiply $60,000 by the factor as follows:

$60,000 × .0219 = $1,314

This states that if Moore Company pays $1,314 at the end of each period for 18 years, then $60,000 will be available to pay off the bond issue at maturity.

We can check this by using Table 13.1 on p. 320 (the ordinary annuity table):

$1,314 × 45.5992 = $59,917.35[8]

It's time to try the following Practice Quiz.

LU 13–3	**PRACTICE QUIZ**

Complete this **Practice Quiz** to see how you are doing

Today, Arrow Company issued bonds that will mature to a value of $90,000 in 10 years. Arrow's controller is planning to set up a sinking fund. Interest rates are 12% compounded semiannually. What will Arrow Company have to set aside to meet its obligation in 10 years? Check your answer. Your answer will be off due to the rounding of Table 13.3.

✓ **Solution**

10 years × 2 = 20 periods $\dfrac{12\%}{2} = 6\%$ $90,000 × .0272 = $2,448

Check $2,448 × 36.7855 = $90,050.90

---

[8]Off due to rounding.

LU 13–3a   EXTRA PRACTICE QUIZ

Need more practice? Try this
Extra Practice Quiz (check
figures in Chapter Organizer,
p. 329)

Today Arrow Company issued bonds that will mature to a value of $120,000 in 20 years. Arrow's controller is planning to set up a sinking fund. Interest rates are 6% compounded semiannually. What will Arrow Company have to set aside to meet its obligation in 10 years? Check your answer. Your answer will be off due to rounding of Table 13.3.

CHAPTER ORGANIZER AND STUDY GUIDE
WITH CHECK FIGURES FOR EXTRA PRACTICE QUIZZES

Topic	Key point, procedure, formula	Example(s) to illustrate situation
Ordinary annuities (find future value), p. 319	Invest money at end of each period. Find future value at maturity. Answers question of how much money accumulates. $\dfrac{\text{Future}}{\text{value of}} \text{ordinary} = \dfrac{\text{Annuity}}{\text{payment}} \times \dfrac{\text{Ordinary}}{\text{annuity}}$ $\text{annuity} \quad \text{each} \quad \text{table}$ $\text{period} \quad \text{factor}$ $FV = PMT\left[\dfrac{(1 + i)^n - 1}{i}\right]$	Use Table 13.1: 2 years, $4,000 ordinary annuity at 8% annually. Value = $4,000 × 2.0800 = $8,320 (2 periods, 8%) $FV = 4,000\left[\dfrac{(1 + .08)^2 - 1}{.08}\right] = \$8,320$
Annuities due (find future value), p. 321	Invest money at beginning of each period. Find future value at maturity. Should be higher than ordinary annuity since it is invested at beginning of each period. Use Table 13.1, but add one period and subtract one payment from answer. $\dfrac{\text{Future}}{\text{value}} \text{of an} = \left(\dfrac{\text{Annuity}}{\text{payment}} \times \dfrac{\text{Ordinary*}}{\text{annuity}}\right) - 1 \text{ Payment}$ $\text{annuity} \quad \text{each} \quad \text{table}$ $\text{due} \quad \text{period} \quad \text{factor}$ *Add 1 period. $FV_{due} = PMT\left[\dfrac{(1 + i)^n - 1}{i}\right](1 + i)$	*Example:* Same example as above but invest money at beginning of period. $4,000 × 3.2464 = $12,985.60 − 4,000.00 $ 8,985.60 (3 periods, 8%) $FV_{due} = 4,000\left(\dfrac{(1 + .08)^2 - 1}{.08}\right)(1 + .08)$ $= \$8,985.60$
Present value of an ordinary annuity (find present value), p. 323	Calculate number of periods and rate per period. Use Table 13.2 to find table factor for present value of $1. Multiply withdrawal for each period by table factor to get present value of an ordinary annuity. $\dfrac{\text{Present}}{\text{value of an}} \text{ordinary} = \dfrac{\text{Annuity}}{\text{payment}} \times \dfrac{\text{Present}}{\text{value of}} \text{ordinary}$ $\text{annuity} \quad \text{annuity}$ $\text{payment} \quad \text{table}$ $PV = PMT\left[\dfrac{1 - (1 + i)^{-n}}{i}\right]$	*Example:* Receive $10,000 for 5 years. Interest is 10% compounded annually. Table 13.2: 5 periods, 10% 3.7908 × $10,000 What you put in today = $37,908 $PV = 10,000\left[\dfrac{1 - (1 + .1)^{-5}}{.1}\right] = \$37,907.88$

(continues)

CHAPTER ORGANIZER AND STUDY GUIDE
WITH CHECK FIGURES FOR EXTRA PRACTICE QUIZZES (concluded)

Topic	Key point, procedure, formula	Example(s) to illustrate situation
Sinking funds (find periodic payment), p. 326	Paying a particular amount of money for a set number of periodic payments to accumulate a specific sum. We know the future and must calculate the periodic payments needed. Answer can be proved by ordinary annuity table. $$\begin{array}{l}\text{Sinking} \\ \text{fund} \\ \text{payment}\end{array} = \begin{array}{c}\text{Future} \\ \text{value}\end{array} \times \begin{array}{c}\text{Sinking} \\ \text{fund table} \\ \text{factor}\end{array}$$	*Example:* $200,000 bond to retire 15 years from now. Interest is 6% compounded annually. By Table 13.3: $200,000 × .0430 = $8,600 Check by Table 13.1: $8,600 × 23.2759 = $200,172.74
KEY TERMS	Annuities certain, *p. 318* Annuity, *p. 317* Annuity due, *p. 318* Contingent annuities, *p. 318*	Future value of an annuity, *p. 318* Ordinary annuity, *p. 318* Payment periods, *p. 318*	Present value of an annuity, *p. 323* Sinking fund, *p. 326* Term of the annuity, *p. 318*

CHECK FIGURES FOR EXTRA PRACTICE QUIZZES WITH PAGE REFERENCES	LU 13–1a (p. 323)
	1. a. $42,914.50
	  b. $43,773
	  c. $36,544.50
		LU 13–2a (p. 326)
		1. $175,042
		2. $121,663.50
		3. $1,352,584.40
			LU 13–3a (p. 328)
			$1,596

Critical Thinking Discussion Questions

1. What is the difference between an ordinary annuity and an annuity due? If you were to save money in an annuity, which would you choose and why?

2. Explain how you would calculate ordinary annuities and annuities due by table lookup. Create an example to explain the meaning of a table factor from an ordinary annuity.

3. What is a present value of an ordinary annuity? Create an example showing how one of your relatives might plan for retirement by using the present value of an ordinary annuity. Would you ever have to use lump-sum payments in your calculation from Chapter 12?

4. What is a sinking fund? Why could an ordinary annuity table be used to check the sinking fund payment?

Classroom Notes

Name _____ Date _____

DRILL PROBLEMS

Complete the ordinary annuities for the following using tables in the *Business Math Handbook:*

	Amount of payment	Payment payable	Years	Interest rate	Value of annuity
13–1.	$10,000	Quarterly	7	4%	
13–2.	$7,000	Semiannually	8	7%	

Redo Problem 13–1 as an annuity due:

13–3.

Calculate the value of the following annuity due without a table. Check your results by Table 13.1 or the *Business Math Handbook* (they will be slightly off due to rounding):

	Amount of payment	Payment payable	Years	Interest rate
13–4.	$2,000	Annually	3	6%

Complete the following using Table 13.2 or the *Business Math Handbook* for the present value of an ordinary annuity:

	Amount of annuity expected	Payment	Time	Interest rate	Present value (amount needed now to invest to receive annuity)
13–5.	$900	Annually	4 years	6%	
13–6.	$15,000	Quarterly	4 years	8%	

13–7. Check Problem 13–5 without the use of Table 13.2.

Using the sinking fund Table 13.3 or the *Business Math Handbook,* complete the following:

	Required amount	Frequency of payment	Length of time	Interest rate	Payment amount end of each period
13–8.	$25,000	Quarterly	6 years	8%	
13–9.	$15,000	Annually	8 years	8%	

13–10. Check the answer in Problem 13–9 by Table 13.1.

WORD PROBLEMS (Use Tables in the *Business Math Handbook*)

13–11. John Regan, an employee at Home Depot, made deposits of $800 at the end of each year for 4 years. Interest is 4% compounded annually. What is the value of Regan's annuity at the end of 4 years?

13–12. Pete King promised to pay his son $300 semiannually for 9 years. Assume Pete can invest his money at 8% in an ordinary annuity. How much must Pete invest today to pay his son $300 semiannually for 9 years?

13–13. "The most powerful force in the universe is compound interest," according to an article in the *Morningstar Column* dated February 13, 2007. Patricia Wiseman is 30 years old and she invests $2,000 in an annuity, earning 5% compound annual return at the beginning of each period, for 18 years. What is the cash value of this annuity due at the end of 18 years?

13–14. The *Toronto Star* on February 15, 2007, described getting rich slowly, but surely. You have 40 years to save. If you start early, with the power of compounding, what a situation you would be in. Valerie Wise is 25 years old and invests $3,000 for only six years in an ordinary annuity at 8% interest compounded annually. What is the final value of Valerie's investment at the end of year 6?

13–15. "Pay Dirt; It's time for a Clean Sweep", was the title of an article that appeared in the Minneapolis, *Star Tribune* on March 15, 2007. Plant your coins in the bank: during a traditional spring cleaning, coins sprout from couch cushions and junk drawers. The average American has $99 lying about. Stick $99 in an ordinary annuity account each year for 10 years at 5% interest and watch it grow. What is the cash value of this annuity at the end of year 10? Round to the nearest dollar.

13–16. Patricia and Joe Payne are divorced. The divorce settlement stipulated that Joe pay $525 a month for their daughter Suzanne until she turns 18 in 4 years. How much must Joe set aside today to meet the settlement? Interest is 6% a year.

13–17. Josef Company borrowed money that must be repaid in 20 years. The company wants to make sure the loan will be repaid at the end of year 20. So it invests $12,500 at the end of each year at 12% interest compounded annually. What was the amount of the original loan?

13–18. Jane Frost wants to receive yearly payments of $15,000 for 10 years. How much must she deposit at her bank today at 11% interest compounded annually?

13–19. Toby Martin invests $2,000 at the end of each year for 10 years in an ordinary annuity at 11% interest compounded annually. What is the final value of Toby's investment at the end of year 10?

13–20. Alice Longtree has decided to invest $400 quarterly for 4 years in an ordinary annuity at 8%. As her financial adviser, calculate for Alice the total cash value of the annuity at the end of year 4.

13–21. At the beginning of each period for 10 years, Merl Agnes invests $500 semiannually at 6%. What is the cash value of this annuity due at the end of year 10?

13–22. Jeff Associates borrowed $30,000. The company plans to set up a sinking fund that will repay the loan at the end of 8 years. Assume a 12% interest rate compounded semiannually. What must Jeff pay into the fund each period of time? Check your answer by Table 13.1.

13–23. On Joe Martin's graduation from college, Joe's uncle promised him a gift of $12,000 in cash or $900 every quarter for the next 4 years after graduation. If money could be invested at 8% compounded quarterly, which offer is better for Joe?

13–24. You are earning an average of $46,500 and will retire in 10 years. If you put 20% of your gross average income in an ordinary annuity compounded at 7% annually, what will be the value of the annuity when you retire?

13–25. GU Corporation must buy a new piece of equipment in 5 years that will cost $88,000. The company is setting up a sinking fund to finance the purchase. What will the quarterly deposit be if the fund earns 8% interest?

13–26. Mike Macaro is selling a piece of land. Two offers are on the table. Morton Company offered a $40,000 down payment and $35,000 a year for the next 5 years. Flynn Company offered $25,000 down and $38,000 a year for the next 5 years. If money can be invested at 8% compounded annually, which offer is better for Mike?

13–27. Al Vincent has decided to retire to Arizona in 10 years. What amount should Al invest today so that he will be able to withdraw $28,000 at the end of each year for 15 years *after* he retires? Assume he can invest the money at 8% interest compounded annually.

13–28. Victor French made deposits of $5,000 at the end of each quarter to Book Bank, which pays 8% interest compounded quarterly. After 3 years, Victor made no more deposits. What will be the balance in the account 2 years after the last deposit?

13–29. Janet Woo decided to retire to Florida in 6 years. What amount should Janet invest today so she can withdraw $50,000 at the end of each year for 20 years after she retires? Assume Janet can invest money at 6% compounded annually.

CHALLENGE PROBLEMS

13–30. David Stokke must determine how much money he needs to set aside now for future home repairs. He has determined his roof has only 10 more years of useful life. His roof would require 15 bundles of shingles. The roof he prefers costs $145 per bundle for total replacement. Assume a 1.5% inflation rate per year over the next 10 years. David is placing his money in a sinking fund at 6% compounded semiannually. **(a)** What is today's cost of replacing the roof? **(b)** What is the cost of replacing the roof in 10 years? **(c)** What amount will David have to put away each year to have enough money to replace the roof?

13–31. Ajax Corporation has hired Brad O'Brien as its new president. Terms included the company's agreeing to pay retirement benefits of $18,000 at the end of each semiannual period for 10 years. This will begin in 3,285 days. If the money can be invested at 8% compounded semiannually, what must the company deposit today to fulfill its obligation to Brad?

 SUMMARY PRACTICE TEST (Use Tables in the *Business Math Handbook*)

1. Lin Lowe plans to deposit $1,800 at the end of every 6 months for the next 15 years at 8% interest compounded semiannually. What is the value of Lin's annuity at the end of 15 years? *(p. 319)*

2. On Abby Ellen's graduation from law school, Abby's uncle, Bull Brady, promised her a gift of $24,000 or $2,400 every quarter for the next 4 years after graduating from law school. If the money could be invested at 6% compounded quarterly, which offer should Abby choose? *(p. 325)*

3. Sanka Blunck wants to receive $8,000 each year for 20 years. How much must Sanka invest today at 4% interest compounded annually? *(p. 325)*

4. In 9 years, Rollo Company will have to repay a $100,000 loan. Assume a 6% interest rate compounded quarterly. How much must Rollo Company pay each period to have $100,000 at the end of 9 years? *(p. 325)*

5. Lance Industries borrowed $130,000. The company plans to set up a sinking fund that will repay the loan at the end of 18 years. Assume a 6% interest rate compounded semiannually. What amount must Lance Industries pay into the fund each period? Check your answer by Table 13.1 *(p. 326)*

6. Joe Jan wants to receive $22,000 each year for the next 22 years. Assume a 6% interest rate compounded annually. How much must Joe invest today? *(p. 325)*

7. Twice a year for 15 years, Warren Ford invested $1,700 compounded semiannually at 6% interest. What is the value of this annuity due? *(p. 321)*

8. Scupper Molly invested $1,800 semiannually for 23 years at 8% interest compounded semiannually. What is the value of this annuity due? *(p. 321)*

9. Nelson Collins decided to retire to Canada in 10 years. What amount should Nelson deposit so that he will be able to withdraw $80,000 at the end of each year for 25 years after he retires? Assume Nelson can invest money at 7% interest compounded annually. *(p. 325)*

10. Bob Bryan made deposits of $10,000 at the end of each quarter to Lion Bank, which pays 8% interest compounded quarterly. After 9 years, Bob made no more deposits. What will be the account's balance 4 years after the last deposit? *(p. 319)*

Classroom Notes

Special Supplement*

Time-Value Relationship Using Plastic Overlays
Contents

One Lump Sum (Single Amount)

EXHIBIT 13.1   Compound (future value) of $.68 at 10% for 4 periods

EXHIBIT 13.2   Present value of $1.00 at 10% for 4 periods

Annuity (Stream of Payments)

EXHIBIT 13.3   Present value of a 4-year annuity of $1.00 at 10%

EXHIBIT 13.4   Future value of a 4-year annuity of $1.00 at 10%

*Note the Kiplinger Article, Business Scrapbook, and Cumulative Review follow this supplement starting on page 337.

Turn transparency over to see relationship of compounding to present value.

EXHIBIT 13.1 Compound (future value) of $.68 at 10% for 4 periods

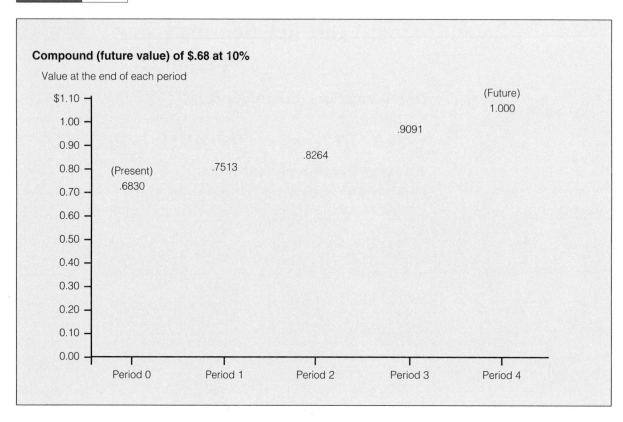

Compound (future value) of $.68 at 10%

Value at the end of each period

68¢ today will grow to $1.00 in the future.

What Exhibit 13.1 Means

If you take $.68 to a bank that pays 10% after 4 periods you will be able to get $1.00. The $.68 is the present value, and the $1.00 is the compound value or future value. Keep in mind that the $.68 is a one lump-sum investment.

EXHIBIT **13.2** Present value of $1.00 at 10% for 4 periods

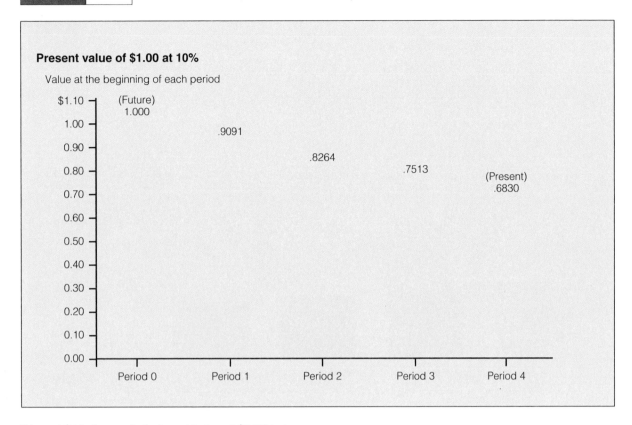

Present value of $1.00 at 10%

Value at the beginning of each period

If I need $1 in four periods, I need to invest $0.68 today.

What Exhibit 13.2 Means

If you want to receive $1.00 at the end of 4 periods at a bank paying 10%, you will have to deposit $.68 in the bank today. The longer you have to wait for your money, the less it is worth. The $1.00 is the compound or future amount, and the $.68 is the present value of a dollar that you will not receive for 4 periods.

EXHIBIT **13.3** Present value of a 4-year annuity of $1.00 at 10%

Present value of $1.00 at 10%

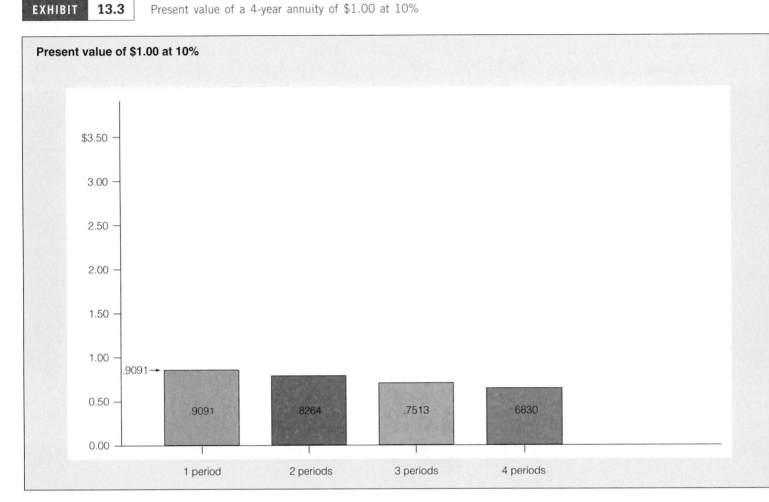

EXHIBIT **13.4** Future value of a 4-year annuity of $1.00 at 10%

Future value of $1.00 at 10%

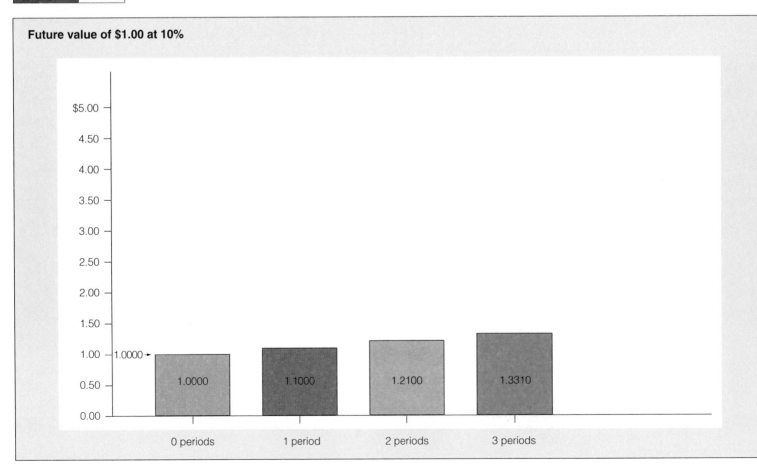

What Exhibit 13.3 Means*

BLUE BOX
(Top box)

Blue shows how to receive $1.00 after 1 period. You must put in $.91 today.

PURPLE BOX
(2nd box from top)

Purple shows how to receive $1.00 after 2 periods. You must put in $.83 today to get $1.00 for 2 periods. You must put in the bank today $1.74 ($.91 + $.83) to take out $1.00 for 2 periods.

YELLOW BOX
(3rd box from top)

Yellow shows how to receive $1.00 after 3 periods. You must put in $.75 today to get $1.00 for 3 periods. You also must put in the bank today $2.49 ($.91 + $.83 + $.75) to take out $1.00 for 3 periods.

GREEN BOX
(4th box from top)

Green shows how to receive $1.00 after 4 periods. You must put in $.68 today to get $1.00 for 4 periods. You also must put in the bank today $3.17 ($.91 + $.83 + $.75 + $.68) to take out $1.00 for 4 periods.

What Exhibit 13.4 Means*

BLUE BOX
(Top box)

Blue shows $1.00 invested at the end of each period. The $1.00 has no time to earn interest.

PURPLE BOX
(2nd box from top)

Purple shows the value of $1.00 after the end of 2nd period. The $1.00 is now worth $1.10 due to compounding for 1 period.

YELLOW BOX
(3rd box from top)

Yellow shows the value of $1.00 after the end of 3rd period. The $1.00 is now worth $1.21 due to the compounding for 2 periods.

GREEN BOX
(4th box from top)

Green shows that the value of $1.00 after the end of 4 periods is $1.33 due to compounding for 3 periods. If you put $1.00 in the bank at 10% for 4 years, the $4.00 grows to $4.64.

*From table in Handbook for 10%.

Periods	Amount of annuity	Present value of an annuity
1	1. 1.0000	. 9091
2	2. 2.1000	1. 7355
3	3. 3100	2. 4869
4	4. 6410	3. 1699

PORTFOLIO DOCTOR A retiree ponders converting his traditional IRA. *By Jeffrey R. Kosnett*

An overlooked way to **SHEAR** your taxes

LIKE MOST people, Tom Berry wants to pay less tax. Tom, a retired 63-year-old computer engineer from Edwardsville, Ill., has a plan that may enable him to do just that: He's considering converting his $165,000 traditional IRA to a Roth IRA.

Traditional IRA distributions are taxable; Roth distributions aren't. Tom must begin taking distributions from his traditional IRA at age 70½. At that point, Tom figures, the combination of taxable withdrawals, pension income and Social Security would push him and his wife, Paula, into the 25% federal tax bracket. Converting his IRA to a Roth now could keep him in a lower tax bracket later. "Why waste that 15% bracket?" Tom asks.

Tom says he has no pressing financial needs and does not intend to draw on his traditional IRA until the law requires him to. Tom, who could live into his nineties based on his family history, invests in an assortment of mutual funds, with about two-thirds in stock funds.

Stumped by your investments? Write to us at portfoliodoc @kiplinger.com.

PHOTOGRAPH BY ANNA KNOTT

Assuming a 7% annual return, Tom's traditional IRA could reach nearly $300,000 by the time he's 70½. Tom would have to take out a minimum of about $11,000 that year, based on an IRS schedule designed to deplete the account over 27 years.

Beyond the sweet smell of tax-free withdrawals in retirement, converting to a Roth is appealing because Tom could avoid those mandatory withdrawals. The original owner of a Roth never has to tap the account, so investments can grow indefinitely. To be eligible to convert to a Roth, your income (on a single or joint return) must be less than $100,000. Tom qualifies. (The $100,000 limit disappears in 2010.)

The drawback with Tom's plan is that he would have to pay taxes on all of the money he moves from his traditional IRA to a Roth. And if Tom switched all the money at once, he would catapult from the 15% bracket to the 33% bracket, and he'd lose one-third of his $165,000 kitty. But there's a way to limit the pain. Tom can convert to a Roth gradually so that he's not pushed into a higher tax bracket in any given year.

It's important to figure out how much you can convert each year without "pushing yourself into an outrageous tax bracket," says Curtis Chen, a financial planner in Belmont, Cal. That amount will vary with your other income and with tweaks in tax brackets.

Test case. If Tom and Paula's taxable income this year before any Roth conversion is, say, $50,000, Tom could move $11,300 to a Roth before tripping into the 25% bracket. Want to try Tom's strategy yourself? For an idea of your own "conversion capacity," compare your estimated taxable income for the year with the income stepping stones in the tax brackets. (To find the latest brackets, search "tax rates" at www.irs.gov.)

Converting to a Roth also holds promise for your heirs: Avoiding mandatory payouts means there might be more money left for them. Even better, money in an inherited Roth IRA is tax-free while cash in a traditional IRA is taxed in the beneficiary's top tax bracket. "If you want to leave money to someone, you'll leave a bigger amount" with a Roth because the taxes have already been paid, says Donald Duncan, a planner with D3 Financial Counselors, in Downers Grove, Ill. He adds that the conversion strategy works best if you pay the taxes on the converted money from other sources rather than from the IRA. That enables more of your money to grow tax-free.

BUSINESS MATH ISSUE

Changing to a Roth is silly because you have to pay taxes upfront.

1. List the key points of the article and information to support your position.
2. Write a group defense of your position using math calculations to support your view.

PROJECT A
Go to the Internet to find the latest change to the Roth 401 since this article was published.

A New Flavor For Retirement

It's Called a Roth 401(k) Plan, And It May Be Better for Some, Like Younger Workers, Parents

By JEFF D. OPDYKE

GET READY for yet another retirement-savings plan.

Come Jan. 1, a new entrant joins the list of options: the Roth 401(k). Workers considering this route must answer a simple question from Uncle Sam: Do you want to pay me now or pay me later?

Traditional 401(k) plans allow investors to sock away part of their income before it is taxed by federal, state or local authorities; the government takes its cut as retirees withdraw the money.

With Roth 401(k) plans, the money that is contributed is taxed now, but the withdrawals are tax-free.

So far, neither workers nor employers have shown much interest in the Roth plans. For workers, paying into a Roth 401(k) means less take-home pay than if they contributed a like sum to a traditional 401(k). For employers, offering the new plan means additional administrative chores.

Still, while Roth 401(k) plans aren't right for everyone, they are advantageous to lots of people in a variety of situations, including younger workers, folks with big estates to leave their heirs and even parents and grandparents saving for children's college education.

At its core, the Roth 401(k) is similar to the Roth IRA, which has grown into a popular way to supplement employer-sponsored retirement plans since it was introduced in 1998. You save after-tax dollars during your working years in a mutual fund or other investments and then withdraw the money—including all the profits the savings generated—tax-free, so long as the account has been open five years or more and you are at least 59½ years old. (Unlike Roth IRAs, which aren't available to high-income folks, there are no income limits with Roth 401(k) plans.)

That tax-free growth is what differentiates the new Roth 401(k) from the old-fashioned 401(k). You will owe Uncle Sam nothing on years of compounded profits, which are likely to be the largest chunk of your account. With traditional 401(k) plans, you skip taxes today, but when you withdraw the money, you pay taxes at ordinary rates not just on the contributions but also on all of the compounded profits. That means a traditional 401(k) ultimately would provide a smaller amount of after-tax dollars to live on in retirement.

Wall Street Journal © 2005

Internet Projects: See text Web site (www.mhhe.com/slater9e) and The Business Math Internet Resource Guide.

A Word Problem Approach—Chapters 10, 11, 12, 13

1. Amy O'Mally graduated from high school. Her uncle promised her as a gift a check for $2,000 or $275 every quarter for 2 years. If money could be invested at 6% compounded quarterly, which offer is better for Amy? (Use the tables in the *Business Math Handbook*.) *(p. 325)*

2. Alan Angel made deposits of $400 semiannually to Sag Bank, which pays 10% interest compounded semiannually. After 4 years, Alan made no more deposits. What will be the balance in the account 3 years after the last deposit? (Use the tables in the *Business Math Handbook*.) *(pp. 319, 299)*

3. Roger Disney decides to retire to Florida in 12 years. What amount should Roger invest today so that he will be able to withdraw $30,000 at the end of each year for 20 years *after* he retires? Assume he can invest money at 8% interest compounded annually. (Use tables in the *Business Math Handbook*.) *(p. 325)*

4. On September 15, Arthur Westering borrowed $3,000 from Vermont Bank at $10\frac{1}{2}\%$ interest. Arthur plans to repay the loan on January 25. Assume the loan is based on exact interest. How much will Arthur totally repay? *(p. 260)*

5. Sue Cooper borrowed $6,000 on an $11\frac{3}{4}\%$, 120-day note. Sue paid $300 toward the note on day 50. On day 90, Sue paid an additional $200. Using the U.S. Rule, Sue's adjusted balance after her first payment is the following. *(p. 261)*

6. On November 18, Northwest Company discounted an $18,000, 12%, 120-day note dated September 8. Assume a 10% discount rate. What will be the proceeds? Use ordinary interest. *(p. 279)*

7. Alice Reed deposits $16,500 into Rye Bank, which pays 10% interest compounded semiannually. Using the appropriate table, what will Alice have in her account at the end of 6 years? *(p. 299)*

8. Peter Regan needs $90,000 in 5 years from today to retire in Arizona. Peter's bank pays 10% interest compounded semiannually. What will Peter have to put in the bank today to have $90,000 in 5 years? *(p. 304)*

Classroom Notes

CHAPTER 14

Installment Buying, Rule of 78, and Revolving Charge Credit Cards

Quick Fix

Refunds on Canceled Cards

■ **The Problem:** You cancel a credit card and then later return an item bought using that card—how do you get the refund?

■ **The Solution:** With more people switching to lower-interest-rate credit cards, some consumers are finding themselves in this position. Credit-card companies like American Express and Citibank say they will automatically reimburse you via check, as long as you've complied with store return policies and had a zero balance when the card was canceled.

Chase says it issues a refund check about a month after the return is processed, while at Citibank, it's generally within 60 days. At MBNA, it can be anywhere from a week to more than 30 days. Sometimes nudging the card company can help speed up the process. When former AmEx cardholders call about oustanding credits, they can receive checks in around a week—as opposed to the normal process time of one to two months—a spokeswoman said. Citibank has roughly the same policy.

—Hope Glassberg

Wall Street Journal © 2005

LEARNING UNIT OBJECTIVES

LU 14–1: Cost of Installment Buying

- Calculate the amount financed, finance charge, and deferred payment (p. 342).
- Calculate the estimated APR by table lookup (p. 343).
- Calculate the monthly payment by formula and by table lookup (p. 346).

LU 14–2: Paying Off Installment Loans before Due Date

- Calculate the rebate and payoff for Rule of 78 (p. 347).

LU 14–3: Revolving Charge Credit Cards

- Calculate the finance charges on revolving charge credit card accounts (pp. 350–352).

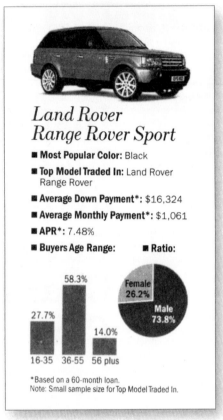

Land Rover
Range Rover Sport

■ **Most Popular Color:** Black

■ **Top Model Traded In:** Land Rover Range Rover

■ **Average Down Payment*:** $16,324

■ **Average Monthly Payment*:** $1,061

■ **APR*:** 7.48%

■ **Buyers Age Range:**   ■ **Ratio:**

Are you interested in buying a Land Rover Range Rover Sport car? The *Wall Street Journal* clipping shows that the car has an APR of 7.48%. In this chapter we will explain what APR means and how you can calculate APR. This chapter also discusses the cost of buying products by installments (closed-end credit) and the revolving credit card (open-end credit).

58.3%

27.7%

14.0%

16-35   36-55   56 plus

Female 26.2%

Male 73.8%

*Based on a 60-month loan.
Note: Small sample size for Top Model Traded In.

Wall Street Journal © 2005

Learning Unit 14–1: Cost of Installment Buying

Installment buying, a form of *closed-end credit,* can add a substantial amount to the cost of big-ticket purchases. To illustrate this, we follow the procedure of buying a pickup truck, including the amount financed, finance charge, and deferred payment price. Then we study the effect of the Truth in Lending Act.

Amount Financed, Finance Charge, and Deferred Payment

This advertisement for the sale of a pickup truck appeared in a local paper. As you can see from this advertisement, after customers make a **down payment,** they can buy the truck with

Ford Motor Company/AP Wide World

4X4 Pickup

9,345

$194.38 MONTH

With $300 down cash or trade for 60 months at Annual Percentage Rate of 10.5%. Amt. financed—$9,045.00. Finance chg.—$2,617.80. Total note—$11,662.80. Total deferred payment price—$11,962.80. Taxes, title, insurance additional.

an **installment loan.** This loan is paid off with a series of equal periodic payments. These payments include both interest and principal. The payment process is called **amortization.** In the promissory notes of earlier chapters, the loan was paid off in one ending payment. Now let's look at the calculations involved in buying a pickup truck.

Checking Calculations in Pickup Advertisement

Calculating Amount Financed The **amount financed** is what you actually borrow. To calculate this amount, use the following formula:

Amount financed = Cash price − Down payment

$9,045   = $9,345   − $300

Calculating Finance Charge The words **finance charge** in the advertisement represent the **interest** charge. The interest charge resulting in the finance charge includes the cost of credit reports, mandatory bank fees, and so on. You can use the following formula to calculate the total interest on the loan:

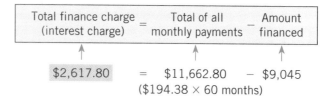

$$\underset{\$2,617.80}{\underset{\text{(interest charge)}}{\text{Total finance charge}}} = \underset{\$11,662.80}{\underset{\text{monthly payments}}{\text{Total of all}}} - \underset{\$9,045}{\underset{\text{financed}}{\text{Amount}}}$$
$$(\$194.38 \times 60 \text{ months})$$

Calculating Deferred Payment Price The **deferred payment price** represents the total of all monthly payments plus the down payment. The following formula is used to calculate the deferred payment price:

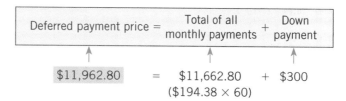

$$\text{Deferred payment price} = \underset{\text{monthly payments}}{\text{Total of all}} + \underset{\text{payment}}{\text{Down}}$$
$$\$11,962.80 \quad = \quad \$11,662.80 \quad + \quad \$300$$
$$(\$194.38 \times 60)$$

Truth in Lending: APR Defined and Calculated

In 1969, the Federal Reserve Board established the **Truth in Lending Act** (Regulation Z). The law doesn't regulate interest charges; its purpose is to make the consumer aware of the true cost of credit.

The Truth in Lending Act requires that creditors provide certain basic information about the actual cost of buying on credit. Before buyers sign a credit agreement, creditors must inform them in writing of the amount of the finance charge and the **annual percentage rate (APR).** The APR represents the true or effective annual interest creditors charge. This is helpful to buyers who repay loans over different periods of time (1 month, 48 months, and so on).

To illustrate how the APR affects the interest rate, assume you borrow $100 for 1 year and pay a finance charge of $9. Your interest rate would be 9% if you waited until the end of the year to pay back the loan. Now let's say you pay off the loan and the finance charge in 12 monthly payments. Each month that you make a payment, you are losing some of the value or use of that money. So the true or effective APR is actually greater than 9%.

The APR can be calculated by formula or by tables. We will use the table method since it is more exact.

Calculating APR Rate by Table 14.1 (p. 344)

Note the following steps for using a table to calculate APR:

CALCULATING APR BY TABLE
Step 1. Divide the finance charge by amount financed and multiply by $100 to get the table lookup factor.
Step 2. Go to APR Table 14.1. At the left side of the table are listed the number of payments that will be made.
Step 3. When you find the number of payments you are looking for, move to the right and look for the two numbers closest to the table lookup number. This will indicate the APR.

Now let's determine the APR for the pickup truck advertisement given earlier in the chapter.

TABLE 14.1   Annual percentage rate table per $100

NUMBER OF PAYMENTS	10.00%	10.25%	10.50%	10.75%	11.00%	11.25%	11.50%	11.75%	12.00%	12.25%	12.50%	12.75%	13.00%	13.25%	13.50%	13.75%
	(FINANCE CHARGE PER $100 OF AMOUNT FINANCED)															
1	0.83	0.85	0.87	0.90	0.92	0.94	0.96	0.98	1.00	1.02	1.04	1.06	1.08	1.10	1.12	1.15
2	1.25	1.28	1.31	1.35	1.38	1.41	1.44	1.47	1.50	1.53	1.57	1.60	1.63	1.66	1.69	1.72
3	1.67	1.71	1.76	1.80	1.84	1.88	1.92	1.96	2.01	2.05	2.09	2.13	2.17	2.22	2.26	2.30
4	2.09	2.14	2.20	2.25	2.30	2.35	2.41	2.46	2.51	2.57	2.62	2.67	2.72	2.78	2.83	2.88
5	2.51	2.58	2.64	2.70	2.77	2.83	2.89	2.96	3.02	3.08	3.15	3.21	3.27	3.34	3.40	3.46
6	2.94	3.01	3.08	3.16	3.23	3.31	3.38	3.45	3.53	3.60	3.68	3.75	3.83	3.90	3.97	4.05
7	3.36	3.45	3.53	3.62	3.70	3.78	3.87	3.95	4.04	4.12	4.21	4.29	4.38	4.47	4.55	4.64
8	3.79	3.88	3.98	4.07	4.17	4.26	4.36	4.46	4.55	4.65	4.74	4.84	4.94	5.03	5.13	5.22
9	4.21	4.32	4.43	4.53	4.64	4.75	4.85	4.96	5.07	5.17	5.28	5.39	5.49	5.60	5.71	5.82
10	4.64	4.76	4.88	4.99	5.11	5.23	5.35	5.46	5.58	5.70	5.82	5.94	6.05	6.17	6.29	6.41
11	5.07	5.20	5.33	5.45	5.58	5.71	5.84	5.97	6.10	6.23	6.36	6.49	6.62	6.75	6.88	7.01
12	5.50	5.64	5.78	5.92	6.06	6.20	6.34	6.48	6.62	6.76	6.90	7.04	7.18	7.32	7.46	7.60
13	5.93	6.08	6.23	6.38	6.53	6.68	6.84	6.99	7.14	7.29	7.44	7.59	7.75	7.90	8.05	8.20
14	6.36	6.52	6.69	6.85	7.01	7.17	7.34	7.50	7.66	7.82	7.99	8.15	8.31	8.48	8.64	8.81
15	6.80	6.97	7.14	7.32	7.49	7.66	7.84	8.01	8.19	8.36	8.53	8.71	8.88	9.06	9.23	9.41
16	7.23	7.41	7.60	7.78	7.97	8.15	8.34	8.53	8.71	8.90	9.08	9.27	9.46	9.64	9.83	10.02
17	7.67	7.86	8.06	8.25	8.45	8.65	8.84	9.04	9.24	9.44	9.63	9.83	10.03	10.23	10.43	10.63
18	8.10	8.31	8.52	8.73	8.93	9.14	9.35	9.56	9.77	9.98	10.19	10.40	10.61	10.82	11.03	11.24
19	8.54	8.76	8.98	9.20	9.42	9.64	9.86	10.08	10.30	10.52	10.74	10.96	11.18	11.41	11.63	11.85
20	8.98	9.21	9.44	9.67	9.90	10.13	10.37	10.60	10.83	11.06	11.30	11.53	11.76	12.00	12.23	12.46
21	9.42	9.66	9.90	10.15	10.39	10.63	10.88	11.12	11.36	11.61	11.85	12.10	12.34	12.59	12.84	13.08
22	9.86	10.12	10.37	10.62	10.88	11.13	11.39	11.64	11.90	12.16	12.41	12.67	12.93	13.19	13.45	13.70
23	10.30	10.57	10.84	11.10	11.37	11.63	11.90	12.17	12.44	12.71	12.97	13.24	13.51	13.78	14.05	14.32
24	10.75	11.02	11.30	11.58	11.86	12.14	12.42	12.70	12.98	13.26	13.54	13.82	14.10	14.38	14.66	14.95
25	11.19	11.48	11.77	12.06	12.35	12.64	12.93	13.22	13.52	13.81	14.10	14.40	14.69	14.98	15.28	15.57
26	11.64	11.94	12.24	12.54	12.85	13.15	13.45	13.75	14.06	14.36	14.67	14.97	15.28	15.59	15.89	16.20
27	12.09	12.40	12.71	13.03	13.34	13.66	13.97	14.29	14.60	14.92	15.24	15.56	15.87	16.19	16.51	16.83
28	12.53	12.86	13.18	13.51	13.84	14.16	14.49	14.82	15.15	15.48	15.81	16.14	16.47	16.80	17.13	17.46
29	12.98	13.32	13.66	14.00	14.33	14.67	15.01	15.35	15.70	16.04	16.38	16.72	17.07	17.41	17.75	18.10
30	13.43	13.78	14.13	14.48	14.83	15.19	15.54	15.89	16.24	16.60	16.95	17.31	17.66	18.02	18.38	18.74
31	13.89	14.25	14.61	14.97	15.33	15.70	16.06	16.43	16.79	17.16	17.53	17.90	18.27	18.63	19.00	19.38
32	14.34	14.71	15.09	15.46	15.84	16.21	16.59	16.97	17.35	17.73	18.11	18.49	18.87	19.25	19.63	20.02
33	14.79	15.18	15.57	15.95	16.34	16.73	17.12	17.51	17.90	18.29	18.69	19.08	19.47	19.87	20.26	20.66
34	15.25	15.65	16.05	16.44	16.85	17.25	17.65	18.05	18.46	18.86	19.27	19.67	20.08	20.49	20.90	21.31
35	15.70	16.11	16.53	16.94	17.35	17.77	18.18	18.60	19.01	19.43	19.85	20.27	20.69	21.11	21.53	21.95
36	16.16	16.58	17.01	17.43	17.86	18.29	18.71	19.14	19.57	20.00	20.43	20.87	21.30	21.73	22.17	22.60
37	16.62	17.06	17.49	17.93	18.37	18.81	19.25	19.69	20.13	20.58	21.02	21.46	21.91	22.36	22.81	23.25
38	17.08	17.53	17.98	18.43	18.88	19.33	19.78	20.24	20.69	21.15	21.61	22.07	22.52	22.99	23.45	23.91
39	17.54	18.00	18.46	18.93	19.39	19.86	20.32	20.79	21.26	21.73	22.20	22.67	23.14	23.61	24.09	24.56
40	18.00	18.48	18.95	19.43	19.90	20.38	20.86	21.34	21.82	22.30	22.79	23.27	23.76	24.25	24.73	25.22
41	18.47	18.95	19.44	19.93	20.42	20.91	21.40	21.89	22.39	22.88	23.38	23.88	24.38	24.88	25.38	25.88
42	18.93	19.43	19.93	20.43	20.93	21.44	21.94	22.45	22.96	23.47	23.98	24.49	25.00	25.51	26.03	26.55
43	19.40	19.91	20.42	20.94	21.45	21.97	22.49	23.01	23.53	24.05	24.57	25.10	25.62	26.15	26.68	27.21
44	19.86	20.39	20.91	21.44	21.97	22.50	23.03	23.57	24.10	24.64	25.17	25.71	26.25	26.79	27.33	27.88
45	20.33	20.87	21.41	21.95	22.49	23.03	23.58	24.12	24.67	25.22	25.77	26.32	26.88	27.43	27.99	28.55
46	20.80	21.35	21.90	22.46	23.01	23.57	24.13	24.69	25.25	25.81	26.37	26.94	27.51	28.08	28.65	29.22
47	21.27	21.83	22.40	22.97	23.53	24.10	24.68	25.25	25.82	26.40	26.98	27.56	28.14	28.72	29.31	29.89
48	21.74	22.32	22.90	23.48	24.06	24.64	25.23	25.81	26.40	26.99	27.58	28.18	28.77	29.37	29.97	30.57
49	22.21	22.80	23.39	23.99	24.58	25.18	25.78	26.38	26.98	27.59	28.19	28.80	29.41	30.02	30.63	31.24
50	22.69	23.29	23.89	24.50	25.11	25.72	26.33	26.95	27.56	28.18	28.80	29.42	30.04	30.67	31.29	31.92
51	23.16	23.78	24.40	25.02	25.64	26.26	26.89	27.52	28.15	28.78	29.41	30.05	30.68	31.32	31.96	32.60
52	23.64	24.27	24.90	25.53	26.17	26.81	27.45	28.09	28.73	29.38	30.02	30.67	31.32	31.98	32.63	33.29
53	24.11	24.76	25.40	26.05	26.70	27.35	28.00	28.66	29.32	29.98	30.64	31.30	31.97	32.63	33.30	33.97
54	24.59	25.25	25.91	26.57	27.23	27.90	28.56	29.23	29.91	30.58	31.25	31.93	32.61	33.29	33.98	34.66
55	25.07	25.74	26.41	27.09	27.77	28.44	29.13	29.81	30.50	31.18	31.87	32.56	33.26	33.95	34.65	35.35
56	25.55	26.23	26.92	27.61	28.30	28.99	29.69	30.39	31.09	31.79	32.49	33.20	33.91	34.62	35.33	36.04
57	26.03	26.73	27.43	28.13	28.84	29.54	30.25	30.97	31.68	32.39	33.11	33.83	34.56	35.28	36.01	36.74
58	26.51	27.23	27.94	28.66	29.37	30.10	30.82	31.55	32.27	33.00	33.74	34.47	35.21	35.95	36.69	37.43
59	27.00	27.72	28.45	29.18	29.91	30.65	31.39	32.13	32.87	33.61	34.36	35.11	35.86	36.62	37.37	38.13
60	27.48	28.22	28.96	29.71	30.45	31.20	31.96	32.71	33.47	34.23	34.99	35.75	36.52	37.29	38.06	38.83

Note: For a more detailed set of tables from 2% to 21.75%, see the reference tables in the *Business Math Handbook*.

As stated in Step 1 on p. 343, we begin by dividing the finance charge by the amount financed and multiply by $100:

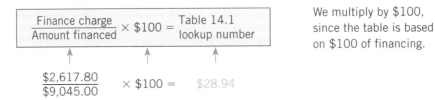

$$\frac{\text{Finance charge}}{\text{Amount financed}} \times \$100 = \text{Table 14.1 lookup number}$$

We multiply by $100, since the table is based on $100 of financing.

$$\frac{\$2,617.80}{\$9,045.00} \times \$100 = \$28.94$$

To look up $28.94 in Table 14.1, we go down the left side of the table until we come to 60 payments (the advertisement states 60 months). Then, moving to the right, we look for $28.94 or the two numbers closest to it. The number $28.94 is between $28.22 and $28.96.

| TABLE | 14.1 | (concluded) |

ANNUAL PERCENTAGE RATE

(FINANCE CHARGE PER $100 OF AMOUNT FINANCED)

NUMBER OF PAYMENTS	14.00%	14.25%	14.50%	14.75%	15.00%	15.25%	15.50%	15.75%	16.00%	16.25%	16.50%	16.75%	17.00%	17.25%	17.50%	17.75%
1	1.17	1.19	1.21	1.23	1.25	1.27	1.29	1.31	1.33	1.35	1.37	1.40	1.42	1.44	1.46	1.48
2	1.75	1.78	1.82	1.85	1.88	1.91	1.94	1.97	2.00	2.04	2.07	2.10	2.13	2.16	2.19	2.22
3	2.34	2.38	2.43	2.47	2.51	2.55	2.59	2.64	2.68	2.72	2.76	2.80	2.85	2.89	2.93	2.97
4	2.93	2.99	3.04	3.09	3.14	3.20	3.25	3.30	3.36	3.41	3.46	3.51	3.57	3.62	3.67	3.73
5	3.53	3.59	3.65	3.72	3.78	3.84	3.91	3.97	4.04	4.10	4.16	4.23	4.29	4.35	4.42	4.48
6	4.12	4.20	4.27	4.35	4.42	4.49	4.57	4.64	4.72	4.79	4.87	4.94	5.02	5.09	5.17	5.24
7	4.72	4.81	4.89	4.98	5.06	5.15	5.23	5.32	5.40	5.49	5.58	5.66	5.75	5.83	5.92	6.00
8	5.32	5.42	5.51	5.61	5.71	5.80	5.90	6.00	6.09	6.19	6.29	6.38	6.48	6.58	6.67	6.77
9	5.92	6.03	6.14	6.25	6.35	6.46	6.57	6.68	6.78	6.89	7.00	7.11	7.22	7.32	7.43	7.54
10	6.53	6.65	6.77	6.88	7.00	7.12	7.24	7.36	7.48	7.60	7.72	7.84	7.96	8.08	8.19	8.31
11	7.14	7.27	7.40	7.53	7.66	7.79	7.92	8.05	8.18	8.31	8.44	8.57	8.70	8.83	8.96	9.09
12	7.74	7.89	8.03	8.17	8.31	8.45	8.59	8.74	8.88	9.02	9.16	9.30	9.45	9.59	9.73	9.87
13	8.36	8.51	8.66	8.81	8.97	9.12	9.27	9.43	9.58	9.73	9.89	10.04	10.20	10.35	10.50	10.66
14	8.97	9.13	9.30	9.46	9.63	9.79	9.96	10.12	10.29	10.45	10.62	10.78	10.95	11.11	11.28	11.45
15	9.59	9.76	9.94	10.11	10.29	10.47	10.64	10.82	11.00	11.17	11.35	11.53	11.71	11.88	12.06	12.24
16	10.20	10.39	10.58	10.77	10.95	11.14	11.33	11.52	11.71	11.90	12.09	12.28	12.46	12.65	12.84	13.03
17	10.82	11.02	11.22	11.42	11.62	11.82	12.02	12.22	12.42	12.62	12.83	13.03	13.23	13.43	13.63	13.83
18	11.45	11.66	11.87	12.08	12.29	12.50	12.72	12.93	13.14	13.35	13.57	13.78	13.99	14.21	14.42	14.64
19	12.07	12.30	12.52	12.74	12.97	13.19	13.41	13.64	13.86	14.09	14.31	14.54	14.76	14.99	15.22	15.44
20	12.70	12.93	13.17	13.41	13.64	13.88	14.11	14.35	14.59	14.82	15.06	15.30	15.54	15.77	16.01	16.25
21	13.33	13.58	13.82	14.07	14.32	14.57	14.82	15.06	15.31	15.56	15.81	16.06	16.31	16.56	16.81	17.07
22	13.96	14.22	14.48	14.74	15.00	15.26	15.52	15.78	16.04	16.30	16.57	16.83	17.09	17.36	17.62	17.88
23	14.59	14.87	15.14	15.41	15.68	15.96	16.23	16.50	16.78	17.05	17.32	17.60	17.88	18.15	18.43	18.70
24	15.23	15.51	15.80	16.08	16.37	16.65	16.94	17.22	17.51	17.80	18.09	18.37	18.66	18.95	19.24	19.53
25	15.87	16.17	16.46	16.76	17.06	17.35	17.65	17.95	18.25	18.55	18.85	19.15	19.45	19.75	20.05	20.36
26	16.51	16.82	17.13	17.44	17.75	18.06	18.37	18.68	18.99	19.30	19.62	19.93	20.24	20.56	20.87	21.19
27	17.15	17.47	17.80	18.12	18.44	18.76	19.09	19.41	19.74	20.06	20.39	20.71	21.04	21.37	21.69	22.02
28	17.80	18.13	18.47	18.80	19.14	19.47	19.81	20.15	20.48	20.82	21.16	21.50	21.84	22.18	22.52	22.86
29	18.45	18.79	19.14	19.49	19.83	20.18	20.53	20.89	21.23	21.58	21.94	22.29	22.64	22.99	23.35	23.70
30	19.10	19.45	19.81	20.17	20.54	20.90	21.26	21.62	21.99	22.35	22.72	23.08	23.45	23.81	24.18	24.55
31	19.75	20.12	20.49	20.87	21.24	21.61	21.99	22.37	22.74	23.12	23.50	23.88	24.26	24.64	25.02	25.40
32	20.40	20.79	21.17	21.56	21.95	22.33	22.72	23.11	23.50	23.89	24.28	24.68	25.07	25.46	25.86	26.25
33	21.06	21.46	21.85	22.25	22.65	23.06	23.46	23.86	24.26	24.67	25.07	25.48	25.88	26.29	26.70	27.11
34	21.72	22.13	22.54	22.95	23.37	23.78	24.19	24.61	25.03	25.44	25.86	26.28	26.70	27.12	27.54	27.97
35	22.38	22.80	23.23	23.65	24.08	24.51	24.94	25.36	25.79	26.23	26.66	27.09	27.52	27.96	28.39	28.83
36	23.04	23.48	23.92	24.35	24.80	25.24	25.68	26.12	26.57	27.01	27.46	27.90	28.35	28.80	29.25	29.70
37	23.70	24.16	24.61	25.06	25.51	25.97	26.42	26.88	27.34	27.80	28.26	28.72	29.18	29.64	30.10	30.57
38	24.37	24.84	25.30	25.77	26.24	26.70	27.17	27.64	28.11	28.59	29.06	29.53	30.01	30.49	30.96	31.44
39	25.04	25.52	26.00	26.48	26.96	27.44	27.92	28.41	28.89	29.38	29.87	30.36	30.85	31.34	31.83	32.32
40	25.71	26.20	26.70	27.19	27.69	28.18	28.68	29.18	29.68	30.18	30.69	31.19	31.69	32.19	32.69	33.20
41	26.39	26.89	27.40	27.91	28.41	28.92	29.44	29.95	30.46	30.97	31.49	32.01	32.52	33.04	33.56	34.08
42	27.06	27.58	28.10	28.62	29.15	29.67	30.19	30.72	31.25	31.78	32.31	32.84	33.37	33.90	34.44	34.97
43	27.74	28.27	28.81	29.34	29.88	30.42	30.96	31.50	32.04	32.58	33.13	33.67	34.22	34.76	35.31	35.86
44	28.42	28.97	29.52	30.07	30.62	31.17	31.72	32.28	32.83	33.39	33.95	34.51	35.07	35.63	36.19	36.76
45	29.11	29.67	30.23	30.79	31.36	31.92	32.49	33.06	33.63	34.20	34.77	35.35	35.92	36.50	37.08	37.66
46	29.79	30.36	30.94	31.52	32.10	32.68	33.26	33.84	34.43	35.01	35.60	36.19	36.78	37.37	37.96	38.56
47	30.48	31.07	31.66	32.25	32.84	33.44	34.03	34.63	35.23	35.83	36.43	37.04	37.64	38.25	38.86	39.46
48	31.17	31.77	32.37	32.98	33.59	34.20	34.81	35.42	36.03	36.65	37.27	37.88	38.50	39.13	39.75	40.37
49	31.86	32.48	33.09	33.71	34.34	34.96	35.59	36.21	36.84	37.47	38.10	38.74	39.37	40.01	40.65	41.29
50	32.55	33.18	33.82	34.45	35.09	35.73	36.37	37.01	37.65	38.30	38.94	39.59	40.24	40.89	41.55	42.20
51	33.25	33.89	34.54	35.19	35.84	36.49	37.15	37.81	38.46	39.12	39.79	40.45	41.11	41.78	42.45	43.12
52	33.95	34.61	35.27	35.93	36.60	37.27	37.94	38.61	39.28	39.96	40.63	41.31	41.99	42.67	43.36	44.04
53	34.65	35.32	36.00	36.68	37.36	38.04	38.72	39.41	40.10	40.79	41.48	42.17	42.87	43.57	44.27	44.97
54	35.35	36.04	36.73	37.42	38.12	38.82	39.52	40.22	40.92	41.63	42.33	43.04	43.75	44.47	45.18	45.90
55	36.05	36.76	37.46	38.17	38.88	39.60	40.31	41.03	41.74	42.47	43.19	43.91	44.64	45.37	46.10	46.83
56	36.76	37.48	38.20	38.92	39.65	40.38	41.11	41.84	42.57	43.31	44.05	44.79	45.53	46.27	47.02	47.77
57	37.47	38.20	38.94	39.68	40.42	41.16	41.91	42.65	43.40	44.15	44.91	45.66	46.42	47.18	47.94	48.71
58	38.18	38.93	39.68	40.43	41.19	41.95	42.71	43.47	44.23	45.00	45.77	46.54	47.32	48.09	48.87	49.65
59	38.89	39.66	40.42	41.19	41.96	42.74	43.51	44.29	45.07	45.85	46.64	47.42	48.21	49.01	49.80	50.60
60	39.61	40.39	41.17	41.95	42.74	43.53	44.32	45.11	45.91	46.71	47.51	48.31	49.12	49.92	50.73	51.55

So we look at the column headings and see a rate between 10.25% and 10.5% . The Truth in Lending Act requires that when creditors state the APR, it must be accurate to the nearest $\frac{1}{4}$ of 1%.[1]

Calculating the Monthly Payment by Formula and Table 14.2 (p. 346)

The pickup truck advertisement showed a $194.38 monthly payment. We can check this by formula and by table lookup.

---

[1] If we wanted an exact reading of APR when the number is not exactly in the table, we would use the process of interpolating. We do not cover this method in this course.

| TABLE 14.2 | Loan amortization table (monthly payment per $1,000 to pay principal and interest on installment loan) |

Terms in months	7.50%	8%	8.50%	9%	10.00%	10.50%	11.00%	11.50%	12.00%
6	$170.34	$170.58	$170.83	$171.20	$171.56	$171.81	$172.05	$172.30	$172.55
12	86.76	86.99	87.22	87.46	87.92	88.15	88.38	88.62	88.85
18	58.92	59.15	59.37	59.60	60.06	60.29	60.52	60.75	60.98
24	45.00	45.23	45.46	45.69	46.14	46.38	46.61	46.84	47.07
30	36.66	36.89	37.12	37.35	37.81	38.04	38.28	38.51	38.75
36	31.11	31.34	31.57	31.80	32.27	32.50	32.74	32.98	33.21
42	27.15	27.38	27.62	27.85	28.32	28.55	28.79	29.03	29.28
48	24.18	24.42	24.65	24.77	25.36	25.60	25.85	26.09	26.33
54	21.88	22.12	22.36	22.59	23.07	23.32	23.56	23.81	24.06
60	20.04	20.28	20.52	20.76	21.25	21.49	21.74	21.99	22.24

By Formula

$$\frac{\text{Finance charge} + \text{Amount financed}}{\text{Number of payments of loan}} = \frac{\$2,617.80 + \$9,045}{60} = \$194.38$$

By Table 14.2 The **loan amortization table** (many variations of this table are available) in Table 14.2 can be used to calculate the monthly payment for the pickup truck. To calculate a monthly payment with a table, use the following steps:

CALCULATING MONTHLY PAYMENT BY TABLE LOOKUP

Step 1. Divide the loan amount by $1,000 (since Table 14.2 is per $1,000):

$$\frac{\$9,045}{\$1,000} = 9.045$$

Step 2. Look up the rate (10.5%) and number of months (60). At the intersection is the table factor showing the monthly payment per $1,000.

Step 3. Multiply quotient in Step 1 by the table factor in Step 2:

$$9.045 \times \$21.49 = \$194.38 .$$

Remember that this $194.38 fixed payment includes interest and the reduction of the balance of the loan. As the number of payments increases, interest payments get smaller and the reduction of the principal gets larger.[2]

Now let's check your progress with the Practice Quiz.

| LU 14–1 | PRACTICE QUIZ |

Complete this **Practice Quiz** to see how you are doing

Courtesy Brunswick Corporation

From the partial advertisement at the right calculate the following:

1. **a.** Amount financed.
    b. Finance charge.
    c. Deferred payment price.
    d. APR by Table 14.1.
    e. Monthly payment by formula.

$288 per month	
Sale price	$14,150
Down payment	$ 1,450
Term/Number of payments	60 months

2. Jay Miller bought a New Brunswick boat for $7,500. Jay put down $1,000 and financed the balance at 10% for 60 months. What is his monthly payment? Use Table 14.2.

[2]In Chapter 15 we give an amortization schedule for home mortgages that shows how much of each fixed payment goes to interest and how much reduces the principal. This repayment schedule also gives a running balance of the loan.

| TABLE | 14.2 | (concluded) |

Terms in months	12.50%	13.00%	13.50%	14.00%	14.50%	15.00%	15.50%	16.00%
6	$172.80	$173.04	$173.29	$173.54	$173.79	$174.03	$174.28	$174.53
12	89.08	89.32	89.55	89.79	90.02	90.26	90.49	90.73
18	61.21	61.45	61.68	61.92	62.15	62.38	62.62	62.86
24	47.31	47.54	47.78	48.01	48.25	48.49	48.72	48.96
30	38.98	39.22	39.46	39.70	39.94	40.18	40.42	40.66
36	33.45	33.69	33.94	34.18	34.42	34.67	34.91	35.16
42	29.52	29.76	30.01	30.25	30.50	30.75	31.00	31.25
48	26.58	26.83	27.08	27.33	27.58	27.83	28.08	28.34
54	24.31	24.56	24.81	25.06	25.32	25.58	25.84	26.10
60	22.50	22.75	23.01	23.27	23.53	23.79	24.05	24.32

✓ **Solutions**

1. a. $14,150 − $1,450 = $12,700
    b. $17,280 ($288 × 60) − $12,700 = $4,580
    c. $17,280 ($288 × 60) + $1,450 = $18,730
    d. $\frac{\$4,580}{\$12,700} \times \$100 = \$36.06$; between 12.75% and 13%
    e. $\frac{\$4,580 + \$12,700}{60} = \$288$

2. $\frac{\$6,500}{\$1,000} = 6.5 \times \$21.25 = \$138.13$ (10%, 60 months)

| LU 14-1a | EXTRA PRACTICE QUIZ |

Need more practice? Try this **Extra Practice Quiz** (check figures in Chapter Organizer, p. 355)

From the partial advertisement at the right calculate the following:
1. a. Amount financed.
    b. Finance charge.
    c. Deferred payment price.
    d. APR by Table 14.1.
    e. Monthly payment by formula.

2. Jay Miller bought a New Brunswick boat for $8,000. Jay puts down $1,000 and financed the balance at 8% for 60 months. What is his monthly payment? Use Table 14.2.

> **$295 per month**
>
> Sale price: $13,999
> Down payment: $1,480
> Term/Number of payments: 60 months

Learning Unit 14-2: Paying Off Installment Loans before Due Date

In Learning Unit 10-3 (p. 264), you learned about the U.S. Rule. This rule applies partial payments to the interest *first,* and then the remainder of the payment reduces the principal. Many states and the federal government use this rule.

Some states use another method for prepaying a loan called the **Rule of 78.** It is a variation of the U.S. Rule. The Rule of 78 got its name because it bases the finance charge rebate and the payoff on a 12-month loan. (Any number of months can be used.) The Rule of 78 is used less today. However, GMAC says that about 50% of its auto loans still use the Rule of 78. For loans of 61 months or longer, the Rule of 78 is not allowed (some states have even shorter requirements).

TABLE 14.3

Rebate fraction table based on Rule of 78

Months to go	Sum of digits	Months to go	Sum of digits	
1	1	31	496	
2	3	32	528	
3	6	33	561	→ 33 months to go
4	10	34	595	
5	15	35	630	
6	21	36	666	
7	28	37	703	
8	36	38	741	
9	45	39	780	
10	55	40	820	
11	66	41	861	
12	78	42	903	
13	91	43	946	
14	105	44	990	
15	120	45	1,035	
16	136	46	1,081	
17	153	47	1,128	
18	171	48	1,176	
19	190	49	1,225	
20	210	50	1,275	
21	231	51	1,326	
22	253	52	1,378	
23	276	53	1,431	
24	300	54	1,485	
25	325	55	1,540	
26	351	56	1,596	
27	378	57	1,653	
28	406	58	1,711	
29	435	59	1,770	
30	465	60	1,830	→ 60 months = 1,830

With the Rule of 78, the finance charge earned the first month is $\frac{12}{78}$. The 78 comes from summing the digits of 12 months. The finance charge for the second month would be $\frac{11}{78}$, and so on. Table 14.3 simplifies these calculations.

When the installment loan is made, a larger portion of the interest is charged to the earlier payments. As a result, when a loan is paid off early, the borrower is entitled to a **rebate,** which is calculated as follows:

CALCULATING REBATE AND PAYOFF FOR RULE OF 78
Step 1. Find the balance of the loan outstanding.
Step 2. Calculate the total finance charge.
Step 3. Find the number of payments remaining.
Step 4. Set up the rebate fraction from Table 14.3.
Step 5. Calculate the rebate amount of the finance charge.
Step 6. Calculate the payoff.

Let's see what the rebate of the finance charge and payoff would be if the pickup truck loan were paid off after 27 months (instead of 60).

To find the finance charge rebate and the final payoff, we follow six specific steps listed below. Let's begin.

Step 1. Find the balance of the loan outstanding:

Total of monthly payments (60 × $194.38)	$11,662.80
Payments to date: 27 × $194.38	− 5,248.26
Balance of loan outstanding	$ 6,414.54

Step 2. Calculate the total finance charge:

$11,662.80	Total of all payments (60 × $194.38)
− 9,045.00	Amount financed ($9,345 − $300)
$ 2,617.80	Total finance charge

Step 3. Find the number of payments remaining:

$$60 - 27 = 33$$

Step 4. Set up the **rebate fraction** from Table 14.3.[3]

$$\frac{\text{Sum of digits based on number of months to go}}{\text{Sum of digits based on total number of months of loan}} = \frac{561}{1,830} \begin{array}{l} \leftarrow 33 \text{ months to go} \\ \leftarrow 60 \text{ months in loan} \end{array}$$

Note: If this loan were for 12 months, the denominator would be 78.

Step 5. Calculate the rebate amount of the finance charge:

$$\text{Rebate fraction} \times \text{Total finance charge} = \text{Rebate amount}$$

$$\underset{\textbf{(Step 4)}}{\frac{561}{1,830}} \times \underset{\textbf{(Step 2)}}{\$2,617.80} = \$802.51$$

Step 6. Calculate the payoff:

$$\text{Balance of loan outstanding} - \text{Rebate} = \text{Payoff}$$

$$\underset{\textbf{(Step 1)}}{\$6,414.54} - \underset{\textbf{(Step 5)}}{\$802.51} = \boxed{\$5,612.03}$$

LU 14–2 PRACTICE QUIZ

Complete this **Practice Quiz** to see how you are doing

Calculate the finance charge rebate and payoff (calculate all six steps):

Loan	Months of loan	End-of-month loan is repaid	Monthly payment	Finance charge rebate	Final payoff
$5,500	12	7	$510		

✓ Solutions

Step 1.

12 × $510 =	$6,120
7 × $510 =	− 3,570
	$2,550

(balance outstanding)

Step 2.

12 × $510 =	$6,120
	− 5,500
	$ 620

(total finance charge)

---

[3]If no table is available, the following formula is available:

$$\frac{\frac{N(N+1)}{2}}{\frac{T(T+1)}{2}} = \frac{\frac{33(33+1)}{2}}{\frac{60(60+1)}{2}} = \frac{561}{1,830}$$

In the numerator, *N* stands for number of months to go, and in the denominator, *T* is total months of the loan.

Step 3. $12 - 7 = 5$ Step 4. $\frac{15}{78}$ (by Table 14.3)

Step 5. $\frac{15}{78} \times \$620 = \boxed{\$119.23 \text{ rebate}}$ Step 6. **Step 1 − Step 5**

(Step 4) (Step 2) $\$2,550 - \$119.23$

$= \boxed{\$2,430.77 \text{ payoff}}$

LU 14–2a EXTRA PRACTICE QUIZ

Need more practice? Try this
Extra Practice Quiz (check
figures in Chapter Organizer,
p. 355)

Calculate the finance charge rebate and payoff (calculate steps):

Loan	Months of loan	End-of-month loan is repaid	Monthly payment	Finance charge rebate	Final payoff
$6,900	12	5	$690		

Learning Unit 14–3: Revolving Charge Credit Cards

Credit Cards Raise Minimums Due

Wall Street Journal © 2005

The above *Wall Street Journal* heading "Credit Cards Raise Minimums Due" affects revolving charge credit card users who pay the minimum interest on what they owe. As a revolving charge user, it is probably not news to you that in 2006, credit card companies have been required to raise the minimum amount due on your account. You should be aware that the higher minimum amount due can give you the problem of *negative amortization*. This means if you only pay the minimum amount and interest costs and fees rise, the end result is your principal could go up.

Let's look at how long it will take to pay off your credit card balance payments with the minimum amount. Study the following clipping "Pay Just the Minimum, and Get Nowhere Fast."

Pay Just the Minimum, and Get Nowhere Fast

THE COST—IN YEARS AND DOLLARS—OF PAYING THE MINIMUM 2% OF BALANCES ON CREDIT CARDS CHARGING 17% ANNUAL INTEREST

Balance	Total Cost	Total Time
$1,000	$2,590.35	17 years, 3 months
$2,500	$7,733.49	30 years, 3 months
$5,000	$16,305.34	40 years, 2 months

SOURCE: WWW.BANKRATE.COM

The clipping assumes that the minimum rate on the balance of a credit card is 2%. Note that if the annual interest cost is 17%, it will take 17 years, 3 months to pay off a balance of $1,000, and the total cost will be $2,590.35. If the balance on your revolving charge credit card is more than $1,000, you can see how fast the total cost rises. If you cannot afford the total cost of paying only the minimum, it is time for you to reconsider how you use your revolving credit card. This is why when you have financial difficulties, experts often advise you first to work on getting rid of your revolving credit card debt.

Do you know why revolving credit cards are so popular? Businesses encourage customers to use credit cards because consumers tend to buy more when they can use a credit card for their purchases. Consumers find credit cards convenient to use and valuable in establishing credit. The problem is that when consumers do not pay their balance in full each month, they do not realize how expensive it is to pay only the minimum of their balance.

To protect consumers, Congress passed the **Fair Credit and Charge Card Disclosure Act of 1988.**[4] This act requires that for direct-mail application or solicitation, credit card companies must provide specific details involving all fees, grace period, calculation of finance charges, and so on.

We begin the unit by seeing how Moe's Furniture Store calculates the finance charge on Abby Jordan's previous month's credit card balance. Then we learn how to calculate the average daily balance on the partial bill of Joan Ring.

Calculating Finance Charge on Previous Month's Balance

Abby Jordan bought a dining room set for $8,000 on credit. She has a **revolving charge account** at Moe's Furniture Store. A revolving charge account gives a buyer **open-end credit.** Abby can make as many purchases on credit as she wants until she reaches her maximum $10,000 credit limit.

Often customers do not completely pay their revolving charge accounts at the end of a billing period. When this occurs, stores add interest charges to the customers' bills. Moe's furniture store calculates its interest using the *unpaid balance method.* It charges $1\frac{1}{2}\%$ on the *previous month's balance,* or 18% per year. Moe's has no minimum monthly payment (many stores require $10 or $15, or a percent of the outstanding balance).

Abby has no other charges on her revolving charge account. She plans to pay $500 per month until she completely pays off her dining room set. Abby realizes that when she makes a payment, Moe's Furniture Store first applies the money toward the interest and then reduces the **outstanding balance** due. (This is the U.S. Rule we discussed in Chapter 10.) For her own information, Abby worked out the first 3-month schedule of payments, shown in Table 14.4. Note how the interest payment is the rate times the outstanding balance.

Today, most companies with credit card accounts calculate the finance charge, or interest, as a percentage of the average daily balance. Interest on credit cards can be very expensive for consumers; however, interest is a source of income for credit card companies.

Calculating Average Daily Balance

Let's look at the following steps for calculating the **average daily balance.** Remember that a **cash advance** is a cash loan from a credit card company.

[4]An update to this act was made in 1997.

TABLE   14.4   Schedule of payments

Monthly payment number	Outstanding balance due	$1\frac{1}{2}\%$ interest payment	Amount of monthly payment	Reduction in balance due	Outstanding balance due
1	$8,000.00	$120.00	$500.00	$380.00	$7,620.00
		(.015 × $8,000.00)		($500.00 − $120.00)	($8,000.00 − $380.00)
2	$7,620.00	$114.30	$500.00	$385.70	$7,234.30
		(.015 × $7,620.00)		($500.00 − $114.30)	($7,620.00 − $385.70)
3	$7,234.30	$108.51	$500.00	$391.49	$6,842.81
		(.015 × $7,234.30)		($500.00 − $108.51)	($7,234.30 − $391.49)

CALCULATING AVERAGE DAILY BALANCE

Step 1. Calculate the daily balance or amount owed at the end of each day during the billing cycle:

$$\frac{\text{Daily}}{\text{balance}} = \frac{\text{Previous}}{\text{balance}} + \frac{\text{Cash}}{\text{advances}} + \text{Purchases} - \text{Payments}$$

Step 2. When the daily balance is the same for more than one day, multiply it by the number of days the daily balance remained the same, or the number of days of the current balance. This gives a cumulative daily balance.

Step 3. Add the cumulative daily balances.

Step 4. Divide the sum of the cumulative daily balances by the number of days in the billing cycle.

Step 5. Finance charge = Rate per month × Average daily balance.

Following is the partial bill of Joan Ring and an explanation of how Joan's average daily balance and finance charge was calculated. Note how we calculated each **daily balance** and then multiplied each daily balance by the number of days the balance remained the same. Take a moment to study how we arrived at 8 days. The total of the cumulative daily balances was $16,390. To get the average daily balance, we divided by the number of days in the billing cycle—30. Joan's finance charge is $1\frac{1}{2}\%$ per month on the average daily balance.

30-day billing cycle

6/20	Billing date	Previous balance	$450
6/27	Payment		$ 50 cr.
6/30	Charge: JCPenney		200
7/9	Payment		40 cr.
7/12	Cash advance		60

7 days had a balance of $450

	No. of days of current balance	Current daily balance	Extension
Step 1 →	7	$450	$ 3,150 ← Step 2
	3	400 ($450 − $50)	1,200
	9	600 ($400 + $200)	5,400
	3	560 ($600 − $40)	1,680
	8	620 ($560 + $60)	4,960
	30		$16,390 ← Step 3

30-day cycle − 22 (7 + 3 + 9 + 3) equals 8 days left with a balance of $620.

$$\text{Average daily balance} = \frac{\$16,390}{30} = \$546.33 \leftarrow \text{Step 4}$$

Step 5 → Finance charge = $546.33 × .015 = $8.19

Now try the following Practice Quiz to check your understanding of this unit.

LU 14–3 PRACTICE QUIZ

Complete this **Practice Quiz** to see how you are doing

1. Calculate the balance outstanding at the end of month 2 (use U.S. Rule) given the following: purchased $600 desk; pay back $40 per month; and charge of $2\frac{1}{2}\%$ interest on unpaid balance.

2. Calculate the average daily balance and finance charge from the information that follows.

31-day billing cycle			
8/20	Billing date	Previous balance	$210
8/27	Payment		$50 cr.
8/31	Charge: Staples		30
9/5	Payment		10 cr.
9/10	Cash advance		60

Rate = 2% per month on average daily balance.

✓ **Solutions**

1.

Month	Balance due	Interest	Monthly payment	Reduction in balance	Balance outstanding
1	$600	$15.00 (.025 × $600)	$40	$25.00 ($40 − $15)	$575.00
2	$575	$14.38 (.025 × $575)	$40	$25.62	$549.38

2. Average daily balance calculated as follows:

No. of days of current balance	Current balance	Extension
7	$210	$1,470
4	160 ($210 − $50)	640
5	190 ($160 + $30)	950
5	180 ($190 − $10)	900
10	240 ($180 + $60)	2,400
31		$6,360

31 − 21 (7 + 4 + 5 + 5) ⟶ 10

$$\text{Average daily balance} = \frac{\$6,360}{31} = \$205.16$$

Finance charge = $4.10 ($205.16 × .02)

LU 14–3a   EXTRA PRACTICE QUIZ

Need more practice? Try this **Extra Practice Quiz** (check figures in Chapter Organizer, p. 355)

1. Calculate the balance outstanding at the end of month 2 (use U.S. Rule) given the following: purchased $300 desk; pay back $20 per month; and charge of $1\frac{1}{4}\%$ interest on unpaid balance.

2. Calculate the average daily balance and finance charge from the following information:

31-day billing cycle

8/21	Billing date Previous balance		$400
8/24	Payment	100 cr.	
8/31	Charge: Staples	60	
9/5	Payment	20 cr.	
9/10	Cash Advance	200	

Finance charge is 2% on average daily balance.

CHAPTER ORGANIZER AND STUDY GUIDE
WITH CHECK FIGURES FOR EXTRA PRACTICE QUIZZES

Topic	Key point, procedure, formula	Example(s) to illustrate situation
Amount financed, p. 342	$\dfrac{\text{Amount}}{\text{financed}} = \dfrac{\text{Cash}}{\text{price}} - \dfrac{\text{Down}}{\text{payment}}$	60 payments at $125.67 per month; cash price $5,295 with a $95 down payment Cash price $5,295 − Down payment − 95 = Amount financed $5,200
Total finance charge (interest), p. 343	$\dfrac{\text{Total}}{\text{finance}} = \dfrac{\text{Total of}}{\text{all monthly}} - \dfrac{\text{Amount}}{\text{financed}}$ charge payments	*(continued from above)* $\dfrac{\$125.67}{\text{per month}} \times \dfrac{60}{\text{months}} = \$7,540.20$ − Amount financed − 5,200.00 = Finance charge $2,340.20
Deferred payment price, p. 343	$\dfrac{\text{Deferred}}{\text{payment}} = \dfrac{\text{Total of}}{\text{all monthly}} + \dfrac{\text{Down}}{\text{payment}}$ price payments	*(continued from above)* $7,540.20 + $95 = $7,635.20
Calculating APR by Table 14.1, p. 344	$\dfrac{\text{Finance charge}}{\text{Amount financed}} \times \$100 = \dfrac{\text{Table 14.1}}{\text{lookup number}}$	*(continued from above)* $\dfrac{\$2,340.20}{\$5,200.00} \times \$100 = \$45.004$ Search in Table 14.1 between 15.50% and 15.75% for 60 payments.
Monthly payment, p. 346	*By formula:* $\dfrac{\text{Finance charge} + \text{Amount financed}}{\text{Number of payments of loan}}$ *By table:* $\dfrac{\text{Loan}}{\$1,000} \times \dfrac{\text{Table}}{\text{factor}}$ (rate, months)	*(continued from above)* $\dfrac{\$2,340.20 + \$5,200.00}{60} = \$125.67$ Given: 15.5% 60 months $5,200 loan $\dfrac{\$5,200}{\$1,000} = 5.2 \times \$24.05 = \$125.06\text{*}$ *Off due to rounding of rate.
Paying off installment loan before due date, p. 348	1. Find balance of loan outstanding (Total of monthly payments − Payments to date). 2. Calculate total finance charge. 3. Find number of payments remaining. 4. Set up rebate fraction from Table 14.3. 5. Calculate rebate amount of finance charge. 6. Calculate payoff.	*Example:* Loan, $8,000; 20 monthly payments of $420; end of month repaid 7. 1. $8,400 (20 × $420) − 2,940 (7 × $420) $5,460 (balance of loan outstanding) 2. $8,400 (total payments) − 8,000 (amount financed) $ 400 (total finance charge) 3. 20 − 7 = 13 4 and 5. $\dfrac{91}{210} \times \$400 = \$173.33$ 6. $5,460.00 (Step 1) − 173.33 rebate (Step 5) $5,286.67 payoff
Open-end credit, p. 350	Monthly payment applied to interest first before reducing balance outstanding.	$4,000 purchase $250 a month payment $2\frac{1}{2}$% interest on unpaid balance $4,000 × .025 = $100 interest $250 − $100 = $150 to lower balance $4,000 − $150 = $3,850 Balance outstanding after month 1.

(continues)

CHAPTER ORGANIZER AND STUDY GUIDE
WITH CHECK FIGURES FOR EXTRA PRACTICE QUIZZES (concluded)

Topic	Key point, procedure, formula	Example(s) to illustrate situation
Average daily balance and finance charge, p. 352	$\dfrac{\text{Daily}}{\text{balance}} = \dfrac{\text{Previous}}{\text{balance}} + \dfrac{\text{Cash}}{\text{advances}}$ $+ \text{ Purchases} - \text{Payments}$ $\dfrac{\text{Average}}{\text{daily}} = \dfrac{\text{Sum of cumulative}}{\dfrac{\text{daily balances}}{\text{Number of days}}}$ $\text{balance} \quad\quad \text{in billing cycle}$ 30-day billing cycle less the 8 and 14. ◀ $\dfrac{\text{Finance}}{\text{charge}} = \dfrac{\text{Monthly}}{\text{rate}} \times \dfrac{\text{Average}}{\text{daily}}$ balance	*30-day billing cycle; $1\frac{1}{2}$% per month* *Example:* 8/21 Balance $100 8/29 Payment $10 9/12 Charge 50 *Average daily balance equals:* 8 days × $100 = $ 800 14 days × 90 = 1,260 8 days × 140 = 1,120 $3,180 ÷ 30 Average daily balance = $106 Finance charge = $106 × .015 = $1.59

KEY TERMS	Amortization, *p. 346*
	 Amount financed, *p. 342*
	 Annual percentage rate
	    (APR), *p. 343*
	 Average daily balance, *p. 351*
	 Cash advance, *p. 351*
	 Daily balance, *p. 352*
	 Deferred payment price, *p. 343*
		Down payment, *p. 342*
		 Fair Credit and Charge Card
		    Disclosure Act of
		    1988, *p. 351*
		 Finance charge, *p. 343*
		 Installment loan, *p. 342*
		 Loan amortization table, *p. 346*
		 Open-end credit, *p. 351*
		
		 Outstanding balance, *p. 351*
		 Rebate, *p. 349*
		 Rebate fraction, *p. 349*
		 Revolving charge
		    account, *p. 351*
		 Rule of 78, *p. 347*
		 Truth in Lending Act, *p. 343*

CHECK FIGURES FOR EXTRA PRACTICE QUIZZES WITH PAGE REFERENCES	LU 14–1a (p. 347)
	 1. a. $12,519
	    b. $5,181
	    c. $19,180
	    d. Bet. 14.50%–14.75%
	    e. $295
	 2. $141.96
		LU 14–2a (p. 350)
		 $4,334.62
		 payoff; $495.38 rebate
			LU 14–3a (p. 353)
			 1. $267.30
			    end of month 2
			 2. $410.97
			    $8.22

Critical Thinking Discussion Questions

1. Explain how to calculate the amount financed, finance charge, and APR by table lookup. Do you think the Truth in Lending Act should regulate interest charges?

2. Explain how to use the loan amortization table. Check with a person who owns a home and find out what part of each payment goes to pay interest versus the amount that reduces the loan principal.

3. What are the six steps used to calculate the rebate and payoff for the Rule of 78? Do you think it is right for the Rule of 78 to charge a larger portion of the finance charges to the earlier payments?

4. What steps are used to calculate the average daily balance? Many credit card companies charge 18% annual interest. Do you think this is a justifiable rate? Defend your answer.

Classroom Notes

Name _____ Date _____

DRILL PROBLEMS

Complete the following table:

	Purchase price of product	Down payment	Amount financed	Number of monthly payments	Amount of monthly payments	Total of monthly payments	Total finance charge
14–1.	Ford Explorer $36,900	$10,000		60	$499		
14–2.	Sony digital camera $700	$100		10	$80.50		

Calculate (a) the amount financed, (b) the total finance charge, and (c) APR by table lookup.

	Purchase price of a used car	Down payment	Number of monthly payments	Amount financed	Total of monthly payments	Total finance charge	APR
14–3.	$5,673	$1,223	48		$5,729.76		
14–4.	$4,195	$95	60		$5,944.00		

Calculate the monthly payment for Problems 14–3 and 14–4 by table lookup and formula. (Answers will not be exact due to rounding of percents in table lookup.)

14–5. (14–3) (Use 13% for table lookup.)

14–6. (14–4) (Use 15.5% for table lookup.)

Calculate the finance charge rebate and payoff:

	Loan	Months of loan	End-of-month loan is repaid	Monthly payment	Finance charge rebate	Final payoff
14–7.	$7,000	36	10	$210		
	Step 1.			**Step 2.**		

	Loan	Months of loan	End-of-month loan is repaid	Monthly payment	Finance charge rebate	Final payoff

Step 3.   **Step 4.**

Step 5.   **Step 6.**

	Loan	Months of loan	End-of-month loan is repaid	Monthly payment	Finance charge rebate	Final payoff
14–8.	$9,000	24	9	$440		

Step 1.   **Step 2.**

Step 3.   **Step 4.**

Step 5.   **Step 6.**

14–9. Calculate the average daily balance and finance charge

30-day billing cycle		
9/16	Billing date Previous balance	$2,000
9/19	Payment	$ 60
9/30	Charge: Home Depot	1,500
10/3	Payment	60
10/7	Cash advance	70
Finance charge is $1\frac{1}{2}$% on average daily balance		

WORD PROBLEMS

14–10. The 2007 edition of *Edmunds* showed the manufacturer's suggested retail price for a 2007 BMW 3 series was $35,300. Audrey McKeown is planning to put 10 percent down and finance the BMW for 60 months. Her bank has agreed to finance the car at 8 percent. She plans to budget no more than $650.00 per month for car payments. **(a)** What is her monthly payment to nearest cent (use loan amortization table)? **(b)** Will her budgeted amount be enough to purchase the BMW?

14–11. The February 26, 2007 issue of *American Banker* reported the average interest rate charged by commercial banking companies for new car loans rose to 7.72%. Some analysts remain concerned that rising credit costs will create a headache for lenders. Jane Stocker plans to finance a new car, in the amount of $23,600, at 7.5% for 60 months. **(a)** What is her monthly payment to nearest cent (use loan amortization table)? **(b)** How much interest will Jane pay on her loan?

14–12. Ramon Hernandez saw the following advertisement for a used Volkswagen Bug and decided to work out the numbers to be sure the ad had no errors. Please help Ramon by calculating **(a)** the amount financed, **(b)** the finance charge, **(c)** APR by table lookup, **(d)** the monthly payment by formula, and **(e)** the monthly payment by table lookup (will be off slightly).

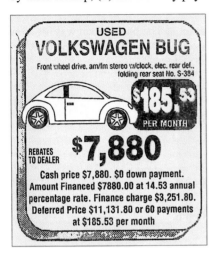

USED
VOLKSWAGEN BUG
Front wheel drive, am/fm stereo w/clock, elec. rear def., folding rear seat No. S-384

$185.53
PER MONTH

REBATES TO DEALER $7,880

Cash price $7,880. $0 down payment. Amount Financed $7880.00 at 14.53 annual percentage rate. Finance charge $3,251.80. Deferred Price $11,131.80 or 60 payments at $185.53 per month

a. Amount financed:

b. Finance charge:

c. APR by table lookup:

d. Monthly payment by formula:

e. Monthly payment by table lookup (use 14.50%):

14–13. From this partial advertisement calculate:

$95.10 per month
#43892 Used car. Cash price $4,100. Down payment $50. For 60 months.

a. Amount financed.

b. Finance charge.

c. Deferred payment price.

d. APR by Table 14.1.

e. Check monthly payment (by formula).

14–14. Paula Westing borrowed $6,200 to travel to Sweden to see her son Arthur. Her loan was to be paid in 48 monthly installments of $170. At the end of 9 months, Paula's daughter Irene convinced her that she should pay off the loan early. What are Paula's rebate and her payoff amount?

Step 1.

Step 2.

Step 3.

Step 4.

Step 5.

Step 6.

14–15. Park Plaza Dodge placed an ad in the *Chicago Sun-Times* on March 28, 2007 stating a new Dodge Nitro SXT was on sale for $18,999, with $2,000 down. Shirley Stewart plans to finance the car. Citizens' Financial Bank quoted a finance charge at 8% for 48 months - Charter One bank quoted her a finance charge at 7.50% for 60 months. **(a)** What would be her monthly payment to Citizens' Financial Bank to nearest cent? **(b)** What would be her monthly payment to Charter One Bank to nearest cent? Use loan amortization table. **(c)** How much more would her monthly payment be on the 48 month loan?

14–16. Joanne Flynn bought a new boat for $14,500. She put a $2,500 down payment on it. The bank's loan was for 48 months. Finance charges totaled $4,400.16. Assume Joanne decided to pay off the loan at the end of the 28th month. What rebate would she be entitled to and what would be the actual payoff amount?

Step 1.

Step 2.

Step 3.

Step 4.

Step 5.

Step 6.

14–17. First America Bank's monthly payment charge on a 48-month $20,000 loan is $488.26. The U.S. Bank's monthly payment fee is $497.70 for the same loan amount. What would be the APR for an auto loan for each of these banks? (Use the *Business Math Handbook*.)

14–18. From the following facts, Molly Roe has requested you to calculate the average daily balance. The customer believes the average daily balance should be $877.67. Respond to the customer's concern.

70,000	140
48,778	89
76,551	117
33,737	74

28-day billing cycle		
3/18	Billing date Previous balance	$800
3/24	Payment	$ 60
3/29	Charge: Sears	250
4/5	Payment	20
4/9	Charge: Macy's	200

14–19. Jill bought a $500 rocking chair. The terms of her revolving charge are $1\frac{1}{2}\%$ on the unpaid balance from the previous month. If she pays $100 per month, complete a schedule for the first 3 months like Table 14.4. Be sure to use the U.S. Rule.

Monthly payment number	Outstanding balance due	$1\frac{1}{2}\%$ interest payment	Amount of monthly payment	Reduction in balance due	Outstanding balance due

14–20. The base price of a Mitsubishi Endeavor XLS AWD is $29,897. With added options, the vehicle is priced at $32,142. Linda Lennon has set aside a down payment of 10% and will finance the balance at 8% for 60 months. Linda's net pay is $3,800 a month. She has budgeted 15% of her net pay toward the monthly payment. **(a)** If Linda purchases the vehicle at the base price, what will be her monthly payment? **(b)** How much over or under budget will Linda be? **(c)** If Linda purchases the vehicle with the options, what will be her monthly payments? **(d)** How much over or under budget will Linda be?

14–21. You have a $1,100 balance on your 15% credit card. You have lost your job and been unemployed for 6 months. You have been unable to make any payments on your balance. However, you received a tax refund and want to pay off the credit card. How much will you owe on the credit card, and how much interest will have accrued? What will be the effective rate of interest after the 6 months (to nearest hundredth percent)?

 SUMMARY PRACTICE TEST

1. Walter Lantz buys a Volvo SUV for $42,500. Walter made a down payment of $16,000 and paid $510 monthly for 60 months. What are the total amount financed and the total finance charge that Walter paid at the end of the 60 months? (p. *343*)

2. Joyce Mesnic bought an HP laptop computer at Staples for $699. Laura made a $100 down payment and financed the balance at 10% for 12 months. What is her monthly payment? (Use the loan amortization table.) (p. *346*)

3. Lee Remick read the following partial advertisement: price, $22,500; down payment, $1,000 cash or trade; and $399.99 per month for 60 months. Calculate **(a)** the total finance charge and **(b)** the APR by Table 14.1 (use the tables in *Business Math Handbook*) to the nearest hundredth percent. (p. 344)

4. Nancy Billows bought a $7,000 desk at Furniture.com. Based on her income, Nancy could only afford to pay back $700 per month. The charge on the unpaid balance is 3%. The U.S. Rule is used in the calculation. Calculate the balance outstanding at the end of month 2. (p. *351*)

Month	Balance due	Interest	Monthly payment	Reduction in balance	Balance outstanding

5. Joan Hart borrowed $9,800 to travel to France to see her son Dick. Joan's loan was to be paid in 50 monthly installments of $250. At the end of 7 months, Joan's daughter Abby convinced her that she should pay off the loan early. What are Joan's rebate and payoff amount? (p. *349*)

Step 1.   **Step 2.**

Step 3.   **Step 4.**

                                               Step 6.

Step 5.

6. Calculate the average daily balance and finance charge on the statement below. (p. *353*)

30-day billing cycle		
7/3	Balance	$400
7/18	Payment	100
7/27	Charge Wal-Mart	250

Assume 2% finance charge on average daily balance.

Personal Finance

Should I take a 0% **CREDIT CARD** offer?

THE SHORT answer is easy. Go for a credit card with a 0% teaser rate if you can pay off the balance before the rate expires—typically in six to 12 months. If you'll need longer to pay off your debt, look for a card with a low fixed rate.

Lest you strike a Faustian bargain, however, read the fine print. Some cards waive fees only on your first balance transfer. If you want to make additional transfers, you may have to pay a fee of up to 4%—or $400 on a balance transfer of $10,000.

Not everyone qualifies for the deal advertised in bold print on the credit application. A bank might bump a 3.99% rate to 5.99% if your credit is less than perfect. And with interest rates rising, it's tougher to get a low-rate offer. "I used to be able to call my card issuers and ask for lower rates," says Eleni Christianson of Mont-

● **Eleni Christianson is using low-rate offers to pay off $18,000 in debt.**

AMANDA FRIEDMAN

clair, Cal. "Now they tell me I have to wait for them to send me offers in the mail."

Low-rate cards can give you a breather, but you have to use the time to pay off your debt. And card issuers won't make it easy to pay down debt quickly. Christianson and her musician husband, John, are focused on paying off $18,000 in credit-card debt—and are frustrated that Chase allows them to make only four payments per month. "They let you use your cards limitlessly, but they limit how often you can pay," says Eleni, a project coordinator for a contractor.

Be careful if you accept a low-rate transfer offer on an existing card that already has a balance. Your payments will be used to pay down the lower-rate balance first, and interest will continue to accrue on the initial balance at the higher rate.
—**THOMAS M. ANDERSON**

I'm living paycheck to paycheck. Can I **INVEST**?

GIVING UP one latte a day will give you plenty of money to get started. You can put it in a high-yield savings account until you have enough to invest in a mutual fund with a minimum deposit of $1,000 or more.

Or, if you don't want to wait, a number of fund companies—Ariel Mutual Funds, Investment Company of America, TIAA-CREF

and T. Rowe Price—will let you invest as little as $50 a month if you set up automatic deductions from your bank account or paycheck.

Your best strategy is to put your money in a fund with a diversified mix of stocks and investing styles. For instance, **T. Rowe Price Spectrum Growth** (symbol PRSGX; 800-638-5660) invests in ten other T. Rowe Price funds. Spectrum

Growth has an annualized return of 9% over the past ten years and 6% over the past five years. Investors pay only the expenses of the underlying funds; investing $600 a year will cost you $5.

Another one-stop alternative is a target-retirement fund, which shifts its asset mix to become more conservative as you get closer to retirement. **T. Rowe Price Retirement 2040**

(TRRDX), launched in 2002, has returned an annualized 14% over the past three years.

Think of it: If you invest $50 a month in an account that earns 8% annually, you will have $74,518 in 30 years. Not a bad start for living paycheck to paycheck—and you can always bump up your investments as that paycheck gets bigger.
—**THOMAS M. ANDERSON**

BUSINESS MATH ISSUE

Paying off debt with low-rate offers is not a good financial decision.

1. List the key points of the article and information to support your position.
2. Write a group defense of your position using math calculations to support your view.

Slater's Business Math Scrapbook

with Internet Application

Putting Your Skills to Work

PROJECT A

Calculate the following for the Ion-2: **(a)** monthly payment, **(b)** amount financed, **(c)** finance charge, and **(d)** APR.

SL1
$0 Down
$119/mo.
With A/C Auto. Sunroof
or **$5975**
Certified Used #8259A, 2 to choose from

ION-1
With A/C CD
$179 Down
$179/mo.
You-Own-It
Stk. # 9023 10 to choose from

CLEARANCE
$4500 OFF
For everyone and up to $6500 off for qualified buyers!
ON ALL NEW 2003 L SERIES

ION-2
Auto. A/C CD
$199 Down
$199/mo.
You-Own-It
Stk. # 9117 10 to choose from

Used Specials 60 months @ 6.9% Annual percentage Rate total of payments $7140. $4,500 off on all L-Series + $1,000 GM Card + $1000 Olds. Loyalty for qualified buyers. ION 1 - MSRP $12,245 - $650 Rebate, 72 payments @ 3.9% Annual Percentage Rate total $12,888. ION 2 - MSRP $15200 - $1500 Rebate 72 Payments @ 1.9% Annual Percentage Rate total: $14,328.

Number of payments	ANNUAL PERCENTAGE RATE								
	2.00	2.50	3.00	3.50	4.00	4.50	5.00	5.50	6.00
61	5.25	6.54	7.94	9.34	10.69	12.04	13.46	14.92	16.24
62	5.34	6.62	8.09	9.38	10.81	12.26	13.71	15.09	16.57
63	5.44	6.70	8.21	9.59	11.06	12.43	13.90	15.37	16.89
64	5.51	6.81	8.34	9.72	11.22	12.67	14.16	15.59	17.12
65	5.58	6.89	8.46	9.92	11.39	12.83	16.36	15.89	17.34
66	5.71	7.02	8.58	10.05	11.60	13.09	14.54	16.11	17.68
67	5.76	7.15	8.74	10.19	11.73	13.30	14.85	16.33	17.94
68	5.87	7.25	8.89	10.40	11.92	13.50	15.07	16.69	18.20
69	5.89	7.46	9.00	10.57	12.14	13.70	15.27	16.89	18.45
70	6.05	7.55	9.13	10.71	12.29	13.88	15.52	17.16	18.73
71	6.14	7.68	9.25	10.87	12.52	14.05	15.73	17.45	19.01
72	6.18	7.78	9.34	11.02	12.70	14.30	15.97	17.68	19.29

Internet Projects: See text Web site (www.mhhe.com/slater9e) and The Business Math Internet Resource Guide.

CHAPTER 15

The Cost of Home Ownership

Risk...and Reward?

Comparing three types of $300,000 mortgages over the first five and 10 years

LOAN	INTEREST RATE	MONTHLY PAYMENT	TOTAL PAYMENTS	PRINCIPAL PAID	LOAN BALANCE
FIRST FIVE YEARS					
30-year fixed	5.5%	$1,703	$102,202	$22,618	$277,382
5/1 ARM	4.5%	1,520	91,203	26,526	273,438
5/1 interest-only ARM [1]	4.5%	1,125	67,500	None	300,000
SECOND FIVE YEARS					
30-year fixed	5.5%	$1,703	$102,202	$29,759	$247,623
5/1 ARM	6.5% [2]	1,847	110,791	25,810	247,664
5/1 interest-only ARM [1]	6.5% [2]	2,026	121,537	28,314	271,686

[1] Interest-only period is for the first five years. [2] Assumes rate on both ARMs rises to 6.5% for years 6 to 10 of the loan. After the first five years, the rate on the ARMs can change annually. ARM=adjustable-rate mortgage.

Note: Figures for total payments and principal paid are for each five-year period; loan balances are for the end of each period. All loans have 30-year terms. Figures are rounded to the nearest dollar.

Source: IndyMac Bank

Wall Street Journal © 2005

LEARNING UNIT OBJECTIVES

LU 15–1: Types of Mortgages and the Monthly Mortgage Payment

- List the types of mortgages available (pp. 367–368).
- Utilize an amortization chart to compute monthly mortgage payments (p. 368).
- Calculate the total cost of interest over the life of a mortgage (p. 369).

LU 15–2: Amortization Schedule—Breaking Down the Monthly Payment

- Calculate and identify the interest and principal portion of each monthly payment (p. 370).
- Prepare an amortization schedule (p. 371).

FIGURE 15.1	Types of mortgages available

Loan types	Advantages	Disadvantages
30-year fixed rate mortgage	A predictable monthly payment.	If interest rates fall, you are locked in to higher rate unless you refinance. (Application and appraisal fees along with other closing costs will result.)
15-year fixed rate mortgage	Interest rate lower than 30-year fixed (usually $\frac{1}{4}$ to $\frac{1}{2}$ of a percent). Your equity builds up faster while interest costs are cut by more than one-half.	A larger down payment is needed. Monthly payment will be higher.
Graduated-payment mortgage (GPM)	Easier to qualify for than 30- or 15-year fixed rate. Monthly payments start low and increase over time.	May have higher APR than fixed or variable rates.
Biweekly mortgage*	Shortens term loan; saves substantial amount of interest; 26 biweekly payments per year. Builds equity twice as fast.	Not good for those not seeking an early loan payoff. Extra payment per year
Adjustable rate mortgage (ARM)	Lower rate than fixed. If rates fall, could be adjusted down without refinancing. Caps available that limit how high rate could go for each adjustment period over term of loan.	Monthly payment could rise if interest rates rise. Riskier than fixed rate mortgage in which monthly payment is stable.
Home equity loan	Cheap and reliable accessible lines of credit backed by equity in your home. Tax-deductible. Rates can be locked in. Reverse mortgages may be available to those 62 or older.	Could lose home if not paid. No annual or interest caps.
Interest-only mortgages	Borrowers pay interest but no principal in the early years (5 to 15) of the loan.	Early years build up no equity.

*A different type of mortgage loan, called a **mortgage accelerator** loan, has come to the United States. It uses home equity borrowing and the borrower's paycheck to shorten the time until a mortgage is paid off, saving tens of thousands in interest expense. The biweekly mortgage loan shortens a mortgage by paying an extra mortgage payment once a year, the mortgage accelerator loan program is based on an approach common in Australia and the United Kingdom, where borrowers deposit their paychecks into an account that, every month, applies every unspent dime against the mortgage loan balance.

Figure 15.1 indicates that lenders now offer a new type of mortgage loan to home buyers—the **interest-only mortgage.** It would seem that to many borrowers, delaying building equity in their home will be an important disadvantage.

When buying a home, purchasers can be concerned about how much a home appreciates in value and which mortgage would be best for them. The *Wall Street Journal* clipping "Sticker Shock" shows that home-price appreciation for a 3-year change increases 95% in South Africa versus 29% in the United States. The *Wall Street Journal* clipping "How the Payments Stack Up" shows how the monthly payment for a U.S. mortgage varies for three different loan types.

Sticker Shock

Home-price appreciation over the past year and three years.

	1-yr. change	3-yr. change
South Africa	28%	95%
China (Shanghai)	27	68
Spain	17	63
Australia	-3	56
U.K.	11	50
France	15	48
Canada	10	31
U.S.	11	29
Thailand	13	29
Sweden	10	27
Hong Kong	19	27
South Korea	-2	20

Note: Data are based on latest available statistics updated through fourth-quarter 2004 or first-quarter 2005.
Sources: Bank for International Settlements, Economy.com, CEIC Data Co., Shanghai Municipal Statistics Bureau

How the Payments Stack Up

Here's what a borrower could pay per $100,000 with three different mortgage products:

MORTGAGE	RATE	MONTHLY PAYMENT
30-year fixed-rate	5.56%	$572.00
30-year fixed-rate with interest-only feature	5.69%	$474.00*
40-year fixed-rate	5.81%	$537.00

*Monthly payment during the initial interest-only period.
Source: Credit Suisse First Boston

Wall Street Journal © 2005

Purchasing a home usually involves paying a large amount of interest. Note how your author was able to save $70,121.40.

Over the life of a 30-year **fixed rate mortgage** (Figure 15.1) of $100,000, the interest would have cost $207,235. Monthly payments would have been $849.99. This would not include taxes, insurance, and so on.

Your author chose a **biweekly mortgage** (Figure 15.1). This meant that every two weeks (26 times a year) the bank would receive $425. By paying every two weeks instead of once a month, the mortgage would be paid off in 23 years instead of 30—a $70,121.40 *savings* on interest. Why? When a payment is made every two weeks, the principal is reduced more quickly, which substantially reduces the interest cost.

Learning Unit 15–1: Types of Mortgages and the Monthly Mortgage Payment

In the past several years, interest rates have been low, which has caused an increase in home sales. Today, more people are buying homes than are renting homes. The question facing prospective buyers concerns which type of **mortgage** will be best for them. Figure 15.1 lists the types of mortgages available to home buyers. Depending on how interest rates are moving when you purchase a home, you may find one type of mortgage to be the most advantageous for you.

Have you heard that elderly people who are house-rich and cash-poor can use their home to get cash or monthly income? The Federal Housing Administration makes it possible for older homeowners to take out a **reverse mortgage** on their homes. Under reverse mortgages, senior homeowners borrow against the equity in their property, often getting fixed monthly checks. The debt is repaid only when the homeowners or their estate sells the home.

Now let's learn how to calculate a monthly mortgage payment and the total cost of loan interest over the life of a mortgage. We will use the following example in our discussion.

EXAMPLE Gary bought a home for $200,000. He made a 20% down payment. The 9% mortgage is for 30 years (30 × 12 = 360 payments). What are Gary's monthly payment and total cost of interest?

Computing the Monthly Payment for Principal and Interest

You can calculate the principal and interest of Gary's **monthly payment** using the **amortization table** shown in Table 15.1 (p. 368) and the following steps. (Remember that this is the same type of amortization table used in Chapter 14 for installment loans.)

COMPUTING MONTHLY PAYMENT BY USING AN AMORTIZATION TABLE
Step 1. Divide the amount of the mortgage by $1,000.
Step 2. Look up the rate and term in the amortization table. At the intersection is the table factor.
Step 3. Multiply Step 1 by Step 2.

For Gary, we calculate the following:

$$\frac{\$160,000 \text{ (amount of mortgage)}}{\$1,000} = 160 \times \$8.05 \text{ (table rate)} = \boxed{\$1,288}$$

So $160,000 is the amount of the mortgage ($200,000 less 20%). The $8.05 is the table factor of 9% for 30 years per $1,000. Since Gary is mortgaging 160 units of $1,000, the factor of $8.05 is multiplied by 160. Remember that the $1,288 payment does not include taxes, insurance, and so on.

| TABLE | 15.1 | Amortization table (mortgage principal and interest per $1,000) |

Term in years	5%	5½%	6%	6½%	7%	7½%	8%	8½%	9%	9½%	10%	10½%	11%
10	10.61	10.86	11.11	11.36	11.62	11.88	12.14	12.40	12.67	12.94	13.22	13.50	13.78
12	9.25	9.51	9.76	10.02	10.29	10.56	10.83	11.11	11.39	11.67	11.96	12.25	12.54
15	7.91	8.18	8.44	8.72	8.99	9.28	9.56	9.85	10.15	10.45	10.75	11.06	11.37
17	7.29	7.56	7.84	8.12	8.40	8.69	8.99	9.29	9.59	9.90	10.22	10.54	10.86
20	6.60	6.88	7.17	7.46	7.76	8.06	8.37	8.68	9.00	9.33	9.66	9.99	10.33
22	6.20	6.51	6.82	7.13	7.44	7.75	8.07	8.39	8.72	9.05	9.39	9.73	10.08
25	5.85	6.15	6.45	6.76	7.07	7.39	7.72	8.06	8.40	8.74	9.09	9.45	9.81
30	5.37	5.68	6.00	6.33	6.66	7.00	7.34	7.69	8.05	8.41	8.78	9.15	9.53
35	5.05	5.38	5.71	6.05	6.39	6.75	7.11	7.47	7.84	8.22	8.60	8.99	9.37

| TABLE | 15.2 | Effect of interest rates on monthly payments |

	9%	11%	Difference
Monthly payment	$1,288	$1,524.80	$236.80 per month
	(160 × $8.05)	(160 × $9.53)	
Total cost of interest	$303,680	$388,928	$85,248
	($1,288 × 360) − $160,000	($1,524.80 × 360) − $160,000	($236.80 × 360)

What Is the Total Cost of Interest?

We can use the following formula to calculate Gary's total interest cost over the life of the mortgage:

$$\text{Total cost of interest} = \text{Total of all monthly payments} - \text{Amount of mortgage}$$

$$\$303,680 = \underset{(\$1,288 \times 360)}{\$463,680} - \$160,000$$

Effects of Interest Rates on Monthly Payment and Total Interest Cost

Table 15.2 shows the effect that an increase in interest rates would have on Gary's monthly payment and his total cost of interest. Note that if Gary's interest rate rises to 11%, the 2% increase will result in Gary paying an additional $85,248 in total interest.

For most people, purchasing a home is a major lifetime decision. Many factors must be considered before this decision is made. One of these factors is how to pay for the home. The purpose of this unit is to tell you that being informed about the types of available mortgages can save you thousands of dollars.

In addition to the mortgage payment, buying a home can include the following costs:

- *Closing costs:* When property passes from seller to buyer, **closing costs** may include fees for credit reports, recording costs, lawyer's fees, points, title search, and so on. A **point** is a one-time charge that is a percent of the mortgage. Two points means 2% of the mortgage. On the following page you can see a sample of closing costs for a $125,000 mortgage in the *Wall Street Journal* clipping "Add-ons."

- *Escrow amount:* Usually, the lending institution, for its protection, requires that each month 1/12 of the insurance cost and 1/12 of the real estate taxes be kept in a special account called the **escrow account.** The monthly balance in this account will change depending on the cost of the insurance and taxes. Interest is paid on escrow accounts.

TABLE	15.1	(concluded)

	INTEREST												
Term in years	$11\frac{1}{2}\%$	$11\frac{3}{4}\%$	12%	$12\frac{1}{2}\%$	$12\frac{3}{4}\%$	13%	$13\frac{1}{2}\%$	$13\frac{3}{4}\%$	14%	$14\frac{1}{2}\%$	$14\frac{3}{4}\%$	15%	$15\frac{1}{2}\%$
10	14.06	14.21	14.35	14.64	14.79	14.94	15.23	15.38	15.53	15.83	15.99	16.14	16.45
12	12.84	12.99	13.14	13.44	13.60	13.75	14.06	14.22	14.38	14.69	14.85	15.01	15.34
15	11.69	11.85	12.01	12.33	12.49	12.66	12.99	13.15	13.32	13.66	13.83	14.00	14.34
17	11.19	11.35	11.52	11.85	12.02	12.19	12.53	12.71	12.88	13.23	13.41	13.58	13.94
20	10.67	10.84	11.02	11.37	11.54	11.72	12.08	12.26	12.44	12.80	12.99	13.17	13.54
22	10.43	10.61	10.78	11.14	11.33	11.51	11.87	12.06	12.24	12.62	12.81	12.99	13.37
25	10.17	10.35	10.54	10.91	11.10	11.28	11.66	11.85	12.04	12.43	12.62	12.81	13.20
30	9.91	10.10	10.29	10.68	10.87	11.07	11.46	11.66	11.85	12.25	12.45	12.65	13.05
35	9.77	9.96	10.16	10.56	10.76	10.96	11.36	11.56	11.76	12.17	12.37	12.57	12.98

Add-ons

A sample of closing costs. Average amounts on a $125,000 mortgage.

CHARGES	PRICE
Administration fee	$413.46
Application fee	$266.40
Attorney or settlement fees	$373.71
Commitment fee	$268.00
Document preparation	$162.22
Flood certification	$22.21
Funding fee	$125.57

Mortgage broker fee	$344.17
Processing	$302.71
Pest and other inspection	$86.07
Recording fee	$72.27
Title insurance	$460.23
Title work*	$220.37

*Includes title search, plat drawing and name search
Source: Bankrate.com

- *Repairs and maintenance*: This includes paint, wallpaper, landscaping, plumbing, electrical expenses, and so on.

As you can see, the cost of owning a home can be expensive. But remember that all interest costs of your monthly payment and your real estate taxes are deductible. For many, owning a home can have advantages over renting.

Before you study Learning Unit 15–2, let's check your understanding of Learning Unit 15–1.

LU 15–1	PRACTICE QUIZ

Complete this **Practice Quiz** to see how you are doing

Given: Price of home, $225,000; 20% down payment; 9% interest rate; 25-year mortgage. Solve for:

1. Monthly payment and total cost of interest over 25 years.
2. If rate fell to 8%, what would be the total decrease in interest cost over the life of the mortgage?

✓ Solutions

1. $225,000 − $45,000 = $180,000

$$\frac{\$180,000}{\$1,000} = 180 \times \$8.40 = \boxed{\$1,512}$$

$$\boxed{\$273,600} = \quad \$453,600 \quad - \$180,000$$
$$(\$1,512 \times 300) \quad \text{25 years} \times \text{12 payments per year}$$

2. 8% = $1,389.60 monthly payment
   (180 × $7.72)

   Total interest cost $236,880 = ($1,389.60 × 300) − $180,000

   Savings $36,720 = ($273,600 − $236,880)

LU 15–1a | EXTRA PRACTICE QUIZ

Need more practice? Try this
Extra Practice Quiz (check
figures in Chapter Organizer,
p. 373)

Given: Price of home, $180,000; 30% down payment; 7% interest rate; 30-year mortgage.
Solve for:

1. Monthly payment and total cost of interest over 30 years.
2. If rate fell to 5%, what would be the total decrease in interest cost over the life of the mortgage?

Learning Unit 15–2: Amortization Schedule—Breaking Down the Monthly Payment

In Learning Unit 15–1, we saw that over the life of Gary's $160,000 loan, he would pay $303,680 in interest. Now let's use the following steps to determine what portion of Gary's first monthly payment reduces the principal and what portion is interest.

CALCULATING INTEREST, PRINCIPAL, AND NEW BALANCE OF MONTHLY PAYMENT
Step 1. Calculate the interest for a month (use current principal): Interest = Principal × Rate × Time.
Step 2. Calculate the amount used to reduce the principal: Principal reduction = Monthly payment − Interest (Step 1).
Step 3. Calculate the new principal: Current principal − Reduction of principal (Step 2) = New principal.

Step 1. Interest (I) = Principal (P) × Rate (R) × Time (T)

$$\$1,200 = \$160,000 \times .09 \times \frac{1}{12}$$

Step 2. The reduction of the $160,000 principal each month is equal to the payment less interest. So we can calculate Gary's new principal balance at the end of month 1 as follows:

Monthly payment at 9% (from Table 15.1)	$1,288 (160 × $8.05)
− Interest for first month	− 1,200
= Principal reduction	$ 88

Step 3. As the years go by, the interest portion of the payment decreases and the principal portion increases.

Principal balance	$160,000
Principal reduction	− 88
Balance of principal	$159,912

Let's do month 2:

Step 1. Interest = Principal × Rate × Time

$$= \$159,912 \times .09 \times \frac{1}{12}$$

$$= \$1,199.34$$

| TABLE | 15.3 | Partial amortization schedule |

		MONTHLY PAYMENT, $1,288		
Payment number	Principal (current)	Interest	Principal reduction	Balance of principal
1	$160,000.00 $\left(\$160,000 \times .09 \times \frac{1}{12}\right)$	$1,200.00 ($1,288 − $1,200)	$88.00 ($160,000 − $88)	$159,912.00
2	$159,912.00 $\left(\$159,912 \times .09 \times \frac{1}{12}\right)$	$1,199.34 ($1,288 − $1,199.34)	$88.66 ($159,912 − $88.66)	$159,823.34
3	$159,823.34	$1,198.68	$89.32	$159,734.02
4	$159,734.02	$1,198.01	$89.99	$159,644.03
5	$159,644.03	$1,197.33	$90.67	$159,553.36
6	$159,553.36	$1,196.65	$91.35	$159,462.01
7	$159,462.01	$1,195.97*	$92.04	$159,369.97

*Off 1 cent due to rounding.

Step 2.
$1,288.00 monthly payment
− 1,199.34 interest for month 2
$ 88.66 principal reduction

Step 3.
$159,912.00 principal balance
−   88.66 principal reduction
$159,823.34 balance of principal

Note that in month 2, interest costs drop 66 cents ($1,200.00 − $1,199.34). So in 2 months, Gary has reduced his mortgage balance by $176.66 ($88.00 + $88.66). After 2 months, Gary has paid a total interest of $2,399.34 ($1,200.00 + $1,199.34).

Example of an Amortization Schedule

The partial **amortization schedule** given in Table 15.3 shows the breakdown of Gary's monthly payment. Note the amount that goes toward reducing the principal and toward payment of actual interest. Also note how the outstanding balance of the loan is reduced. After 7 months, Gary still owes $159,369.97. Often when you take out a mortgage loan, you will receive an amortization schedule from the company that holds your mortgage.

In the future, you may want to consider when it would be a good time to refinance your mortgage. The two *Wall Street Journal* clippings "The Costs of Refinancing" and "Running the Numbers" should be helpful in making this decision.

The Costs of Refinancing

Here are some common charges for refinancing a $300,000 mortgage.

- Application fee: $0 to $495
- Appraisal: $300 to $450
- Attorney or settlement fee: $400
- Credit report: $35
- Documentation preparation: $125 to $250
- Processing fee: $300
- Title Insurance: $1,000

Source: LendingTree Inc.

Running the Numbers

If you're still on the fence about refinancing, here are the monthly payments at various interest rates on a 30-year fixed-rate mortgage for every $100,000 you owe:

RATES	MONTHLY PAYMENT
5.50%	$567.79
5.75%	$583.57
6.00%	$599.55
6.25%	$615.72
6.50%	$632.07
6.75%	$648.59
7.00%	$665.30

Source: HSH Associates

It's time to test your knowledge of Learning Unit 15–2 with a Practice Quiz.

LU 15–2   PRACTICE QUIZ

Complete this **Practice Quiz** to see how you are doing

$100,000 mortgage; monthly payment, $953 (100 × $9.53)

Prepare an amortization schedule for first three periods for the following: mortgage, $100,000; 11%; 30 years.

✓ **Solutions**

		PORTION TO—		
Payment number	Principal (current)	Interest	Principal reduction	Balance of principal
1	$100,000	$916.67 $\left(\$100,000 \times .11 \times \frac{1}{12}\right)$	$36.33 ($953.00 − $916.67)	$99,963.67 ($100,000 − $36.33)
2	$99,963.67	$916.33 $\left(\$99,963.67 \times .11 \times \frac{1}{12}\right)$	$36.67 ($953.00 − $916.33)	$99,927.00 ($99,963.67 − $36.67)
3	$99,927	$916.00 $\left(\$99,927 \times .11 \times \frac{1}{12}\right)$	$37.00 ($953.00 − $916.00)	$99,890.00 ($99,927.00 − $37.00)

LU 15–2a   EXTRA PRACTICE QUIZ

Need more practice? Try this **Extra Practice Quiz** (check figures in Chapter Organizer, p. 373)

Prepare an amortization schedule for the first two periods for the following: mortgage, $70,000; 7%; 30 years.

CHAPTER ORGANIZER AND STUDY GUIDE
WITH CHECK FIGURES FOR EXTRA PRACTICE QUIZZES

Topic	Key point, procedure, formula	Example(s) to illustrate situation
Computing monthly mortgage payment, p. 367	Based on per $1,000 Table 15.1: $\dfrac{\text{Amount of mortgage}}{\$1,000} \times$ Table rate	Use Table 15.1: 12% on $60,000 mortgage for 30 years. $\dfrac{\$60,000}{\$1,000} = 60 \times \$10.29$ $= \$617.40$
Calculating total interest cost, p. 368	$\begin{array}{c}\text{Total of all} \\ \text{monthly payments}\end{array} - \begin{array}{c}\text{Amount of} \\ \text{mortgage}\end{array}$	Using example above: 30 years = 360 (payments) × $617.40 $222,264 − 60,000 $162,264 (mortgage interest over life of mortgage)
Amortization schedule, p. 371	$I = P \times R \times T$ $\left(I \text{ for month} = P \times R \times \frac{1}{12}\right)$ $\begin{array}{c}\text{Principal} \\ \text{reduction}\end{array} = \begin{array}{c}\text{Monthly} \\ \text{payment}\end{array} - \text{Interest}$ $\begin{array}{c}\text{New} \\ \text{principal}\end{array} = \begin{array}{c}\text{Current} \\ \text{principal}\end{array} - \begin{array}{c}\text{Reduction of} \\ \text{principal}\end{array}$	Using same example:

Using same example:

		Portion to—	
Payment number	Interest	Principal reduction	Balance of principal
1	$600 $\left(\$60,000 \times .12 \times \frac{1}{12}\right)$	$17.40 $\left(\begin{array}{c}\$617.40 \\ -\$600.00\end{array}\right)$	$59,982.60 $\left(\begin{array}{c}\$60,000.00 \\ -\$17.40\end{array}\right)$
2	$599.83 $\left(\$59,982.60 \times .12 \times \frac{1}{12}\right)$	$17.57 $\left(\begin{array}{c}\$617.40 \\ -\$599.83\end{array}\right)$	$59,965.03 $\left(\begin{array}{c}\$59,982.60 \\ -\$17.57\end{array}\right)$

(continues)

CHAPTER ORGANIZER AND STUDY GUIDE
WITH CHECK FIGURES FOR EXTRA PRACTICE QUIZZES (concluded)

Topic	Key point, procedure, formula		Example(s) to illustrate situation	
KEY TERMS	Adjustable rate mortgage, (ARM), *p. 366* Amortization schedule, *p. 371* Amortization table, *p. 367* Biweekly mortgage, *p. 367* Closing costs, *p. 368*	Escrow account, *p. 368* Fixed rate mortgage, *p. 367* Graduated-payment mortgages (GPM), *p. 366* Home equity loan, *p. 366* Interest-only mortgage, *p. 366*	Mortgage accelerator *p. 366* Monthly payment, *p. 367* Mortgages, *p. 367* Points, *p. 368* Reverse mortgage, *p. 367*	

CHECK FIGURES FOR EXTRA PRACTICE QUIZZES WITH PAGE REFERENCES	LU 15–1a (p. 370)
	1. $839.16
	   $176,097.60
	2. $117,583.20
	   $58,514.40
			LU 15–2a (p. 372)
			$408.33 $57.87 $69,942.13
			$408.00 $58.20 $69,833.93	

Critical Thinking Discussion Questions

1. Explain the advantages and disadvantages of the following loan types: 30-year fixed rate, 15-year fixed rate, graduated-payment mortgage, biweekly mortgage, adjustable rate mortgage, and home equity loan. Why might a bank require a home buyer to establish an escrow account?

2. How is an amortization schedule calculated? Is there a best time to refinance a mortgage?

3. What is a point? Is paying points worth the cost?

4. Would you ever consider a jumbo mortgage?

Classroom Notes

Name _____ Date _____

DRILL PROBLEMS

Complete the following amortization chart by using Table 15.1.

	Selling price of home	Down payment	Principal (loan)	Rate of interest	Years	Payment per $1,000	Monthly mortgage payment
15–1.	$140,000	$10,000		7%	25		
15–2.	$90,000	$5,000		$5\frac{1}{2}\%$	30		
15–3.	$340,000	$70,000		6%	35		

15–4. What is the total cost of interest in Problem 15–2?

15–5. If the interest rate rises to 7% in Problem 15–2, what is the total cost of interest?

Complete the following:

	Selling price	Down payment	Amount mortgage	Rate	Years	Monthly payment	First Payment Broken Down Into— Interest	Principal	Balance at end of month
15–6.	$125,000	$5,000		7%	30				
15–7.	$199,000	$40,000		$12\frac{1}{2}\%$	35				

15–8. Bob Jones bought a new log cabin for $70,000 at 11% interest for 30 years. Prepare an amortization schedule for first 3 periods.

Payment number	Portion to— Interest	Principal	Balance of loan outstanding

15–9. The March 9, 2007 edition of the *Amarillo Globe-News* reported mortgage rates at a low for the year. The local rates for a 30 year mortgage at the Citibank are 6.00% and the First United Bank at 6.50%. Tom Burke plans to purchase a $350,000 home with 20 percent down. **(a)** What would Tom's monthly payment be at the Citibank? **(b)** What would Tom's monthly payment be at the First United Bank?

15–10. Oprah Winfrey has closed on a 42-acre estate near Santa Barbara, California, for $50,000,000. If Oprah puts 20% down and finances at 7% for 30 years, what would her monthly payment be?

15–11. Joe Levi bought a home in Arlington, Texas, for $140,000. He put down 20% and obtained a mortgage for 30 years at $5\frac{1}{2}\%$. What is Joe's monthly payment? What is the total interest cost of the loan?

	70,000	14
	48,778	89
	76,551	117
	33,737	74

15–12. If in Problem 15–11 the rate of interest is $7\frac{1}{2}\%$, what is the difference in interest cost?

15–13. Mike Jones bought a new split-level home for $150,000 with 20% down. He decided to use Victory Bank for his mortgage. They were offering $13\frac{3}{4}\%$ for 25-year mortgages. Provide Mike with an amortization schedule for the first three periods.

| Payment number | Portion to— | | Balance of loan outstanding |
	Interest	Principal	

15–14. Harriet Marcus is concerned about the financing of a home. She saw a small cottage that sells for $50,000. If she puts 20% down, what will her monthly payment be at **(a)** 25 years, $11\frac{1}{2}\%$; **(b)** 25 years, $12\frac{1}{2}\%$; **(c)** 25 years, $13\frac{1}{2}\%$; **(d)** 25 years, 15%? What is the total cost of interest over the cost of the loan for each assumption? **(e)** What is the savings in interest cost between $11\frac{1}{2}\%$ and 15%? **(f)** If Harriet uses 30 years instead of 25 for both $11\frac{1}{2}\%$ and 15%, what is the difference in interest?

15–15. The *Los Angeles Times* on March 10, 2007 listed a home in BelAir at $12,850,000. Willard Paine is interested in purchasing this home. **(a)** if he put 20% down and finances at 7% for 30 years, what would be his monthly payment? **(b)** If he put 30% down at 7% for 30 years, what would be his monthly payment?

15–16. On January 9, 2007 the *New York Times* reported mortgage applications were up as home buyers see a break in rates. Daniel and Jan were part of that surge. Last month, the couple agreed to pay $560,000 for a four-bedroom colonial home in Waltham, Mass., with $60,000 down payment. They have a 30 year mortgage at a fixed rate of 6.00%. **(a)** How much is their monthly payment? **(b)** After the first payment, what would be the balance of the principal?

CHALLENGE PROBLEMS

15–17. A Boston historical home built in 1903 has an appraised price of $625,000 and $3,900 yearly property taxes. A Chicago historical home built in 1889 has a price of $425,000 and $5,020 yearly property taxes. Ronald Albert is offered employment in both Boston and Chicago at $125,000 a year. Ron loves historical homes, and his job acceptance will be based to a large extent on which home he is able to afford. His local banker will finance either home at $7\frac{1}{2}$% interest with 20% down for 30 years. Ron does not want to spend more than 35% of his gross salary on monthly payments. **(a)** What would be the monthly payments for the home in Boston? **(b)** What would be the monthly payments for the home in Chicago? **(c)** How much more are the monthly payments for the Boston home? **(d)** Can Ron afford either home?

15–18. Sharon Fox decided to buy a home in Marblehead, Massachusetts, for $275,000. Her bank requires a 30% down payment. Sue Willis, an attorney, has notified Sharon that besides the 30% down payment there will be the following additional costs:

Recording of the deed	$ 30.00
A credit and appraisal report	155.00
Preparation of appropriate documents	48.00

A transfer tax of 1.8% of the purchase price and a loan origination fee of 2.5% of the mortgage amount

Assume a 30-year mortgage at a rate of 10%.

   a. What is the initial amount of cash Sharon will need?

   b. What is her monthly payment?

   c. What is the total cost of interest over the life of the mortgage?

 SUMMARY PRACTICE TEST

1. Pat Lavoie bought a home for $180,000 with a down payment of $10,000. Her rate of interest is 6% for 30 years. Calculate her **(a)** monthly payment; **(b)** first payment, broken down into interest and principal; and **(c)** balance of mortgage at the end of the month. *(pp. 367, 368)*

2. Jen Logan bought a home in Iowa for $110,000. She put down 20% and obtained a mortgage for 30 years at $5\frac{1}{2}\%$. What are Jen's monthly payment and total interest cost of the loan? *(p. 368)*

3. Christina Sanders is concerned about the financing of a home. She saw a small Cape Cod–style house that sells for $90,000. If she puts 10% down, what will her monthly payment be at **(a)** 30 years, 5%; **(b)** 30 years, $5\frac{1}{2}$% **(c)** 30 years, 6%; and **(d)** 30 years, $6\frac{1}{2}$% What is the total cost of interest over the cost of the loan for each assumption? *(p. 368)*

4. Loretta Scholten bought a home for $210,000 with a down payment of $30,000. Her rate of interest is 6% for 35 years. Calculate Loretta's payment per $1,000 and her monthly mortgage payment. *(p. 367)*

5. Using Problem 4, calculate the total cost of interest for Loretta Scholten. *(p. 368)*

Personal Finance

A KIPLINGER APPROACH

GOOD TIMING—and maybe a short-term rental—can help smooth the transition from one home to another.

Should you buy or sell first?

IF SELLERS are having trouble finding a buyer, they might consider your offer to buy their home contingent on selling your current home. You can make this contingency more palatable by including a "kick-out" clause, which allows the sellers to continue to market their home while you search for a buyer for yours.

But most sellers don't like to see a home-sale continency in a purchase offer. It ties them up with an offer that is by no means a sure thing.

Selling first

REAL-ESTATE agents prefer that you sell your current home first and put off serious shopping until after you've accepted an offer. That's safer for them: There's more risk that an offer encumbered by a home-sale contingency will fall through—and take the agent's paycheck with it.

Trouble is, if you've already agreed to vacate your home in 60 days, you could feel tremendous pressure to settle for a house that falls short of your ideal. And if the sellers of the house you want know you need to find a home quickly, it can be that much harder to negotiate a good price.

If you sell first, you can take some of the heat off by negotiating better terms for your home sale.

Aim for a longer period until closing—say, 90 days instead of 60—or ask the buyers if they would consider a short-term rent-back to you for another month or two after closing. Offer a security deposit—say, a couple of thousand dollars—and a daily rent that covers their new mortgage costs. Both parties should also check with their homeowners insurance company to make sure their homes and possessions are covered during a temporary rent-back.

Buying first

THIS STRATEGY makes the most sense if you're in a hot market where you're likely to encounter a bidding war over prime real estate.

But in a slowing market, if you buy a new home first, you could get stuck making payments on two houses if your current home doesn't sell fast enough. Plus, you will have to come up with cash for a down payment on the new house.

Many people use their home-equity line of credit as a "bridge" loan to supply the down payment on a new home. But you need a robust income to qualify for payments on the old mortgage, the bridge loan and the mortgage on your new home.

The lender will probably turn you down for the new mortgage if the payments on all three (plus any other outstanding debt) total more than 36% of your gross income. The burden of three mortgages could also force you to jump at a low-ball offer on your current house—and you can expect such offers once buyers tour the empty house and realize you need to sell.

Renting out your current home is another option, and it may be a better financial move provided the rent checks more than cover the mortgage and the expense of upkeep. Tax deductions could even put you ahead of the game.

If you rent out your current house, most mortgage lenders will consider up to 75% of the rent payments as income, as long as you have a signed lease. **K**

BUSINESS MATH ISSUE

From Kiplinger's Buying and Selling a Home: Make the Right Choice in any Market April, 2006, Kaplan Business 8e (ISBN 1419535781) p. 5.

A bridge loan is the only way to buy and sell a home.

1. List the key points of the article and information to support your position.
2. Write a group defense of your position using math calculations to support your view.

PROJECT A

Explain the relationship between interest rates and points.

Green Thumb / *Growing Your Money* ◆ *By Ron Lieber*

Deciphering Mortgage Points

Research Shows Few Do It Right; Calculating the Unknown

AN OFFER TO pay more now in order to pay less later can be a real head-scratcher. But it's a key part of mortgage negotiations—and there's evidence that people often make the wrong choice.

Lenders frequently let borrowers pay "points" to lower the interest rate on their mortgage. Each point costs one percent of the mortgage amount, and you pay up front (or roll the points into the loan and pay over time). In return, the loan's interest rate drops permanently, often from one-eighth to one-quarter of a percentage point for every "point" paid.

Points were popular in the 1970s, when interest rates were high. As rates have fallen to historic lows recently, fewer people have bothered. Buying points can still make sense, however, if you play the numbers right.

Start with a basic question: How long do you think you will hold the loan? If you hold it long enough, the savings on the monthly payments from the lower interest rate will more than cover the cost of the points. Most of the time, it takes years to get there.

Doing the math involves other issues, too, such as whether you intend to invest any savings, like the money not spent on points. Plus, there are tax breaks for points buyers. There's a good calculator for figuring it all out at mtgprofessor.com. Scroll down, click on "Mortgage Calculators," then scroll to the points calculators.

Say you seek a $500,000, 30-year, fixed-rate mortgage and can get a 6% rate with one point or a 6.25% rate with no points. You would have to keep that loan for 57 months to break even on the points (assuming you are in the 33% tax bracket and your savings earn 7%).

To see how points have worked out for borrowers, Penn State professor Abdullah Yavas and one of his graduate students, Yan Chang, who is now a senior economist at mortgage giant Freddie Mac, tracked 3,785 fixed-rate mortgages between 1996 and 2003. The two researchers obtained their data from Freddie, but the company didn't fund the research or assist in any other way, says Mr. Yavas.

The pair found that just 1.4% of borrowers held their mortgages long enough to break even on the points they paid. The rest paid off their loans more than three years, on average, before they would have hit that break-even point.

How could so many people get it wrong? Interest rates fell during the period, and home values rose, so those who refinanced had good reason to seek a new deal.

But that highlights the risk in paying points in the first place: No one can predict which way interest rates are headed. That said, rates remain low, which means that people currently paying points are somewhat less likely to need to refinance later just to obtain a lower rate.

Other unknowns are closer to home: Maybe you unexpectedly have twins, or your aging parents need to move in, necessitating more space. Or a big promotion enables you to upgrade your suburb.

Getty Images

Extra Points

A primer on points, the discount that lenders often offer people applying for mortgages:

■ **Each point** costs 1% of the mortgage amount

■ **You get** a discount on your interest rate, often from one eighth to one fourth of a percentage point

■ **Various tax** deductions are available to people who buy points

Wall Street Journal © 2006

Internet Projects: See text Web site (www.mhhe.com/slater9e) and The Business Math Internet Resource Guide.

CHAPTER 16

How to Read, Analyze, and Interpret Financial Reports

LEARNING UNIT OBJECTIVES

LU 16–1: Balance Sheet—Report as of a Particular Date

- Explain the purpose and the key items on the balance sheet (*pp. 383–386*).

- Explain and complete vertical and horizontal analysis (*pp. 386–388*).

LU 16–2: Income Statement—Report for a Specific Period of Time

- Explain the purpose and the key items on the income statement (*pp. 389–392*).

- Explain and complete vertical and horizontal analysis (*p. 392–394*).

LU 16–3: Trend and Ratio Analysis

- Explain and complete a trend analysis (*p. 394*).

- List, explain, and calculate key financial ratios (*p. 394*).

Coach's Net Income Jumps 37%, Driven by Strong Japanese Sales

Dow Jones Newswires

Handbag and leather-goods maker **Coach Inc.** posted a 37% increase in fiscal second-quarter earnings, helped by strong sales in Japan and fewer markdowns.

The news sent the company's shares up 8.8%, or $2.82, to $34.89 in 4 p.m. New York Stock Exchange composite trading.

The New York company said net income rose to $174.2 million, or 45 cents a share, for the quarter ended Dec. 31, from $126.9 million, or 32 cents a share, in the year-earlier period. Sales rose 22% to $650.3 million from $531.8 million.

"They're just hitting on all cylinders," said Christine Chen, an analyst at Pacific Growth Equities.

Morgan Keegan & Co. analyst Brad Stephens was similarly impressed with the company's ability to shoehorn its way into Japan's luxury-handbag market and said it could reap substantial gains if Japanese consumers begin to ratchet up their spending.

Coach has said it is the No. 2 luxury brand in Japan behind Louis Vuitton, part of the French luxury-goods house **LVMH Moët Hennessy Louis Vuitton** SA, with an 8% share of the market.

Direct-to-consumer sales, which include Coach Japan, increased 21% to $504 million. U.S. same-store sales, or sales at stores open at least a year, rose 20%. In Japan, sales rose only 7% because of a weaker yen; Japanese sales rose 20% on a constant-currency basis.

Coach said January is off to a strong start, driven by consumer response to early spring offerings.

This spring Coach will add about 15 more retail stores in the U.S., bringing the total to about 25 new retail stores for the full fiscal year. It plans to add at least six new locations in Japan during the second half, for a full-year total of at least 12 new shops.

Wall Street Journal © 2006

"*Next...an in-depth report on corporate corruption...
excluding, of course, our parent company.*"

Barron's © 2005

Living With Sarbanes-Oxley

Wall Street Journal © 2005

The *Wall Street Journal* article that follows the heading "Living with Sarbanes-Oxley" states that after a wave of business scandals (Enron and world.com), the Sarbanes-Oxley Act was passed to ensure public companies are accurately reporting their financial statements. As you will see in this chapter, an understatement of expenses overstates the reported earnings or net income of a company. This overstatement presents a false picture of the company's financial position.

This chapter explains how to analyze two key financial reports: the *balance sheet* (shows a company's financial condition at a particular date) and the *income statement* (shows a company's profitability over a time period).[1] Business owners must understand their financial statements to avoid financial difficulties. This includes knowing how to read, analyze, and interpret financial reports.

Learning Unit 16–1: Balance Sheet—Report As of a Particular Date

Moving the Goalposts

The centerpiece of Sarbanes-Oxley is internal controls: the checks and balances that make sure public companies record assets, liabilities and other items accurately on financial statements. Under Sarbanes-Oxley, companies must make sure their controls are sound, then have an auditor sign off on them.

Wall Street Journal © 2005

The *Wall Street Journal* clipping "Moving the Goalposts" is a subheading of the clipping "Living with Sarbanes-Oxley." Under the sub-head it is stated that Sarbanes-Oxley requires internal controls so that public companies record assets, liabilities, and other item accurately on financial statements.

[1]The third key financial report is the statement of cash flows. We do not discuss this statement. For more information on the statement of cash flows, check your accounting text.

David Young Wolff/PhotoEdit

The **balance sheet** gives a financial picture of what a company is worth as of a particular date, usually at the end of a month or year. This report lists (1) how much the company owns (assets), (2) how much the company owes (liabilities), and (3) how much the owner (owner's equity) is worth.

Note that assets and liabilities are divided into two groups: current (*short term,* usually less than one year); and *long term,* usually more than one year. The basic formula for a balance sheet is as follows:

$$\text{Assets} - \text{Liabilities} = \text{Owner's equity}$$

Like all formulas, the items on both sides of the equal sign must balance.

By reversing the above formula, we have the following common balance sheet layout:

$$\boxed{\text{Assets} = \text{Liabilities} + \text{Owner's equity}}$$

To introduce you to the balance sheet, let's assume that you collect baseball cards and decide to open a baseball card shop. As the owner of The Card Shop, your investment, or owner's equity, is called **capital.** Since your business is small, your balance sheet is short. After the first year of operation, The Card Shop balance sheet looks like this below. The heading gives the name of the company, title of the report, and date of the report. Note how the totals of both sides of the balance sheet are the same. This is true of all balance sheets.

Capital does not mean cash. It is the owner's investment in the company.

THE CARD SHOP Balance Sheet December 31, 2009		Report as of a particular date	
Assets		**Liabilities**	
Cash	$ 3,000	Accounts payable	$ 2,500
Merchandise inventory (baseball cards)	4,000	**Owner's Equity**	
Equipment	3,000	E. Slott, capital	7,500
Total assets	$10,000	Total liabilities and owner's equity	$10,000

We can take figures from the balance sheet of The Card Shop and use our first formula to determine how much the business is worth:

$$\boxed{\text{Assets} - \text{Liabilities} = \text{Owner's equity (capital)}}$$

$$\$10,000 - \$2,500 = \$7,500$$

Since you are the single owner of The Card Shop, your business is a **sole proprietorship.** If a business has two or more owners, it is a **partnership.** A **corporation** has many owners or stockholders, and the equity of these owners is called **stockholders' equity.** Now let's study the balance sheet elements of a corporation.

Elements of the Balance Sheet

The format and contents of all corporation balance sheets are similar. Figure 16.1 (p. 385) shows the balance sheet of Mool Company. As you can see, the formula Assets = Liabilities + Stockholders' equity (we have a corporation in this example) is also the framework of this balance sheet.

To help you understand the three main balance sheet groups (assets, liabilities, and stockholders' equity) and their elements, we have labeled them in Figure 16.1. An explanation of these groups and their elements follows. Do not try to memorize the elements. Just try to understand their meaning. Think of Figure 16.1 as a reference aid. You will find that the more you work with balance sheets, the easier it is for you to understand them.

1. **Assets:** Things of value *owned* by a company (economic resources of the company) that can be measured and expressed in monetary terms.
   a. **Current assets:** Assets that companies consume or convert to cash *within 1 year* or a normal operating cycle.

| FIGURE | **16.1** | Balance sheet |

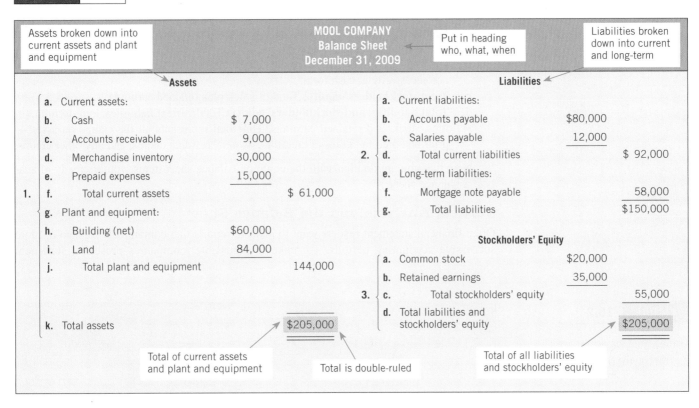

b. **Cash:** Total cash in checking accounts, savings accounts, and on hand.

c. **Accounts receivable:** Money *owed* to a company by customers from sales on account (buy now, pay later).

d. **Merchandise inventory:** Cost of goods in stock for resale to customers.

e. **Prepaid expenses:** The purchases of a company are assets until they expire (insurance or rent) or are consumed (supplies).

f. **Total current assets:** Total of all assets that the company will consume or convert to cash within 1 year.

g. **Plant and equipment:** Assets that will last longer than 1 year. These assets are used in the operation of the company.

h. **Building (net):** The cost of the building minus the depreciation that has accumulated. Usually, balance sheets show this as "Building less accumulated depreciation." In Chapter 17 we discuss accumulated depreciation in greater detail.

i. **Land:** An asset that does not depreciate, but it can increase or decrease in value.

j. **Total plant and equipment:** Total of building and land, including machinery and equipment.

k. **Total assets:** Total of current assets and plant and equipment.

2. **Liabilities:** Debts or obligations of the company.

   a. **Current liabilities:** Debts or obligations of the company that are *due within 1 year.*

   b. **Accounts payable:** A current liability that shows the amount the company owes to creditors for services or items purchased.

   c. **Salaries payable:** Obligations that the company must pay within 1 year for salaries earned but unpaid.

   d. **Total current liabilities:** Total obligations that the company must pay within 1 year.

   e. **Long-term liabilities:** Debts or obligations that the company does not have to pay within 1 year.

   f. **Mortgage note payable:** Debt owed on a building that is a long-term liability; often the building is the collateral.

   g. **Total liabilities:** Total of current and long-term liabilities.

3. **Stockholders' equity (owner's equity):** The rights or interest of the stockholders to assets of a corporation. If the company is not a corporation, the term *owner's equity* is used. The word *capital* follows the owner's name under the title *Owner's Equity*.
   a. **Common stock:** Amount of the initial and additional investment of corporation owners by the purchase of stock.
   b. **Retained earnings:** The amount of corporation earnings that the company retains, not necessarily in cash form.
   c. **Total stockholders' equity:** Total of stock plus retained earnings.
   d. **Total liabilities and stockholders' equity:** Total current liabilities, long-term liabilities, stock, and retained earnings. This total represents all the claims on assets—prior and present claims of creditors, owners' residual claims, and any other claims.

Now that you are familiar with the common balance sheet items, you are ready to analyze a balance sheet.

Vertical Analysis and the Balance Sheet

Often financial statement readers want to analyze reports that contain data for two or more successive accounting periods. To make this possible, companies present a statement

FIGURE 16.2

Comparative balance sheet: Vertical analysis

We divide each item by the total of assets.

Portion ($8,000)

Base ($85,000) × Rate (?)

We divide each item by the total of liabilities and stockholders' equity.

Portion ($20,000)

Base ($85,000) × Rate (?)

ROGER COMPANY Comparative Balance Sheet December 31, 2008 and 2009				
	2009		2008	
	Amount	Percent	Amount	Percent
Assets				
Current assets:				
Cash	$22,000	25.88	$18,000	22.22
Accounts receivable	8,000	9.41	9,000	11.11
Merchandise inventory	9,000	10.59	7,000	8.64
Prepaid rent	4,000	4.71	5,000	6.17
Total current assets	$43,000	50.59	$39,000	48.15*
Plant and equipment:				
Building (net)	$18,000	21.18	$18,000	22.22
Land	24,000	28.24	24,000	29.63
Total plant and equipment	$42,000	49.41*	$42,000	51.85
Total assets	$85,000	100.00	$81,000	100.00
Liabilities				
Current liabilities:				
Accounts payable	$14,000	16.47	$8,000	9.88
Salaries payable	18,000	21.18	17,000	20.99
Total current liabilities	$32,000	37.65	$25,000	30.86*
Long-term liabilities:				
Mortgage note payable	12,000	14.12	20,000	24.69
Total liabilities	$44,000	51.76*	$45,000	55.56*
Stockholders' Equity				
Common stock	$20,000	23.53	$20,000	24.69
Retained earnings	21,000	24.71	16,000	19.75
Total stockholders' equity	$41,000	48.24	$36,000	44.44
Total liabilities and stockholders' equity	$85,000	100.00	$81,000	100.00

Note: All percents are rounded to the nearest hundredth percent.
*Due to rounding.

showing the data from these periods side by side. As you might expect, this statement is called a **comparative statement.**

Comparative reports help illustrate changes in data. Financial statement readers should compare the percents in the reports to industry percents and the percents of competitors.

Figure 16.2 (p. 386) shows the comparative balance sheet of Roger Company. Note that the statement analyzes each asset as a percent of total assets for a single period. The statement then analyzes each liability and equity as a percent of total liabilities and stockholders' equity. We call this type of analysis **vertical analysis.**

The following steps use the portion formula to prepare a vertical analysis of a balance sheet.

PREPARING A VERTICAL ANALYSIS OF A BALANCE SHEET
Step 1. Divide each asset (the portion) as a percent of total assets (the base). Round as indicated.
Step 2. Round each liability and stockholders' equity (the portions) as a percent of total liabilities and stockholders' equity (the base). Round as indicated.

We can also analyze balance sheets for two or more periods by using **horizontal analysis.** Horizontal analysis compares each item in one year by amount, percent, or both with the same item of the previous year. Note the Abby Ellen Company horizontal analysis

FIGURE	16.3

Comparative balance sheet: Horizontal analysis

Difference between 2008 and 2009

Portion
−($1,000)

Base × Rate
($6,000)   (?)

2008

ABBY ELLEN COMPANY
Comparative Balance Sheet
December 31, 2008 and 2009

	2009	2008	Increase (decrease) Amount	Increase (decrease) Percent
Assets				
Current assets:				
Cash	$ 6,000	$ 4,000	$2,000	50.00*
Accounts receivable	5,000	6,000	(1,000)	− 16.67
Merchandise inventory	9,000	4,000	5,000	125.00
Prepaid rent	5,000	7,000	(2,000)	− 28.57
Total current assets	$25,000	$21,000	$4,000	19.05
Plant and equipment:				
Building (net)	$12,000	$12,000	–0–	–0–
Land	18,000	18,000	–0–	–0–
Total plant and equipment	$30,000	$30,000	–0–	–0–
Total assets	$55,000	$51,000	$4,000	7.84
Liabilities				
Current liabilities:				
Accounts payable	$ 3,200	$ 1,800	$1,400	77.78
Salaries payable	2,900	3,200	(300)	− 9.38
Total current liabilities	$ 6,100	$ 5,000	$1,100	22.00
Long-term liabilities:				
Mortgage note payable	17,000	15,000	2,000	13.33
Total liabilities	$23,100	$20,000	$3,100	15.50
Owner's Equity				
Abby Ellen, capital	$31,900	$31,000	$ 900	2.90
Total liabilities and owner's equity	$55,000	$51,000	$4,000	7.84

*The percents are not summed vertically in horizontal analysis.

shown in Figure 16.3 (p. 387). To make a horizontal analysis, we use the portion formula and the steps that follow.

PREPARING A HORIZONTAL ANALYSIS OF A COMPARATIVE BALANCE SHEET
Step 1. Calculate the increase or decrease (portion) in each item from the base year.
Step 2. Divide the increase or decrease in Step 1 by the old or base year.
Step 3. Round as indicated.

You can see the difference between vertical analysis and horizontal analysis by looking at the example of vertical analysis in Figure 16.2 (p. 386). The percent calculations in Figure 16.2 are for each item of a particular year as a percent of that year's total assets or total liabilities and stockholders' equity.

Horizontal analysis needs comparative columns because we take the difference *between* periods. In Figure 16.3, for example, the accounts receivable decreased $1,000 from 2008 to 2009. Thus, by dividing $1,000 (amount of change) by $6,000 (base year), we see that Abby's receivables decreased 16.67%.

Let's now try the following Practice Quiz.

LU 16–1   PRACTICE QUIZ

Complete this **Practice Quiz**
to see how you are doing

1. Complete this partial comparative balance sheet by vertical analysis. Round percents to the nearest hundredth.

	2009		2008	
	Amount	**Percent**	**Amount**	**Percent**
Assets				
Current assets:				
a. Cash	$ 42,000		$ 40,000	
b. Accounts receivable	18,000		17,000	
c. Merchandise inventory	15,000		12,000	
d. Prepaid expenses	17,000		14,000	
•	•		•	
•	•		•	
•	•		•	
Total current assets	$160,000		$150,000	

2. What is the amount of change in merchandise inventory and the percent increase?

✓ Solutions

		2009		**2008**	
1.	**a.** Cash	$\dfrac{\$42,000}{\$160,000} =$	26.25%	$\dfrac{\$40,000}{\$150,000} =$	26.67%
	b. Accounts receivable	$\dfrac{\$18,000}{\$160,000} =$	11.25%	$\dfrac{\$17,000}{\$150,000} =$	11.33%
	c. Merchandise inventory	$\dfrac{\$15,000}{\$160,000} =$	9.38%	$\dfrac{\$12,000}{\$150,000} =$	8.00%
	d. Prepaid expenses	$\dfrac{\$17,000}{\$160,000} =$	10.63%	$\dfrac{\$14,000}{\$150,000} =$	9.33%

2.

$$\begin{array}{r} \$15,000 \\ -\ 12,000 \\ \hline \end{array}$$

Amount = $ 3,000

Percent $= \dfrac{\$3,000}{\$12,000} = 25\%$

LU 16–1a EXTRA PRACTICE QUIZ

Need more practice? Try this **Extra Practice Quiz** (check figures in Chapter Organizer, p. 398)

1. Complete this partial comparative balance sheet by vertical analysis. Round percents to the nearest hundredth.

	2009		2008	
	Amount	Percent	Amount	Percent
Assets				
Current assets:				
a. Cash	$ 38,000		$ 35,000	
b. Accounts receivable	$ 19,000		$ 18,000	
c. Merchandise inventory	$ 16,000		$ 11,000	
d. Prepaid expenses	$ 20,000		$ 16,000	
•	•		•	
•	•		•	
•	•		•	
Total current assets	$180,000		$140,000	

2. What is the amount of change in merchandise inventory and the percent increase?

Learning Unit 16–2: Income Statement—Report for a Specific Period of Time

The McGraw-Hill Companies, Jill Braaten photographer

One of the most important departments in a company is its accounting department. The job of the accounting department is to determine the financial results of the company's operations. Is the company making money or losing money? Are the numbers presented by the accounting department correct? What happens if the accounting department has made accounting errors?

The *Wall Street Journal* clipping "Kodak Restates Losses on Accounting Errors" answers these questions. As you can see, the Kodak accounting department made errors; as a result, the errors will affect the company's losses.

Kodak Restates Losses on Accounting Errors

ROCHESTER, N.Y.—**Eastman Kodak** Co. said that as a result of accounting errors involving restructuring charges, its third-quarter net loss was wider than previously reported by $9 million, or three cents a share. It is restating previously reported results for the first and second quarters to slightly reduce net losses in those periods.

The camera and film maker is involved in a long-running restructuring of its operations as the imaging industry converts from film to digital products. It has said the restructuring involves complex accounting issues as it

closes plants and lays off workers.

Kodak said the latest restatement involved noncash accounting errors in recording severance and pension-related costs, partially offset by a gain on real estate. As a result, its net loss in the third quarter was $1.038 billion, or $3.61 a share, instead of $1.029 billion, or $3.58 a share.

It said that as a result of the restatements, its first-quarter restated net loss was $140 million, or 49 cents a share, instead of $142 million, or 50 cents; its second-quarter restated net loss was $141 million, or 49 cents, instead of $154 million, or 54 cents.

Wall Street Journal © 2005

In this learning unit we look at the **income statement**—a financial report that tells how well a company is performing (its profitability or net profit) during a specific period of time (month, year, etc.). In general, the income statement reveals the inward flow of revenues (sales) against the outward or potential outward flow of costs and expenses.

The form of income statements varies depending on the company's type of business. However, the basic formula of the income is the same:

$$\text{Revenues} - \text{Operating expenses} = \text{Net income}$$

In a merchandising business like The Card Shop, we can enlarge on this formula:

FIGURE 16.4 | Income statement

MOOL COMPANY Income Statement For Month Ended December 31, 2009			

Report for a specific period → [heading]

Put in heading who, what, when → [heading]

Revenues:

1.	a.	Gross sales		$22,080
	b.	Less: Sales returns and allowances	$ 1,082	
	c.	Sales discounts	432	1,514
	d.	Net sales		$20,566

Actual sales after discounts and returns

Cost of merchandise (goods) sold:

2.	a.	Merchandise inventory December 1, 2009		$1,248
	b.	Purchases		$10,512
	c.	Less: Purchase returns and allowances	$336	
	d.	Less: Purchase discounts	204	540
	e.	Cost of net purchases		9,972
	f.	Cost of merchandise (goods available for sale)		$11,220
	g.	Less: Merchandise inventory, December 31, 2009		1,600
	h.	Cost of merchandise (goods) sold		9,620

Inventory not yet sold

3. {		Gross profit from sales		$10,946

Net sales − Cost of merchandise (goods) sold

Operating expenses:

4.	a.	Salary	$ 2,200	
	b.	Insurance	1,300	
	c.	Utilities	400	
	d.	Plumbing	120	
	e.	Rent	410	
	f.	Depreciation	200	
	g.	Total operating expenses		4,630
5. {		Net income		$ 6,316

Gross profit − Operating expenses

Note: Numbers are subtotaled from left to right.

Revenues (sales) ← After any returns, allowances, or discounts
− Cost of merchandise or goods ← Baseball cards
= Gross profit from sales
− Operating expenses
= Net income (profit)

THE CARD SHOP Income Statement For Month Ended December 31, 2009	
Revenues (sales)	$8,000
Cost of merchandise (goods) sold	3,000
Gross profit from sales	$5,000
Operating expenses	750
Net income	$4,250

Now let's look at The Card Shop's income statement to see how much profit The Card Shop made during its first year of operation. For simplicity, we assume The Card Shop sold all the cards it bought during the year. For its first year of business, The Card Shop made a profit of $4,250.

We can now go more deeply into the income statement elements as we study the income statement of a corporation.

Elements of the Corporation Income Statement

Figure 16.4 (p. 390) gives the format and content of the Mool Company income statement—a corporation. The five main items of an income statement are revenues, cost of merchandise (goods) sold, gross profit on sales, operating expenses, and net income. We will follow the same pattern we used in explaining the balance sheet and define the main items and the letter-coded subitems.

1. **Revenues:** Total earned sales (cash or credit) less any sales returns and allowances or sales discounts.

    a. **Gross sales:** Total earned sales before sales returns and allowances or sales discounts. Note in the *Wall Street Journal* clipping "Heinz Profit Falls 19% Despite Sales Increase" that sales increased for Heinz but its profits were down.

Toby Talbot/AP Wide World

Heinz Profit Falls 19% Despite Sales Increase

Dow Jones Newswires

H.J. Heinz Co. reported a 19% decline in its fiscal first-quarter profit, as strong North American consumer sales were offset by weak European earnings.

The Pittsburgh maker of Heinz ketchup and Ore-Ida frozen fries said net income in the three months ended July 27 fell to $157.3 million, or 45 cents a share, from $194.8 million, or 55 cents a share, a year earlier. Results included $24.5 million in costs for workforce reductions and strategic reviews for potential sales of assets.

Wall Street Journal © 2005

b. **Sales returns and allowances:** Reductions in price or reductions in revenue due to goods returned because of product defects, errors, and so on. When the buyer keeps the damaged goods, an allowance results.

c. **Sales (not trade) discounts:** Reductions in the selling price of goods due to early customer payment. For example, a store may give a 2% discount to a customer who pays a bill within 10 days.

d. **Net sales:** Gross sales less sales returns and allowances less sales discounts.

2. **Cost of merchandise (goods) sold:** All the costs of getting the merchandise that the company sold. The cost of all unsold merchandise (goods) will be subtracted from this item (ending inventory).

    a. **Merchandise inventory, December 1, 2009:** Cost of inventory in the store that was for sale to customers at the beginning of the month.

    b. **Purchases:** Cost of additional merchandise brought into the store for resale to customers.

    c. **Purchase returns and allowances:** Cost of merchandise returned to the store due to damage, defects, errors, and so on. Damaged goods kept by the buyer result in a cost reduction called an *allowance.*

    d. **Purchase discounts:** Savings received by the buyer for paying for merchandise before a certain date. These discounts can result in a substantial savings to a company.

    e. **Cost of net purchases:** Cost of purchases less purchase returns and allowances less purchase discounts.

    f. **Cost of merchandise (goods available for sale):** Sum of beginning inventory plus cost of net purchases.

g. **Merchandise inventory, December 31, 2009:** Cost of inventory remaining in the store to be sold.

h. **Cost of merchandise (goods) sold:** Beginning inventory plus net purchases less ending inventory.

3. **Gross profit from sales:** Net sales less cost of merchandise (goods) sold.

4. **Operating expenses:** Additional costs of operating the business beyond the actual cost of inventory sold.

a.–f. **Expenses:** Individual expenses broken down.

g. **Total operating expenses:** Total of all the individual expenses.

5. **Net income:** Gross profit less operating expenses.

In the next section you will learn some formulas that companies use to calculate various items on the income statement.

Calculating Net Sales, Cost of Merchandise (Goods) Sold, Gross Profit, and Net Income of an Income Statement

It is time to look closely at Figure 16.4 (p. 390) and see how each section is built. Use the previous vocabulary as a reference. We will study Figure 16.4 step by step.

Step 1. Calculate the net sales—what Mool earned:

$$\text{Net sales} = \text{Gross sales} - \frac{\text{Sales returns}}{\text{and allowances}} - \text{Sales discounts}$$

$$\$20{,}566 = \$22{,}080 - \$1{,}082 - \$432$$

Step 2. Calculate the cost of merchandise (goods) sold:

$$\begin{array}{c}\text{Cost of}\\\text{merchandise}\\\text{(goods) sold}\end{array} = \begin{array}{c}\text{Beginning}\\\text{inventory}\end{array} + \begin{array}{c}\text{Net purchases}\\\text{(purchases less}\\\text{returns and discounts)}\end{array} - \begin{array}{c}\text{Ending}\\\text{inventory}\end{array}$$

$$\$9{,}620 = \$1{,}248 + \$9{,}972 - \$1{,}600$$

Step 3. Calculate the gross profit from sales—profit before operating expenses:

$$\begin{array}{c}\text{Gross profit}\\\text{from sales}\end{array} = \text{Net sales} - \begin{array}{c}\text{Cost of merchandise}\\\text{(goods) sold}\end{array}$$

$$\$10{,}946 = \$20{,}566 - \$9{,}620$$

Step 4. Calculate the net income—profit after operating expenses:

$$\text{Net income} = \text{Gross profit} - \text{Operating expenses}$$

$$\$6{,}316 = \$10{,}946 - \$4{,}630$$

Analyzing Comparative Income Statements

We can apply the same procedures of vertical and horizontal analysis to the income statement that we used in analyzing the balance sheet. Let's first look at the vertical analysis for Royal Company, Figure 16.5 (p. 393). Then we will look at the horizontal analysis of Flint Company's 2008 and 2009 income statements shown in Figure 16.6 (p. 393). Note in the margin how numbers are calculated.

The following Practice Quiz will test your understanding of this *unit*.

| FIGURE | 16.5 |

Vertical analysis

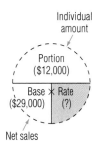

Individual
amount

Portion
($12,000)

Base × Rate
($29,000)   (?)

Net sales

ROYAL COMPANY Comparative Income Statement For Years Ended December 31, 2008 and 2009				
	2009	Percent of net	2008	Percent of net
Net sales	$45,000	100.00	$29,000	100.00*
Cost of merchandise sold	19,000	42.22	12,000	41.38
Gross profit from sales	$26,000	57.78	$17,000	58.62
Operating expenses:				
Depreciation	$ 1,000	2.22	$ 500	1.72
Selling and advertising	4,200	9.33	1,600	5.52
Research	2,900	6.44	2,000	6.90
Miscellaneous	500	1.11	200	.69
Total operating expenses	$ 8,600	19.11†	$ 4,300	14.83
Income before interest and taxes	$17,400	38.67	$12,700	43.79
Interest expense	6,000	13.33	3,000	10.34
Income before taxes	$11,400	25.33†	$ 9,700	33.45
Provision for taxes	5,500	12.22	3,000	10.34
Net income	$ 5,900	13.11	$ 6,700	23.10†

*Net sales = 100%
†Off due to rounding.

| FIGURE | 16.6 |

Horizontal analysis

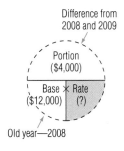

Difference from
2008 and 2009

Portion
($4,000)

Base × Rate
($12,000)   (?)

Old year—2008

FLINT COMPANY Comparative Income Statement For Years Ended December 31, 2008 and 2009				
			INCREASE (DECREASE)	
	2009	2008	Amount	Percent
Sales	$90,000	$80,000	$10,000	
Sales returns and allowances	2,000	2,000	–0–	
Net sales	$88,000	$78,000	$10,000	+ 12.82
Cost of merchandise (goods) sold	45,000	40,000	5,000	+ 12.50
Gross profit from sales	$43,000	$38,000	$ 5,000	+ 13.16
Operating expenses:				
Depreciation	$ 6,000	$ 5,000	$ 1,000	+ 20.00
Selling and administrative	16,000	12,000	4,000	+ 33.33
Research	600	1,000	(400)	− 40.00
Miscellaneous	1,200	500	700	+ 140.00
Total operating expenses	$23,800	$18,500	$ 5,300	+ 28.65
Income before interest and taxes	$19,200	$19,500	$ (300)	− 1.54
Interest expense	4,000	4,000	–0–	
Income before taxes	$15,200	$15,500	$ (300)	− 1.94
Provision for taxes	3,800	4,000	(200)	− 5.00
Net income	$11,400	$11,500	$ (100)	− .87

| LU 16–2 | PRACTICE QUIZ |

Complete this **Practice Quiz**
to see how you are doing

From the following information, calculate:

a. Net sales.

b. Cost of merchandise (goods) sold.

c. Gross profit from sales.

d. Net income.

Given Gross sales, $35,000; sales returns and allowances, $3,000; beginning inventory, $6,000; net purchases, $7,000; ending inventory, $5,500; operating expenses, $7,900.

✓ **Solutions**

a. $35,000 − $3,000 = $32,000 (Gross sales − Sales returns and allowances)

b. $6,000 + $7,000 − $5,500 = $7,500 (Beginning inventory + Net purchases − Ending inventory)

c. $32,000 − $7,500 = $24,500 (Net sales − Cost of merchandise sold)

d. $24,500 − $7,900 = $16,600 (Gross profit from sales − Operating expenses)

LU 16–2a EXTRA PRACTICE QUIZ

Need more practice? Try this **Extra Practice Quiz** (check figures in Chapter Organizer, p. 398)

From the following information, calculate:

a. Net sales

b. Cost of merchandise (goods) sold

c. Gross profit from sales

d. Net income

Given: Gross sales, $36,000; sales returns and allowances, $2,800; beginning inventory, $5,900; net purchases, $6,800; ending inventory, $5,200; operating expenses, $8,100.

Learning Unit 16–3: Trend and Ratio Analysis

Now that you understand the purpose of balance sheets and income statements, you are ready to study how experts look for various trends as they analyze the financial reports of companies. This learning unit discusses trend analysis and ratio analysis. The study of these trends is valuable to businesses, financial institutions, and consumers.

Trend Analysis

Many tools are available to analyze financial reports. When data cover several years, we can analyze changes that occur by expressing each number as a percent of the base year. The base year is a past period of time that we use to compare sales, profits, and so on, with other years. We call this **trend analysis.**

Using the following example of Rose Company, we complete a trend analysis with the following steps:

COMPLETING A TREND ANALYSIS
Step 1. Select the base year (100%).
Step 2. Express each amount as a percent of the base year amount (rounded to the nearest whole percent).

GIVEN (BASE YEAR 2007)			
	2010	2009	2008	2007
Sales	$621,000	$460,000	$340,000	$420,000
Gross profit	182,000	141,000	112,000	124,000
Net income	48,000	41,000	22,000	38,000

TREND ANALYSIS			
	2010	2009	2008	2007
Sales	148%	110%	81%	100%
Gross profit	147	114	90	100
Net income	126	108	58	100

How to Calculate Trend Analysis

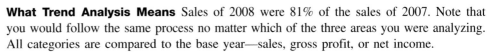

$$\frac{\text{Each item}}{\text{Base amount}} = \frac{\$340,000}{\$420,000} = 80.95\% = \boxed{81\%}$$

Sales for 2008

Sales for 2007

What Trend Analysis Means Sales of 2008 were 81% of the sales of 2007. Note that you would follow the same process no matter which of the three areas you were analyzing. All categories are compared to the base year—sales, gross profit, or net income.

We now will examine **ratio analysis**—another tool companies use to analyze performance.

Ratio Analysis

A *ratio* is the relationship of one number to another. Many companies compare their ratios with those of previous years and with ratios of other companies in the industry. Companies can get ratios of the performance of other companies from their bankers, accountants, local small business center, libraries, and newspaper articles. For example, ratios at McDonald's will be different than at Toys "R" Us. McDonald's sells more perishable products.

Percentage ratios are used by companies to determine the following:

1. How well the company manages its assets—*asset management ratios.*
2. The company's debt situation—*debt management ratios.*
3. The company's profitability picture—*profitability ratios.*

Each company must decide the true meaning of what the three types of ratios (asset management, debt management, and profitability) are saying. Table 16.1 (p. 396) gives a summary of the key ratios, their calculations (rounded to the nearest hundredth), and what they mean. All calculations are from Figures 16.1 (p. 385) and 16.4 (p. 390).

Now you can check your knowledge with the Practice Quiz that follows.

Portion ($340,000)

Base ($420,000) × Rate (?)

2009

LU 16–3 PRACTICE QUIZ

Complete this **Practice Quiz** to see how you are doing

1. Prepare a trend analysis from the following sales, assuming a base year of 2007. Round to the nearest whole percent.

	2010	**2009**	**2008**	**2007**
Sales	$29,000	$44,000	$48,000	$60,000

2. **Given** Total current assets (CA), $15,000; accounts receivable (AR), $6,000; total current liabilities (CL), $10,000; inventory (Inv), $4,000; net sales, $36,000; total assets, $30,000; net income (NI), $7,500.
   Calculate
   a. Current ratio.
   b. Acid test.
   c. Average day's collection.
   d. Profit margin on sales (round to the nearest hundredth percent).

✓ **Solutions**

		2010	**2009**	**2008**	**2007**
1.	Sales	48%	73%	80%	100%

$$\left(\frac{\$29,000}{\$60,000}\right) \quad \left(\frac{\$44,000}{\$60,000}\right) \quad \left(\frac{\$48,000}{\$60,000}\right)$$

2. a. $\dfrac{CA}{CL} = \dfrac{\$15,000}{\$10,000} = \boxed{1.5}$

b. $\dfrac{CA - Inv}{CL} = \dfrac{\$15,000 - \$4,000}{\$10,000} = \boxed{1.1}$

c. $\dfrac{AR}{\dfrac{\text{Net sales}}{360}} = \dfrac{\$6,000}{\dfrac{\$36,000}{360}} = \boxed{60 \text{ days}}$

d. $\dfrac{NI}{\text{Net sales}} = \dfrac{\$7,500}{\$36,000} = \boxed{20.83\%}$

LU 16–3a EXTRA PRACTICE QUIZ

Need more practice? Try this **Extra Practice Quiz** (check figures in Chapter Organizer, p. 398)

1. Prepare a trend analysis from the following sales, assuming a base year of 2007. Round to the nearest whole percent.

	2010	**2009**	**2008**	**2007**
Sales	$25,000	$60,000	$50,000	$70,000

2. **Given:** Total current assets (CA), $14,000; accounts receivable (AR), $5,500; total current liabilities (CL), $9,000; inventory (Inv), $3,900; net sales, $36,500; total assets, $32,000; net income (NI), $8,000. Calculate:
   a. Current ratio.
   b. Acid test.
   c. Average day's collection.
   d. Profit margin on sales (round to the nearest hundredth percent).

TABLE 16.1 Summary of key ratios: A reference guide*

Ratio	Formula	Actual calculations	What it says	Questions that could be raised
1. Current ratio[†]	$\dfrac{\text{Current assets}}{\text{Current liabilities}}$ (Current assets include cash, accounts receivable, and marketable securities.)	$\dfrac{\$61,000}{\$92,000} = .66{:}1$ Industry average, 2 to 1	Business has 66¢ of current assets to meet each $1 of current debt.	Not enough current assets to pay off current liabilities. Industry standard is $2 for each $1 of current debt.
2. Acid test (quick ratio) Top of fraction often → referred to as *quick assets*	$\dfrac{\text{Current assets} - \text{Inventory} - \text{Prepaid expenses}}{\text{Current liabilities}}$ (Inventory and prepaid expenses are excluded because it may not be easy to convert these to cash.)	$\dfrac{\$61,000 - \$30,000 - \$15,000}{\$92,000}$ $= .17{:}1$ Industry average, 1 to 1	Business has only 17¢ to cover each $1 of current debt. This calculation excludes inventory and prepaid expenses.	Same as above but more severe.
3. Average day's collection	$\dfrac{\text{Accounts receivable}}{\dfrac{\text{Net sales}}{360}}$	$\dfrac{\$9,000}{\dfrac{\$20,566}{360}} = 158 \text{ days}$ Industry average, 90–120 days	On the average, it takes 158 days to collect accounts receivable.	Could we speed up collection since industry average is 90–120 days?
4. Total debt to total assets	$\dfrac{\text{Total liabilities}}{\text{Total assets}}$	$\dfrac{\$150,000}{\$205,000} = 73.17\%$ Industry average, 50%–70%	For each $1 of assets, the company owes 73¢ in current and long-term debt.	73% is slightly higher than industry average.
5. Return on equity	$\dfrac{\text{Net income}}{\text{Stockholders' equity}}$	$\dfrac{\$6,316}{\$55,000} = 11.48\%$ Industry average, 15%–20%	For each $1 invested by the owner, a return of 11¢ results.	Could we get a higher return on money somewhere else?
6. Asset turnover	$\dfrac{\text{Net sales}}{\text{Total assets}}$	$\dfrac{\$20,566}{\$205,000} = 10\text{¢}$ Industry average, 3¢ to 8¢	For each $1 invested in assets, it returns 10¢ in sales.	Are assets being utilized efficiently?
7. Profit margin on net sales	$\dfrac{\text{Net income}}{\text{Net sales}}$	$\dfrac{\$6,316}{\$20,566} = 30.71\%$ Industry average, 25%–40%	For each $1 of sales, company produces 31¢ in profit.	Compared to competitors, are we showing enough profits versus our increased sales?

*Inventory turnover is discussed in Chapter 18.
[†]For example, Wal-Mart Stores, Inc., has a current ratio of 1.51.

CHAPTER ORGANIZER AND STUDY GUIDE
WITH CHECK FIGURES FOR EXTRA PRACTICE QUIZZES

Topic	Key point, procedure, formula	Example(s) to illustrate situation
Balance sheet		
Vertical analysis, p. 386	Process of relating each figure on a financial report (down the column) to a total figure.	Current assets $520 52% Plant and equipment 480 48 Total assets $1,000 100%
Horizontal analysis, p. 388	Analyzing comparative financial reports shows rate and amount of change across columns item by item.	<table><tr><td></td><td>2009</td><td>2008</td><td>Change</td><td>%</td></tr><tr><td>Cash,</td><td>$5,000</td><td>$4,000</td><td>$1,000</td><td>25%</td></tr></table> $\left(\dfrac{\$1,000}{\$4,000}\right)$
Income statement formulas, p. 392	(Horizontal and vertical analysis can also be done for income statements.)	
Net sales, p. 392	$\dfrac{\text{Gross}}{\text{sales}} - \dfrac{\text{Sales returns}}{\text{and allowances}} - \dfrac{\text{Sales}}{\text{discounts}}$	$200 gross sales − 10 sales returns and allowances − 2 sales discounts $188 net sales
Cost of merchandise (goods) sold, p. 392	$\dfrac{\text{Beginning}}{\text{inventory}} + \dfrac{\text{Net}}{\text{purchases}} - \dfrac{\text{Ending}}{\text{inventory}}$	$50 + $100 − $20 = $130 Beginning inventory + Net purchases − Ending inventory = Cost of merchandise (goods) sold
Gross profit from sales, p. 392	Net sales − $\dfrac{\text{Cost of merchandise}}{\text{(goods) sold}}$	$188 − $130 = $58 gross profit from sales Net sales − Cost of merchandise (goods) sold = Gross profit from sales
Net income, p. 392	Gross profit − Operating expenses	$58 − $28 = $30 Gross profit from sales − Operating expenses = Net income
Trend analysis, p. 394	Each number expressed as a percent of the base year. $\dfrac{\text{Each item}}{\text{Base amount}}$	<table><tr><td></td><td>2010</td><td>2009</td><td>2008</td></tr><tr><td>Sales</td><td>$200</td><td>$300</td><td>$400 ← Base year</td></tr><tr><td></td><td>50%</td><td>75%</td><td>100%</td></tr></table> $\left(\dfrac{\$200}{\$400}\right)\ \left(\dfrac{\$300}{\$400}\right)$
Ratios, p. 395	Tools to interpret items on financial reports.	Use this example for calculating the following ratios: current assets, $30,000; accounts receivable, $12,000; total current liabilities, $20,000; inventory, $6,000; prepaid expenses, $2,000; net sales, $72,000; total assets, $60,000; net income, $15,000; total liabilities, $30,000.
Current ratio, p. 396	$\dfrac{\text{Current assets}}{\text{Current liabilities}}$	$\dfrac{\$30,000}{\$20,000} = 1.5$
Acid test (quick ratio), p. 396	$\dfrac{\text{Current assets} - \text{Inventory} - \text{Prepaid expenses}}{\text{Current liabilities}}$ Called quick assets	$\dfrac{\$30,000 - \$6,000 - \$2,000}{\$20,000} = 1.1$

(continues)

CHAPTER ORGANIZER AND STUDY GUIDE
WITH CHECK FIGURES FOR EXTRA PRACTICE QUIZZES (concluded)

Topic	Key point, procedure, formula	Example(s) to illustrate situation
Average day's collection, p. 396	$\dfrac{\dfrac{\text{Accounts receivable}}{\text{Net sales}}}{360}$	$\dfrac{\$12,000}{\dfrac{\$72,000}{360}} = 60 \text{ days}$
Total debt to total assets, p. 396	$\dfrac{\text{Total liabilities}}{\text{Total assets}}$	$\dfrac{\$30,000}{\$60,000} = 50\%$
Return on equity, p. 396	$\dfrac{\text{Net income}}{\text{Stockholders' equity (A} - \text{L)}}$	$\dfrac{\$15,000}{\$30,000} = 50\%$
Asset turnover, p. 396	$\dfrac{\text{Net sales}}{\text{Total assets}}$	$\dfrac{\$72,000}{\$60,000} = 1.2$
Profit margin on net sales, p. 396	$\dfrac{\text{Net income}}{\text{Net sales}}$	$\dfrac{\$15,000}{\$72,000} = .2083 = 20.83\%$

KEY TERMS	Accounts payable, p. 385 Accounts receivable, p. 385 Acid test, p. 396 Assets, p. 384 Asset turnover, p. 396 Balance sheet, p. 384 Capital, p. 384 Common stock, p. 386 Comparative statement, p. 387 Corporation, p. 384 Cost of merchandise (goods) sold, p. 391 Current assets, p. 384 Current liabilities, p. 385 Current ratio, p. 396 Expenses, p. 392 Gross profit from sales, p. 392 Gross sales, p. 391	Horizontal analysis, p. 388 Income statement, p. 389 Liabilities, p. 385 Long-term liabilities, p. 385 Merchandise inventory, p. 385 Mortgage note payable, p. 385 Net income, p. 392 Net purchases, p. 392 Net sales, p. 391 Operating expenses, p. 392 Owner's equity, p. 386 Partnership, p. 384 Plant and equipment, p. 385 Prepaid expenses, p. 385 Purchase discounts, p. 391 Purchase returns and allowances, p. 391 Purchases, p. 391 Quick assets, p. 396 Quick ratio, p. 396 Ratio analysis, p. 395 Retained earnings, p. 386 Return on equity, p. 396 Revenues, p. 391 Salaries payable, p. 385 Sales (not trade) discounts, p. 391 Sales returns and allowances, p. 391 Sole proprietorship, p. 384 Stockholders' equity, p. 384 Trend analysis, p. 394 Vertical analysis, p. 387
CHECK FIGURES FOR EXTRA PRACTICE QUIZZES WITH PAGE REFERENCES	LU 16–1a (p. 389) 1. a. 21.11%; 25% b. 10.56%; 12.86% c. 8.89%; 7.86% d. 11.11%; 11.43% 2. 45.45%	LU 16–2a (p. 394) 1. a. $33,200 b. $7,500 c. $25,700 d. $17,600 LU 16–3a (p. 396) 1. 36%; 86%; 71%; 100% 2. a. 1.6 b. 1.12 c. 54.2 d. 21.92%

Critical Thinking Discussion Questions

1. What is the difference between current assets and plant and equipment? Do you think land should be allowed to depreciate?

2. What items make up stockholders' equity? Why might a person form a sole proprietorship instead of a corporation?

3. Explain the steps to complete a vertical or horizontal analysis relating to balance sheets. Why are the percents not summed vertically in horizontal analysis?

4. How do you calculate net sales, cost of merchandise (goods) sold, gross profit, and net income? Why do we need two separate figures for inventory in the cost of merchandise (goods) sold section?

5. Explain how to calculate the following: current ratios, acid test, average day's collection, total debt to assets, return on equity, asset turnover, and profit margin on net sales. How often do you think ratios should be calculated?

6. What is trend analysis? Explain how the portion formula assists in preparing a trend analysis.

Name _____ Date _____

DRILL PROBLEMS

16–1. As the accountant for Vic's Grooming, prepare a December 31, 2010, balance sheet like that for The Card Shop (LU 16–1) from the following: cash, $28,000; accounts payable, $16,000; merchandise inventory, $10,000; Vic Sullivan, capital, $39,000; and equipment, $17,000.

16–2. From the following, prepare a classified balance sheet for Lowell Company as of December 31, 2010, Ending merchandise inventory was $3,000 for the year.

Cash	$2,000	Accounts payable	$1,200
Prepaid rent	1,200	Salaries payable	1,500
Prepaid insurance	2,000	Note payable (long term)	2,000
Office equipment (net)	3,000	J. Lowell, capital*	6,500

*What the owner supplies to the business. Replaces common stock and retained earnings section.

16–3. Complete a horizontal analysis for Brown Company (round percents to the nearest hundredth):

			INCREASE (DECREASE)	
BROWN COMPANY Comparative Balance Sheet December 31, 2009 and 2010	2010	2009	Amount	Percent
Assets				
Current assets:				
Cash	$ 15,750	$10,500		
Accounts receivable	18,000	13,500		
Merchandise inventory	18,750	22,500		
Prepaid advertising	54,000	45,000		
Total current assets	$106,500	$ 91,500		
Plant and equipment:				
Building (net)	$120,000	$126,000		
Land	90,000	90,000		
Total plant and equipment	$210,000	$216,000		
Total assets	$316,500	$307,500		
Liabilities				
Current liabilities:				
Accounts payable	$132,000	$120,000		
Salaries payable	22,500	18,000		
Total current liabilities	$154,500	$138,000		
Long-term liabilities:				
Mortgage note payable	99,000	87,000		
Total liabilities	$253,500	$225,000		
Owner's Equity				
J. Brown, capital	63,000	82,500		
Total liabilities and owner's equity	$316,500	$307,500		

16–4. Prepare an income statement for Munroe Sauce for the year ended December 31, 2010. Beginning inventory was $1,248. Ending inventory was $1,600.

Sales	$34,900
Sales returns and allowances	1,092
Sales discount	1,152
Purchases	10,512
Purchase discounts	540
Depreciation expense	115
Salary expense	5,200
Insurance expense	2,600
Utilities expense	210
Plumbing expense	250
Rent expense	180

16–5. The following is a partial list of financial highlights from a Motorola annual report:

	2008	2007
	(dollars in millions)	
Net sales	$37,580	$33,075
Earnings before taxes	2,231	1,283
Net earnings	1,318	891

Complete a horizontal and vertical analysis from the above information. Round to the nearest hundredth percent.

16–6. From the Lowell Instrument Corporation second-quarter report ended 2010, do a vertical analysis for the second quarter of 2010.

LOWELL INSTRUMENT CORPORATION AND SUBSIDIARIES Consolidated Statements of Operation (Unaudited) (In thousands of dollars, except share data)			
	SECOND QUARTER		
	2010	2009	Percent of net
Net sales	$6,698	$6,951	
Cost of sales	4,089	4,462	
Gross margin	2,609	2,489	
Expenses:			
Selling, general and administrative	1,845	1,783	
Product development	175	165	
Interest expense	98	123	
Other (income), net	(172)	(99)	
Total expenses	1,946	1,972	
Income before income taxes	663	517	
Provision for income taxes	265	209	
Net income	$398	$308	
Net income per common share*	$.05	$.03	
Weighted average number of common shares and equivalents	6,673,673	6,624,184	

*Income per common share reflects the deduction of the preferred stock dividend from net income.
†Off due to rounding.

16–7. Complete the comparative income statement and balance sheet for Logic Company (round percents to the nearest hundredth):

LOGIC COMPANY Comparative Income Statement For Years Ended December 31, 2010 and 2011				
			INCREASE (DECREASE)	
	2011	2010	Amount	Percent
Gross sales	$19,000	$15,000		
Sales returns and allowances	1,000	100		
Net sales	$18,000	$14,900		
Cost of merchandise (goods) sold	12,000	9,000		
Gross profit	$ 6,000	$ 5,900		
Operating expenses:				
Depreciation	$ 700	$ 600		
Selling and administrative	2,200	2,000		
Research	550	500		
Miscellaneous	360	300		
Total operating expenses	$ 3,810	$ 3,400		
Income before interest and taxes	$ 2,190	$ 2,500		
Interest expense	560	500		
Income before taxes	$ 1,630	$ 2,000		
Provision for taxes	640	800		
Net income	$ 990	$ 1,200		

LOGIC COMPANY Comparative Balance Sheet December 31, 2010 and 2011				
	2011		2010	
	Amount	Percent	Amount	Percent
Assets				
Current assets:				
Cash	$12,000		$ 9,000	
Accounts receivable	16,500		12,500	
Merchandise inventory	8,500		14,000	
Prepaid expenses	24,000		10,000	
Total current assets	$61,000		$45,500	
Plant and equipment:				
Building (net)	$14,500		$11,000	
Land	13,500		9,000	
Total plant and equipment	$28,000		$20,000	
Total assets	$89,000		$65,500	
Liabilities				
Current liabilities:				
Accounts payable	$13,000		$ 7,000	
Salaries payable	7,000		5,000	
Total current liabilities	$20,000		$12,000	
Long-term liabilities:				
Mortgage note payable	22,000		20,500	
Total liabilities	$42,000		$32,500	
Stockholders' Equity				
Common stock	$21,000		$21,000	
Retained earnings	26,000		12,000	
Total stockholders' equity	$47,000		$33,000	
Total liabilities and stockholders' equity	$89,000		$65,500	

*Due to rounding.

From Problem 16–7, your supervisor has requested that you calculate the following ratios (round to the nearest hundredth):

	2011	**2010**
16–8. Current ratio.		
16–9. Acid test.		
16–10. Average day's collection.		
16–11. Asset turnover.		
16–12. Total debt to total assets.		
16–13. Net income (after tax) to the net sales.		
16–14. Return on equity (after tax).		

16–8.

16–9.

16–10.

16–11.

16–12.

16–13.

16–14.

WORD PROBLEMS

16–15. The *St. Joseph News-Press* (MO) on November 10, 2006 reported net income to producers of ethanol soared. Sales of fuel-grade alcohol grew from $3.55 million to $4.3 million. What was the percent increase in sales? Round to the nearest hundredth percent.

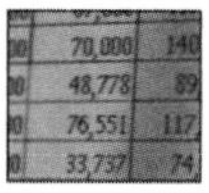

16–16. In the February 12, 2007 issue of *Forbes,* it was reported that net income at Texex, a construction equipment company, shot up 95% to $299 million on sales of $5.6 billion. **(a)** What was the net income last year? Round to nearest tenth million. **(b)** Net income is what percent of total sales? Round to the nearest hundredth percent.

16 – 17. Find the following ratios for Motorola Credit Corporation's annual report: **(a)** total debt to total assets, **(b)** return on equity, **(c)** asset turnover (to nearest cent), and **(d)** profit margin on net sales. Round to the nearest hundredth percent.

(dollars in millions)

Net revenue (sales)	$ 265
Net earnings	147
Total assets	2,015
Total liabilities	1,768
Total stockholders' equity	427

16–18. In the December 2006 edition of *Chicago* magazine, sales figures were presented for the past 5 years on merchandise sold at Chicago department and discount stores ($million) Sales in 2005 were $3,154; 2004 $3,414; in 2003 $3,208; in 2002 $3,152 and in 2001 $3,216. Using 2001 as the base year, complete a trend analysis, round each percent to the nearest whole percent.

16–19. Don Williams received a memo requesting that he complete a trend analysis of the following numbers using 2009 as the base year and rounding each percent to the nearest whole percent. Could you help Don with the request?

	2012	2011	2010	2009
Sales	$340,000	$400,000	$420,000	$500,000
Gross profit	180,000	240,000	340,000	400,000
Net income	70,000	90,000	40,000	50,000

CHALLENGE PROBLEMS

16–20. The *Federal Express Annual Report* reported the following financial highlights in millions for the years 2003 and 2002. Madeleine Paine is a stockholder and is trying to analyze this report.

	2003	2002
Revenues	$22,487	$20,607
Net income	830	710
Total assets	15,385	13,812
Common stockholders' investment	7,288	6,545

REVENUE (IN BILLIONS)				
2003	2002	2001	2000	1999
$22.5	$20.6	$19.6	$18.3	$16.8

(a) What was the percent increase/decrease for each of the above? Round to the nearest hundredth percent. **(b)** What is the return on equity for each year? Round to nearest hundredth percent. **(c)** What was the asset turnover for each year? Round to nearest hundredth. **(d)** What is the profit margin on sales for each year? Round to nearest hundredth percent. **(e)** Using 1999 as the base year, prepare a trend analysis. Round to the nearest whole percent.

16 – 21. As the accountant for Tootsie Roll, you are asked to calculate the current ratio and the quick ratio for the following partial financial statement. Round to the nearest tenth.

Assets		Liabilities	
Current assets:		Current liabilities:	
Cash and cash equivalents (Note 1)	$ 4,224,190	Notes payable to banks	$ 672,221
Investments (Note 1)	32,533,769	Accounts payable	7,004,075
Accounts receivable, less allowances of $748,000 and $744,000	16,206,648	Dividends payable	576,607
		Accrued liabilities (Note 5)	9,826,534
Inventories (Note 1):		Income taxes payable	4,471,429
Finished goods and work in progress	12,650,955		
Raw materials and supplies	10,275,858		
Prepaid expenses	2,037,710		

SUMMARY PRACTICE TEST

1. Given: Gross sales, $170,000; sales returns and allowances, $9,000; beginning inventory, $8,000; net purchases, $18,000; ending inventory, $5,000; and operating expenses, $56,000. Calculate (a) net sales, (b) cost of merchandise (goods) sold, (c) gross profit from sales, and (d) net income. *(p. 392)*

2. Complete the following partial comparative balance sheet by filling in the total current assets and percent column; assume no plant and equipment (round to the nearest hundredth percent as needed). *(p. 386)*

	Amount	Percent	Amount	Percent
Assets				
Current assets:				
Cash	$ 9,000		$ 8,000	
Accounts receivable	5,000		7,500	
Merchandise inventory	12,000		6,900	
Prepaid expenses	7,000		8,000	
Total current assets				

*Due to rounding.

3. Calculate the amount of increase or decrease and the percent change of each item (round to the nearest hundredth percent as needed). *(p. 387)*

	2011	2010	Amount	Percent
Cash	$19,000	$ 8,000		
Land	70,000	30,000		
Accounts payable	21,000	10,000		

4. Complete a trend analysis for sales (round to the nearest whole percent and use 2010 as the base year). *(p. 395)*

	2013	2012	2011	2010
Sales	$140,000	$350,000	$210,000	$190,000

5. From the following, prepare a balance sheet for True Corporation as of December 31, 2011. *(p. 385)*

Building	$40,000	Mortgage note payable	$70,000
Merchandise inventory	12,000	Common stock	10,000
Cash	15,000	Retained earnings	37,000
Land	90,000	Accounts receivable	9,000
Accounts payable	50,000	Salaries payable	8,000
Prepaid rent	9,000		

6. Solve from the following facts (round to the nearest hundredth). *(p. 396)*

Current assets	$14,000	Net sales	$40,000
Accounts receivable	5,000	Total assets	$38,000
Current liabilities	20,000	Net income	$10,100
Inventory	4,000		

   a. Current ratio

   b. Acid test

   c. Average day's collection

   d. Asset turnover

   e. Profit margin on sales

As a job reference, tell the whole TRUTH

MONEY & ETHICS
by Knight Kiplinger

I *was recently called by a human-resources manager checking the references of an applicant who used to work for me. The person had been a poor performer and was "counseled out" of our firm. What's the most ethical way to respond?*

In these litigious times, employment lawyers often advise against saying anything negative about a former employee, lest you be vulnerable to a defamation charge. They suggest that you confirm nothing more than dates of employment and job description. Although that's the safe thing to do, it leads to poor performers being passed along from one job to the next. I prefer to give a balanced account of the former employee's work, sticking to the facts—and trusting in confidentiality. Wouldn't you appreciate this candor if you were the one making the hiring decision?

I have a friend who uses his corporate stationery for virtually all his correspondence, including consumer complaints, college-alumni work and club-membership recommendations, even soliciting friends' support for charities. Is this acceptable?

Not only is it poor etiquette, but it's also unethical to trade on the stature of his employer for his own purposes (especially in a personal consumer complaint). Companies should make it clear that their letterhead is for business correspondence only.

Have a money-and-ethics question you'd like answered in this column? Write editor in chief Knight Kiplinger at ethics@kiplinger.com.

FAQ | Are cash-balance pension plans protected if the employer goes bankrupt?

Pension PROTECTION

YES, THEY are insured by the Pension Benefit Guaranty Corp. Cash-balance pensions resemble 401(k)s in that you have an account that builds until you retire or leave the company. Usually, you're credited with a percentage of your pay each year and earn a fixed or variable interest rate. Unlike 401(k)s, though, you don't contribute your own money or direct the investments. The company is obligated to pay the benefit that you're due. If the employer terminates the plan for lack of money, the PBGC will assume trusteeship and pay benefits within certain limits. The maximum annual benefit in plans terminating in 2007 is $49,500. The PBGC cannot guarantee more than what your firm pays at normal retirement age (in other words, it won't support early-out inducements), and it won't guaran-

● **You won't be left high and dry by your cash-balance plan, thanks to Uncle Sam's pension guaranty.**

tee benefit increases made within five years of the plan's termination. Recent court decisions and provisions in the pension-reform law enacted last year make it likely that more firms will adopt cash-balance plans.

STOCK TO WATCH
That GREAT STREET

It used to be a commercial bank, and the name suggests real estate, but State Street Corp. (symbol STT) is the glue for capital markets. It runs exchange-traded funds, it's custodian for pension funds and mutual funds, and it manages institutional money. State Street prospers from the worldwide expansion of investing and fund management: It does 40% of its business in foreign countries, which has Michael Mayo of Prudential Securities, a bear on ordinary banks, recommending State Street *con mucho gusto*. Or is it *élan?*

STATE STREET

State Street Corp.
SYMBOL: STT
PRICE: $71
2006 TOTAL RETURN: 23.2%

22 PERCENT of U.S. workers are covered by cash-balance pension plans. The money accounts for 26% of all pension assets.

BUSINESS MATH ISSUE

Corporations have no ethics—strictly the bottom line motivates them.

1. List the key points of the article and information to support your position.
2. Write a group defense of your position using math calculations to support your view.

Slater's Business Math Scrapbook

with Internet Application

Putting Your Skills to Work

PROJECT A
Find out what *impairment* means.

TV-Tube Venture of Philips, LG Plans to Take Impairment Charge

By Yun-Hee Kim
Dow Jones Newswires

SEOUL, South Korea—LG.Philips Displays said it will take a $725 million impairment charge in the fourth quarter related to a sales slump in cathode-ray-tube television sets.

The Hong Kong joint venture, between **LG Electronics** Inc. of South Korea and **Philips Electronics** NV of the Netherlands, said that capacity increases and "very strong" price erosion of flat-panel TV sets have created "adverse market conditions" for CRTs in markets such as Europe. The joint venture makes CRTs for TV sets and computer monitors.

"The resulting reduction in demand for CRTs has adversely affected LG.Philips Displays operations," LG.Philips Displays said, adding that "several options" are being evaluated to improve its business position and financial structure. The company didn't elaborate on the options, and a company representative couldn't immediately be reached for comment.

CRT manufacturers such as LG.Philips Displays and **Samsung SDI** Co. of South Korea have seen demand for their main products wane as consumers replace bulky CRT TV sets with slimmer and more-fashionable flat-panel alternatives such as plasma and liquid-crystal displays, prices for which have fallen sharply during recent months.

Both Philips and LG Electronics retain a 50% stake in LG.Philips Displays, which has been struggling from dwindling demand for CRTs.

Brian Sohn, manager of LG Electronics' investor relations, said the charge to be incurred by the joint venture is expected to have "limited" impact on LG Electronics' fourth-quarter earnings.

A representative at Philips, based in Amsterdam, couldn't immediately be reached for comment.

According to figures released by LG Electronics, LG.Philips Displays posted an operating profit of $15 million on sales of $690 million in the third quarter.

Wall Street Journal © 2005

Hitting the Spot
Retail giant Wal-Mart still towers over Target. For fiscal year ended Jan.31, 2004:

COMPANY	NET SALES (IN BILLIONS)	SALES PER SQ. FOOT	NET INCOME, (IN BILLIONS)	TOTAL U.S. AD SPENDING (IN MILLIONS)	U.S. DISCOUNT STORES[2]	U.S. SUPER STORES[2]	EMPLOYEES
Wal-Mart	$256	$433	$9.1	$487	1,362	1,671	1,200,000
Target	$48[1]	$282	$1.8	$474	1,313	136	273,000

[1] Includes credit card revenues   [2] Wal-Mart stores as of Oct. 31; Target stores as of Nov. 4

Source: the companies; Sanford C. Bernstein, LLC; TNS Media Intelligence/CMR

Wall Street Journal © 2004

PROJECT B
Calculate profit margin on net sales. Round to nearest hundredth percent.

 Internet Projects: See text Web site (www.mhhe.com/slater9e) and The Business Math Internet Resource Guide.

Video Case

As a child, Jalem Getz, the CEO of Buycostumes.com put little thought into his Halloween costumes. Now he thinks about costumes all year long.

Jalem Getz founded online business Buycostumes in a warehouse in the Milwaukee suburbs in 1999 taking advantage of Wisconsin's central U.S. location and cheap rent. Getz used to dislike the lack of seasons in his native California. Now, he uses the extreme seasonality of the Halloween business to turn a big profit.

The company got its start as brick-and-mortar retail business owned by Getz and partner Jon Majdoch. While still in their early 20s, the two began operating a chain of seasonal Halloween Express franchise stores, and then branched out into a couple of lamp and home accessory shops.

In 2001, the company changed its name to Buyseasons, Inc. to reflect its new broader focus. "Rather than just focus on one season, we target consumers in different seasons," said Jalem Getz. The Buycostumes name is still in broad use.

Being an e-tailer means not having to open a retail space for just two months of the year, or stock other items. Money saved on storefronts goes to maintaining a stock of 10,000 Halloween items – 100 times what most retailers carry for the season.

"Our selection sets us apart," Getz said. "A lot of customers are looking for something unique, by having that large selection we immediately build that additional goodwill."

The key to Buyseasons' success limiting the choice of merchandise to items that can't readily be found in neighborhood stores. That means less price competition and higher margins for Byseasons, which has been maintaining a 47.5 percent gross margin rate on the buycostumes.com site.

In July 2006, Liberty Media announced plans to acquire Buycostumes.com Inc. 500 company, for an undisclosed sum. Getz will stay on as CEO.

Buycostumes.com is the biggest online seller of costumes. It was ranked on October 2005 in Inc. magazine as the 75th –fastest growing U.S. private firm, with revenue of $17.6 million last year and three-year growth of 1,046 percent. Sales this year are expected to hit $25 million to $28 million, according to Getz.

Other online Halloween firms also predicted double-digit growth in 2005 – according to a forecast by the National Retail Federation the entire industry would have a 5% gain, leading to a record $3.3 billion in sales for the entire industry.

BuySeasons' sales reached nearly $30 million in 2005, Getz said, up from $17.6 million in 2004. The company's sales are expected to post 50% annual growth over the next three year. The company bills itself as the world's largest Internet retailer of Halloween costumes and accessories.

PROBLEM 1

The video stated the shipment of packages will increase from a normal 500 packages per day to as many as 30,000 packages per day. Phone calls would increase from 1,600 per week to 30,000 a week. **(a)** What is the percent of increase in packages per day? Round to the nearest hundredth percent. **(b)** What is the percent of increase in phone calls per week?

PROBLEM 2

The video advertises the "Mrs. Franklin Adult" costume with a retail value of $149.99 and Buycostumes.com price of $99.99. The "American Revolutionary Adult" costume with a retail value $314.99 and Buycostumes.com price of $239.99. **(a)** What is the dollar amount of savings achieved by purchasing on-line for each costume? **(b)** What is the percent savings by purchasing on-line for each costume? Round to the nearest hundredth percent.

PROBLEM 3

On March 26, 2006, the *Milwaukee Journal Sentinel* reported BuySeasons, which now leases 81,000 square feet in a business park, wanted to move to a 200,000-square-foot building. The May 3, 2006 issue reported the Zoning, Neighborhoods & Development Committee voted 3-1 to recommend the sale of 9.2 acres in Menomonee Valley Industrial Center to house a new headquarters for BuySeasons, operative of Buycostumes.com., at a price of $110,000 per acre. **(a)** What would be the percent increase in space for BuySeasons? Round to the nearest hundredth percent. **(b)** What would be the total price for the land?

PROBLEM 4

In 2007, the company expects to have just over 600 seasonal employees. The number of seasonal employees is expected to exceed 800 in 2008 and 900 in 2009. In 2007, the company would employ 90 full employees, 126 in 2008, and 161 in 2009. **(a)** Complete a trend analysis of seasonal employees for the three years. **(b)** Complete a trend analysis of full time employees for the three years using 2007 as the base year. Round to the nearest whole percent.

PROBLEM 5

On October 30, 2006, *USA Today* reported on the booming number of young adults who treat themselves to Halloween fun. The 18- to 24-year old group is spending an average of $30.38 on costumes this year, a 38% increase over 2005, according to the National Federation and BIGresearch. Those 25 to 34 will spend an average of $31.33 up 17%. National Costumers Association President Debbie Lyn Owens says college students suiting up for parties are fueling much of the costume growth. **(a)** What was the average amount spent on costumes for the 18- to 24-year old group in 2004? **(b)** What was the average amount spent on costumes for the 26–34 group in 2004? Round your answer to the nearest cent.

PROBLEM 6

The company's seasonal employees earn between $9.00 to $16.00 per hour, the company is required to pay time and one half for overtime. A seasonal worker works 43 hours the first week of his employment. He is married and has no children. His hourly pay is $14.50 per hour. **(a)** What is his gross pay for the week? **(b)** How much is deducted for Social Security? **(c)** How much is deducted for Medicare? (d) How much is withheld for Federal Income Tax? Round your answers to the nearest cents. (Note: See Chapter 9 on Payroll or Math Handbook)

PROBLEM 7

Buycostumes.com had annual sales in 2005 of $30 million, mostly in the months before Halloween. The company had a 31% share of the online Halloween market. According to Hitwise, an Internet tracking company, the company is expected to hit $50 million in sales in 2006. **(a)** with 31% of the market, what would be the total dollar amount spent for costumes? Round to the nearest million dollars. **(b)** What is the anticipated percent increase next year for Buycostumers? Round to the nearest hundredth percent.

PROBLEM 8

Sales reached nearly $30 million in 2005, said the company CEO up from $17.6 millions in 2004. What was the percent increase? Round to the nearest hundredth percent.

PROBLEM 9

The National Retail Federation predicted a 5 percent gain to a record $3.3 billion for 2005. **(a)** What would have been the sales for 2004? The Halloween firms predicted at least a 10 percent gain for 2005. *(b)* What is the amount the Halloween firms predicted for 2005? **(c)** How much of an increase would this be? Round your answers to the nearest hundredth.

PROBLEM 10

In 2001 Buycostumes.com had sales of approximately $4 million with 11 full-time employees. In 2005 sales grew nearly $30 million and in 2009 full-time employees are expected to grow to 161. **(a)** What was the percent growth in sales? **(b)** What is the expected percent growth of full-time employees? Round to the nearest percent.

CHAPTER 17

Depreciation

LEARNING UNIT OBJECTIVES

LU 17–1: Concept of Depreciation and the Straight-Line Method

- Explain the concept and causes of depreciation (*p. 413*).
- Prepare a depreciation schedule and calculate partial-year depreciation (*p. 414–415*).

LU 17–2: Units-of-Production Method

- Explain how use affects the units-of-production method (*p. 415*).
- Prepare a depreciation schedule (*p. 416*).

LU 17–3: Declining-Balance Method

- Explain the importance of residual value in the depreciation schedule (*p. 417*).
- Prepare a depreciation schedule (*p. 417*).

LU 17–4: Modified Accelerated Cost Recovery System (MACRS) with Introduction to ACRS

- Explain the goals of ACRS and MACRS and their limitations (*p. 418*).
- Calculate depreciation using the MACRS guidelines (*p. 419*).

This chapter concentrates on depreciation—a business operating expense. In Learning Units 17–1 to 17–3, we discuss methods of calculating depreciation for financial reporting. In Learning Unit 17–4, we look at how tax laws force companies to report depreciation for tax purposes. Financial reporting methods and the tax-reporting methods are both legal.

Learning Unit 17–1: Concept of Depreciation and the Straight-Line Method

Companies frequently buy assets such as equipment or buildings that will last longer than 1 year. JCPenney would be an example of this. As time passes, these assets depreciate, or lose some of their market value. The total cost of these assets cannot be shown in *1 year* as an expense of running the business. In a systematic and logical way, companies must estimate the asset cost they show as an expense of a particular period. This process is called **depreciation.**

Remember that depreciation *does not* measure the amount of deterioration or decline in the market value of the asset. Depreciation is simply a means of recognizing that these assets are depreciating. For example, the *Wall Street Journal* clipping "IRS to Allow Depreciation of Some Golf-Green Costs" reports that some golf greens are depreciated for tax purposes.

IRS to Allow Depreciation Of Some Golf-Green Costs

Dow Jones Newswires

WASHINGTON—Certain land-improvement costs associated with "modern" golf greens are depreciable for tax purposes, the Internal Revenue Service said.

In a ruling released yesterday, the IRS said old-fashioned "push up" or natural-soil greens will remain nondepreciable but that certain costs incurred in the original construction or reconstruction of "modern" golf-course greens, which feature substantial integrated drainage systems, will be depreciable.

According to the IRS's ruling, "push up or natural soil greens are essentially landscaping that involves some reshaping or regrading of the land." Those greens may have limited irrigation systems, such as hoses and sprinklers adjacent, but a subsurface drainage system isn't used.

The IRS said modern greens make use of technological changes in green design and construction and contain sophisticated drainage systems.

Reprinted by permission of The Wall Street Journal, © 2000 Dow Jones & Company, Inc. All Rights Reserved Worldwide.

The depreciation process results in **depreciation expense** that involves three key factors: (1) **asset cost**—amount the company paid for the asset including freight and charges relating to the asset; (2) **estimated useful life**—number of years or time periods for which the company can use the asset; and (3) **residual value (salvage** or **trade-in value)**—expected cash value at the end of the asset's useful life. For example, the useful life of JCPenney's buildings is estimated at 50 years.

Depreciation expense is listed on the income statement. The **accumulated depreciation** title on the balance sheet gives the amount of the asset's depreciation taken to date. Asset cost less accumulated depreciation is the asset's book value. The **book value** shows the unused amount of the asset cost that the company may depreciate in future accounting periods. At the end of the asset's life, the asset's book value is the same as its residual value—book value cannot be less than residual value.

Depending on the amount and timetable of an asset's depreciation, a company can increase or decrease its profit. If a company shows greater depreciation in earlier years, the company will have a lower reported profit and pay less in taxes. Thus, depreciation can be an indirect tax savings for the company.

Later in the chapter we will discuss the different methods of computing depreciation that spread the cost of an asset over specified periods of time. However, first let's look at some of the major causes of depreciation.

Causes of Depreciation

As assets, all machines have an estimated amount of usefulness simply because as companies use the assets, the assets gradually wear out. The cause of this depreciation is *physical deterioration.*

The growth of a company can also cause depreciation. Many companies begin on a small scale. As the companies grow, they often find their equipment and buildings inadequate. The use of depreciation enables these businesses to "write off" their old, inadequate equipment and buildings. Companies cannot depreciate land. For example, a garbage dump can be depreciated but not the land.

Harry Cabluck/AP Wide World

Another cause of depreciation is the result of advances in technology. The computers that companies bought a few years ago may be in perfect working condition but outdated. Companies may find it necessary to replace these old computers with more sophisticated, faster, and possibly more economical machines. Thus, *product obsolescence* is a key factor contributing to depreciation.

Now we are ready to begin our study of depreciation methods. The first method we will study is straight-line depreciation. It is also the most common of the three depreciation methods (straight line, units of production, and declining balance). In a survey of 600 corporations, 81% responded that they used straight-line depreciation.

Straight-Line Method

The **straight-line method** of depreciation is used more than any other method. It tries to distribute the same amount of expense to each period of time. Most large companies, such as Gillette Corporation, Southwest Airlines, Campbell's Soup, and General Mills use the straight-line method. *Today, more than 90% of U.S. companies depreciate by straight line.* For example, let's assume Ajax Company bought equipment for $2,500. The company estimates that the equipment's period of "usefulness"—or *useful life*—will be 5 years. After 5 years the equipment will have a residual value (salvage value) of $500. The company decides to calculate its depreciation with the straight-line method and uses the following formula:

$$\frac{\text{Depreciation expense}}{\text{each year}} = \frac{\text{Cost} - \text{Residual value}}{\text{Estimated useful life in years}}$$

$$\frac{\$2,500 - \$500}{5 \text{ years}} = \$400 \text{ depreciation expense taken each year}$$

Table 17.1 gives a summary of the equipment depreciation that Ajax Company will take over the next 5 years. Companies call this summary a **depreciation schedule.** A corporation like Southwest Airlines depreciates its flight equipment 20 to 25 years.

TABLE 17.1

Depreciation schedule for straight-line method

$$\frac{100\%}{\text{Number of years}} = \frac{100\%}{5} = 20\%$$

Thus, the company is depreciating the equipment at a 20% rate each year.

End of year	Cost of equipment	Depreciation expense for year	Accumulated depreciation at end of year	Book value at end of year (Cost − Accumulated depreciation)
1	$2,500	$400	$ 400	$2,100 ($2,500 − $400)
2	2,500	400	800	1,700
3	2,500	400	1,200	1,300
4	2,500	400	1,600	900
5	2,500	400	2,000	500
	↑	↑	↑	↑
	Cost stays the same.	Depreciation expense is same each year.	Accumulated depreciation increases by $400 each year.	Book value is lowered by $400 until residual value of $500 is reached.

Depreciation for Partial Years

If a company buys an asset before the 15th of the month, the company calculates the asset's depreciation for a full month. Companies do not take the full month's depreciation for assets bought after the 15th of the month. For example, assume Ajax Company (Table 17.1) bought the equipment on May 6. The company would calculate the depreciation for the first year as follows:

$$\frac{\$2,500 - \$500}{5 \text{ years}} = \$400 \times \frac{8}{12} = \$266.67$$

Now let's check your progress with the Practice Quiz before we look at the next depreciation method.

LU 17–1   PRACTICE QUIZ

Complete this **Practice Quiz** to see how you are doing

1. Prepare a depreciation schedule using straight-line depreciation for the following:
   Cost of truck $16,000
   Residual value   1,000
   Life   5 years
2. If the truck were bought on February 3, what would the depreciation expense be in the first year?

✓ Solutions

1.

End of year	Cost of truck	Depreciation expense for year	Accumulated depreciation at end of year	Book value at end of year (Cost − Accumulated depreciation)
1	$16,000	$3,000	$ 3,000	$13,000 ($16,000 − $3,000)
2	16,000	3,000	6,000	10,000
3	16,000	3,000	9,000	7,000
4	16,000	3,000	12,000	4,000
5	16,000	3,000	15,000	1,000 ← Note that we are down to residual value

2. $\frac{\$16,000 - \$1,000}{5} = \$3,000 \times \frac{11}{12} = \boxed{\$2,750}$

LU 17–1a   EXTRA PRACTICE QUIZ

Need more practice? Try this **Extra Practice Quiz** (check figures in Chapter Organizer, p. 421)

1. Prepare a depreciation schedule using straight-line depreciation for the following:
   Cost of truck $20,000
   Residual value   2,000
   Life   3 years
2. If the truck were bought on February 3, what would the depreciation expense be in the first year?

Learning Unit 17–2: Units-of-Production Method

Unlike in the straight-line depreciation method, in the **units-of-production method** the passage of time is not used to determine an asset's depreciation amount. Instead, the company determines the asset's depreciation according to how much the company uses the asset. This use could be miles driven, tons hauled, or units that a machine produces. For example, when a company such as Ajax Company (in Learning Unit 17–1) buys equipment, the company estimates how many units the equipment can produce. Let's assume the equipment has a useful life of 4,000 units. The following formulas are used to calculate the equipment's depreciation for the units-of-production method.

TABLE	17.2	Depreciation schedule for units-of-production method

End of year	Cost of equipment	Units produced	Depreciation expense for year	Accumulated depreciation at end of year	Book value at end of year (Cost − Accumulated depreciation)
1	$2,500	300	$ 150 (300 × $.50)	$ 150	$2,350 ($2,500 − $150)
2	2,500	400	200	350	2,150
3	2,500	600	300	650	1,850
4	2,500	2,000	1,000	1,650	850
5	2,500	700 ↑ At the end of 5 years, the equipment produced 4,000 units. If in year 5 the equipment produced 1,500 units, only 700 could be used in the calculation, or it will go below the equipment's residual value.	350 ↑ Units produced per year times $.50 equals depreciation expense.	2,000	500 ↑ Residual value of $500 is reached. (Be sure depreciation is not taken below the residual value.)

$$\frac{\text{Depreciation}}{\text{per unit}} = \frac{\text{Cost} - \text{Residual value}}{\text{Total estimated units produced}} = \frac{\$2,500 - \$500}{4,000 \text{ units}} = \$.50 \text{ per unit}$$

$$\frac{\text{Depreciation}}{\text{amount}} = \frac{\text{Unit}}{\text{depreciation}} \times \frac{\text{Units}}{\text{produced}} = \$.50 \text{ times actual number of units}$$

Now we can complete Table 17.2. Note that the table gives the units produced each year. Let's check your understanding of this unit with the Practice Quiz.

LU 17–2	PRACTICE QUIZ

Complete this **Practice Quiz** to see how you are doing

$$\frac{\$20,000 - \$4,000}{16,000} = \$1$$

From the following facts prepare a depreciation schedule:

Machine cost	$20,000
Residual value	4,000

Expected to produce 16,000 units over its expected life

	2006	2007	2008	2009	2010
Units produced:	2,000	8,000	3,000	1,800	1,600

✓ **Solutions**

End of year	Cost of machine	Units produced	Depreciation expense for year	Accumulated depreciation at end of year	Book value at end of year (Cost − Accumulated depreciation)
1	$20,000	2,000	$2,000 (2,000 × $1)	$ 2,000	$18,000
2	20,000	8,000	8,000	10,000	10,000
3	20,000	3,000	3,000	13,000	7,000
4	20,000	1,800	1,800	14,800	5,200
5	20,000	1,600	1,200*	16,000	4,000

*Note that we only can depreciate 1,200 units since we cannot go below the residual value of $4,000.

Need more practice? Try this **Extra Practice Quiz** (check figures in Chapter Organizer, p. 421)

From the following facts prepare a depreciation expense:

Machine cost	$30,000
Residual value	2,000

Expected to produce 56,000 units over its expected life

	2006	2007	2008	2009	2010
Units produced	1,000	6,000	4,000	2,000	2,500

Learning Unit 17–3: Declining-Balance Method

In the declining-balance method, we cannot depreciate below the residual value.

The **declining-balance method** is another type of accelerated depreciation that takes larger amounts of depreciation expense in the earlier years of the asset. The straight-line method, you recall, estimates the life of the asset and distributes the same amount of depreciation expense to each period. To take larger amounts of depreciation expense in the asset's earlier years, the declining-balance method uses up to *twice* the **straight-line rate** in the first year of depreciation. A key point to remember is that the declining-balance method does not deduct the residual value in calculating the depreciation expense. Today, the declining-balance method is the basis of current tax depreciation.

For all problems, we will use double the straight-line rate unless we indicate otherwise. Today, the rate is often 1.5 or 1.25 times the straight-line rate. Again we use our $2,500 equipment with its estimated useful life of 5 years. As we build the depreciation schedule in Table 17.3, note the following steps:

Step 1. Rate is equal to $\dfrac{100\%}{5 \text{ years}} \times 2 = 40\%$.

Or another way to look at it is that the straight-line rate is $\frac{1}{5} \times 2 = \frac{2}{5} = 40\%$.

Step 2.

$$\dfrac{\text{Depreciation expense}}{\text{each year}} = \dfrac{\text{Book value of equipment}}{\text{at beginning of year}} \times \dfrac{\text{Depreciation}}{\text{rate}}$$

TABLE 17.3 Depreciation schedule for declining-balance method

End of year	Cost of equipment	Accumulated depreciation at beginning of year	Book value at beginning of year (Cost − Accumulated depreciation)	Depreciation (Book value at beginning of year × Rate)	Accumulated depreciation at end of year	Book value at end of year (Cost − Accumulated depreciation)
1	$2,500	—	$2,500	$1,000 ($2,500 × .40)	$1,000	$1,500 ($2,500 − $1,000)
2	2,500	$1,000	1,500	600 ($1,500 × .40)	1,600	900
3	2,500	1,600	900	360 ($900 × .40)	1,960	540
4	2,500	1,960	540	40	2,000	500
5	2,500	2,000	500		2,000	500
	↑ Original cost of $2,500 does not change. Residual value was not subtracted.	↑ Ending accumulated depreciation of 1 year becomes next year's beginning.	↑ Cost less accumulated depreciation	↑ *Note:* In year 4, only $40 is taken since we cannot depreciate below residual value of $500. In year 5, no depreciation is taken.	↑ Accumulated depreciation balance plus depreciation expense this year.	↑ Book value now equals residual value.

Step 3. We cannot depreciate the equipment below its residual value ($500). The straight-line method automatically reduced the asset's book value to the residual value. This is not true with the declining-balance method. So you must be careful when you prepare the depreciation schedule.

Now let's check your progress again with another Practice Quiz.

LU 17–3 | PRACTICE QUIZ

Complete this **Practice Quiz** to see how you are doing

Prepare a depreciation schedule from the following:

Cost of machine: $16,000   Estimated life: 5 years
Rate: 40% (this is twice the straight-line rate)   Residual value: $1,000

✓ **Solutions**

End of year	Cost of machine	Accumulated depreciation at beginning of year	Book value at beginning of year (Cost − Accumulated depreciation)	Depreciation (Book value at beginning of year × Rate)	Accumulated depreciation at end of year	Book value at end of year (Cost − Accumulated depreciation)
1	$16,000	$ –0–	$16,000.00	$6,400.00	$ 6,400.00	$9,600.00
2	16,000	6,400.00	9,600.00	3,840.00	10,240.00	5,760.00
3	16,000	10,240.00	5,760.00	2,304.00	12,544.00	3,456.00
4	16,000	12,544.00	3,456.00	1,382.40	13,926.40	2,073.60
5	16,000	13,926.40	2,073.60	829.44*	14,755.84	1,244.16

*Since we do not reach the residual value of $1,000, another $244.16 could have been taken as depreciation expense to bring it to the estimated residual value of $1,000.

LU 17–3a | EXTRA PRACTICE QUIZ

Need more practice? Try this **Extra Practice Quiz** (check figures in Chapter Organizer, p. 421)

Prepare a depreciation schedule from the following:

Cost of machine: $31,000   Estimated life: 3 years
Rate: 40% (this is twice the straight-line rate)   Residual value: $1,000

Learning Unit 17–4: Modified Accelerated Cost Recovery System (MACRS) with Introduction to ACRS

In Learning Units 17–1 to 17–3, we discussed the depreciation methods used for financial reporting. Since 1981, federal tax laws have been passed that state how depreciation must be taken for income tax purposes. Assets put in service from 1981 through 1986 fell under the federal **Accelerated Cost Recovery System (ACRS)** tax law enacted in 1981. The Tax Reform Act of 1986 established the **Modified Accelerated Cost Recovery System (MACRS)** for all property placed into service after December 31, 1986. Both these federal laws provide users with tables giving the useful lives of various assets and the depreciation rates. We look first at the MACRS and then at a 1989 update.

Depreciation for Tax Purposes Based on the Tax Reform Act of 1986 (MACRS)

Tables 17.4 and 17.5 give the classes of recovery and annual depreciation percentages that MACRS established in 1986. The key points of MACRS are:

1. It calculates depreciation for tax purposes.
2. It ignores residual value.

TABLE	17.4

Modified Accelerated Cost Recovery System (MACRS) for assets placed in service after December 31, 1986

Class recovery period (life)	Asset types
3-year*	Racehorses more than 2 years old or any horse other than a racehorse that is more than 12 years old at the time placed into service; special tools of certain industries.
5-year*	Automobiles (not luxury); taxis; light general-purpose trucks; semiconductor manufacturing equipment; computer-based telephone central-office switching equipment; qualified technological equipment; property used in connection with research and experimentation.
7-year*	Railroad track; single-purpose agricultural (pigpens) or horticultural structures; fixtures; equipment; furniture.
10-year*	New law doesn't add any specific property under this class.
15-year†	Municipal wastewater treatment plants; telephone distribution plants and comparable equipment used for two-way exchange of voice and data communications.
20-year†	Municipal sewers.
27.5-year‡	Only residential rental property.
31.5-year‡	Only nonresidential real property.

*These classes use a 200% declining-balance method switching to the straight-line method.
†These classes use a 150% declining-balance method switching to the straight-line method.
‡These classes use a straight-line method.

TABLE	17.5	Annual recovery for MACRS

Recovery year	3-year class (200% D.B.)	5-year class (200% D.B.)	7-year class (200% D.B.)	10-year class (200% D.B.)	15-year class (150% D.B.)	20-year class (150% D.B.)
1	33.00	20.00	14.28	10.00	5.00	3.75
2	45.00	32.00	24.49	18.00	9.50	7.22
3	15.00*	19.20	17.49	14.40	8.55	6.68
4	7.00	11.52*	12.49	11.52	7.69	6.18
5		11.52	8.93*	9.22	6.93	5.71
6		5.76	8.93	7.37	6.23	5.28
7			8.93	6.55*	5.90*	4.89
8			4.46	6.55	5.90	4.52
9				6.55	5.90	4.46*
10				6.55	5.90	4.46
11				3.29	5.90	4.46
12					5.90	4.46
13					5.90	4.46
14					5.90	4.46
15					5.90	4.46
16					3.00	4.46

*Identifies when switch is made to straight line.

3. Depreciation in the first year (for personal property) is based on the assumption that the asset was purchased halfway through the year. (A new law adds a midquarter convention for all personal property if more than 40% is placed in service during the last 3 months of the taxable year.)

4. Classes 3, 5, 7, and 10 use a 200% declining-balance method for a period of years before switching to straight-line depreciation. You do not have to determine the year in which to switch since Table 17.5 builds this into the calculation.

5. Classes 15 and 20 use a 150% declining-balance method before switching to straight-line depreciation.

6. Classes 27.5 and 31.5 use straight-line depreciation.

EXAMPLE Using the same equipment cost of $2,500 for Ajax, prepare a depreciation schedule under MACRS assuming the equipment is a 5-year class and not part of the tax bill of 1989. Use Table 17.5. Note that percent figures from Table 17.5 have been converted to decimals.

End of year	Cost	Depreciation expense	Accumulated depreciation	Book value at end of year
1	$2,500	$500 (.20 × $2,500)	$ 500	$2,000
2	2,500	800 (.32 × $2,500)	1,300	1,200
3	2,500	480 (.1920 × $2,500)	1,780	720
4	2,500	288 (.1152 × $2,500)	2,068	432
5	2,500	288 (.1152 × $2,500)	2,356	144
6	2,500	144 (.0576 × $2,500)	2,500	–0–

Update on MACRS: The 1989 Tax Bill

Before the 1989 tax bill (**Omnibus Budget Reconciliation Act of 1989**), cellular phones and similar equipment were depreciated under MACRS. Since cellular phones are subject to personal use, the 1989 act now treats them as "listed" property. This means that unless business use is greater than 50%, the straight-line method of depreciation is required.

Let's try another Practice Quiz.

LU 17–4 PRACTICE QUIZ

Complete this **Practice Quiz** to see how you are doing

1. In 1991, Rancho Corporation bought semiconductor equipment for $80,000. Using MACRS, what is the depreciation expense in year 3?
2. What would depreciation be the first year for a wastewater treatment plant that cost $800,000?

✓ **Solutions**

1. $80,000 × .1920 = $15,360
2. $800,000 × .05 = $40,000

LU 17–4a EXTRA PRACTICE QUIZ

Need more practice? Try this **Extra Practice Quiz** (check figures in Chapter Organizer, p. 421)

1. In 1991, Rancho Corporation bought semiconductor equipment for $90.000. Using MACRS, what is the depreciation expense in year 3?
2. What would depreciation be the first year for a wastewater treatment plan that cost $900,000?

CHAPTER ORGANIZER AND STUDY GUIDE
WITH CHECK FIGURES FOR EXTRA PRACTICE QUIZZES

Topic	Key point, procedure, formula	Example(s) to illustrate situation
Straight-line method, p. 413	Depreciation expense each year $= \dfrac{\text{Cost} - \text{Residual value}}{\text{Estimated useful life in years}}$ For partial years if purchased before 15th of month depreciation is taken.	Truck, $25,000; $5,000 residual value, 4-year life. $\dfrac{\text{Depreciation}}{\text{expense}} = \dfrac{\$25,000 - \$5,000}{4}$ $= \$5,000$ per year

(continues)

CHAPTER ORGANIZER AND STUDY GUIDE
WITH CHECK FIGURES FOR EXTRA PRACTICE QUIZZES (concluded)

Topic	Key point, procedure, formula	Example(s) to illustrate situation
Units-of-production method, p. 415	$$\frac{\text{Depreciation}}{\text{per unit}} = \frac{\text{Cost} - \text{Residual value}}{\text{Total estimated units produced}}$$ Do not depreciate below residual value even if actual units are greater than estimate.	Machine, $5,000; estimated life in units, 900; residual value, $500. Assume first year produced 175 units. $$\text{Depreciation expense} = \frac{\$5,000 - \$500}{900}$$ $$= \frac{\$4,500}{900}$$ $$= \$5 \text{ depreciation per unit}$$ 175 units $\times$ $5 = $875 depreciation expense
Declining-balance method, p. 417	An accelerated method. Residual value not subtracted from cost in depreciation schedule. Do not depreciate below residual value. $$\begin{array}{c}\text{Depreciation}\\\text{expense}\\\text{each year}\end{array} = \begin{array}{c}\text{Book}\\\text{value of}\\\text{equipment}\\\text{at beginning}\\\text{of year}\end{array} \times \begin{array}{c}\text{Depreciation}\\\text{rate}\end{array}$$	Truck, 50,000; estimated life, 5 years; residual value, $10,000. $\frac{1}{5} = 20\% \times 2 = 40\%$ (assume double the straight-line rate) | Year	Cost	Depreciation expense	Book value at end of year
---	---	---	---
1	$50,000	$20,000 ($50,000 $\times$ .40)	$30,000 ($50,000 − $20,000)
2	50,000	12,000 ($30,000 $\times$ .40)	18,000 ($50,000 − $32,000)	
MACRS/Tax Bill of 1989, p. 418	After December 31, 1986, depreciation calculation is modified. Tax Act of 1989 modifies way to depreciate cellular phones and similar equipment.	Auto: $8,000, 5 years. First year, .20 $\times$ $8,000 = $1,600 depreciation expense
KEY TERMS	Accelerated Cost Recovery System (ACRS), *p. 418* Accelerated depreciation method, *p. 418* Accumulated depreciation, *p. 413* Asset cost, *p. 413* Book value, *p. 413* Declining-balance method, *p. 417*	Depreciation, *p. 413* Depreciation expense, *p. 413* Depreciation schedule, *p. 414* Estimated useful life, *p. 413* Modified Accelerated Cost Recovery System (MACRS), *p. 418* Omnibus Budget Reconciliation Act of 1989, *p. 420* Residual value, *p. 413* Salvage value, *p. 413* Straight-line method, *p. 414* Straight-line rate, *p. 414* Trade-in value, *p. 413* Units-of-production method, *p. 415*
CHECK FIGURES FOR EXTRA PRACTICE QUIZZES WITH PAGE REFERENCES	LU 17–1a (p. 415) 1. Book value EOY 3 $2,000 2. $5,500 LU 17–2a (p. 417) $.50; Book value EOY 5 $22,250	LU 17–3a (p. 418) $$\frac{\text{Depreciation expense}}{\text{year}}$$ 1 $12,400 2 $7,440 3 4,464 LU 17–4a (p. 420) 1. $17,280 2. $45,000	

Critical Thinking Discussion Questions

1. What is the difference between depreciation expense and accumulated depreciation? Why does the book value of an asset never go below the residual value?

2. Compare the straight-line method to the units-of-production method. Should both methods be based on the passage of time?

3. Why is it possible in the declining-balance method for a person to depreciate below the residual value by mistake?

4. Explain the Modified Accelerated Cost Recovery System. Do you think this system will be eliminated in the future?

Classroom Notes

Name _____   Date _____

DRILL PROBLEMS

From the following facts, complete a depreciation schedule using the straight-line method:

Given   Cost of Range Rover $90,000
        Residual value   10,000
        Estimated life   8 years

End of year	Cost of Range Rover	Depreciation expense for year	Accumulated depreciation at end of year	Book value at end of year
17–1.				
17–2.				
17–3.				
17–4.				
17–5.				
17–6.				
17–7.				
17–8.				

Given   Volvo truck $25,000
        Residual value   5,000
        Estimated life   5 years

End of year	Cost of truck	Accumulated depreciation at beginning of year	Book value at beginning of year	Depreciation expense for year	Accumulated depreciation at end of year	Book value at end of year
17–9.						
17–10.						
17–11.						
17–12.						

For the first 2 years, calculate the depreciation expense for a $7,000 car under MACRS. This is a nonluxury car.

              MACRS   **MACRS**

17–13. Year 1   **17–14.**   Year 2

Complete the following table given this information:

Cost of machine	$94,000	Estimated units machine will produce	100,000
Residual value	4,000	Actual production:	
Useful life	5 years		Year 1 Year 2
			60,000 15,000

	Depreciation Expense	
Method	**Year 1**	**Year 2**
17–15. Straight line		
17–16. Units of production		
17–17. Declining balance		
17–18. MACRS (5-year class)		

WORD PROBLEMS

17–19. The January 2007 issue of *Focus* reported on the Tax Reform Act of 1986 (MACRS) as compared to the Economic Recovery Act of 1981 (ACRS). The ACRS required real estate to be depreciated over a 15-year life, but that did not last long. The (MACRS) increased the depreciable life to 31.5 years. Dwight Welch has property valued at $1,350,000. During the first year, how much was Dwight able to depreciate using MACRS (assume a 15-year life class)?

17–20. Pat Brown bought a Chevy truck for $28,000 with an estimated life of 5 years. The residual value of the truck is $3,000. Assume a straight-line method of depreciation. **(a)** What will be the book value of the truck at the end of year 3? **(b)** If the Chevy truck was bought the first year on April 12, how much depreciation would be taken the first year?

17–21. Jim Company bought a machine for $36,000 with an estimated life of 5 years. The residual value of the machine is $6,000. Calculate **(a)** the annual depreciation and **(b)** the book value at the end of year 3. Assume straight-line depreciation.

17–22. Using Problem 17–21, calculate the first 2 years' depreciation, assuming the units-of-production method. This machine is expected to produce 120,000 units. In year 1, it produced 19,000 units, and in year 2, 38,000 units.

17–23. On October 9, 2006, *U.S. News & World Report* discussed resale value of Recreational Vehicles. Jim Clinnin purchased a used RV with 19,000 miles for $46,900. Originally the RV sold for $70,000 with a residual value of $20,000. After subtracting the residual value, depreciation allowance per mile was $.86. How much was Jim's purchase price over or below the book value?

17–24. *Tax Adviser* reported on reclassification of properties under the modified acceleration cost recovery system. Brookshire Bros. had been classifying property as nonresidential real property with a 39-year recovery period on its tax returns. The company filed amended returns, reclassifying the property as 15-year property. If the property has a value of $325,000, what would be the amount of depreciation for the first year?

17–25. An article in the July 2006 issue of *Overdrive* magazine reported on straight line and accelerated methods of depreciation. Perry Wiseman of Truckers Accounting Service in Omaha, Nebraska likes to use the straight line method and take a little bit extra the first year, so there are three good years of depreciation. The cost of his truck was $108,000, with a useful life of 3 years and a residual value of $35,000. What would be the book value of the truck after the first year? Round your answers to the nearest dollar.

CHALLENGE PROBLEMS

17–26. *Construction Equipment* ran an article on calculating equipment depreciation. The delivered price (including attachments) of a crawler dozer tractor is $135,000 with a residual value of 35%. The useful life of the tractor is 7,700 hours. **(a)** What is the total amount of depreciation allowed? **(b)** What is the amount of depreciation per hour? **(c)** Operating the tractor an average of $7\frac{1}{4}$ hours a day for 5 days a week, what would be the depreciation for the first year? **(d)** If the hours of operation were the same each year, what would be the total number of years of useful life for the tractor? Round years to the nearest whole number.

17–27. A piece of equipment was purchased July 26, 2009, at a cost of $72,000. The estimated residual value is $5,400 with the useful life of 5 years. Assume a production life of 60,000 units. Compute the depreciation for years 2009 and 2010 using **(a)** straight-line; **(b)** units-of-production (in 2009, 5,000 units produced and in 2010, 18,000 units produced).

 SUMMARY PRACTICE TEST

1. Leo Lucky, owner of a Pizza Hut franchise, bought a delivery truck for $30,000. The truck has an estimated life of 5 years with a residual value of $10,000. Leo wants to know which depreciation method will be the best for his truck. He asks you to prepare a depreciation schedule using the declining-balance method at twice the straight-line rate. *(p. 417)*

2. Using MACRS, what is the depreciation for the first year on furniture costing $12,000? *(p. 418)*

3. Abby Matthew bought a new Jeep Commander for $30,000. The Jeep Commander has a life expectancy of 5 years with a residual value of $10,000. Prepare a depreciation schedule for the straight-line-method. *(p. 414)*

4. Car.com bought a Toyota for $28,000. The Toyota has a life expectancy of 10 years with a residual value of $3,000. After 3 years, the Toyota was sold for $19,000. What was the difference between the book value and the amount received from selling the car if Car.com used the straight-line method of depreciation? *(p. 414)*

5. A machine cost $70,200; it had an estimated residual value of $6,000 and an expected life of 300,000 units. What would be the depreciation in year 3 if 60,000 units were produced?
(Round to nearest cent.) *(p. 415)*

Buy a 2006 car ON SALE?

CARMAKERS' incentives on 2006 cars may tempt you to skip the 2007 models just coming into showrooms. At first blush, it seems like a smart financial move. You get the same warranty and the same new-car smell. But it could be a mistake: Unless you get a big discount on the '06, you'll likely come out ahead buying an '07 model.

The reason is depreciation. As they've sat on the lot, the 2006s have bled resale value. For example, in July a 2007 Ford Mustang GT convertible had a three-year resale value equal to 63% of the sticker price, according to *Kelley Blue Book*. But a new 2006 model was expected to be worth only 58% of its sticker price after three years. The 2007 costs just $160 more than the 2006, but after three years it could be worth nearly $1,700 more. In other words, to save $160 now, you'd surrender $1,700 at trade-in time.

This isn't an exercise in crystal-ball gazing, but a tried-and-true fact of auto economics. Here's an example from the recent past: If you bought a 2003 Mercedes-Benz C240 three years ago just as the 2004 models became available, you would have saved $1,755 over the newer model. But if you traded it in today, you'd get $2,700 less, according to average prices dealers pay.

When older is better. If you can get a low enough price for a 2006 model—through incentives, dealer discounts or your negotiating skills— you can erase the depreciation gap. For example, the 2007 Chevrolet Equinox LT has a sticker price $275 higher than the 2006 model and is expected to be worth about $1,500 more after three years. So if you go with the '07, you should be ahead by $1,225. But recent sales data show that the 2006 is selling for about $1,100 less than sticker, which means you're really ahead by

DRIVE TIME
by Mark K. Solheim

❝ Unless you get a big discount on the '06, you'll likely come out ahead buying an '07 model. ❞

● Buy the 2007 Mustang and you could be up $1,500 at trade-in time.

only $125. If you negotiate an extra $125 or more off the sticker price, the 2006 is a better deal.

In general, the lower the price of the vehicle—and the longer you keep the car— the narrower the depreciation gap between newer and older models. If you don't care about resale value because you plan to keep the car until it sputters and dies, buying the older model at whatever discount probably makes sense, says Jack Nerad, executive editorial director of *Kelley Blue Book*.

Another factor: Some new models may include standard equipment that used to be optional, which adds value to new vehicles without raising prices much. For example, Chevy made stability control, which helps prevent skids, standard equipment on the 2007 Equinox.

If the new model is a total makeover, comparisons no longer apply. Redesigned models don't just look different; they usually have powertrain and interior improvements that boost quality.

Mind the gap. Run the numbers yourself on any 2006 versus 2007 model. The resale value, also known as the residual value, is hard to come by (*Kiplinger's* publishes resale values once a year, in the December issue). But dealers should be willing to share up-to-date figures that they get from leasing companies for three, four or five years down the road. Multiply the resale-value percentage by the sticker price to see what the vehicle is likely to be worth to a dealer when you're ready to sell. Or simply estimate the gap. A difference of $1,000 after three years is typical for vehicles under $30,000; after five years, figure on $500. For $40,000 vehicles, the spreads are closer to $2,000 for three years and $1,500 for five. If the combination of incentives and the discount you negotiate for the 2006 beats the gap—and you love the color—drive the older model off the lot.

Got a question? Ask Mark at kiplinger.com/drivetime, or write to him at 1729 H Street, N.W., Washington, DC 20006.

WALTER SMITH (TOP)

BUSINESS MATH ISSUE

Depreciation has no real effect on car sales.

1. List the key points of the article and information to support your position.
2. Write a group defense of your position using math calculations to support your view.

Slater's Business Math Scrapbook

with Internet Application

Putting Your Skills to Work

PROJECT A
Is there any bonus
depreciation available
today? Search the Web.

Big Tax Break Prompts SUV Sales

Shoppers Scramble to Buy Before Dec. 31 Deadline; What It Takes to Qualify

By MICHELLE HIGGINS

Two months ago, President Bush signed into law a bill that includes a sharp cut in a special tax deduction for many new SUVs. But, thanks to another wrinkle in the tax code, some car shoppers who buy a large SUV before the end of this year can still get a sizable deduction.

The new law pares a special deduction for many SUVs purchased after Oct. 22 from a maximum of $102,000 for this year to just $25,000. The provision applies to small businesses. But even with that limit, a company can still write off a substantial portion of a new vehicle's cost in the first year.

Including the new limit and "bonus depreciation" rules, a typical small business can still deduct as much as $52,000 on a new $70,000 SUV if the vehicle was used for business 100% of the time.

This provides a potential sales boost for the much-criticized SUV, and car dealers are eager to promote the loophole. Earlier this month, the National Automobile Dealers Association sent out a bulletin telling its members about the Dec. 31 bonus-depreciation deadline. BMW North America also alerted its dealers, pointing out the rules apply to its X5 SUV, which starts at about $42,000.

Accountants, meanwhile, have also

*The **BMW X5** qualifies for the deduction*

been spreading the word to their small-business clients. In November, Rob Johanson, a certified public accountant at NBS Financial Services Inc. in Westlake Village, Calif., sent out an e-mail about the last-minute opportunity. Out of about 350 small-business clients, at least a handful have followed the advice.

To qualify for the SUV deduction, a vehicle must have a gross vehicle weight—the weight when fully loaded—of more than 6,000 pounds. This includes popular pickups such as the Ford F-150, Dodge Ram and Chevy Silverado. It can also kick in when doctors, lawyers or other professionals use an SUV for work such as the Hummer, BMW X5 or Cadillac Escalade. But to get the full tax break, they have to use it 100% of the time.

The tax incentive comes as full-size SUV sales have been flattening despite aggressive discounting by auto makers. Truck-based SUV sales are down 2.2%

year to date through November, and have been flat much of the past three years, says Paul Taylor, chief economist at the National Automobile Dealers Association. Truck-based SUVs have sold at a rate just under three million units a year for the past three years, and are on a track to do that again this year, he says.

The bonus depreciation deduction typically applies only to equipment that the business is actually using before Jan. 1, 2005. (You can't pay for the SUV before the end of the year, pick it up in early January and then get the full tax break.)

After that, the write-off on that $70,000 SUV would typically drop to $34,000, says Martin Nissenbaum, national director of personal income-tax planning at Ernst & Young in New York.

Not all small companies are eligible for the $25,000 SUV deduction. Once a company's annual spending on business equipment exceeds a certain amount, the deduction begins to drop.

**Internet Projects: See text Web site
(www.mhhe.com/slater9e) and The
Business Math Internet Resource Guide.**

CHAPTER 18

Inventory and Overhead

Just-in-Time Inventories Make U.S. Vulnerable in a Pandemic

Low Stockpiles at Hospitals
Boost Efficiency but Leave
No Extras for Flu Outbreak

A Run on Protective Masks

By BERNARD WYSOCKI JR.
And SARAH LUECK

Like many big hospitals, the University of Utah Hospital carries a 30-day supply of drugs, in part because it would be too costly or wasteful to stockpile more. Some of its hepatitis vaccine supply has been diverted to the hurricane-ravaged Gulf, leaving it vulnerable should an outbreak occur closer to home. About 77 other drugs are in short supply because of manufacturing and other glitches, such as a drug maker shutting down a factory.

Wall Street Journal © 2006

LEARNING UNIT OBJECTIVES

LU 18–1: Assigning Costs to Ending Inventory—Specific Identification; Weighted Average; FIFO; LIFO

- List the key assumptions of each inventory method (pp. 431–436).
- Calculate the cost of ending inventory and cost of goods sold for each inventory method (pp. 431–436).

LU 18–2: Retail Method; Gross Profit Method; Inventory Turnover; Distribution of Overhead

- Calculate the cost ratio and ending inventory at cost for the retail method (p. 437).
- Calculate the estimated inventory using the gross profit method (p. 437).
- Explain and calculate inventory turnover (p. 438).
- Explain overhead; allocate overhead according to floor space and sales (p. 439).

Have you ever wondered how a company keeps track of its inventory? The two methods that a company can use to monitor its inventory are the *perpetual* method and the *periodic* method.

The perpetual inventory system should be familiar to most consumers. Today, it is common for cashiers to run scanners across the product code of each item sold. These scanners read pertinent information into a computer terminal, such as the item's number, department, and price. The computer then uses the **perpetual inventory system** as it subtracts outgoing merchandise from inventory and adds incoming merchandise to inventory. However, as you probably know, the computer cannot be completely relied on to maintain an accurate count of merchandise in stock. Since some products may be stolen or lost, periodically a physical count is necessary to verity the computer count.

Did you know that Wal-Mart wants suppliers to use radio-transmitter tags to improve the flow of products in and out of their stores? Note in the following *Wall Street Journal* clipping "Suppliers Struggle with Wal-Mart ID-Tag Plan" that Wal-Mart suppliers have to begin adopting Wal-Mart's radio-transmitter tag plan to monitor inventory.

Suppliers Struggle With Wal-Mart ID-Tag Plan

By Susan Warren

SUPPLIERS OF PRODUCTS sold by **Wal-Mart Stores** Inc. say they will meet the retail giant's January deadline to begin using a new electronic-labeling technology—but most are doing as little as they can to meet the goal.

Wal-Mart set the deadline hoping to speed up adoption of radio-transmitter tags, which promise to revolutionize how products flow in and out of stores. The world's largest retailer asked its top 100 suppliers to begin using the tags on at least some products they deliver to Wal-Mart by the end of January.

But manufacturers are growing concerned that they are being pushed too far, too fast, and worry they'll be forced to sink large sums into unproven "radio ID" technology for no reason other than pleasing Wal-Mart. As a result, many suppliers are looking to meet the retailer's deadline without committing any more time or money than they absolutely must.

Wall Street Journal © 2004

David Buffington/Getty Images

With the increased use of computers, many companies are changing to a perpetual inventory system of maintaining inventory records. Some small stores, however, still use the **periodic inventory system.** This system usually does not keep a running account of its inventory but relies only on a physical inventory count taken at least once a year. The store then uses various accounting methods to value the cost of its merchandise. In this chapter we discuss the periodic method of inventory.

You may wonder why a company should know the status of its inventory. In Chapter 16 we introduced you to the balance sheet and the income statement. Companies cannot accurately prepare these statements unless they have placed the correct value on their inventory. To do this, a company must know (1) the cost of its ending inventory (found on the balance sheet) and (2) the cost of the goods (merchandise) sold (found on the income statement).

Frequently, the same type of merchandise flows into a company at different costs. The value assumptions a company makes about the merchandise it sells affects the cost assigned to its ending inventory. Remember that different costs result in different levels of profit on a firm's financial reports.

This chapter begins by using the Blue Company to discuss four common methods (specific identification, weighted average, FIFO, and LIFO) that companies use to calculate costs of ending inventory and the cost of goods sold. In these methods, the flow of costs does not always match the flow of goods. The chapter

<table>
<tr><td rowspan="2">FIGURE 18.1</td><td></td><td>Number of
units purchased</td><td>Cost
per unit</td><td>Total
cost</td></tr>
<tr><td>Beginning inventory</td><td>40</td><td>$ 8</td><td>$ 320</td></tr>
</table>

<table>
<tr><th></th><th>Number of
units purchased</th><th>Cost
per unit</th><th>Total
cost</th></tr>
<tr><td>Beginning inventory</td><td>40</td><td>$ 8</td><td>$ 320</td></tr>
<tr><td>First purchase (April 1)</td><td>20</td><td>9</td><td>180</td></tr>
<tr><td>Second purchase (May 1)</td><td>20</td><td>10</td><td>200</td></tr>
<tr><td>Third purchase (October 1)</td><td>20</td><td>12</td><td>240</td></tr>
<tr><td>Fourth purchase (December 1)</td><td>20</td><td>13</td><td>260</td></tr>
<tr><td>Goods (merchandise) available for sale</td><td>120</td><td></td><td>$1,200 ← Step 1</td></tr>
<tr><td>Units sold</td><td>72</td><td></td><td></td></tr>
<tr><td>Units in ending inventory</td><td>48</td><td></td><td></td></tr>
</table>

Blue Company—a case study

continues with a discussion of two methods of estimating ending inventory (retail and gross profit methods), inventory turnover, and the distribution of overhead.

Learning Unit 18–1: Assigning Costs to Ending Inventory—Specific Identification; Weighted Average; FIFO; LIFO

Blue Company is a small artist supply store. Its beginning inventory is 40 tubes of art paint that cost $320 (at $8 a tube) to bring into the store. As shown in Figure 18.1, Blue made additional purchases in April, May, October, and December. Note that because of inflation and other competitive factors, the cost of the paint rose from $8 to $13 per tube. At the end of December, Blue had 48 unsold paint tubes. During the year, Blue had 120 paint tubes to sell. Blue wants to calculate (1) the cost of ending inventory (not sold) and (2) the cost of goods sold.

Specific Identification Method

Companies that sell high-cost items such as autos, jewelry, antiques, and so on, usually use the specific identification method.

Companies use the **specific identification method** when they can identify the original purchase cost of an item with the item. For example, Blue Company color codes its paint tubes as they come into the store. Blue can then attach a specific invoice price to each paint tube. This makes the flow of goods and flow of costs the same. Then, when Blue computes its ending inventory and cost of goods sold, it can associate the actual invoice cost with each item sold and in inventory.

To help Blue calculate its inventory with the specific identification method, use the steps that follow.

CALCULATING THE SPECIFIC IDENTIFICATION METHOD
Step 1. Calculate the cost of goods (merchandise available for sale).
Step 2. Calculate the cost of the ending inventory.
Step 3. Calculate the cost of goods sold (Step 1 – Step 2).

First, Blue must actually count the tubes of paint on hand. Since Blue coded these paint tubes, it can identify the tubes with their purchase cost and multiply them by this cost to arrive at a total cost of ending inventory. Let's do this now.

	Cost per unit	Total cost
20 units from April 1	$ 9	$180
20 units from October 1	12	240
8 units from December 1	13	104
Cost of ending inventory		$524 ← Step 2

Blue uses the following cost of goods sold formula to determine its cost of goods sold:

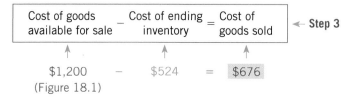

(Figure 18.1)

Note that the $1,200 for cost of goods available for sale comes from Figure 18.1 (p. 431). Remember, we are focusing our attention on Blue's *purchase costs*. Blue's actual *selling price* does not concern us.

Now let's look at how Blue would use the weighted-average method.

Weighted-Average Method[1]

The **weighted-average method** prices the ending inventory by using an average unit cost. Let's replay Blue Company and use the weighted-average method to find the average unit cost of its ending inventory and its cost of goods sold. Blue would use the steps that follow.

CALCULATING THE WEIGHTED-AVERAGE METHOD
Step 1. Calculate the average unit cost.
Step 2. Calculate the cost of the ending inventory.
Step 3. Calculate the cost of goods sold.

In the table that follows, Blue makes the calculation.

	Number of units purchased	Cost per unit	Total cost
Beginning inventory	40	$ 8	$ 320
First purchase (April 1)	20	9	180
Second purchase (May 1)	20	10	200
Third purchase (October 1)	20	12	240
Fourth purchase (December 1)	20	13	260
Goods (merchandise) available for sale	120		$1,200
Units sold	72		
Units in ending inventory	48		

$$\text{Weighted average unit cost} = \frac{\text{Total cost of goods available for sale}}{\text{Total number of units available for sale}} = \frac{\$1,200}{120 \text{ units}} = \$10 \text{ average unit cost}$$ ← **Step 1**

Average cost of ending inventory: 48 units at $10 = $480 ← **Step 2**

$$\text{Cost of goods available for sale} - \text{Cost of ending inventory} = \text{Cost of goods sold}$$

$1,200 − $480 = $720 ← **Step 3**

Remember that some of the costs we used to determine the average unit cost were higher and others were lower. The weighted-average method, then, calculates an *average unit price* for goods. Companies with similar units of goods, such as rolls of wallpaper, often use the weighted-average method. Also, companies with homogeneous products such as fuels and grains may use the weighted-average method.

Now let's see how Blue Company would value its inventory with the FIFO method.

---

[1] Virtually all countries permit the use of the weighted-average method.

FIFO—First-In, First-Out Method[2]

The **first-in, first-out (FIFO)** inventory valuation method assumes that the first goods (paint tubes for Blue) brought into the store are the first goods sold. Thus, FIFO assumes that each sale is from the oldest goods in inventory. FIFO also assumes that the inventory remaining in the store at the end of the period is the most recently acquired goods. This cost flow assumption may or may not hold in the actual physical flow of the goods. An example of a corporation's using the FIFO method is Gillette Corporation.

Use the following steps to calculate inventory with the FIFO method.

CALCULATING THE FIFO INVENTORY
Step 1. List the units to be included in the ending inventory and their costs.
Step 2. Calculate the cost of the ending inventory.
Step 3. Calculate the cost of goods sold.

In the table that follows, we show how to calculate FIFO for Blue using the above steps.

FIFO (bottom up)	Number of units purchased	Cost per unit	Total cost
Beginning inventory	40	$ 8	$ 320
First purchase (April 1)	20	9	180
Second purchase (May 1)	20	10	200
Third purchase (October 1)	20	12	240
Fourth purchase (December 1)	20	13	260
Goods (merchandise) available for sale	120		$1,200
Units sold	72		
Units in ending inventory	48		

20 units from December 1 purchased at $13		$260
20 units from October 1 purchased at $12	← Step 1 →	240
8 units from May 1 purchased at $10		80
48 units result in an ending inventory cost of		$580 ← Step 2

$$\underset{\$1{,}200}{\text{Cost of goods available for sale}} - \underset{\$580}{\text{Cost of ending inventory}} = \underset{\$620}{\text{Cost of goods sold}} \;\;\leftarrow \text{Step 3}$$

In FIFO, the cost flow of goods tends to follow the physical flow. For example, a fish market could use FIFO because it wants to sell its old inventory first. Note that during inflation, FIFO produces a higher income than other methods. So companies using FIFO during this time must pay more taxes.

We conclude this unit by using the LIFO method to value Blue Company's inventory.

LIFO—Last-In, First-Out Method[3]

If Blue Company chooses the **last-in, first-out (LIFO)** method of inventory valuation, then the goods sold by Blue will be the last goods brought into the store. The ending inventory would consist of the old goods that Blue bought earlier.

You can calculate inventory with the LIFO method by using the steps that follow.

---

[2]Virtually all countries permit the use of the FIFO method.
[3]Many countries, such as Australia, Hong Kong, South Africa, and the United Kingdom, do not permit the use of LIFO.

	CALCULATING THE LIFO INVENTORY		
Step 1.	List the units to be included in the ending inventory and their costs.		
Step 2.	Calculate the cost of the ending inventory.		
Step 3.	Calculate the cost of goods sold.		

Now we use the above steps to calculate LIFO for Blue.

LIFO (top down)	Number of units purchased	Cost per unit	Total cost
Beginning inventory	40	$ 8	$ 320
First purchase (April 1)	20	9	180
Second purchase (May 1)	20	10	200
Third purchase (October 1)	20	12	240
Fourth purchase (December 1)	20	13	260
Goods (merchandise) available for sale	120		$1,200
Units sold	72		
Units in ending inventory	48		

40 units of beginning inventory at $8 $320

8 units from April at $9   ← **Step 1** →   72

48 units result in an ending inventory cost of $392 ← **Step 2**

Cost of goods available for sale	−	Cost of ending inventory	=	Cost of goods sold
$1,200	−	$392	=	$808 ← **Step 3**

Although LIFO doesn't always match the physical flow of goods, companies do still use it to calculate the flow of costs for products such as DVDs and computers, which have declining replacement costs. Also, during inflation, LIFO produces less income than other methods. This results in lower taxes for companies using LIFO.

Before concluding this unit, we will make a summary for the cost of ending inventory and cost of goods sold under the weighted-average, FIFO, and LIFO methods. From this summary, you can see that in times of rising prices, LIFO gives the highest cost of goods sold ($808). This results in a tax savings for Blue. The weighted-average method tends to smooth out the fluctuations between LIFO and FIFO and falls in the middle.

The key to this discussion of inventory valuation is that different costing methods produce different results. So management, investors, and potential investors should understand the different inventory costing methods and should know which method a particular company uses. For example, Fruit of the Loom, Inc., changed its inventories from LIFO to FIFO due to cost reductions.

Let's check your understanding of this unit with a Practice Quiz.

Inventory method	Cost of goods available for sale	Cost of ending inventory	Cost of goods sold
Weighted average	$1,200	**$480** **Step 1:** Total goods, $1,200 Total units, 120 $\dfrac{\$1,200}{120} = \$10$ **Step 2:** $10 \times 48 = \$480$	$1,200 − $480 = **$720**

FIFO	$1,200	Bottom up to inventory level (48)
		20 × $13 = $260
		20 × $12 = 240
		  8 × $10 = 80
		                $580
			$1,200 − $580 = **$620**

LIFO	$1,200	Top down to inventory level (48)
		40 × $8 = $320
		  8 × $9 = 72
		              $392
			$1,200 − $392 = **$808**

LU 18–1   PRACTICE QUIZ

Complete this **Practice Quiz** to see how you are doing

From the following, calculate **(a)** the cost of ending inventory and **(b)** the cost of goods sold under the assumption of (1) weighted-average method, (2) FIFO, and (3) LIFO (ending inventory shows 72 units):

	Number of books purchased for resale	Cost per unit	Total
January 1 inventory	30	$3	$ 90
March 1	50	2	100
April 1	20	4	80
November 1	60	6	360

✓ **Solutions**

1.   a.   72 units of ending inventory × $3.94 = $283.68 cost of ending inventory
($630 ÷ 160)

   b.

$$\underset{\downarrow}{\substack{\text{Cost of goods} \\ \text{available for sale}}} - \underset{\downarrow}{\substack{\text{Cost of ending} \\ \text{inventory}}} = \underset{\downarrow}{\substack{\text{Cost of} \\ \text{goods sold}}}$$

$630   − $283.68   =   **$346.32**

2.   a.

60 units from November 1 purchased at $6	$360
12 units from April 1 purchased at $4	48
72 units Cost of ending inventory	$408

   b.

$$\underset{\downarrow}{\substack{\text{Cost of goods} \\ \text{available for sale}}} - \underset{\downarrow}{\substack{\text{Cost of ending} \\ \text{inventory}}} = \underset{\downarrow}{\substack{\text{Cost of} \\ \text{goods sold}}}$$

$630   − $408   =   **$222**

3.   a.

30 units from January 1 purchased at $3	$ 90
42 units from March 1 purchased at $2	84
72 Cost of ending inventory	$174

b.

$$\underset{\downarrow}{\text{Cost of goods available for sale}} - \underset{\downarrow}{\text{Cost of ending inventory}} = \underset{\downarrow}{\text{Cost of goods sold}}$$

$$\$630 \quad - \quad \$174 \quad = \quad \boxed{\$456}$$

LU 18–1a EXTRA PRACTICE QUIZ

Need more practice? Try this **Extra Practice Quiz** (check figures in Chapter Organizer, p. 444)

From the following, calculate (a) the cost of ending inventory and (b) the cost of goods sold under the assumption of (1) weighted-average, (2) FIFO, and LIFO (ending inventory shows 58 units):

	Number of books purchased for resale	Cost per unit	Total
January 1 inventory	20	$4	$ 80
March 1	60	3	180
April 1	40	5	200
November 1	50	7	350

Learning Unit 18–2: Retail Method; Gross Profit Method; Inventory Turnover; Distribution of Overhead

Customers want stores to have products available for sale as soon as possible. This has led to outsourced warehouses offshore where tens of thousands of products can be stored ready to be quickly shipped to various stores. The following *Wall Street Journal* "Outsourced Warehouses Boom as Factories Move Offshore, People Expect Quick Shipping" shows new trends in outsourcing and controlling costs relating to warehouse costs and distribution.

Outsourced Warehouses Boom As Factories Move Offshore, People Expect Quick Shipping

By KRIS MAHER

Columbus, Ohio

IN A CAVERNOUS building here, workers speed around on motorized vehicles between rows of cardboard boxes. They rise up on hydraulic lifts to reach the tops of stacks stretching 28 feet high. A man on a foot-powered scooter races to check inventories of products ranging from DVD players to antiwrinkle cream and heart-surgery devices. Forklift drivers honk as they make their way across the dusky building the size of five football fields.

This warehouse and several others operated by **ODW Logistics** Inc. are the temporary home to tens of thousands of products made in 120 locations around the world by hundreds of manufacturers. They supply ODW's 80 customers, such as **Deere** & Co. and **Limited Brands** Inc. Each week, for example, 750,000 pounds of khaki pants, T-shirts and other apparel arrive from China, the Philippines, Sri Lanka, Indonesia and India. After stopping here, they are bound for Victoria's Secret, Eddie Bauer and the Limited. Two other vast warehouses are devoted almost entirely to cereal.

Such omnibus facilities are increasingly important way stations in the global, just-in-time economy. Cost-cutting and shifting of production offshore are driving growing numbers of manufacturers, retailers and suppliers to outsource their warehouses and distribution needs to the $89.4 billion third-party logistics industry.

Wall Street Journal © 2005

Courtesy ODW Logistics, Inc.

When retailers receive their products, they go into one of their most important assets—their inventory. When the product is sold, it must be removed from inventory so it can be replaced or discontinued. Often these transactions occur electronically at the registers that customers use to pay for products. How is inventory controlled when the register of the store cannot perform the task of adding and subtracting products from inventory?

Convenience stores often try to control their inventory by taking physical inventories. This can be time consuming and expensive. Some stores draw up monthly financial reports but do not want to spend the time or money to take a monthly physical inventory.

Many stores estimate the amount of inventory on hand. Stores may also have to estimate their inventories when they have a loss of goods due to fire, theft, flood, and the like. This unit begins with two methods of estimating the value of ending inventory—the *retail method* and the *gross profit method.*

Retail Method

Many companies use the **retail method** to estimate their inventory. As shown in Figure 18.2, this method does not require that a company calculate an inventory cost for each item. To calculate the $3,500 ending inventory in Figure 18.2, Green Company used the steps that follow.

CALCULATING THE RETAIL METHOD
Step 1. Calculate the cost of goods available for sale at cost and retail: $6,300; $9,000.
Step 2. Calculate a cost ratio using the following formula:
$$\frac{\text{Cost of goods available for sale at cost}}{\text{Cost of goods available for sale at retail}} = \frac{\$6,300}{\$9,000} = .70$$
Step 3. Deduct net sales from cost of goods available for sale at retail: $9,000 − $4,000.
Step 4. Multiply the cost ratio by the ending inventory at retail: .70 × $5,000.

FIGURE 18.2

Estimating inventory with the retail method

	Cost	Retail	
Beginning inventory	$4,000	$6,000	
Net purchases during month	2,300	3,000	
Cost of goods available for sale **(Step 1)**	$6,300	$9,000	
Less net sales for month		4,000	**(Step 3)**
Ending inventory at retail		$5,000	
Cost ratio ($6,300 ÷ $9,000) **(Step 2)**		70%	
Ending inventory at cost (.70 × $5,000) **(Step 4)**		$3,500	

Now let's look at the gross profit method.

Gross Profit Method

To use the **gross profit method** to estimate inventory, the company must keep track of (1) average gross profit rate, (2) net sales at retail, (3) beginning inventory, and (4) net purchases. You can use the following steps to calculate the gross profit method:

CALCULATING THE GROSS PROFIT METHOD
Step 1. Calculate the cost of goods available for sale (Beginning inventory + Net purchases).
Step 2. Multiply the net sales at retail by the complement of the gross profit rate. This is the estimated cost of goods sold.
Step 3. Calculate the cost of estimated ending inventory (Step 1 − Step 2).

EXAMPLE   Assume Radar Company has the following information in its records:

Gross profit on sales	30%
Beginning inventory, January 1, 2009	$20,000
Net purchases	8,000
Net sales at retail for January	12,000

If you use the gross profit method, what is the company's estimated inventory?

The gross profit method calculates Radar's estimated cost of ending inventory at the end of January as follows:

Goods available for sale			
Beginning inventory, January 1, 2009		$20,000	
Net purchases		8,000	
Cost of goods available for sale		$28,000	← Step 1
Less estimated cost of goods sold:			
Net sales at retail	$12,000		
Cost percentage (100% − 30%)	Step 2 → .70		
Estimated cost of goods sold		8,400	
Estimated ending inventory, January 31, 2009		$19,600	← Step 3

Note that the cost of goods available for sale less the estimated cost of goods sold gives the estimated cost of ending inventory.

Since this chapter has looked at inventory flow, let's discuss inventory turnover—a key business ratio.

Inventory Turnover

Inventory turnover is the number of times the company replaces inventory during a specific time. Companies use the following two formulas to calculate inventory turnover:

$$\text{Inventory turnover at retail} = \frac{\text{Net sales}}{\text{Average inventory at retail}}$$

$$\text{Inventory turnover at cost} = \frac{\text{Cost of goods sold}}{\text{Average inventory at cost}}$$

You should note that inventory turnover at retail is usually lower than inventory turnover at cost. This is due to theft, markdowns, spoilage, and so on. Also, retail outlets and grocery stores usually have a higher turnover, but jewelry and appliance stores have a low turnover.

Now let's use an example to calculate the inventory turnover at retail and at cost.

EXAMPLE   The following facts are for Abby Company, a local sporting goods store (rounded to the nearest hundredth):

Net sales	$32,000	Cost of goods sold	$22,000
Beginning inventory at retail	11,000	Beginning inventory at cost	7,500
Ending inventory at retail	8,900	Ending inventory at cost	5,600

With these facts, we can make the following calculations:

$$\textbf{Average inventory} = \frac{\text{Beginning inventory} + \text{Ending inventory}}{2}$$

$$\text{At retail: } \frac{\$32,000}{\dfrac{\$11,000 + \$8,900}{2}} = \frac{\$32,000}{\$9,950} = \boxed{3.22}$$

$$\text{At cost: } \frac{\$22,000}{\dfrac{\$7,500 + \$5,600}{2}} = \frac{\$22,000}{\$6,550} = \boxed{3.36}$$

What Turnover Means

Inventory is often a company's most expensive asset. The turnover of inventory can have important implications. Too much inventory results in the use of needed space, extra insurance coverage, and so on. A low inventory turnover could indicate customer dissatisfaction, too much tied-up capital, and possible product obsolescence. A high inventory turnover might mean insufficient amounts of inventory causing stockouts that may lead to future lost sales. If inventory is moving out quickly, perhaps the company's selling price is too low compared to that of its competitors.

In recent years the **just-in-time (JIT) inventory system** from Japan has been introduced in the United States. Under ideal conditions, manufacturers must have suppliers that will provide materials daily as the manufacturing company needs them, thus eliminating inventories. The companies that are using this system, however, have often not been able to completely eliminate the need to maintain some inventory.

Distribution of Overhead

In Chapter 16 we studied the cost of goods sold and operating expenses shown on the income statement. The operating expenses included **overhead expenses**—expenses that are *not* directly associated with a specific department or product but that contribute indirectly to the running of the business. Examples of such overhead expenses are rent, taxes, and insurance.

Companies must allocate their overhead expenses to the various departments in the company. The two common methods of calculating the **distribution of overhead** are by (1) floor space (square feet) or (2) sales volume.

Calculations by Floor Space

To calculate the distribution of overhead by floor space, use the steps that follow.

CALCULATING THE DISTRIBUTION OF OVERHEAD BY FLOOR SPACE

Step 1. Calculate the total square feet in all departments.

Step 2. Calculate the ratio for each department based on floor space.

Step 3. Multiply each department's floor space ratio by the total overhead.

EXAMPLE   Roy Company has three departments with the following floor space:

Department A	6,000 square feet
Department B	3,000 square feet
Department C	1,000 square feet

The accountant's job is to allocate $90,000 of overhead expenses to the three departments. To allocate this overhead by floor space:

	Floor space in square feet	**Ratio**	
Department A	6,000	$\dfrac{6,000}{10,000} = 60\%$	
Department B	3,000	$\dfrac{3,000}{10,000} = 30\%$	← **Steps 1 and 2**
Department C	$\dfrac{1,000}{10,000}$ total square feet	$\dfrac{1,000}{10,000} = 10\%$	

Department A	.60 × $90,000 =	$54,000	
Department B	.30 × $90,000 =	27,000	← **Step 3**
Department C	.10 × $90,000 =	9,000	
		$90,000	

Calculations by Sales

To calculate the distribution of overhead by sales, use the steps that follow.

> **CALCULATING THE DISTRIBUTION OF OVERHEAD BY SALES**
>
> **Step 1.** Calculate the total sales in all departments.
> **Step 2.** Calculate the ratio for each department based on sales.
> **Step 3.** Multiply each department's sales ratio by the total overhead.

EXAMPLE Morse Company distributes its overhead expenses based on the sales of its departments. For example, last year Morse's overhead expenses were $60,000. Sales of its two departments were as follows, along with its ratio calculation.

Since Department A makes 80% of the sales, it is allocated 80% of the overhead expenses.

	Sales	**Ratio**	
Department A	$ 80,000	$\frac{\$80,000}{\$100,000} = .80$	
Department B	20,000	$\frac{\$20,000}{\$100,000} = .20$	← **Steps 1 and 2**
Total sales	$100,000		

These ratios are then multiplied by the overhead expense to be allocated.

Department A	.80 × $60,000 =	$48,000	
Department B	.20 × $60,000 =	12,000	← **Step 3**
		$60,000	

It's time to try another Practice Quiz.

LU 18–2 PRACTICE QUIZ

*Complete this **Practice Quiz** to see how you are doing*

1. From the following facts, calculate the cost of ending inventory using the retail method (round the cost ratio to the nearest tenth percent):

January 1—inventory at cost	$ 18,000
January 1—inventory at retail	$ 58,000
Net purchases at cost	$220,000
Net purchases at retail	$376,000
Net sales at retail	$364,000

2. Given the following, calculate the estimated cost of ending inventory using the gross profit method:

Gross profit on sales	40%
Beginning inventory, January 1, 2009	$27,000
Net purchases	$ 7,500
Net sales at retail for January	$15,000

3. Calculate the inventory turnover at cost and at retail from the following (round the turnover to the nearest hundredth):

Average inventory at cost	Average inventory at retail	Net sales	Cost of goods sold
$10,590	$19,180	$109,890	$60,990

4. From the following, calculate the distribution of overhead to Departments A and B based on floor space.

Amount of overhead expense to be allocated	Square footage
$70,000	10,000 Department A
	30,000 Department B

✓ Solutions

		Cost	Retail
1.	Beginning inventory	$ 18,000	$ 58,000
	Net purchases during the month	220,000	376,000
	Cost of goods available for sale	$238,000	$434,000
	Less net sales for the month		364,000
	Ending inventory at retail		$ 70,000
	Cost ratio ($238,000 ÷ $434,000)		54.8%
	Ending inventory at cost (.548 × $70,000)		$ 38,360
2.	**Goods available for sale**		
	Beginning inventory, January 1, 2009		$ 27,000
	Net purchases		7,500
	Cost of goods available for sale		$ 34,500
	Less estimated cost of goods sold:		
	Net sales at retail	$ 15,000	
	Cost percentage (100% − 40%)	.60	
	Estimated cost of goods sold		9,000
	Estimated ending inventory, January 31, 2009		$ 25,500

3. Inventory turnover at cost $= \dfrac{\text{Cost of goods sold}}{\text{Average inventory at cost}} = \dfrac{\$60,900}{\$10,590} = 5.76$

Inventory turnover at retail $= \dfrac{\text{Net sales}}{\text{Average inventory at retail}} = \dfrac{\$109,890}{\$19,180} = 5.73$

4.

		Ratio			
Department A	10,000	$\dfrac{10,000}{40,000}$	= .25 × $70,000 =	$17,500
Department B	$\dfrac{30,000}{40,000}$	$\dfrac{30,000}{40,000}$	= .75 × $70,000 =	52,500
				$70,000

LU 18–2a EXTRA PRACTICE QUIZ

Need more practice? Try this **Extra Practice Quiz** (check figures in Chapter Organizer, p. 444)

1. From the following, calculate the cost of ending inventory using the retail method (round the cost ratio to the nearest tenth percent):

January 1—inventory at cost	$19,000
January 1—inventory at retail	$60,000
Net purchases at cost	$265,000
Net purchases at retail	$392,000
Net sales at retail	$375,000

2. Given the following, calculate the estimated cost of ending inventory using the gross profit method:

Gross profit on sales	30%
Beginning inventory, January 1, 2009	$30,000
Net purchases	$8,000
Net sales at retail for January	$16,000

3. Calculate the inventory turnover at cost and at retail from the following (round the turnover to the nearest hundredth):

Average inventory at cost	Average inventory at retail	Net sales	Cost of goods sold
$11,200	$21,800	$129,500	$76,500

4. From the following, calculate the distribution of overhead to Departments A and B based on floor space.

Amount of overhead expense to be allocated	Square footage
$60,000	10,000 Department A
	50,000 Department B

CHAPTER ORGANIZER AND STUDY GUIDE
WITH CHECK FIGURES FOR EXTRA PRACTICE QUIZZES

Topic	Key point, procedure, formula	Example(s) to illustrate situation
Specific identification method, p. 431	Identification could be by serial number, physical description, or coding. The flow of goods and flow of costs are the same.	<table><tr><td></td><td>Cost per unit</td><td>Total cost</td></tr><tr><td>April 1, 3 units at</td><td>$7</td><td>$21</td></tr><tr><td>May 5, 4 units at</td><td>8</td><td>32</td></tr><tr><td></td><td></td><td>$53</td></tr></table> If 1 unit from each group is left, ending inventory is: $1 \times \$7 = \$7$ $+ 1 \times 8 = 8$ $\$15$ Cost of goods available for sale $-$ Cost of ending inventory $=$ Cost of goods sold $\$53 \quad - \quad \$15 \quad = \quad \$38$
Weighted-average method, p. 432	Weighted average unit cost $= \dfrac{\text{Total cost of goods available for sale}}{\text{Total number of units available for sale}}$	<table><tr><td></td><td>Cost per unit</td><td>Total cost</td></tr><tr><td>1/XX, 4 units at</td><td>$4</td><td>$16</td></tr><tr><td>5/XX, 2 units at</td><td>5</td><td>10</td></tr><tr><td>8/XX, 3 units at</td><td>6</td><td>18</td></tr><tr><td></td><td></td><td>$44</td></tr></table> Unit cost $= \dfrac{\$44}{9} = \$4.89$ If 5 units left, cost of ending inventory is 5 units $\times$ \$4.89 $=$ $24.45
FIFO—first-in, first-out method, p. 433	Sell old inventory first. Ending inventory is made up of last merchandise brought into store.	Using example above: 5 units left: (Last into store) 3 units at $6 $18 2 units at $5 10 Cost of ending inventory $28
LIFO—last-in, first-out method, p. 433	Sell last inventory brought into store first. Ending inventory is made up of oldest merchandise in store.	Using weighted-average example: 5 units left: (First into store) 4 units at $4 $16 1 unit at $5 5 Cost of ending inventory $21

(continues)

CHAPTER ORGANIZER AND STUDY GUIDE
WITH CHECK FIGURES FOR EXTRA PRACTICE QUIZZES (continued)

Topic	Key point, procedure, formula	Example(s) to illustrate situation
Retail method, p. 436	Ending inventory at cost equals: $\dfrac{\text{Cost of goods available at cost}}{\text{Cost of goods available at retail}} \times$ Ending inventory at retail (This is cost ratio.)	
Gross profit method, p. 437	$\dfrac{\text{Beg.}}{\text{inv.}} + \dfrac{\text{Net}}{\text{purchases}} - \dfrac{\text{Estimated cost of goods sold}}{} = \dfrac{\text{Estimated ending inventory}}{}$	
Inventory turnover at retail and at cost, p. 438	$\dfrac{\text{Net sales}}{\text{Average inventory at retail}}$ or $\dfrac{\text{Cost of goods sold}}{\text{Average inventory at cost}}$	
Distribution of overhead, p. 439	Based on floor space or sales volume, calculate: 1. Ratios of department floor space or sales to the total. 2. Multiply ratios by total amount of overhead to be distributed.	

Retail method example:

	Cost	Retail
Beginning inventory	$52,000	$ 83,000
Net purchases	28,000	37,000
Cost of goods available for sale	$80,000	$120,000
Less net sales for month		80,000
Ending inventory at retail		$ 40,000

Cost ratio $= \dfrac{\$80,000}{\$120,000} = .67 = 67\%$

Rounded to nearest percent.
Ending inventory at cost, $26,800
(.67 × $40,000)

Gross profit method example:

Goods available for sale

Beginning inventory	$30,000
Net purchases	3,000
Cost of goods available for sale	$33,000

Less: Estimated cost of goods sold:

Net sales at retail	$18,000
Cost percentage (100% − 30%)	.70
Estimated cost of goods sold	12,600
Estimated ending inventory	$20,400

Inventory turnover example:

Inventory, January 1 at cost	$20,000
Inventory, December 31 at cost	48,000
Cost of goods sold	62,000

At cost:

$\dfrac{\$62,000}{\dfrac{\$20,000 + \$48,000}{2}} = 1.82$ (inventory turnover at cost)

Distribution of overhead example:

Total overhead to be distributed, $10,000

	Floor space
Department A	6,000 sq. ft.
Department B	2,000 sq. ft.
	8,000 sq. ft.

Ratio A $= \dfrac{6,000}{8,000} = .75$

Ratio B $= \dfrac{2,000}{8,000} = .25$

Dept. A = .75 × $10,000 = $7,500
Dept. B = .25 × $10,000 = $2,500

(continues)

CHAPTER ORGANIZER AND STUDY GUIDE
WITH CHECK FIGURES FOR EXTRA PRACTICE QUIZZES (concluded)

Topic	Key point, procedure, formula		Example(s) to illustrate situation

KEY TERMS	Average inventory, *p. 438*
	Distribution of
	  overhead, *p. 439*
	First-in, first-out (FIFO)
	  method, *p. 433*
	Gross profit method, *p. 437*
	Inventory turnover, *p. 438*
		Just-in-time (JIT) inventory
		  system, *p. 439*
		Last-in, first-out (LIFO)
		  method, *p. 433*
		Overhead expenses, *p. 439*
		Periodic inventory
		  system, *p. 430*
			Perpetual inventory
			  system, *p. 430*
			Retail method, *p. 437*
			Specific identification
			  method, *p. 431*
			Weighted-average
			  method, *p. 432*

CHECK FIGURES FOR **EXTRA PRACTICE QUIZZES** **WITH PAGE REFERENCES**	LU 18–1a (p. 436) 1. a. $276.08; b. $533.92 2. a. $390; b. $420 3. a. $194 b. $616		LU 18–2a (p. 441) 1. $48,356 2. $26,800 3. 6.83; 5.94 4. $10,000; $50,000

Critical Thinking Discussion Questions

1. Explain how you would calculate the cost of ending inventory and cost of goods sold for specific identification, FIFO, LIFO, and weighted-average methods. Explain why during inflation, LIFO results in a tax savings for a business.

2. Explain the cost ratio in the retail method of calculating inventory. What effect will the increased use of computers have on the retail method?

3. What is inventory turnover? Explain the effect of a high inventory turnover during the Christmas shopping season.

4. How is the distribution of overhead calculated by floor space or sales? Give an example of why a store in your area cut back one department to expand another. Did it work?

Name _____   Date _____

DRILL PROBLEMS

18–1. Using the specific identification method, calculate (a) the ending inventory and (b) the cost of goods sold given the following:

Date	Units purchased	Cost per iPod	Ending inventory
June 1	15 Apple iPods	$150	3 iPods from June 1
October 1	25 Apple iPods	175	6 iPods from Oct. 1
December 1	35 Apple iPods	200	9 iPods from Dec. 1

From the following, (a) calculate the cost of ending inventory (round the average unit cost to the nearest cent) and (b) cost of goods sold using the weighted-average method, FIFO, and LIFO (ending inventory shows 61 units).

	Number purchased	Cost per unit	Total
January 1 inventory	40	$4	$160
April 1	60	7	420
June 1	50	8	400
November 1	55	9	495

18–2. Weighted average:

18–3. FIFO:

18–4. LIFO:

From the following, (18–5 to 18–12) calculate the cost of ending inventory and cost of goods sold for LIFO (18–13), FIFO (18–14), and the weighted-average (18–15) methods (make sure to first find total cost to complete the table); ending inventory is 49 units:

Beginning inventory and purchases	Units	Unit cost	Total dollar cost
18–5. Beginning inventory, January 1	5	$2.00	
18–6. April 10	10	2.50	
18–7. May 15	12	3.00	
18–8. July 22	15	3.25	
18–9. August 19	18	4.00	
18–10. September 30	20	4.20	
18–11. November 10	32	4.40	
18–12. December 15	16	4.80	

18–13. LIFO:

Cost of ending inventory   **Cost of goods sold**

18–14. FIFO:

Cost of ending inventory   **Cost of goods sold**

18–15. Weighted average:

Cost of ending inventory   **Cost of goods sold**

18–16. From the following, calculate the cost ratio (round to the nearest hundredth percent) and the cost of ending inventory to the nearest cent under the retail method.

Net sales at retail for year	$40,000	Purchases—cost	$14,000
Beginning inventory—cost	27,000	Purchases—retail	19,000
Beginning inventory—retail	49,000		

18–17. Complete the following (round answers to the nearest hundredth):

a. Average inventory at cost	b. Average inventory at retail	c. Net sales	d. Cost of goods sold	e. Inventory turnover at cost	f. Inventory turnover at retail
$14,000	$21,540	$70,000	$49,800		

Complete the following (assume $90,000 of overhead to be distributed):

		Square feet	Ratio	Amount of overhead allocated
18–18.	Department A	10,000		
18–19.	Department B	30,000		

18–20. Given the following, calculate the estimated cost of ending inventory using the gross profit method.

Gross profit on sales	55%	Net purchases	$ 3,900
Beginning inventory	$29,000	Net sales at retail	$17,000

WORD PROBLEMS

18–21. Comparing LIFO and FIFO inventory valuation methods was the topic in the May 8, 2006 issue of the *Grand Rapids Business Journal*. The purpose of LIFO is to match current costs of products produced or held for resale with the income earned from the current sale of the product. LIFO assumes the last inventory purchased during the period is sold first. 10 units were purchased on January 1, 2005, for $9.00 each and 5 units were purchased on December 1, 2005 at $10.00. Seven units were sold. **(a)** What would be the inventory amount using LIFO? **(b)** What would be the inventory amount using FIFO?

18–22. Marvin Company has a beginning inventory of 12 sets of paints at a cost of $1.50 each. During the year, the store purchased 4 sets at $1.60, 6 sets at $2.20, 6 sets at $2.50, and 10 sets at $3.00. By the end of the year, 25 sets were sold. Calculate **(a)** the number of paint sets in stock and **(b)** the cost of ending inventory under LIFO, FIFO, and the weighted-average methods. Round to nearest cent for the weighted average.

18–23. On August 23, 2006 *The Daily Oklahoman* reported a change in the inventory accounting method used by LSB Industries. The company changed from "last in, first out," to "first in, first out" method of rotating inventory to use the oldest product first. Using LIFO, ending inventory is $30,000. Switching to FIFO, ending inventory would be calculated at $25,000, with $150,000 inventory available for sale. The change would not only be reflected on the balance sheet, the income statement would also show a change in cost of merchandise (goods) sold. This would also cause a change in net income, therefore having a bearing on taxes paid by the firm. **(a)** What would be the cost of merchandise sold using LIFO? **(b)** What would be the cost of merchandise sold using FIFO?

18–24. The *Fairfield County Business Journal* on August 21, 2006, suggested one way for companies to improve cash flow would be increasing inventory turnover. A company needs to work on keeping inventory low, without hurting its ability to deliver within reasonable time frames. Too much inventory ties up cash that may be needed. By using a just-in-time inventory system, J.W. Collins would have been able to decrease his inventory by 10%. Collins' cost of goods sold is $120,000. Beginning inventory (at cost) is $80,000 and ending inventory (at cost) is $65,000. **(a)** What is J.W. Collins' inventory turnover (at cost) not using a just-in-time inventory system? **(b)** Using a just-in-time inventory system, what would be the inventory turnover (at cost)? Round to the nearest hundredth.

18–25. May's Dress Shop's inventory at cost on January 1 was $39,000. Its retail value is $59,000. During the year, May purchased additional merchandise at a cost of $195,000 with a retail value of $395,000. The net sales at retail for the year were $348,000. Could you calculate May's inventory at cost by the retail method? Round the cost ratio to the nearest whole percent.

18–26. A sneaker shop has made the following wholesale purchases of new running shoes: 11 pairs at $24, 20 pairs at $2.50, and 16 pairs at $26.50. An inventory taken last week indicates that 17 pairs are still in stock. Calculate the cost of this inventory by FIFO.

18–27. Over the past 3 years, the gross profit rate for Jini Company was 35%. Last week a fire destroyed all Jini's inventory. Using the gross profit method, estimate the cost of inventory destroyed in the fire, given the following facts that were recorded in a fireproof safe:

Beginning inventory	$ 6,000
Net purchases	64,000
Net sales at retail	49,000

CHALLENGE PROBLEMS

18–28. Patrick McMahon is selling shares in a company whose stock he had never purchased. Patrick had owned 800 shares of Pitney Bowes for many years. In a spin-off, Pitney stockholders received 8 shares of Imagistics for each 100 Pitney shares they owned. Pitney Bowes told its shareholders that their basis in Imagistics was 2.25% of their basis in Pitney. That is, for every $100 shareholders had spent to buy Pitney in the first place, $2.25 was allocated to Imagistics. Patrick decides to sell his complete inventory of Imagistics at $17.55 per share. **(a)** How many shares does Patrick have in his inventory? **(b)** What is his cost basis for these shares? **(c)** What is his capital gain (assume no commission involved)?

18–29. Logan Company uses a perpetual inventory system on a FIFO basis. Assuming inventory on January 1 was 800 units at $8 each, what is the cost of ending inventory at the end of October 5?

Received			Sold	
Date	**Quantity**	**Cost per unit**	**Date**	**Quantity**
Apr. 15	220	$5	Mar. 8	500
Nov. 12	1,900	9	Oct. 5	200

 SUMMARY PRACTICE TEST

1. Writing.com has a beginning inventory of 16 sets of pens at a cost of $2.12 each. During the year, Writing.com purchased 8 sets at $2.15, 9 sets at $2.25, 14 sets at $3.05, and 13 sets at $3.20. By the end of the year, 29 sets were sold. Calculate **(a)** the number of pen sets in stock and **(b)** the cost of ending inventory under LIFO, FIFO, and weighted-average methods. *(pp. 431–434)*

2. Lee Company allocates overhead expenses to all departments on the basis of floor space (square feet) occupied by each department. The total overhead expenses for a recent year were $200,000. Department A occupied 8,000 square feet; Department B, 20,000 square feet; and Department C, 7,000 square feet. What is the overhead allocated to Department C? In your calculations, round to the nearest whole percent. *(p. 439)*

3. A local college bookstore has a beginning inventory costing $80,000 and an ending inventory costing $84,000. Sales for the year were $300,000. Assume the bookstore markup rate on selling price is 70%. Based on the selling price, what is the inventory turnover at cost? Round to the nearest hundredth. *(p. 438)*

4. Dollar Dress Shop's inventory at cost on January 1 was $82,800. Its retail value is $87,500. During the year, Dollar purchased additional merchandise at a cost of $300,000 with a retail value of $325,000. The net sales at retail for the year were $295,000. Calculate Dollar's inventory at cost by the retail method. Round the cost ratio to the nearest whole percent. *(p. 437)*

5. On January 1, Randy Company had an inventory costing $95,000. During January, Randy had net purchases of $118,900. Over recent years, Randy's gross profit in January has averaged 45% on sales. The company's net sales in January were $210,800. Calculate the estimated cost of ending inventory using the gross profit method. *(p. 438)*

Personal Finance

STOCKS | This company is why you can buy silk ties on the street. Its shares may be a good deal, too. *By Andrew Tanzer*

CHINA go-between

SAY YOU'RE AN importer sitting in Chicago. You could be a retailer, a wholesaler or a manufacturer in search of cheap goods. Whether you seek electronics, fashion accessories, toys or hardware, the supplier of choice is probably a low-cost factory in China. But how can you find that competitive but anonymous Chinese manufacturer?

Merle Hinrichs, a native of Nebraska and longtime resident of Hong Kong, has built a surging and highly profitable business around just that challenge. Hinrichs's **Global Sources Ltd.** (symbol GSOL) operates a vast electronic marketplace that connects factories in China and elsewhere in Asia with buyers around the globe.

Some statistics tell the story of the Globalsources.com community. The Web site, divided into 13 product sections, such as children's products, security and auto parts, hosts information on 1.8 million products from 130,000 suppliers. More than 560,000 buyers from 230 countries submit millions of sales leads each year through the site. Global Sources earns its keep not through transaction fees but by selling ad space to thousands of manufacturers.

Hinrichs, 65, is no Internet geek.

- **Market capitalization:** $661 million
- **Revenues:** $155 million*
- **Earnings per share:** 2006, $0.51†; 2007, $0.71†
- **Shareholder services:** 415-433-3777

Data to February 14. *Estimate for 2006. †Estimate. SOURCES: Thomson, Yahoo, Citigroup.

He made his first fortune in print media, publishing unglamorous but ad-rich trade magazines before migrating online. He established Asian Sources publications (as it was then called) in Hong Kong in 1970 and shrewdly provided an initial ad medium for no-name small and midsize exporters in Taiwan, Hong Kong and Korea. Later, he tapped into the staggering industrial growth in China, where Global Sources operates 44 offices that are replete with ad salespeople.

When the Internet sprang up in the mid 1990s, Hinrichs seized the opportunity. A bulky trade magazine takes weeks to produce and wing its way to a buyer in Chicago. With Global Sources Online, a factory in China can change its product ad instantaneously. "Our total focus is on helping businesses market their products globally," says Hinrichs. "We're media-agnostic."

Although electronic media account for almost half of Global Sources' revenues, Hinrichs still publishes a dozen print trade publications. "Print is the hidden secret," he says. "You cannot build brands just online."

Global's fastest-growing business is the China sourcing fairs it hosts each spring and fall in Hong Kong. Last year, it sponsored six such product fairs, which attracted nearly 150,000 buyers from around the world. Global Sources sold nearly 13,000 booths to Chinese manufacturers for an average of $3,700 per booth. Hinrichs explains that because importers are "buying container-loads of products, most of which are made to specifications," they want to meet their suppliers in person.

Global Sources, a nice proxy for growth in global trade, is finally moving onto investors' radar screens. The stock has risen 70% since October, to $17, aided by favorable comments by CNBC's Jim Cramer. Citigroup expects Global to earn $40 million in 2008, three times its 2005 profits. It rates the stock, which trades at 24 times estimated 2007 profits, a "buy," with a one-year target of $22.50.

MICHAEL S. YAMASHITA/CORBIS

BUSINESS MATH ISSUE

Just-in-time inventory is just a fad.

1. List the key points of the article and information to support your position.
2. Write a group defense of your position using math calculations to support your view.

Slater's Business Math Scrapbook

with Internet Application
Putting Your Skills to Work

PROJECT A
Should Ryerson Tull change to
FIFO? Why?

Tracking the Numbers / *Short Order*

Costly Inventory Lesson For Some Short-Sellers

*Why Did Fall in Steel Prices
Fail to Dent Ryerson Tull?
It's a Matter of FIFO, LIFO*

By KAREN RICHARDSON
And PAUL GLADER

A LITTLE EXTRA TIME spent with the Inventory Accounting 101 textbook would have saved short-sellers a lot of pain—and millions of dollars—on their bet against **Ryerson Tull Inc.**

Ryerson Tull, one of the largest and most visible metal-service centers—which distribute steel and other metal—has the dubious distinction of being one of the 10 most-heavily shorted stocks on the New York Stock Exchange. Shorts—who sell borrowed shares on a bet the stock will fall—reckoned the company would face big losses as falling steel prices ate into the value of its inventories. So far, they've been wrong.

"I think there is a lot that people don't get about this company," says Marc Cohodes of the hedge fund Rocker Partners. Though best known for short-selling, Rocker actually owns just over 5% of Ryerson's stock, according to a July 29 securities filing. "We short fads, frauds and failures—and we buy situations that are not well understood or not well followed," Mr. Cohodes explains.

The shorts and other skeptics are raising questions about why Ryerson doesn't employ FIFO—"first-in, first-out"—accounting for its inventory. Under FIFO, the method employed by dealers in perishable goods such as food, rising market prices lead to "inventory holding gains," a rise in the value of inventory that boosts earnings. Likewise, a fall in market prices can lead to inventory-holding losses that hit earnings.

Ryerson instead uses LIFO—last-in, first-out—which is more common for inventories of products, like steel, that don't spoil easily over time. There's good economic reason for Ryerson to do so. Companies that use LIFO don't record an increase in inventory value as market prices rise, or inventory-holding losses when market prices fall. So in an inflationary cycle they report lower earnings, and pay lower taxes, than if they used FIFO. Lower taxes means more money in the bank. In a deflationary environment, LIFO firms tend to report higher earnings than their FIFO counterparts.

But in a July 29 conference call to discuss second-quarter earnings, five of the 12 investment analysts participating asked Ryerson executives variations on the same question, about how to compare the company's LIFO results to those of FIFO companies.

"We've been using LIFO since 1949," says Terence Rogers, Ryerson's vice president of finance and treasurer. "[The question] always comes up in a sharply inflationary or deflationary environment," adds Jay Gratz, Ryerson's chief financial officer.

Steel Yourself, Shorts

Ryerson Tull has 25 million freely trading shares outstanding. Short interest, in millions of shares:

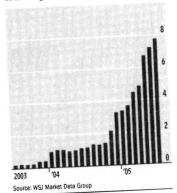

Source: WSJ Market Data Group

As steel spot prices fell 50% over the past 10 months from their 2004 peaks because of a steel surplus, short-sellers set their sights on industry middlemen, like Ryerson, that buy and process steel and other metals from steel mills and aluminum plants to store in warehouses and resell to manufacturers.

Shorts accounted for 31% of the publicly available shares of Ryerson Tull as of mid-July, the latest data available. The short-selling activity, in fact, helped pressure the company's market value to just below $500 million.

Mr. Gratz estimates that about half of that short interest is from trading related to $175 million in convertible bonds the company issued in November. So-called arbitrage traders often buy a convertible bond and sell the issuing company's underlying stock as a hedge. Mr. Gratz says he suspects the rest of the shorts are betting against the company's stock specifically because of the LIFO accounting

Internet Projects: See text Web site (www.mhhe.com/slater9e) and The Business Math Internet Resource Guide.

CHAPTER 19

Sales, Excise, and Property Taxes

Quick Fix

Checking on Sales Tax

■ **The Problem:** You're shopping online and want to know if you will be charged state sales tax on your purchase.

■ **The Solution:** Online retailers are required to charge tax on items shipped to states where they have a physical presence. Check to see whether the retailer has a store in your state either by browsing the retailer's store locations online or by giving it a call. This should give a pretty good sense of what to expect at the checkout. But it isn't foolproof. Offices and warehouses often count as physical locations, and they may be more difficult to locate. (Check out the corporate address.) And online retailers can choose to charge sales tax regardless of whether they have a store or warehouse in a particular state. Many also provide a list of states where they charge sales tax off the bottom of their home page or in a footnote on the price that appears at checkout. And you can always do a dry run and abandon your purchase before completing the transaction if you don't like what you see.
— *Jessica E. Vascellaro*

Wall Street Journal © 2005

LEARNING UNIT OBJECTIVES

LU 19–1: Sales and Excise Taxes

• Compute sales tax on goods sold involving trade and cash discounts and shipping charges *(pp. 454–455).*

• Explain and calculate excise tax *(p. 455).*

LU 19–2: Property Tax

• Calculate the tax rate in decimal *(p. 456).*

• Convert tax rate in decimal to percent, per $100 of assessed value, per $1,000 of assessed value, and in mills *(p. 457).*

• Compute property tax due *(p. 457).*

Do you like to go to the Internet to make your purchases because you save on state and local sales taxes? The following *Wall Street Journal* clipping "Some States Push to Collect Sales Tax" shows how much state and local sales tax revenue has been lost from Internet sales. Times are changing, and more taxes are being collected.

Some States Push to Collect Sales Tax

By Robert Guy Matthews

FOR YEARS, states and online retailers have bickered over whether the retailers should—and, if so, could—collect local and state sales taxes on purchases made over the Internet. The states have said they should and could. The retailers have argued that the complexity of different tax rates and categories among states and localities made it very difficult to do so.

Hoping to put an end to that argument, 18 states tomorrow will implement a long-planned move to remove obstacles that the retailers have cited. Architects of the Streamlined Sales Tax Project are devising a computer program that tracks the tax rates of the 18 states and their localities and automatically adds that rate to the bill of every online purchase. The states will also entice online retailers to collect state and local sales taxes by offering amnesty on taxes the retailers haven't collected in the years since the Internet retail boom began.

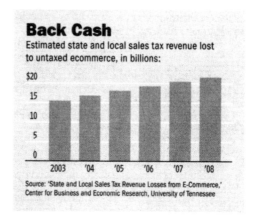

Back Cash
Estimated state and local sales tax revenue lost to untaxed ecommerce, in billions:

Source: 'State and Local Sales Tax Revenue Losses from E-Commerce,' Center for Business and Economic Research, University of Tennessee

As you know, sales tax rates vary from state to state. Four state capitals (Concord, New Hampshire; Dover, Delaware; Helena, Montana; and Salem, Oregon) do not impose a sales tax. However, if you live in California, Florida, Texas, or Washington, your combined state and local tax rate reaches 7% or more.

In Learning Unit 19–1 you will learn how sales taxes are calculated. This learning unit also discusses the excise tax that is collected in addition to the sales tax. Learning Unit 19–2 explains the use of property tax.

Learning Unit 19–1: Sales and Excise Taxes

Today, many states have been raising their sales tax and excise tax. Also, states have been gradually dropping some of their sales tax exemptions. In Connecticut, a 6% sales tax was imposed on newspapers sold at newsstands but not through subscriptions. Connecticut also imposes a 6% sales tax at vending machines.

Sales Tax

In many cities, counties, and states, the sellers of certain goods and services collect **sales tax** and forward it to the appropriate government agency. Forty-five states have a sales tax. Of the 45 states, 28 states and the District of Columbia exempt food; 44 states and the District of Columbia exempt prescription drugs.

Sales taxes are usually computed electronically by the new cash register systems and scanners. However, it is important to know how sellers calculate sales tax manually. The following example of a car battery will show you how to manually calculate sales tax.

EXAMPLE

Selling price of a Sears battery	$32.00	Shipping charge	$3.50
Trade discount to local garage	10.50	Sales tax	5%

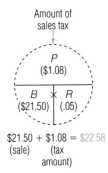

Amount of
sales tax

P
($1.08)

B   *R*
($21.50)   (.05)

$21.50 + $1.08 = $22.58
(sale)   (tax
amount)

Manual calculation

$32.00 − $10.50 =

$21.50 taxable
×   .05
$ 1.08 tax
+ 21.50 taxable
+ 3.50 shipping
$26.08 total price with tax and shipping

Check

100% is base + 5% is tax = 105%
1.05 × $21.50 = $22.58
+ 3.50 shipping
$26.08

In this example, note how the trade discount is subtracted from the selling price before any cash discounts are taken. If the buyer is entitled to a 6% cash discount, it is calculated as follows:

$$.06 \times \$21.50 = \$1.29$$

Also, remember that we do not take cash discounts on the sales tax or shipping charges.

Calculating Actual Sales

Managers often use the cash register to get a summary of their total sales for the day. The total sales figure includes the sales tax. So the sales tax must be deducted from the total sales. To illustrate this, let's assume the total sales for the day were $40,000, which included a 7% sales tax. What were the actual sales?

Hint: $40,000 is 107% of actual sales

$$\text{Actual sales} = \frac{\text{Total sales}}{1 + \text{Tax rate}}$$

Total sales

$$\text{Actual sales} = \frac{\$40,000}{1.07} = \$37,383.18$$

100% sales
+ 7% tax
107% → 1.07

Thus, the store's actual sales were $37,383.18. The actual sales plus the tax equal $40,000.

Check

$37,383.18 × .07 =

$ 2,616.82 sales tax
+ 37,383.18 actual sales
$40,000.00 total sales including sales tax

Excise Tax

Governments (local, federal, and state) levy **excise tax** on particular products and services. This can be a sizable source of revenue for these governments.

Consumers pay the excise tax in addition to the sales tax. The excise tax is based on a percent of the *retail* price of a product or service. This tax, which varies in different states, is imposed on luxury items or nonessentials. Examples of products or services subject to the excise tax include airline travel, telephone service, alcoholic beverages, jewelry, furs, fishing rods, tobacco products, and motor vehicles. Although excise tax is often calculated as a percent of the selling price, the tax can be stated as a fixed amount per item sold. The following example calculates excise tax as a percent of the selling price.[1]

EXAMPLE On June 1, Angel Rowe bought a fur coat for a retail price of $5,000. Sales tax is 7% with an excise tax of 8%. Her total cost is as follows:

$5,000
+   350 sales tax (.07 × $5,000)
+   400 excise tax (.08 × $5,000)
$5,750

Let's check your progress with a Practice Quiz.

---

[1]If excise tax were a stated fixed amount per item, it would have to be added to the cost of goods or services before any sales tax were taken. For example, a $100 truck tire with a $4 excise tax would be $104 before the sales tax was calculated.

LU 19–1 PRACTICE QUIZ

Complete this **Practice Quiz** to see how you are doing

From the following shopping list, calculate the total sales tax (food items are excluded from sales tax, which is 8%):

Chicken	$6.10	Orange juice	$1.29	Shampoo	$4.10
Lettuce	$ .75	Laundry detergent	$3.65		

✓ **Solutions**

Shampoo	$4.10
Laundry detergent	+ 3.65
	$7.75 × .08 = $.62

LU 9–1a EXTRA PRACTICE QUIZ

Need more practice? Try this **Extra Practice Quiz** (check figures in Chapter Organizer, p. 459)

From the following shopping list, calculate the total sales tax (food items are excluded from sales tax, which is 7%):

Chicken	$7.90	Orange juice	$1.50	Shampoo	$5.90
Lettuce	$ .85	Laundry detergent	$4.10		

Learning Unit 19–2: Property Tax

When you own property, you must pay property tax. In this unit we listen in on a conversation between a property owner and a tax assessor.

Defining Assessed Value

Bill Adams was concerned when he read in the local paper that the property tax rate had been increased. Bill knows that the revenue the town receives from the tax helps pay for fire and police protection, schools, and other public services. However, Bill wants to know how the town set the new rate and the amount of the new property tax.

Bill went to the town assessor's office to get specific details. The assessor is a local official who estimates the fair market value of a house. Before you read the summary of Bill's discussion, note the following formula:

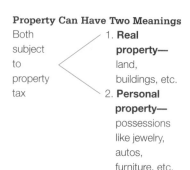

Property Can Have Two Meanings
Both subject to property tax
1. **Real property—** land, buildings, etc.
2. **Personal property—** possessions like jewelry, autos, furniture, etc.

$$\text{Assessed value} = \text{Assessment rate} \times \text{Market value}$$

Bill: What does **assessed value** mean?

Assessor: *Assessed value* is the value of the property for purposes of computing property taxes. We estimated the market value of your home at $210,000. In our town, we assess property at 30% of the market value. Thus, your home has an assessed value of $63,000 ($210,000 × .30). Usually, assessed value is rounded to the nearest dollar.

Bill: I know that the **tax rate** multiplied by my assessed value ($63,000) determines the amount of my property tax. What I would like to know is how did you set the new tax rate?

Determining the Tax Rate

Assessor: In our town first we estimate the total amount of revenue needed to meet our budget. Then we divide the total of all assessed property into this figure to get the *tax rate*. The formula looks like this:

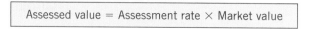

$$\text{Tax rate} = \frac{\text{Budget needed}}{\text{Total assessed value}^2}$$

Our town budget is $125,000, and we have a total assessed property value of $1,930,000. Using the formula, we have the following:

$$\frac{\$125,000}{\$1,930,000} = \$.0647668 = \boxed{.0648} \text{ tax rate per dollar}$$

---

[2]Remember that exemptions include land and buildings used for educational and religious purposes and the like.

Note that the rate should be rounded up to the indicated digit, *even if the digit is less than 5.* Here we rounded to the nearest ten thousandth.

How the Tax Rate Is Expressed

Assessor: We can express the .0648 tax rate per dollar in the following forms:

By percent	Per $100 of assessed value	Per $1,000 of assessed value	In mills
6.48%	$6.48	$64.80	64.80
(Move decimal two places to right.)	(.0648 × 100)	(.0648 × 1,000)	$\left(\dfrac{.0648}{.001}\right)$

A **mill** is $\frac{1}{10}$ of a cent or $\frac{1}{1,000}$ of a dollar (.001). To represent the number of mills as a tax rate per dollar, we divide the tax rate in decimal by .001. Rounding practices vary from state to state. Colorado tax bills are now rounded to the thousandth mill. An alternative to finding the rate in mills is to multiply the rate per dollar by 1,000, since a dollar has 1,000 mills. In the problems in this text, we round the mills per dollar to nearest hundredth.

How to Calculate Property Tax Due[3]

Assessor: The following formula will show you how we arrive at your **property tax:**

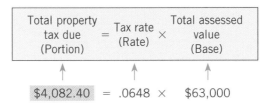

$$
\begin{array}{c}
\text{Total property tax due (Portion)} = \text{Tax rate (Rate)} \times \text{Total assessed value (Base)} \\
\uparrow \qquad\qquad \uparrow \qquad\qquad \uparrow \\
\$4{,}082.40 = .0648 \times \$63{,}000
\end{array}
$$

We can use the other forms of the decimal tax rate to show you how the property tax will not change even when expressed in various forms:

By percent	Per $100	Per $1,000	Mills
6.48% × $63,000	$\dfrac{\$63{,}000}{\$100} = 630$	$\dfrac{\$63{,}000}{\$1{,}000} = 63$	Property tax due
= **$4,082.40**	630 × $6.48	63 × $64.80	= Mills × .001 × Assessed value
	= $4,082.40	= $4,082.40	= 64.80 × .001 × $63,000
			= $4,082.40

Now it's time to try the Practice Quiz.

LU 19–2   PRACTICE QUIZ

Complete this **Practice Quiz** to see how you are doing

From the following facts: (1) calculate assessed value of Bill's home; (2) calculate the tax rate for the community in decimal (to nearest ten thousandths); (3) convert the decimal to **(a)** %, **(b)** per $100 of assessed value, **(c)** per $1,000 of assessed value, and **(d)** in mills (to nearest hundredth); and (4) calculate the property tax due on Bill's home in decimal, per $100, per $1,000, and in mills.

Given

Assessed market value	40%	Total budget needed	$ 176,000
Market value of Bill's home	$210,000	Total assessed value	$1,910,000

✓ **Solutions**

1. .40 × $210,000 = **$84,000**   2. $\dfrac{\$176{,}000}{\$1{,}910{,}000} = $ .0922 per dollar

---

[3]Some states have credits available to reduce what the homeowner actually pays. For example, 42 out of 50 states give tax breaks to people over age 65. In Alaska, the state's homestead exemption reduces the property tax of a $168,000 house from $1,512 to $253.

3. a. .0922 = 9.22%   **b.** .0922 × 100 = $9.22

   c. .0922 × 1,000 = $92.20   **d.** $\frac{.0922}{.001}$ = 92.2 mills   (or .0922 × 1,000)

4. .0922 × $84,000 = $7,744.80

   $9.22 × 840 = $7,744.80

   $92.20 × 84 = $7,744.80

   92.20 × .001 × $84,000 = $7,744.80

LU 19–2a   EXTRA PRACTICE QUIZ

Need more practice? Try this **Extra Practice Quiz** (check figures in Chapter Organizer, p. 459)

From the following facts: (1) calculate assessed value of Bill's home; (2) calculate the tax rate for the community in decimal (to nearest ten thousandths); (3) convert the decimal to **(a)** %, **(b)** per $100 of assessed value, **(c)** per $1,000 of assessed value, and **(d)** in mills (to nearest hundredth); and (4) calculate the property tax due on Bill's home in decimal, per $100, per $1,000, and in mills.

Given

Assessed market value	40%	Total budget needed	$ 159,000
Market value of Bill's home	$150,000	Total assessed value	$1,680,000

CHAPTER ORGANIZER AND STUDY GUIDE
WITH CHECK FIGURES FOR EXTRA PRACTICE QUIZZES

Topic	Key point, procedure, formula	Example(s) to illustrate situation
Sales tax, p. 454	Sales tax is not calculated on trade discounts. Shipping charges, etc., also are not subject to sales tax. Actual sales = $\frac{\text{Total sales}}{1 + \text{Tax rate}}$ Cash discounts are calculated on sale price before sales tax is added on.	Calculate sales tax: Purchased 12 bags of mulch at $59.40; 10% trade discount; 5% sales tax. $59.40 − $5.94 = $53.46 $53.46 × .05 $2.67 sales tax Any cash discount would be calculated on $53.46.
Excise tax, p. 455	Excise tax is calculated separately from sales tax and is an additional tax. It is based as a percent of the selling price. It could be stated as a fixed amount per item sold. In that case, the excise tax would be added to the cost of the item before any sales tax calculations. Rate for excise tax will vary.	Jewelry $4,000 retail price Sales tax 7% Excise tax 10% $4,000 + 280 sales tax + 400 excise tax $4,680
Assessed value, p. 456	Assessment rate × Market value	$100,000 house; rate, 30%; $30,000 assessed value.

(continues)

CHAPTER ORGANIZER AND STUDY GUIDE
WITH CHECK FIGURES FOR EXTRA PRACTICE QUIZZES (concluded)

Topic	Key point, procedure, formula	Example(s) to illustrate situation
Tax rate, p. 456	$\dfrac{\text{Budget needed}}{\text{Total assessed value}} = \text{Tax rate}$ (Round rate up to indicated digit even if less than 5.)	$\dfrac{\$800{,}000}{\$9{,}200{,}000} = .08695 = \boxed{.0870}$ tax rate per \$1
Expressing tax rate in other forms, p. 457	1. Percent: Move decimal two places to right. Add % sign. 2. Per \$100: Multiply by 100. 3. Per \$1,000: Multiply by 1,000. 4. Mills: Divide by .001.	1. $.0870 = \boxed{8.7\%}$ 2. $.0870 \times 100 = \boxed{\$8.70}$ 3. $.0870 \times 1{,}000 = \boxed{\$87}$ 4. $\dfrac{.0870}{.001} = \boxed{87 \text{ mills}}$
Calculating property tax, p. 457	$\dfrac{\text{Total property}}{\text{tax due}} = \text{Tax rate} \times \dfrac{\text{Total assessed}}{\text{value}}$ Various forms: 1. Percent × Assessed value 2. Per \$100: $\dfrac{\text{Assessed value}}{\$100} \times \text{Rate}$ 3. Per \$1,000: $\dfrac{\text{Assessed value}}{\$1{,}000} \times \text{Rate}$ 4. Mills: Mills × .001 × Assessed value	*Example:* Rate, .0870 per \$1; $30,000 assessed value 1. $(.087)8.7\% \times \$30{,}000 = \boxed{\$2{,}610}$ 2. $\dfrac{\$30{,}000}{\$100} = 300 \times \$8.70 = \boxed{\$2{,}610}$ 3. $\dfrac{\$30{,}000}{\$1{,}000} = 30 \times \$87 = \boxed{\$2{,}610}$ 4. $\dfrac{.0870}{.001} = 87$ mills 87 mills × .001 × \$30,000 = $\boxed{\$2{,}610}$
KEY TERMS	Assessed value, *p. 456*　　Personal property, *p. 456*　　Sales tax, *p. 454* Excise tax, *p. 455*　　Property tax, *p. 457*　　Tax rate, *p. 456* Mill, *p. 457*　　Real property, *p. 456*	
CHECK FIGURES FOR EXTRA PRACTICE QUIZZES WITH PAGE REFERENCES	LU 19–1a (p. 459) \$.70	LU 19–2a (p. 458) 1. \$60,000 2. \$.0946 3. a. 9.46%　　b. \$9.46; 　　c. 94.60;　　d. 94.6 mills 4. \$5,676

Critical Thinking Discussion Questions

1. Explain sales and excise taxes. Should all states have the same tax rate for sales tax?

2. Explain how to calculate actual sales when the sales tax was included in the sales figure. Is a sales tax necessary?

3. How is assessed value calculated? If you think your value is unfair, what could you do?

4. What is a mill? When we calculate property tax in mills, why do we use .001 in the calculation?

Classroom Notes

Name _____ Date _____

DRILL PROBLEMS

Calculate the following:

	Retail selling price	Sales tax (4%)	Excise tax (8%)	Total price including taxes
19–1.	$1,400			
19–2.	$1,900			

Calculate the actual sales since the sales and sales tax were rung up together; assume a 6% sales tax (round your answer to the nearest cent):

19–3. $90,000

19–4. $26,000

Calculate the assessed value of the following pieces of property:

	Assessment rate	Market value	Assessed value
19–5.	40%	$180,000	
19–6.	80%	$210,000	

Calculate the tax rate in decimal form to the nearest ten thousandth:

	Required budget	Total assessed value	Tax rate per dollar
19–7.	$920,000	$39,500,000	

Complete the following:

	Tax rate per dollar	In percent	Per $100	Per $1,000	Mills
19–8.	.0956				
19–9.	.0699				

Complete the amount of property tax due to the nearest cent for each situation:

	Tax rate	Assessed value	Amount of property tax due
19–10.	40 mills	$ 65,000	
19–11.	$42.50 per $1,000	105,000	
19–12.	$8.75 per $100	125,000	
19–13.	$94.10 per $1,000	180,500	

WORD PROBLEMS

19–14. Maggie Grace went to Photo Inc. and bought a $700 digital camera that is subject to 6% sales tax and 7% excise tax. What is the total amount Maggie paid?

19–15. Don Chather bought a new Dell computer for $1,995. This included a 6% sales tax. What is the amount of sales tax and the selling price before the tax?

19–16. According to the March 4, 2007 *Waterloo-Cedar Falls Courier*, the city council is set to consider cutting homeowners taxes. The property tax rate would fall from $18.85 to $18.78 per $1,000 of assessed taxable property valuation. Kay Hall has a $350,000 home, with an assessed rate of 60%. **(a)** What would her tax bill be under the present rate? **(b)** What would her tax bill be under the proposed cut?

19–17. In the community of Revere, the market value of a home is $180,000. The assessment rate is 30%. What is the assessed value?

19–18. On November 10, 2006, the *Connecticut Post* reported Bridgeport's tax assessment is based on 70% of a home's appraised value. Dolly Curtis who lives in a Victorian house on Flat Rock Road said her assessment rose to $468,230 from half that amount. **(a)** What is the value of Dolly's home? **(b)** What had been the value of dolly's home before the reassessment?

19–19. Lois Clark bought a ring for $6,000. She must still pay a 5% sales tax and a 10% excise tax. The jeweler is shipping the ring, so Lois must also pay a $40 shipping charge. What is the total purchase price of Lois's ring?

19–20. Blunt County needs $700,000 from property tax to meet its budget. The total value of assessed property in Blunt is $110,000,000. What is the tax rate of Blunt? Round to the nearest ten thousandth. Express the rate in mills.

19–21. Bill Shass pays a property tax of $3,200. In his community, the tax rate is 50 mills. What is Bill's assessed value?

19–22. The home of Bill Burton is assessed at $80,000. The tax rate is 18.50 mills. What is the tax on Bill's home?

19–23. *The Blade* (OH), on February 7, 2007, reported on property revaluations. Jesse Garza has a home assessed at $285,000. The tax rate is 7.9 mills. What is the tax on Jesse's home?

19–24. Bill Blake pays a property tax of $2,500. In his community, the tax rate is 55 mills. What is Bill's assessed value? Round to the nearest dollar.

19–25. A new comparative property tax study by the executive director of a Minneapolis group of landlords showed that the Wells Fargo Center in downtown Minneapolis pays four times the taxes as the Wells Fargo Center in downtown Denver. The property tax rate for Minneapolis is $8.73 per square foot, and the Denver rate is $2.14 a square foot. If 3,500 square feet is occupied at each location, what is the difference paid in property taxes?

19–26. The Newton County commissioners have approved a $9.3 million budget for the year 2006. Kathy Griffin's home has a market value of $150,000 and a 30% assessment rate. The total assessed property value for Newton County is $1,339,150,719, the same as it was last year. **(a)** What is the tax rate per dollar for 2006? **(b)** Last year the tax rate per dollar was .0065. What was the county's total budget last year? Round to the nearest hundred thousands. **(c)** What was the amount of Kathy's county taxes last year? **(d)** How much will Kathy pay in county taxes for 2006? **(e)** How much have Kathy's taxes increased?

19–27. Art Neuner, an investor in real estate, bought an office condominium. The market value of the condo was $250,000 with a 70% assessment rate. Art feels that his return should be 12% per month on his investment after all expenses. The tax rate is $31.50 per $1,000. Art estimates it will cost $275 per month to cover general repairs, insurance, and so on. He pays a $140 condo fee per month. All utilities and heat are the responsibility of the tenant. Calculate the monthly rent for Art. Round your answer to the nearest dollar (at intermediate stages).

DVD SUMMARY PRACTICE TEST

1. Carol Shan bought a new Apple iPod at Best Buy for $299. The price included a 5% sales tax. What are the sales tax and the selling price before the tax? *(p. 455)*

2. Jeff Jones bought a ring for $4,000 from Zales. He must pay a 7% sales tax and 10% excise tax. Since the jeweler is shipping the ring, Jeff must also pay a $30 shipping charge. What is the total purchase of Jeff's ring? *(p. 455)*

3. The market value of a home in Boston, Massachusetts, is $365,000. The assessment rate is 40%. What is the assessed value? *(p. 456)*

4. Jan County needs $910,000 from its property tax to meet the budget. The total value of assessed property in Jan is $180,000,000. What is Jan's tax rate? Round to the nearest ten-thousandth. Express the rate in mills (to the nearest tenth). *(p. 456)*

5. The home of Nancy Billows is assessed at $250,000. The tax rate is 4.95 mills. What is the tax on Nancy's home? *(p. 456)*

6. V's Warehouse has a market value of $880,000. The property in V's area is assessed at 35% of the market value. The tax rate is $58.90 per $1,000 of assessed value. What is V's property tax? *(p. 457)*

Cut your **PROPERTY** tax

T HE RURAL county where I live has just reassessed real estate values, and my home's assessment more than tripled, as did most others in the county. The assessed value is now more than my most recent

ASK KIM
by Kimberly Lankford

property appraisal. Should I appeal? What information would I have to present? —**TIM TAGLAUER**, *via e-mail*

Go for it. As many as 60% of homes are assessed for too much, estimates Pete Sepp, of the National Taxpayers Union, and about 33% of property-tax appeals succeed.

Procedures vary, but you generally have 30 to 60 days after receiving an assessment notice to file an appeal. Ask the assessor's office for a copy of your property card, which documents the information on which the assessment was based. If the card lists the wrong number of rooms or square footage, for example, you may be able to get your assessment changed without a formal appeal.

If the information is accurate, go to Zillow.com to see how your home's assessment stacks up against others in your neighborhood. If you find that similar homes are assessed at a lower value, you may have a strong case.

If you spot big discrepancies, check your local assessor's office's records for more details on homes with similar features and lower assessments. Or find comparable assessments and explain why your home's value should be lower, says Sepp, whose organization publishes the helpful brochure *How to Fight Property Taxes* ($6.95; www.ntu.org). Some jurisdictions also allow you to submit as evidence market-value information, such as your recent appraisal.

> **❝ As many as 60% of homes are assessed for too much, and about 33% of appeals succeed. ❞**

BUSINESS MATH ISSUE

Kiplinger's © 2007

All homes are not fairly assessed.

1. List the key points of the article and information to support your position.
2. Write a group defense of your position using math calculations to support your view.

Slater's Business Math Scrapbook

with Internet Application

Putting Your Skills to Work

Bartering to Avoid Taxes

Popular Real-Estate Strategy Is Increasingly Used to Defer Capital Gains on Other Assets

By RACHEL EMMA SILVERMAN

Procrastination: *This Louisville Slugger used by Joe DiMaggio was part of a recent 1031 exchange that deferred $80,000 in taxes.*

JOHN A. HILLERICH IV recently helped his company make a big trade—and hold off tens of thousands of dollars in taxes.

His business, **Hillerich & Bradsby** Co., which makes Louisville Slugger bats and operates a baseball museum, bought a bat valued at nearly $350,000 that was used by Joe DiMaggio during his 1941 56-game hitting streak. In exchange, the company sold a collection of baseball memorabilia, including a Ty Cobb bat and several original photos of Mickey Mantle.

Simply selling off the memorabilia and pocketing the cash would have meant a big capital-gains hit. But the deal was structured in a special way—as a "like-kind" trade of similar assets—which helped the company defer some $80,000 in taxes.

It is bartering for the well-to-do. Using a section of the tax code called 1031, a growing number of wealthy individuals and companies are participating in so-called like-kind, or 1031, exchanges. The strategy allows participants to defer, or sometimes even avoid, capital-gains taxes when they quickly replace business or investment assets with similar property of equal or greater value.

In recent years, 1031 exchanges have soared in popularity, mostly with real estate, as investors have flocked into the real-estate market and prices have skyrocketed, leading to big capital gains that investors have been eager to put off. But as people grow familiar with the tactic, and are diversifying into a wider variety of investment assets, some are now doing trades with other types of property, including art, collectibles, private jets, collector cars, yachts, copyrights, race horses, even Web site addresses.

The total value of all property involved in 1031 exchanges jumped to $175 billion in 2003, the latest figures available, compared with roughly $90 billion in 1999, according to estimates from Deloitte Tax LLP, a unit of Deloitte & Touche USA LLP.

The idea behind the tax break, which has been around for decades, is to encourage capital reinvestment; the taxes you defer are like a loan from the government to buy new investment or business assets. So the assets involved must be purchased for investment or business purposes, rather than personal use. Investors can conduct a direct, cashless trade with one party—say, swapping a horse for a horse. But most sellers do "deferred exchanges," whereby a property is sold to one party, and then replaced with a similar asset that may be purchased from another party.

India Introduces A Value-Added Tax

Reuters News Service

NEW DELHI—India introduced a value-added tax Friday, its most significant tax change in years, despite protests from wholesale and retail sectors.

The VAT replaces a complex web of Indian state sales taxes and forms the centerpiece of the government's tax measures to simplify the system and raise revenue for cash-strapped regions.

Shopkeepers across India kept their shutters down for a third straight day Friday in protest against the levy, which they worry is complex, poorly prepared and set to burden them with higher payments. Eight states, five of them ruled by the main opposition Bharatiya Janata Party, also oppose the tax. However, a senior government official said the tax—in place in 130 countries—had been adopted in a majority of India's 29 states.

Implementation of the VAT here has been delayed five times in nearly 10 years.

CHAPTER 20

Life, Fire, and Auto Insurance

LEARNING UNIT OBJECTIVES

LU 20–1: Life Insurance

- Explain the types of life insurance; calculate life insurance premiums (pp. 468–470).
- Explain and calculate cash value and other nonforfeiture options (pp. 470–471).

LU 20–2: Fire Insurance

- Explain and calculate premiums for fire insurance of buildings and their contents (pp. 472–473).
- Calculate refunds when the insured and the insurance company cancel fire insurance (pp. 473–474).
- Explain and calculate insurance loss when coinsurance is not met (p. 474).

LU 20–3: Auto Insurance

- Explain and calculate the cost of auto insurance (pp. 475–479).

Ask Personal Journal.

Q: *My insurer says the maximum deductible for my auto-insurance policy in Connecticut is $1,000, citing state law. Is this true?* –MANUEL HIDALGO, WEST HARTFORD, CONN.

A: The amount of the deductible you pay before your auto-insurance policy kicks in is typically set by you and the insurance company. According to Connecticut's Department of Insurance, there is no state law that sets the maximum deductible for auto policies. State Farm Insurance Cos., for example, offers deductible options of $2,000 for comprehensive and collision coverage. (Drivers who only purchase liability coverage typically aren't required to pay a deductible on claims.) By requesting higher deductibles, you can lower your costs substantially. Boosting your policy's deductible to $1,000 could save you 40% or more a year by lowering the price of collision and comprehensive coverage, according to the Insurance Information Institute Inc.

—*Jane J. Kim*

We answer readers' questions here each Thursday. Send your questions to **PersonalJournal@WSJ.com**

Wall Street Journal © 2005

Is Long-Term Care Worth the Price?

Premiums Are Now Lower, But Out-of-Pocket Costs May Be Too Much for Some

By CHRISTOPHER OSTER

INSURERS ARE OFFERING long-term-care policies with long-term deductibles in order to lower premiums and increase sales. But the policies have been slow to catch on.

Long-term-care insurance pays for care for individuals with chronic illnesses or disabilities that leave them unable to care for themselves. Typical policies will pay for three years to six years of care, but premiums are pricey, some-times more than $2,000 a year.

That has turned off some potential customers who would prefer to take the risk that they can afford to cover their own care. One potential solution is for policyholders to take on longer "elimination periods," which are similar to deductibles on auto and home policies. As with those policies, the more a policyholder is willing to pay out of pocket for long-term care, the lower the premiums.

Making Use of Savings

By buying a policy with a long deductible period, consumers are betting they can afford to pay for six months, a full year, or as much as four years of their own care. But with nursing-home care averaging more than $100,000 a year in some states, that's an expensive bet.

For those able to afford the bigger out-of-pocket expense, though, the premiums savings could be used to extend coverage to possibly lifetime coverage.

Even taking on a deductible period of 90 days, instead of 30, can mean considerable savings. Consider a policy issued to a healthy 40-year-old man, with a maximum benefit of $150 a day and three-year coverage. With a 30-day deductible, a policy issued by John Hancock Financial Services, a unit of **Manulife Financial** Corp., carries an annual premium of $1,398. Lengthen the deductible to 90 days and the premium drops to $1,165. A full year gets a premium of $932.

Given the same scenario, **UnumProvident** Corp. charges $794 for a policy with a 30-day deductible and $529 for one with a full-year deductible, according to Long

Wall Street Journal © 2004

If you are thinking of purchasing a long-term care insurance policy, you have to consider the effect of your decision. The *Wall Street Journal* clipping "Is Long-Term Care Worth the Price?" may help you make your decision. You must weigh the cost of long-term care insurance against your estimate of your future financial position. Remember that the actual care could cost you over $500 per day. On the other hand, if you are in good health and your future looks good, your premium savings could be used to extend coverage to possibly lifetime coverage.

Regardless of the type of insurance you buy—nursing home, property, life, fire, or auto—be sure to read and understand the policy before you buy the insurance. It has been reported that half of the people in the United States who have property insurance have not read their policy and 60% do not understand their policy. If you do not understand your life, fire, or auto insurance policies, this chapter should answer many of your questions. We begin by studying life insurance.

Learning Unit 20–1: Life Insurance

Bob Brady owns Bob's Deli. He is 40 years of age, married, and has three children. Bob wants to know what type of life insurance protection will best meet his needs. Following is a discussion between an insurance agent, Rick Jones, and Bob.

Bob: I would like to buy a life insurance policy that will pay my wife $200,000 in the event of my death. My problem is that I do not have much cash. You know, bills, bills, bills. Can you explain some types of life insurance and their costs?

Rick: Let's begin by explaining some life insurance terminology. The **insured** is you—the **policyholder** receiving coverage. The **insurer** is the company selling the insurance policy. Your wife is the **beneficiary.** As the beneficiary, she is the person named in the policy to receive the insurance proceeds at the death of the insured (that's you, Bob). The amount stated in the policy, say, $200,000, is the **face amount** of the policy. The **premium** (determined by **statisticians** called *actuaries*) is the periodic payments you agree to make for the cost of the insurance policy. You can pay premiums annually, semiannually, quarterly, or monthly. The more frequent the payment, the higher the total cost due to increased paperwork, billing, and so on. Now we look at the different types of insurance.

Types of Insurance

In this section Rick explains term insurance, straight life (ordinary life), 20-payment life, 20-year endowment, and universal life insurance.

Term Insurance

Rick: The cheapest type of life insurance is **term insurance,** but it only provides *temporary* protection. Term insurance pays the face amount to your wife (beneficiary) only if you die within the period of the insurance (1, 5, 10 years, and so on).

For example, let's say you take out a 5-year term policy. The insurance company automatically allows you to renew the policy at increased rates until age 70. A new policy called **level premium term** may be less expensive than an annual term policy since each year for, say, 50 years, the premium will be fixed.

The policy of my company lets you convert to other insurance types without a medical examination. To determine your rates under 5-year term insurance, check this table (Table 20.1). The annual premium at 40 years per $1,000 of insurance is $3.52. We use the following steps to calculate the total yearly premium.

CALCULATING ANNUAL LIFE INSURANCE PREMIUMS
Step 1. Look up the age of the insured and the type of insurance in Table 20.1 (for females, subtract 3 years). This gives the premium cost per $1,000.
Step 2. Divide the amount of coverage by $1,000 and multiply the answer by the premium cost per $1,000.

TABLE **20.1**

Life insurance rates for males (for females, subtract 3 years from the age)*

Age	Five-year term	Age	Straight life	Age	Twenty-payment life	Age	Twenty-year endowment
20	1.85	20	5.90	20	8.28	20	13.85
21	1.85	21	6.13	21	8.61	21	14.35
22	1.85	22	6.35	22	8.91	22	14.92
23	1.85	23	6.60	23	9.23	23	15.54
24	1.85	24	6.85	24	9.56	24	16.05
25	1.85	25	7.13	25	9.91	25	17.55
26	1.85	26	7.43	26	10.29	26	17.66
27	1.86	27	7.75	27	10.70	27	18.33
28	1.86	28	8.08	28	11.12	28	19.12
29	1.87	29	8.46	29	11.58	29	20.00
30	1.87	30	8.85	30	12.05	30	20.90
31	1.87	31	9.27	31	12.57	31	21.88
32	1.88	32	9.71	32	13.10	32	22.89
33	1.95	33	10.20	33	13.67	33	23.98
34	2.08	34	10.71	34	14.28	34	25.13
35	2.23	35	11.26	35	14.92	35	26.35
36	2.44	36	11.84	36	15.60	36	27.64
37	2.67	37	12.46	37	16.30	37	28.97
38	2.95	38	13.12	38	17.04	38	30.38
39	3.24	39	13.81	39	17.81	39	31.84
40	3.52	40	14.54	40	18.61	40	33.36
41	3.79	41	15.30	41	19.44	41	34.94
42	4.04	42	16.11	42	20.31	42	36.59
43	4.26	43	16.96	43	21.21	43	38.29
44	4.50	44	17.86	44	22.15	44	40.09

*Note that these tables are a sampling of age groups, premium costs, and insurance coverage that are available under 45 years of age.

$$\frac{\$200,000 \text{ (coverage)}}{\$1,000} = 200 \times \$3.52 = \boxed{\$704}$$

Number of   Cost per   Annual
thousands $1,000   premium
                   for age 40

Airport flight insurance is a type of term insurance.

From this formula you can see that for $704 per year for the next 5 years, we, your insurance company, offer to pay your wife $200,000 in the event of your death. At the end of the 5th year, you are not entitled to any cash from your paid premiums. If you do not renew your policy (at a higher rate) and die in the 6th year, we will not pay your wife anything. Term insurance provides protection for only a specific period of time.

Bob: Are you telling me that my premium does not build up any cash savings that you call **cash value**?

Rick: The term insurance policy does not build up cash savings. Let me show you a policy that does build up cash value. This policy is straight life.

Straight Life (Ordinary Life)

Rick: Straight life insurance provides *permanent* protection rather than the temporary protection provided by term insurance. The insured pays the same premium each year or until death.[1] The premium for straight life is higher than that for term insurance because straight life provides both protection and a built-in cash savings feature. According to our table (Table 20.1, p. 000), your annual premium, Bob, would be:

Face value is usually the amount paid to the beneficiary at the time of insured's death.

$$\frac{\$200,000}{\$1,000} = 200 \times \$14.54 = \boxed{\$2,908} \text{ annual premium}$$

Bob: Compared to term, straight life is quite expensive.

Rick: Remember that term insurance has no cash value accumulating, as straight life does. Let me show you another type of insurance—20-payment life—that builds up cash value.

Twenty-Payment Life

Rick: A **20-payment life** policy is similar to straight life in that 20-payment life provides permanent protection and cash value, but you (the insured) pay premiums for only the first 20 years. After 20 years you own **paid-up insurance.** According to my table (Table 20.1), your annual premium would be:

$$\frac{\$200,000}{\$1,000} = 200 \times \$18.61 = \boxed{\$3,722} \text{ annual premium}$$

Bob: The 20-payment life policy is more expensive than straight life.

Rick: This is because you are only paying for 20 years. The shorter period of time does result in increased yearly costs. Remember that in straight life you pay premiums over your entire life. Let me show you another alternative that we call 20-year endowment.

Twenty-Year Endowment

Rick: The **20-year endowment** insurance policy is the most expensive. It is a combination of term insurance and cash value. For example, from age 40 to 60, you receive term insurance protection in that your wife would receive $200,000 should you die. At age 60, your protection *ends* and you receive the face value of the policy that equals the $200,000 cash value. Let's use my table again (Table 20.1) to see how expensive the 20-year endowment is:

$$\frac{\$200,000}{\$1,000} = 200 \times \$33.36 = \boxed{\$6,672} \text{ annual premium}$$

In summary, Bob, following is a review of the costs for the various types of insurance we have talked about:

---

[1] In the following section on nonforfeiture values, we show how a policyholder in later years can stop making payments and still be covered by using the accumulated cash value built up.

FIGURE **20.1**

Nonforfeiture options

Option 1: Cash value (cash surrender value)

a. Receive cash value of policy.

b. Policy is terminated.

The longer the policy has been in effect, the higher the cash value because more premiums have been paid in.

Option 2: Reduced paid-up insurance

a. Cash value buys protection without paying new premiums.

b. Face amount of policy is related to cash value buildup and age of insured. The **face amount is less than original policy.**

c. Policy continues for life (at a reduced face amount).

Option 3: Extended term insurance

a. Original face amount of policy continues for a certain period of time.

b. Length of policy depends on cash value built up and on insured's age.

c. This option results automatically if policyholder doesn't pay premiums and fails to elect another option.

	5-year term	Straight life	20-payment life	20-year endowment
Premium cost per year	$704	$2,908	$3,722	$6,672

Before we proceed, I have another policy that may interest you—universal life.

Universal Life Insurance

Rick: Universal life is basically a **whole-life** insurance plan with flexible premium schedules and death benefits. Under whole life, the premiums and death benefits are fixed. Universal has limited guarantees with greater risk on the holder of the policy. For example, if interest rates fall, the policyholder must pay higher premiums, increase the number of payments, or switch to smaller death benefits in the future.

Bob: That policy is not for me—too much risk. I'd prefer fixed premiums and death benefits.

Rick: OK, let's look at how straight life, 20-payment life, and 20-year endowment can build up cash value and provide an opportunity for insurance coverage without requiring additional premiums. We call these options **nonforfeiture values.**

Nonforfeiture Values

Rick: Except for term insurance, the other types of life insurance build up cash value as you pay premiums. These policies provide three options should you, the policyholder, ever want to cancel your policy, stop paying premiums, or collect the cash value. My company lists these options here (Figure 20.1).

For example, Bob, let's assume that at age 40 we sell you a $200,000 straight-life policy. Assume that at age 55, after the policy has been in force for 15 years, you want to stop paying premiums. From this table (Table 20.2, p. 471), I can show you the options that are available.

Insight into Health and Business Insurance Often people who interview for a new job are more concerned with the salary offered than the whole health care package such as eye care, dental care, hospital and doctor care, and so on. Be sure you know exactly what the new job offers in health insurance. For employees, company health insurance and life insurance benefits can be an important job consideration.

Some of the key types of business insurance that you may need as a business owner include fire insurance, business interruption insurance (business loss until physical damages are fixed), casualty insurance (insurance against a customer's suing your business due to an accident on company property), workers' compensation (insurance against injuries or sickness from being on the job), and group insurance (life, health, and accident). The following *Wall Street Journal* clipping "Terror Insurance Act Extended by Senate" reminds business owners that insurers are required to offer terrorism insurance to businesses:

| TABLE | 20.2 | Nonforfeiture options based on $1,000 face value |

	STRAIGHT LIFE				20-PAYMENT LIFE				20-YEAR ENDOWMENT			
Years insurance policy in force	Cash value	Amount of paid-up insurance	EXTENDED TERM Years	EXTENDED TERM Day	Cash value	Amount of paid-up insurance	EXTENDED TERM Years	EXTENDED TERM Day	Cash value	Amount of paid-up insurance	EXTENDED TERM Years	EXTENDED TERM Day
5	29	86	9	91	71	220	19	190	92	229	23	140
10	96	259	18	76	186	521	28	195	319	520	30	160
15	148	371	20	165	317	781	32	176	610	790	35	300
20	265	550	21	300	475	1,000	Life		1,000	1,000	Life	

Option 1: Cash value

$$\frac{\$200,000}{\$1,000} = 200 \times \$148 = \$29,600$$

Option 2: Reduced paid-up insurance

$$\frac{\$200,000}{\$1,000} = 200 \times \$371 = \$74,200$$

Option 3: Extended term insurance

Bob could continue this $200,000 policy for 20 years and 165 days.

Terror Insurance Act Extended by Senate

The Senate approved a two-year extension of the soon-to-expire federal program that covers big insurance claims caused by terrorist attacks.

The chamber, on a voice vote, approved a revised version of the Terrorism Risk Insurance Act of 2002. The new legislation would require insurers to pick up a bigger share of damages from terrorism attacks in the U.S. The House is expected to take up the issue in early December, setting the stage for President Bush to sign a final bill before the program expires Dec. 31.

Under the current law, insurers are required to offer terrorism insurance to businesses. In return, the government limits the industry's losses in the case of attacks by foreign terrorists.

At the urging of the White House, the Senate agreed to reduce coverage in the program by excluding commercial vehicles, theft, surety and other items, and to raise the deductibles for insurers. After the industry pays the equivalent of damages caused by the Sept. 11, 2001, attacks, or about $32 billion, the federal government would cover 90% of the remaining insured losses in 2006.

Wall Street Journal © 2005

Although group health insurance costs have soared today, many companies still pay the major portion of the cost. Some companies also provide health insurance benefits for retirees. As health costs continue to rise, we can expect to see some changes in this employee benefit.

Companies vary in the type of life insurance benefits they provide to their employees. This insurance can be a percent of the employee's salary with the employee naming the beneficiary; or in the case of key employees, the company can be the beneficiary.

If as an employer you need any of the types of insurance mentioned in this section, be sure to shop around for the best price. If you are in the job market, consider the benefits offered by a company as part of your salary and make your decisions accordingly.

In the next unit, we look specifically at fire insurance. Now let's check your understanding of this unit with a Practice Quiz.

LU 20-1   PRACTICE QUIZ

Complete this **Practice Quiz** to see how you are doing

1. Bill Boot, age 39, purchased a $60,000, 5-year term life insurance policy. Calculate his annual premium from Table 20.1. After 4 years, what is his cash value?

2. Ginny Katz, age 32, purchased a $78,000, straight life policy. Calculate her annual premium. If after 10 years she wants to surrender her policy, what options and what amounts are available to her?

✓ **Solutions**

1. $\dfrac{\$60,000}{\$1,000} = 60 \times \$3.24 = \boxed{\$194.40}$ No cash value in term insurance.

2. $\dfrac{\$78,000}{\$1,000} = 78 \times \$8.46^* = \boxed{\$659.88}$

Option 1: Cash value $78 \times \$96 = \boxed{\$7,488}$

Option 2: Paid up $78 \times \$259 = \boxed{\$20,202}$

Option 3: Extended term $\boxed{18 \text{ years } 76 \text{ days}}$

*For females we subtract 3 years.

LU 20–1a EXTRA PRACTICE QUIZ

Need more practice? Try this **Extra Practice Quiz** (check figures in Chapter Organizer, p. 482)

1. Bill Boot, age 37, purchased a $70,000, 5-year term life insurance policy. Calculate his annual premium from Table 20.1. After 3 years, what is his cash value?
2. Ginny Katz, age 30, purchased a $95,000, straight-life policy. Calculate her annual premium. If after 5 years she wants to surrender her policy, what options and what amounts are available to her?

Learning Unit 20–2: Fire Insurance

Periodically, some areas of the United States, especially California, have experienced drought followed by devastating fires. These fires spread quickly and destroy wooded areas and homes. When the fires occur, the first thought of the owners is the adequacy of their **fire insurance.** Homeowners are made more aware of the importance of fire insurance that provides for the replacement value of their home. Out-of-date fire insurance policies can result in great financial loss.

This unit looks at Alice Swan and the discussion with her insurance agent about her fire insurance needs for her new dress shop at 4 Park Plaza. (Alice owns the building.)

Alice: What is *extended coverage?*

Bob: Your basic fire insurance policy provides financial protection if fire or lightning damages your property. However, the extended coverage protects you from smoke, chemicals, water, or other damages that firefighters may cause to control the fire. We have many options available.

Alice: What is the cost of a fire insurance policy?

Bob: Years ago, if you bought a policy for 2, 3, 5, or more years, reduced rates were available. Today, with rising costs of reimbursing losses from fires, most insurance companies write policies for 1 to 3 years. The cost of a 3-year policy premium is 3 times the annual premium. Because of rising insurance premiums, your total costs are cheaper if you buy one 3-year policy than three 1-year policies.

Alice: For my purpose, I will need coverage for 1 year. Before you give me the premium rates, what factors affect the cost of my premium?

Bob: In your case, you have several factors in your favor that will result in a lower premium. For example, (1) your building is brick, (2) the roof is fire-resistant, (3) the building is located next to a fire hydrant, (4) the building is in a good location (not next to a gas station) with easy access for the fire department, and (5) the goods within your store are not as flammable as, say, those of a paint store. I have a table here (Table 20.3, p. 000) that gives an example of typical fire insurance rates for buildings and contents (furniture, fixtures, etc.).

Jonathan Gruenke/The Saginaw News/AP Wide World

TABLE   20.3

Fire insurance rates per $100 of coverage for buildings and contents

| | CLASSIFICATION OF BUILDING | | | |
| | CLASS A | | CLASS B | |
Rating of area	Building	Contents	Building	Contents
1	.28	.35	.41	.54
2	.33	.47	.50	.60
3	.41	.50	.61	.65

Fire insurance premium equals premium for building and premium for contents.

Let's assume your building has an insured value of $190,000 and is rated Class B, Area No. 2, and we insure your contents for $80,000. Then we calculate your total annual premium for building and contents as follows:

$$\text{Premium} = \frac{\text{Insured value}}{\$100} \times \text{Rate}$$

Building

$$\frac{\$190,000}{\$100} = 1,900 \times \$.50 = \$950$$

Contents

$$\frac{\$80,000}{\$100} = 800 \times \$.60 = \$480$$

Total premium = $950 + $480 = **$1,430**

For our purpose, we round all premiums to the nearest cent. In practice, the premium is rounded to the nearest dollar.

Canceling Fire Insurance

Alice: What if my business fails in 7 months? Do I get back any portion of my premium when I cancel?

Bob: If the insured—that's you, Alice—cancels or wants a policy for less than 1 year, we use this **short-rate table** (Table 20.4, p. 474). The rates in the short-rate table will cost you more. For example, if you cancel at the end of 7 months, the premium cost is 67% of the annual premium. These rates are higher because it is more expensive to process a policy for a short time. We would calculate your refund as follows:

Short-rate premium = Annual premium × Short rate

$958.10   = $1,430   ×   .67

Refund = Annual premium − Short-rate premium

$471.90 = $1,430   − $958.10

Alice: Let's say that I don't pay my premium or follow the fire codes. What happens if your insurance company cancels me?

Bob: If the insurance company cancels you, the company is *not* allowed to use the short-rate table. To calculate what part of the premium the company may keep,[2] you can prorate the premium based on the actual days that have elapsed. We can illustrate the amount of your refund by assuming you are canceled after 7 months:

Note that when the insurance company cancels the policy, the refund ($595.83) is greater than if the insured cancels ($471.90).

For insurance company:

$$\text{Charge} = \$1,430 \text{ annual premium} \times \frac{7 \text{ months elapsed}}{12}$$

Charge = $834.17

For insured:

Refund = $1,430 annual premium − $834.17 charge

Refund = **$595.83**

[2]Many companies use $\frac{\text{Days}}{365}$

TABLE 20.4

Fire insurance short-rate and cancellation table

Time policy is in force		Percent of annual rate to be charged	Time policy is in force		Percent of annual rate to be charged
Days:	5	8%	Months:	5	52%
	10	10		6	61
	20	15		7	67
	25	17		8	74
Months:	1	19		9	81
	2	27		10	87
	3	35		11	96
	4	44		12	100

TABLE 20.4

Fire insurance short-rate and cancellation table

Coinsurance

Alice: My friend tells me that I should meet the coinsurance clause. What is coinsurance?

Bob: Usually, fire does not destroy the entire property. **Coinsurance** means that you and the insurance company *share* the risk. The reason for this coinsurance clause[3] is to encourage property owners to purchase adequate coverage.

Alice: What is adequate coverage?

Bob: In the fire insurance industry, the usual rate for coinsurance is 80% of the current replacement cost. This cost equals the value to replace what was destroyed. If your insurance coverage is 80% of the current value, the insurance company will pay all damages up to the face value of the policy.

Alice: Hold it Bob! Will you please show me how this coinsurance is figured?

Bob: Yes, Alice, I'll be happy to show you how we figure coinsurance. Let's begin by looking at the following steps so you can see what amount of the insurance the company will pay.

CALCULATING WHAT INSURANCE COMPANY PAYS WITH COINSURANCE CLAUSE

Step 1. Set up a fraction. The numerator is the actual amount of the insurance carried on the property. The denominator is the amount of insurance you should be carrying on the property to meet coinsurance (80% times the replacement value).

Step 2. Multiply the fraction by the amount of loss (up to the face value of the policy).

Let's assume for this example that you carry $60,000 fire insurance on property that will cost $100,000 to replace. If the coinsurance clause in your policy is 80% and you suffer a loss of $20,000, your insurance company will pay the following:

Insurance coverage

Loss

$$\text{Step 1} \rightarrow \frac{\$60,000}{\$80,000} \times \$20,000 = \boxed{\$15,000}^{[4]}$$

What you should have carried

($100,000 × .80) **Step 2**

If you had had actual insurance coverage of $80,000, then the insurance company would have paid $20,000. Remember that if the coinsurance clause is met, the most an insurance company will pay is the face value of the policy.

You are now ready for the following Practice Quiz.

Although there are many types of property and homeowner's insurance policies, they usually include fire protection.

---

[3]In some states (including Wisconsin), the clause is not in effect for losses under $1,000.

[4]This kind of limited insurance payment for a loss is often called an **indemnity.**

LU 20–2 | PRACTICE QUIZ

1. Calculate the total annual premium of a warehouse that has an area rating of 2 with a building classification of B. The value of the warehouse is $90,000 with contents valued at $30,000.

2. If insured cancels in Problem 1 at the end of month 9, what are the cost of the premium and the refund?

3. Jones insures a building for $120,000 with an 80% coinsurance clause. The replacement value is $200,000. Assume a loss of $60,000 from fire. What will the insurance company pay? If the loss was $160,000 and coinsurance *was* met, what will the insurance company pay?

✓ **Solutions**

1. $\dfrac{\$90,000}{\$100} = 900 \times \$.50 = \$450$

   $\dfrac{\$30,000}{\$100} = 300 \times \$.60 = \underline{180}$

   $\$630$ ← total premium

2. $\$630 \times .81 = \boxed{\$510.30}$ $\$630 - \$510.30 = \boxed{\$119.70}$

3. $\dfrac{\$120,000}{\$160,000} = \dfrac{3}{4} \times \$60,000 = \boxed{\$45,000}$

   $\uparrow$

   $(.80 \times \$200,000)$ $\boxed{\$160,000}$ never more than face value

LU 20–2a | EXTRA PRACTICE QUIZ

1. Calculate the total annual fire insurance premium of a warehouse that has an area rating of 3 with a building classification of A. The value of the warehouse is $80,000 with contents valued at $20,000.

2. If the insured from problem 1 cancels at the end of month 8, what are the costs of the premium and the refund?

3. Jones insures a building for $140,000 with an 80% coinsurance clause. The replacement value is $250,000. Assume a loss of $50,000 from fire. What will the insurance company pay? If the loss was $170,000 and coinsurance was met, what will the insurance company pay?

Learning Unit 20–3: Auto Insurance

If you own an auto, you have had some experience purchasing auto insurance. Often first-time auto owners do not realize that auto insurance can be a substantial expense. Remember that the cost of auto insurance varies from state to state. Also, what would you do for insurance if you want to rent a truck?

The *Boston Globe* clipping "The 10,000-pound question" has some important information for those who want to rent a truck from home improvement stores like Home Depot or Lowe's.

Douglas C. Pizac/AP Wide World

The 10,000-pound question

When renting a truck from home improvement stores like Home Depot or Lowe's, here are a few points to remember:

- Neither company sells insurance.
- Both companies tell customers they don't need extra insurance.
- If the truck's weight exceeds 10,000 pounds, the renter's personal car insurance won't provide coverage.
- Even with a truck weighing less than 10,000 pounds, there may be gaps in insurance coverage.

Note that your auto insurance may cover you when you rent a truck. Be sure to check on this with the home improvement store where you rent the truck and your auto insurance company.

Insurance rates often increase when a driver is involved in an accident. Some insurance companies give reduced rates to accident-free drivers—a practice that has encouraged drivers to be more safety conscious. For example, State Farm Insurance offers a discount to drivers who maintain a safety record. An important factor in safe driving is the use of a seat belt. Make it a habit to always put on your seat belt.

In this unit we follow Shirley as she learns about auto insurance. Shirley, who just bought a new auto, has never purchased auto insurance. So she called her insurance agent, Bob Long, who agreed to meet her for lunch. We will listen in on their conversation.

Shirley: Bob, where do I start?

Liability insurance includes
1. **Bodily injury**—injury or death to people in passenger car or other cars, etc.
2. **Property damage**—injury to other people's autos, trees, buildings, hydrants, etc.

Bob: Our state has two kinds of **liability insurance, or compulsory insurance,** that by law you must buy (regulations and requirements vary among states). Liability insurance covers any physical damages that you inflict on others or their property. You must buy liability insurance for the following:

1. **Bodily injury** to others: 10/20. This means that the insurance company will pay damages to people injured or killed by your auto up to $10,000 for injury to one person per accident or a total of $20,000 for injuries to two or more people per accident.

2. **Property damage** to someone else's property: 5. The insurance company will pay up to $5,000 for damages that you have caused to the property of others.

Now we leave Shirley and Bob for a few moments as we calculate Shirley's premium for compulsory insurance.

Calculating Premium for Compulsory Insurance[5]

Insurance companies base auto insurance rates on the territory you live in, the class of driver (class 10 is experienced driver with driver training), whether auto is for business use, how much you drive the car, the age of the car, and the make of the car (symbol). Shirley lives in Territory 5 (suburbia). She is classified as 17 because she is an inexperienced operator licensed for less than 6 years. Her car is age 3 and symbol 4 (make of car). We use Table 20.5 (p. 477) to calculate Shirley's compulsory insurance. Note that the table rates in this unit are not representative of all areas of the country. In case of lawsuits, the minimum coverage may not be adequate. Some states add surcharges to the premium if the person has a poor driving record. The tables are designed to show how rates are calculated. From Table 20.5, we have the following:

The tables we use in this unit are for Territory 5. Other tables are available for different territories.

Bodily	$ 98
+ Property	160
	$258

Remember that the $258 premium represents minimum coverage. Assume Shirley hits two people and the courts award them $13,000 and $5,000, respectively. Shirley would be responsible for $3,000 because the insurance company would pay only up to $10,000 per person and a total of $20,000 per accident.

Although total damages of $18,000 are less than $20,000, the insurance company pays only $15,000.

	(1)	**(2)**	
	$13,000	+ $5,000 =	$18,000
Paid by insurance company	− 10,000	− 5,000 =	− 15,000
Paid by Shirley	$ 3,000	+ $ 0 =	$ 3,000

We return to Shirley and Bob. Bob now shows Shirley how to calculate her optional insurance coverage. Remember that optional insurance coverages (Tables 20.6 to 20.10) are added to the costs in Table 20.5 (p. 477).

Calculating Optional Insurance Coverage

Bob: In our state, you can add optional bodily injury to the compulsory amount. If you finance your car, the lender may require specific amounts of optional insurance to protect its

[5]Some states may offer medical payment insurance (a supplement to policyholders' health and accident insurance) as well as personal injury protection against uninsured or underinsured motorists.

TABLE 20.5

Compulsory insurance (based on class of driver)

BODILY INJURY TO OTHERS		DAMAGE TO SOMEONE ELSE'S PROPERTY	
Class	10/20	Class	5M*
10	$ 55	10	$129
17	98	17	160
18	80	18	160
20	116	20	186

Explanation of 10/20 and 5

10	20	5
Maximum paid to one person per accident for bodily injury	Maximum paid for total bodily injury per accident	Maximum paid for property damage per accident

*M means thousands.

investment. I have two tables (Tables 20.6 and 20.7) here that we use to calculate the option of 250/500/50. This means that in an accident the insurance company will pay $250,000 per person, up to $500,000 per accident, and up to $50,000 for property damage.

Bob then explains the tables to Shirley. By studying the tables, you can see how insurance companies figure bodily injury and damage to someone else's property. Shirley is Class 17:

Bodily

250/500 = $228

Property

50M = + 168

$396 premium for optional bodily injury and property damage

Note: These are additional amounts to compulsory.

Collision and comprehensive are optional insurance types that pay only the insured. Note that Tables 20.8 and 20.9 are based on territory, age, and car symbol. The higher the symbol, the more expensive the car.

Shirley: Is that all I need?

Bob: No, I would recommend two more types of optional coverage: **collision** and **comprehensive.** Collision provides protection against damages to your car caused by a moving vehicle. It covers the cost of repairs less **deductibles** (amount of repair you cover first before the insurance company pays the rest) and depreciation.[6] In collision, insurance companies pay the resale or book value. So as the car gets older, after 5 or more years, it

TABLE 20.6

Bodily injury

Class	15/30	20/40	20/50	25/50	25/60	50/100	100/300	250/500	500/1,000
10	27	37	40	44	47	69	94	144	187
17	37	52	58	63	69	104	146	228	298
18	33	46	50	55	60	89	124	193	251
20	41	59	65	72	78	119	168	263	344

TABLE 20.7

Damage to someone else's property

Class	10M	25M	50M	100M
10	132	134	135	136
17	164	166	168	169
18	164	166	168	169
20	191	193	195	197

[6]In some states, repair to glass has no deductible and many insurance companies now use a $500 deductible instead of $300.

might make sense to drop the collision. The decision depends on how much risk you are willing to assume. Comprehensive covers damages resulting from theft, fire, falling objects, and so on. Now let's calculate the cost of these two types of coverage—assuming a $100 deductible for collision and a $200 deductible for comprehensive—with some more of my tables (Tables 20.8 and 20.9).

	Class	Age	Symbol	Premium	
Collision	17	3	4	$191 ($148 + $43)	Cost to
Comprehensive	17	3	4	+ 56 ($52 + $4)	reduce deductibles
				$247	

Total premium
for collision and
comprehensive

Shirley: Anything else?

Bob: I would also recommend that you buy towing and substitute transportation coverage. The insurance company will pay up to $25 for each tow. Under substitute transportation, the insurance company will pay you $12 a day for renting a car, up to $300 total. Again, from

TABLE   20.8   Collision

Classes	Age group	Symbols 1–3 $300 ded.	Symbol 4 $300 ded.	Symbol 5 $300 ded.	Symbol 6 $300 ded.	Symbol 7 $300 ded.	Symbol 8 $300 ded.	Symbol 10 $300 ded.
10–20	1	180	180	187	194	214	264	279
	2	160	160	166	172	190	233	246
	3	148	148	154	166	183	221	233
	4	136	136	142	160	176	208	221
	5	124	124	130	154	169	196	208

These classes would use all this information.

To find the premium, use the age and symbol only.

Additional cost to reduce deductible

Class	From $300 to $200	From $300 to $100
10	13	27
17	20	43
18	16	33
20	26	55

TABLE   20.9   Comprehensive

Classes	Age group	Symbols 1–3 $300 ded.	Symbol 4 $300 ded.	Symbol 5 $300 ded.	Symbol 6 $300 ded.	Symbol 7 $300 ded.	Symbol 8 $300 ded.	Symbol 10 $300 ded.
10–25	1	61	61	65	85	123	157	211
	2	55	55	58	75	108	138	185
	3	52	52	55	73	104	131	178
	4	49	49	52	70	99	124	170
	5	47	47	49	67	94	116	163

Additional cost to reduce deductible: From $300 to $200 add $4

TABLE 20.10

Transportation and towing

Substitute transportation	$16
Towing and labor	4

TABLE 20.11

Worksheet for calculating Shirley's auto premium

Compulsory insurance	Limits	Deductible	Premium
Bodily injury to others	$10,000 per person $20,000 per accident	None	$ 98 (Table 20.5)
Damage to someone else's property	$5,000 per accident	None	$160 (Table 20.5)
Options			
Optional bodily injury to others	$250,000 per person $500,000 per accident	None	$228 (Table 20.6)
Optional property damage	$50,000 per accident	None	$168 (Table 20.7)
Collision	Actual cash value	$100	$191 (Table 20.8) ($148 + $43)
Comprehensive	Actual cash value	$200	$ 56 (Table 20.9) ($52 + $4)
Substitute transportation	Up to $12 per day or $300 total	None	$ 16 (Table 20.10)
Towing and labor	$25 per tow	None	$ 4 (Table 20.10)
			$921 Total premium

another table (Table 20.10), we find the additional premium for towing and substitute transportation is $20 ($16 + $4).

We leave Shirley and Bob now as we make a summary of Shirley's total auto premium in Table 20.11.

Premiums for collision, property damage, and comprehensive are not reduced by no fault.

No-Fault Insurance Some states have **no-fault insurance,** a type of auto insurance that was intended to reduce premium costs on bodily injury. With no fault, one forfeits the right to sue for *small* claims involving medical expense, loss of wages, and so on. Each person collects the bodily injury from his or her insurance company no matter who is at fault. In reality, no-fault insurance has not reduced premium costs, due to large lawsuits, fraud, and operating costs of insurance companies. Many states that were once considering no fault are no longer pursuing its adoption. Note that states with no-fault insurance require the purchase of *personal-injury protection (PIP)*. The most successful no-fault law seems to be in Michigan, since it has tough restrictions on the right to sue along with unlimited medical and rehabilitation benefits.

It's time to take your final Practice Quiz in this chapter.

LU 20–3   PRACTICE QUIZ

Complete this **Practice Quiz** *to see how you are doing*

Calculate the annual auto premium for Mel Jones who lives in Territory 5, is a driver classified 18, and has a car with age 4 and symbol 7. His state has compulsory insurance, and Mel wants to add the following options:

1. Bodily injury, 100/300.
2. Damage to someone else's property, 10M.
3. Collision, $200 deductible.
4. Comprehensive, $200 deductible.
5. Towing.

✓ Solutions

Compulsory

Bodily	$ 80	(Table 20.5)
Property	160	(Table 20.5)

Options

Bodily	124		(Table 20.6)
Property	164		(Table 20.7)
Collision	192	($176 + $16)	(Table 20.8)
Comprehensive	103	($99 + $4)	(Table 20.9)
Towing	4		(Table 20.10)
Total annual premium	**$827**		

LU 20–3a EXTRA PRACTICE QUIZ

Need more practice? Try this **Extra Practice Quiz** (check figures in Chapter Organizer, p. 482)

Calculate the annual auto premium for Mel Jones who lives in Territory 5, is a driver classified 17, and has a car with age 5 and symbol 6. His state has compulsory insurance, and Mel wants to add the following options:

1. Bodily injury, 100/300.
2. Damage to someone else's property, 10M.
3. Collision, $200 deductible.
4. Comprehensive, $200 deductible.
5. Towing.

CHAPTER ORGANIZER AND STUDY GUIDE WITH CHECK FIGURES FOR EXTRA PRACTICE QUIZZES

Topic	Key point, procedure, formula	Example(s) to illustrate situation
Life insurance, p. 467	Using Table 20.1, per $1,000: $$\frac{\text{Coverage desired}}{\$1,000} \times \text{Rate}$$ For females, subtract 3 years.	**Given** $80,000 of insurance desired; age 34; male. 1. Five-year term: $$\frac{\$80,000}{\$1,000} = 80 \times \$2.08 = \boxed{\$166.40}$$ 2. Straight life: $$\frac{\$80,000}{\$1,000} = 80 \times \$10.71 = \boxed{\$856.80}$$ 3. Twenty-payment life: $$\frac{\$80,000}{\$1,000} = 80 \times \$14.28 = \boxed{\$1,142.40}$$ 4. Twenty-year endowment: $$\frac{\$80,000}{\$1,000} = 80 \times \$25.13 = \boxed{\$2,010.40}$$
Nonforfeiture values, p. 471	**By Table 20.2** Option 1: Cash surrender value. Option 2: Reduced paid-up insurance policy continues for life at reduced face amount. Option 3: Extended term—original face policy continued for a certain period of time.	A $50,000 straight-life policy was issued to Jim Rose at age 28. At age 48 Jim wants to stop paying premiums. What are his nonforfeiture options? Option 1: $\frac{\$50,000}{\$1,000} = 50 \times \$265$ $ = \boxed{\$13,250}$ Option 2: $50 \times \$550 = \boxed{\$27,500}$ Option 3: $\boxed{21 \text{ years } 300 \text{ days}}$

(continues)

CHAPTER ORGANIZER AND STUDY GUIDE
WITH CHECK FIGURES FOR EXTRA PRACTICE QUIZZES (continued)

Topic	Key point, procedure, formula	Example(s) to illustrate situation
Fire insurance, p. 472	Per $100 $\text{Premium} = \dfrac{\text{Insurance value}}{\$100} \times \text{Rate}$ Rate can be for buildings or contents.	**Given** Area 3; Class B; building insured for $90,000; contents, $30,000. Building: $\dfrac{\$90,000}{\$100} = 900 \times \$.61$ $= \$549$ Contents: $\dfrac{\$30,000}{\$100} = 300 \times \$.65$ $= \$195$ Total: $549 + $195 = $744
Canceling fire insurance—short-rate Table 20.4 (canceling by policyholder), p. 473	$\dfrac{\text{Short-rate}}{\text{premium}} = \dfrac{\text{Annual}}{\text{premium}} \times \dfrac{\text{Short}}{\text{rate}}$ $\text{Refund} = \dfrac{\text{Annual}}{\text{premium}} - \dfrac{\text{Short-rate}}{\text{premium}}$ If insurance company cancels, do not use Table 20.4.	Annual premium is $400. Short rate is .35 (cancel end of 3 months). $400 × .35 = $140 Refund = $400 − $140 = $260
Canceling by insurance company, p. 473	$\text{Annual premium} \times \dfrac{\text{Months elapsed}}{12}$ (Refund is higher since company cancels.)	Using example above but if insurance company cancels at end of 3 months. $400 \times \frac{1}{4} = $100 Refund = $400 − $100 = $300
Coinsurance, p. 474	Amount insurance company pays: Actual ⟶ Insurance carried insurance (Face value) $\overline{} \times$ Loss What Insurance required coverage ⟶ to meet coinsurance should (Rate × Replacement value) have been Insurance company never pays more than the face value.	**Given** Face value, $30,000; replacement value, $50,000; coinsurance rate, 80%; loss, $10,000; insurance to meet required coinsurance, $40,000. $\dfrac{\$30,000}{\$40,000} \times \$10,000 = \$7,500$ paid by insurance company ($50,000 × .80)

Auto insurance, p. 476	**Compulsory** Required insurance.
	Optional Added to cost of compulsory.
	Bodily injury—pays for injury to person caused by insured.
	Property damage—pays for property damage (not for insured auto).
	Collision—pays for damages to insured auto.
	Comprehensive—pays for damage to insured auto for fire, theft, etc.
	Towing.
	Substitute transportation.
		Calculate the annual premium.
		Driver class 10; compulsory 10/20/5.
		Optional
		Bodily—100/300
		Property—10M
		Collision—age 3, symbol 10, $100 deductible
		Comprehensive—$300 deductible
		          ($55 + $129)
		
		10/20/5 $184 Table 20.5
		Bodily 94 Table 20.6
		Property 132 Table 20.7
		          ($233 + $27)
		
		Collision 260 Table 20.8
		Comprehensive 178 Table 20.9
		Total premium $848

(continues)

CHAPTER ORGANIZER AND STUDY GUIDE
WITH CHECK FIGURES FOR EXTRA PRACTICE QUIZZES (concluded)

Topic	Key point, procedure, formula		Example(s) to illustrate situation
KEY TERMS	Beneficiary, *p. 467* Bodily injury, *p. 467* Cash value, *p. 469* Coinsurance, *p. 474* Collision, *p. 477* Comprehensive insurance, *p. 477* Compulsory insurance, *p. 476* Deductibles, *p. 477* Extended term insurance, *p. 470* Face amount, *p. 467*	Fire insurance, *p. 472* Indemnity, *p. 474* Insured, *p. 467* Insurer, *p. 467* Level premium term, *p. 468* Liability insurance, *p. 476* No-fault insurance, *p. 479* Nonforfeiture values, *p. 471* Paid-up insurance, *p. 469* Policyholder, *p. 467* Premium, *p. 467* Property damage, *p. 476*	Reduced paid-up insurance, *p. 470* Short-rate table, *p. 473* Statisticians, *p. 467* Straight life insurance, *p. 469* Term insurance, *p. 468* 20-payment life, *p. 469* 20-year endowment, *p. 469* Universal life, *p. 470* Whole life, *p. 470*
CHECK FIGURES FOR EXTRA PRACTICE QUIZZES WITH PAGE REFERENCES	LU 20–1a (p. 472) 1. $186.90; no cash value 2. $736.25 Opt. 1. $2,755 2. $8,170 3. 9 years 91 days	LU 20–2a (p. 475) 1. $428 2. $111.28; $316.72 3. $35,000 Never more than $170,000	LU 20–3a (p. 480) $817

Critical Thinking Discussion Questions

1. Compare and contrast term insurance versus whole-life insurance. At what age do you think people should take out life insurance?

2. What is meant by *nonforfeiture values?* If you take the cash value option, should it be paid in a lump sum or over a number of years?

3. How do you use a short-rate table? Explain why an insurance company gets less in premiums if it cancels a policy than if the insured cancels.

4. What is coinsurance? Do you feel that an insurance company should pay more than the face value of a policy if a catastrophe resulted?

5. Explain compulsory auto insurance, collision, and comprehensive. If your car is stolen, explain the steps you might take with your insurance company.

6. "Health insurance is not that important. It would not be worth the premiums." Please take a stand.

Name _____   Date _____

DRILL PROBLEMS

Calculate the annual premium for the following policies using Table 20.1 (for females subtract 3 years from the table).

	Amount of coverage (face value of policy)	Age and sex of insured	Type of insurance policy	Annual premium
20–1.	$140,000	28 F	Straight life	
20–2.	$90,000	40 M	20-payment life	
20–3.	$150,000	29 F	5-year term	
20–4.	$50,000	27 F	20-year endowment	

Calculate the following nonforfeiture options for Lee Chin, age 42, who purchased a $200,000 straight-life policy. At the end of year 20, Lee stopped paying premiums.

20–5. Option 1: Cash surrender value

20–6. Option 2: Reduced paid-up insurance

20–7. Option 3: Extended term insurance

Calculate the total cost of a fire insurance premium for a building and contents given the following (round to nearest cent):

	Rating of area	Class	Building	Contents	Total premium cost
20–8.	3	B	$90,000	$40,000	

Calculate the short-rate premium and refund of the following:

	Annual premium	Canceled after	Short-rate premium	Refund
20–9.	$700	8 months by insured		
20–10.	$360	4 months by insurance company		

Complete the following:

	Replacement value of property	Amount of insurance	Kind of policy	Actual fire loss	Amount insurance company will pay
20–11.	$100,000	$60,000	80% coinsurance	$22,000	
20–12.	$60,000	$40,000	80% coinsurance	$42,000	

Calculate the annual auto insurance premium for the following:

20–13. Britney Sper, Territory 5
Class 17 operator
Compulsory, 10/20/5   _____

Optional

a. Bodily injury, 500/1,000   _____

b. Property damage, 25M   _____

c. Collision, $100 deductible   _____

   Age of car is 2; symbol of car is 7

d. Comprehensive, $200 deductible   _____

   Total annual premium   _____

WORD PROBLEMS

20–14. On March 10, 2007 the *Houston Chronicle* reported on the statewide average cost for a homeowners' fire insurance policy in Texas. The average price of a homeowners' policy is now $1,138. Joyce Maris was recently transferred to Illinois and has cancelled her policy after 8 months. The amount of the policy was $1,038.00. What is the amount of Joyce's refund?

20–15. Mike Reno, age 44, saw an Insurance Solutions Direct advertisement stating that its $500,000 term policy costs $395 per year. Compare this to Table 20.1 in the text. How much would he save by going with Insurance Solutions Direct?

20–16. Margie Rale, age 38, a well-known actress, decided to take out a limited-payment life policy. She chose this since she expects her income to decline in future years. Margie decided to take out a 20-year payment life policy with a coverage amount of $90,000. Could you advise Margie about what her annual premium will be? If she decides to stop paying premiums after 15 years, what will be her cash value?

20–17. Janette Raffa has two young children and wants to take out an additional $300,000 of 5-year term insurance. Janette is 40 years old. What will be her additional annual premium? In 3 years, what cash value will have been built up?

20–18. Roger's office building has a $320,000 value, a 2 rating, and a B building classification. The contents in the building are valued at $105,000. Could you help Roger calculate his total annual premium?

20–19. Abby Ellen's toy store is worth $400,000 and is insured for $200,000. Assume an 80% coinsurance clause and that a fire caused $190,000 damage. What is the liability of the insurance company?

20–20. Escalating insurance premiums in Florida was the topic in the March 16, 2007 edition of *The Palm Beach Post.* Because of Florida's Hurricane damages, homeowners saw companies like State Farm putting into effect a 52.9% rate hike. Tammy Sears owns a $235,000 building with contents valued at $90,000. The rating is Class B, Area No. 3. **(a)** What had been Tammy's total premium before the increase? **(b)** What is Tammy's total premium after the increase?

20–21. As given via the Internet, auto insurance quotes gathered online could vary from $947 to $1,558. A class 18 operator carries compulsory 10/20/5 insurance. He has the following optional coverage: bodily injury, 500/1,000; property damage, 50M; and collision, $200 deductible. His car is 1 year old, and the symbol of the car is 8. He has comprehensive insurance with a $200 deductible. Using your text, what is the total annual premium?

20–22. Dan Miller insured his pizza shop for $100,000 for fire insurance at an annual rate per $100 of $.66. At the end of 11 months, Earl canceled the policy since his pizza shop went out of business. What was the cost of Earl's premium and his refund?

20–23. Warren Ford insured his real estate office with a fire insurance policy for $95,000 at a cost of $.59 per $100. Eight months later the insurance company canceled his policy because of a failure to correct a fire hazard. What did Warren have to pay for the 8 months of coverage? Round to the nearest cent.

20–24. On July 20, *The Dispatch* (Gilroy, CA) compared the insurance bills of Gilroy and San Jose drivers. Gilroy drivers saw an 11% increase in automobile insurance, whereas San Jose drivers saw a 6% decrease. Marvin Braun lives in Gilroy and is comparing the cost of collision insurance. He is also thinking about relocating to San Jose. Based on Class 18, age 4, symbol 5, **(a)** what is his present premium for collision? **(b)** What will his premium be if he stays in Gilroy? **(c)** What will his premium be if he moves to San Jose?

20–25. Tina Grey bought a new Honda Civic and insured it with only 10/20/5 compulsory insurance. Driving up to her ski chalet one snowy evening, Tina hit a parked van and injured the couple inside. Tina's car had damage of $4,200, and the van she struck had damage of $5,500. After a lengthy court suit, the injured persons were awarded personal injury judgments of $16,000 and $7,900, respectively. What will the insurance company pay for this accident, and what is Tina's responsibility?

20–26. Rusty Reft, who lives in Territory 5, carries 10/20/5 compulsory liability insurance along with optional collision that has a $300 deductible. Rusty was at fault in an accident that caused $3,600 damage to the other auto and $900 damage to his own. Also, the courts awarded $15,000 and $7,000, respectively, to the two passengers in the other car for personal injuries. How much will the insurance company pay, and what is Rusty's share of the responsibility?

20–27. Marika Katz bought a new Blazer and insured it with only compulsory insurance 10/20/5. Driving up to her summer home one evening, Marika hit a parked car and injured the couple inside. Marika's car had damage of $7,500, and the car she struck had damage of $5,800. After a lengthy court suit, the couple struck were awarded personal injury judgments of $18,000 and $9,000, respectively. What will the insurance company pay for this accident, and what is Marika's responsibility?

CHALLENGE PROBLEMS

20–28. Using an electronic spreadsheet, it was determined the Ford family would need $985,000 of insurance on John's life and $375,000 on Cindy's life. John and Cindy are both 36 years old. John and Cindy are torn between straight life and 20-payment life. John earns a salary of $80,000. Cindy works part-time earning $11,000. They have disposable income (after taxes) of 60%. **(a)** What will be John's annual premium for straight life? **(b)** What will be Cindy's annual premium for straight life? **(c)** What will be John's annual premium for 20-payment life? **(d)** What will be Cindy's premium for 20-payment life? **(e)** What percent of their disposable income would go toward the straight life policy? Round to the nearest hundredth percent. **(f)** What percent of their disposable income would go toward the 20-payment life? Round to the nearest hundredth percent.

20–29. Bill, who understands the types of insurance that are available, is planning his life insurance needs. At this stage of his life (age 35), he has budgeted $200 a year for life insurance premiums. Could you calculate for Bill the amount of coverage that is available under straight life and for a 5-year term? Could you also show Bill that if he were to die at age 40, how much more his beneficiary would receive if he'd been covered under the 5-year term? Round to the nearest thousand.

 SUMMARY PRACTICE TEST

1. Howard Slater, age 44, an actor, expects his income to decline in future years. He decided to take out a 20-year payment life policy with a $90,000 coverage. What will be Howard's annual premium? If he decides to stop paying premiums after 15 years, what will be his cash value? *(p. 468)*

2. J.C. Monahan, age 40, bought a straight-life insurance policy for $210,000. Calculate her annual premium. If after 20 years J.C. no longer pays her premiums, what nonforfeiture options will be available to her? *(p. 471)*

3. The property of Pote's Garage is worth $900,000. Pote has a $375,000 fire insurance policy that contains an 80% coinsurance clause. What will the insurance company pay on a fire that causes $450,000 damage? If Pote meets the coinsurance, how much will the insurance company pay? *(p. 474)*

4. Lee Collins insured her pizza shop with an $90,000 fire insurance policy at a $1.10 annual rate per $100. At the end of 7 months, Lee's pizza shop went out of business so she canceled the policy. What is the cost of Lee's premium and her refund? *(p. 474)*

5. Charles Prose insured his real estate office with a $300,000 fire insurance policy at $.78 annual rate per $100. Nine months later the insurance company canceled his policy because Charles failed to correct a fire hazard. What was Charles's cost for the 9-month coverage? Round to the nearest cent. *(p. 473)*

6. Roger Laut, who lives in Territory 5, carries 10/20/5 compulsory liability insurance along with optional collision that has a $1,000 deductible. Roger was at fault in an accident that caused $4,800 damage to the other car and $8,800 damage to his own car. Also, the courts awarded $19,000 and $9,000, respectively, to the two passengers in the other car for personal injuries. How much does the insurance company pay, and what is Roger's share of the responsibility? *(pp. 475–479)*

Personal Finance

Cut **INSURANCE** costs

Paying too much for insurance?
SIMPLE SOLUTION: Shop online and switch policies.

ETHAN ROBERTS, who owns a catering
business in Los Angeles, was skeptical
about pitches from life-insurance companies
offering super-low rates. To check them out,
Roberts, 39, went to online insurance broker
AccuQuote.com and typed in information about
his medical history and activities.

Within minutes he received several companies'
rate quotes. As a result, he bought a 20-year,
$250,000 term-life policy from GE Capital, cut-
ting his premium in half compared with the cost
of a similar State Farm policy he purchased just a
year and a half ago.

Roberts's experience isn't a fluke. Rates on
term-life policies have plummeted over the

past decade. In 1994, a healthy 40-year-old man
would have paid at least $995 per year for a
$500,000 term-life policy with a 20-year rate
guarantee. Several companies offer the same policy
today for less than $400, according to Byron
Udell, chief executive officer of AccuQuote.
"Overall, term-life prices remain at all-time
lows," says Bob Bland, CEO of Insure.com.

Many big-name companies have jumped on the
low-rate bandwagon. Even if you bought a policy
just a few years ago, as long as you're healthy, you
can probably find a much better rate or lock in
the same premium for a longer period. You may
also save on a policy purchased more recently if
you neglected to shop around the first time.

That's the lesson Ethan Roberts learned. To buy
his life insurance, he originally turned to the State
Farm agent he works with for auto and homeowners coverage, without bothering to compare rates.

But thanks to online-shopping sites, such as
AccuQuote.com, Insure.com and InsWeb (www
.insweb.com), it's easy to get price quotes (and
arrange to purchase a policy) from dozens of companies. It may also be worth your while to get online price quotes for auto insurance. A number of
insurers are changing the way they calculate premiums, which can mean substantial savings for
low-risk drivers.

In the past, auto-insurance rates were based on
a handful of variables, such as the type of car you
own, your age and your driving record. Now companies are using advanced computing capabilities
to look at dozens of variables.

Allstate, for example, went from seven pricing
tiers to 384, says spokesman Michael Trevino.
To determine premiums, the company uses many
variables in your credit report, as well as the cor-
relation between the type of car you drive and
your potential liability. "We were able to lower
rates by about 25% for people who are the best
risks," says Trevino.

New pricing rules also mean that some high-
risk drivers can get coverage from insurers that
shunned them in the past. Premiums may be
high, but at least you won't be turned down.

Some individuals who aren't the best risks under the new system (such as those with poor credit
records) may do better with a company that hasn't
changed the way it determines prices. Whatever
your situation, you can shop more efficiently at
Allstate.com, Progressive.com, StateFarm.com
and InsWeb, which works with a number of insurance companies. —**KIMBERLY LANKFORD**

BUSINESS MATH ISSUE

Going online will always save you money for cutting insurance costs.

1. List the key points of the article and information to support your position.
2. Write a group defense of your position using math calculations to support your view.

Slater's Business Math Scrapbook

with Internet Application

Putting Your Skills to Work

PROJECT A
Go to the Web and visit the companies listed in the clipping to see what they offer now for auto insurance.

Cranky Consumer / By Ron Lieber

Shopping for Auto Insurance

MOST CONSUMERS select their auto insurer based on price, but at least some players in the industry would like that to change.

Allstate Corp. is rolling out "gold" and "platinum" plans that allow drivers who pay a bit more to qualify for one or more free accidents; if they get in a wreck, their insurance premiums wouldn't automatically go up.

The strategy seems logical as premium increases moderate. Earlier this year, the Insurance Information Institute predicted car-insurance premiums would rise by 1.5% this year, the lowest such increase since 2000. When prices aren't rising, consumers have fewer reasons to shop around, which means companies have to offer new services to entice them to switch providers.

Still, it seems as if the industry can't resist price-touting. **Berkshire Hathaway Inc.'s** Geico spends millions on ads promising big savings. And **Progressive** Corp. continues to promote a tool on its Web site that lets users compare Progressive's rates with rivals.

Having just purchased a 2003 Toyota Highlander, we decided to shop around for coverage. We looked into Allstate's offering and checked out **Amica Mutual Insurance Co.**, which scored the highest in the J.D. Power & Associates National Auto Insurance Study.

There were some twists, too: We hadn't owned a car or had car insurance in more than a decade. Plus, we live in Brooklyn, N.Y., where theft and insurance fraud are common and can send rates spiraling skyward.

Sure enough, Allstate refused to cover

Lisa Haney

us at any price when we called a local agent. She said we'd have to move to Manhattan if we wanted a policy.

A company spokesman said that anyone in New York state who hadn't had insurance within the past year would be declined. The company might have made an exception in our case if we had garaged the car in Manhattan.

Meanwhile, Progressive's price-comparison tool helped us realize just how high its quote was. The Web site quoted us $2,408 for six months of Progressive coverage. This seemed expensive, given that we'd set two deductibles at $1,000 (we provided the same parameters to each company). Two of the providers listed by the tool had much lower prices.

Oddly, Progressive's comparison rates included Allstate. The tool noted it would likely charge us $903 or $956 for six months. A Progressive spokeswoman says it uses rates on file with insurance regulators but can't always predict how

companies will apply their underwriting standards, which are generally secret.

Amica gets J.D. Power's highest grade for "overall experience." But Amica's Web site wouldn't even let us set our own deductibles before it quoted us a price, which came back at $2,811 for a year. A call to the 800 number yielded a further $350 or so in savings.

Then we tried two online brokers, which didn't bring the price down much. Insureone.com, a unit of **Affirmative Insurance Holdings** Inc., wouldn't touch New York state residents. Another one, youdecide.com, a unit of **Vbenx** Corp., came back with just one annual quote for $5,975, the highest price of all.

Geico, however, lived up to its marketing. Its slick Web site was easy to use and returned a quote of $711.90 for six months. USAA, which covers only current and former members of the U.S. military and their families (that's us), came in at about $10 more when we called. But the rep noted USAA offers a $50 rebate to customers who buy child car seats. Plus, he told us, it pays an annual dividend averaging 7% to all policyholders depending on how the company performed that year. USAA also had a high J.D. Power ranking.

After we signed up with USAA, things didn't go smoothly. Turns out you can't get that car-seat rebate until the baby is born. She isn't here yet, and the company dropped the program after we called. Plus, USAA told us we had to get our car inspected within 30 days—but then sent us a note threatening to cut off our insurance when we didn't get it done within a week or so. A USAA spokesman says our rep is new and the deadline is shorter in New York. One error in our favor: The rep was also wrong about the dividend—it's actually averaged 9.3% since it began in 1995.

Write to cranky@wsj.com

COMPANY	PRICE QUOTE	PROS	CONS	COMMENT
Allstate	Declined coverage	New plans offer unique features for more money	Told us we had to move from Brooklyn to Manhattan to get a policy	We wished the local agent had been able to provide a better explanation for the denial.
Amica Mutual Insurance	$2,811 for a year	Topped J.D. Power & Associates satisfaction index	Its Web site wouldn't let us adjust our deductibles	When we called, we managed to make changes to save $350.
Progressive	$2,408 for six months	A nifty price-comparison tool that shows competitors' rates	The tool pointed out just how uncompetitive its rates actually were	The company has doubled business in our area recently, but our profile was too risky
USAA	$722.25 for six months	Low rate and a friendly phone representative	The worst Web site we used, and the rep gave us wrong information	USAA is improving the Web site soon; the rep, it turns out, was new
Youdecide.com	$5,975 for a year (from Travelers)	This online brokerage offers quotes from multiple insurers	Only one of them was interested in bidding for our business	Our lack of insurance and problematic address haunted us here, too

Wall Street Journal © 2005

Internet Projects: See text Web site (www.mhhe.com/slater9e) and The Business Math Internet Resource Guide.

CHAPTER 21

Stocks, Bonds, and Mutual Funds

LEARNING UNIT OBJECTIVES

LU 21–1: Stocks

- Read and explain stock quotations (p. 491).
- Calculate dividends of preferred and common stocks; calculate return on investment (p. 493).

LU 21–2: Bonds

- Read and explain bond quotations (p. 496).
- Compare bond yields to bond premiums and discounts (pp. 496–497).

LU 21–3: Mutual Funds

- Explain and calculate net asset value and mutual fund commissions (p. 498).
- Read and explain mutual fund quotations (p. 498).

Ask Personal Journal.

Q: Can net capital losses that exceed $3,000 a year be carried over into future years? —L.H., Tucson, Ariz.

A: Yes, in most cases. Capital losses from the sale of stocks and other investments can first be used to offset capital gains. Then if your losses exceed your gains, you can apply up to $3,000 a year—or $1,500 if you're married filing separately—against wages and other ordinary income. Losses above that can be carried over.

A taxpayer with a $10,000 net capital loss in 2004 would use $3,000 of it to offset ordinary income in 2004 and carry over $7,000 to 2005, says Bob Scharin, editor of RIA's "Practical Tax Strategies." If you have a capital loss, consider selling an investment with a capital gain before year end—if you are inclined to sell it anyway—since it can cut your tax liability, says Mark Luscombe of CCH Inc., a tax publisher. —Jane J. Kim

We answer readers' questions here each Thursday. Send your questions to **PersonalJournal@WSJ.com**

Wall Street Journal © 2005

Do you shop at Home Depot? Did you know that because Home Depot has difficulty finding places to build more stores and its stock price is stagnant, the company is going to broaden its business operations? The following *Wall Street Journal* clipping "Home Depot Slows Store Openings, Looks to Build Industrial Business" discusses how Home Depot plans to compensate for its slower retail growth and stagnant stock price by capturing a large share of the professional supply and maintenance industry.

Home Depot Slows Store Openings, Looks to Build Industrial Business

By Chad Terhune

Home Depot Inc., faced with fewer places for U.S. expansion and a stagnant stock price, plans to cut retail-store openings by nearly half over the next five years and rely more heavily on sales to commercial and industrial customers.

"There are retailers who got locked into the traditional retail model and ran out of square footage. Game over," Bob Nardelli, Home Depot's chairman and chief executive, said in an interview following the Atlanta retailer's yearly presentation to analysts and investors yesterday. "We knew we had to broaden our playing field to provide some solid business growth."

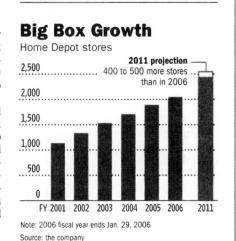

Big Box Growth
Home Depot stores

Note: 2006 fiscal year ends Jan. 29, 2006
Source: the company

Wall Street Journal © 2006

If you check the stock prices of your favorite stores from time to time and some stock prices are stagnant, you can sometimes forecast that these stores may be planning to change their future goals. Also, when you realize that the stock market is an indication of the health of our economy, you may become interested in becoming an investor.

Before you become an investor, you should follow these general principles: (1) know your risk tolerance and the risk of the investments you are considering—determine whether you are a low-risk conservative investor or a high-risk speculative investor; (2) know your time frame—how soon you need your money; (3) know the liquidity of the investments you are considering—how easy it is to get your money; (4) know the return you can expect on your money—how much your money should earn; and (5) do not put "all your eggs in one basket"—diversity with a mixture of stocks, bonds, and cash equivalents. It is most important that before you seek financial advice from others, you go to the library and/or the Internet for information. When you do your own research first, you can judge the advice you receive from others.

This chapter introduces you to the major types of investments—stocks, bonds, and mutual funds. These investments indicate the performance of the companies they represent and the economy of the country at home and abroad.

Learning Unit 21-1: Stocks

We begin this unit with an introduction to the basic stock terms. Then we explain the reason why people buy stocks, newspaper stock quotations, dividends on preferred and common stocks, and return on investment.

Introduction to Basic Stock Terms

Companies sell shares of ownership in their company to raise money to finance operations, plan expansion, and so on. These ownership shares are called **stocks.** The buyers of the

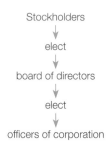

FIGURE 21.1

New York Stock Exchange

Stockholders
↓
elect
↓
board of directors
↓
elect
↓
officers of corporation

NYSE Mel Nudelman/AP Wide World

If you own 50 shares of common stock, you are entitled to 50 votes in company elections. Preferred stockholders do not have this right.

stock (**stockholders**) receive **stock certificates** verifying the number of shares of stock they own.

The two basic types of stock are **common stock** and **preferred stock.** Common stockholders have voting rights. Preferred stockholders do not have voting rights, but they receive preference over common stockholders in **dividends** (payments from profit) and in the company's assets if the company goes bankrupt. **Cumulative preferred stock** entitles its owners to a specific amount of dividends in 1 year. Should the company fail to pay these dividends, the **dividends in arrears** accumulate. The company pays no dividends to common stockholders until the company brings the preferred dividend payments up to date.

Why Buy Stocks?

Some investors own stock because they think the stock will become more valuable, for example, if the company makes more profit, new discoveries, and the like. Other investors own stock to share in the profit distributed by the company in dividends (cash or stock).

For various reasons, investors at different times want to sell their stock or buy more stock. Strikes, inflation, or technological changes may cause some investors to think their stock will decline in value. These investors may decide to sell. Then the law of supply and demand takes over. As more people want to sell, the stock price goes down. Should more people want to buy, the stock price would go up.

How Are Stocks Traded?

Stock exchanges (see Figure 21.1) provide an orderly trading place for stock. You can think of these exchanges as an auction place. Only **stockbrokers** and their representatives are allowed to trade on the floor of the exchange. Stockbrokers charge commissions for stock trading—buying and selling stock for investors. As you might expect, in this age of the Internet, stock trades can also be made on the Internet.

How to Read Stock Quotations in the Newspaper's Financial Section*

We will use Home Depot stock to learn how to read the stock quotations found in your newspaper. Note the following newspaper listing of Home Depot stock:

52 WEEKS		STOCK (SYM)	DIV	YLD %	PE	VOL 100's	CLOSE	NET CHG
HI	LO							
43.95	32.85	Home DPT	.90	2.3	14	178416	39.92	+0.55

The highest price at which Home Depot stock traded during the past 52 weeks was $43.95 per share. This means that during the year someone was willing to pay $43.95 for a share of stock.

---

*For centuries, stocks were traded and reported in fraction form as shown in the chapter opening photo. In 2001 the New York Stock Exchange and NASDAQ began the conversion to decimals, which is how it is reported today.

The lowest price at which Home Depot stock traded during the year was $32.85 per share.

The newspaper lists the company name. The symbol that Home Depot uses for trading is DPT. Home Depot paid a dividend of $.90 per share to stock owners last year. So if you owned 100 shares, you received a **cash dividend** of $90 (100 shares × $.90).

The **stock yield** percent tells stockholders that the dividend per share is returning a rate of 2.3% to investors. This 2.3% is based on the closing price. The calculation is:

$$\frac{\text{Stock}}{\text{yield}} = \frac{\text{Annual dividend per share}}{\text{Today's closing price per share}} = \frac{\$.90}{\$39.92} = 2.25\% \text{ or } 2.3\% \text{ (rounded to nearest tenth percent)}$$

The 2.3% return may seem low to people who could earn a better return on their money elsewhere. Remember that if the stock price rises and you sell, your investment may result in a high rate of return.

The Home Depot stock is selling at $39.92; it is selling at 14 times its **earning per share (EPS).** Earnings per share are not listed on the stock quote.

$$\text{Earnings per share} = \text{Annual earnings} \div \text{Total number of shares outstanding}$$

The **price-earnings ratio,** or **PE ratio,** measures the relationship between the closing price per share of stock and the annual earnings per share. For Home Depot we calculate the following price-earnings ratio. (Assume Home Depot earns $2.85 per share. This is not listed in the newspaper.)

Round PE to the nearest whole number.

$$\text{PE ratio} = \frac{\text{Closing price per share of stock}}{\text{Annual earnings per share}} = \frac{\$39.92}{\$2.85} = 14$$

If the PE ratio column shows ". . . ," this means the company has no earnings. The PE ratio will often vary depending on quality of stock, future expectations, economic conditions, and so on.

In the newspaper stock quotations for Home Depot, the number in the volume column is in the 100s. Thus, to 178,416, you add two zeros to get 17,841,600. This indicates that 17,841,600 shares were traded on this day. Remember that shares of stock need a buyer and a seller to trade.

The last trade of the day, called the closing price, was at $39.92 per share.

On the *previous day,* the closing price was $39.37 (not given). The *new* close is $39.92. The result is that the closing price is up $.55 from the *previous day.*

Dividends on Preferred and Common Stocks

If you own stock in a company, the company may pay out dividends. (Not all companies pay dividends.) The amount of the dividend is determined by the net earnings of the company listed in its financial report.

Earlier we stated that cumulative preferred stockholders must be paid all past and present dividends before common stockholders can receive any dividends. Following is an example to illustrate the calculation of dividends on preferred and common stocks for 2009 and 2010.

EXAMPLE The stock records of Jason Corporation show the following:

Preferred stock issued: 20,000 shares.   In 2009, Jason paid no dividends.

Preferred stock cumulative at $.80 per share.   In 2010, Jason paid $512,000 in dividends.

Common stock issued: 400,000 shares.

Remember that common stockholders do not have the cumulative feature as preferred do.

Since Jason declared no dividends in 2009, the company has $16,000 (20,000 shares × $.80 = $16,000) dividends in arrears to preferred stockholders. The dividend of $512,000 in 2010 is divided between preferred and common stocks as follows:

	2009		2010	
Dividends paid	0		$512,000	
Preferred stockholders*	Paid: 0		Paid for 2009 (20,000 shares × $.80)	$ 16,000
	Owe: Preferred, $16,000 (20,000 shares × $.80)		Paid for 2010	16,000
				$ 32,000
Common stockholders	0		Total dividend	$512,000
			Paid preferred for 2009 and 2010	− 32,000
			To common	$480,000
			$\dfrac{\$480,000}{400,000 \text{ shares}}$ = $1.20 per share	

*For a discussion of par value (arbitrary value placed on stock for accounting purposes) and cash and stock dividend distribution, check your accounting text.

Calculating Return on Investment

Now let's learn how to calculate a return on your investment of Home Depot stock, assuming the following:

Bought 200 shares at $35.75.

Sold at end of 1 year 200 shares at $42.80.

1% commission rate on buying and selling stock.

Current $.90 dividend per share in effect.

Bought		**Sold**	
200 shares at $35.75	$7,150.00	200 shares at $42.80	$8,560.00
+ Broker's commission (.01 × $7,150)	+ 71.50	− Broker's commission (.01 × $8,560)	− 85.60
Total cost	$7,221.50	Total receipt	$8,474.40

Note: A commission is charged on both the buying and selling of stock.

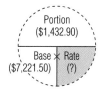

Total receipt	$8,474.40	
Total cost	− 7,221.50	
Net gain	$1,252.90	
Dividends	+ 180.00	(200 shares × $.90)
Total gain	$1,432.90	

Portion ↗ $\dfrac{\$1,432.90}{\$7,221.50}$ = 19.84% rate of return (to nearest hundredth percent)

↑
Base

It's time for another Practice Quiz.

LU 21–1 **PRACTICE QUIZ**

Complete this **Practice Quiz** to see how you are doing

1. From the following Texaco stock quotation **(a)** explain the letters, **(b)** estimate the company's earnings per share, and **(c)** show how "YLD %" was calculated.

52 WEEKS				YLD		VOL		NET
HI	LO	STOCK (SYM)	DIV	%	PE	100's	CLOSE	CHG
73.90	48.25	Texaco TX	1.80	2.5	14	13020	72.25	+0.46
(A)	(B)	(C)	(D)	(E)	(F)	(G)	(H)	(I)

2. **Given:** 30,000 shares of preferred cumulative stock at $.70 per share; 200,000 shares of common; 2009, no dividend; 2010, $109,000. How much is paid to each class of stock in 2010?

✓ **Solutions**

1. **a.** (A) Highest price traded in last 52 weeks.
   (B) Lowest price traded in past 52 weeks.
   (C) Name of corporation is Texaco (symbol TX).
   (D) Dividend per share per year is $1.80.
   (E) Yield for year is 2.5%.
   (F) Texaco stock sells at 14 times its earnings.
   (G) Sales volume for the day is 1,302,000 shares.
   (H) The last price (closing price for the day) is $72.25.
   (I) Stock is up $.46 from closing price yesterday.

   b. $\text{EPS} = \dfrac{\$72.25}{14} = \$5.16$ per share

   c. $\dfrac{\$1.80}{\$72.25} = 2.5\%$

2. **Preferred:** 30,000 × $.70 = $21,000   Arrears 2009
                                  +   21,000   2010
                                    ─────────
                                     $42,000

   Common: $67,000 ($109,000 − $42,000)

LU 21–1a EXTRA PRACTICE QUIZ

Need more practice? Try this **Extra Practice Quiz** (check figures in Chapter Organizer, p. 500)

1. From the following Circuit City stock quotation **(a)** explain the letters, **(b)** estimate the company's earnings per share, and **(c)** show how YLD % was calculated.

| 52 WEEKS | | | | YLD | | VOL | | NET |
HI	LO	STOCK (SYM)	DIV	%	PE	100'S	CLOSE	CHG
38.69	8.69	CirCty CC	.07	.4	23	11187	16.68	+0.57
(A)	(B)	(C)	(D)	(E)	(F)	(G)	(H)	(I)

2. **Given:** 40,000 shares of preferred cumulative stock at a $.60 per share; 300,000 shares; 300,000 shares of common; 2009, no dividend; 2010, $210,000. How much is paid to each class of stock in 2010?

Learning Unit 21–2: Bonds

Have you heard of the Rule of 115? This rule is used as a rough measure to show how quickly an investment will triple in value. To use the rule, divide 115 by the rate of return your money earns. For example, if a bond earns 5% interest, divide 115 by 5. This measure estimates that your money in the bond will triple in 23 years.

This unit begins by explaining the difference between bonds and stocks. Then you will learn how to read bond quotations and calculate bond yields.

Reading Bond Quotations

Goodyear, Despite SEC Probe, Plans $650 Million Bond Sale

Sometimes companies raise money by selling bonds instead of stock. When you buy stock, you become a part owner in the company. To raise money, companies may not want to sell

Bond quotes are stated in percents of the face value of the bond and not in dollars as stock is. Interest is paid semiannually.

more stock and thus dilute the ownership of their current stock owners, so they sell bonds. **Bonds** represent a promise from the company to pay the face amount to the bond owner at a future date, along with interest payments at a stated rate.

Once a company issues bonds, they are traded as stock is. If a company goes bankrupt, bondholders have the first claim to the assets of the corporation—before stockholders. As with stock, changes in bond prices vary according to supply and demand. Brokers also charge commissions on bond trading. These commissions vary.

How to Read the Bond Section of the Newspaper

The bond section of the newspaper shows the bonds that are traded that day. The information given on bonds differs from the information given on stocks. The newspaper states bond prices in *percents of face amount, not in dollar amounts* as stock prices are stated. Also, bonds are usually in denominations of $1,000 (the face amount).

When a bond sells at a price below its face value, the bond is sold at a discount. Why? The interest that the bond pays may not be as high as the current market rate. When this happens, the bond is not as attractive to investors, and it sells for a **discount.** The opposite could, of course, also occur. The bond may sell at a **premium,** which means that the bond sells for more than its face value or the bond interest is higher than the current market rate.

Let's look at this newspaper information given for IBM bonds:

Bonds	Current yield	Vol.	Close	Net change
IBM $8\frac{3}{8}$ 19	7.0	5	$120\frac{1}{2}$	+1

Note: Bond prices are stated as a percent of face amount.

The name of the company is IBM. It produces a wide range of computers. The interest on the bond is $8\frac{3}{8}\%$. The company pays the interest semiannually. The bond matures (comes due) in 2019. The total interest for the year is $83.75 (.08375 × $1,000). Remember that the face value of the bond is $1,000. Now let's show this with the following formula:

Yearly interest = Face value of bond × Stated yearly interest rate

$83.75 = $1,000 × .08375

We calculate the 7.0% yield by dividing the total annual interest of the bond by the total cost of the bond. (For our purposes, we will omit the commission cost.) All bond yields are rounded to the nearest tenth percent.

Note this bond is selling for more than $1,000 since its interest is very attractive compared to other new offerings.

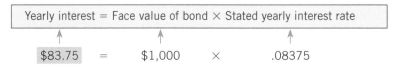

$$\frac{\text{Yearly interest}}{\text{Cost of bond at closing}} = \frac{\$83.75 \,(.08375 \times \$1,000)}{\$1,205 \,(1.205 \times \$1,000)}$$
$$= 6.95\% = \boxed{7.0\%} \qquad \text{This is same as 120.5\%.}$$

Five $1,000 bonds were traded. Note that we do *not* add two zeros as we did to the sales volume of stock.

The last bond traded on this day was 120.5% of face value, or in dollars, $1,205 ($120\frac{1}{2}\%$ = 120.5% = 1.205).

The last trade of the day was up 1% of the face value from the last trade of yesterday. In dollars this is 1% = $10.

1% = .01 × $1,000 = $10

Thus, the closing price on this day, 120.5% − 1%, equals yesterday's close of 119.5% ($1,195). Note that *yesterday's close is not listed in today's quotations.*

Calculating Bond Yields

The IBM bond (selling at a premium) pays $8\frac{3}{8}\%$ interest when it is yielding investors 7%.

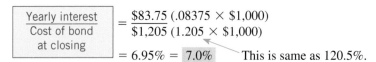

$$\text{Bond yield} = \frac{\text{Total annual interest of bond}}{\text{Total current cost of bond at closing*}}$$

*We assume this to be the buyer's purchase price.

The following example will show us how to calculate **bond yields.**

EXAMPLE Jim Smith bought 5 bonds of IBM at the closing price of $120\frac{1}{2}$ (remember that in dollars $120\frac{1}{2}$ is $1,205). Jim's total cost excluding commission is:

$$5 \times \$1,205 = \$6,025$$

What is Jim's interest?

No matter what Jim pays for the bonds, he will still receive interest of $83.75 per bond ($.08375 \times \$1,000$). Jim bought the bonds at $1,205 each, resulting in a bond yield of 7%. Let's calculate Jim's yield to the nearest tenth percent:

(5 bonds $\times$ $83.75 interest per bond per year)

$$\frac{\$418.75}{\$6,025} = 6.95\% = \boxed{7\%}$$

The yield is 7% since Jim paid more for the bonds and still receives 8% of the face value.

Now let's try another Practice Quiz.

LU 21-2 PRACTICE QUIZ

Complete this **Practice Quiz** to see how you are doing

Bonds		Yield	Sales	Close	Net change
Aetna $6\frac{3}{8}$	03	6.4	20	$100\frac{3}{8}$	$+\frac{7}{8}$

From the above bond quotation, **(1)** calculate the cost of 5 bonds at closing (disregard commissions) and **(2)** check the current yield of 6.4%.

✓ **Solutions**

1. $100\frac{3}{8}\% = 100.375\% = 1.00375 \times \$1,000 = \$1,003.75 \times 5 = \boxed{\$5,018.75}$
2. $6.375\% = .06375 \times \$1,000 = \$63.75$ annual interest

$$\frac{\$63.75}{\$1,003.75} = 6.35\% = \boxed{6.4\%}$$

LU 21-2a EXTRA PRACTICE QUIZ

Need more practice? Try this **Extra Practice Quiz** (check figures in Chapter Organizer, p. 500)

Bonds		Yield	Sales	Close	Net change
Aetna $7\frac{1}{2}$	08	7.4%	20	$100\frac{1}{4}$	$+\frac{3}{4}$

From the above bond quotation, **(1)** calculate the cost of 5 bonds at closing (disregard commissions) and **(2)** check the current yield of 7.5%.

Learning Unit 21-3: Mutual Funds

Steve Senne/AP Wide World

In recent years, mutual funds have increased dramatically and people in the United States have invested billions in mutual funds. Investors can choose from several fund types—stock funds, bond funds, international funds, balanced (stocks and bonds) funds, and so on. This learning unit tells you why investors choose mutual funds and discusses the net asset value of mutual funds, mutual fund commissions, and how to read a mutual fund quotation.

Why Investors Choose Mutual Funds

The main reasons investors choose mutual funds are the following:

1. **Diversification.** When you invest in a mutual fund, you own a small portion of many different companies. This protects you against the poor performance of a single company but not against a sell-off in the market (stock and bond exchanges) or fluctuations in the interest rate.

2. **Professional management.** You are hiring a professional manager to look after your money when you own shares in mutual funds. The success of a particular fund is often due to the person(s) managing the fund.

3. **Liquidity.** Most funds will buy back your fund shares whenever you decide to sell.

4. **Low fund expenses.** Competition forces funds to keep their expenses low to maximize their performance. Because stocks and bonds in a mutual fund represent thousands of shareholders, funds can trade in large blocks, reducing transaction costs.

5. **Access to foreign markets.** Through mutual funds, investors can conveniently and inexpensively invest in foreign markets.

Net Asset Value

Investing in a **mutual fund** means that you buy shares in the fund's portfolio (group of stocks and/or bonds). The value of your mutual fund share is expressed in the share's **net asset value (NAV),** which is the dollar value of one mutual fund share. You calculate the NAV by subtracting the fund's current liabilities from the current market value of the fund's investments and dividing this by the number of shares outstanding.

$$NAV = \frac{\text{Current market value of fund's investments} - \text{Current liabilities}}{\text{Number of shares outstanding}}$$

The NAV helps investors track the value of their fund investment. After the market closes on each business day, the fund uses the closing prices of the investments it owns to find the dollar value of one fund share, or NAV. This is the price investors receive if they sell fund shares on that day or pay if they buy fund shares on that day.

Commissions When Buying Mutual Funds

The following table is a quick reference for the cost of buying mutual fund shares. Commissions vary from 0% to $8\frac{1}{2}$% depending on how the mutual fund is classified.

Classification	Commission charge*	Offer price to buy
No-load (NL) fund	No sales charge	NAV (buy directly from investment company)
Low-load (LL) fund	3% or less	NAV + commission % (buy directly from investment company or from a broker)
Load fund	$8\frac{1}{2}$% or less	NAV + commission % (buy from a broker)

*On a front-end load, you pay commission when you purchase the fund shares, while on a back-end load, you pay when you redeem or sell. In general, if you hold the shares for more than 5 years, you pay no commission charge.

The offer price to buy a share for a low-load or load fund is the NAV plus the commission. Now let's look at how to read a mutual fund quotation.

Putnam Funds Class A								
AmGv p	8.94	−0.01	3.7	2.5	Inv p	15.39	0.03	13.7	13.4
AABal p	12.39	...	12.4	10.4	MidCapVal p	15.09	0.01	17.1	16.8
AAGr p	14.14	...	16.0	14.2	NwOp p	50.37	0.04	10.3	10.9
CATx p	8.29	...	4.9	4.6	NwValA p	19.08	...	14.9	14.0
CapApr p	22.74	0.01	13.0	13.1	NYTx p	8.73	−0.01	4.9	4.1
ClassicEq p	14.89	0.04	12.9	10.9	OTC p	9.14	−0.01	15.4	10.7
Conv p	19.64	0.01	14.8	10.7	Research p	16.16	−0.02	11.7	9.6
DiscGr p	20.76	...	12.6	9.3	SmCapVal p	16.43	−0.03	18.1	18.6
Dvrln p	10.08	...	7.0	6.8	TFHY	13.17	...	6.3	6.6
EqIn p	17.49	0.01	17.8	13.8	TxEx p	8.84	...	4.6	4.4
Geo p	18.01	0.01	12.1	9.2	USGv p	13.14	−0.01	4.2	3.3
GlblEqty p	11.03	−0.02	21.1	16.0	Util p	13.58	−0.04	26.0	20.0
Grln p	19.87	0.02	15.1	12.3	Vsta p	11.53	0.02	8.2	13.7
Hlth p	58.22	0.31	3.1	9.2	Voy p	18.53	...	6.5	6.7
HiYd p	8.10	...	9.2	8.5					
Incm p	6.80	−0.01	4.7	3.8					
IntGrln p	16.78	...	24.6	22.1					
IntCaO p	37.21	0.05	29.6	27.8					
IntlEq p	32.73	0.02	25.3	19.7					
IntlNop p	16.76	−0.01	23.4	20.0					

How to Read a Mutual Fund Quotation

We will be studying the Putnam Mutual Funds. Cindy Joelson has invested in the Growth and Income Fund with the hope that over the years this will provide her with financial security when she retires. On December 7, Cindy turns to *the Wall Street Journal* and looks up the Putnam Growth Income Fund quotation.

The name of the fund is Growth and Income, which has the investment objective of growth and income securities as set forth in the fund's prospectus (document giving information about the fund). Note that this is only one fund in the Putnam family of funds.

- The $19.87 figure is the NAV plus the sales commission.
- The fund has increased $.02 from the NAV quotation of the previous day.
- The fund has a 15.1% return this year (January through December 7). This assumes reinvestments of all distributions. Sales charges are not reflected.
- The three-year return is 12.3%.

Now let's check your understanding of this unit with a Practice Quiz.

LU 21–3 | PRACTICE QUIZ

Complete this **Practice Quiz** to see how you are doing

From the mutual fund quotation of the Smith Barney Aggressive Growth Fund shown below, complete the following:

1. NAV

   _____

2. NAV change

   _____

3. Total return, YTD

   _____

✓ **Solutions**

1. 92.97
2. −0.51
3. 8.1%

```
Smith Barney A
 Adjlnc p      9.71    ...   0.5   3.2
 AgGrA p      92.97  -0.51   8.1  -1.3
 ApprA p      14.29  -0.09   3.6   1.5
 CaMuA p      16.94   0.01   0.8   5.1
 DivlncA p    12.18  -0.06   2.6  -0.5
 DvLgCpA      14.37  -0.11   2.1  -3.0
 DvsInA p      6.84    ...   1.1   5.3
 FdValA p     14.81  -0.05   5.6   1.4
 GrIncA p     14.86  -0.11   3.6  -0.8
 GvScA         9.96  -0.01   1.4   5.8
 HiIncA t      6.97    ...   1.4   3.3
 InAlCpGrA p  13.12  -0.09   6.3  -6.1
 IntNYA        9.14  -0.01   0.9   5.6
 InvGdA       13.15  -0.05   2.6   8.8
 LgCapGA p    22.51  -0.18   3.2   1.9
 LgCapV A p   15.77  -0.07   6.8  -1.6
 LgCpCoA p    17.34  -0.14   3.5  -5.2
```

Reprinted by permission of The Wall Street Journal, © 2004 Dow Jones & Company, Inc. All Rights Reserved Worldwide.

LU 21–3a | EXTRA PRACTICE QUIZ

Need more practice? Try this **Extra Practice Quiz** (check figures in Chapter Organizer, p. 500)

From the mutual fund quotation of the Smith Barney Aggressive Balance A Fund shown below, complete the following:

1. NAV

   _____

2. NAV change

   _____

3. Total return, YTD

   _____

```
 GrInc 1....... 15.65  -0.14 -  3.6
 LgCpCo1..... 20.91  -0.18 -  5.3
Smith Barney A
 AdjGvA p...... 9.82    ... +  3.3
 AgGrA p...... 103.51 -1.26 +  5.0
 ApprA p...... 14.93  -0.12 +  2.6
 BalancA p.... 13.25  -0.09 -  5.2
 CaMuA p..... 16.56  -0.01 +  1.2
 DvLgCpA..... 16.28  -0.19 -  6.1
 DvsInA p..... 6.85   -0.01 +  1.8
 FdValA p..... 15.10  -0.10 +  2.7
 GlGvtA p..... 10.43  -0.01 +  2.5
 GrInc A p.... 15.64  -0.13 -  3.7
 GvScA........ 9.41   -0.02 +  1.8
 HiIncA t...... 8.04   -0.02 +  2.0
 InAgGrA p ... 27.46  -0.31 - 21.9
 InAlCpGrA p. 15.32  -0.10 - 16.0
 IntNYA........ 8.68    ... +  2.3
 InvGdA....... 11.94  -0.03 +  4.5
 LgCapGA p.. 21.75  -0.32 -  5.1
 LgCapV A p.. 17.62  -0.06 +  0.5
 LgCpCoA p.. 20.80  -0.18 -  5.5
 MdCpCoA p.. 21.13  -0.22 -  2.9
```

Reprinted by permission of The Wall Street Journal, © 2001 Dow Jones & Company, Inc. All Rights Reserved Worldwide.

CHAPTER ORGANIZER AND STUDY GUIDE
WITH CHECK FIGURES FOR EXTRA PRACTICE QUIZZES

Topic	Key point, procedure, formula	Example(s) to illustrate situation
Stock yield, p. 493	$\dfrac{\text{Annual dividend per share}}{\text{Today's closing price per share}}$ (Round yield to nearest tenth percent.)	Annual dividend, $.72 Today's closing price, $42.375 $\dfrac{\$.72}{\$42.375} = 1.7\%$
Price-earnings ratio, p. 493	$PE = \dfrac{\text{Closing price per share of stock}}{\text{Annual earnings per share}}$ (Round answer to nearest whole number.)	From previous example: Closing price, $42.375 Annual earnings per share, $4.24 $\dfrac{\$42.375}{\$4.24} = 9.99 = 10$

(continues)

CHAPTER ORGANIZER AND STUDY GUIDE
WITH CHECK FIGURES FOR EXTRA PRACTICE QUIZZES (concluded)

Topic	Key point, procedure, formula	Example(s) to illustrate situation
Dividends with cumulative preferred, p. 493	Cumulative preferred stock is entitled to all dividends in arrears before common stock receives dividend.	2009 dividend omitted; in 2010, $400,000 in dividends paid out. Preferred is cumulative at $.90 per share; 20,000 shares of preferred issued and 100,000 shares of common issued. To preferred: 20,000 shares × $.90 = $18,000 In arrears 2009: 20,000 shares × .90 = 18,000 Dividend to preferred $36,000 To common: $364,000 ($400,000 − $36,000) $\frac{\$364,000}{100,000 \text{ shares}}$ = $3.64 dividend to common per share
Cost of a bond, p. 496	Bond prices are stated as a percent of the face value. Bonds selling for less than face value result in bond discounts. Bonds selling for more than face value result in bond premiums.	Bill purchases 5 $1,000, 12% bonds at closing price of $103\frac{1}{4}$. What is his cost (omitting commissions)? $103\frac{1}{4}$% = 103.25% = 1.0325 in decimal 1.0325 × $1,000 bond = $1,032.50 per bond 5 bonds × $1,032.50 = $5,162.50
Bond yield, p. 496	$\frac{\text{Total annual interest of bond}}{\text{Total current cost of bond at closing}}$ (Round to nearest tenth percent.)	Calculate bond yield from last example on one bond. ($1,000 × .12) $\frac{\$120}{\$1,032.50}$ = 11.6%
NAV, p. 498	$NAV = \frac{\text{Current market value of fund's investment} - \text{Current liabilities}}{\text{Number of shares outstanding}}$	The NAV of the Scudder Income Bond Fund was $12.84. The NAV change was 0.01. What was the NAV yesterday? $12.83

KEY TERMS	Bonds, *p. 495* Bond yield, *p. 496* Cash dividend, *p. 493* Common stocks, *p. 492* Cumulative preferred stock, *p. 492* Discount, *p. 496* Dividends, *p. 495*	Dividends in arrears, *p. 492* Earnings per share (EPS), *p. 493* Mutual fund, *p. 498* Net asset value (NAV), *p. 498* PE ratio, *p. 493* Preferred stock, *p. 492*	Premium, *p. 496* Price-earnings ratio, *p. 493* Stockbrokers, *p. 492* Stock certificate, *p. 492* Stockholders, *p. 492* Stocks, *p. 492* Stock yield, *p. 493*
CHECK FIGURES FOR EXTRA PRACTICE QUIZZES WITH PAGE REFERENCES	LU 21–1a (p. 495) 1. b. $.73 per share c. .4% 2. Pref. $48,000 Com. $168,000	LU 21–2a (p. 497) 1. $5,012.50 2. $\frac{\$75}{\$1,002.50}$ = 7.48%	LU 21–3a (p. 499) 1. 13.25 2. −.09 3. −5.2%

Critical Thinking Discussion Questions

1. Explain how to read a stock quotation. What are some of the red flags of buying stock?

2. What is the difference between odd and round lots? Explain why the commission on odd lots could be quite expensive.

3. Explain how to read a bond quote. What could be a drawback of investing in bonds?

4. Compare and contrast stock yields and bond yields. As a conservative investor, which option might be better? Defend your answer.

5. Explain what NAV means. What is the difference between a load and a no-load fund? How safe are mutual funds?

Name _____ Date _____

DRILL PROBLEMS

Calculate the cost (omit commission) of buying the following shares of stock:

21–1. 300 shares of Google at $382.99

21–2. 900 shares of eBay at $86.10

Calculate the yield of each of the following stocks (round to the nearest tenth percent):

Company	Yearly dividend	Closing price per share	Yield
21–3. Boeing	$.68	$64.63	____
21–4. Circuit City	$.07	$9.56	____

Calculate the earnings per share, price-earnings ratio (to nearest whole number), or stock price as needed:

Company	Earnings per share	Closing price per share	Price-earnings ratio
21–5. BellSouth	$3.15	$40.13	____
21–6. American Express	$3.85	_____	26

21–7. Calculate the total cost of buying 400 shares of CVS at $59.38. Assume a 2% commission.

21–8. If in Problem 21–1 the 300 shares of Google stock were sold at $360.00, what would be the loss? Commission is omitted.

21–9. Given: 20,000 shares cumulative preferred stock ($2.25 dividend per share): 40,000 shares common stock. Dividends paid: 2009, $8,000; 2010, 0; and 2011, $160,000. How much will preferred and common receive each year?

For each of these bonds, calculate the total dollar amount you would pay at the quoted price (disregard commission or any interest that may have accrued):

Company	Bond price	Number of bonds purchased	Dollar amount of purchase price
21–10. Petro	$87\frac{3}{4}$	3	_____
21–11. Wang	114	2	_____

For the following bonds, calculate the total annual interest, total cost, and current yield (to the nearest tenth percent):

Bond	Number of bonds purchased	Selling price	Total annual interest	Total cost	Current yield
21–12. Sharn $11\frac{3}{4}$ 09	2	115	_____	_____	_____
21–13. Wang $6\frac{1}{2}$ 07	4	$68\frac{1}{8}$	_____	_____	_____

21–14. From the following calculate the net asset values. Round to the nearest cent.

	Current market value of fund investment	Current liabilities	Number of shares outstanding	NAV
a.	$5,550,000	$770,000	600,000	_____
b.	$13,560,000	$780,000	840,000	_____

21–15. From the following mutual fund quotation, complete the blanks:

				TOTAL RETURN		
Inv. obj.	NAV	NAV chg.	YTD	4 wks.	1 yr.	
EuGr ITL	12.04	−0.06	+8.2	+0.9	+9.6	

NAV _____   NAV change _____

Total return, 1 year _____

WORD PROBLEMS

21–16. Lee Stone bought 800 shares of Disney at $21.50 per share. Assume a commission of 2% of the purchase price. What is the total cost to Lee?

21–17. Assume in Problem 21–16 that Lee sells the stock for $26.10 with the same 2% commission rate. What is the bottom line for Lee?

21–18. Jim Corporation pays its cumulative preferred stockholders $1.60 per share. Jim has 30,000 shares of preferred and 75,000 shares of common. In 2009, 2010, and 2011, due to slowdowns in the economy, Jim paid no dividends. Now in 2012, the board of directors decided to pay out $500,000 in dividends. How much of the $500,000 does each class of stock receive as dividends?

21–19. Maytag Company earns $4.80 per share. Today the stock is trading at $59.25. The company pays an annual dividend of $1.40. Calculate **(a)** the price-earnings ratio (round to the nearest whole number) and **(b)** the yield on the stock (to the nearest tenth percent).

21–20. "Investing in Bonds", was the topic of the February 12, 2007 issue of *Forbes*. Buying at a discount helps you by raising your yield. Nancy Kartman is purchasing a U.S. Industries corporate bond. The bond is paying 4% interest and closed at 97. **(a)** What is Nancy's purchase price for this bond? **(b)** How much interest will she receive each year? **(c)** What is the current yield of this bond? Round to the nearest hundredth percent.

21–21. The following bond was quoted in the *Wall Street Journal:*

Bonds	Curr. yld.	Vol.	Close	Net chg.
NY Tel $7\frac{1}{4}$ 11	7.2	10	$100\frac{7}{8}$	$+1\frac{1}{8}$

Five bonds were purchased yesterday, and 5 bonds were purchased today. How much more did the 5 bonds cost today (in dollars)?

21–22. The February 2007 issue of *Money* suggested investors look for stocks that are priced near their 2006 high, a low price/earnings ratio, and a dividend yield of 3% or more. Chris Luna is researching the DuPont Corporation. The following is the current stock listing: Price is $48.75, and the 52 week range $39–$49. Average earnings per share is $3.20 and the dividend is $1.47 **(a)** What is the P/E ratio to the nearest whole number? **(b)** What is the yield to the nearest hundredth?

21–23. Ron bought a bond of Bee Company for $79\frac{1}{4}$. The original bond was $5\frac{3}{4}$ 08. Ron wants to know the current yield (to the nearest tenth percent). Please help Ron with the calculation.

21–24. Abby Sane decided to buy corporate bonds instead of stock. She desired to have the fixed-interest payments. She purchased 5 bonds of Meg Corporation $11\frac{3}{4}$ 09 at $88\frac{1}{4}$. As the stockbroker for Abby (assume you charge her a $5 commission per bond), please provide her with the following: **(a)** the total cost of the purchase, **(b)** total annual interest to be received, and **(c)** current yield (to nearest tenth percent).

21–25. Mary Blake is considering whether to buy stocks or bonds. She has a good understanding of the pros and cons of both. The stock she is looking at is trading at $59.25, with an annual dividend of $3.99. Meanwhile, the bond is trading at $96\frac{1}{4}$, with an annual interest rate of $11\frac{1}{2}\%$. Calculate for Mary her yield (to the nearest tenth percent) for the stock and the bond.

21–26. The *St. Louis Post-Dispatch*, dated January 16, 2007, reported on local company earnings. MEMC Electronic Materials Inc. on Thursday closed at $43.62 and an increase of $2.08. Robert Hunt purchased 200 shares on Wednesday and 200 shares on Thursday; he paid a 3% commission. **(a)** What was Robert's total price for the stock purchased on Thursday? **(b)** What was Robert's total price for the stock purchased on Wednesday?

21–27. Louis Hall read in the paper that Fidelity Growth Fund has a NAV of $16.02. He called Fidelity and asked them how the NAV was calculated. Fidelity gave him the following information:

Current market value of fund investment	$8,550,000
Current liabilities	$ 860,000
Number of shares outstanding	480,000

Did Fidelity provide Louis with the correct information?

21–28. Lee Ray bought 130 shares of a mutual fund with a NAV of $13.10. This fund also has a load charge of $8\frac{1}{2}\%$. **(a)** What is the offer price and **(b)** what did Lee pay for his investment?

21–29. Ron and Madeleine Couple received their 2005 Form 1099-DIV (dividends received) in the amount of $1,585. Ron and Madeleine are in the 28% bracket. What would be their tax liability on the dividends received?

CHALLENGE PROBLEMS

21–30. Here's an example of how breakpoint discounts on sales commissions for mutual fund investors work:

Sales charge

Less than $25,000, 5.75%

$25,000 to $49,999, 5.50%

$50,000 to $99,999, 4.75%

$100,000 to $249,999, 3.75%

Nancy Dolan is interested in the T Rowe Price Mid Cap Fund. On November 7, 2003, the NAV was 19.43. **(a)** What minimum amount of shares must Nancy purchase to have a sales charge of 5.50%? **(b)** What are the minimum shares Nancy must purchase to have a sales charge of 4.75%? **(c)** What are the minimum shares Nancy must purchase to have a sales charge of 3.75%? **(d)** What would be the total purchase price for **(a)**, **(b)**, or **(c)**? Round up to the nearest share even if it is less than 5.

21–31. On September 6, Irene Westing purchased one bond of Mick Corporation at $98\frac{1}{2}$. The bond pays $8\frac{3}{4}$ interest on June 1 and December 1. The stockbroker told Irene that she would have to pay the accrued interest and the market price of the bond and a $6 brokerage fee. What was the total purchase price for Irene? Assume a 360-day year (each month is 30 days) in calculating the accrued interest. (*Hint:* Final cost = Cost of bond + Accrued interest + Brokerage fee. Calculate time for accrued interest.)

 SUMMARY PRACTICE TEST

1. Russell Slater bought 700 shares of Disney stock at $24.90 per share. Assume a commission of 4% of the purchase price. What is the total cost to Russell? *(p. 491)*

2. Avis Company earns $2.50 per share. Today, the stock is trading at $18.99. The company pays an annual dividend of $.25. Calculate **(a)** the price-earnings ratio (to the nearest whole number) and **(b)** the yield on the stock (to the nearest tenth percent). *(p. 493)*

3. The stock of Aware is trading at $4.90. The price-earnings ratio is 4 times earnings. Calculate the earnings per share (to the nearest cent) for Sapient. *(p. 493)*

4. Tom Fox bought 8 bonds of UXY Company $3\frac{1}{2}$ 09 at 84 and 4 bonds of Foot Company $4\frac{1}{8}$ 10 at 93. Assume the commission on the bonds is $3 per bond. What was the total cost of all the purchases? *(p. 496)*

5. Leah Long bought one bond of Vick Company for 147. The original bond was $8\frac{1}{4}$ 10. Leah wants to know the current yield to the nearest tenth percent. Help Leah with the calculation. *(p. 496)*

6. Cumulative preferred stockholders of Rale Company receive $.80 per share. The company has 70,000 shares outstanding. For the last 9 years, Rale paid no dividends. This year, Rale paid $400,000 in dividends. What is the amount of dividends in arrears that is still owed to preferred stockholders? *(p. 493)*

7. Bill Roundy bought 800 shares of a mutual fund with a NAV of $14.10. This fund has a load charge of 3%. **(a)** What is the offer price and **(b)** what did Bill pay for the investment? *(p. 498)*

JEFF CHIU/AP PHOTO

STOCKS | Despite a triple-digit price, shares of the leading search-engine company aren't overvalued. *By David Landis*

What's **GOOGLE** worth?

NEARLY everyone agrees that Google is a great company. But at what price? The market isn't sure. Shares have lurched from a high of $475 in January to $338 in mid March. Analysts aren't much help. Their target prices range from $255 to $600.

Google's 41% share of the U.S. on-line-search market leads the pack and is growing, and it collects $6 billion of the $500 billion spent worldwide each year on advertising. So it might seem a good bet that the company will grow more than enough to justify whatever price you pay today. But some Cisco investors must surely have felt the same way when they paid $80 for shares of the world's leading networking company in 2000, after five years of astonishing growth. Cisco now trades for $20.

Still, Google looks relatively inexpensive based on several measures of value. For example, it trades at 38 times the $8.89 per share that analysts, on average, expect the company to earn in 2006 and 28 times next year's expected earnings of $12. That's cheap compared with Yahoo's price-earnings ratio of 57 for this year and 42 based on next year's earnings. Piper Jaffray analyst Safa Rashtchy says market-leading technology companies such as Google can justifiably trade at P/Es ranging from 50 to 60. His $600 one-year target price assumes 2007 earnings per share of $11.98 and a P/E of 50.

Another way to measure Google's value is using the PEG ratio, which compares the P/E to expected long-term profit growth. The faster the growth, the more justifiable a high P/E. In Google's case, the *G*—the expected growth rate—is 31%. So its PEG is 1.2 based on this year's earnings forecast and 0.9 based on next year's. Generally, a PEG ratio close to one is considered cheap. Goldman Sachs analyst Anthony Noto says a leading growth company like Google should trade at a PEG of 1.5 to 2. His $500 one-year target is based on a PEG of 1.8. By contrast, Yahoo's PEG is 2.2 on '06 profit estimates and 1.6 on next year's.

Better measure. If you want to take your analysis to a higher level of sophistication—and complexity—forget the P/E. Because various accounting maneuvers can distort reported earnings, many analysts rely on a purer measure of profitability that goes by the acronym Ebitda, or earnings before interest, taxes, depreciation and amortization. Many analysts also believe that enterprise value—a company's stock-market capitalization plus outstanding debt minus its cash holdings—is a better measure than stock-market value alone of how investors value a company.

So if you divide Google's enterprise value (think of it as its price) by its Ebitda (think of it as a proxy for earnings) based on '06 estimates, you get 23. The number by itself is meaningless, but compared with Yahoo's 24, it seems to suggest once again that Google is reasonably priced. Citigroup analyst Mark Mahaney argues that since Google has the higher estimated growth rate (Yahoo's is 26%), its EV/Ebitda ratio should be higher. He sees Google reaching $471 in a year.

Why does Google trade so far below many analysts' target prices? Perhaps it's because much of its share price represents the promise of future earnings, and investors seem to have lost confidence lately that the company can live up to such lofty expectations. But at today's share price, odds are that a show of faith in Google will eventually be rewarded.

GOOGLE Then and now

REVENUES | **2001**: $86 million
TODAY: $6.1 billion*

PROFITS | **2001**: $7 million
TODAY: 1.5 billion*

EMPLOYEES | **2001**: 284
TODAY: 5,680†

MARKET VALUE | **2001**: Not publicly traded **TODAY**: $99.8 billion‡

*For 2005. †Year-end 2005. ‡To March 13.
SOURCE: Google.

BUSINESS MATH ISSUE

Google stock is way overpriced.

1. List the key points of the article and information to support your position.
2. Write a group defense of your position using math calculations to support your view.

PROJECT A
How is Viacom stock
doing today?

Viacom Plays to Be Market Prize

*New Management Woos Investors
After Shake-Up Rattles Shares;
MTV Networks Questions Linger*

By Matthew Karnitschnig

VIACOM INC. CHAIRMAN Sumner Redstone thought he would be greeted as a conquering hero by Wall Street when he booted Tom Freston as chief executive last week. Instead, an investor-led insurgency nearly broke out as Viacom stock tumbled 8%.

But after an intensive effort by Viacom's new CEO, Philippe Dauman, and his No. 2, Tom Dooley, to calm nerves, the stock has recovered most of the ground it lost, to $35.79 apiece yesterday for the more-active Class B shares. And there are signs Mr. Redstone's drastic action may have the effect it intended—to renew confidence in Viacom's prospects and jump-start a rally in Viacom stock.

Many investors say Viacom is a buy. The stock is down 12% from where it started in January after Viacom was split from **CBS** Corp. Some on Wall Street believe the arrival of new top management promising a more aggressive Web strategy means the stock may be headed upward.

"We're very confident holding on to the stock and will perhaps add to our position," says Kurt Funderburg, a money manager with Harris Associates, which had about 21.5 million Viacom shares as of June 30.

That optimism, echoed by a number of major investors, is reinforced by the stock's relative cheapness compared with its peer group. Viacom trades at about 16 times projected 2007 earnings, below the comparable multiple of 18 at which both **Walt Disney** Co. and **News Corp.** trade. Even **Time Warner** Inc., another underperformer, is more highly valued, with a multiple of 16.6. CBS is cheaper, its stock trading at 15.6 times next year's earnings, but the company's businesses are concentrated in the slower-growing broadcasting industry.

A plunge into Viacom isn't without risk. The firing of Mr. Freston has created turmoil within MTV Networks, Viacom's cable-network division, which accounts for 70% of the company's revenue and nearly all its profit. Mr. Freston led the division for two decades, building it into one of the most successful businesses in the entertainment industry and creating much loyalty within the division's management ranks.

Not only does Viacom's new CEO, Mr. Dauman, not have the same experience, but Mr. Freston's exit also prompted speculation that other talented executives may follow him out the door. The biggest question hung over Judy McGrath, the head of MTV Networks, who has a close relationship with Mr. Freston.

Viacom rings *up gains. Depicted from its stable: a* **Neopet**, *Comedy Central's* **Jon Stewart**, *Nick Jr.'s* **Dora the Explorer** *and Nickelodeon's* **SpongeBob SquarePants**.

HEARD ON THE STREET

Wall Street Journal © 2006

Internet Projects: See text Web site (www.mhhe.com/slater9e) and The Business Math Internet Resource Guide.

Video Case

Federal Signal Corporation began its operations in 1901. The company is a manufacturer and worldwide supplier of safety, signaling, and communications equipment; hazardous area lighting; fire rescue vehicles; vehicle-mounted aerial access platforms; and street sweeping and vacuum loader vehicles. The four major operating groups are Safety Products, Tool, Environmental Products, and Fire Rescue.

U.S. fire departments buy 3,000 to 4,000 fire trucks every year, priced from $110,000 for a small pumper to more than $600,000 for an elaborate aerial ladder. Federal Signal, a publicly held corporation, is one of the largest national players with an estimated 20% of the U.S. market, but its share of the crowded international market is still only about 20%.

While the economic downshift has hurt most manufacturers of trucks and heavy equipment, it appears to have helped Federal Signal by making available the raw materials the company needs. Four years ago, Federal Signal was struggling to get enough chassis to manufacture a growing backlog of fire truck orders at its three North American fire truck plants. The chassis shortage pulled down profits for the company's Fire Rescue Group. Federal Signal began turning the corner on the chassis shortage, primarily because of its suppliers' bad fortune.

Now the market for big trucks is oversaturated. That's bad news for truck manufacturers but good news for Federal Signal, which is whittling down some of its backorders for fire trucks and, as a result, picking up its bottom line and stock price.

One factor that protects Federal Signal during economic downturns is municipal budgeting. Generally, municipalities have longer lead time for spending on bigger capital equipment. Since Federal Signal is not dependent on private industry for business, the future does look as bright as Federal's warning lights.

PROBLEM 1

The Fire Rescue Group is Federal Signal's biggest sales generator with revenue of $310 million, followed by the Safety Products Group with $262 million and the Environment Products Group with $247 million. What percent are the sales of the Fire Rescue Group to the total sales? Round to the nearest hundredth percent.

PROBLEM 2

With Federal Signal stock selling at $23.22, there were 58,200 shares traded in one day on the New York Stock Exchange. What was the total value of the stock traded?

PROBLEM 3

Federal Signal's current assets were as follows:

Cash and cash equivalents	$ 15,336
Trade accounts receivable	162,878
Inventories	176,892
Prepaid expenses	10,745

Current liabilities totaled $362,457. What is Federal Signal's current ratio? Round to the nearest hundredth.

PROBLEM 4

With a share price of $23.22 for Federal Signal stock: (a) What would be the price of 300 shares with a 2% commission? (b) Earnings per share (EPS) are $1.23; what would be the price-earnings (PE) ratio? Round to the nearest whole number.

PROBLEM 5

With a $23.22 closing price and an annual dividend of $.78, what would be Federal Signal's dividend yield? Round to the nearest hundredth percent.

PROBLEM 6

Federal Signal has a quarterly EPS of $.26. The company expects the quarterly EPS to grow by 14%. What is the expected dollar amount for the quarterly EPS? Round to the nearest cent.

PROBLEM 7

Federal Signal's interest expense increased to $7.8 million from $7.0 million, largely as a result of increased financial services assets. What was the percent increase in interest expense? Round to the nearest hundredth percent.

PROBLEM 8

Net cash provided by operations for the first quarter was $21.9 million, up 30% from last year. What was last year's cash flow?

CHAPTER 22

Business Statistics

LEARNING UNIT OBJECTIVES

LU 22–1: Mean, Median, and Mode

- Define and calculate the mean *(p. 511)*.
- Explain and calculate a weighted mean *(p. 512)*.
- Define and calculate the median *(p. 513)*.
- Define and identify the mode *(p. 513)*.

LU 22–2: Frequency Distributions and Graphs

- Prepare a frequency distribution *(pp. 514–515)*.
- Prepare bar, line, and circle graphs *(pp. 515–517)*.
- Calculate price relatives and cost comparisons *(p. 518)*.

LU 22–3: Measures of Dispersion (Optional Section)

- Explain and calculate the range *(p. 520)*.
- Define and calculate the standard deviation *(p. 520)*.
- Estimate percentage of data by using standard deviations *(p. 521)*.

Go Figure / *Think Retirement Now*

The finances of younger Americans are worse off than those of people their age 20 years ago, according to a study commissioned by the American Institute of Certified Public Accountants. Americans ages 25 to 34 years old had a median net worth of $3,746 in 2004, down from $6,788 in 1985. Their average debt climbed to $4,733 from $3,118.

—*Terri Cullen*

Spendthrifts

A study commissioned by the American Institute of Certified Public Accountants found the spending habits of Americans aged 25 to 34 have left them in poor financial shape. Among the findings*:

- Average credit-card debt: **$4,088**
- Average student loan: **$20,000**
- Percentage of income spent on debt payments: **24%**
- Percentage maintaining an interest-bearing savings account in 2004: **47%**
- Percentage maintaining an interest-bearing savings account in 1985: **61%**
- Median net worth in 2004: **$3,746**
- Median net worth in 1985: **$6,788**

Source: The American Institute of Certified Public Accountants.
* Numbers are for 2004 unless otherwise specified.

Getty Images

What To Do

- **Save it:** Building a nest egg may be last on your priority list, behind living expenses and paying off debt. But saving a little today in a tax-advantaged retirement account such as a 401(k) can reap big returns later. Calculate your worth: http://online.wsj.com/page/2_0401.html

- **Max it:** Increased contributions usually mean lower taxes, since all or part of your contributions will generally be deducted from your taxable salary. That means the net amount in your paycheck may decline less than the additional amount you choose to contribute. Do the math:

http://online.wsj.com/page/2_0423.html

- **Match it:** "Workers," says Jack Callahan, president of Fidelity Institutional Retirement Services Co., "should always contribute enough to 401(k) plans to receive 100% of their employer's match." It's free money—take advantage of it.

- **Target it:** Consider investing in so-called target mutual funds, which gradually shift assets to more-conservative investments as you near retirement. Among the top performers: Freedom Fidelity 2025, T. Rowe Price Retirement 2035, Vanguard Target Retirement 2045.

Wall Street Journal © 2006

Getting Going / *By Kelly K. Spors*

Counting on Getting an Inheritance? Better Make Other Retirement Plans

IF YOU'RE COUNTING ON an inheritance from your parents to rescue your under-funded retirement plan, you could be playing a dangerous game.

Despite predictions of a massive transfer of wealth between generations, many baby boomers can expect to get little or nothing from their parents.

Economists and financial experts can't agree on how much money baby boomers and their offspring are likely to inherit. In fact, their predictions of the total sum involved vary widely. But many agree that a small number of wealthy families are likely to receive the bulk of the windfall, and that many other would-be heirs will end up disappointed.

About 64% of those who receive bequests of $100,000 or more are already well off, ranking in the top quintile of net worth, according to an AARP study analyzing the Federal Reserve Board's 2001 Survey of Consumer Finances, the most recent figures available. The median inheritance baby boomers received was about $48,000, but 83% of them said they'd received no inheritance to date.

"It's fair to say that expectation is greater than reality," says Paul G. Schervish, director of Boston College's Center on Wealth and Philanthropy. The Center estimates that at least $45 trillion will be disbursed by estates over the next five decades, though others argue that projection is too high.

Wall Street Journal © 2005

You may have heard that it is wise for people to plan ahead and begin early to put money away for their retirement. The *Wall Street Journal* clipping "Counting on Getting an Inheritance? Better Make Other Retirement Plans" enforces the idea to begin early to provide for your retirement. The clipping states that the median inheritance baby boomers received was about $48,000.

In this chapter we look at various techniques that analyze and graphically represent business statistics. Learning Unit 22–1 discusses the mean, median, and mode. Learning Unit 22–2 explains how to gather data by using frequency distributions and to express these data visually in graphs. Emphasis is placed on whether graphs are indeed giving accurate information. The chapter concludes with an introduction to index numbers—an application of statistics—and an optional learning unit on measures of dispersion.

Learning Unit 22–1: Mean, Median, and Mode

Companies frequently use averages and measurements to guide their business decisions. The mean and median are the two most common averages used to indicate a single value that represents an entire group of numbers. The mode can also be used to describe a set of data.

Mean

The accountant of Bill's Sport Shop told Bill, the owner, that the average daily sales for the week were $150.14. The accountant stressed that $150.14 was an average and did not represent specific daily sales. Bill wanted to know how the accountant arrived at $150.14.

The accountant went on to explain that he used an arithmetic average, or **mean** (a measurement), to arrive at $150.14 (rounded to the nearest hundredth). He showed Bill the following formula:

$$\text{Mean} = \frac{\text{Sum of all values}}{\text{Number of values}}$$

The accountant used the following data:

	Sun.	Mon.	Tues.	Wed.	Thur.	Fri.	Sat.
Sport Shop sales	$400	$100	$68	$115	$120	$68	$180

To compute the mean, the accountant used these data:

$$\text{Mean} = \frac{\$400 + \$100 + \$68 + \$115 + \$120 + \$68 + \$180}{7} = \boxed{\$150.14}$$

When values appear more than once, businesses often look for a **weighted mean.** The format for the weighted mean is slightly different from that for the mean. The concept, however, is the same except that you weight each value by how often it occurs (its frequency). Thus, considering the frequency of the occurrence of each value allows a weighting of each day's sales in proper importance. To calculate the weighted mean, use the following formula:

$$\text{Weighted mean} = \frac{\text{Sum of products}}{\text{Sum of frequencies}}$$

Let's change the sales data for Bill's Sport Shop and see how to calculate a weighted mean:

	Sun.	Mon.	Tues.	Wed.	Thur.	Fri.	Sat.
Sport Shop sales	$400	$100	$100	$80	$80	$100	$400

Value	Frequency	Product
$400	2	$ 800
100	3	300
80	2	160
		$1,260

The weighted mean is $\dfrac{\$1,260}{7} = \boxed{\$180}$

Note how we multiply each value by its frequency of occurrence to arrive at the product. Then we divide the sum of the products by the sum of the frequencies.

When you calculate your grade point average (GPA), you are using a weighted average. The following formula is used to calculate GPA:

$$\text{GPA} = \frac{\text{Total points}}{\text{Total credits}}$$

Now let's show how Jill Rivers calculated her GPA to the nearest tenth.

Given   A = 4; B = 3; C = 2; D = 1; F = 0

Courses	Credits attempted	Grade received	Points (Credits × Grade)	
Introduction to Computers	4	A	16 (4 × 4)	
Psychology	3	B	9 (3 × 3)	
English Composition	3	B	9 (3 × 3)	
Business Law	3	C	6 (2 × 3)	
Business Math	3	B	9 (3 × 3)	
	16		49	$\dfrac{49}{16} = \boxed{3.1}$

When high or low numbers do not significantly affect a list of numbers, the mean is a good indicator of the center of the data. If high or low numbers do have an effect, the median may be a better indicator to use.

Median

The **median** is another measurement that indicates the center of the data. An average that has one or more extreme values is not distorted by the median. For example, let's look at the following yearly salaries of the employees of Rusty's Clothing Shop.

Alice Knight	$95,000	Jane Wang	$67,000
Jane Hess	27,000	Bill Joy	40,000
Joel Floyd	32,000		

Note how Alice's salary of $95,000 will distort an average calculated by the mean.

$$\frac{\$95,000 + \$27,000 + \$32,000 + \$67,000 + \$40,000}{5} = \boxed{\$52,200}$$

The $52,200 average salary is considerably more than the salary of three of the employees. So it is not a good representation of the store's average salary. Let's use the following steps to find the median.

FINDING THE MEDIAN OF A GROUP OF VALUES
Step 1. Orderly arrange values from the smallest to the largest.
Step 2. Find the middle value.
a. *Odd number of values:* Median is the middle value. You find this by first dividing the total number of numbers by 2. The next-higher number is the median.
b. *Even number of values:* Median is the average of the two middle values.

For Rusty's Clothing Shop, we find the median as follows:

1. Arrange values from smallest to largest:
    $27,000; $32,000; $40,000 ; $67,000; $95,000

2. Since the middle value is an odd number, $40,000 is the median. Note that half of the salaries fall below the median and half fall above ($5 \div 2 = 2\frac{1}{2}$—next number is the median).

If Jane Hess ($27,000) were not on the payroll, we would find the median as follows:

1. Arrange values from smallest to largest:
    $32,000; $40,000; $67,000; $95,000

2. Average the two middle values:

$$\frac{\$40,000 + \$67,000}{2} = \boxed{\$53,500}$$

Note that the median results in two salaries below and two salaries above the average.
Now we'll look at another measurement tool—the mode.

Mode

The **mode** is a measurement that also records values. In a series of numbers, the value that occurs most often is the mode. If all the values are different, there is no mode. If two or more numbers appear most often, you may have two or more modes. Note that we do not have to arrange the numbers in the lowest-to-highest order, although this could make it easier to find the mode.

EXAMPLE   3, 4, 5, 6, 3, 8, 9, 3, 5, 3

3 is the mode since it is listed 4 times.

Now let's check your progress with a Practice Quiz.

LU 22–1 | PRACTICE QUIZ

Complete this **Practice Quiz**
to see how you are doing

Barton Company's sales reps sold the following last month:

Sales rep	Sales volume	Sales rep	Sales volume
A	$16,500	C	$12,000
B	15,000	D	48,900

Calculate the mean and the median. Which is the better indicator of the center of the data?
Is there a mode?

✓ Solutions

$$\text{Mean} = \frac{\$16,500 + \$15,000 + \$12,000 + \$48,900}{4} = \boxed{\$23,100}$$

$$\text{Median} = \frac{\$15,000 + \$16,500}{2} = \boxed{\$15,750}$$

$12,000, $15,000, $16,500,
$48,900. Note how we arrange
numbers from smallest to highest
to calculate median.

Median is the better indicator since in calculating the mean, the $48,900 puts the average
of $23,100 much too high. There is no mode.

LU 22–1a | EXTRA PRACTICE QUIZ

Need more practice? Try this
Extra Practice Quiz (check
figures in Chapter Organizer,
p. 524)

Barton's Company sales reps sold the following last month:

Sales rep	Sales volume	Sales rep	Sales volume
A	$17,000	C	$11,000
B	14,000	D	51,000

Calculate the mean and median. Which is the better indicator of the center of the data? Is
there a mode?

Learning Unit 22–2: Frequency Distributions and Graphs

In this unit you will learn how to gather data and illustrate these data. Today, computer software programs can make beautiful color graphics. But how accurate are these graphics? This
Wall Street Journal clipping gives an example of graphics that did not agree with the numbers
beneath them. The clipping reminds all readers to check the numbers illustrated by the graphics.

What's Wrong With this Picture?
Utility's Glasses Are Never Empty

By KATHLEEN DEVENY
Staff Reporter of THE WALL STREET JOURNAL

When Les Waas, an investor in Philadelphia Suburban Corp., paged through
the company's 1994 annual report, he was
impressed by what he saw.

The water utility had used a series of
charts to represent its revenues, net income and book value per share, among
other results. Each figure was represented
by the level of water in a glass. Each chart
showed strong growth.

Then Mr. Waas looked a little more
carefully. The bars in the chart seemed to
indicate far more impressive growth than
the numbers beneath them. A chart showing the growth in the number of Philadelphia Suburban's water customers, for ex-

ample, seemed to indicate the company's
customer base had more than tripled since
1990. But the numbers actually increased
only 6.4%.

The reason for the disparity: The
charts don't begin at zero. Even an empty
glass in the accompanying chart would
represent a customer base of 230,000.

	1990	1991	1992	1993	1994
Number of Metered Water Customers (thousands)	235	237	245	247	250

Collecting raw data and organizing the data is a prerequisite to presenting statistics graphically. Let's illustrate this by looking at the following example.

A computer industry consultant wants to know how much college freshmen are willing to spend to set up a computer in their dormitory rooms. After visiting a local college dorm, the consultant gathered the following data on the amount of money 20 students spent on computers:

$1,000	$7,000	$4,000	$1,000	$ 5,000	$1,000	$3,000
5,000	2,000	3,000	3,000	3,000	8,000	9,000
3,000	6,000	6,000	1,000	10,000	1,000	

Price of computer	Tally	Frequency
$ 1,000	ЖН	5
2,000	I	1
3,000	ЖН	5
4,000	I	1
5,000	II	2
6,000	II	2
7,000	I	1
8,000	I	1
9,000	I	1
10,000	I	1

Note that these raw data are not arranged in any order. To make the data more meaningful, the consultant made the **frequency distribution** table. Think of this distribution table as a way to organize a list of numbers to show the patterns that may exist.

As you can see, 25% ($\frac{5}{20} = \frac{1}{4} = 25\%$) of the students spent $1,000 and another 25% spent $3,000. Only four students spent $7,000 or more.

Now let's see how we can use bar graphs.

Bar Graphs

Bar graphs help readers see the changes that have occurred over a period of time. This is especially true when the same type of data is repeatedly studied. Note the following example of the use of bar graphs.

Did you know that Mexican-made Coke has such a popular taste and look of home for many immigrants that stores in Hispanic communities cannot keep it in stock? Meanwhile, sales of Coca-Cola Classic are down. The following *Wall Street Journal* clipping "U.S. Thirst for Mexican Cola Poses Sticky Problem for Coke" gives two bar graphs to illustrate this problem.

Ric Feld/AP Wide World

U.S. Thirst for Mexican Cola Poses Sticky Problem for Coke

Though It's the Real Thing,
   Soda's Route Across Border
   Breaks Company Rules

Investigating an 'Irritation'

By Chad Terhune

The middle shelf in the soft-drink aisle at Las Tarascas, a Latino supermarket in Lawrenceville, Ga., was bare last week. But store manager Erik Carvallo couldn't call the local Coca-Cola bottler to replenish his stock of Coke.

The Coke Mr. Carvallo's customers had snapped up comes in scuffed glass bottles stamped "Hecho en Mexico"—made in Mexico. It found its way to this Atlanta suburb through an underground supply chain that flouts Coca-Cola Co.'s long-established distribution system.

Mexican-made Coke is such a popular taste of home for many immigrants that Las Tarascas sells about 20 cases a week, or nearly 500 12-ounce bottles at $1.25 apiece. "It's what they grew up with," says Mr. Carvallo.

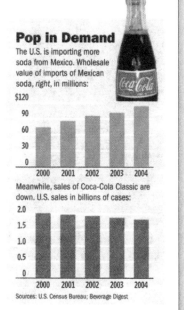

Pop in Demand

The U.S. is importing more soda from Mexico. Wholesale value of imports of Mexican soda, *right*, in millions:

Meanwhile, sales of Coca-Cola Classic are down. U.S. sales in billions of cases:

Sources: U.S. Census Bureau; Beverage Digest

Let's return to our computer consultant example and make a bar graph of the computer purchases data collected by the consultant. Note that the height of the bar represents the frequency of each purchase. Bar graphs can be vertical or horizontal.

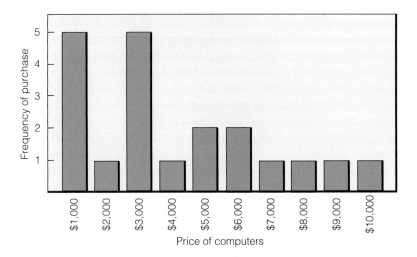

We can simplify this bar graph by grouping the prices of the computers. The grouping, or *intervals,* should be of equal sizes.

Class	Frequency
$1,000–$ 3,000.99	11
3,001– 5,000.99	3
5,001– 7,000.99	3
7,001– 9,000.99	2
9,001– 11,000.99	1

A bar graph for the grouped data follows.

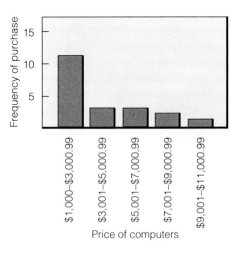

Next, let's see how we can use line graphs.

Line Graphs

A **line graph** shows trends over a period of time. Often separate lines are drawn to show the comparison between two or more trends.

Have you noticed that the trend is for college textbooks to increase in price? The following clipping "Percentage Increase in College Tuition and Fees and Textbook Prices, 1986–2004" shows the steady increase in the cost of college textbooks. You can also see the upward price trend of college tuition and fees.

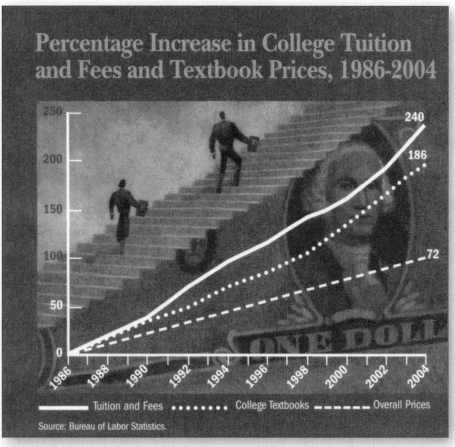

National Education Association © 2005 *Higher Education Advocate*

We conclude our discussion of graphics with the use of the circle graph.

Circle Graphs

.15 × 360° =   54.0
.11 × 360° =   39.6
.36 × 360° = 129.6
.38 × 360° = 136.8
360.0

Circle graphs, often called *pie charts,* are especially helpful for showing the relationship of parts to a whole. The entire circle represents 100%, or 360°; the pie-shaped pieces represent the subcategories. Note at the top of the following page (p. 518) how the circle graph in the *Wall Street Journal* clipping "Wal-Mart Stakes India Claim—Ahead of Possible Market Opening, Foreign Retailers Gear Up" uses the percentage of anticipated sales breakdown of the retail sector in India to estimate future sales.

To draw a circle graph (or pie chart), begin by drawing a circle. Then take the percentages and convert each percentage to a decimal. Next multiply each decimal by 360° to get the degrees represented by the percentage. Circle graphs must total 360°.

We conclude this unit with a brief discussion of index numbers.

An Application of Statistics: Index Numbers

The financial section of a newspaper often gives different index numbers describing the changes in business. These **index numbers** express the relative changes in a variable compared with some base, which is taken as 100. The changes may be measured from time to time or from place to place. Index numbers function as percents and are calculated like percents.

Wal-Mart Stakes India Claim

Ahead of Possible Market Opening, Foreign Retailers Gear Up

Sizing Up the Competition

Wal-Mart and other big chains are eagerly anticipating liberalization of the retail sector in India, where more than 95% of retail sales are made through 12 million mom-and-pop shops, newspaper stalls and tea stands like those pictured above.

Sales growth by division
Year-to-year percentage change

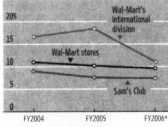

FY2006* sales breakdown

*First 48 weeks only. Fiscal years end Jan. 31

Source: the company

Frequently, a business will use index numbers to make comparisons of a current price relative to a given year. For example, a calculator may cost \$9 today relative to a cost of \$75 some 30 years ago. The **price relative** of the calculator is $\frac{\$9}{\$75} \times 100 = 12\%$. The calculator now costs 12% of what it cost some 30 years ago. A price relative, then, is the current price divided by some previous year's price—the base year—multiplied by 100.

$$\text{Price relative} = \frac{\text{Current price}}{\text{Base year's price}} \times 100$$

Index numbers can also be used to estimate current prices at various geographic locations. The frequently quoted Consumer Price Index (CPI), calculated and published monthly by the U.S. Bureau of Labor Statistics, records the price relative percentage cost of many goods and services nationwide compared to a base period. Table 22.1 (p. 519) gives a portion of the CPI that uses 1982–84 as its base period. Note that the table shows, for example, that the price relative for housing in Los Angeles is 139.3% of what it cost in 1982–84. Thus, Los Angeles housing costs amounting to \$100.00 in 1982–84 now cost \$139.30. So if you built a \$90,000 house in 1982–84, it is worth \$125,370 today. (Convert 139.3% to the decimal 1.393; multiply \$90,000 by 1.393 = \$125,370.)

Once again, we complete the unit with a Practice Quiz.

TABLE 22.1	Expense	Atlanta	Chicago	New York	Los Angeles
	Food	131.9	130.3	139.6	130.9
Consumer Price Index (in percent)	Housing	128.8	131.4	139.3	139.3
	Clothing	133.8	124.3	121.8	126.4
	Medical care	177.6	163.0	172.4	163.3

LU 22–2 PRACTICE QUIZ

Complete this **Practice Quiz** to see how you are doing

1. The following is the number of sales made by 20 salespeople on a given day. Prepare a frequency distribution and a bar graph. Do not use intervals for this example.

    5   8   9   1   4   4   0   3   2   8
    8   9   5   1   9   6   7   5   9   10

2. Assuming the following market shares for diapers 5 years ago, prepare a circle graph:

Pampers	32%	Huggies	24%
Luvs	20%	Others	24%

3. Today a new Explorer costs $30,000. In 1991 the Explorer cost $19,000. What is the price relative? Round to the nearest tenth percent.

✓ **Solutions**

1.

Number of sales	Tally	Frequency
0	I	1
1	II	2
2	I	1
3	I	1
4	II	2
5	III	3
6	I	1
7	I	1
8	III	3
9	IIII	4
10	I	1

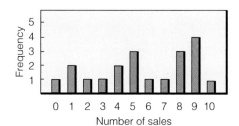

2.
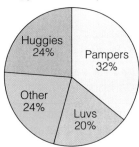

$.32 \times 360° = 115.20°$
$.20 \times 360° = 72.00°$
$.24 \times 360° = 86.40°$
$.24 \times 360° = 86.40°$

3. $\dfrac{\$30,000}{\$19,000} \times 100 = 157.9$

LU 22–2a EXTRA PRACTICE QUIZ

Need more practice? Try this **Extra Practice Quiz** (check figures in Chapter Organizer, p. 524)

1. The following is the number of sales made by 20 salespeople on a given day. Prepare a frequency distribution and a bar graph. Do not use intervals for this example.

    0   8   9   1   4   4   0   3   2   8
    8   9   0   1   9   6   7   0   9   10

2. Assuming the following market shares for diapers 5 years ago, prepare a circle graph.

Pampers	40%	Huggies	25%
Luvs	20%	Others	15%

3. Today a new Explorer costs $35,000. In 1991, the Explorer cost $19,000. What is the price relative? Round to the nearest tenth percent.

Learning Unit 22–3: Measures of Dispersion (Optional)

In Learning Unit 22–1 you learned how companies use the mean, median, and mode to indicate a single value, or number, that represents an entire group of numbers, or data. Often it is valuable to know how the information is scattered (spread or dispersed) within a data set. A **measure of dispersion** is a number that describes how the numbers of a set of data are spread out or dispersed.

This learning unit discusses three measures of dispersion—range, standard deviation, and normal distribution. We begin with the range—the simplest measure of dispersion.

Range

The **range** is the difference between the two extreme values (highest and lowest) in a group of values or a set of data. For example, often the actual extreme values of hourly temperature readings during the past 24 hours are given but not the range or difference between the high and low readings. To find the range in a group of data, subtract the lowest value from the highest value.

> Range = Highest value − Lowest value

Thus, if the high temperature reading during the past 24 hours was 90° and the low temperature reading was 60° the range is 90° − 60°, or 30°.

The range is difficult to use since it depends only on the values of the extremes and not on other values in the data set. Also, the range depends on the *number* of values on which it is based; that is, the larger the number of values, the larger the range is apt to be. The range gives only a general idea of the spread of values in a data set.

EXAMPLE   Find the range of the following values: 83.6, 77.3, 69.2, 93.1, 85.4, 71.6.

Range = 93.1 − 69.2 = 23.9

Standard Deviation

Since the **standard deviation** is intended to measure the spread of data around the mean, you must first determine the mean of a set of data. The following diagram shows two sets of data—A and B. In the diagram, the means of A and B are equal. Now look at how the data in these two sets are spread or dispersed.

Data set A	Data set B
x x x x x 0 1 2 3 4 5 6 7 8 9 10 11 12 13	x x x x x 0 1 2 3 4 5 6 7 8 9 10 11 12 13
Mean = (1 + 2 + 5 + 10 + 12) ÷ 5 = 6	Mean = (4 + 4 + 5 + 8 + 9) ÷ 5 = 6

Note that although the means of data sets A and B are equal, A is more widely dispersed, which means B will have a smaller standard deviation than A.

To find the standard deviation of an ungrouped set of data, use the following steps:

FINDING THE STANDARD DEVIATION
Step 1. Find the mean of the set of data.
Step 2. Subtract the mean from each piece of data to find each deviation.
Step 3. Square each deviation (multiply the deviation by itself).
Step 4. Sum all squared deviations.
Step 5. Divide the sum of the squared deviations by $n − 1$, where n equals the number of pieces of data.
Step 6. Find the square root ($\sqrt{}$) of the number obtained in Step 5 (use a calculator). This is the standard deviation. (The square root is a number that when multiplied by itself equals the amount shown inside the square root symbol.)

Two additional points should be made. First, Step 2 sometimes results in negative numbers. Since the sum of the deviations obtained in Step 2 should always be zero, we would not be able to find the average deviation. This is why we square each deviation—to generate positive quantities only. Second, the standard deviation we refer to is used with *sample* sets of data, that is, a collection of data from a population. The population is the *entire* collection of data. When the standard deviation for a population is calculated, the sum of the squared deviations is divided by n instead of by $n - 1$. In all problems that follow, sample sets of data are being examined.

EXAMPLE Calculate the standard deviations for the sample data sets A and B given in the diagram on p. 520. Round the final answer to the nearest tenth. Note that Step 1—find the mean—is given in the diagram.

Standard deviation of data sets A and B: The table on the left uses Steps 2 through 6 to find the standard deviation of data set A, and the table on the right uses Steps 2 through 6 to find the standard deviation of data set B.

Data	Step 2 Data − Mean	Step 3 (Data − Mean)^2
1	$1 - 6 = -5$	25
2	$2 - 6 = -4$	16
5	$5 - 6 = -1$	1
10	$10 - 6 = 4$	16
12	$12 - 6 = 6$	36
	Total 0	94 **(Step 4)**

Step 5: Divide by $n - 1$: $\dfrac{94}{5 - 1} = \dfrac{94}{4} = 23.5$

Step 6: The square root of $\sqrt{23.5}$ is 4.8 (rounded).

The standard deviation of data set A is 4.8.

Data	Step 2 Data − Mean	Step 3 (Data − Mean)^2
4	$4 - 6 = -2$	4
4	$4 - 6 = -2$	4
5	$5 - 6 = -1$	1
8	$8 - 6 = 2$	4
9	$9 - 6 = 3$	9
	Total 0	22 **(Step 4)**

Step 5: Divide by $n - 1$: $\dfrac{22}{5 - 1} = \dfrac{22}{4} = 5.5$

Step 6: The square root of $\sqrt{5.5}$ is 2.3.

The standard deviation of data set B is 2.3.

As suspected, the standard deviation of data set B is less than that of set A. The standard deviation value reinforces what we see in the diagram.

Normal Distribution

One of the most important distributions of data is the **normal distribution.** In a normal distribution, data are spread *symmetrically* about the mean. A graph of such a distribution looks like the bell-shaped curve in Figure 22.1. Many data sets are normally distributed. Examples are the life span of automobile engines, women's heights, and intelligence quotients.

FIGURE   22.1

Standard deviation and the normal distribution

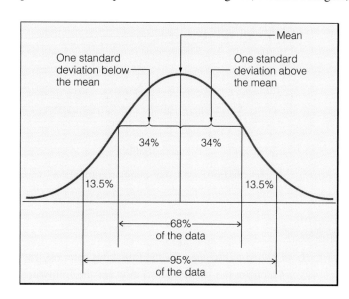

In a normal distribution, the data are spread out symmetrically—50% of the data lie above the mean, and 50% of the data lie below the mean. Additionally, if the data are normally distributed, 68% of the data should be found within one standard deviation above and below the mean. About 95% of the data should be found within two standard deviations above and below the mean. Figure 22.1 illustrates these facts.

EXAMPLE Assume that the mean useful life of a particular lightbulb is 2,000 hours and is normally distributed with a standard deviation of 300 hours. Calculate the useful life of the lightbulb with **(a)** one standard deviation of the mean and **(b)** two standard deviations of the mean; also **(c)** calculate the percent of lightbulbs that will last 2,300 hours or longer.

a. The useful life of the lightbulb one standard deviation from the mean is one standard deviation above *and* below the mean.

$$2,000 \pm 300 = 1,700 \text{ and } 2,300 \text{ hours}$$

The useful life is somewhere between 1,700 and 2,300 hours.

b. The useful life of the lightbulb within two standard deviations of the mean is within two standard deviations above *and* below the mean.

$$2,000 \pm 2(300) = 1,400 \text{ and } 2,600 \text{ hours}$$

c. Since 50% of the data in a normal distribution lie below the mean and 34% represent the amount of data one standard deviation above the mean, we must calculate the percent of data that lies beyond one standard deviation above the mean.

$$100\% - (50\% + 34\%) = \boxed{16\%}$$

So 16% of the bulbs should last 2,300 hours or longer.

It's time for another Practice Quiz.

LU 22–3 PRACTICE QUIZ

Complete this **Practice Quiz** to see how you are doing

1. Calculate the range for the following data: 58, 13, 17, 26, 5, 41.
2. Calculate the standard deviation for the following sample set of data: 113, 92, 77, 125, 110, 93, 111. Round answers to the nearest tenth.

✓ **Solutions**

1. $58 - 5 = \boxed{53 \text{ range}}$
2.

Data	Data − Mean	(Data − Mean)^2
113	113 − 103 = 10	100
92	92 − 103 = −11	121
77	77 − 103 = −26	676
125	125 − 103 = 22	484
110	110 − 103 = 7	49
93	93 − 103 = −10	100
111	111 − 103 = 8	64
	Total	1,594

$$1,594 \div (7 - 1) = 265.6666667$$

$$\sqrt{265.6666667} = \boxed{16.3} \text{ standard deviation}$$

LU 22–3 EXTRA PRACTICE QUIZ

Need more practice? Try this **Extra Practice Quiz** (check figures in Chapter Organizer, p. 524)

1. Calculate the range for the following data: 60, 13, 17, 26, 5, 41.
2. Calculate the standard deviation for the following sample set of data: 120, 88, 77, 125, 110, 93, 111. Round answers to the nearest tenth.

CHAPTER ORGANIZER AND STUDY GUIDE
WITH CHECK FIGURES FOR EXTRA PRACTICE QUIZZES

Topic	Key point, procedure, formula	Example(s) to illustrate situation
Mean, p. 511	$\dfrac{\text{Sum of all values}}{\text{Number of values}}$	Age of basketball team: 22, 28, 31, 19, 15 $\text{Mean} = \dfrac{22 + 28 + 31 + 19 + 15}{5}$ $= \boxed{23}$
Weighted mean, p. 512	$\dfrac{\text{Sum of products}}{\text{Sum of frequencies}}$	(see table below)

For the Weighted mean example:

	S.	M.	T.	W.	Th.	F.	S.
Sales	$90	$75	$80	$75	$80	$90	$90

Value	Frequency	Product
$90	3	$270
75	2	150
80	2	160
	7	$580

$\text{Mean} = \dfrac{\$580}{7} = \boxed{\$82.86}$

Topic	Key point, procedure, formula	Example(s) to illustrate situation

Median, p. 513	1. Arrange values from smallest to largest.
	 2. Find the middle value.
	   a. Odd number of values: median is middle value.
	   $\left(\dfrac{\text{Total number of numbers}}{2}\right)$
	   Next-higher number is median.
	   b. Even number of values: average of two middle values.
		12, 15, 8, 6, 3
		 1. 3 6 8 12 15
		 2. $\dfrac{5}{2} = 2.5$
		 Median is third number, $\boxed{8.}$

Topic	Key point, procedure, formula	Example(s) to illustrate situation
Frequency distribution, p. 515	Method of listing numbers or amounts not arranged in any particular way by columns for numbers (amounts), tally, and frequency	Number of sodas consumed in one day: 1, 5, 4, 3, 4, 2, 2, 3, 2, 0

Number of sodas	Tally	Frequency
0	I	1
1	I	1
2	III	3
3	II	2
4	II	2
5	I	1

Topic	Key point, procedure, formula	Example(s) to illustrate situation
Bar graphs, p. 516	Height of bar represents frequency. Bar graph used for grouped data. Bar graphs can be vertical or horizontal.	From soda example above:
Line graphs, p. 517	Shows trend. Helps to put numbers in order.	**Sales** 2005 $1,000 2006 2,000 2007 3,000

(continues)

CHAPTER ORGANIZER AND STUDY GUIDE
WITH CHECK FIGURES FOR EXTRA PRACTICE QUIZZES (concluded)

Topic	Key point, procedure, formula	Example(s) to illustrate situation
Circle graphs, p. 517	Circle = 360° % × 360° = Degrees of pie to represent percent Total should = 360°	60% favor diet soda 40% favor sugared soda 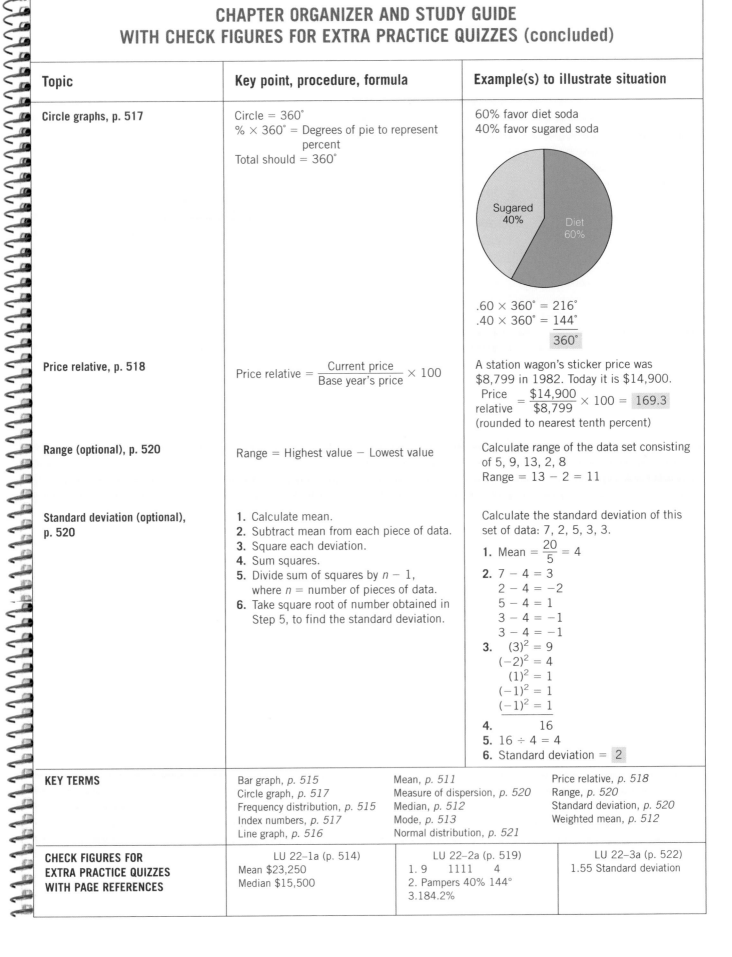 .60 × 360° = 216° .40 × 360° = $\underline{144°}$ $\boxed{360°}$
Price relative, p. 518	Price relative = $\dfrac{\text{Current price}}{\text{Base year's price}} \times 100$	A station wagon's sticker price was $8,799 in 1982. Today it is $14,900. $\dfrac{\text{Price}}{\text{relative}} = \dfrac{\$14,900}{\$8,799} \times 100 = \boxed{169.3}$ (rounded to nearest tenth percent)
Range (optional), p. 520	Range = Highest value − Lowest value	Calculate range of the data set consisting of 5, 9, 13, 2, 8 Range = 13 − 2 = 11

Standard deviation (optional), p. 520	1. Calculate mean.
	2. Subtract mean from each piece of data.
	3. Square each deviation.
	4. Sum squares.
	5. Divide sum of squares by $n - 1$, where n = number of pieces of data.
	6. Take square root of number obtained in Step 5, to find the standard deviation.
		Calculate the standard deviation of this set of data: 7, 2, 5, 3, 3.
		1. Mean = $\dfrac{20}{5} = 4$
		2. $7 - 4 = 3$
		   $2 - 4 = -2$
		   $5 - 4 = 1$
		   $3 - 4 = -1$
		   $3 - 4 = -1$
		3. $(3)^2 = 9$
		   $(-2)^2 = 4$
		   $(1)^2 = 1$
		   $(-1)^2 = 1$
		   $(-1)^2 = \underline{1}$
		4. $\qquad 16$
		5. $16 \div 4 = 4$
		6. Standard deviation = $\boxed{2}$

KEY TERMS	Bar graph, *p. 515* Circle graph, *p. 517* Frequency distribution, *p. 515* Index numbers, *p. 517* Line graph, *p. 516*	Mean, *p. 511* Measure of dispersion, *p. 520* Median, *p. 512* Mode, *p. 513* Normal distribution, *p. 521*	Price relative, *p. 518* Range, *p. 520* Standard deviation, *p. 520* Weighted mean, *p. 512*

CHECK FIGURES FOR EXTRA PRACTICE QUIZZES WITH PAGE REFERENCES	LU 22–1a (p. 514) Mean $23,250 Median $15,500	LU 22–2a (p. 519) 1. 9 1111 4 2. Pampers 40% 144° 3.184.2%	LU 22–3a (p. 522) 1.55 Standard deviation

Critical Thinking Discussion Questions

1. Explain the mean, median, and mode. Give an example that shows you must be careful when you read statistics in an article.

2. Explain frequency distributions and the types of graphs. Locate a company annual report and explain how the company shows graphs to highlight its performance. Does the company need more or fewer of these visuals? Could price relatives be used?

3. Explain the statement that standard deviations are not accurate.

Classroom Notes

Name _____ Date _____

Calculate the mean (to the nearest hundredth):

22–1. 8, 9, 8, 3

22–2. 8, 11, 19, 17, 15

22–3. $55.83, $66.92, $108.93

22–4. $1,001, $68.50, $33.82, $581.95

22–5. Calculate the grade-point average: A = 4, B = 3, C = 2, D = 1, F = 0 (to nearest tenth).

Courses	Credits	Grade
Computer Principles	3	B
Business Law	3	C
Logic	3	D
Biology	4	A
Marketing	3	B

22–6. Find the weighted mean (to the nearest tenth):

Value	Frequency	Product
4	7	
8	3	
2	9	
4	2	

Find the median:

22–7. 55, 10, 19, 38, 100, 25

22–8. 95, 103, 98, 62, 31, 15, 82

Find the mode:

22–9. 8, 9, 3, 4, 12, 8, 8, 9

22–10. 22, 19, 15, 16, 18, 18, 5, 18

22–11. Given: Truck cost   2007 $30,000
                    Truck cost   2004 $21,000

Calculate the price relative (round to the nearest tenth percent).

22–12. Given the following sales of Lowe Corporation, prepare a line graph (run sales from $5,000 to $20,000).

2009	$ 8,000
2010	11,000
2011	13,000
2012	18,000

22–13. Prepare a frequency distribution from the following weekly salaries of teachers at Moore Community College. Use the following intervals:

$200–$299.99
300– 399.99
400– 499.99
500– 599.99

$210	$505	$310	$380	$275
290	480	550	490	200
286	410	305	444	368

22–14. Prepare a bar graph from the frequency distribution in Problem 22–13.

22–15. How many degrees on a pie chart would each be given from the following?

Wear digital watch	42%
Wear traditional watch	51%
Wear no watch	7%

WORD PROBLEMS

22–16. The March 2007 issue of *AARP Bulletin*, cited the following data provided by the U.S. Census Bureau. The data showed median ages—the age at which half the residents are younger and half older in several states.

39.7	40.2	37.5	38.4
40.7	38	37.4	38.5
38.2	41.2	39.1	
37.3	37.9	39.5	
37.6	39.1	39.3	

(a) What is the mean? **(b)** What is the Mode? **(c)** What is the Median?

22–17. "Anatomy of an A380", was the featured story in the March 5, 2007 issue of *Fortune*. EADS is the parent company of Airbus. EADS major shareholders are as follow: SEPI (Spanish) 5.5% DaimlerChrsler 22.5%, SOGEADE (Lagardere; French government) 30% and Public Shares at 42%. Prepare a pie chart for the EADS' Annual Report.

22–18. On March 15, 2007, *Pfizer Inc.* issued the company's 2006 Financial Report. Net income for the past 6 years, shown in millions, is as follows:

Year	Net Income
2001	1.22
2002	1.48
2003	.54
2004	1.51
2005	1.10
2006	2.67

Prepared a bar graph for the past 6 years (use .25 increments)

22–19. Bill Small, a travel agent, provided Alice Hall with the following information regarding the cost of her upcoming vacation:

Transportation	35%
Hotel	28%
Food and entertainment	20%
Miscellaneous	17%

Construct a circle graph for Alice.

22–20. Jim Smith, a marketing student, observed how much each customer spent in a local convenience store. Based on the following results, prepare **(a)** a frequency distribution and **(b)** a bar graph. Use intervals of $0–$5.99, $6.00–$11.99, $12.00–$17.99, and $18.00–$23.99.

$18.50	$18.24	$ 6.88	$9.95
16.10	3.55	14.10	6.80
12.11	3.82	2.10	
15.88	3.95	5.50	

22–21. Angie's Bakery bakes bagels. Find the weighted mean (to the nearest whole bagel) given the following daily production for June:

200	150	200	150	200
150	190	360	360	150
190	190	190	200	150
360	400	400	150	200
400	360	150	400	360
400	400	200	150	150

22–22. Melvin Company reported sales in 2011 of $300,000. This compared to sales of $150,000 in 2010 and $100,000 in 2009. Construct a line graph for Melvin Company.

CHALLENGE PROBLEMS

22–23. The *Chicago Sun-Times* listed average monthly earnings for various careers requiring a bachelor's degree.

a. Prepare a frequency distribution from the following data.

Accountant	$3,321	Occupational therapist	$4,113
Architect	4,103	Physician assistant	4,427
Computer programmer	4,255	Public relations specialist	3,056
Flight attendant	3,560	Sales representative	4,530
Graphic designer	2,765	Social worker	2,500
Insurance agent	3,225		

Use the following intervals:

$2,500–$2,999.99
$3,000– 3,499.99
$3,500– 3,999.99
$4,000– 4,499.99
$4,500– 4,999.99

b. Prepare a bar graph from the frequency distribution.

c. From the above averages, find the mean and median. Round to the nearest whole number.

22–24. The following circle graph is a suggested budget for Ron Rye and his family for a month:

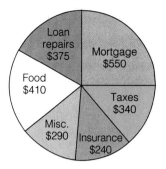

Ron would like you to calculate the percent (to the hundredth) for each part of the circle graph along with the appropriate number of degrees.

Classroom Notes

Name _____ Date _____

DRILL PROBLEMS

1. Calculate the range for the following set of data: 117, 98, 133, 52, 114, 35.

Calculate the standard deviation for the following sample sets of data. Round the final answers to the nearest tenth.

2. 83.6, 92.3, 56.5, 43.8, 77.1, 66.7

3. 7, 3, 12, 17, 5, 8, 9, 9, 13, 15, 6, 6, 4, 5

4. 41, 41, 38, 27, 53, 56, 28, 45, 47, 49, 55, 60

WORD PROBLEMS

5. The mean useful life of car batteries is 48 months. They have a standard deviation of 3. If the useful life of batteries is normally distributed, calculate (a) the percent of batteries with a useful life of less than 45 months and (b) the percent of batteries that will last longer than 54 months.

6. The average weight of a particular box of crackers is 24.5 ounces with a standard deviation of 0.8 ounce. The weights of the boxes are normally distributed. What percent of the boxes (a) weighs more than 22.9 ounces and (b) weighs less than 23.7 ounces?

7. An examination is normally distributed with a mean score of 77 and a standard deviation of 6. Find the percent of individuals scoring as indicated below.

   a. Between 71 and 83
   b. Between 83 and 65
   c. Above 89
   d. Less than 65
   e. Between 77 and 65

8. Listed below are the sales figures in thousands of dollars for a group of insurance salespeople. Calculate the mean sales figure and the standard deviation.

$117	$350	$400	$245	$420
223	275	516	265	135
486	320	285	374	190

9. The time in seconds it takes for 20 individual sewing machines to stitch a border onto a particular garment is listed below. Calculate the mean stitching time and the standard deviation to the nearest hundredth.

67	69	64	71	73
58	71	64	62	67
62	57	67	60	65
60	63	72	56	64

 SUMMARY PRACTICE TEST

1. In July, Lee Realty sold 10 homes at the following prices: $140,000; $166,000; $80,000; $98,000; $185,000; $150,000; $108,000; $114,000; $142,000; and $250,000. Calculate the mean and median. *(pp. 511, 513)*

2. Lowes counted the number of customers entering the store for a week. The results were 1,100; 950; 1,100; 1,700; 880; 920; and 1,100. What is the mode? *(p. 513)*

3. This semester Hung Lee took four 3-credit courses at Riverside Community College. She received a A in accounting and C's in history, psychology, and algebra. What is her cumulative grade point average (assume A = 4 and B = 3) to the nearest hundredth? *(p. 512)*

4. Pete's Variety Shop reported the following sales for the first 20 days of May. *(p. 515)*

$100	$400	$600	$400	$600
100	600	300	500	700
200	600	700	500	200
100	600	100	700	700

Prepare a frequency distribution for Pete.

5. Leeds Company produced the following number of maps during the first 5 weeks of last year. Prepare a bar graph. *(p. 516)*

Week	Maps
1	800
2	600
3	400
4	700
5	300

6. Laser Corporation reported record profits of 30%. It stated in the report that the cost of sales was 40% with expenses of 30%. Prepare a circle graph for Laser. *(p. 517)*

7. Today a new Explorer costs $39,900. In 1990, Explorers cost $24,000. What is the price relative to the nearest tenth percent? *(p. 518)*

*8. Calculate the standard deviation for the following set of data: 7, 2, 5, 3, 3, 10. Round final answer to nearest tenth. *(p. 520)*

*Optional problem.

Personal Finance

APPLE VS. MICROSOFT

Why two **TECH TITANS** will please shareholders in the coming year

Apple Inc.'s TV advertising campaign cleverly portrays its products as hip alternatives to stodgy old Microsoft's. In a way, the portrayal fits the two companies' stocks as well. Apple shares (symbol AAPL) have risen more than 1,200% in the past four years to a recent $97, and they trade for 32 times expected calendar '07 earnings of $3.03 per share. By comparison, investors seem uninterested in Microsoft's shares, which have done little for five years. At $31, they can be had for just 19 times estimated calendar '07 earnings of $1.68 per share, way below their heyday price-earnings ratios. We think both stocks have promise, but for different reasons.

Apple's shares are "not ridiculously expensive," says Ryan Jacob, who counts the maker of two iconic products, the iPod and the Mac computer, among the top holdings of his Jacob Internet fund. "They have a lot of new products coming out next year, and that could increase their sales and earnings numbers considerably." In January, the Cupertino, Cal., company announced a potential blockbuster, a product that combines an iPod and a cell phone, as well as a device that lets you play computer-downloaded movies on your TV. Owning Apple is a bet that the company will continue to come up with hit products.

Microsoft's new-product schedule, which features updates of Office and the Windows operating system, has been known for some time. These products will be hits by virtue of Microsoft's huge base of users. Robert Millen, co-manager of Jensen fund, says the Redmond, Wash., company is entering the "most significant product cycle in its 30-year history." Curiously, Jensen fund's managers, who favor stocks with high returns on equity (a measure of profitability), had never bought Microsoft (MSFT) because it had always been too expensive and they were concerned about the company's antitrust problems. With the legal concerns now mostly resolved and the share price lagging, they began buying last September at about $27. Millen says he doesn't have a target price, but Jensen managers try to buy stocks when they are undervalued by 30% to 40%. That implies he thinks the shares could fetch $39 to $45 if fully valued.

BUSINESS MATH ISSUE

The statistics in this article are misleading.

1. List the key points of the article and information to support your position.
2. Write a group defense of your position using math calculations to support your view.

Slater's Business Math Scrapbook

with Internet Application

Putting Your Skills to Work

PROJECT A

Go to the Web and find today the annual revenues for Exxon, Wal-Mart, General Motors, Ford Motor, and General Electric.

BY THE NUMBERS

Net income

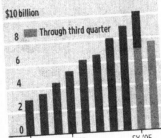

$10 billion

Through third quarter

8

6

4

2

0

FY 1997   FY 2000   FY '05

Fiscal years end Jan. 31

Work force

Approximate number of U.S. employees

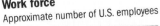

Federal government	1.9 million*
Wal-Mart	1.3 million
Target	292,000
Kmart	133,000
Costco	86,900

*Civilian work force; excludes postal employees

Stores by country
As of Oct. 31, 2005

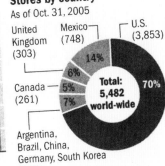

United Kingdom (303)   Mexico (748)   U.S. (3,853)

14%

6%

5%

7%

Canada (261)

Total: 5,482 world-wide   70%

Argentina, Brazil, China, Germany, South Korea (317)

Annual revenue
Top five U.S. companies by revenue for most recent fiscal year, in billions

Exxon Mobil	$298.0
Wal-Mart	285.2
General Motors	193.5
Ford Motor	170.8
General Electric	152.4

Growing larger
Current and planned approximate U.S. selling space in Wal-Mart stores:

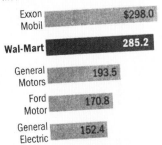

19 square miles   21 square miles   Approximate area of Manhattan: 22.7 square miles

2005   2006

Note: Data represent totals for Wal-Mart Stores, Wal-Mart Supercenters, Sam's Clubs, Wal-Mart Neighborhood Markets and Wal-Mart International

Sources: the companies; feddesk.com

Wall Street Journal © 2005

Internet Projects: See text Web site (www.mhhe.com/slater9e) and The Business Math Internet Resource Guide.

APPENDIX

Additional Homework
by Learning Unit

Name _____   Date _____

Learning Unit 1–1:   Reading, Writing, and Rounding Whole Numbers

DRILL PROBLEMS

1. Express the following numbers in verbal form:

   a. 7,521 _____

     _____

   b. 160,501 _____

     _____

   c. 2,098,767 _____

     _____

   d. 58,003 _____

     _____

   e. 50,025,212,015 _____

     _____

2. Write in numeric form:

   a. Ninety thousand, two hundred eighty-one _____

   b. Fifty-eight thousand, three _____

   c. Two hundred eighty thousand, five _____

   d. Three million, ten _____

   e. Sixty-seven thousand, seven hundred sixty _____

3. Round the following numbers:

   a. To the nearest ten:

     42 _____   379 _____   855 _____   5,981 _____   206 _____

   b. To the nearest hundred:

     9,664 _____   2,074 _____   888 _____   271 _____   75 _____

   c. To the nearest thousand:

     21,486 _____   621 _____   3,504 _____   9,735 _____

4. Round off each number to the nearest ten, nearest hundred, nearest thousand, and round all the way. (Remember that you are rounding the original number each time.)

		Nearest ten	Nearest hundred	Nearest thousand	Round all the way
a.	4,752	_____	_____	_____	_____
b.	70,351	_____	_____	_____	_____
c.	9,386	_____	_____	_____	_____
d.	4,983	_____	_____	_____	_____
e.	408,119	_____	_____	_____	_____
f.	30,051	_____	_____	_____	_____

5. Name the place position (place value) of the underlined digit.

   a. 8,3̲48 _____

   b. 9̲,734 _____

   c. 34̲7,107 _____

   d. 72̲3 _____

       e. 28,200,000,121 _____

       f. 706,359,005 _____

       g. 27,563,530 _____

WORD PROBLEMS

  6. Ken Lawler was shopping for a computer. He went to three different Web sites and found the computer he wanted at three different prices. At Web site A the price was $2,115, at Web site B the price was $1,990, and at Web site C the price was $2,050. What is the approximate price Ken will have to pay for the computer? Round to the nearest thousand. (Just one price.)

  7. Amy Parker had to write a check at the bookstore when she purchased her books for the new semester. The total cost of the books was $384. How will she write this amount in verbal form on her check?

  8. Matt Schaeffer was listening to the news and heard that steel production last week was one million, five hundred eighty-seven thousand tons. Express this amount in numeric form.

  9. Jackie Martin is the city clerk and must go to the aldermen's meetings and take notes on what is discussed. At last night's meeting, they were discussing repairs for the public library, which will cost three hundred seventy-five thousand, nine hundred eighty-five dollars. Write this in numeric form as Jackie would.

10. A government survey revealed that 25,963,400 people are employed as office workers. To show the approximate number of office workers, round the number all the way.

11. Bob Donaldson wished to present his top student with a certificate of achievement at the end of the school year in 2004. To make it appear more official, he wanted to write the year in verbal form. How did he write the year?

12. Nancy Morrissey has a problem reading large numbers and determining place value. She asked her brother to name the place value of the 4 in the number 13,542,966. Can you tell Nancy the place value of the 4? What is the place value of the 3?

     The 4 is in the _____ place.

     The 3 is in the _____ place.

Name _____   Date _____

Learning Unit 1–2: Adding and Subtracting Whole Numbers

DRILL PROBLEMS

1. Add by totaling each separate column:

	a.	**b.**	**c.**	**d.**	**e.**	**f.**	**g.**	**h.**
	659	43	493	36	716	535	751	75,730
	322	58	826	76	458	107	378	48,531
		96		43	397	778	135	15,797
				24	139	215	747	
					478	391	368	

2. Estimate by rounding all the way, then add the actual numbers:

a.	**b.**	**c.**
580	1,470	475
971	7,631	837
548	4,383	213
430		775
506		432

d.	**e.**	**f.**
442	2,571	10,928
609	3,625	9,321
766	4,091	12,654
410	928	15,492
128		

3. Estimate by rounding all the way, then subtract the actual numbers:

a.	**b.**	**c.**
81	91	68
− 42	− 33	− 59

d.	**e.**	**f.**
981	622	1,125
− 283	− 328	− 913

4. Subtract and check:

a.	**b.**	**c.**
4,947	3,724	474,820
− 4,362	− 2,138	− 85,847

d.	**e.**	**f.**
50,000	65,003	15,715
− 21,762	− 24,987	− 3,503

5. In the following sales report, total the rows and the columns, then check that the grand total is the same both horizontally and vertically.

Salesperson	Region 1	Region 2	Region 3	Total
a. Becker	$ 5,692	$ 7,403	$ 3,591	
b. Edwards	7,652	7,590	3,021	
c. Graff	6,545	6,738	4,545	
d. Jackson	6,937	6,950	4,913	
e. Total				

WORD PROBLEMS

6. Joy Jill owes $6,500 on her car loan, plus interest of $499. How much will it cost her to pay off this loan?

7. Sales at Rich's Convenience Store were $3,587 on Monday, $3,944 on Tuesday, $4,007 on Wednesday, $3,890 on Thursday, and $4,545 on Friday. What were the total sales for the week?

8. Poor's Variety Store sold $5,000 worth of lottery tickets in the first week of August; it sold $289 less in the second week. How much were the lottery ticket sales in the second week of August?

9. A truck weighed 9,550 pounds when it was empty. After being filled with rubbish, it was driven to the dump where it weighed in at 22,347 pounds. How much did the rubbish weigh?

10. Lynn Jackson had $549 in her checking account when she went to the bookstore. Lynn purchased an accounting book for $62, the working papers for $28, a study guide for $25, and a mechanical pencil for $5. After Lynn writes a check for the entire purchase, how much money will remain in her checking account?

11. A new hard-body truck is advertised with a base price of $6,986 delivered. However, the window sticker on the truck reads as follows: tinted glass, $210; automatic transmission, $650; power steering, $210; power brakes, $215; safety locks, $95; air conditioning, $1,056. Estimate the total price, including the accessories, by rounding all the way and *then* calculating the exact price.

12. Four different stores are offering the same make and model of camcorder:

Store A	Store B	Store C	Store D
$1,285	$1,380	$1,440	$1,355

Find the difference between the highest price and the lowest price. Check your answer.

13. A Xerox XC830 copy machine has a suggested retail price of $1,395. The net price is $649. How much is the discount on the copy machine?

Name _____   Date _____

Learning Unit 1–3: Multiplying and Dividing Whole Numbers

DRILL PROBLEMS

1. In the following problems, first estimate by rounding all the way, then work the actual problems and check:

Actual   **Estimate**   **Check**

a.   160
    $\times$ 15

b.   4,216
    $\times$ 45

c.   52,376
    $\times$ 309

d.   3,106
    $\times$ 28

2. Multiply (use the shortcut when applicable):

a.   4,072   b.   5,100
    $\times$ 100 $\times$ 40

c.   76,000   d. 93 $\times$ 100,000
    $\times$ 1,200

3. Divide by rounding all the way; then do the actual calculation and check showing the remainder as a whole number.

Actual   **Estimate**   **Check**

a. 8)7,709

b. 26)5,910

	Actual	Estimate	Check
c.	151)3,783		

d. 46)19,550

4. Divide by the shortcut method:

   a. 200)5,400   **b.** 50)5,650

   c. 1,200)43,200   **d.** 17,000)510,000

WORD PROBLEMS

5. Mia Kaminsky sells state lottery tickets in her variety store. If Mia's Variety Store sells 410 lottery tickets per day, how many tickets will be sold in a 7-day period?

6. Arlex Oil Company employs 100 people who are eligible for profit sharing. The financial manager has announced that the profits to be shared amount to $64,000. How much will each employee receive?

7. John Duncan's employer withheld $4,056 in federal taxes from his pay for the year. If equal deductions are made each week, what is John's weekly deduction?

8. Anne Domingoes drives a Volvo that gets 32 miles per gallon of gasoline. How many miles can she travel on 25 gallons of gas?

9. How many 8-inch pieces of yellow ribbon can be cut from a spool of ribbon that contains 6 yards (1 yard = 36 inches)?

10. The number of commercials aired per day on a local television station is 672. How many commercials are aired in 1 year?

11. The computer department at City College purchased 18 computers at a cost of $2,400 each. What was the total price for the computer purchase?

12. Net income for Goodwin's Partnership was $64,500. The five partners share profits and losses equally. What was each partner's share?

13. Ben Krenshaw's supervisor at the construction site told Ben to divide a load of 1,423 bricks into stacks containing 35 bricks each. How many stacks will there be when Ben has finished the job? How many "extra" bricks will there be?

Name _____ Date _____

Learning Unit 2–1: Types of Fractions and Conversion Procedures

DRILL PROBLEMS

1. Identify the type of fraction—proper, improper, or mixed number:

  a. $9\frac{1}{5}$ **b.** $\frac{29}{28}$ **c.** $\frac{29}{27}$

  d. $9\frac{3}{11}$ **e.** $\frac{18}{5}$ **f.** $\frac{30}{37}$

2. Convert to a mixed number:

  a. $\frac{29}{4}$ **b.** $\frac{137}{8}$ **c.** $\frac{27}{5}$

  d. $\frac{29}{9}$ **e.** $\frac{71}{8}$ **f.** $\frac{43}{6}$

3. Convert the mixed number to an improper fraction:

  a. $7\frac{1}{5}$ **b.** $12\frac{3}{11}$ **c.** $4\frac{3}{7}$

  d. $20\frac{4}{9}$ **e.** $10\frac{11}{12}$ **f.** $17\frac{2}{3}$

4. Tell whether the fractions in each pair are equivalent or not:

  a. $\frac{3}{4}$ $\frac{9}{12}$ _____   **b.** $\frac{2}{3}$ $\frac{12}{18}$ _____   **c.** $\frac{7}{8}$ $\frac{15}{16}$ _____

  d. $\frac{4}{5}$ $\frac{12}{15}$ _____   **e.** $\frac{3}{2}$ $\frac{9}{4}$ _____   **f.** $\frac{5}{8}$ $\frac{7}{11}$ _____

  g. $\frac{7}{12}$ $\frac{7}{24}$ _____   **h.** $\frac{5}{4}$ $\frac{30}{24}$ _____   **i.** $\frac{10}{26}$ $\frac{12}{26}$ _____

5. Find the greatest common divisor by the step approach and reduce to lowest terms:

  a. $\frac{36}{42}$

  b. $\frac{30}{75}$

  c. $\frac{74}{148}$

  d. $\frac{15}{600}$

  e. $\frac{96}{132}$

f. $\dfrac{84}{154}$

6. Convert to higher terms:

   a. $\dfrac{8}{10} = \dfrac{}{70}$

   b. $\dfrac{2}{15} = \dfrac{}{30}$

   c. $\dfrac{6}{11} = \dfrac{}{132}$

   d. $\dfrac{4}{9} = \dfrac{}{36}$

   e. $\dfrac{7}{20} = \dfrac{}{100}$

   f. $\dfrac{7}{8} = \dfrac{}{560}$

WORD PROBLEMS

7. Ken drove to college in $3\frac{1}{4}$ hours. How many quarter-hours is that? Show your answer as an improper fraction.

8. Mary looked in the refrigerator for a dozen eggs. When she found the box, only 5 eggs were left. What fractional part of the box of eggs was left?

9. At a recent meeting of a local Boosters Club, 17 of the 25 members attending were men. What fraction of those in attendance were men?

10. By weight, water is two parts out of three parts of the human body. What fraction of the body is water?

11. Three out of 5 students who begin college will continue until they receive their degree. Show in fractional form how many out of 100 beginning students will graduate.

12. Tina and her friends came in late to a party and found only $\frac{3}{4}$ of a pizza remaining. In order for everyone to get some pizza, she wanted to divide it into smaller pieces. If she divides the pizza into twelfths, how many pieces will she have? Show your answer in fractional form.

13. Sharon and Spunky noted that it took them 35 minutes to do their exercise routine. What fractional part of an hour is that? Show your answer in lowest terms.

14. Norman and his friend ordered several pizzas, which were all cut into eighths. The group ate 43 pieces of pizza. How many pizzas did they eat? Show your answer as a mixed number.

Name _____   Date _____

Learning Unit 2-2: Adding and Subtracting Fractions

DRILL PROBLEMS

1. Find the least common denominator (LCD) for each of the following groups of denominators using the prime numbers:

   a. 8, 16, 32

   b. 9, 15, 20

   c. 12, 15, 32

   d. 7, 9, 14, 28

2. Add and reduce to lowest terms or change to a mixed number if needed:

   a. $\dfrac{1}{8} + \dfrac{4}{8}$

   b. $\dfrac{5}{12} + \dfrac{8}{15}$

   c. $\dfrac{7}{8} + \dfrac{5}{12}$

   d. $7\dfrac{2}{3} + 5\dfrac{1}{4}$

   e. $\dfrac{2}{3} + \dfrac{4}{9} + \dfrac{1}{4}$

3. Subtract and reduce to lowest terms:

   a. $\dfrac{5}{9} - \dfrac{2}{9}$

   b. $\dfrac{14}{15} - \dfrac{4}{15}$

   c. $\dfrac{8}{9} - \dfrac{5}{6}$

   d. $\dfrac{7}{12} - \dfrac{9}{16}$

   e. $33\dfrac{5}{8} - 27\dfrac{1}{2}$

   f. $9 - 2\dfrac{3}{7}$

   g. $15\dfrac{1}{3} - 9\dfrac{7}{12}$

   h. $92\dfrac{3}{10} - 35\dfrac{7}{15}$

   i. $93 - 57\dfrac{5}{12}$

   j. $22\dfrac{5}{8} - 17\dfrac{1}{4}$

WORD PROBLEMS

4. Dan Lund took a cross-country trip. He drove $5\frac{3}{8}$ hours on Monday, $6\frac{1}{2}$ hours on Tuesday, $9\frac{3}{4}$ hours on Wednesday, $6\frac{3}{8}$ hours on Thursday, and $10\frac{1}{4}$ hours on Friday. Find the total number of hours Dan drove in the first 5 days of his trip.

5. Sharon Parker bought 20 yards of material to make curtains. She used $4\frac{1}{2}$ yards for one bedroom window, $8\frac{3}{5}$ yards for another bedroom window, and $3\frac{7}{8}$ yards for a hall window. How much material did she have left?

6. Molly Ring visited a local gym and lost $2\frac{1}{4}$ pounds the first weekend and $6\frac{1}{8}$ pounds in week 2. What is Molly's total weight loss?

7. Bill Williams had to drive $46\frac{1}{4}$ miles to work. After driving $28\frac{5}{6}$ miles he noticed he was low on gas and had to decide whether he should stop to fill the gas tank. How many more miles does Bill have to drive to get to work?

8. Albert's Lumber Yard purchased $52\frac{1}{2}$ cords of lumber on Monday and $48\frac{3}{4}$ cords on Tuesday. It sold $21\frac{3}{8}$ cords on Friday. How many cords of lumber remain at Albert's Lumber Yard?

9. At Arlen Oil Company, where Dave Bursett is the service manager, it took $42\frac{1}{3}$ hours to clean five boilers. After a new cleaning tool was purchased, the time for cleaning five boilers was reduced to $37\frac{4}{9}$ hours. How much time was saved?

Name _____   Date _____

Learning Unit 2–3:   Multiplying and Dividing Fractions

DRILL PROBLEMS

1. Multiply (use cancellation technique):

a. $\dfrac{6}{13} \times \dfrac{26}{12}$

b. $\dfrac{3}{8} \times \dfrac{2}{3}$

c. $\dfrac{5}{7} \times \dfrac{9}{10}$

d. $\dfrac{3}{4} \times \dfrac{9}{13} \times \dfrac{26}{27}$

e. $6\dfrac{2}{5} \times 3\dfrac{1}{8}$

f. $2\dfrac{2}{3} \times 2\dfrac{7}{10}$

g. $45 \times \dfrac{7}{9}$

h. $3\dfrac{1}{9} \times 1\dfrac{2}{7} \times \dfrac{3}{4}$

i. $\dfrac{3}{4} \times \dfrac{7}{9} \times 3\dfrac{1}{3}$

j. $\dfrac{1}{8} \times 6\dfrac{2}{3} \times \dfrac{1}{10}$

2. Multiply (do not use canceling; reduce by finding the greatest common divisor):

a. $\dfrac{3}{4} \times \dfrac{8}{9}$

b. $\dfrac{7}{16} \times \dfrac{8}{13}$

3. Multiply or divide as indicated:

a. $\dfrac{25}{36} \div \dfrac{5}{9}$

b. $\dfrac{18}{8} \div \dfrac{12}{16}$

c. $2\dfrac{6}{7} \div 2\dfrac{2}{5}$

d. $3\dfrac{1}{4} \div 16$

e. $24 \div 1\dfrac{1}{3}$

f. $6 \times \dfrac{3}{2}$

g. $3\frac{1}{5} \times 7\frac{1}{2}$

h. $\frac{3}{8} \div \frac{7}{4}$

i. $9 \div 3\frac{3}{4}$

j. $\frac{11}{24} \times \frac{24}{33}$

k. $\frac{12}{14} \div 27$

l. $\frac{3}{5} \times \frac{2}{7} \div \frac{3}{10}$

WORD PROBLEMS

4. Mary Smith plans to make 12 meatloafs to store in her freezer. Each meatloaf requires $2\frac{1}{4}$ pounds of ground beef. How much ground beef does Mary need?

5. Judy Carter purchased a real estate lot for $24,000. She sold it 2 years later for $1\frac{5}{8}$ times as much as she had paid for it. What was the selling price?

6. Lynn Clarkson saw an ad for a camcorder that cost $980. She knew of a discount store that would sell it to her for a markdown of $\frac{3}{20}$ off the advertised price. How much is the discount she can get?

7. To raise money for their club, the members of the Marketing Club purchased 68 bushels of popcorn to resell. They plan to repackage the popcorn in bags that hold $\frac{2}{21}$ of a bushel each. How many bags of popcorn will they be able to fill?

8. Richard Tracy paid a total of $375 for lumber costing $9\frac{3}{8}$ per foot. How many feet did he purchase?

9. While training for a marathon, Kristin Woods jogged $7\frac{3}{4}$ miles per hour for $2\frac{2}{3}$ hours. How many miles did Kristin jog?

10. On a map, 1 inch represents 240 miles. How many miles are represented by $\frac{3}{8}$ of an inch?

11. In Massachusetts, the governor wants to allot $\frac{1}{6}$ of the total sales tax collections to public education. The total sales tax collected is $2,472,000; how much will go to education?

Name _____   Date _____

Learning Unit 3–1:   Rounding Decimals; Fraction and Decimal Conversions

DRILL PROBLEMS

1. Write in decimal:
   a. Sixty-two hundredths _____

   b. Nine tenths _____

   c. Nine hundred fifty-three thousandths _____

   d. Four hundred one thousandths _____

   e. Six hundredths _____

2. Round each decimal to the place indicated:
   a. .4326 to the nearest thousandth _____

   b. .051 to the nearest tenth _____

   c. 8.207 to the nearest hundredth _____

   d. 2.094 to the nearest hundredth _____

   e. .511172 to the nearest ten thousandth _____

3. Name the place position of the underlined digit:
   a. .8$\underline{2}$6 _____

   b. .91$\underline{4}$ _____

   c. 3.$\underline{1}$169 _____

   d. 53.17$\underline{5}$ _____

   e. 1.017$\underline{4}$ _____

4. Convert to fractions (do not reduce):

   a. .83 _____   b. .426 _____   c. 2.516 _____

   d. .62$\frac{1}{2}$ _____   e. 13.007 _____   f. 5.03$\frac{1}{4}$ _____

5. Convert to fractions and reduce to lowest terms:

   a. .4   b. .44   c. .53

   d. .336   e. .096   f. .125

   g. .3125   h. .008   i. 2.625

   j. 5.75   k. 3.375   l. 9.04

6. Convert the following fractions to decimals and round your answer to the nearest hundredth:

   a. $\frac{1}{8}$ b. $\frac{7}{16}$

   c. $\frac{2}{3}$ d. $\frac{3}{4}$

e. $\dfrac{9}{16}$

f. $\dfrac{5}{6}$

g. $\dfrac{7}{9}$

h. $\dfrac{38}{79}$

i. $2\dfrac{3}{8}$

j. $9\dfrac{1}{3}$

k. $11\dfrac{19}{50}$

l. $6\dfrac{21}{32}$

m. $4\dfrac{83}{97}$

n. $1\dfrac{2}{5}$

o. $2\dfrac{2}{11}$

p. $13\dfrac{30}{42}$

WORD PROBLEMS

7. Alan Angel got 2 hits in his first 7 times at bat. What is his average to the nearest thousandths place?

8. Bill Breen earned $1,555, and his employer calculated that Bill's total FICA deduction should be $118.9575. Round this deduction to the nearest cent.

9. At the local college, .566 of the students are men. Convert to a fraction. Do not reduce.

10. The average television set is watched 2,400 hours a year. If there are 8,760 hours in a year, what fractional part of the year is spent watching television? Reduce to lowest terms.

11. On Saturday, the employees at the Empire Fish Company work only $\frac{1}{3}$ of a day. How could this be expressed as a decimal to nearest thousandths?

12. The North Shore Cinema has 610 seats. At a recent film screening there were 55 vacant seats. Show as a fraction the number of filled seats. Reduce as needed.

13. Michael Sullivan was planning his marketing strategy for a new product his company had produced. He was fascinated to discover that Rhode Island, the smallest state in the United States, was only twenty thousand, five hundred seven ten millionths the size of the largest state, Alaska. Write this number in decimal.

14. Bull Moose Company purchased a new manufacturing plant, located on an acre of land, for a total price of $2,250,000. The accountant determined that $\frac{3}{7}$ of the total price should be allocated as the price of the building. What decimal portion is the price of the building? Round to the nearest thousandth.

Name _____   Date _____

Learning Unit 3–2: Adding, Subtracting, Multiplying, and Dividing Decimals

DRILL PROBLEMS

1. Rearrange vertically and add:

   a. 8.88 + 7.4 + 14.006 + 2.94   **b.** 1.0625 + 4.0881 + .0775

   c. .903 + .078 + .17 + .1 + .96   **d.** 3.38 + .175 + .0186 + .2

2. Rearrange and subtract:

   a. .86 − .43   **b.** .885 − .069

   c. 11.67 − .935   **d.** 261.2 − 8.08

3. Multiply and round to the nearest tenth:

   a. 13.6 × .02   **b.** 1.73 × .069

   c. 400 × 3.7   **d.** 0.025 × 5.6

4. Divide and round to the nearest hundredth:

   a. 13.869 ÷ .6   **b.** 1.0088 ÷ .14   **c.** 18.7 ÷ 2.16   **d.** 15.64 ÷ .34

5. Complete by the shortcut method:

   a. 6.87 × 1,000   **b.** 927,530 ÷ 100   **c.** 27.2 ÷ 1,000

   d. .21 × 1,000   **e.** 347 × 100   **f.** 347 ÷ 100

   g. .0021 ÷ 10   **h.** 85.44 × 10,000   **i.** 83.298 × 100

   j. 23.0109 ÷ 100

WORD PROBLEMS (Use Business Math Handbook Tables as Needed.)

6. Bill Blum noted his FJ cruiser odometer reading of 17,629.3 at the beginning of his vacation. At the end of his vacation the reading was 20,545.1. How many miles did he drive during his vacation?

7. Jeanne Allyn purchased 12.25 yards of ribbon for a craft project. The ribbon cost 37¢ per yard. What was the total cost of the ribbon?

8. Leo Green wanted to find out the gas mileage for his company truck. When he filled the gas tank, he wrote down the odometer reading of 9,650.7. The next time he filled the gas tank the odometer reading was 10,112.2. He looked at the gas pump and saw that he had taken 18.5 gallons of gas. Find the gas mileage per gallon for Leo's truck. Round to the nearest tenth.

9. At Halley's Rent-a-Car, the cost per day to rent a medium-size car is $35.25 plus 37¢ a mile. What would be the charge to rent this car for 1 day if you drove 205.4 miles?

10. A trip to Mexico costs 6,000 pesos. What is this in U.S. dollars? Check your answer.

11. If a commemorative gold coin weighs 7.842 grams, find the number of coins that can be produced from 116 grams of gold. Round to the nearest whole number.

Name _____   Date _____

Learning Unit 4–1:   The Checking Account; Credit Card Transactions

DRILL PROBLEMS

1. The following is a deposit slip made out by Fred Young of the F. W. Young Company.

  a. How much cash did Young deposit?   _____

  b. How many checks did Young deposit?   _____

  c. What was the total amount deposited?   _____

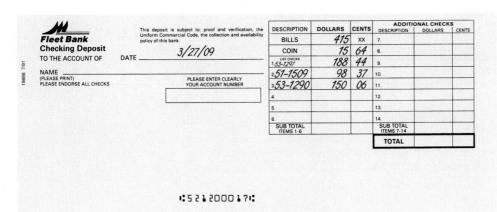

2. Blackstone Company had a balance of $2,173.18 in its checking account. Henry James, Blackstone's accountant, made a deposit that consisted of 2 fifty-dollar bills, 120 ten-dollar bills, 6 five-dollar bills, 14 one-dollar bills, $9.54 in change, plus two checks they had accepted, one for $16.38 and the other for $102.50. Find the amount of the deposit and the new balance in Blackstone's checking account.

3. Answer the following questions using the illustration:

No. 113	$ 750 00/100		Jones Company		No. 113

October 4 20 XX
To Neuner Realty
For real estate

Jones Company
22 Aster Road
Salem, MA 01970

	DOLLARS	CENTS
BALANCE	1,020	93
AMT. DEPOSITED	2,756	80
TOTAL	3,777	73
AMT. THIS CHECK	750	00
BALANCE FORWARD	3,027	73

October 4 20 XX   5-13/110

PAY
TO THE
ORDER
OF   Neuner Realty Company $ 750 00/100

Seven Hundred Fifty and 00/100   DOLLARS

Fleet Bank   FLEET BANK OF MASSACHUSETTS,
NATIONAL ASSOCIATION
BOSTON, MASSACHUSETTS   Kevin Jones

MEMO   real estate

⑆011000138⑆   14 0380 113

  a. Who is the payee?   _____

  b. Who is the drawer?   _____

  c. Who is the drawee?   _____

  d. What is the bank's identification number   _____

     e. What is Jones Company's account number? _____

     f. What was the balance in the account on September 30? _____

     g. For how much did Jones write Check No. 113? _____

     h. How much was deposited on October 1? _____

     i. How much was left after Check No. 113 was written? _____

4. Write each of the following amounts in verbal form as you would on a check:

     a. $25 _____

     b. $245.75 _____

     c. $3.98 _____

     d. $1,205.05 _____

     e. $3,013 _____

     f. $510.10 _____

Name _____   Date _____

Learning Unit 4-2: Bank Statement and Reconciliation Process; Trends in Online Banking

WORD PROBLEMS

1. Find the bank balance on January 31.

Date	Checks and payments			Deposits	Balance
January 1					401.17
January 2	108.64				_____
January 5	116.50			432.16	_____
January 6	14.92	150.00	10.00		_____
January 11	12.29			633.89	_____
January 18	108.64	18.60			_____
January 25	43.91	23.77		657.22	_____
January 26	75.00				_____
January 31	6.75 sc				_____

2. Joe Madruga, of Madruga's Taxi Service, received a bank statement for the month of May showing a balance of $932.36. His records show that the bank had not yet recorded two of his deposits, one for $521.50 and the other for $98.46. There are outstanding checks in the amounts of $41.67, $135.18, and $25.30. The statement also shows a service charge of $3.38. The balance in the check register is $1,353.55. Prepare a bank reconciliation for Madruga's as of May 31.

3. In reconciling the checking account for Nasser Enterprises, Beth Accomando found that the bank had collected a $3,000 promissory note on the company's behalf and had charged a $15 collection fee. There was also a service charge of $7.25. What amount should be added/subtracted from the checkbook balance to bring it up to date?

   Add: _____   Deduct: _____

4. In reconciling the checking account for Colonial Cleaners, Steve Papa found that a check for $34.50 had been recorded in the check register as $43.50. The bank returned an NSF check in the amount of $62.55. Interest income of $8.25 was earned and a service charge of $10.32 was assessed. What amount should be added/subtracted from the checkbook balance to bring it up to date?

   Add: _____   Deduct: _____

5. Matthew Stokes was completing the bank reconciliation for Parker's Tool and Die Company. The check register balance was $1,503.67. Matthew found that a $76.00 check had been recorded in the check register as $67.00; that a note for $1,500 had been collected by the bank for Parker's and the collection fee was $12.00; that $15.60 interest was earned on the account; and that an $8.35 service charge had been assessed. What should the check register balance be after Matthew updates it with the bank reconciliation information?

6. Consumers, community activists, and politicians are decrying the new line of accounts because several include a $3 service charge for some customers who use bank tellers for transactions that can be done through an automated teller machine. Bill Wade banks at a local bank that charges this fee. He was having difficulty balancing his checkbook because he did not notice this fee on his bank statement. His bank statement showed a balance of $822.18. Bill's checkbook had a balance of $206.48. Check No. 406 for $116.08 and Check No. 407 for $12.50 were outstanding. A $521 deposit was not on the statement. Bill has his payroll check electronically deposited to his checking account—the payroll check was for $1,015.12 (Bill's payroll checks vary each month). There are also a $1 service fee and a teller fee of $6. Complete Bill's bank reconciliation.

7. At First National Bank in San Diego, some customers have to pay $25 each year as an ATM card fee. John Levi banks at First National Bank and just received his bank statement showing a balance of $829.25; his checkbook balance is $467.40. The bank statement shows an ATM card fee of $25.00, teller fee of $9.00, interest of $1.80, and John's $880 IRS refund check, which was processed by the IRS and deposited to his account. John has two checks that have not cleared—No. 112 for $620.10 and No. 113 for $206.05. There is also a deposit in transit for $1,312.10. Prepare John's bank reconciliation.

Name _____   Date _____

Learning Unit 5–1:   Solving Equations for the Unknown

DRILL PROBLEMS

1. Write equations for the following situations. Use N for the unknown number. Do not solve the equations.
   a. Three times a number is 90.

   b. A number increased by 13 equals 25.

   c. Seven less than a number is 5.

   d. Fifty-seven decreased by 3 times a number is 21.

   e. Fourteen added to one-third of a number is 18.

   f. Twice the sum of a number and 4 is 32.

   g. Three-fourths of a number is 9.

   h. Two times a number plus 3 times the same number plus 8 is 68.

2. Solve for the unknown number:
   a. $B + 12 = 38$

   b. $29 + M = 44$

   c. $D - 77 = 98$

   d. $7N = 63$

   e. $\dfrac{X}{12} = 11$

   f. $3Q + 4Q + 2Q = 108$

   g. $H + 5H + 3 = 57$

   h. $2(N - 3) = 62$

   i. $\dfrac{3R}{4} = 27$

   j. $E - 32 = 41$

   k. $5(2T - 2) = 120$

   l. $12W - 5W = 98$

m. $49 - X = \quad 37$

n. $12(V + 2) = \quad 84$

o. $7D + 4 = \quad 5D + 14$

p. $7(T - 2) = \quad 2T - 9$

Name _____   Date _____

Learning Unit 5–2:   Solving Word Problems for the Unknown

WORD PROBLEMS

1. A blue denim shirt at the Old Navey was marked down $20. The sale price was $40. What was the original price?

Unknown(s)	Variables(s)	Relationship

2. Goodwin's Corporation found that $\frac{2}{3}$ of its employees were vested in their retirement plan. If 124 employees are vested, what is the total number of employees at Goodwin's?

Unknown(s)	Variables(s)	Relationship

3. Eileen Haskin's utility and telephone bills for the month totaled $180. The utility bill was 3 times as much as the telephone bill. How much was each bill?

Unknown(s)	Variables(s)	Relationship

4. Ryan and his friends went to the golf course to hunt for golf balls. Ryan found 15 more than $\frac{1}{3}$ of the total number of golf balls that were found. How many golf balls were found if Ryan found 75 golf balls?

Unknown(s)	Variables(s)	Relationship

5. Linda Mills and Sherry Somers sold 459 tickets for the Advertising Club's raffle. If Linda sold 8 times as many tickets as Sherry, how many tickets did each one sell?

Unknown(s)	Variables(s)	Relationship

6. Jason Mazzola wanted to buy a suit at Giblee's. Jason did not have enough money with him, so Mr. Giblee told him he would hold the suit if Jason gave him a deposit of $\frac{1}{5}$ of the cost of the suit. Jason agreed and gave Mr. Giblee $79. What was the price of the suit?

Unknown(s)	Variables(s)	Relationship

7. Peter sold watches ($7) and necklaces ($4) at a flea market. Total sales were $300. People bought 3 times as many watches as necklaces. How many of each did Peter sell? What were the total dollar sales of each?

Unknown(s)	Variables(s)	Price	Relationship

8. Peter sold watches ($7) and necklaces ($4) at a flea market. Total sales for 48 watches and necklaces were $300. How many of each did Peter sell? What were the total dollar sales of each?

Unknown(s)	Variables(s)	Price	Relationship

9. A 3,000 piece of direct mailing cost $1,435. Printing cost is $550, about $3\frac{1}{2}$ times the cost of typesetting. How much did the typesetting cost? Round to the nearest cent.

Unknown(s)	Variables(s)	Relationship

10. In 2009, Tony Rigato, owner of MRM, saw an increase in sales to $13.5 million. Rigato states that since 2006, sales have more than tripled. What were his sales in 2006?

Unknown(s)	Variables(s)	Relationship

Name _____   Date _____

Learning Unit 6–1:   Conversions

DRILL PROBLEMS

1. Convert the following to percents (round to the nearest tenth of a percent if needed):

a.	.07	_____ %	**b.**	.645	_____ %	**c.**	.009	_____ %
d.	8.3	_____ %	**e.**	5.26	_____ %	**f.**	6	_____ %
g.	.0105	_____ %	**h.**	.1180	_____ %	**i.**	5.0375	_____ %
j.	.862	_____ %	**k.**	.2615	_____ %	**l.**	.8	_____ %
m.	.025	_____ %	**n.**	.06	_____ %			

2. Convert the following to decimals (do not round):

a.	46%	_____	**b.**	.09%	_____
c.	4.7%	_____	**d.**	9.67%	_____
e.	.2%	_____	**f.**	$\frac{1}{4}$%	_____
g.	.76%	_____	**h.**	110%	_____
i.	$12\frac{1}{2}$%	_____	**j.**	5%	_____
k.	.004%	_____	**l.**	$7\frac{5}{10}$%	_____
m.	$\frac{3}{4}$%	_____	**n.**	1%	_____

3. Convert the following to percents (round to the nearest tenth of a percent if needed):

a.	$\frac{7}{10}$	_____ %	**b.**	$\frac{1}{5}$	_____ %
c.	$1\frac{5}{8}$	_____ %	**d.**	$\frac{2}{7}$	_____ %
e.	2	_____ %	**f.**	$\frac{14}{100}$	_____ %
g.	$\frac{1}{6}$	_____ %	**h.**	$\frac{1}{2}$	_____ %
i.	$\frac{3}{5}$	_____ %	**j.**	$\frac{3}{25}$	_____ %
k.	$\frac{5}{16}$	_____ %	**l.**	$\frac{11}{50}$	_____ %
m.	$4\frac{3}{4}$	_____ %	**n.**	$\frac{3}{200}$	_____ %

4. Convert the following to fractions in simplest form:

a.	40%	_____	**b.**	15%	_____
c.	50%	_____	**d.**	75%	_____
e.	35%	_____	**f.**	85%	_____
g.	$12\frac{1}{2}$%	_____	**h.**	$37\frac{1}{2}$%	_____
i.	$33\frac{1}{3}$%	_____	**j.**	3%	_____
k.	8.5%	_____	**l.**	$5\frac{3}{4}$%	_____
m.	100%	_____	**n.**	10%	_____

5. Complete the following table by finding the missing fraction, decimal, or percent equivalent:

	Fraction	Decimal	Percent		Fraction	Decimal	Percent
a.	_____	.25	25%	**h.**	$\frac{1}{6}$	.16$\overline{6}$	_____
b.	$\frac{3}{8}$	_____	$37\frac{1}{2}\%$	**i.**	_____	.083$\overline{3}$	$8\frac{1}{3}\%$
c.	$\frac{1}{2}$	.5	_____	**j.**	$\frac{1}{9}$	_____	$11\frac{1}{9}\%$
d.	$\frac{2}{3}$	_____	$66\frac{2}{3}\%$	**k.**	_____	.3125	$31\frac{1}{4}\%$
e.	_____	.4	40%	**l.**	$\frac{3}{40}$	.075	_____
f.	$\frac{3}{5}$	.6	_____	**m.**	$\frac{1}{5}$	_____	20%
g.	$\frac{7}{10}$	_____	70%	**n.**	_____	1.125	$112\frac{1}{2}\%$

WORD PROBLEMS

6. In 2009, Mutual of New York reported an overwhelming 60% of its new sales came from existing clients. What fractional part of its new sales came from existing clients? Reduce to simplest form.

7. Six hundred ninety corporations and design firms competed for the Industrial Design Excellence Award (IDEA). Twenty were selected as the year's best and received gold awards. Show the gold award winners as a fraction; then show what percent of the entrants received gold awards. Round to the nearest tenth of a percent.

8. In the first half of 2009, stock prices in the Standard & Poor's 500-stock index rose 17.5%. Show the increase in decimal.

9. In the recent banking crisis, many banks were unable to cover their bad loans. Citicorp, the nation's largest real estate lender, was reported as having only enough reserves to cover 39% of its bad loans. What fractional part of its loan losses was covered?

10. Dave Mattera spent his vacation in Las Vegas. He ordered breakfast in his room, and when he went downstairs to the coffee shop, he discovered that the same breakfast was much less expensive. He had paid 1.884 times as much for the breakfast in his room. What was the percent of increase for the breakfast in his room?

11. Putnam Management Company of Boston recently increased its management fee by .09%. What is the increase as a decimal? What is the same increase as a fraction?

12. Joel Black and Karen Whyte formed a partnership and drew up a partnership agreement, with profits and losses to be divided equally after each partner receives a $7\frac{1}{2}\%$ return on his or her capital contribution. Show their return on investment as a decimal and as a fraction. Reduce.

Name _____   Date _____

Learning Unit 6–2:   Application of Percents—Portion Formula

DRILL PROBLEMS

1. Fill in the amount of the base, rate, and portion in each of the following statements:
   a. The Johnsons spend $3,600 a month on food, which is 30% of their monthly income of $12,000.
      Base _____   Rate _____   Portion _____

   b. Rocky Norman got a $15 discount when he purchased a new camera. This was 20% off the sticker price of $75.
      Base _____   Rate _____   Portion _____

   c. Mary Burns got a 12% senior citizens discount when she bought a $7.00 movie ticket. She saved $0.84.
      Base _____   Rate _____   Portion _____

   d. Arthur Bogey received a commission of $13,500 when he sold the Brown's house for $225,000. His commission rate is 6%.
      Base _____   Rate _____   Portion _____

   e. Leo Davis deposited $5,000 in a certificate of deposit (CD). A year later he received an interest payment of $450 which was a yield of 9%.
      Base _____   Rate _____   Portion _____

   f. Grace Tremblay is on a diet that allows her to eat 1,600 calories per day. For breakfast she had 600 calories, which is $37\frac{1}{2}$% of her allowance.
      Base _____   Rate _____   Portion _____

2. Find the portion; round to the nearest hundredth if necessary:
   a. 7% of 74 _____   b. 12% of 205 _____   c. 16% of 630 _____
   d. 7.5% of 920 _____   e. 25% of 1,004 _____   f. 10% of 79 _____
   g. 103% of 44 _____   h. 30% of 78 _____   i. .2% of 50 _____
   j. 1% of 5,622 _____   k. $6\frac{1}{4}$% of 480 _____   l. 150% of 10 _____
   m. 100% of 34 _____   n. $\frac{1}{2}$% of 27 _____

3. Find the rate; round to the nearest tenth of a percent as needed:

   a. 30 is what percent of 90? _____   b. 6 is what percent of 200? _____
   c. 275 is what percent of 1,000? _____   d. .8 is what percent of 44? _____
   e. 67 is what percent of 2,010? _____   f. 550 is what percent of 250? _____
   g. 13 is what percent of 650? _____   h. $15 is what percent of $455? _____
   i. .05 is what percent of 100? _____   j. $6.25 is what percent of $10? _____

4. Find the base; round to the nearest tenth as needed:

   a. 63 is 30% of _____   b. 60 is 33% of _____   c. 150 is 25% of _____
   d. 47 is 1% of _____   e. $21 is 120% of _____   f. 2.26 is 40% of _____
   g. 75 is $12\frac{1}{2}$% of _____   h. 18 is 22.2% of _____   i. $37.50 is 50% of _____
   j. 250 is 100% of _____

5. Find the percent of increase or decrease. Round to nearest tenth percent as needed:

	Last year	This year	Amount of change	Percent of change
a.	5,962	4,378	_____	_____
b.	$10,995	$12,250	_____	_____
c.	120,000	140,000	_____	_____
d.	120,000	100,000	_____	_____

WORD PROBLEMS

6. A machine that originally cost $2,400 was sold for $600 at the end of 5 years. What percent of the original cost is the selling price?

7. Joanne Byrne invested $75,000 in a candy shop and is making 12% per year on her investment. How much money per year is she making on her investment?

8. There was a fire in Bill Porper's store that caused 2,780 inventory items to be destroyed. Before the fire, 9,565 inventory items were in the store. What percent of inventory was destroyed? Round to nearest tenth percent.

9. Elyse's Dress Shoppe makes 25% of its sales for cash. If the cash receipts on January 21 were $799, what were the total sales for the day?

10. The YMCA is holding a fund-raiser to collect money for a new gym floor. So far it has collected $7,875, which is 63% of the goal. What is the amount of the goal? How much more money must the YMCA collect?

11. Leslie Tracey purchased her home for $51,500. She sold it last year for $221,200. What percent profit did she make on the sale? Round to nearest tenth percent.

12. Maplewood Park Tool & Die had an annual production of 375,165 units this year. This is 140% of the annual production last year. What was last year's annual production?

Name _____ Date _____

Learning Unit 7–1: Trade Discounts—Single and Chain*

DRILL PROBLEMS

1. Calculate the trade discount amount for each of the following items:

Item	List price	Trade discount	Trade discount amount
a. Apple iPod	$ 300	40%	_____
b. Flat-screen TV	$1,200	30%	_____
c. Suit	$ 500	10%	_____
d. Bicycle	$ 800	$12\frac{1}{2}$	_____
e. David Yurman bracelet	$ 950	40%	_____

2. Calculate the net price for each of the following items:

Item	List price	Trade discount amount	Net price
a. Home Depot table	$600	$250	_____
b. Bookcase	$525	$129	_____
c. Rocking chair	$480	$ 95	_____

3. Fill in the missing amount for each of the following items:

Item	List price	Trade discount amount	Net price
a. Sears electric saw	_____	$19	$56.00
b. Electric drill	$90	_____	$68.50
c. Ladder	$56	$15.25	_____

4. For each of the following, find the percent paid (complement of trade discount) and the net price:

List price	Trade discount	Percent paid	Net price
a. $45	15%	_____	_____
b. $195	12.2%	_____	_____
c. $325	50%	_____	_____
d. $120	18%	_____	_____

5. In each of the following examples, find the net price equivalent rate and the single equivalent discount rate:

Chain discount	Net price equivalent rate	Single equivalent discount rate
a. 25/5	_____	_____
b. 15/15	_____	_____
c. 15/10/5	_____	_____
d. 12/12/6	_____	_____

*Freight problems to be shown in LU 7–2 material.

6. In each of the following examples, find the net price and the trade discount:

List price	Chain discount	Net price	Trade discount
a. $5,000	10/10/5	_____	_____
b. $7,500	9/6/3	_____	_____
c. $898	20/7/2	_____	_____
d. $1,500	25/10	_____	_____

7. The list price of a handheld calculator is $19.50, and the trade discount is 18%. Find the trade discount amount.

8. The list price of a silver picture frame is $29.95, and the trade discount is 15%. Find the trade discount amount and the net price.

9. The net price of a set of pots and pans is $65, and the trade discount is 20%. What is the list price?

10. Jennie's Variety Store has the opportunity to purchase candy from three different wholesalers; each of the wholesalers offers a different chain discount. Company A offers 25/5/5, Company B offers 20/10/5, and Company C offers 15/20. Which company should Jennie deal with? *Hint:* Choose the company with the highest single equivalent discount rate.

11. The list price of a television set is $625. Find the net price after a series discount of 30/20/10.

12. Mandy's Accessories Shop purchased 12 purses with a total list price of $726. What was the net price of each purse if the wholesaler offered a chain discount of 25/20?

13. Kransberg Furniture Store purchased a bedroom set for $1,097.25 from Furniture Wholesalers. The list price of the set was $1,995. What trade discount rate did Kransberg receive?

14. Susan Monk teaches second grade and receives a discount at the local art supply store. Recently she paid $47.25 for art supplies after receiving a chain discount of 30/10. What was the regular price of the art supplies?

Name _____   Date _____

Learning Unit 7–2:   Cash Discounts, Credit Terms, and Partial Payments

DRILL PROBLEMS

1. Complete the following table:

	Date of invoice	Date goods received	Terms	Last day of discount period	End of credit period
a.	February 8		2/10, n/30		
b.	August 26		2/10, n/30		
c.	October 17		3/10, n/60		
d.	March 11	May 10	3/10, n/30, ROG		
e.	September 14		2/10, EOM		
f.	May 31		2/10, EOM		

2. Calculate the cash discount and the net amount paid.

	Invoice amount	Cash discount rate	Discount amount	Net amount paid
a.	$75	3%		
b.	$1,559	2%		
c.	$546.25	2%		
d.	$9,788.75	1%		

3. Use the complement of the cash discount to calculate the net amount paid. Assume all invoices are paid within the discount period.

	Terms of invoice	Amount of invoice	Complement	Net amount paid
a.	2/10, n/30	$1,125		
b.	3/10, n/30 ROG	$4,500		
c.	2/10, EOM	$375.50		
d.	1/15, n/45	$3,998		

4. Calculate the amount of cash discount and the net amount paid.

	Date of invoice	Terms of invoice	Amount of invoice	Date paid	Cash discount	Amount paid
a.	January 12	2/10, n/30	$5,320	January 22		
b.	May 28	2/10, n/30	$975	June 7		
c.	August 15	2/10, n/30	$7,700	August 26		
d.	March 8	2/10, EOM	$480	April 10		
e.	January 24	3/10, n/60	$1,225	February 3		

5. Complete the following table:

	Total invoice	Freight charges included in invoice total	Date of invoice	Terms of invoice	Date of payment	Cash discount	Amount paid
a.	$852	$12.50	3/19	2/10, n/30	3/29		
b.	$669.57	$15.63	7/28	3/10, EOM	9/10		
c.	$500	$11.50	4/25	2/10, n/60	6/5		
d.	$188	$9.70	1/12	2/10, EOM	2/10		

6. In the following table, assume that all the partial payments were made within the discount period.

	Amount of invoice	Terms of invoice	Partial payment	Amount to be credited	Balance outstanding
a.	$481.90	2/10, n/30	$90.00	_____	_____
b.	$1,000	2/10, EOM	$500.00	_____	_____
c.	$782.88	3/10, n/30, ROG	$275.00	_____	_____
d.	$318.80	2/15, n/60	$200.00	_____	_____

WORD PROBLEMS

7. Northwest Chemical Company received an invoice for $12,480, dated March 12, with terms of 2/10, n/30. If the invoice was paid March 22, what was the amount due?

8. On May 27, Trotter Hardware Store received an invoice for trash barrels purchased for $13,650 with terms of 3/10, EOM; the freight charge, which is included in the price, is $412. What are (a) the last day of the discount period and (b) the amount of the payment due on this date?

9. The Glass Sailboat received an invoice for $930.50 with terms 2/10, n/30 on April 19. On April 29, it sent a payment of $430.50. (a) How much credit will be given on the total due? (b) What is the new balance due?

10. Dallas Ductworks offers cash discounts of 2/10, 1/15, n/30 on all purchases. If an invoice for $544 dated July 18 is paid on August 2, what is the amount due?

11. The list price of a DVD player is $299.90 with trade discounts of 10/20 and terms of 3/10, n/30. If a retailer pays the invoice within the discount period, what amount must the retailer pay?

12. The invoice of a sneakers supplier totaled $2,488.50, was dated February 7, and offered terms 2/10, ROG. The shipment of sneakers was received on March 7. What are (a) the last date of the discount period and (b) the amount of the discount that will be lost if the invoice is paid after that date?

13. Starburst Toy Company receives an invoice amounting to $1,152.30 with terms of 2/10, EOM and dated November 6. If a partial payment of $750 is made on December 8, what are (a) the credit given for the partial payment and (b) the balance due on the invoice?

14. Todd's Sporting Goods received an invoice for soccer equipment dated July 26 with terms 3/10, 1/15, n/30 in the amount of $3,225.83, which included shipping charges of $375.50. If this bill is paid on August 5, what amount must be paid?

Name _____   Date _____

Learning Unit 8–1: Markups Based on Cost (100%)

DRILL PROBLEMS

1. Fill in the missing numbers:

	Cost	Dollar markup	Selling price
a.	$11.80	$2.50	_____
b.	$8.32	_____	$11.04
c.	$25.27	_____	$29.62
d.	_____	$75.00	$165.00
e.	$86.54	$29.77	_____

2. Calculate the markup based on cost (round to the nearest cent).

	Cost	Markup (percent of cost)	Dollar markup
a.	$425.00	30%	_____
b.	$1.52	20%	_____
c.	$9.90	$12\frac{1}{2}$	_____
d.	$298.10	50%	_____
e.	$74.25	38%	_____
f.	$552.25	100%	_____

3. Calculate the dollar markup and rate of the markup as a percent of cost (round percents to nearest tenth percent). Verify your result, which may be slightly off due to rounding.

	Cost	Selling price	Dollar markup	Markup (percent of cost)	Verify
a.	$2.50	$4.50	_____	_____	_____
b.	$12.50	$19.00	_____	_____	_____
c.	$0.97	$1.25	_____	_____	_____
d.	$132.25	$175.00	_____	_____	_____
e.	$65.00	$89.99	_____	_____	_____

4. Calculate the dollar markup and the selling price.

	Cost	Markup (percent of cost)	Dollar markup	Selling price
a.	$2.20	40%	_____	_____
b.	$2.80	16%	_____	_____
c.	$840.00	$12\frac{1}{2}\%$	_____	_____
d.	$24.36	30%	_____	_____

5. Calculate the cost (round to the nearest cent).

	Selling price	Rate of markup based on cost	Cost
a.	$1.98	30%	_____
b.	$360.00	60%	_____
c.	$447.50	20%	_____
d.	$1,250.00	100%	_____

6. Find the missing numbers. Round money to the nearest cent and percents to the nearest tenth percent.

	Cost	Dollar markup	Percent markup on cost	Selling price
a.	$72.00	_____	40%	_____
b.	_____	$7.00	_____	$35.00
c.	$8.80	$1.10	_____	_____
d.	_____	_____	28%	$19.84
e.	$175.00	_____	_____	$236.25

WORD PROBLEMS

7. The cost of an recliner chair is $399 and the markup rate is 35% of the cost. What are **(a)** the dollar markup and **(b)** the selling price?

8. If Barry's Furniture Store purchased a floor lamp for $120 and plans to add a markup of $90, **(a)** what will the selling price be and **(b)** what is the markup as a percent of cost?

9. If Lesjardin's Jewelry Store is selling a gold bracelet for $349, which includes a markup of 35% on cost, what are **(a)** Lesjardin's cost and **(b)** the amount of the dollar markup?

10. Toll's Variety Store sells an alarm clock for $14.75. The alarm clock cost Toll's $9.90. What is the markup amount as a percent of cost? Round to the nearest whole percent.

11. Swanson's Audio Supply marks up its merchandise by 40% on cost. If the markup on a cassette player is $85, what are **(a)** the cost of the cassette player and **(b)** the selling price?

12. Brown's Department Store is selling a shirt for $55. If the markup is 70% on cost, what is Brown's cost (to the nearest cent)?

13. Ward's Greenhouse purchased tomato flats for $5.75 each. Ward's has decided to use a markup of 42% on cost. Find the selling price.

Name _____   Date _____

Learning Unit 8–2:   Markups Based on Selling Price (100%)

DRILL PROBLEMS

1. Calculate the markup based on the selling price.

	Selling price	Markup (percent of selling price)	Dollar markup
a.	$16.00	40%	_____
b.	$230.00	25%	_____
c.	$81.00	42.5%	_____
d.	$72.88	$37\frac{1}{2}\%$	_____
e.	$1.98	$7\frac{1}{2}\%$	_____

2. Calculate the dollar markup and the markup as a percent of selling price (to the nearest tenth percent). Verify your answer, which may be slightly off due to rounding.

	Cost	Selling price	Dollar markup	Markup (percent of selling price)	Verify
a.	$2.50	$4.25	_____	_____	_____
b.	$16.00	$24.00	_____	_____	_____
c.	$45.25	$85.00	_____	_____	_____
d.	$0.19	$0.25	_____	_____	_____
e.	$5.50	$8.98	_____	_____	_____

3. Given the *cost* and the markup as a percent of *selling price*, calculate the selling price.

	Cost	Markup (percent of selling price)	Selling price
a.	$5.90	15%	_____
b.	$600	32%	_____
c.	$15	50%	_____
d.	$120	30%	_____
e.	$0.29	20%	_____

4. Given the selling price and the percent markup on selling price, calculate the cost.

	Cost	Markup (percent of selling price)	Selling price
a.	_____	40%	$6.25
b.	_____	20%	$16.25
c.	_____	19%	$63.89
d.	_____	$62\frac{1}{2}\%$	$44.00

5. Calculate the equivalent rate of markup (round to the nearest hundredth percent).

	Markup on cost	**Markup on selling price**		**Markup on cost**	**Markup on selling price**
a.	40%	_____	b.	50%	_____
c.	_____	50%	d.	_____	35%
e.	_____	40%			

WORD PROBLEMS

6. Fisher Equipment is selling a Wet/Dry Shop Vac for $49.97. If Fisher's markup is 40% of the selling price, what is the cost of the Shop Vac?

7. Gove Lumber Company purchased a 10-inch table saw for $225 and will mark up the price 35% on the selling price. What will the selling price be?

8. To realize a sufficient gross margin, City Paint and Supply Company marks up its paint 27% on the selling price. If a gallon of Latex Semi-Gloss Enamel has a markup of $4.02, find **(a)** the selling price and **(b)** the cost.

9. A Magnavox 20-inch color TV cost $180 and sells for $297. What is the markup based on the selling price? Round to the nearest hundredth percent.

10. Bargain Furniture sells a five-piece country maple bedroom set for $1,299. The cost of this set is $700. What are **(a)** the markup on the bedroom set, **(b)** the markup percent on cost, and **(c)** the markup percent on the selling price? Round to the nearest hundredth percent.

11. Robert's Department Store marks up its sundries by 28% on the selling price. If a 6.4-ounce tube of toothpaste costs $1.65, what will the selling price be?

12. To be competitive, Tinker Toys must sell the Nintendo Control Deck for $89.99. To meet expenses and make a sufficient profit, Tinker Toys must add a markup on the selling price of 23%. What is the maximum amount that Tinker Toys can afford to pay a wholesaler for Nintendo?

13. Nicole's Restaurant charges $7.50 for a linguini dinner that costs $2.75 for the ingredients. What rate of markup is earned on the selling price? Round to the nearest hundredth percent.

Name _____   Date _____

Learning Unit 8–3:   Markdowns and Perishables

DRILL PROBLEMS

1. Find the dollar markdown and the sale price.

	Original selling price	Markdown percent	Dollar markdown	Sale price
a.	$100	30%	_____	_____
b.	$2,099.98	25%	_____	_____
c.	$729	30%	_____	_____

2. Find the dollar markdown and the markdown percent on original selling price.

	Original selling price	Sale price	Dollar markdown	Markdown percent
a.	$19.50	$9.75	_____	_____
b.	$250	$175	_____	_____
c.	$39.95	$29.96	_____	_____

3. Find the original selling price.

	Sale price	Markdown percent	Original selling price
a.	$328	20%	_____
b.	$15.85	15%	_____

4. Calculate the final selling price.

	Original selling price	First markdown	Second markdown	Final markup	Final selling price
a.	$4.96	25%	8%	5%	_____
b.	$130	30%	10%	20%	_____

5. Find the missing amounts.

Number of units	Unit cost	Total cost	Estimated* spoilage	Desired markup (percent of cost)	Total selling price	Selling price per unit
a. 72	$3	_____	12%	50%	_____	_____
b. 50	$0.90	_____	16%	42%	_____	_____

*Round to the nearest whole unit as needed.

WORD PROBLEMS

6. Speedy King is having a 30%-off sale on their box springs and mattresses. A queen-size, back-supporter mattress is priced at $325. What is the sale price of the mattress?

7. Murray and Sons sell a personal fax machine for $602.27. It is having a sale, and the fax machine is marked down to $499.88. What is the percent of the markdown?

8. Coleman's is having a clearance sale. A lamp with an original selling price of $249 is now selling for $198. Find the percent of the markdown. Round to the nearest hundredth percent.

9. Johnny's Sports Shop has advertised markdowns on certain items of 22%. A soccer ball is marked with a sale price of $16.50. What was the original price of the soccer ball?

10. Sam Grillo sells seasonal furnishings. Near the end of the summer a five-piece patio set that was priced $349.99 had not been sold, so he marked it down by 12%. As Labor Day approached, he still had not sold the patio set, so he marked it down an additional 18%. What was the final selling price of the patio set?

11. Calsey's Department Store sells their down comforters for a regular price of $325. During its white sale the comforters were marked down 22%. Then, at the end of the sale, Calsey's held a special promotion and gave a second markdown of 10%. When the sale was over, the remaining comforters were marked up 20%. What was the final selling price of the remaining comforters?

12. The New Howard Bakery wants to make a 60% profit on the cost of its pies. To calculate the price of the pies, it estimated that the usual amount of spoilage is 5 pies. Calculate the selling price for each pie if the number of pies baked each day is 24 and the cost of the ingredients for each pie is $1.80.

13. Sunshine Bakery bakes 660 loaves of bread each day and estimates that 10% of the bread will go stale before it is sold and will have to be discarded. The owner of the bakery wishes to realize a 55% markup on cost on the bread. If the cost to make a loaf of bread is $0.46, what should the owner sell each loaf for?

Name _____ Date _____

Learning Unit 8–4: Break Even Analysis

DRILL PROBLEMS

1. Calculate the contribution margin.

	Selling Price per unit	Variable cost per unit	Contribution margin
a.	$12.00	$5.00	
b.	$15.99	$4.88	
c.	$18.99	$4.99	
d.	$251.86	$110.00	
e.	$510.99	$310.00	
f.	$1,000.10	$410.00	

2. Calculate the selling price per unit.

	Selling price per unit	Variable cost per unit	Contribution margin
a.		$12.18	$ 4.10
b.		$19.19	$ 5.18
c.		$21.00	$13.00
d.		$41.00	$14.88
e.		$128.10	$79.50
f.		$99.99	$60.00

3. Calculate the breakeven point (round to nearest whole unit)

	Break even point	Fixed cost	Selling price per unit	Variable cost per unit
a.		$50,000	$4.00	$1.00
b.		$30,000	$6.00	$2.00
c.		$20,000	$9.00	$3.00
d.		$100,000	$12.00	$4.00
e.		$120,000	$14.00	$5.00
f.		$90,000	$26.00	$8.00

WORD PROBLEMS

4. Jones Co. Produces bay of candy. Each bay sells for 3.99. The variable cost per unit is $2.85. What is the contribution margin for Jones Co.?

5. Logan Co. produces stuffed animals. They have $40,000 in fixed costs. Logan sells each animal for $19.99 with a $12.10 cost per unit. What is the break even point for Logan? Round to the nearest whole number.

6. Ranyo Company produces lawn mowers. It has a breakeven point $6,000 lawn mowers. If its contribution margin is $150. What is Ranyo's fixed cost?

7. Moore company has $100,000 in fixed costs. Its contribution margin is $4.50. Calculate the break even point for Moore to nearest whole number.

Name _____   Date _____

Learning Unit 9–1: Calculating Various Types of Employees' Gross Pay

DRILL PROBLEMS

1. Fill in the missing amounts for each of the following employees. Do not round the overtime rate in your calculations and round your final answers to the nearest cent.

Employee	Total hours	Rate per hour	Regular pay	Overtime pay	Gross pay
a. Ben Badger	40	$7.60	_____	_____	_____
b. Casey Guitare	43	$9.00	_____	_____	_____
c. Norma Harris	37	$7.50	_____	_____	_____
d. Ed Jackson	45	$12.25	_____	_____	_____

2. Calculate each employee's gross from the following data. Do not round the overtime rate in your calculation but round your final answers to the nearest cent.

Employee	S	M	Tu	W	Th	F	S	Total hours	Rate per hour	Regular pay	Overtime pay	Gross pay
a. L. Adams	0	8	8	8	8	8	0	____	$8.10	_____	_____	_____
b. M. Card	0	9	8	9	8	8	4	____	$11.35	_____	_____	_____
c. P. Kline	2	$7\frac{1}{2}$	$8\frac{1}{4}$	8	$10\frac{3}{4}$	9	2	____	$10.60	_____	_____	_____
d. J. Mack	0	$9\frac{1}{2}$	$9\frac{3}{4}$	$9\frac{1}{2}$	10	10	4	____	$9.95	_____	_____	_____

3. Calculate the gross wages of the following production workers.

Employee	Rate per unit	No. of units produced	Gross pay
a. A. Bossie	$0.67	655	_____
b. J. Carson	$0.87\frac{1}{2}$	703	_____

4. Using the given differential scale, calculate the gross wages of the following production workers.

Units produced	Amount per unit
From 1–50	$.55
From 51–100	.65
From 101–200	.72
More than 200	.95

Employee	Units produced	Gross pay
a. F. Burns	190	_____
b. B. English	210	_____
c. E. Jackson	200	_____

5. Calculate the following salespersons' gross wages.
   a. Straight commission:

Employee	Net sales	Commission	Gross pay
M. Salley	$40,000	13%	_____

b. Straight commission with draw:

Employee	Net sales	Commission	Draw	Commission minus draw
G. Gorsbeck	$38,000	12%	$600	_____

c. Variable commission scale:

Up to $25,000	8%
Excess of $25,000 to $40,000	10%
More than $40,000	12%

Employee	Net sales	Gross pay
H. Lloyd	$42,000	_____

d. Salary plus commission:

Employee	Salary	Commission	Quota	Net sales	Gross pay
P. Floyd	$2,500	3%	$400,000	$475,000	_____

WORD PROBLEMS

For all problems with overtime, be sure to round only the final answer.

6. In the first week of December, Dana Robinson worked 52 hours. His regular rate of pay is $11.25 per hour. What was Dana's gross pay for the week?

7. Davis Fisheries pays its workers for each box of fish they pack. Sunny Melanson receives $.30 per box. During the third week of July, Sunny packed 2,410 boxes of fish. What is Sunny's gross pay?

8. Maye George is a real estate broker who receives a straight commission of 6%. What would her commission be for a house that sold for $197,500?

9. Devon Company pays Eileen Haskins a straight commission of $12\frac{1}{2}$% on net sales. In January, Devon gave Eileen a draw of $600. She had net sales that month of $35,570. What was Eileen's commission minus draw?

10. Parker and Company pays Selma Stokes on a variable commission scale. In a month when Selma had net sales of $155,000, what was her gross pay based on the following schedule?

Net sales	Commission rate
Up to $40,000	5%
Excess of $40,000 to $75,000	5.5%
Excess of $75,000 to $100,000	6%
More than $100,000	7%

11. Marsh Furniture Company pays Joshua Charles a monthly salary of $1,900 plus a commission of $2\frac{1}{2}$% on sales over $12,500. Last month, Joshua had net sales of $17,799. What was Joshua's gross pay for the month?

12. Amy McWha works at Lamplighter Bookstore where she earns $7.75 per hour plus a commission of 2% on her weekly sales in excess of $1,500. Last week, Amy worked 39 hours and had total sales of $2,250. What was Amy's gross pay for the week?

Name _____   Date _____

Learning Unit 9–2: Computing Payroll Deductions for Employees' Pay; Employers' Responsibilities

DRILL PROBLEMS

Use tables in the *Business Math Handbook* (assume FICA rates in text).

Employee	Allowances and marital status	Cumulative earnings	Salary per week	Taxable earnings S.S.	Taxable earnings Medicare
1. Pete Small	M—3	$97,000	$2,300	a. _____	b. _____
2. Alice Hall	M—1	$90,000	$1,100	c. _____	d. _____
3. Jean Rose	M—2	$100,000	$2,000	e. _____	f. _____

4. What is the tax for Social Security and Medicare for Pete in Problem 1?

5. Calculate Pete's FIT by the percentage method.

6. What would employees contribute for this week's payroll for SUTA and FUTA?

WORD PROBLEMS

7. Cynthia Pratt has earned $96,000 thus far this year. This week she earned $3,500. Find her total FICA tax deduction (Social Security and Medicare).

8. If Cynthia (Problem 7) earns $1,050 the following week, what will be her new total FICA tax deduction?

9. Roger Alley, a service dispatcher, has weekly earnings of $750. He claimed four allowances on his W-4 form and is married. Besides his FIT and FICA deductions, he has deductions of $35.16 for medical insurance and $17.25 for union dues. Calculate his net earnings for the third week in February. Use the percentage method.

10. Nicole Mariotte is unmarried and claimed one withholding allowance on her W-4 form. In the second week of February, she earned $707.35. Deductions from her pay included federal withholding, Social Security, Medicare, health insurance for $47.75, and $30.00 for the company meal plan. What is Nicole's net pay for the week? Use the percentage method.

11. Gerald Knowlton had total gross earnings of $97,200 in the last week of November. His earnings for the first week in December were $804.70. His employer uses the percentage method to calculate federal withholding. If Gerald is married, claims two allowances, and has medical insurance of $52.25 deducted each week from his pay, what is his net pay for the week?

Name _____   Date _____

Learning Unit 10–1: Calculation of Simple Interest and Maturity Value

DRILL PROBLEMS

1. Find the simple interest for each of the following loans:

Principal	Rate	Time	Interest
a. $6,000	4%	1 year	_____
b. $3,000	12%	3 years	_____
c. $18,000	$8\frac{1}{2}\%$	10 months	_____

2. Find the simple interest for each of the following loans; use the exact interest method. Use the days-in-a-year calendar in the text when needed.

Principal	Rate	Time	Interest
a. $900	4%	30 days	_____
b. $4,290	8%	250 days	_____
c. $1,500	8%	Made March 11 Due July 11	_____

3. Find the simple interest for each of the following loans using the ordinary interest method (Banker's Rule).

Principal	Rate	Time	Interest
a. $5,250	$7\frac{1}{2}\%$	120 days	_____
b. $700	3%	70 days	_____
c. $2,600	11%	Made on June 15 Due October 17	_____

WORD PROBLEMS

4. On October 17, Nina Verga borrowed $4,500 at a rate of 3%. She promised to repay the loan in 10 months. What are **(a)** the amount of the simple interest and **(b)** the total amount owed upon maturity?

5. Marjorie Folsom borrowed $5,500 to purchase a computer. The loan was for 9 months at an annual interest rate of $12\frac{1}{2}\%$. What are **(a)** the amount of interest Marjorie must pay and **(b)** the maturity value of the loan?

6. Eric has a loan for $1,200 at an ordinary interest rate of 9.5% for 80 days. Julie has a loan for $1,200 at an exact interest rate of 9.5% for 80 days. Calculate **(a)** the total amount due on Eric's loan and **(b)** the total amount due on Julie's loan.

7. Roger Lee borrowed $5,280 at $13\frac{1}{2}\%$ on May 24 and agreed to repay the loan on August 24. The lender calculates interest using the exact interest method. How much will Roger be required to pay on August 24?

8. On March 8, Jack Faltin borrowed $10,225 at $9\frac{3}{4}\%$. He signed a note agreeing to repay the loan and interest on November 8. If the lender calculates interest using the ordinary interest method, what will Jack's repayment be?

9. Dianne Smith's real estate taxes of $641.49 were due on November 1, 2007. Due to financial difficulties, Dianne was unable to pay her tax bill until January 15, 2008. The penalty for late payment is $13\frac{3}{8}\%$ ordinary interest. What is the penalty Dianne will have to pay, and what is Dianne's total payment on January 15?

10. On August 8, Rex Eason had a credit card balance of $550, but he was unable to pay his bill. The credit card company charges interest of $18\frac{1}{2}\%$ annually on late payments. What amount will Rex have to pay if he pays his bill 1 month late?

11. An issue of *Your Money* discussed average consumers who carry a balance of $2,000 on one credit card. If the yearly rate of interest is 18%, how much are consumers paying in interest per year?

12. AFBA Industrial Bank of Colorado Springs, Colorado, charges a credit card interest rate of 11% per year. If you had a credit card debt of $1,500, what would your interest amount be after 3 months?

Name _____   Date _____

Learning Unit 10-2:   Finding Unknown in Simple Interest Formula

DRILL PROBLEMS

1. Find the principal in each of the following. Round to the nearest cent. Assume 360 days. *Calculator hint:* Do denominator calculation first, do not round; when answer is displayed, save it in memory by pressing [M+]. Now key in the numerator (interest amount), [÷], [MR], [=] for the answer. Be sure to clear memory after each problem by pressing [MR] again so that the M is no longer in the display.

	Rate	Time	Interest	Principal
a.	8%	70 days	$68	_____
b.	11%	90 days	$125	_____
c.	9%	120 days	$103	_____
d.	$8\frac{1}{2}\%$	60 days	$150	_____

2. Find the rate in each of the following. Round to the nearest tenth of a percent. Assume 360 days.

	Principal	Time	Interest	Rate
a.	$7,500	120 days	$350	_____
b.	$975	60 days	$25	_____
c.	$20,800	220 days	$910	_____
d.	$150	30 days	$2.10	_____

3. Find the time (to the nearest day) in each of the following. Assuming ordinary interest, use 360 days.

	Principal	Rate	Interest	Time (days)	Time (years) (Round to nearest hundredth)
a.	$400	11%	$7.33	_____	_____
b.	$7,000	12.5%	$292	_____	_____
c.	$1,550	9.2%	$106.95	_____	_____
d.	$157,000	10.75%	$6,797.88	_____	_____

4. Complete the following. Assume 360 days for all examples.

	Principal	Rate (nearest tenth percent)	Time (nearest day)	Simple interest
a.	$345	_____	150 days	$14.38
b.	_____	12.5%	90 days	$46.88

c. $750	12.2%	_____	$19.06
d. $20,260	16.7%	110 days	_____

WORD PROBLEMS

Use 360 days.

5. In June, Becky opened a $20,000 bank CD paying 6% interest, but she had to withdraw the money in a few days to cover one child's college tuition. The bank charged her $600 in penalties for the withdrawal. What percent of the $20,000 was she charged?

6. Dr. Vaccarro invested his money at $12\frac{1}{2}\%$ for 175 days and earned interest of $760. How much money did Dr. Vaccarro invest?

7. If you invested $10,000 at 5% interest in a 6-month CD compounding interest daily, you would earn $252.43 in interest. How much would the same $10,000 invested in a bank paying simple interest earn?

8. Thomas Kyrouz opened a savings account and deposited $750 in a bank that was paying 7.2% simple interest. How much were his savings worth in 200 days?

9. Mary Millitello paid the bank $53.90 in interest on a 66-day loan at 9.8%. How much money did Mary borrow? Round to the nearest dollar.

10. If Anthony Lucido deposits $2,400 for 66 days and makes $60.72 in interest, what interest rate is he receiving?

11. Find how long in days David Wong must invest $23,500 of his company's cash at 8.4% in order to earn $652.50 in interest.

Name _____   Date _____

Learning Unit 10–3: U.S. Rule—Making Partial Note Payments Before Due Date

DRILL PROBLEMS

1. A merchant borrowed $3,000 for 320 days at 11% (assume a 360-day year). Use the U.S. Rule to complete the following table:

Payment number	Payment day	Amount paid	Interest to date	Principal payment	Adjusted balance
					$3,000
1	75	$500	_____	_____	_____
2	160	$750	_____	_____	_____
3	220	$1,000	_____	_____	_____
4	320	_____	_____	_____	_____

2. Use the U.S. Rule to solve for total interest costs, balances, and final payments (use ordinary interest).

   Given
   Principal, $6,000, 5%, 100 days
   Partial payments on 30th day, $2,000
   on 70th day, $1,000

WORD PROBLEMS

3. John Joseph borrowed $10,800 for 1 year at 14%. After 60 days, he paid $2,500 on the note. On the 200th day, he paid an additional $5,000. Use the U.S. Rule and ordinary interest to find the final balance due.

4. Doris Davis borrowed $8,200 on March 5 for 90 days at $8\frac{3}{4}\%$. After 32 days, Doris made a payment on the loan of $2,700. On the 65th day, she made another payment of $2,500. What is her final payment if you use the U.S. Rule with ordinary interest?

5. David Ring borrowed $6,000 on a 13%, 60-day note. After 10 days, David paid $500 on the note. On day 40, David paid $900 on the note. What are the total interest and ending balance due by the U.S. Rule? Use ordinary interest.

Name _____ Date _____

Learning Unit 11–1: Structure of Promissory Notes; the Simple Discount Note

DRILL PROBLEMS

1. Identify each of the following characteristics of promissory notes with an **I** for simple interest note, a **D** for simple discount note, or a **B** if it is true for both.

    ___ Interest is computed on face value, or what is actually borrowed.

    ___ A promissory note for a loan usually less than 1 year.

    ___ Borrower receives proceeds = Face value − Bank discount.

    ___ Maturity value = Face value + Interest.

    ___ Maturity value = Face value.

    ___ Borrower receives the face value.

    ___ Paid back by one payment at maturity.

    ___ Interest computed on maturity value, or what will be repaid, and not on actual amount borrowed.

2. Find the bank discount and the proceeds for the following (assume 360 days):

	Maturity value	Discount rate	Time (days)	Bank discount	Proceeds
a.	$8,000	3%	60	_____	_____
b.	$4,550	8.1%	110	_____	_____
c.	$19,350	12.7%	55	_____	_____
d.	$63,400	10%	90	_____	_____
e.	$13,490	7.9%	200	_____	_____
f.	$780	$12\frac{1}{2}\%$	65	_____	_____

3. Find the effective rate of interest for each of the loans in Problem 2. Use the answers you calculated in Problem 2 to solve these problems (round to the nearest tenth percent).

	Maturity value	Discount rate	Time (days)	Effective rate
a.	$8,000	.03	60	_____
b.	$4,550	8.1%	110	_____
c.	$19,350	12.7%	55	_____
d.	$63,400	10%	90	_____

e. $13,490	7.9%	200	_____
f. $780	$12\frac{1}{2}\%$	65	_____

WORD PROBLEMS

Assume 360 days.

4. Mary Smith signed a $9,000 note for 135 days at a discount rate of 4%. Find the discount and the proceeds Mary received.

5. The Salem Cooperative Bank charges an $8\frac{3}{4}\%$ discount rate. What are the discount and the proceeds for a $16,200 note for 60 days?

6. Bill Jackson is planning to buy a used car. He went to City Credit Union to take out a loan for $6,400 for 300 days. If the credit union charges a discount rate of $11\frac{1}{2}\%$, what will the proceeds of this loan be?

7. Mike Drislane goes to the bank and signs a note for $9,700. The bank charges a 15% discount rate. Find the discount and the proceeds if the loan is for 210 days.

8. Flora Foley plans to have a deck built on the back of her house. She decides to take out a loan at the bank for $14,300. She signs a note promising to pay back the loan in 280 days. If the note was discounted at 9.2%, how much money will Flora receive from the bank?

9. At the end of 280 days, Flora (Problem 8) must pay back the loan. What is the maturity value of the loan?

10. Dave Cassidy signed a $7,855 note at a bank that charges a 14.2% discount rate. If the loan is for 190 days, find **(a)** the proceeds and **(b)** the effective rate charged by the bank (to the nearest tenth percent).

11. How much money must Dave (Problem 10) pay back to the bank?

Name _____   Date _____

Learning Unit 11–2: Discounting an Interest-Bearing Note Before Maturity

DRILL PROBLEMS

1. Calculate the maturity value for each of the following promissory notes (use 360 days):

Date of note	Principal of note	Length of note (days)	Interest rate	Maturity value
a. April 12	$5,000	150	6%	_____
b. August 23	$15,990	85	13%	_____
c. December 10	$985	30	11.5%	_____

2. Find the maturity date and the discount period for the following; assume no leap years. *Hint:* See Exact Days-in-a-Year Calendar, Chapter 7.

Date of note	Length of note (days)	Date of discount	Maturity date	Discount period
a. March 11	200	June 28	_____	_____
b. January 22	60	March 2	_____	_____
c. April 19	85	June 6	_____	_____
d. November 17	120	February 15	_____	_____

3. Find the bank discount for each of the following (use 360 days):

Date of note	Principal of note	Length of note	Interest rate	Bank discount rate	Date of discount	Bank discount
a. October 5	$2,475	88 days	11%	9.5%	December 10	_____
b. June 13	$9,055	112 days	15%	16%	August 11	_____
c. March 20	$1,065	75 days	12%	11.5%	May 24	_____

4. Find the proceeds for each of the discounted notes in Problem 3.

   a. _____

   b. _____

   c. _____

WORD PROBLEMS

5. Connors Company received a $4,000, 90-day, 10% note dated April 6 from one of its customers. Connors Company held the note until May 16, when the company discounted it at a bank at a discount rate of 12%. What were the proceeds that Connors Company received?

6. Souza & Sons accepted a 9%, $22,000, 120-day note from one of its customers on July 22. On October 2, the company discounted the note at Cooperative Bank. The discount rate was 12%. What were (a) the bank discount and (b) the proceeds?

7. The Fargate Store accepted an $8,250, 75-day, 9% note from one of its customers on March 18. Fargate discounted the note at Parkside National Bank at $9\frac{1}{2}$% on March 29. What proceeds did Fargate receive?

8. On November 1, Marjorie's Clothing Store accepted a $5,200, $8\frac{1}{2}$%, 90-day note from Mary Rose in granting her a time extension on her bill. On January 13, Marjorie discounted the note at Seawater Bank, which charged a 10% discount rate. What were the proceeds that Majorie received?

9. On December 3, Duncan's Company accepted a $5,000, 90-day, 12% note from Al Finney in exchange for a $5,000 bill that was past due. On January 29, Duncan discounted the note at The Sidwell Bank at 13.1%. What were the proceeds from the note?

10. On February 26, Sullivan Company accepted a 60-day, 10% note in exchange for a $1,500 past-due bill from Tabot Company. On March 28, Sullivan Company discounted at National Bank the note received from Tabot Company. The bank discount rate was 12%. What are (a) the bank discount and (b) the proceeds?

11. On June 4, Johnson Company received from Marty Russo a 30-day, 11% note for $720 to settle Russo's debt. On June 17, Johnson discounted the note at Eastern Bank whose discount rate was 15%. What proceeds did Johnson receive?

12. On December 15, Lawlers Company went to the bank and discounted a 10%, 90-day, $14,000 note dated October 21. The bank charged a discount rate of 12%. What were the proceeds of the note?

Name _____   Date _____

Learning Unit 12–1:   Compound Interest (Future Value)—The Big Picture

DRILL PROBLEMS

1. In the following examples, calculate manually the amount at year-end for each of the deposits, assuming that interest is compounded annually. Round to the nearest cent each year.

	Principal	Rate	Number of years	Year 1	Year 2	Year 3	Year 4
a.	$530	4%	2	_____	_____		
b.	$1,980	12%	4	_____	_____	_____	_____

2. In the following examples, calculate the simple interest, the compound interest, and the difference between the two. Round to the nearest cent; do not use tables.

	Principal	Rate	Number of years	Simple interest	Compound interest	Difference
a.	$4,600	10%	2	_____	_____	_____
b.	$18,400	9%	4	_____	_____	_____
c.	$855	$7\frac{1}{5}$%	3	_____	_____	_____

3. Find the future value and the compound interest using the Future Value of $1 at Compound Interest table or the Compound Daily table. Round to the nearest cent.

	Principal	Investment terms	Future value	Compound interest
a.	$10,000	6 years at 8% compounded annually	_____	_____
b.	$10,000	6 years at 8% compounded quarterly	_____	_____
c.	$8,400	7 years at 12% compounded semiannually	_____	_____
d.	$2,500	15 years at 10% compounded daily	_____	_____
e.	$9,600	5 years at 6% compounded quarterly	_____	_____
f.	$20,000	2 years at 6% compounded monthly	_____	_____

4. Calculate the effective rate (APY) of interest using the Future Value of $1 at Compound Interest table.

Investment terms	Effective rate (annual percentage yield)
a. 12% compounded quarterly	_____
b. 12% compounded semiannually	_____
c. 6% compounded quarterly	_____

WORD PROBLEMS

5. John Mackey deposited $5,000 in his savings account at Salem Savings Bank. If the bank pays 6% interest compounded quarterly, what will be the balance of his account at the end of 3 years?

6. Pine Valley Savings Bank offers a certificate of deposit at 12% interest, compounded quarterly. What is the effective rate (APY) of interest?

7. Jack Billings loaned $6,000 to his brother-in-law Dan, who was opening a new business. Dan promised to repay the loan at the end of 5 years, with interest of 8% compounded semiannually. How much will Dan pay Jack at the end of 5 years?

8. Eileen Hogarty deposits $5,630 in City Bank, which pays 12% interest, compounded quarterly. How much money will Eileen have in her account at the end of 7 years?

9. If Kevin Bassage deposits $3,500 in Scarsdale Savings Bank, which pays 8% interest, compounded quarterly, what will be in his account at the end of 6 years? How much interest will he have earned at that time?

10. Arlington Trust pays 6% compounded semiannually. How much interest would be earned on $7,200 for 1 year?

11. Paladium Savings Bank pays 9% compounded quarterly. Find the amount and the interest on $3,000 after three quarters. Do not use a table.

12. David Siderski bought a $7,500 bank certificate paying 16% compounded semiannually. How much money did he obtain upon cashing in the certificate 3 years later?

13. An issue of *Your Money* showed that the more frequently the bank compounds your money, the better. Just how much better is a function of time. A $10,000 investment for 6% in a 5-year certificate of deposit at three different banks can result in different interest being earned.
   a. Bank A (simple interest, no compounding)
   b. Bank B (quarterly compounding)
   c. Bank C (daily compounding)
       What would be the interest for each bank?

Name _____   Date _____

Learning Unit 12–2:   Present Value—The Big Picture

DRILL PROBLEMS

1. Use the *Business Math Handbook* to find the table factor for each of the following:

	Future value	Rate	Number of years	Compounded	Table value
a.	$1.00	10%	5	Annually	_____
b.	$1.00	12%	8	Semiannually	_____
c.	$1.00	6%	10	Quarterly	_____
d.	$1.00	12%	2	Monthly	_____
e.	$1.00	8%	15	Semiannually	_____

2. Use the *Business Math Handbook* to find the table factor and the present value for each of the following:

	Future value	Rate	Number of years	Compounded	Table value	Present value
a.	$1,000	14%	6	Semiannually	_____	_____
b.	$1,000	16%	7	Quarterly	_____	_____
c.	$1,000	8%	7	Quarterly	_____	_____
d.	$1,000	8%	7	Semiannually	_____	_____
e.	$1,000	8%	7	Annually	_____	_____

3. Find the present value and the interest earned for the following:

	Future value	Number of years	Rate	Compounded	Present value	Interest earned
a.	$2,500	6	8%	Annually	_____	_____
b.	$4,600	10	6%	Semiannually	_____	_____
c.	$12,800	8	10%	Semiannually	_____	_____
d.	$28,400	7	8%	Quarterly	_____	_____
e.	$53,050	1	12%	Monthly	_____	_____

4. Find the missing amount (present value or future value) for each of the following:

	Present value	Investment terms	Future value
a.	$3,500	5 years at 8% compounded annually	_____
b.	_____	6 years at 12% compounded semiannually	$9,000
c.	$4,700	9 years at 14% compounded semiannually	_____

WORD PROBLEMS

Solve for future value or present value.

5. Paul Palumbo assumes that he will need to have a new roof put on his house in 4 years. He estimates that the roof will cost him $18,000 at that time. What amount of money should Paul invest today at 8%, compounded semiannually, to be able to pay for the roof?

6. Tilton, a pharmacist, rents his store and has signed a lease that will expire in 3 years. When the lease expires, Tilton wants to buy his own store. He wants to have a down payment of $35,000 at that time. How much money should Tilton invest today at 6% compounded quarterly to yield $35,000?

7. Brad Morrissey loans $8,200 to his brother-in-law. He will be repaid at the end of 5 years, with interest at 10% compounded semiannually. Find out how much he will be repaid.

8. The owner of Waverly Sheet Metal Company plans to buy some new machinery in 6 years. He estimates that the machines he wishes to purchase will cost $39,700 at that time. What must he invest today at 8% compounded semiannually to have sufficient money to purchase the new machines?

9. Paul Stevens's grandparents want to buy him a car when he graduates from college in 4 years. They feel that they should have $27,000 in the bank at that time. How much should they invest at 12% compounded quarterly to reach their goal?

10. Gilda Nardi deposits $5,325 in a bank that pays 12% interest, compounded quarterly. Find the amount she will have at the end of 7 years.

11. Mary Wilson wants to buy a new set of golf clubs in 2 years. They will cost $775. How much money should she invest today at 9% compounded annually so that she will have enough money to buy the new clubs?

12. Jack Beggs plans to invest $30,000 at 10% compounded semiannually for 5 years. What is the future value of the investment?

13. Ron Thrift has a 2000 Honda that he expects will last 3 more years. Ron does not like to finance his purchases. He went to First National Bank to find out how much money he should put in the bank to purchase a $20,300 car in 3 years. The bank's 3-year CD is compounded quarterly with a 4% rate. How much should Ron invest in the CD?

14. The Downers Grove YMCA had a fund-raising campaign to build a swimming pool in 6 years. Members raised $825,000; the pool is estimated to cost $1,230,000. The money will be placed in Downers Grove Bank, which pays daily interest at 6%. Will the YMCA have enough money to pay for the pool in 6 years?

Name _____   Date _____

Learning Unit 13–1: Annuities: Ordinary Annuity and Annuity Due (Find Future Value)

DRILL PROBLEMS

1. Find the value of the following ordinary annuities (calculate manually):

Amount of each annual deposit	Interest rate	Value at end of year 1	Value at end of year 2	Value at end of year 3
a. $1,000	8%	_____	_____	_____
b. $2,500	12%	_____	_____	_____
c. $7,200	10%	_____	_____	_____

2. Use the Ordinary Annuity Table: Compound Sum of an Annuity of $1 to find the value of the following ordinary annuities:

Annuity payment	Payment period	Term of annuity	Interest rate	Value of annuity
a. $650	Semiannually	5 years	6%	_____
b. $3,790	Annually	13 years	12%	_____
c. $500	Quarterly	1 year	8%	_____

3. Find the annuity due (deposits are made at beginning of period) for each of the following using the Ordinary Annuity Table:

Amount of payment	Payment period	Interest rate	Time (years)	Amount of annuity
a. $900	Annually	7%	6	_____
b. $1,200	Annually	11%	4	_____
c. $550	Semiannually	10%	9	_____

4. Find the amount of each annuity:

Amount of payment	Payment period	Interest rate	Time (years)	Type of annuity	Amount of annuity
a. $600	Semiannually	12%	8	Ordinary	_____
b. $600	Semiannually	12%	8	Due	_____
c. $1,100	Annually	9%	7	Ordinary	_____

WORD PROBLEMS

5. At the end of each year for the next 9 years, D'Aldo Company will deposit $25,000 in an ordinary annuity account paying 9% interest compounded annually. Find the value of the annuity at the end of the 9 years.

6. David McCarthy is a professional baseball player who expects to play in the major leagues for 10 years. To save for the future, he will deposit $50,000 at the beginning of each year into an account that pays 11% interest compounded annually. How much will he have in this account at the end of 10 years?

7. Tom and Sue plan to get married soon. Because they hope to have a large wedding, they are going to deposit $1,000 at the end of each month into an account that pays 24% compounded monthly. How much will they have in this account at the end of 1 year?

8. Chris Dennen deposits $15,000 at the end of each year for 13 years into an account paying 7% interest compounded annually. What is the value of her annuity at the end of 13 years? How much interest will she have earned?

9. Amanda Blinn is 52 years old today and has just opened an IRA. She plans to deposit $500 at the end of each quarter into her account. If Amanda retires on her 62nd birthday, what amount will she have in her account if the account pays 8% interest compounded quarterly?

10. Jerry Davis won the citywide sweepstakes and will receive a check for $2,000 at the beginning of each 6 months for the next 5 years. If Jerry deposits each check in an account that pays 8% compounded semiannually, how much will he have at the end of 5 years?

11. Mary Hynes purchased an ordinary annuity from an investment broker at 8% interest compounded semiannually. If her semiannual deposit is $600, what will be the value of the annuity at the end of 15 years?

Learning Unit 13–2: Present Value of an Ordinary Annuity (Find Present Value)

DRILL PROBLEMS

1. Use the Present Value of an Annuity of $1 table to find the amount to be invested today to receive a stream of payments for a given number of years in the future. Show the manual check of your answer. (Check may be a few pennies off due to rounding.)

Amount of expected payments	Payment period	Interest rate	Term of annuity	Present value of annuity
a. $1,500	Yearly	9%	2 years	_____
b. $2,700	Yearly	13%	3 years	_____
c. $2,700	Yearly	6%	3 years	_____

2. Find the present value of the following annuities. Use the Present Value of an Annuity of $1 table.

Amount of each payment	Payment period	Interest rate	Time (years)	Compounded	Present value of annuity
a. $2,000	Year	7%	25	Annually	_____
b. $7,000	Year	11%	12	Annually	_____
c. $850	6 months	12%	5	Semiannually	_____
d. $1,950	6 months	14%	9	Semiannually	_____
e. $500	Quarter	12%	10	Quarterly	_____

WORD PROBLEMS

3. Tom Hanson would like to receive $200 each quarter for the 4 years he is in college. If his bank account pays 8% compounded quarterly, how much must he have in his account when he begins college?

4. Jean Reith has just retired and will receive a $12,500 retirement check every 6 months for the next 20 years. If her employer can invest money at 12% compounded semiannually, what amount must be invested today to make the semiannual payments to Jean?

5. Tom Herrick will pay $4,500 at the end of each year for the next 7 years to pay the balance of his college loans. If Tom can invest his money at 7% compounded annually, how much must he invest today to make the annual payments?

6. Helen Grahan is planning an extended sabbatical for the next 3 years. She would like to invest a lump sum of money at 10% interest so that she can withdraw $6,000 every 6 months while on sabbatical. What is the amount of the lump sum that Helen must invest?

7. Linda Rudd has signed a rental contract for office equipment, agreeing to pay $3,200 at the end of each quarter for the next 5 years. If Linda can invest money at 12% compounded quarterly, find the lump sum she can deposit today to make the payments for the length of the contract.

8. Sam Adams is considering lending his brother John $6,000. John said that he would repay Sam $775 every 6 months for 4 years. If money can be invested at 8%, calculate the equivalent cash value of the offer today. Should Sam go ahead with the loan?

9. The State Lotto Game offers a grand prize of $1,000,000 paid in 20 yearly payments of $50,000. If the state treasurer can invest money at 9% compounded annually, how much must she invest today to make the payments to the grand prize winner?

10. Thomas Martin's uncle has promised him upon graduation a gift of $20,000 in cash or $2,000 every quarter for the next 3 years. If money can be invested at 8%, which offer will Thomas accept? (Thomas is a business major.)

11. Paul Sasso is selling a piece of land. He has received two solid offers. Jason Smith has offered a $60,000 down payment and $50,000 a year for the next 5 years. Kevin Bassage offered $35,000 down and $55,000 a year for the next 5 years. If money can be invested at 7% compounded annually, which offer should Paul accept? (To make the comparison, find the equivalent cash price of each offer.)

12. Abe Hoster decided to retire to Spain in 10 years. What amount should Abe invest today so that he will be able to withdraw $30,000 at the end of each year for 20 years after he retires? Assume he can invest money at 8% interest compounded annually.

Learning Unit 13-3: Sinking Funds (Find Periodic Payments)

DRILL PROBLEMS

1. Given the number of years and the interest rate, use the Sinking Fund Table based on $1 to calculate the amount of the periodic payment.

Frequency of payment	Length of time	Interest rate	Future amount	Sinking fund payment
a. Annually	19 years	5%	$125,000	_____
b. Annually	7 years	10%	$205,000	_____
c. Semiannually	10 years	6%	$37,500	_____
d. Quarterly	9 years	12%	$12,750	_____
e. Quarterly	6 years	8%	$25,600	_____

2. Find the amount of each payment into the sinking fund and the amount of interest earned.

Maturity value	Interest rate	Term (years)	Frequency of payment	Sinking fund payment	Interest earned
a. $45,500	5%	13	Annually	_____	_____
b. $8,500	10%	20	Semiannually	_____	_____
c. $11,000	8%	5	Quarterly	_____	_____
d. $66,600	12%	$7\frac{1}{2}$	Semiannually	_____	_____

WORD PROBLEMS

3. To finance a new police station, the town of Pine Valley issued bonds totaling $600,000. The town treasurer set up a sinking fund at 8% compounded quarterly in order to redeem the bonds in 7 years. What is the quarterly payment that must be deposited into the fund?

4. Arlex Oil Corporation plans to build a new garage in 6 years. To finance the project, the financial manager established a $250,000 sinking fund at 6% compounded semianually. Find the semiannual payment required for the fund.

5. The City Fisheries Corporation sold $300,000 worth of bonds that must be redeemed in 9 years. The corporation agreed to set up a sinking fund to accumulate the $300,000. Find the amount of the periodic payments made into the fund if payments are made annually and the fund earns 8% compounded annually.

6. Gregory Mines Corporation wishes to purchase a new piece of equipment in 4 years. The estimated price of the equipment is $100,000. If the corporation makes periodic payments into a sinking fund with 12% interest compounded quarterly, find the amount of the periodic payments.

7. The Best Corporation must buy a new piece of machinery in $4\frac{1}{2}$ years that will cost $350,000. If the firm sets up a sinking fund to finance this new machine, what will the quarterly deposits be assuming the fund earns 8% interest compounded quarterly?

8. The Lowest-Price-in-Town Company needs $75,500 in 6 years to pay off a debt. The company makes a decision to set up a sinking fund and make semiannual deposits. What will their payments be if the fund pays 10% interest compounded semiannually?

9. The WIR Company plans to renovate their offices in 5 years. They estimate that the cost will be $235,000. If they set up a sinking fund that pays 12% quarterly, what will their quarterly payments be?

Name _____ Date _____

Learning Unit 14–1: Cost of Installment Buying

DRILL PROBLEMS

1. For the following installment problems, find the amount financed and the finance charge.

	Sale price	Down payment	Number of monthly payments	Monthly payment	Amount financed	Finance charge
a.	$1,500	$300	24	$58	_____	_____
b.	$12,000	$3,000	30	$340	_____	_____
c.	$62,500	$4,700	48	$1,500	_____	_____
d.	$4,975	$620	18	$272	_____	_____
e.	$825	$82.50	12	$67.45	_____	_____

2. For each of the above purchases, find the deferred payment price.

	Sale price	Down payment	Number of monthly payments	Monthly payment	Deferred payment price
a.	$1,500	$300	24	$58	_____
b.	$12,000	$3,000	30	$340	_____
c.	$62,500	$4,700	48	$1,500	_____
d.	$4,975	$620	18	$272	_____
e.	$825	$82.50	12	$67.45	_____

3. Use the Annual Percentage Rate Table per $100 to calculate the estimated APR for each of the previous purchases.

	Sale price	Down payment	Number of monthly payments	Monthly payment	Annual percentage rate
a.	$1,500	$300	24	$58	_____
b.	$12,000	$3,000	30	$340	_____
c.	$62,500	$4,700	48	$1,500	_____
d.	$4,975	$620	18	$272	_____
e.	$825	$82.50	12	$67.45	_____

4. Given the following information, calculate the monthly payment by the loan amortization table.

	Amount financed	Interest rate	Number of months of loan	Monthly payment
a.	$12,000	10%	18	_____
b.	$18,000	11%	36	_____
c.	$25,500	13.50%	54	_____

WORD PROBLEMS

5. Jill Walsh purchases a bedroom set for a cash price of $3,920. The down payment is $392, and the monthly installment payment is $176 for 24 months. Find (a) the amount financed, (b) the finance charge, and (c) the deferred payment price.

6. An automaker promotion loan on a $20,000 automobile and a down payment of 20% are being financed for 48 months. The monthly payments will be $367.74. What will be the APR for this auto loan? Use the table in the *Business Math Handbook*.

7. David Nason purchased a recreational vehicle for $25,000. David went to City Bank to finance the purchase. The bank required that David make a 10% down payment and monthly payments of $571.50 for 4 years. Find **(a)** the amount financed, **(b)** the finance charge, and **(c)** the deferred payment that David paid.

8. Calculate the estimated APR that David (Problem 7) was charged per $100 using the Annual Percentage Rate Table.

9. Young's Motors advertised a new car for $16,720. They offered an installment plan of 5% down and 42 monthly payments of $470. What are **(a)** the deferred payment price and **(b)** the estimated APR for this car (use the table)?

10. Angie French bought a used car for $9,000. Angie put down $2,000 and financed the balance at 11.50% for 36 months. What is her monthly payment? Use the loan amortization table.

Learning Unit 14–2: Paying Off Installment Loan Before Due Date

DRILL PROBLEMS

1. Find the balance of each loan outstanding and the total finance charge.

Amount financed	Monthly payment	Number of payments	Payments to date	Balance of loan outstanding	Finance charge
a. $1,500	$125	15	10	_____	_____
b. $21,090	$600	40	24	_____	_____
c. $895	$60	18	10	_____	_____
d. $4,850	$150	42	30	_____	_____

2. For the loans in Problem 1, find the number of payments remaining and calculate the rebate amount of the finance charge (use Rebate Fraction Table Based on Rule of 78).

Amount financed	Monthly payment	Number of payments	Payments to date	Number of payments remaining	Finance charge rebate
a. $1,500	$125	15	10	_____	_____
b. $21,090	$600	40	24	_____	_____
c. $895	$60	18	10	_____	_____
d. $4,850	$150	42	30	_____	_____

3. For the loans in Problems 1 and 2, show the remaining balance of the loan and calculate the payoff amount to retire the loan at this time.

Amount financed	Monthly payment	Number of payments	Payments to date	Balance of loan outstanding	Final payoff
a. $1,500	$125	15	10	_____	_____
b. $21,090	$600	40	24	_____	_____
c. $895	$60	18	10	_____	_____
d. $4,850	$150	42	30	_____	_____

4. Complete the following; show all the steps.

Loan	Months of loan	Monthly payment	End of month loan is repaid	Final payoff
a. $6,200	36	$219	24	_____
b. $960	12	$99	8	_____

WORD PROBLEMS

5. Maryjane Hannon took out a loan for $5,600 to have a swimming pool installed in her backyard. The note she signed required 21 monthly payments of $293. At the end of 15 months, Maryjane wants to know the balance of her loan outstanding and her total finance charge.

6. After calculating the above data (Problem 5), Maryjane is considering paying off the rest of the loan. To make her decision, Maryjane wants to know the finance charge rebate she will receive and the final payoff amount.

7. Ben Casey decided to buy a used car for $7,200. He agreed to make monthly payments of $225 for 36 months. What is Ben's total finance charge?

8. After making 20 payments, Ben (Problem 7) wants to pay off the rest of the loan. What will be the amount of Ben's final payoff?

9. Jeremy Vagos took out a loan to buy a new boat that cost $12,440. He agreed to pay $350 a month for 48 months. After 24 monthly payments, he calculates that he has paid $8,400 on his loan and has 24 payments remaining. Jeremy's friend Luke tells Jeremy that he will pay off the rest of the loan (in a single payment) if he can be half owner of the boat. What is the amount that Luke will have to pay?

Learning Unit 14–3:   Revolving Charge Credit Cards

DRILL PROBLEMS

1. Use the U.S. Rule to calculate the outstanding balance due for each of the following independent situations:

Monthly payment number	Outstanding balance due	$1\frac{1}{2}\%$ interest payment	Amount of monthly payment	Reduction in balance due	Outstanding balance due
a. 1	$9,000.00	_____	$600	_____	_____
b. 5	$5,625.00	_____	$1,000	_____	_____
c. 4	$926.50	_____	$250	_____	_____
d. 12	$62,391.28	_____	$1,200	_____	_____
e. 8	$3,255.19	_____	$325	_____	_____

2. Complete the missing data for a $6,500 purchase made on credit. The annual interest charge on this revolving charge account is 18%, or $1\frac{1}{2}\%$ interest on previous month's balance. Use the U.S. Rule.

Monthly payment number	Outstanding balance due	$1\frac{1}{2}\%$ interest payment	Amount of monthly payment	Reduction in balance due	Outstanding balance due
1	$6,500	_____	$700	_____	_____
2	_____	_____	$700	_____	_____
3	_____	_____	$700	_____	_____

3. Calculate the average billing daily balance for each of the monthly statements for the following revolving credit accounts (assume a 30-day billing cycle):

Billing date	Previous balance	Payment date	Payment amount	Charge date(s)	Charge amount(s)	Average daily balance
a. 4/10	$329	4/25	$35	4/29	$56	_____
b. 6/15	$573	6/25	$60	6/26 6/30	$25 $72	_____
c. 9/15	$335.50	9/20	$33.55	9/25 9/26	$12.50 $108	_____

4. Find the finance charge for each monthly statement (Problem 3) if the annual percentage rate is 15%.

   a. _____   b. _____   c. _____

WORD PROBLEMS

5. Niki Marshall is going to buy a new bedroom set at Scottie's Furniture Store, where she has a revolving charge account. The cost of the bedroom set is $5,500. Niki does not plan to charge anything else to her account until she has completely paid for the bedroom set. Scottie's Furniture Store charges an annual percentage rate of 18%, or $1\frac{1}{2}$% per month. Niki plans to pay $1,000 per month until she has paid for the bedroom set. Set up a schedule for Niki to show her outstanding balance at the end of each month after her $1,000 payment and also the amount of her final payment. Use the U.S. Rule.

6. Frances Dollof received her monthly statement from Brown's Department Store. The following is part of the information contained on that statement. Finance charge is calculated on the average daily balance.

Date	Reference	Department	Description	Amount
Dec. 15	5921	359	Petite sportswear	84.98
Dec. 15	9612	432	Footwear	55.99
Dec. 15	2600	126	Women's fragrance	35.18
Dec. 23	6247	61	Ralph Lauren towels	20.99
Dec. 24	0129	998	Payment received—thank you	100.00CR

Previous balance	Annual percentage rate	Billing date
719.04 12/13	18%	JAN 13

Brown's Charge Account Terms
Payment is required in monthly installments upon receipt of monthly statement in accordance with Brown's payment terms.

When my new balance is:	My minimum required payment is:	When my new balance is:	My minimum required payment is:
Up to $20.00	New Balance	$350.01 to $400.00	$40.00
$ 20.01 to $200.00	$20.00	$400.01 to $450.00	$45.00
$200.01 to $250.00	$25.00	$450.01 to $500.00	$50.00
$250.01 to $300.00	$30.00	More than $500.00	$50.00 plus
$300.01 to $350.00	$35.00		$10.00 for each $50.00 (or fraction thereof) of New Balance over $500.00

    a. Calculate the average daily balance for the month.

    b. What is Ms. Dollof's finance charge?

    c. What is the new balance for Ms. Dollof's account?

    d. What is the minimum payment Frances is required to pay according to Brown's payment terms?

7. What is the finance charge for a Brown's customer who has an average daily balance of $3,422.67?

8. What is the minimum payment for a Brown's customer with a new balance of $522.00?

9. What is the minimum payment for a Brown's customer with a new balance of $325.01?

10. What is the new balance for a Brown's customer with a previous balance of $309.35 whose purchases totaled $213.00, given that the customer made a payment of $75.00 and the finance charge was $4.65?

RECAP OF WORD PROBLEMS IN LU 14–1

11. A home equity loan on a $20,000 automobile with a down payment of 20% is being financed for 48 months. The interest is tax deductible. The monthly payments will be $401.97. What is the APR on this loan? Use the table in the *Business Math Handbook*. If the person is in the 28% income tax bracket, what will be the tax savings with this type of a loan?

12. An automobile with a total transaction price of $20,000 with a down payment of 20% is being financed for 48 months. Banks and credit unions require a monthly payment of $400.36. What is the APR for this auto loan? Use the table in the *Business Math Handbook*.

13. Assume you received a $2,000 rebate that brought the price of a car down to $20,000; the financing rate was for 48 months, and your total interest was $3,279. Using the table in the *Business Math Handbook*, what was your APR?

Classroom Notes

Name _____ Date _____

Learning Unit 15–1: Types of Mortgages and the Monthly Mortgage Payment

DRILL PROBLEMS

1. Use the table in the *Business Math Handbook* to calculate the monthly payment for principal and interest for the following mortgages:

Price of home	Down payment	Interest rate	Term in years	Monthly payment
a. $200,000	15%	6%	25	_____
b. $200,000	15%	$5\frac{1}{2}\%$	30	_____
c. $450,000	10%	$11\frac{3}{4}\%$	30	_____
d. $450,000	10%	11%	30	_____

2. For each of the mortgages, calculate the amount of interest that will be paid over the life of the loan.

Price of home	Down payment	Interest rate	Term in years	Total interest paid
a. $200,000	15%	$6\frac{1}{2}\%$	25	_____
b. $200,000	15%	$10\frac{1}{2}\%$	30	_____
c. $450,000	10%	$11\frac{3}{4}\%$	30	_____
d. $450,000	10%	11%	30	_____

3. Calculate the increase in the monthly mortgage payments for each of the rate increases in the following mortgages. Also calculate what percent of change the increase represents (round to the tenth percent).

Mortgage amount	Term in years	Interest rate	Increase in interest rate	Increase in monthly payment	Percent change
a. $175,000	22	9%	1%	_____	_____
b. $300,000	30	$11\frac{3}{4}\%$	$\frac{3}{4}\%$	_____	_____

4. Calculate the increase in total interest paid for the increase in interest rates in Problem 3.

Mortgage amount	Term in years	Interest rate	Increase in interest rate	Increase in total interest paid
a. $175,000	22	9%	1%	_____
b. $300,000	30	$11\frac{3}{4}\%$	$\frac{3}{4}\%$	_____

WORD PROBLEMS

5. The Counties are planning to purchase a new home that costs $150,000. The bank is charging them 6% interest and requires a 20% down payment. The Counties are planning to take a 25-year mortgage. How much will their monthly payment be for principal and interest?

6. The MacEacherns wish to buy a new house that costs $299,000. The bank requires a 15% down payment and charges $11\frac{1}{2}\%$ interest. If the MacEacherns take out a 15-year mortgage, what will their monthly payment for principal and interest be?

7. Because the monthly payments are so high, the MacEacherns (Problem 6) want to know what the monthly payments would be for **(a)** a 25-year mortgage and **(b)** a 30-year mortgage. Calculate these two payments.

8. If the MacEacherns choose a 30-year mortgage instead of a 15-year mortgage, **(a)** how much money will they "save" monthly and **(b)** how much more interest will they pay over the life of the loan?

9. If the MacEacherns choose the 25-year mortgage instead of the 30-year mortgage, **(a)** how much more will they pay monthly and **(b)** how much less interest will they pay over the life of the loan?

10. Larry and Doris Davis plan to purchase a new home that costs $415,000. The bank that they are dealing with requires a 20% down payment and charges $12\frac{3}{4}\%$. The Davises are planning to take a 25-year mortgage. What will the monthly payment be?

11. How much interest will the Davises (Problem 10) pay over the life of the loan?

Learning Unit 15–2: Amortization Schedule—Breaking Down the Monthly Payment

DRILL PROBLEMS

1. In the following, calculate the monthly payment for each mortgage, the portion of the first monthly payment that goes to interest, and the portion of the payment that goes toward the principal.

Amount of mortgage	Interest rate	Term in years	Monthly payment	Portion to interest	Portion to principal
a. $170,000	8%	22	_____	_____	_____
b. $222,000	$11\frac{3}{4}\%$	30	_____	_____	_____
c. $167,000	$10\frac{1}{2}\%$	25	_____	_____	_____
d. $307,000	13%	15	_____	_____	_____
e. $409,500	$12\frac{1}{2}\%$	20	_____	_____	_____

2. Prepare an amortization schedule for the first 3 months of a 25-year, 12% mortgage on $265,000.

Payment number	Monthly payment	Portion to interest	Portion to principal	Balance of loan outstanding
1	_____	_____	_____	_____
2	_____	_____	_____	_____
3	_____	_____	_____	_____

3. Prepare an amortization schedule for the first 4 months of a 30-year, $10\frac{1}{2}\%$ mortgage on $195,500.

Payment number	Monthly payment	Portion to interest	Portion to principal	Balance of loan outstanding
1	_____	_____	_____	_____
2	_____	_____	_____	_____
3	_____	_____	_____	_____
4	_____	_____	_____	_____

WORD PROBLEMS

4. Jim and Janice Hurst are buying a new home for $235,000. The bank which is financing the home requires a 20% down payment and charges a $13\frac{1}{2}\%$ interest rate. Janice wants to know **(a)** what the monthly payment for the principal and interest will be if they take out a 30-year mortgage and **(b)** how much of the first payment will be for interest on the loan.

5. The Hursts (Problem 4) thought that a lot of their money was going to interest. They asked the banker just how much they would be paying for interest over the life of the loan. Calculate the total amount of interest that the Hursts will pay.

6. The banker told the Hursts (Problem 4) that they could, of course, save on the interest payments if they took out a loan for a shorter period of time. Jim and Janice decided to see if they could afford a 15-year mortgage. Calculate how much more the Hursts would have to pay each month for principal and interest if they took a 15-year mortgage for their loan.

7. The Hursts (Problem 4) thought that they might be able to afford this, but first wanted to see **(a)** how much of the first payment would go to the principal and **(b)** how much total interest they would be paying with a 15-year mortgage.

8.

	1980	2009
Cost of median-priced new home	$44,200	$136,600
10% down payment	$4,420	
Fixed-rate, 30-year mortgage		
Interest rate	8.9%	$7\frac{1}{2}\%$
Total monthly principal and interest	$316	

Complete the 2009 year.

9. You can't count on your home mortgage lender to keep you from getting in debt over your head. The old standards of allowing 28% of your income for mortgage debt (including taxes and insurance) usually still apply. If your total monthly payment is $1,033, what should be your annual income to buy a home?

10. Assume that a 30-year fixed-rate mortgage for $100,000 was 9% at one date as opposed to 7% the previous year. What is the difference in monthly payments for these 2 years?

11. If you had a $100,000 mortgage with $7\frac{1}{2}\%$ interest for 25 years and wanted a $7\frac{1}{2}\%$ loan for 35 years, what would be the change in monthly payments? How much more would you pay in interest?

Classroom Notes

Name _____   Date _____

Learning Unit 16–1:   Balance Sheet—Report as of a Particular Date

DRILL PROBLEMS

1. Complete the balance sheet for David Harrison, Attorney, and show that

Assets = Liabilities + Owner's equity

Account totals are as follows: accounts receivable, $4,800; office supplies, $375; building (net), $130,000; accounts payable, $1,200; notes payable, $137,200; cash, $2,250; prepaid insurance, $1,050; office equipment (net), $11,250; land, $75,000; capital, $85,900; and salaries payable, $425.

DAVID HARRISON, ATTORNEY
Balance Sheet
December 31, 2009

Assets

Current assets:
 Cash   _____

 Accounts receivable   _____

 Prepaid insurance   _____

 Office supplies   _____

  Total current assets   _____

Plant and equipment:

 Office equipment (net)   _____

 Building (net)   _____

 Land   _____

  Total plant and equipment   _____

Total assets   _____

Liabilities

Current liabilities:

 Accounts payable   _____

 Salaries payable   _____

  Total current liabilities   _____

Long-term liabilities:

 Notes payable   _____

  Total liabilities   _____

Owner's Equity

David Harrison, capital, December 31, 2007   _____

Total liabilities and owner's equity   _____

2. Given the amounts in each of the accounts of Fisher-George Electric Corporation, fill in these amounts on the balance sheet to show that

Assets = Liabilities + Stockholders' equity

Account totals are as follows: cash, $2,500; merchandise inventory, $1,325; automobiles (net), $9,250; common stock, $10,000; accounts payable, $275; office equipment (net), $5,065; accounts receivable, $300; retained earnings, $6,895; prepaid insurance, $1,075; salaries payable, $175; and mortgage payable, $2,170.

FISHER-GEORGE ELECTRIC CORPORATION Balance Sheet December 31, 2009		
Assets		
Current assets:		
Cash	_____	
Accounts receivable	_____	
Merchandise inventory	_____	
Prepaid insurance	_____	
Total current assets		_____
Plant and equipment:		
Office equipment (net)	_____	
Automobiles (net)	_____	
Total plant and equipment		_____
Total assets		═══════
Liabilities		
Current liabilities:		
Accounts payable	_____	
Salaries payable	_____	
Total current liabilities		_____
Long-term liabilities:		
Mortgage payable	_____	
Total liabilities		_____
Stockholders' Equity		
Common stock	_____	
Retained earnings	_____	
Total stockholders' equity		_____
Total liabilities and stockholders' equity		═══════

3. Complete a vertical analysis of the following partial balance sheet (round all percents to the nearest hundredth percent).

THREEMAX, INC. Comparative Balance Sheet Vertical Analysis At December 31, 2008 and 2009				
	2008		**2009**	
	Amount	Percent	Amount	Percent
Assets				
Cash	$ 8,500	_____	$ 10,200	_____
Accounts receivable (net)	11,750	_____	15,300	_____
Merchandise inventory	55,430	_____	54,370	_____
Store supplies	700	_____	532	_____
Office supplies	650	_____	640	_____
Prepaid insurance	2,450	_____	2,675	_____
Office equipment (net)	12,000	_____	14,300	_____
Store equipment (net)	32,000	_____	31,000	_____
Building (net)	75,400	_____	80,500	_____
Land	200,000	_____	150,000	_____
Total assets	$398,880	_____	$359,517	_____

4. Complete a horizontal analysis of the following partial balance sheet (round all percents to the nearest hundredth percent).

THREEMAX, INC. Comparative Balance Sheet Horizontal Analysis At December 31, 2008 and 2009				
	2009	2008	Change	Percent
Assets				
Cash	$ 8,500	$ 10,200	_____	_____
Accounts receivable (net)	11,750	15,300	_____	_____
Merchandise inventory	55,430	54,370	_____	_____
Store supplies	700	532	_____	_____
Office supplies	650	640	_____	_____
Prepaid insurance	2,450	2,675	_____	_____
Office equipment (net)	12,000	14,300	_____	_____
Store equipment (net)	32,000	31,000	_____	_____
Building (net)	75,400	80,500	_____	_____
Land	200,000	150,000	_____	_____
Total assets	$398,880	$359,517		

Learning Unit 16–2: Income Statement—Report for a Specific Period of Time

DRILL PROBLEMS

1. Complete the income statement for Foley Realty, doing all the necessary addition. Account totals are as follows: office salaries expense, $15,255; advertising expense, $2,400; rent expense, $18,000; telephone expense, $650; insurance expense, $1,550; office supplies, $980; depreciation expense, office equipment, $990; depreciation expense, automobile, $2,100; sales commissions earned, $98,400; and management fees earned, $1,260.

FOLEY REALTY Income Statement For the Year Ended December 31, 2009	
Revenues:	
Sales commissions earned	_____
Management fees earned	_____
Total revenues	
Operating expenses:	
Office salaries expense	_____
Advertising expense	_____
Rent expense	_____
Telephone expense	_____
Insurance expense	_____
Office supplies expense	_____
Depreciation expense, office equipment	_____
Depreciation expense, automobile	_____
Total operating expenses	_____
Net income	_____

2. Complete the income statement for Toll's, Inc., a merchandising concern, doing all the necessary addition and subtraction. Sales were $250,000, sales returns and allowances were $1,400, sales discounts were $2,100, merchandise inventory, December 31, 2008, was $42,000, purchases were $156,000, purchases returns and allowances were $1,100, purchases discounts were $3,000, merchandise inventory, December 31, 2009, was $47,000, selling expenses were $37,000, and general and administrative expenses were $29,000.

TOLL'S, INC.
Income Statement
For the Year Ended December 31, 2009

Revenues:
 Sales _____
  Less: Sales return and allowances _____
   Sales discounts _____ _____
 Net sales _____
Cost of goods sold:
 Merchandise inventory, December 31, 2008 _____
 Purchases _____
  Less: Purchases returns and allowances _____
   Purchase discounts _____ _____
 Cost of net purchases _____
 Goods available for sale _____
 Merchandise inventory, December 31, 2009 _____
  Total cost of goods sold _____
Gross profit from sales _____
Operating expenses:
 Selling expenses _____
 General and administrative expenses _____
  Total operating expenses _____
Net income ===========

3. Complete a vertical analysis of the following partial income statement (round all percents to the nearest hundredth percent). Note net sales are 100%.

THREEMAX, INC.
Comparative Income Statement Vertical Analysis
For Years Ended December 31, 2008 and 2009

	2009		2008	
	Amount	Percent	Amount	Percent
Sales	$795,450		$665,532	
Sales returns and allowances	−6,250		−5,340	
Sales discounts	−6,470		−5,125	
Net sales	$782,730		$655,067	
Cost of goods sold:				
Beginning inventory	$ 75,394		$ 81,083	
Purchases	575,980		467,920	
Purchases discounts	−4,976		−2,290	
Goods available for sale	$646,398		$546,713	
Less ending inventory	−66,254		−65,712	
Total costs of goods sold	$580,144		$481,001	
Gross profit	$202,586		$174,066	

4. Complete a horizontal analysis of the following partial income statement (round all percents to the nearest hundredth percent).

THREEMAX, INC. Comparative Income Statement Horizontal Analysis For Years Ended December 31, 2009 and 2008				
	2009	2008	Change	Percent
Sales	$795,450	$665,532	_____	_____
Sales returns and allowances	−6,250	−5,340	_____	_____
Sales discounts	−6,470	−5,125	_____	_____
Net sales	$782,730	$655,067	_____	_____
Cost of goods sold:				
Beginning inventory	$ 75,394	$ 81,083	_____	_____
Purchases	575,980	467,920	_____	_____
Purchases discounts	−4,976	−2,290	_____	_____
Goods available for sale	$646,398	$546,713	_____	_____
Less ending inventory	−66,254	−65,712	_____	_____
Total cost of goods sold	$580,144	$481,001	_____	_____
Gross profit	$202,586	$174,066	_____	_____

Learning Unit 16–3: Trend and Ratio Analysis

DRILL PROBLEMS

1. Express each amount as a percent of the base-year (2007) amount. Round to the nearest tenth percent.

	2010	2009	2008	2007
Sales	$562,791	$560,776	$588,096	$601,982
Percent	_____	_____	_____	_____
Gross profit	$168,837	$196,271	$235,238	$270,891
Percent	_____	_____	_____	_____
Net income	$67,934	$65,927	$56,737	$62,762
Percent	_____	_____	_____	_____

2. If current assets = $42,500 and current liabilities = $56,400, what is the current ratio (to the nearest hundredth)?

3. In Problem 2, if inventory = $20,500 and prepaid expenses = $9,750, what is the quick ratio, or acid test (to the nearest hundredth)?

4. If accounts receivable = $36,720 and net sales = $249,700, what is the average day's collection (to the nearest whole day)?

5. If total liabilities = $243,000 and total assets = $409,870, what is the ratio of total debt to total assets (to the nearest hundredth percent)?

6. If net income = $55,970 and total stockholders' equity = $440,780, what is the return on equity (to the nearest hundredth percent)?

7. If net sales = $900,000 and total assets = $1,090,000, what is the asset turnover (to the nearest hundredth)?

8. In Problem 7, if the net income is $36,600, what is the profit margin on net sales (to the nearest hundredth percent)?

WORD PROBLEMS

9. Calculate trend percentages for the following items using 2007 as the base year. Round to the nearest hundredth percent.

	2010	2009	2008	2007
Sales	$298,000	$280,000	$264,000	$249,250
Cost of goods sold	187,085	175,227	164,687	156,785
Accounts receivable	29,820	28,850	27,300	26,250

10. According to the balance sheet for Ralph's Market, current assets = $165,500 and current liabilities = $70,500. Find the current ratio (to the nearest hundredth).

11. On the balance sheet for Ralph's Market (Problem 10), merchandise inventory = $102,000. Find the quick ratio (acid test).

12. The balance sheet of Moses Contractors shows cash of $5,500, accounts receivable of $64,500, an inventory of $42,500, and current liabilities of $57,500. Find Moses' current ratio and acid test ratio (both to the nearest hundredth).

13. Moses' income statement shows gross sales of $413,000, sales returns of $8,600, and net income of $22,300. Find the profit margin on net sales (to the nearest hundredth percent).

14. Given:

Cash	$ 39,000	Retained earnings	$194,000
Accounts receivable	109,000	Net sales	825,000
Inventory	150,000	Cost of goods sold	528,000
Prepaid expenses	48,000	Operating expenses	209,300
Plant and equipment (net)	487,000	Interest expense	13,500
Accounts payable	46,000	Income taxes	32,400
Other current liabilities	43,000	Net income	41,800
Long-term liabilities	225,000		
Common stock	325,000		

Calculate (to nearest hundredth or hundredth percent as needed):

a. Current ratio. **b.** Quick ratio. **c.** Average day's collection.

d. Total debt to total assets. **e.** Return on equity. **f.** Asset turnover.

g. Profit margin on net sales.

15. The Vale Group lost $18.4 million in profits for the year 2008 as sales dropped to $401 million. Sales in 2007 were $450.6 million. What percent is the decrease in Vale's sales? Round to the nearest hundredth percent.

Name _____ Date _____

Learning Unit 17–1: Concept of Depreciation and the Straight-Line Method

DRILL PROBLEMS

1. Find the annual straight-line rate of depreciation, given the following estimated lives.

Life	Annual rate	Life	Annual rate
a. 25 years	_____	**b.** 4 years	_____
c. 10 years	_____	**d.** 5 years	_____
e. 8 years	_____	**f.** 30 years	_____

2. Find the annual depreciation using the straight-line depreciation method (round to the nearest whole dollar).

Cost of asset	Residual value	Useful life	Annual depreciation
a. $2,460	$400	4 years	_____
b. $24,300	$2,000	6 years	_____
c. $350,000	$42,500	12 years	_____
d. $17,325	$5,000	5 years	_____
e. $2,550,000	$75,000	30 years	_____

3. Find the annual depreciation and ending book value for the first year using the straight-line depreciation method. Round to the nearest dollar.

Cost	Residual value	Useful life	Annual depreciation	Ending book value
a. $6,700	$600	3 years	_____	_____
b. $11,600	$500	6 years	_____	_____
c. $9,980	–0–	5 years	_____	_____
d. $36,950	$2,500	12 years	_____	_____
e. $101,690	$3,600	27 years	_____	_____

4. Find the first-year depreciation to nearest dollar for the following assets, which were only owned for part of a year. Round to the nearest whole dollar the annual depreciation for in-between calculations.

Date of purchase	Cost of asset	Residual value	Useful life	First year depreciation
a. April 8	$10,500	$1,200	4 years	_____
b. July 12	$23,900	$3,200	6 years	_____
c. June 19	$8,880	$800	3 years	_____
d. November 2	$125,675	$6,000	17 years	_____
e. May 25	$44,050	–0–	9 years	_____

WORD PROBLEMS

5. North Shore Grinding purchased a lathe for $37,500. This machine has a residual value of $3,000 and an expected useful life of 4 years. Prepare a depreciation schedule for the lathe using the straight-line depreciation method.

6. Colby Wayne paid $7,750 for a photocopy machine with an estimated life of 6 years and a residual value of $900. Prepare a depreciation schedule using the straight-line depreciation method. Round to nearest whole dollar. (Last year's depreciation may have to be adjusted due to rounding.)

7. The Leo Brothers purchased a machine for $8,400 that has an estimated life of 3 years. At the end of 3 years the machine will have no value. Prepare a depreciation schedule for this machine.

8. Fox Realty bought a computer table for $1,700. The estimated useful life of the table is 7 years. The residual value at the end of 7 years is $370. Find **(a)** the annual rate of depreciation to the nearest hundredth percent, **(b)** the annual amount of depreciation, and **(c)** the book value of the table at the end of the *third* year using the straight-line depreciation method.

9. Cashman, Inc., purchased an overhead projector for $560. It has an estimated useful life of 6 years, at which time it will have no remaining value. Find the book value at the end of 5 years using the straight-line depreciation method. Round the annual depreciation to the nearest whole dollar.

10. Shelley Corporation purchased a new machine for $15,000. The estimated life of the machine is 12 years with a residual value of $2,400. Find **(a)** the annual rate of depreciation to the nearest hundredth percent, **(b)** the annual amount of depreciation, **(c)** the accumulated depreciation at the end of 7 years, and **(d)** the book value at the end of 9 years.

11. Wolfe Ltd. purchased a supercomputer for $75,000 on July 7, 2003. The computer has an estimated life of 5 years and will have a residual value of $15,000. Find **(a)** the annual depreciation amount, **(b)** the depreciation amount for 2003, **(c)** the accumulated depreciation at the end of 2004, and **(d)** the book value at the end of 2005.

Learning Unit 17–2: Units-of-Production Method

DRILL PROBLEMS

1. Find the depreciation per unit for each of the following assets. Round to three decimal places.

Cost of asset	Residual value	Estimated production	Depreciation per unit
a. $3,500	$800	9,000 units	_____
b. $309,560	$22,000	1,500,000 units	_____
c. $54,890	$6,500	275,000 units	_____

2. Find the annual depreciation expense for each of the assets in Problem 1.

Cost of asset	Residual value	Estimated production	Depreciation per unit	Units produced	Amount of depreciation
a. $3,500	$800	9,000 units	_____	3,000	_____
b. $309,560	$22,000	1,500,000 units	_____	45,500	_____
c. $54,890	$6,500	275,000 units	_____	4,788	_____

3. Find the book value at the end of the first year for each of the assets in Problems 1 and 2.

Cost of asset	Residual value	Estimated production	Depreciation per unit	Units produced	Book value
a. $3,500	$800	9,000 units	_____	3,000	_____
b. $309,560	$22,000	1,500,000 units	_____	45,500	_____
c. $54,890	$6,500	275,000 units	_____	4,788	_____

4. Calculate the accumulated depreciation at the end of year 2 for each of the following machines. Carry out the unit depreciation to three decimal places.

Cost of machine	Residual value	Estimated life	Hours used during year 1	Hours used during year 2	Accumulated depreciation
a. $67,900	$4,300	19,000 hours	5,430	4,856	_____
b. $3,810	$600	33,000 hours	10,500	9,330	_____
c. $25,000	$4,900	80,000 hours	7,000	12,600	_____

WORD PROBLEMS

5. Prepare a depreciation schedule for the following machine: The machine cost $63,400; it has an estimated residual value of $5,300 and expected life of 290,500 units. The units produced were:

Year 1	95,000 units
Year 2	80,000 units
Year 3	50,000 units
Year 4	35,500 units
Year 5	30,000 units

6. Forsmann & Smythe purchased a new machine that cost $46,030. The machine has a residual value of $2,200 and estimated output of 430,000 hours. Prepare a units-of-production depreciation schedule for this machine (round the unit depreciation to three decimal places). The hours of use were:

Year 1	90,000 hours
Year 2	150,000 hours
Year 3	105,000 hours
Year 4	90,000 hours

7. Young Electrical Company depreciates its vans using the units-of-production method. The cost of its new van was $24,600, the useful life is 125,000 miles, and the trade-in value is $5,250. What are **(a)** the depreciation expense per mile (to three decimal places) and **(b)** the book value at the end of the first year if it drives 29,667 miles?

8. Tremblay Manufacturing Company purchased a new machine for $52,000. The machine has an estimated useful life of 185,000 hours and a residual value of $10,000. The machine was used for 51,200 hours the first year. Find **(a)** the depreciation rate per hour (round to three decimal places), **(b)** the depreciation expense for the first year, and **(c)** the book value of the machine at the end of the first year.

Learning Unit 17–3: Declining-Balance Method

DRILL PROBLEMS

1. Find the declining-balance rate of depreciation, given the following estimated lives.

Life	Declining rate
a. 25 years	_____
b. 10 years	_____
c. 8 years	_____

2. Find the first year depreciation amount for the following assets using the declining-balance depreciation method. Round to the nearest whole dollar.

Cost of asset	Residual value	Useful life	First year depreciation
a. $2,460	$400	4 years	_____
b. $24,300	$2,000	6 years	_____
c. $350,000	$42,500	12 years	_____
d. $17,325	$5,000	5 years	_____
e. $2,550,000	$75,000	30 years	_____

3. Find the depreciation expense and ending book value for the first year, using the declining-balance depreciation method. Round to the nearest dollar.

Cost	Residual value	Useful life	First year depreciation	Ending book value
a. $6,700	$600	3 years	_____	_____
b. $11,600	$500	6 years	_____	_____
c. $9,980	–0–	5 years	_____	_____
d. $36,950	$2,500	12 years	_____	_____
e. $101,690	$3,600	27 years	_____	_____

WORD PROBLEMS

4. North Shore Grinding purchased a lathe for $37,500. This machine has a residual value of $3,000 and an expected useful life of 4 years. Prepare a depreciation schedule for the lathe using the declining-balance depreciation method. Round to the nearest whole dollar.

5. Colby Wayne paid $7,750 for a photocopy machine with an estimated life of 6 years and a residual value of $900. Prepare a depreciation schedule using the declining-balance depreciation method. Round to the nearest whole dollar.

6. The Leo Brothers purchased a machine for $8,400 that has an estimated life of 3 years. At the end of 3 years, the machine will have no value. Prepare a depreciation schedule for this machine. Round to the nearest whole dollar.

7. Fox Realty bought a computer table for $1,700. The estimated useful life of the table is 7 years. The residual value at the end of 7 years is $370. Find **(a)** the declining depreciation rate to the nearest hundredth percent, **(b)** the amount of depreciation at the end of the *third* year, and **(c)** the book value of the table at the end of the *third* year using the declining-balance depreciation method. Round to the nearest whole dollar.

8. Cashman, Inc., purchased an overhead projector for $560. It has an estimated useful life of 6 years, at which time it will have no remaining value. Find the book value at the end of 5 years using the declining-balance depreciation method. Round to the nearest whole dollar.

9. Shelley Corporation purchased a new machine for $15,000. The estimated life of the machine is 12 years with a residual value of $2,400. Find **(a)** the declining-balance depreciation rate as a fraction and as a percent (hundredth percent), **(b)** the amount of depreciation at the end of the first year, **(c)** the accumulated depreciation at the end of 7 years, and **(d)** the book value at the end of 9 years. Round to the nearest dollar.

Learning Unit 17–4: Modified Accelerated Cost Recovery System (MACRS) with Introduction to ACRS

DRILL PROBLEMS

1. Using the MACRS method of depreciation, find the recovery rate, first-year depreciation expense, and book value of the asset at the end of the first year. Round to the nearest whole dollar.

	Cost of asset	Recovery period	Recovery rate	Depreciation expense	End-of-year book value
a.	$2,500	3 years	____	_____	_____
b.	$52,980	3 years	____	_____	_____
c.	$4,250	5 years	____	_____	_____
d.	$128,950	10 years	____	_____	_____
e.	$13,775	5 years	____	_____	_____

2. Find the accumulated depreciation at the end of the second year for each of the following assets. Round to the nearest whole dollar.

	Cost of asset	Recovery period	Accumulated depreciation at end of 2nd year using MACRS	Book value at end of 2nd year using MACRS
a.	$2,500	3 years	_____	_____
b.	$52,980	3 years	_____	_____
c.	$4,250	5 years	_____	_____
d.	$128,950	10 years	_____	_____
e.	$13,775	5 years	_____	_____

WORD PROBLEMS

3. Colby Wayne paid $7,750 for a photocopy machine that is classified as equipment and has a residual value of $900. Prepare a depreciation schedule using the MACRS depreciation method. Round all calculations to the nearest whole dollar.

4. Fox Realty bought a computer table for $1,700. The table is classified as furniture. The residual value at the end of the table's useful life is $370. Using the MACRS depreciation method, find **(a)** the amount of depreciation at the end of the *third* year, **(b)** the total accumulated depreciation at the end of year 3, and **(c)** the book value of the table at the end of the *third* year. Round all calculations to the nearest dollar.

5. Cashman, Inc., purchased an overhead projector for $560. It is classified as office equipment and will have no residual value. Find the book value at the end of 5 years using the MACRS depreciation method. Round to the nearest whole dollar.

6. Shelley Corporation purchased a new machine for $15,000. The machine is comparable to equipment used for two-way exchange of voice and data with a residual value of $2,400. Find **(a)** the amount of depreciation at the end of the first year, **(b)** the accumulated depreciation at the end of 7 years, and **(c)** the book value at the end of 9 years. Round to the nearest dollar.

7.* Wolfe Ltd. purchased a supercomputer for $75,000 at the beginning of 1996. The computer is classified as a 5-year asset and will have a residual value of $15,000. Using MACRS, find **(a)** the depreciation amount for 1996, **(b)** the accumulated depreciation at the end of 1997, **(c)** the book value at the end of 1998, and **(d)** the last year that the asset will be depreciated.

8.* Cummins Engine Company uses a straight-line depreciation method to calculate the cost of an asset of $1,200,000 with a $200,000 residual value and a life expectancy of 15 years. How much would Cummins have for depreciation expense for each of the first 2 years? Round to the nearest dollar for each year.

9. An article in an issue of *Management Accounting* stated that Cummins Engine Company changed its depreciation. The cost of its asset was $1,200,000 with a $200,000 residual value (with a life expectancy of 15 years) and an estimated productive capacity of 864,000 products. Cummins produced 59,000 products this year. What would it write off for depreciation using the units-of-production method?

*These problems are placed here for a quick review.

Classroom Notes

Name _____   Date _____

Learning Unit 18–1:   Assigning Costs to Ending Inventory—Specific Identification; Weighted Average; FIFO; LIFO

DRILL PROBLEMS

1. Given the value of the beginning inventory, purchases for the year, and ending inventory, find the cost of goods available for sale and the cost of goods sold.

	Beginning inventory	Purchases	Ending inventory	Cost of goods available for sale	Cost of goods sold
a.	$1,000	$4,120	$2,100	_____	_____
b.	$52,400	$270,846	$49,700	_____	_____
c.	$205	$48,445	$376	_____	_____
d.	$78,470	$2,788,560	$100,600	_____	_____
e.	$965	$53,799	$2,876	_____	_____

2. Find the missing amounts; then calculate the number of units available for sale and the cost of the goods available for sale.

Date	Category	Quantity	Unit cost	Total cost
January 1	Beginning inventory	1,207	$45	_____
February 7	Purchase	850	$46	_____
April 19	Purchase	700	$47	_____
July 5	Purchase	1,050	$49	_____
November 2	Purchase	450	$52	_____
Goods available for sale		_____		_____

3. Using the *specific identification* method, find the ending inventory and cost of goods sold for the merchandising concern in Problem 2.

Remaining inventory	Unit cost	Total cost
20 units from beginning inventory	_____	_____
35 units from February 7	_____	_____
257 units from July 5	_____	_____
400 units from November 2	_____	_____
Cost of ending inventory		_____
Cost of goods sold		_____

4. Using the *weighted-average* method, find the average cost per unit (to the nearest cent) and the cost of ending inventory.

	Units available for sale	Cost of goods available for sale	Units in ending inventory	Weighted-average unit cost	Cost of ending inventory
a.	2,350	$120,320	1,265	_____	_____
b.	7,090	$151,017	1,876	_____	_____
c.	855	$12,790	989	_____	_____
d.	12,964	$125,970	9,542	_____	_____
e.	235,780	$507,398	239,013	_____	_____

5. Use the *FIFO* method of inventory valuation to determine the value of ending inventory, which consists of 40 units, and the cost of goods sold.

Date	Category	Quantity	Unit cost	Total cost
January 1	Beginning inventory	37	$219.00	_____
March 5	Purchases	18	230.60	_____
June 17	Purchases	22	255.70	_____
October 18	Purchases	34	264.00	_____
Goods available for sale		____		_____

Ending inventory = _____   Cost of goods sold = _____

6. Use the *LIFO* method of inventory valuation to determine the value of the ending inventory, which consists of 40 units, and the cost of goods sold.

Date	Category	Quantity	Unit cost	Total cost
January 1	Beginning inventory	37	$219.00	_____
March 5	Purchases	18	230.60	_____
June 17	Purchases	22	255.70	_____
October 18	Purchases	34	264.00	_____
Goods available for sale		___		_____

Ending inventory = _____   Cost of goods sold = _____

WORD PROBLEMS

7. At the beginning of September, Green's of Gloucester had 13 yellow raincoats in stock. These raincoats cost $36.80 each. During the month, Green's purchased 14 raincoats for $37.50 each and 16 raincoats for $38.40 each, and they sold 26 raincoats. Calculate **(a)** the average unit cost (round to the nearest cent) and **(b)** the ending inventory value using the weighted-average method.

8. If Green's of Gloucester (Problem 7) used the FIFO method, what would the value of the ending inventory be?

9. If Green's of Gloucester (Problem 7) used the LIFO method, what would the value of the ending inventory be?

10. Hobby Caterers purchased recycled-paper sketch pads during the year as follows:

January	350 pads for $.27 each
March	400 pads for $.31 each
July	200 pads for $.36 each
October	850 pads for $.26 each
November	400 pads for $.31 each

    At the end of the year, the company had 775 of these sketch pads in stock. Find the ending inventory value using **(a)** the weighted-average method (round to the nearest cent), **(b)** the FIFO method, and **(c)** the LIFO method.

11. On March 1, Sandler's Shoe Store had the following sports shoes in stock:

    13 pairs running shoes for $33 a pair
    22 pairs walking shoes for $29 a pair
    35 pairs aerobic shoes for $26 a pair
    21 pairs cross-trainers for $52 a pair

    During the month Sandler's sold 10 pairs of running shoes, 15 pairs of walking shoes, 28 pairs of aerobic shoes, and 12 pairs of cross-trainers. Use the specific identification method to find **(a)** the cost of the goods available for sale, **(b)** the value of the ending inventory, and **(c)** the cost of goods sold.

Learning Unit 18–2: Retail Method; Gross Profit Method; Inventory Turnover; Distribution of Overhead

DRILL PROBLEMS

1. Given the following information, calculate **(a)** the goods available for sale at cost and retail, **(b)** the cost ratio (to the nearest thousandth), **(c)** the ending inventory at retail, and **(d)** the cost of the March 31 inventory (to the nearest dollar) by the retail inventory method.

	Cost	Retail
Beginning inventory, March 1	$57,300	$95,500
Purchases during March	$28,400	$48,000
Sales during March		$79,000

2. Given the following information, use the gross profit method to calculate **(a)** the cost of goods available for sale, **(b)** the cost percentage, **(c)** the estimated cost of goods sold, and **(d)** the estimated cost of the inventory as of April 30.

Beginning inventory, April 1	$30,000
Net purchases during April	81,800
Sales during April	98,000
Average gross profit on sales	40%

3. Given the following information, find the average inventory.

Merchandise inventory, January 1, 200A	$82,000
Merchandise inventory, December 31, 200A	$88,000

4. Given the following information, find the inventory turnover for the company in Problem 3 to the nearest hundredth.

Cost of goods sold (12/31/0A) $625,000

5. Given the following information, calculate the **(a)** average inventory at retail, **(b)** average inventory at cost, **(c)** inventory turnover at retail, and **(d)** inventory turnover at cost. Round to the nearest hundredth.

	Cost	Retail
Merchandise inventory, January 1	$ 250,000	$ 355,000
Merchandise inventory, December 31	$ 235,000	$ 329,000
Cost of goods sold	$1,525,000	
Sales		$2,001,000

6. Given the floor space for the following departments, find the entire floor space and the percent each department represents.

		Percent of floor space
Department A	15,000 square feet	_____
Department B	25,000 square feet	_____
Department C	10,000 square feet	_____
Total floor space	50,000 square feet	_____

7. If the total overhead for all the departments (Problem 6) is $200,000, how much of the overhead expense should be allocated to each department?

	Overhead/department
Department A	_____
Department B	_____
Department C	_____

WORD PROBLEMS

8. During the accounting period, Ward's Greenery sold $290,000 of merchandise at marked retail prices. At the end of the period, the following information was available from Ward's records:

	Cost	Retail
Beginning inventory	$ 53,000	$ 79,000
Net purchases	$204,000	$280,000

Use the retail method to estimate Ward's ending inventory at cost. Round the cost ratio to the nearest thousandth.

9. On January 1, Benny's Retail Mart had a $49,000 inventory at cost. During the first quarter of the year, Benny's made net purchases of $199,900. Benny's records show that during the past several years, the store's gross profit on sales has averaged 35%. If Benny's records show $275,000 in sales for the quarter, estimate the ending inventory for the first quarter, using the gross profit method.

10. On April 4, there was a big fire and the entire inventory of R. W. Wilson Company was destroyed. The company records were salvaged. They showed the following information:

Sales (January 1 through April 4)	$127,000
Merchandise inventory, January 1	16,000
Net purchases	71,250

On January 1, the inventory was priced to sell for $38,000 and additional items bought during the period were priced to sell for $102,000. Calculate the cost of the inventory that was destroyed by the fire using the retail method. Round the cost ratio to the nearest thousandth.

11. During the past 4 years, the average gross margin on sales for R. W. Wilson Company was 36% of net sales. Using the data in Problem 10, calculate the cost of the ending inventory destroyed by fire using the gross profit method.

12. Chase Bank has to make a decision on whether to grant a loan to Sally's Furniture store. The lending officer is interested in how often Sally's inventory is turned over. Using selected information from Sally's income statement, calculate the inventory turnover for Sally's Furniture Store (to the nearest hundredth).

Merchandise inventory, January 1, 200A	$ 43,000
Merchandise inventory, December 31, 200A	55,000
Cost of goods sold	128,000

13. Wanting to know more about a business he was considering buying, Jake Paige studied the business's books. He found that beginning inventory for the previous year was $51,000 at cost and $91,800 at retail, ending inventory was $44,000 at cost and $72,600 at retail, sales were $251,000, and cost of goods sold was $154,000. Using this information, calculate for Jake the inventory turnover at cost and the inventory turnover at retail.

14. Ralph's Retail Outlet has calculated its expenses for the year. Total overhead expenses are $147,000. Ralph's accountant must allocate this overhead to four different departments. Given the following information regarding the floor space occupied by each department, calculate how much overhead expense should be allocated to each department.

Department W	12,000 square feet
Department X	9,000 square feet
Department Y	14,000 square feet
Department Z	7,000 square feet

15. How much overhead would be allocated to each department of Ralph's Retail Outlet (Problem 14) if the basis of allocation were the sales of each department? Sales for each of the departments were:

Department W	$110,000
Department X	$120,000
Department Y	$170,000
Department Z	$100,000

Name _____   Date _____

Learning Unit 19–1:   Sales and Excise Taxes

DRILL PROBLEMS

1. Calculate the sales tax and the total amount due for each of the following:

	Total sales	Sales tax rate	Sales tax	Total amount due
a.	$536	5%	_____	_____
b.	$11,980	6%	_____	_____
c.	$3,090	$8\frac{1}{4}\%$	_____	_____
d.	$17.65	$5\frac{1}{2}\%$	_____	_____
e.	$294	7.42%	_____	_____

2. Find the amount of actual sales and amount of sales tax on the following total receipts:

	Total receipts	Sales tax rate	Actual sales	Sales tax
a.	$27,932.15	5.5%	_____	_____
b.	$35,911.53	7%	_____	_____
c.	$115,677.06	$6\frac{1}{2}\%$	_____	_____
d.	$142.96	$5\frac{1}{4}\%$	_____	_____
e.	$5,799.24	4.75%	_____	_____

3. Find the sales tax, excise tax, and total cost for each of the following items:

	Retail price	Sales tax, 5.2%	Excise tax, 11%	Total cost
a.	$399	_____	_____	_____
b.	$22,684	_____	_____	_____
c.	$7,703	_____	_____	_____

4. Calculate the amount, subtotal, sales tax, and total amount due of the following:

Quantity	Description	Unit price	Amount
3	Taxable item	$4.30	_____
2	Taxable item	$5.23	_____
4	Taxable item	$1.20	_____
		Subtotal	_____
		5% sales tax	_____
		Total	_____

5. Given the sales tax rate and the amount of the sales tax, calculate the price of the following purchases (before tax was added):

	Tax rate	Tax amount	Price of purchase
a.	7%	$71.61	_____
b.	$5\frac{1}{2}\%$	$3.22	_____

6. Given the sales tax rate and the total price (including tax), calculate the price of the following purchases (before the tax was added):

	Tax rate	Total price	Price of purchase
a.	5%	$340.20	_____
b.	6%	$1,224.30	_____

WORD PROBLEMS

7. In a state with a 4.75% sales tax, what will be the sales tax and the total price of a video game marked $110?

8. Browning's invoice included a sales tax of $38.15. If the sales tax rate is 6%, what was the total cost of the taxable goods on the invoice?

9. David Bowan paid a total of $2,763 for a new computer. If this includes a sales tax of 5.3%, what was the marked price of the computer?

10. After a 5% sales tax and a 12% excise tax, the total cost of a leather jacket was $972. What was the selling price of the jacket?

11. A customer at the RDM Discount Store purchased four tubes of toothpaste priced at $1.88 each, six toothbrushes for $1.69 each, and three bottles of shampoo for $2.39 each. What did the customer have to pay if the sales tax is $5\frac{1}{2}$%?

12. Bill Harrington purchased a mountain bike for $875. Bill had to pay a sales tax of 6% and an excise tax of 11%. What was the total amount Bill had to pay for his mountain bike?

13. Donna DeCoff received a bill for $754 for a new chair she had purchased. The bill included a 6.2% sales tax and a delivery charge of $26. What was the selling price of the chair?

Learning Unit 19–2: Property Tax

DRILL PROBLEMS

1. Find the assessed value of the following properties (round to the nearest whole dollar):

Market value	Assessment rate	Assessed value
a. $195,000	35%	_____
b. $1,550,900	50%	_____
c. $75,000	75%	_____
d. $2,585,400	65%	_____
e. $349,500	85%	_____

2. Find the tax rate for each of the following municipalities (round to the nearest tenth of a percent):

Budget needed	Total assessed value	Tax rate
a. $2,594,000	$44,392,000	_____
b. $17,989,000	$221,900,000	_____
c. $6,750,000	$47,635,000	_____
d. $13,540,000	$143,555,500	_____
e. $1,099,000	$12,687,000	_____

3. Express each of the following tax rates in all the indicated forms:

	By percent	Per $100 of assessed value	Per $1,000 of assessed value	In mills
a.	7.45%	_____	_____	_____
b.	_____	$14.24	_____	_____
c.	_____	_____	_____	90.8
d.	_____	_____	$62.00	_____

4. Calculate the property tax due for each of the following:

Total assessed value	Tax rate	Total property tax due
a. $12,900	$6.60 per $100	_____
b. $175,400	43 mills	_____
c. $320,500	2.7%	_____
d. $2,480,000	$17.85 per $1,000	_____
e. $78,900	59 mills	_____
f. $225,550	$11.39 per $1,000	_____
g. $198,750	$2.63 per $100	_____

WORD PROBLEMS

5. The county of Chelsea approved a budget of $3,450,000, which had to be raised through property taxation. If the total assessed value of properties in the county of Chelsea was $37,923,854, what will the tax rate be? The tax rate is stated per $100 of assessed valuation.

6. Linda Tawse lives in Camden and her home has a market value of $235,000. Property in Camden is assessed at 55% of its market value, and the tax rate for the current year is $64.75 per $1,000. What is the assessed valuation of Linda's home?

7. Using the information in Problem 6, find the amount of property tax that Linda will have to pay.

8. Mary Faye Souza has property with a fair market value of $219,500. Property in Mary Faye's city is assessed at 65% of its market value and the tax rate is $3.64 per $100. How much is Mary Faye's property tax due?

9. Cagney's Greenhouse has a fair market value of $1,880,000. Property is assessed at 35% by the city. The tax rate is 6.4%. What is the property tax due for Cagney's Greenhouse?

10. In Chester County, property is assessed at 40% of its market value, the residential tax rate is $12.30 per $1,000, and the commercial tax rate is $13.85 per $1,000. What is the property tax due on a home that has a market value of $205,000?

11. Using the information in Problem 10, find the property tax due on a grocery store with a market value of $5,875,000.

12. Bob Rose's home is assessed at $195,900. Last year the tax rate was 11.8 mills, and this year the rate was raised to 13.2 mills. How much more will Bob have to pay in taxes this year?

Classroom Notes

Name _____   Date _____

Learning Unit 20–1:   Life Insurance

DRILL PROBLEMS

1. Use the table in the *Business Math Handbook* to find the annual premium per $1,000 of life insurance and calculate the annual premiums for each policy listed. Assume the insureds are males.

Face value of policy	Type of insurance	Age at issue	Annual premium per $1,000	Number of $1,000s in face value	Annual premium
a. $25,000	Straight life	31	_____	_____	_____
b. $40,500	20-year endowment	40	_____	_____	_____
c. $200,000	Straight life	44	_____	_____	_____
d. $62,500	20-payment life	25	_____	_____	_____
e. $12,250	5-year term	35	_____	_____	_____
f. $42,500	20-year endowment	42	_____	_____	_____

2. Use Table 20.1 to find the annual premium for each of the following life insurance policies. Assume the insured is a 30-year-old male.

Face value of policy	Five-year term policy	Straight life policy	Twenty-payment life policy	Twenty-year endowment
a. $50,000	_____	_____	_____	_____
b. $1,000,000	_____	_____	_____	_____
c. $250,000	_____	_____	_____	_____
d. $72,500	_____	_____	_____	_____

3. Use the table in the *Business Math Handbook* to find the annual premium for each of the following life insurance policies. Assume the insured is a 30-year-old female.

Face value of policy	Five-year term policy	Straight life policy	Twenty-payment life policy	Twenty-year endowment
a. $50,000	_____	_____	_____	_____
b. $1,000,000	_____	_____	_____	_____
c. $250,000	_____	_____	_____	_____
d. $72,500	_____	_____	_____	_____

4. Use the table in the *Business Math Handbook* to find the nonforfeiture options for the following policies:

Years policy in force	Type of policy	Face value	Cash value	Amount of paid-up insurance	Extended term
a. 10	Straight life	$25,000	_____	_____	_____
b. 20	20-year endowment	$500,000	_____	_____	_____
c. 5	20-payment life	$2,000,000	_____	_____	_____
d. 15	Straight life	$750,000	_____	_____	_____
e. 5	20-year endowment	$93,500	_____	_____	_____

WORD PROBLEMS

5. If Mr. Davis, aged 39, buys a $90,000 straight life policy, what is the amount of his annual premium?

6. If Miss Jennie McDonald, age 27, takes out a $65,000 20-year endowment policy, what premium amount will she pay each year?

7. If Gary Thomas decides to cash in his $45,000 20-payment life insurance policy after 15 years, what cash surrender value will he receive?

8. Mary Allyn purchased a $70,000 20-year endowment policy when she was 26 years old. Ten years later, she decided that she could no longer afford the premiums. If Mary decides to convert her policy to paid-up insurance, what amount of paid-up insurance coverage will she have?

9. Peter and Jane Rizzo are both 28 years old and are both planning to take out $50,000 straight life insurance policies. What is the difference in the annual premiums they will have to pay?

10. Paul Nasser purchased a $125,000 straight life policy when he was 30 years old. He is now 50 years old. Two months ago, he slipped in the bathtub and injured his back; he will not be able to return to his regular job for several months. Due to a lack of income, he feels that he can no longer continue to pay the premiums on his life insurance policy. If Paul decides to surrender his policy for cash, how much cash will he receive?

11. If Paul Nasser (Problem 10) chooses to convert his policy to paid-up insurance, what will the face value of his new policy be?

Learning Unit 20–2: Fire Insurance

DRILL PROBLEMS

1. Use the tables in the *Business Math Handbook* to find the premium for each of the following:

	Rating of area	Building class	Building value	Value of contents	Total annual premium
a.	3	A	$80,000	$32,000	_____
b.	2	B	$340,000	$202,000	_____
c.	2	A	$221,700	$190,000	_____
d.	1	B	$96,400	$23,400	_____
e.	3	B	$65,780	$62,000	_____

2. Use the tables in the *Business Math Handbook* to find the short-term premium and the amount of refund due if the insured cancels.

	Annual premium	Months of coverage	Short-term premium	Refund due
a.	$1,860	3	_____	_____
b.	$650	7	_____	_____
c.	$1,200	10	_____	_____
d.	$341	12	_____	_____
e.	$1,051	4	_____	_____

3. Find the amount to be paid for each of the following losses:

	Property value	Coinsurance clause	Insurance required	Insurance carried	Amount of loss	Insurance company pays (indemnity)
a.	$85,000	80%	_____	$70,000	$60,000	_____
b.	$52,000	80%	_____	$45,000	$50,000	_____
c.	$44,000	80%	_____	$33,000	$33,000	_____
d.	$182,000	80%	_____	$127,400	$61,000	_____

WORD PROBLEMS

4. Mary Rose wants to purchase fire insurance for her building, which is rated as Class B; the rating of the area is 2. If her building is worth $225,000 and the contents are worth $70,000, what will her annual premium be?

5. Janet Ambrose owns a Class A building valued at $180,000. The contents of the building are valued at $145,000. The territory rating is 3. What is her annual fire insurance premium?

6. Jack Altshuler owns a building worth $355,500. The contents are worth $120,000. The classification of the building is B, and the rating of the area is 1. What annual premium must Jack pay for his fire insurance?

7. Jay Viola owns a store valued at $460,000. His fire insurance policy (which has an 80% coinsurance clause) has a face value of $345,000. A recent fire resulted in a loss of $125,000. How much will the insurance company pay?

8. The building that is owned by Tally's Garage is valued at $275,000 and is insured for $225,000. The policy has an 80% coinsurance clause. If there is a fire in the building and the damages amount to $220,000, how much of the loss will be paid for by the insurance company?

9. Michael Dannon owns a building worth $420,000. He has a fire insurance policy with a face value of $336,000 (there is an 80% coinsurance clause). There was recently a fire that resulted in a $400,000 loss. How much money will he receive from the insurance company?

10. Rice's Rent-A-Center business is worth $375,000. He has purchased a $250,000 fire insurance policy. The policy has an 80% coinsurance clause. What will Rice's reimbursement be (a) after a $150,000 fire and (b) after a $330,000 fire?

11. If Maria's Pizza Shop is valued at $210,000 and is insured for $147,000 with a policy that contains an 80% coinsurance clause, what settlement is due after a fire that causes (a) $150,000 in damages and (b) $175,000 in damages?

Learning Unit 20–3: Auto Insurance

DRILL PROBLEMS

1. Calculate the annual premium for compulsory coverage for each of the following.

Driver classification	Bodily	Property	Total premium
a. 17	_____	_____	_____
b. 20	_____	_____	_____
c. 10	_____	_____	_____

2. Calculate the amount of money the insurance company and the driver should pay for each of the following accidents, assuming the driver carries compulsory insurance only.

Accident and court award	Insurance company pays	Driver pays
a. Driver hit one person and court awarded $15,000.	_____	_____
b. Driver hit one person and court awarded $12,000 for personal injury.	_____	_____
c. Driver hit two people; court awarded first person $9,000 and the second person $12,000.	_____	_____

3. Calculate the additional premium payment for each of the following options.

Optional insurance coverage	Addition to premium
a. Bodily injury 50/100/25, driver class 20	_____
b. Bodily injury 25/60/10, driver class 17	_____
c. Collision insurance, driver class 10, age group 3, symbol 5, deductible $100	_____
d. Comprehensive insurance, driver class 10, age group 3, symbol 5, deductible $200	_____
e. Substitute transportation, towing, and labor; driver class 10, age group 3, symbol 5	_____

4. Compute the annual premium for compulsory insurance with optional liability coverage for bodily injury and damage to someone else's property.

Driver classification	Bodily coverage	Premium
a. 17	50/100/25	_____
b. 20	100/300/10	_____
c. 10	25/60/25	_____
d. 18	250/500/50	_____
e. 20	25/50/10	_____

5. Calculate the annual premium for each of the following drivers with the indicated options. All drivers must carry compulsory insurance.

Driver classification	Car age	Car symbol	Bodily injury	Collision	Comprehensive	Transportation and towing	Annual premium
a. 10	2	4	50/100/10	$100 deductible	$300 deductible	Yes	_____
b. 18	3	2	25/60/25	$200 deductible	$200 deductible	Yes	_____

WORD PROBLEMS

6. Ann Centerino's driver classification is 10. She carries only compulsory insurance coverage. What annual insurance premium must she pay?

7. Gary Hines is a class 18 driver. He wants to add optional bodily injury and property damage of 250/500/50 to his compulsory insurance coverage. What will be Gary's total annual premium?

8. Sara Goldberg wants optional bodily injury coverage of 50/100/25 and collision coverage with a deductible of $300 in addition to the compulsory coverage her state requires. Sara is a class 17 driver and has a symbol 4 car that is 2 years old. What annual premium must Sara pay?

9. Karen Babson has just purchased a new car with a symbol of 8. She wants bodily injury and property liability of 500/1,000/100, comprehensive and collision insurance with a $200 deductible, and transportation and towing coverage. If Karen is a class 10 driver, what will be her annual insurance premium? There is no compulsory insurance requirement in her state. Assume age group 1.

10. Craig Haberland is a class 18 driver. He has a 5-year-old car with a symbol of 4. His state requires compulsory insurance coverage. In addition, he wishes to purchase collision and comprehensive coverage with the maximum deductible. He also wants towing insurance. What will Craig's annual insurance premium be?

11. Nancy Poland has an insurance policy with limits of 10/20. If Nancy injures a pedestrian and the judge awards damages of $18,000, **(a)** how much will the insurance company pay and **(b)** how much will Nancy pay?

12. Peter Bell carries insurance with bodily injury limits of 25/60. Peter is in an accident and is charged with injuring four people. The judge awards damages of $10,000 to each of the injured parties. How much will the insurance company pay? How much will Peter pay?

13. Jerry Greeley carries an insurance policy with bodily injury limits of 25/60. Jerry is in an accident and is charged with injuring four people. If the judge awards damages of $20,000 to each of the injured parties, **(a)** how much will the insurance company pay and **(b)** how much will Jerry pay?

14. An issue of *Your Money* reported that the Illinois Department of Insurance gave a typical premium for a brick house in Chicago built in 1950, assuming no policy discounts and a replacement cost estimated at $100,000. With a $100 deductible, the annual premium will be $653. Using the rate in your textbook, with a rating area 3 and class B, what would be the annual premium? (This problem reviews fire insurance.)

15. An issue of *Money* ran a story on cutting car insurance premiums. Raising the car insurance deductible to $500 will cut the collision premium 15%. Theresa Mendex insures her car; her age group is 5 and symbol is 5. What would be her reduction if she changed her policy to a $500 deductible? What would the collision insurance now cost?

16. Robert Stuono lost his life insurance when he was downsized from an investment banking company early this year. So Stuono, age 44, enlisted the help of an independent agent who works with several insurance companies. His goal is $350,000 in term coverage with a level premium for 5 years. What will Robert's annual premium be for term insurance? (This problem reviews life insurance.)

Classroom Notes

Name _____   Date _____

Learning Unit 21–1:   Stocks

DRILL PROBLEMS

52 weeks		Stocks	SYM	Div	Yld %	PE	Vol 100s	High	Low	Close	Net chg
Hi	Lo										
43.88	25.51	Disney	DIS	.21	.8	49	49633	27.69	26.50	27.69	+0.63

1. From the listed information for Disney, complete the following:
   a. _____ was the highest price at which Disney stock traded during the year.
   b. _____ was the lowest price at which Disney stock traded during the year.
   c. _____ was the amount of the dividend Disney paid to shareholders last year.
   d. _____ is the dividend amount a shareholder with 100 shares would receive.
   e. _____ is the rate of return the stock yielded to its stockholders.
   f. _____ is how many times the earnings per share the stock is selling for.
   g. _____ is the number of shares traded on the day of this stock quote.
   h. _____ is the highest price paid for Disney stock on this day.
   i. _____ is the lowest price paid for Disney stock on this day.
   j. _____ is the change in price from yesterday's closing price.

2. Use the Disney information to show how the yield percent was calculated.

3. What was the price of the last trade of Disney stock yesterday?

WORD PROBLEMS

4. Assume a stockbroker's commission of 2%. What will it cost to purchase 200 shares of Saplent Corporation at $10.75?

5. In Problem 4, the stockbroker's commission for selling stock is the same as that for buying stock. If the customer who purchased 200 shares at $10.75 sells the 200 shares of stock at the end of the year at $18.12, what will be the gain on investment?

6. Holtz Corporation's records show 80,000 shares of preferred stock issued. The preferred dividend is $2 per share, which is cumulative. The records show 750,000 shares of common stock issued. In 2009, no dividends were paid. In 2010, the board of directors declared a dividend of $582,500. What are **(a)** the total amount of dividends paid to preferred stockholders, **(b)** the total amount of dividends paid to common stockholders, and **(c)** the amount of the common dividend per share?

7. Melissa Tucker bought 300 shares of Delta Air Lines stock listed at $61.22 per share. What is the total amount she paid if the stockbroker's commission is 2.5%?

8. A year later, Melissa (Problem 7) sold the stock she had purchased. The market price of the stock at this time was $72.43. Delta Air Lines had paid its shareholders a dividend of $1.20 per share. If the stockbroker's commission to sell stock is 2.5%, what gain did Melissa realize?

9. The board of directors of Parker Electronics, Inc., declared a $539,000 dividend. If the corporation has 70,000 shares of common stock outstanding, what is the dividend per share?

Learning Unit 21–2: Bonds

DRILL PROBLEMS

Bond	Current yield	Sales	Close	Net change
IBM $10\frac{1}{4}$ 09	10.0	11	$102\frac{1}{2}$	$+\frac{1}{8}$

1. From the bond listing above complete the following:
   a. _____ is the name of the company.
   b. _____ is the percent of interest paid on the bond.
   c. _____ is the year in which the bond matures.
   d. _____ is the total interest for the year.
   e. _____ was yesterday's close on the IBM bond.

2. Show how to calculate the current yield of 10.0% for IBM. (Trade commissions have been omitted.)

3. Use the information for the IBM bonds to calculate (a) the amount the last bond traded for on this day and (b) the amount the last bond traded for yesterday.

4. What will be the annual interest payment (a) to the bondholder assuming he paid $101\frac{3}{4}$ and (b) to the bondholder who purchased the bond for $102\frac{1}{2}$?

5. If Terry Gambol purchased three IBM bonds at this day's closing price, (a) what will be her total cost excluding commission and (b) how much interest will she receive for the year?

6. Calculate the bond yield (to the nearest tenth percent) for each of the following:

Bond interest rate	Purchase price	Bond yield
a. 7%	97	_____
b. $9\frac{1}{2}\%$	$101\frac{5}{8}$	_____
c. $13\frac{1}{4}\%$	$104\frac{1}{4}$	_____

7. For each of the following, state whether the bond sold at a premium or a discount and give the amount of the premium or discount.

Bond interest rate	Purchase price	Premium or discount
a. 7%	97	_____
b. $9\frac{1}{2}\%$	$101\frac{5}{8}$	_____
c. $13\frac{1}{4}\%$	$104\frac{1}{4}$	_____

WORD PROBLEMS

8. Rob Morrisey purchased a $1,000 bond that was quoted at $102\frac{1}{4}$ and paying $8\frac{7}{8}\%$ interest. (a) How much did Rob pay for the bond? (b) What was the premium or discount? (c) How much annual interest will he receive?

9. Jackie Anderson purchased a bond that was quoted at $62\frac{1}{2}$ and paying interest of $10\frac{1}{2}\%$. (a) How much did Jackie pay for the bond? (b) What was the premium or discount? (c) What interest will Jackie receive annually? (d) What is the bond's current annual yield (to the nearest tenth percent)?

10. Swartz Company issued bonds totaling $2,000,000 in order to purchase updated equipment. If the bonds pay interest of 11%, what is the total amount of interest the Swartz Company must pay semiannually?

11. The RJR and ACyan companies have both issued bonds that are paying $7\frac{3}{8}\%$ interest. The quoted price of the RJR bond is $94\frac{1}{8}$, and the quoted price of the ACyan bond is $102\frac{7}{8}$. Find the current annual yield on each (to the nearest tenth percent).

12. Mary Rowe purchased 25 bonds of Chrysler Corporation $8\frac{3}{8}\%$ bonds of 2009. The bonds closed at $93\frac{1}{4}$. Find **(a)** the total purchase price and **(b)** the amount of the first semiannual interest payment Mary will receive.

13. What is the annual yield (to the nearest hundredth percent) of the bonds Mary Rowe purchased?

14. Mary Rowe purchased a $1,000 bond listed as ARch $10\frac{7}{8}$ 09 for $122\frac{3}{4}$. What is the annual yield of this bond (to the nearest tenth percent)?

Learning Unit 21–3: Mutual Funds

DRILL PROBLEMS

From the following, calculate the NAV. Round to the nearest cent.

	Current market value of fund investments	Current liabilities	Number of shares outstanding	NAV
1.	$6,800,000	$850,000	500,000	_____
2.	$11,425,000	$690,000	810,000	_____
3.	$22,580,000	$1,300,000	1,400,000	_____

Complete the following using this information:

NAV	Net change	Fund name	Inv. obj.	YTD %Ret	Total return 1 Yr R
$23.48	+.14	EuroA	Eu	+37.3	+7.6 E

4. NAV _____
5. NAV change _____
6. Total return year to date _____
7. Return for the last 12 months _____
8. What does an E rating mean? _____

Calculate the commission (load) charge and the offer to buy.

	NAV	% commission (load) charge	Dollar amount of commission (load) charge	Offer price
9.	$17.00	$8\frac{1}{2}\%$	_____	_____
10.	$21.55	6%	_____	_____
11.	$14.10	4%	_____	_____

WORD PROBLEMS

12. Paul wanted to know how his Fidelity mutual fund $14.33 NAV in the newspaper was calculated. He called Fidelity, and he received the following information:

Current market value of fund investment	$7,500,000
Current liabilities	$910,000
Number of shares outstanding	460,000

Please calculate the NAV for Paul. Was the NAV in the newspaper correct?

13. Jeff Jones bought 150 shares of Putnam Vista Fund. The NAV of the fund was $9.88. The offer price was $10.49. What did Jeff pay for these 150 shares?

14. Pam Long purchased 300 shares of the no-load Scudder's European Growth Company Fund. The NAV is $12.61. What did Pam pay for the 300 shares?

15. Assume in Problem 14 that 8 years later Pam sells her 300 shares. The NAV at the time of sale was $12.20. What is the amount of her profit or loss on the sale?

16. Financial planner J. Michael Martin recommended that Jim Kelly choose a long-term bond because it gives high income while Kelly waits for better stock market opportunities down the road. The bond Martin recommended matures in 2010 and was originally issued at $8\frac{1}{2}\%$ interest and the current yield is 7.9%. What would be the current selling price for this bond and how would that price appear in the bond quotations?

17.

Bonds	Vol.	Close	Net chg.
Comp USA $9\frac{1}{2}$ 09	70	$102\frac{3}{8}$	$-\frac{1}{8}$
GMA 7 10	5	$101\frac{5}{8}$	$-1\frac{1}{4}$

From the above information, compare the two bonds for:

a. When the bonds expire.
b. The yield of each bond.
c. The current selling price.
d. Whether the bond is selling at a discount or premium.
e. Yesterday's bond close.

Name _____   Date _____

Learning Unit 22–1:   Mean, Median, and Mode

Note: Optional problems for LU 22–3 are found on page 000.

DRILL PROBLEMS

1. Find the mean for the following lists of numbers. Round to the nearest hundredth.
   a. 12, 16, 20, 25, 29   Mean _____
   b. 80, 91, 98, 82, 68, 82, 79, 90   Mean _____
   c. 9.5, 12.3, 10.5, 7.5, 10.1, 18.4, 9.8, 6.2, 11.1, 4.8, 10.6   Mean _____

2. Find the weighted mean for the following. Round to the nearest hundredth.
   a. 4, 4, 6, 8, 8, 13, 4, 6, 8   Weighted mean _____
   b. 82, 85, 87, 82, 82, 90, 87, 63, 100, 85, 87   Weighted mean _____

3. Find the median for the following:
   a. 56, 89, 47, 36, 90, 63, 55, 82, 46, 81   Median _____
   b. 59, 22, 39, 47, 33, 98, 50, 73, 54, 46, 99   Median _____

4. Find the mode for the following:
   24, 35, 49, 35, 52, 35, 52   Mode _____

5. Find the mean, median, and mode for each of the following:
   a. 72, 48, 62, 54, 73, 62, 75, 57, 62, 58, 78
      Mean _____   Median _____   Mode _____
   b. $0.50, $1.19, $0.58, $1.19, $2.83, $1.71, $2.21, $0.58, $1.29, $0.58
      Mean _____   Median _____   Mode _____
   c. $92, $113, $99, $117, $99, $105, $119, $112, $95, $116, $102, $120
      Mean _____   Median _____   Mode _____
   d. 88, 105, 120, 119, 105, 128, 160, 151, 90, 153, 107, 119, 105
      Mean _____   Median _____   Mode _____

WORD PROBLEMS

6. The sales for the year at the 8 Bed and Linen Stores were $1,442,897, $1,556,793, $1,703,767, $1,093,320, $1,443,984, $1,665,308, $1,197,692, and $1,880,443. Find the mean earnings for a Bed and Linen Store for the year.

7. To avoid having an extreme number affect the average, the manager of Bed and Linen Stores (Problem 6) would like you to find the median earnings for the 8 stores.

8. The Bed and Linen Store in Salem sells many different towels. Following are the prices of all the towels that were sold on Wednesday: $7.98, $9.98, $9.98, $11.49, $11.98, $7.98, $12.49, $12.49, $11.49, $9.98, $9.98, $16.00, and $7.98. Find the mean price of a towel.

9. Looking at the towel prices, the Salem manager (Problem 8) decided that he should have calculated a weighted mean. Find the weighted mean price of a towel.

10. The manager of the Salem Bed and Linen Store above would like to find another measure of the central tendency called the *median.* Find the median price for the towels sold.

11. The manager at the Salem Bed and Linen Store would like to know the most popular towel among the group of towels sold on Wednesday. Find the mode for the towel prices for Wednesday.

Learning Unit 22–2: Frequency Distributions and Graphs

DRILL PROBLEMS

1. A local dairy distributor wants to know how many containers of yogurt health club members consume in a month. The distributor gathered the following data:

17	17	22	14	26	23	23	15	18	16
18	15	23	18	29	20	24	17	12	15
18	19	18	20	28	21	25	21	26	14
16	18	15	19	27	15	22	19	19	13
20	17	13	24	28	18	28	20	17	16

Construct a frequency distribution table to organize this data.

2. Construct a bar graph for the Problem 1 data. The height of each bar should represent the frequency of each amount consumed.

3. To simplify the amount of data concerning yogurt consumption, construct a relative frequency distribution table. The range will be from 1 to 30 with five class intervals: 1–6, 7–12, 13–18, 19–24, and 25–30.

4. Construct a bar graph for the grouped data.

5. Prepare a pie chart to represent the above data.

WORD PROBLEMS

6. The women's department of a local department store lists its total sales for the year: January, $39,800; February, $22,400; March, $32,500; April, $33,000; May, $30,000; June, $29,200; July, $26,400; August, $24,800; September, $34,000; October, $34,200; November, $38,400; December, $41,100. Draw a line graph to represent the monthly sales of the women's department for the year. The vertical axis should represent the dollar amount of the sales.

7. The following list shows the number of television sets sold in a year by the sales associates at Souza's TV and Appliance Store.

115	125	139	127	142	153	169	126	141
130	137	150	169	157	146	173	168	156
140	146	134	123	142	129	141	122	141

Construct a relative frequency distribution table to represent the data. The range will be from 115 to 174 with intervals of 10.

8. Use the data in the distribution table for Problem 7 to construct a bar graph for the grouped data.

9. Expenses for Flora Foley Real Estate Agency for the month of June were as follows: salaries expense, $2,790; utilities expense, $280; rent expense, $2,000; commissions expense, $4,800; and other expenses, $340. Present this data in a circle graph. (First calculate the percent relationship between each item and the total, then determine the number of degrees that represents each item.)

10. Today a new Jeep costs $25,000. In 1970, the Jeep cost $4,500. What is the price relative? (Round to nearest tenth percent.)

APPENDIX B

Check Figures

Odd-Numbered Drill and Word Problems for End-of-Chapter Problems.

Challenge Problems.

Summary Practice Tests (all).

Cumulative Reviews (all).

Odd-Numbered Additional Assignments by Learning Unit from Appendix A.

Check Figures to Drill and Word Problems (Odds), Challenge Problems, Summary Practice Tests, and Cumulative Reviews

Chapter 1

End-of-Chapter Problems

1-1. 104
1-3. 158
1-5. 13,580
1-7. 113,690
1-9. 38
1-11. 3,600
1-13. 1,074
1-15. 31,110
1-17. 340,531
1-19. 126,000
1-21. 90
1-23. 86 R4
1-25. 309
1-27. 1,616
1-29. 24,876
1-31. 17,989; 18,000
1-33. 80
1-35. 144
1-37. 216
1-39. 19 R21
1-41. 7,690; 6,990
1-43. 70,470; 72,000
1-45. 700
1-47. $500; $300; $497
1-49. $240; $200; $1,200; $1,080
1-51. $2,436; $3,056; $620 more
1-53. 905,600
1-55. 1,080
1-57. 106
1-59. $547,400
1-61. $1,872,000
1-63. $4,815; $250,380
1-65. $54,872
1-67. 200,000; 10,400,000
1-69. $1,486
1-71. No Avg. $33
1-73. $796
1-75. $600,000, $150,000
1-76. $2,974,400; $800,800
1-77. $12,000 difference

Summary Practice Test

1. 7,017,243
2. Nine million, six hundred twenty-two thousand, three hundred sixty-four
3. a. 70
   b. 900
   c. 8,000
   d. 10,000
4. 17,000; 17,672
5. 8,100,000 $8,011,758
6. 829,412,000
7. 379 R19
8. 100

9. $95
10. $500; no
11. $1,000

Chapter 2

End-of-Chapter Problems

2-1. Improper
2-3. Proper
2-5. $61\frac{2}{5}$
2-7. $\frac{59}{3}$
2-9. $\frac{11}{13}$
2-11. 60 ($2 \times 2 \times 3 \times 5$)
2-13. 96 ($2 \times 2 \times 2 \times 2 \times 2 \times 3$)
2-15. $\frac{13}{21}$
2-17. $15\frac{5}{12}$
2-19. $\frac{5}{6}$
2-21. $7\frac{4}{9}$
2-23. $\frac{5}{16}$
2-25. $\frac{3}{25}$
2-27. $\frac{1}{3}$
2-29. $\frac{7}{18}$
2-31. $408\frac{3}{4}$; $128\frac{1}{4}$
2-33. $35
2-35. $1,200
2-37. $63\frac{1}{4}$ inch; $11\frac{1}{12}$ inch remain
2-39. $119\frac{1}{8}$; $48\frac{7}{8}$
2-41. $6\frac{1}{2}$ gallons
2-43. $525
2-45. $\frac{23}{36}$
2-47. $25
2-49. $3\frac{3}{4}$ lb apple; $8\frac{1}{8}$ cups flour; $\frac{5}{8}$ cup marg.; $5\frac{15}{16}$ cups of sugar; 5 teaspoon cin.
2-51. 400 people
2-53. 92 pieces
2-55. 5,800 books
2-57. $200
2-59. $45\frac{3}{16}$ inch

2-61. $62,500,000; $37,500,000
2-63. $\frac{3}{8}$
2-65. $2\frac{3}{5}$ hours
2-67. 60 sandwiches
2-68. $103\frac{3}{4}$ inch; yes 39 inch left from board #2
2-69. a. 400 homes b. $320,000
   c. 3,000 people; 2,500 people
   d. $112.50
   e. $8,800,000

Summary Practice Test

1. Mixed number
2. Proper
3. Improper
4. $18\frac{1}{9}$
5. $\frac{65}{8}$
6. 9; $\frac{7}{10}$
7. 64
8. 24 ($2 \times 2 \times 3 \times 2 \times 1 \times 1 \times 1$)
9. $6\frac{17}{20}$
10. $\frac{1}{4}$
11. $6\frac{2}{21}$
12. $\frac{1}{14}$
13. $3\frac{5}{6}$ hours
14. 7,840 rolls
15. a. 60,000 veggie
    b. 30,000 regular
16. $39\frac{1}{2}$ hours
17. $26

Chapter 3

End-of-Chapter Problems

3-1. Thousandths
3-3. .8; .76; .758
3-5. 5.8; 5.83; 5.831
3-7. 6.6; 6.56; 6.556
3-9. $4,822.78
3-11. .09
3-13. .09
3-15. .64
3-17. 14.91
3-19. $\frac{62}{100}$

3–21. $\dfrac{125}{10,000}$

3–23. $\dfrac{825}{1,000}$

3–25. $\dfrac{7,065}{10,000}$

3–27. $28\dfrac{48}{100}$

3–29. .004
3–31. .0085
3–33. 818.1279
3–35. 3.4
3–37. 2.32
3–39. 1.2; 1.26791
3–41. 4; 4.0425
3–43. 24,526.67
3–45. 161.29
3–47. 6,824.15
3–49. .04
3–51. .63
3–53. 2.585
3–55. .0086
3–57. 486
3–59. 3.950
3–61. 7,913.2
3–63. .583
3–65. $17.00
3–67. $1.40
3–69. $119.47
3–71. $8.97
3–73. $116 savings
3–75. $399.16
3–77. $105.08
3–79. $210
3–81. $73.52
3–83. $1.58; $3,713
3–85. $6,465.60
3–87. $.90; 589,176,000
3–88. $560.45

Summary Practice Test

1. 767.849
2. .7
3. .07
4. .007
5. $\dfrac{9}{10}$
6. $6\dfrac{97}{100}$
7. $\dfrac{685}{1,000}$
8. .29
9. .13
10. 4.57
11. .08
12. 390.2702
13. 9.2
14. 118.67
15. 34,684.01
16. 62,940

17. 832,224,982.1
18. $24.56
19. $936.30
20. $385.40
21. A $.12
22. $441.35
23. $28.10

Chapter 4

End-of-Chapter Problems

4–1. $4,641.33
4–3. $4,626.33
4–5. $800.72
4–7. $540.82
4–9. $577.95
4–11. $998.86
4–12. $1,862.13
4–13. $3,061.67

Summary Practice Test

1. End Bal. $15,649.21
2. $8,730
3. $1,282.70
4. $10,968.50

Chapter 5

End-of-Chapter Problems

5–1. $D = 81$
5–3. $Q = 300$
5–5. $Y = 15$
5–7. $Y = 12$
5–9. $P = 25$
5–11. 2,325
5–13. Hugh 50; Joe 250
5–15. 50 shorts; 200 T-shirts
5–17. $D = 80$
5–19. $N = 63$
5–21. $Y = 7$
5–23. $P = \$485.99$
5–25. Pete = 90; Bill = 450
5–27. 48 boxes pens;
240 batteries
5–29. $A = 135$
5–31. $M = 60$
5–33. $3,750
5–35. $W = 129$
5–37. Shift 1: 3,360; shift 2: 2,240
5–39. 22 cartons of hammers
18 cartons of wrenches
5–40. 208 children; 229 women;
1,009 total homeless
5–41. $B = 10$; $6B = 30$

Summary Practice Test

1. $541.90
2. $84,000
3. Sears, 70; Buy 560
4. Abby 200; Jill 1,000

5. 13 dishes; 78 pots
6. Pasta 300; 1,300 pizzas

Chapter 6

End-of-Chapter Problems

6–1. 74%
6–3. 90%
6–5. 356.1%
6–7. .08
6–9. .643
6–11. 1.19
6–13. 8.3%
6–15. 87.5%
6–17. $\dfrac{1}{25}$
6–19. $\dfrac{19}{60}$
6–21. $\dfrac{27}{400}$
6–23. 10.5
6–25. 102.5
6–27. 156.6
6–29. 114.88
6–31. 16.2
6–33. 141.67
6–35. 10,000
6–37. 17,777.78
6–39. 108.2%
6–41. 110%
6–43. 400%
6–45. 59.40
6–47. 1,100
6–49. 40%
6–51. −6%
6–53. 75%
6–55. $10,000
6–57. $160
6–59. 677.78%
6–61. $28,175
6–63. 94%
6–65. 19.04%; $1.21; $8.74
6–67. 39.94%
6–69. 12.8%
6–71. 1,000
6–73. $400
6–75. 25%
6–77. $44,444,400
6–79. 1,747,758
6–81. 13.3%
6–83. 40%
6–85. $1,160,000
6–87. $24,000
6–89. 29.79%
6–91. $41,176
6–93. 40%
6–95. 585,000
6–96. $18.76; $11.73; 4.00%
6–97. $55,429

Summary Practice Test

1. 92.1%
2. 40%
3. 1,588%
4. 800%
5. .42
6. .0798
7. 4.0
8. .0025
9. 16.7%
10. 33.3%
11. $\frac{31}{160}$
12. $\frac{31}{500}$
13. $540,000
14. $2,330,000
15. 75%
16. 2.67%
17. $382.61
18. $639
19. $150,000

Chapter 7

End-of-Chapter Problems

7–1. .931; .069; $20.70; $279.30
7–3. .893079; .106921; $28.76; $240.24
7–5. $369.70; $80.30
7–7. $1,392.59; $457.41
7–9. June 28; July 18
7–11. June 15; July 5
7–13. July 10; July 30
7–15. $138; $6,862
7–17. $2; $198
7–19. $408.16; $291.84
7–21. $190; $285
7–23. $1,347.50; $67.38; $1,280.12
7–25. $576.06; $48.94
7–27. $5,100; $5,250
7–29. $5,850
7–31. $8,571.43
7–33. $8,173.20
7–35. $8,333.33; $11,666.67
7–37. $99.99
7–39. $489.90; $711.10
7–41. $4,658.97
7–43. $1,083.46; $116.54
7–45. $5,008.45
7–47. Save $4.27 with Verizon
7–49. $1,500; 8.34%; $164.95; $16,330.05; $1,664.95
7–50. $4,794.99

Summary Practice Test

1. $332.50
2. $211.11
3. $819.89; $79.11

4. **a.** Nov. 14; Dec. 4
   b. March 20; April 9
   c. June 10; June 30
   d. Jan. 10; Jan. 30
5. $15; $285
6. $7,120
7. B: 20.95%
8. $1,938.78; $6,061.22
9. $7,076.35

Chapter 8

End-of-Chapter Problems

8–1. $120; $420
8–3. $4,285.71
8–5. $6.90; 45.70%
8–7. $180; $270
8–9. $110.83
8–11. $34.20; 69.8%
8–13. 11%
8–15. $3,830.40; $1,169.60; 23.39%
8–17. 16,250; $4.00
8–19. $5,000; 50%
8–21. $14.29
8–23. 535%; 84.25%
8–25. $84
8–27. 42.86%
8–29. $3.56
8–31. 20,000
8–33. $558.60
8–35. $195
8–37. $129.99
8–39. $2.31
8–41. 12,000
8–42. $4,629.63; $370.37; $10,204.08; $5,204.08 savings
8–43. $94.98; $20.36; loss

Summary Practice Test

1. $126
2. 30.26%
3. $482.76; $217.24
4. $79; 37.97%
5. $133.33
6. $292.50
7. 27.27%
8. $160
9. 25.9%
10. $1.15
11. 11,500

Cumulative Review 6, 7, 8

1. 650,000
2. $296.35
3. $133
4. $2,562.14
5. $48.75
6. $259.26
7. $1.96; $1.89

Chapter 9

End-of-Chapter Problems

9–1. 39; $292.50
9–3. $12.00; $452
9–5. $1,071
9–7. $60
9–9. $13,000
9–11. $4,500
9–13. $11,900; $6,900; $138; $388
9–15. $465; $116
9–17. $152.54; $86.80; $20.30; $1,140.36
9–19. $752.60; $113.60
9–21. $520.00; $32.24; $7.54; $43.54; $436.68
9–23. $297
9–25. $825
9–27. $1,081.61
9–29. $357; $56
9–31. $233.38; $195.22; $38.16
9–32. Difference $143.34

Summary Practice Test

1. 49; $428
2. $790
3. $24,700
4. $465; $290
5. $293.46
6. $798 SUTA; $112 FUTA; no tax in quarter 2

Chapter 10

End-of-Chapter Problems

10–1. $960; $16,960
10–3. $978.75; $18,978.75
10–5. $28.23; $613.23
10–7. $20.38; $1,020.38
10–9. $73.78; $1,273.78
10–11. $1,904.76
10–13. $4,390.61
10–15. $595.83; $10,595.83
10–17. $2,377.70
10–19. 4.7 years
10–21. $21,596.11
10–23. $714.87; $44.87
10–25. $3,569.27; $3,540.10
10–27. $2,608.65
10–29. $18,720.12
10–31. 12.37%
10–33. 72 days
10–35. 5.6%
10–36. $6,815.10; $6,834.38; $19.28 saved
10–37. $7.82; $275.33

Summary Practice Test

1. $27.23; $2,038.11
2. $86,400

3. $14,901.25
4. $14,888.90
5. $32,516
6. $191.09; $10,191.09

Chapter 11

End-of-Chapter Problems
11–1. $637.50; $17,362.50
11–3. 25 days
11–5. $51,451.39; 57; $733.18; $50,718.21
11–7. 4.04%
11–9. $8,537.50; 9.8%
11–11. $8,937
11–13. 5.06%
11–15. $5,133.33; 56; $71.87; $5,061.46
11–17. $4,836.44
11–18. $329,955.64; $329,524.33; $431.31 more
11–19. $2,127.66; 9.57%

Summary Practice Test
1. $160,000
2. $302.22; $16,697.98; $17,000; 4.1%
3. $61,132.87
4. $71,264.84
5. $57,462.50; 7.6%
6. 5.58%

Chapter 12

End-of-Chapter Problems
12–1. 4; 2%; $1,515.40; $115.40
12–3. $10,404; $404
12–5. 12.55%
12–7. 14; 1%; .8700; $3,915.00
12–9. 28; 3%; .4371; $7,692.96
12–11. 2.2879 × $7,692.96
12–13. $32,987.50
12–15. Mystic $4,775
12–17. $25,734.40
12–19. $3,807
12–21. 5.06%
12–23. $37,644
12–25. Yes, $17,908 (compounding) or $8,376 (p. v.)
12–27. $3,739.20
12–29. $13,883.30
12–31. $471,813.71; $459,313.71 int.
12–32. $689,125; $34,125 Bank B

Summary Practice Test
1. $48,760
2. $31,160
3. $133,123.12
4. No, $26,898 (compounding) or $22,308 (p. v.)

5. 6.14%
6. $46,137
7. $187,470
8. $28,916.10

Chapter 13

End-of-Chapter Problems
13–1. $321,291
13–3. $324,504
13–5. $3,118.59
13–7. End of first year $2,405.71
13–9. $1,410
13–11. $3,397.20
13–13. $59,077.80
13–15. $1,245
13–17. $900,655
13–19. $33,444
13–21. $13,838.25
13–23. Annuity $12,219.11 or $12,219.93
13–25. $3,625.60
13–27. $111,013.29
13–29. $404,313.97
13–30. $2,175; $2,501.25; $93.05
13–31. $120,747.09

Summary Practice Test
1. $100,952.82
2. $33,914.88 or $33,913.57
3. $108,722.40
4. $2,120
5. $2,054
6. $264,915.20
7. $83,304.59
8. $237,501.36
9. $473,811.99
10. $713,776.37

Cumulative Review 10, 11, 12, 13
1. Annuity $2,058.62 or $2,058.59
2. $5,118.70
3. $116,963.02
4. $3,113.92
5. $5,797.92
6. $18,465.20
7. $29,632.35
8. $55,251

Chapter 14

End-of-Chapter Problems
14–1. Finance charge $3,040
14–3. Finance charge $1,279.76; 12.75%–13%
14–5. $119.39; $119.37
14–7. $295.14; $5,164.86
14–9. $2,741; $41.12
14–11. $472.94; $4,776.40

14–13. **a.** $4,050 **b.** $1,656
    c. $5,756
    d. 14.25% to 14.50%
    e. $95.10
14–15. $415.12; $340.66; $74.46
14–17. 8.00% to 8.25%; 8.75% to 9%
14–19. $218.31 outstanding balance
14–20. $545.68; $24.32 under; $586.66; $16.66
14–21. 15.48%

Summary Practice Test
1. $26,500; $4,100
2. $52.66
3. 4.25% to 4.5%
4. $6,005.30
5. $2,003.29; $8,746.71
6. $400; $8

Chapter 15

End-of-Chapter Problems
15–1. $919.10
15–3. $1,541.70
15–5. $118,796
15–7. $1,679.04; $1,656.25; $22.79; $158,977.21
15–9. $1,680.00; $1,772.40
15–11. $636.16; $117,017.60
15–13. Payment 3, $119,857.38
15–15. $68,464.80; $59,906.70
15–17. $3,825; $2,798.33
15–18. $1,690.15; $415,954

Summary Practice Test
1. $1,020; $850; $169,830
2. $499.84; $91,942.40
3. **a.** $434.97; $75,589.20
    b. $460.08; $84,628.80
    c. $486; $93,960
    d. $512.73; $103,582.80
4. $5.71; $1,027.80
5. $251,676

Chapter 16

End-of-Chapter Problems
16–1. Total assets $55,000
16–3. Inventory −16.67%; mortgage note +13.79%
16–5. Net sales 13.62%; earnings 2008 5.94%
16–7. Depreciation $100; + 16.67%
16–9. 1.43; 1.79
16–11. .20; .23
16–13. .06; .08
16–15. 21.13%
16–17. 87.74%; 34.43%; .13; 55.47%
16–19. 2012 68% sales
16–20. Rev. 9.12%; total assets 11.39%
16–21. 3.5; 2.3

Summary Practice Test
1. a. $161,000
   b. $21,000
   c. $140,000
   d. $84,000
2. Acc. rec. 15.15%; 24.67%
3. Cash $11,000; 137.50%
4. 2,013; 74%
5. Total assets $175,000
6. a. .70 b. .50 c. 45 days
   d. 1.05 e. .25

Chapter 17

End-of-Chapter Problems
17–1. Book value (end of year) $80,000
17–3. Book value (end of year) $60,000
17–5. Book value (end of year) $40,000
17–7. Book value (end of year) $20,000
17–9. Book value (end of year) $15,000
17–11. Book value (end of year) $5,400
17–13. $1,400
17–15. $18,000
17–17. $22,560
17–19. $67,500
17–21. $6,000; $18,000
17–23. $6,760 below
17–25. $83,667
17–26. $87,750; $11.40; $21,489; 4 years
17–27. $13,320; 1.11

Summary Practice Test
1. Book value end of year 2: $10,800
2. $1,713.60
3. Acc. Dep., $4,000; $8,000; $12,000; $16,000; $20,000
4. $1,500
5. $12,600

Chapter 18

End-of-Chapter Problems
18–1. $3,300; $10,325
18–3. $543; $932
18–5. $10
18–7. $36
18–9. $72
18–11. $140.80
18–13. $147.75; $345.60
18–15. $188.65; $304.70
18–17. 3.56; 3.25
18–19. .75; $67,500
18–21. $72; $77
18–23. $120,000; $125,000
18–25. $55,120
18–27. $38,150

18–28. $64; $144; $979.20
18–29. $1,900

Summary Practice Test
1. a. 31
   b. $66.87; $93.30; $80.29
2. $40,000
3. 1.10
4. $109,275
5. $97,960

Chapter 19

End-of-Chapter Problems
19–1. $1,568
19–3. $84,905.66
19–5. $72,000
19–7. $.0233
19–9. 6.99%; $6.99; $69.90; 69.90
19–11. $4,462.50
19–13. $16,985.05
19–15. $112.92
19–17. $54,000
19–19. $6,940
19–21. $64,000
19–23. $2,251.50
19–25. $23,065 more in Minn.
19–26. .0069447; $8,700,000; $292.50; $312.51; $20.01
19–27. $979

Summary Practice Test
1. $284.76; $14.24
2. $4,710
3. $146,000
4. 5.1 mills
5. $1,237.50
6. $18,141.20

Chapter 20

End-of-Chapter Problems
20–1. $998.20
20–3. $277.50
20–5. $53,000
20–7. 21 years, 300 days
20–9. $518; $182
20–11. $16,500
20–13. $1,067
20–15. $1,855 cheaper
20–17. $801
20–19. $118,750
20–21. $1,100
20–23. $373.67
20–25. $22,900; $10,700
20–27. $24,000; $16,300
20–28. $11,662.40; $3,825; $15,366; $5,126.25; 28.37%; 37.53%
20–29. $72,000

Summary Practice Test
1. $1,993.50; $28,530

2. $2,616.60; $55,650; $115,500; 21 years 300 days
3. $234,375; $450,000
4. $990; $326.70
5. $1,755
6. Insurance company pays $31,600; Roger pays $10,000

Chapter 21

End-of-Chapter Problems
21–1. $114,897
21–3. 1.1%
21–5. 13
21–7. $24,227.04
21–9. 2009   preferred $8,000
      2010   0
      2011   preferred $127,000
      common $33,000
21–11. $2,280
21–13. $260; $2,725; 9.5%
21–15. $12.04; $−.06; 9.6%
21–17. Gain $2,918.40
21–19. 12; 2.4%
21–21. $5,043.75; $56.25
21–23. 7.3%
21–25. Stock 6.7%; bond 11.9%
21–27. Yes, $16.02
21–29. $443.80
21–30. $1,287 shs.; 2,574 shs.; 5,147 shs.; $103,756.44
21–31. $1,014.33

Summary Practice Test
1. $18,127.26
2. 8; 1.3%
3. $1.23
4. $10,476
5. 5.6%
6. $160,000
7. $14.52; $11,616

Chapter 22

End-of-Chapter Problems
22–1. 7.00
22–3. $77.23
22–5. 2.7
22–7. 31.5
22–9. 8
22–11. 142.9
22–13. $200–$299.99 ⊪
22–15. Traditional watch 183.6°
22–17.

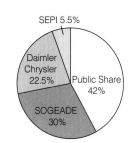

22–19. Transportation   126°
   Hotel   100.8°
   Food   72°
   Miscellaneous   61.2°

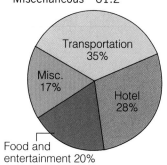

22–21. 250
22–23. (c) $3,623; $3,560
22–24. 24.94%

Optional Assignment
   1. 98
   3. 4.3
   5. 16%; 2.5%
   7. 68%; 81.5%; 2.5%; 2.5%; 47.5%
   9. 5.02

Summary Practice Test
   1. $143,300; $141,000
   2. 1,100
   3. 2.50
   4. 100; llll; 4
   5. Bar 1 on horizontal axis goes up to 800 on vertical axis
   6. Profits   108°
      Cost of sales   144°
      Expense   108°
   7. 166%
   8. 3.0 standard deviation

Check Figures (Odds) to Additional Assignments by Learning Unit from Appendix A

LU 1–1

1. **a.** Seven thousand, five hundred twenty-one
   d. Fifty-eight thousand, three
3. **a.** 40; 380; 860; 5,980; 210
   c. 21,000; 1,000; 4,000; 10,000
5. **a.** Hundreds place
   c. Ten thousands place
   e. Billions place
7. Three hundred eighty-four
9. $375,985
11. Two thousand, four

LU 1–2

1. **a.** 981
   c. 1,319
   d. 179
3. **a.** Estimated 40; 39
   c. Estimated 10; 9
5. $71,577
7. $19,973
9. 12,797 lbs
11. Estimated $9,400; $9,422
13. $746 discount

LU 1–3

1. **a.** Estimated 4,000; actual 2,400
   c. Estimated 15,000,000; actual 16,184,184
3. **a.** Estimated 1,000; actual 963 R5
   c. Estimated 20; actual 25 R8
5. 2,870
7. $78
9. 27
11. $43,200
13. 40 stacks and 23 "extra" bricks

LU 2–1

1. **a.** Mixed
   b. Improper
   c. Improper

   d. Mixed number
   e. Improper
   f. Proper
3. **a.** $\frac{36}{5}$ **c.** $\frac{31}{7}$ **f.** $\frac{53}{3}$
5. **a.** $6; \frac{6}{7}$ **b.** $15; \frac{2}{5}$ **e.** $12; \frac{8}{11}$
7. $\frac{13}{4}$
9. $\frac{17}{25}$
11. $\frac{60}{100}$
13. $\frac{7}{12}$

LU 2–2

1. **a.** 32   **b.** 180   **c.** 480
   d. 252
3. **a.** $\frac{1}{3}$ **b.** $\frac{2}{3}$ **e.** $6\frac{1}{8}$ **h.** $56\frac{5}{6}$
5. $3\frac{1}{40}$ yards
7. $17\frac{5}{12}$ miles
9. $4\frac{8}{9}$ hours

LU 2–3

1. **a.** $\dfrac{\overset{1}{\cancel{6}}}{\underset{1}{\cancel{13}}} \times \dfrac{\overset{2}{\cancel{26}}}{\underset{1}{\cancel{12}}} = 1$
3. **a.** $1\frac{1}{4}$ **b.** 3   **g.** 24   **l.** $\frac{4}{7}$
5. $39,000
7. 714
9. $20\frac{2}{3}$ miles
11. $412,000

LU 3–1

1. **a.** .62   **b.** .9   **c.** .953
   d. .401   **e.** .06
3. **a.** Hundredths place
   d. Thousandths place
5. **a.** $\frac{2}{5}$ **b.** $\frac{11}{25}$
   g. $\frac{5}{16}$ **l.** $9\frac{1}{25}$
7. .286
9. $\frac{566}{1,000}$
11. .333
13. .0020507

LU 3–2

1. **a.** 33.226   **b.** 5.2281   **d.** 3.7736
3. **a.** .3   **b.** .1   **c.** 1,480.0   **d.** .1
5. **a.** 6,870   **c.** .0272
   e. 34,700   **i.** 8,329.8
7. $4.53
9. $111.25
11. 15

LU 4–1

1. **a.** $430.64   **b.** 3   **c.** $867.51
3. **a.** Neuner Realty Co.
   b. Kevin Jones
   h. $2,756.80

LU 4–2

1. $1,435.42
3. Add $3,000; deduct $22.25
5. $2,989.92
7. $1,315.20

LU 5–1

1. **a.** $3N = 90$ **e.** $14 + \frac{N}{3} = 18$
   h. $2N + 3N + 8 = 68$

LU 5-2

1. $60
3. $45 telephone; $135 utility
5. 51 tickets—Sherry;
   408 tickets—Linda
7. 12 necklaces ($48);
   36 watches ($252)
9. $157.14

LU 6-1

1. a. 7% b. 64.5%
   i. 503.8% l. 80%
3. a. 70% c. 162.5%
   h. 50% n. 1.5%
5. a. $\frac{1}{4}$ b. .375 c. 50%
   d. .66$\overline{6}$ n. 1$\frac{1}{8}$
7. 2.9%
9. $\frac{39}{100}$
11. $\frac{9}{10,000}$

LU 6-2

1. a. $12,000; 30%; $3,600
   c. $7.00; 12%; $.84
3. a. 33.3% b. 3%
   c. 27.5%
5. a. −1,584; −26.6%
   d. −20,000; −16.7%
7. $9,000
9. $3,196
11. 329.5%

LU 7-1

1. a. $120 b. $360 c. $50
   d. $100 e. $380
3. a. $75 b. $21.50; $40.75
5. a. .7125; .2875 b. .7225; .2775
7. $3.51
9. $81.25
11. $315
13. 45%

LU 7-2

1. a. February 18; March 10
   d. May 20; June 9
   e. October 10; October 30
3. a. .98; $1,102.50
   c. .98; $367.99
5. a. $16.79; $835.21
7. $12,230.40
9. a. $439.29 b. $491.21
11. $209.45
13. a. $765.31 b. $386.99

LU 8-1

1. a. $14.30 b. $2.72
   c. $4.35 d. $90 e. $116.31

3. a. $2; 80% b. $6.50; 52%
   c. $.28; 28.9%
5. a. $1.52 b. $225
   c. $372.92 d. $625
7. a. $139.65 b. $538.65
9. a. $258.52 b. $90.48
11. a. $212.50 b. $297.50
13. $8.17

LU 8-2

1. a. $6.40 b. $57.50
   c. $34.43 d. $27.33 e. $.15
3. a. $6.94 b. $882.35 c. $30
   d. $171.43
5. a. 28.57% b. 33.33%
   d. 53.85%
7. $346.15
9. 39.39%
11. $2.29
13. 63.33%

LU 8-3

1. a. $30.00; $70
   b. $525; $1,574.98
3. a. $410 b. $18.65
5. a. $216; $324; $5.14
   b. $45; $63.90; $1.52
7. 17%
9. $21.15
11. $273.78
13. $.79

LU 8-4

1. a. $7.00 b. $11.11
3. a. 16,667 b. 7,500
5. 5,070

LU 9-1

1. a. $304; 0; $304
   b. $360; $40.50; $400.50
3. a. $438.85 b. $615.13
5. a. $5,200 b. $3,960
   c. $3,740 d. $4,750
7. $723.00
9. $3,846.25
11. $2,032.48

LU 9-2

1. a. $500; $2,300
3. 0; $2,000
5. $352.12
7. $143.75
9. $604.79
11. $658.94

LU 10-1

1. a. $240 b. $1,080
   c. $1,275
3. a. $131.25 b. $4.08
   c. $98.51

5. a. $515.63 b. $6,015.63
7. a. $5,459.66
9. $659.36
11. $360

LU 10-2

1. a. $4,371.44 b. $4,545.45
   c. $3,433.33
3. a. 60; .17 b. 120; .33
   c. 270; .75 d. 145; .40
5. 3%
7. $250
9. $3,000
11. 119 days

LU 10-3

1. a. $2,568.75; $1,885.47;
   $920.04
3. $4,267.59
5. $4,715.30; $115.30

LU 11-1

1. I; B; D; I; D; I; B; D
3. a. 3%
   c. 13%
5. $15,963.75
7. $848.75; $8,851.25
9. $14,300
11. $7,855

LU 11-2

1. a. $5,125
   b. $16,480.80
   c. $994.44
3. a. $14.76
   b. $223.25
   c. $3.49
5. $4,031.67
7. $8,262.74
9. $5,088.16
11. $721.45

LU 12-1

1. a. $573.25 year 2
   b. $3,115.57 year 4
3. a. $15,869; $5,869
   b. $16,084; $6,084
5. $5,980
7. $8,881.20
9. $2,129.40
11. $3,207.09; $207.09
13. $3,000; $3,469; $3,498

LU 12-2

1. a. .6209 b. .3936 c. .5513
3. a. $1,575,50; $924.50
   b. $2,547.02; $2,052.98
5. $13,152.60
7. $13,356.98

9. $16,826.40
11. $652.32
13. $18,014.22

LU 13–1

1. a. $1,000; $2,080; $3,246.40
3. a. $6,888.60 **b.** $6,273.36
5. $325,525
7. $13,412
9. $30,200.85
11. $33,650.94

LU 13–2

1. a. $2,638.65 **b.** $6,375.24; $7,217.10
3. $2,715.54
5. $24,251.85
7. $47,608
9. $456,425
11. Accept Jason $265,010

LU 13–3

1. a. $4,087.50
3. $16,200
5. $24,030
7. $16,345
9. $8,742

LU 14–1

1. a. $1,200; $192
  b. $9,000; $1,200
3. a. 14.75% **b.** 10%
  c. 11.25%
5. a. $3,528 **b.** $696
  c. $4,616
7. a. $22,500 **b.** $4,932
  c. $29,932
9. a. $20,576 **b.** 12.75%

LU 14–2

1. a. $625; $375
  b. $9,600; $2,910
3. a. $625; $578.12
5. $1,758; $553
7. $900
9. $7,287.76

LU 14–3

1. a. $465; $8,535
  b. $915.62; $4,709.38
3. a. $332.03 **b.** $584.83
  c. $384.28
5. Final payment $784.39
7. $51.34
9. $35
11. $922.49
13. 7.50% to 7.75%

LU 15–1

1. a. $1,096.50 **b.** $965.60; $4,090.50; $3,859.65
3. a. $117.25, 7.7%
  b. $174, 5.7%
5. $774
7. $2,584.71; $2,518.63
9. a. $66.08 **b.** $131,293.80
11. $773,560

LU 15–2

1. a. $1,371.90; $1,133.33; $238.57
3. #4 balance outstanding $195,183.05
5. $587,612.80
7. $327.12; $251,581.60
9. $44,271.43
11. $61,800

LU 16–1

1. Total assets $224,725
3. Merch. inventory 13.90%; 15.12%

LU 16–2

1. Net income $57,765
3. Purchases 73.59%; 71.43%

LU 16–3

1. Sales 2010, 93.5%; 2009, 93.2%
3. .22
5. 59.29%
7. .83
9. COGS 119.33%; 111.76%; 105.04%
11. .90
13. 5.51%
15. 11.01%

LU 17–1

1. a. 4% **b.** 25% **c.** 10%
  d. 20%
3. a. $2,033; $4,667
  b. $1,850; $9,750
5. $8,625 depreciation per year
7. $2,800 depreciation per year
9. $95
11. a. $12,000 **b.** $6,000
  c. $18,000 **d.** $45,000

LU 17–2

1. a. $.300 **b.** $.192 **c.** $.176
3. a. $.300, $2,600
  b. $.192, $300,824
5. $5,300 book value end of year 5
7. a. $.155 **b.** $20,001.61

LU 17–3

1. a. 8% **b.** 20% **c.** 25%
3. a. $4,467; $2,233
  b. $3,867; $7,733
5. $121, year 6
7. a. 28.57% **b.** $248 **c.** $619
9. a. 16.67% **b.** $2,500
  c. $10,814 **d.** $2,907

LU 17–4

1. a. 33%; $825; $1,675
3. Depreciation year 8, $346
5. $125
7. a. $15,000 **b.** $39,000
  c. $21,600 **d.** 2001
9. $68,440

LU 18–1

1. a. $5,120; $3,020
  b. $323,246; $273,546
3. $35,903; $165,262
5. $10,510.20; $16,345
7. $37.62; $639.54
9. $628.40
11. $3,069; $952; $2,117

LU 18–2

1. a. $85,700; $143,500; .597; $64,500; $38,507
3. $85,000
5. $342,000; $242,500; 5.85; 6.29
7. $60,000; $100,000; $40,000
9. $70,150
11. $5,970
13. 3.24; 3.05
15. $32,340; $35,280; $49,980; $29,400

LU 19–1

1. a. $26.80; $562.80
  b. $718.80; $12,698.80
3. a. $20.75; $43.89; $463.64
5. Total is **(a)** $1,023; **(b)** $58.55
7. $5.23; $115.23
9. $2,623.93
11. $26.20
13. $685.50

LU 19–2

1. a. $68,250 **b.** $775,450
3. a. $7.45; $74.50; 74.50
5. $9.10
7. $8,368.94
9. $42,112
11. $32,547.50

LU 20–1

1. **a.** $9.27; 25; $231.75
3. **a.** $93.00; $387.50; $535.00; $916.50
5. $1,242.90
7. $14,265
9. $47.50 more
11. $68,750

LU 20–2

1. **a.** $488 **b.** $2,912
3. **a.** $68,000; $60,000
   b. $41,600; $45,000
5. $1,463
7. $117,187.50
9. $336,000
11. **a.** $131,250 **b.** $147,000

LU 20–3

1. **a.** $98; $160; $258
3. **a.** $312 **b.** $233 **c.** $181
   d. $59; $20
5. **a.** $647 **b.** $706
7. $601
9. $781
11. $10,000; $8,000
13. $60,000; $20,000
15. $19.50; $110.50

LU 21–1

1. **a.** $43.88 **f.** 49
3. $27.06
5. $1,358.52 gain
7. $18,825.15
9. $7.70

LU 21–2

1. **a.** IBM **b.** $10\frac{1}{4}$ **c.** 2009
   d. $102.50 **e.** $102\frac{3}{8}$
3. **a.** $1,025
   b. $1,023.75
5. **a.** $3,075
   b. $307.50
7. **a.** $30 discount **b.** $16.25 premium **c.** $42.50 premium
9. **a.** $625 **b.** $375 discount
   c. $105 **d.** 16.8%
11. 7.8%; 7.2%
13. 8.98%

LU 21–3

1. $11.90
3. $15.20
5. +$.14
7. 7.6%

9. $1.45; $18.45
11. $.56; $14.66
13. $1,573.50
15. $123.00 loss
17. **a.** 2007; 2008
    b. 9.3% Comp USA
       6.9% GMA
    c. $1,023.75 Comp USA
       $1,016.25 GMA
    d. Both at premium
    e. $1,025 Comp USA
       $1,028.75 GMA

LU 22–1

1. **a.** 20.4 **b.** 83.75 **c.** 10.07
3. **a.** 59.5 **b.** 50
5. **a.** 63.7; 62; 62
7. $1,500,388.50
9. $10.75
11. $9.98

LU 22–2

1. 18: ⱖ‖ 7
3. 25–30: ⱖ‖‖ 8
5. 7.2°
7. 145–154: ‖‖‖ 4
9. 98.4°; 9.9°; 70.5°; 169.2°; 11.9°

Classroom Notes

Classroom Notes

Classroom Notes

Classroom Notes

Classroom Notes

Classroom Notes

Classroom Notes

Classroom Notes

Glossary

The Glossary contains a comprehensive list of the key terms used in the text. In many cases, examples are also included in the definitions. Recall that key terms and their page references are listed in the Chapter Organizer and Study Guide for each chapter.

Accelerated Cost Recovery System (ACRS) (p. 418) Tax law enacted in 1981 for assets put in service from 1981 through 1986.

Accelerated depreciation method (p. 418) Computes more depreciation expense in the early years of the asset's life than in the later years.

Accounts payable (p. 385) Amounts owed to creditors for services or items purchased.

Accounts receivable (p. 385) Amount owed by customers to a business from previous sales.

Accumulated depreciation (p. 413) Amount of depreciation that has accumulated on plant and equipment assets.

Acid test (p. 396) Current assets less inventory less prepaid expenses divided by current liabilities.

Addends (p. 8) Numbers that are combined in the addition process. *Example:* 8 + 9 = 17, of which 8 and 9 are the addends.

Adjustable rate mortgage (p. 366) Rate of mortgage is lower than a fixed rate mortgage. Rates adjusted without refinancing. Caps available to limit how high rate can go for each adjustment period over term of loan.

Adjusted bank balance (p. 96) Current balance of checkbook after reconciliation process.

Amortization (p. 346) Process of paying back a loan (principal plus interest) by equal periodic payments (see **amortization schedule**).

Amortization schedule (p. 371) Shows monthly payment to pay back loan at maturity. Payment also includes interest. Note payment is fixed at same amount each month.

Amount financed (p. 342) Cash price less down payment.

Annual percentage rate (APR) (p. 343) True or effective annual interest rate charged by sellers. Required to be stated by Truth in Lending Act.

Annual percentage rate (APR) table (p. 343) Effective annual rate of interest on a loan or installment purchase as shown by table lookup.

Annual percentage yield (APY) (p. 301) Truth in savings law forced banks to report actual interest in form of APY. Interest yield must be calculated on actual number of days bank has the money.

Annuities certain (p. 318) Annuities that have stated beginning and ending dates.

Annuity (p. 317) Stream of equal payments made at periodic times.

Annuity due (p. 318) Annuity that is paid (or received) at the beginning of the time period.

Assessed value (p. 456) Value of a property that an assessor sets (usually a percent of property's market value) that is used in calculating property taxes.

Asset cost (p. 413) Amount company paid for the asset.

Assets (p. 384) Things of value owned by a business.

Asset turnover (p. 396) Net sales divided by total assets.

ATM (p. 89) Automatic teller machine that allows customers of a bank to transfer funds and make deposits or withdrawals.

Average daily balance (p. 352) Sum of daily balances divided by number of days in billing cycle.

Average inventory (p. 458) Total of all inventories divided by number of times inventory taken.

Balance sheet (p. 384) Financial report that lists assets, liabilities, and equity. Report reflects the financial position of the company as of a particular date.

Bank discount (p. 282) The amount of interest charged by a bank on a note. (Maturity value × Bank discount rate × Number of days bank holds note) ÷ 360.

Bank discount rate (p. 280) Percent of interest.

Banker's Rule (p. 260) Time is exact days/360 in calculating simple interest.

Bank reconciliation (p. 96) Process of comparing the bank balance to the checkbook balance so adjustments can be made regarding checks outstanding, deposits in transit, and the like.

Bank statement (p. 95) Report sent by the bank to the owner of the checking account indicating checks processed, deposits made, and so on, along with beginning and ending balances.

Bar graph (p. 515) Visual representation using horizontal or vertical bars to make comparison or to show relationship on items of similar makeup.

Base (p. 144) Number that represents the whole 100%. It is the whole to which something is being compared. Usually follows word *of*.

Beneficiary (p. 467) Person(s) designated to receive the face value of the life insurance when insured dies.

Biweekly (p. 236) Every 2 weeks (26 times in a year).

Biweekly mortgage (p. 367) Mortgage payments made every 2 weeks rather than monthly. This payment method takes years off the life of the mortgage and substantially reduces the cost of interest.

Blank endorsement (p. 91) Current owner of check signs name on back. Whoever presents checks for payment receives the money.

Bodily injury (p. 467) Auto insurance that pays damages to people injured or killed by your auto.

Bond discount (p. 496) Bond selling for less than the face value.

Bond premium (p. 496) Bond selling for more than the face value.

Bonds (p. 495) Written promise by a company that borrows money usually with fixed-interest payment until maturity (repayment time).

Bond yield (p. 496) Total annual interest divided by total cost.

Book value (p. 413) Cost less accumulated depreciation.

Breakeven point (p. 219) Point at which seller has covered all expenses and costs and has made no profit or suffered a loss.

Cancellation (p. 47) Reducing process that is used to simplify the multiplication and division of fractions. *Example:*

$$\frac{\overset{1}{\cancel{4}}}{8} \times \frac{1}{\underset{1}{\cancel{4}}}$$

Capital (p. 384) Owners' investment in the business.

Cash advance (p. 309) Money borrowed by holder of credit card. It is recorded as another purchase and is used in the calculation of the average daily balance.

Cash discount (p. 179) Savings that result from early payment by taking advantage of discounts offered by the seller; discount is not taken on freight or taxes.

Cash dividend (p. 493) Cash distribution of company's profit to owners of stock.

Cash value (p. 469) Except for term insurance, this indicates the value of the policy when terminated. Options fall under the heading of nonforfeiture values.

Centi- (Appendix D) Prefix indicating .01 of a basic metric unit.

Chain or series discount (p. 176) Two or more trade discounts that are applied to the balance remaining after the previous discount is taken. Often called a **series discount.**

Check register (p. 89) Record-keeping device that records checks paid and deposits made by companies using a checking account.

Checks (p. 89) Written documents signed by appropriate person that directs the bank to pay a specific amount of money to a particular person or company.

Check stub (p. 89) Provides a record of checks written. It is attached to the check.

Circle graph (p. 517) A visual representation of the parts to the whole.

Closing costs (p. 368) Costs incurred when property passes from seller to buyer such as for credit reports, recording costs, points, and so on.

CM (p. 97) Abbreviation for **credit memorandum.** The bank is adding to your account. The CM is found on the bank statement. *Example:* Bank collects a note for you.

Coinsurance (p. 474) Type of fire insurance in which the insurer and insured share the risk. Usually there is an 80% coinsurance clause.

Collision (p. 477) Optional auto insurance that pays for the repairs to your auto from an accident after deductible is met. Insurance company will only pay for repairs up to the value of the auto (less deductible).

Commissions (p. 238) Payments based on established performance criteria.

Common denominator (p. 40) To add two or more fractions, denominators must be the same.

Common stocks (p. 386) Units of ownership called shares.

Comparative statement (p. 387) Statement showing data from two or more periods side by side.

Complement (p. 174) 100% less the stated percent. *Example:* 18% → 82% is the complement (100% − 18%).

Compounding (p. 299) Calculating the interest periodically over the life of the loan and adding it to the principal.

Compound interest (p. 299) The interest that is calculated periodically and then added to the principal. The next period the interest is calculated on the adjusted principal (old principal plus interest).

Comprehensive insurance (p. 477) Optional auto insurance that pays for damages to the auto caused by factors other than from collision (fire, vandalism, theft, and the like).

Compulsory insurance (p. 476) Insurance required by law—standard coverage.

Constants (p. 116) Numbers that have a fixed value such as 3 or −7. Placed on right side of equation; also called *knowns.*

Contingent annuities (p. 318) Beginning and ending dates of the annuity are uncertain (not fixed).

Contingent liability (p. 282) Potential liability that may or may not result from discounting a note.

Contribution margin (p. 219) Difference between selling price and variable cost.

Conversion periods (p. 297) How often (a period of time) the interest is calculated in the compounding process. *Example:* Daily—each day; monthly—12 times a year; quarterly—every 3 months; semiannually— every 6 months.

Corporation (p. 384) Company with many owners or stockholders. Equity of these owners is called stockholders' equity.

Cost (p. 204) Price retailers pay to manufacturer or supplier to bring merchandise into store.

Cost of merchandise (goods) sold (p. 391) Beginning inventory + Net purchases − Ending inventory.

Credit card (p. 350) A piece of plastic that allows you to buy on credit.

Credit memo (CM) (p. 97) Transactions of bank that increase customer's account.

Credit period (end) (p. 179) Credit days are counted from date of invoice. Has no relationship to the discount period.

Cumulative preferred stock (p. 492) Holders of preferred stock must receive current year and any dividends in arrears before any dividends are paid out to the holders of common stock.

Current assets (p. 384) Assets that are used up or converted into cash within 1 year or operating cycle.

Current liabilities (p. 385) Obligations of a company due within 1 year.

Current ratio (p. 396) Current assets divided by current liabilities.

Daily balance (p. 352) Calculated to determine customer's finance charge: Previous balance + Any cash advances + Purchases − Payments.

Daily compounding (p. 299) Interest calculated on balance each day.

Debit card (p. 89) Transactions result in money being immediately deducted from customer's checking account.

Debit memo (DM) (p. 97) A debit transaction bank does for customers.

Deca- (Appendix D) Prefix indicating 10 times basic metric unit.

Deci- (Appendix D) Prefix indicating .1 of basic metric unit.

Decimal equivalent (p. 69) Decimal represents the same value as the fraction. *Example:*

$$.05 = \frac{5}{100}$$

Decimal fraction (p. 67) Decimal representing a fraction; the denominator has a power of 10.

Decimal point (p. 2, 65) Center of the decimal system—located between units and tenths. Numbers to left are *whole numbers;* to the right are *decimal numbers.*

Decimal system (p. 2) The U.S. base 10 numbering system that uses the 10 single-digit numbers shown on a calculator.

Decimals (p. 65) Numbers written to the right of a decimal point. *Example:* 5.3, 18.22.

Declining-balance method (p. 417) Accelerated method of depreciation. The depreciation each year is calculated by book value beginning each year times the rate.

Deductibles (p. 477) Amount insured pays before insurance company pays. Usually the higher the deductible, the lower the premium will be.

Deductions (p. 237) Amounts deducted from gross earnings to arrive at net pay.

Deferred payment price (p. 343) Total of all monthly payments plus down payment.

Denominator (p. 35) The number of a common fraction below the division line (bar). *Example:*

$$\frac{8}{9}, \text{ of which 9 is the denominator}$$

Deposit slip (p. 90) Document that shows date, name, account number, and items making up a deposit.

Deposits in transit (p. 97) Deposits not received or processed by bank at the time the bank statement is prepared.

Depreciation (p. 413) Process of allocating the cost of an asset (less residual value) over the asset's estimated life.

Depreciation causes (p. 413) Normal use, product obsolescence, aging, and so on.

Depreciation expense (p. 413) Process involving asset cost, estimated useful life, and residual value (salvage or trade-in value).

Depreciation schedule (p. 414) Table showing amount of depreciation expense, accumulated depreciation, and book value for each period of time for a plant asset.

Difference (p. 9) The resulting answer from a subtraction problem. *Example:* Minuend less subtrahend equals difference.

$$215 - 15 = 200$$

Differential pay schedule (p. 238) Pay rate is based on a schedule of units completed.

Digit (p. 3) Our decimal number system of 10 characters from 0 to 9.

Discounting a note (p. 283) Receiving cash from selling a note to a bank before the due date of a note. Steps to discount include: (1) calculate maturity value, (2) calculate number of days bank waits for money, (3) calculate bank discount, and (4) calculate proceeds.

Discount period (p. 180, 283) Amount of time to take advantage of a cash discount.

Distribution of overhead (p. 439) Companies distribute overhead by floor space or sales volume.

Dividend (p. 14) Number in the division process that is being divided by another. *Example:* 5)15, in which 15 is the dividend.

Dividends (p. 495) Distribution of company's profit in cash or stock to owners of stock.

Dividends in arrears (p. 492) Dividends that accumulate when a company fails to pay dividends to cumulative preferred stockholders.

Divisor (p. 14) Number in the division process that is dividing into another. *Example:* 5)15, in which 5 is the divisor.

DM (p. 97) Abbreviation for **debit memorandum.** The bank is charging your account. The DM is found on the bank statement. *Example:* NSF.

Dollar markdown (p. 216) Original selling price less the reduction to price. Markdown may be stated as a percent of the original selling price. *Example:*

$$\frac{\text{Dollar markdown}}{\text{Original selling price}}$$

Dollar markup (p. 205) Selling price less cost. Difference is the amount of the markup. Markup is also expressed in percent.

Down payment (p. 342) Amount of initial cash payment made when item is purchased.

Drafts (p. 89) Written orders like checks instructing a bank, credit union, or savings and loan institution to pay your money to a person or organization.

Draw (p. 239) The receiving of advance wages to cover business or personal expenses. Once wages are earned, drawing amount reduces actual amount received.

Drawee (p. 90) One ordered to pay the check.

Drawer (p. 90) One who writes the check.

Due date (p. 180) Maturity date or when the note will be repaid.

Earnings per share (p. 493) Annual earnings ÷ Total number of shares outstanding.

Effective rate (p. 281, 301) True rate of interest. The more frequent the compounding, the higher the effective rate.

Electronic deposits (p. 98) Credit card run through terminal which approves (or disapproves) the amount and adds it to company's bank balance.

Electronic funds transfer (EFT) (p. 95) A computerized operation that electronically transfers funds among parties without the use of paper checks.

Employee's Withholding Allowance Certificate (W-4) (p. 241) Completed by employee to indicate allowance claimed to determine amount of FIT that is deducted.

End of credit period (p. 180) Last day from date of invoice when customer can take cash discount.

End of month—EOM (also **proximo**) **(p. 184)** Cash discount period begins at the end of the month invoice is dated. After the 25th discount period, one additional month results.

Endorse (p. 91) Signing the back of the check; thus ownership is transferred to another party.

Endowment life (p. 469) Form of insurance that pays at maturity a fixed amount of money to insured or to the beneficiary. Insurance coverage would terminate when paid—similar to term life.

Equation (p. 116) Math statement that shows equality for expressions or numbers, or both.

Equivalent (fractional) (p. 38) Two or more fractions equivalent in value.

Escrow account (p. 368) Lending institution requires that each month $\frac{1}{12}$ of the insurance cost and real estate taxes be kept in a special account.

Exact interest (p. 260) Calculating simple interest using 365 days per year in time.

Excise tax (p. 455) Tax that government levies on particular products and services. Tax on specific luxury items or nonessentials.

Expression (p. 116) A meaningful combination of numbers and letters called *terms.*

Extended term insurance (p. 470) Resulting from nonforfeiture, it keeps the policy for the full face value going without further premium payments for a specific period of time.

Face amount (p. 467) Dollar amount stated in policy.

Face value (p. 279) Amount of insurance that is stated on the policy. It is usually the maximum amount for which the insurance company is liable.

Fair Credit and Charge Card Disclosure Act of 1988 (p. 351) Act that tightens controls on credit card companies soliciting new business.

Fair Labor Standards Act (p. 237) Federal law has minimum wage standards and the requirement of overtime pay. There are many exemptions for administrative personnel and for others.

Federal income tax (FIT) withholding (p. 242) Federal tax withheld from paycheck.

Federal Insurance Contribution Act (FICA) (p. 241) Percent of base amount of each employee's salary. FICA taxes used to fund retirement, disabled workers, Medicare, and so on. FICA is now broken down into Social Security and Medicare.

Federal Unemployment Tax Act (FUTA) (p. 244) Tax paid by employer. Current rate is .8% on first $7,000 of earnings.

Federal withholding tax (p. 242) See **Income tax.**

Finance charge (p. 343) Total payments − Actual loan cost.

Fire insurance (p. 472) Stipulated percent (normally 80%) of value that is required for insurance company to pay to reimburse one's losses.

First-in, first-out (FIFO) method (p. 433) This method assumes the first inventory brought into the store will be the first sold. Ending inventory is made up of goods most recently purchased.

Fixed cost (p. 219) Costs that do not change with increase or decrease in sales.

Fixed rate mortgage (p. 367) Monthly payment fixed over number of years, usually 30 years.

FOB destination (p. 173) Seller pays cost of freight in getting goods to buyer's location.

FOB shipping point (p. 173) Buyer pays cost of freight in getting goods to his location.

Formula (p. 116) Equation that expresses in symbols a general fact, rule, or principle.

Fraction (p. 35) Expresses a part of a whole number. *Example:*

$\frac{5}{6}$ expresses 5 parts out of 6

Freight terms (p. 173) Determine how freight will be paid. Most common freight terms are **FOB shipping point** and **FOB destination.**

Frequency distribution (p. 515) Shows by table the number of times event(s) occurs.

Full endorsement (p. 91) This endorsement identifies the next person or company to whom the check is to be transferred.

Future value (FV) (p. 299) Final amount of the loan or investment at the end of the last period. Also called *compound amount.*

Future value of annuity (p. 318) Future dollar amount of a series of payments plus interest.

Graduated-payment mortgage (p. 367) Borrower pays less at beginning of mortgage. As years go on, the payments increase.

Graduated plans (p. 367) In beginning years, mortgage payment is less. As years go on, monthly payments rise.

Gram (Appendix D) Basic unit of weight in metric system. An ounce equals about 28 grams.

Greatest common divisor (p. 37) The largest possible number that will divide evenly into both the numerator and denominator.

Gross pay (p. 237) Wages before deductions.

Gross profit (p. 204) Difference between cost of bringing goods into the store and selling price of the goods.

Gross profit from sales (p. 392) Net sales − Cost of goods sold.

Gross profit method (p. 437) Used to estimate value of inventory.

Gross sales (p. 391) Total earned sales before sales returns and allowances or sales discounts.

Hecto- (Appendix D) Prefix indicating 100 times basic metric unit.

Higher terms (p. 38) Expressing a fraction with a new numerator and denominator that is equivalent to the original. *Example:*

$$\frac{2}{9} \to \frac{6}{27}$$

Home equity loan (p. 366) Cheap and readily accessible lines of credit backed by equity in your home; tax-deductible; rates can be locked in.

Horizontal analysis (p. 388) Method of analyzing financial reports where each total this period is compared by amount of percent to the same total last period.

Improper fraction (p. 35) Fraction that has a value equal to or greater than 1; numerator is equal to or greater than the denominator. *Example:*

$$\frac{6}{6}, \frac{14}{9}$$

Income statement (p. 389) Financial report that lists the revenues and expenses for a specific period of time. It reflects how well the company is performing.

Income tax or FIT (p. 242) Tax that depends on allowances claimed, marital status, and wages earned.

Indemnity (p. 474) Insurance company's payment to insured for loss.

Index numbers (p. 517) Express the relative changes in a variable compared with some base, which is taken as 100.

Individual retirement account (IRA) (p. 316) An account established for retirement planning.

Installment cost (p. 342) Down payment + (Number of payments × Monthly payment). Also called deferred payment.

Installment loan (p. 342) Loan paid off with a series of equal periodic payments.

Installment purchases (p. 342) Purchase of an item(s) that requires periodic payments for a specific period of time with usually a high rate of interest.

Insured (p. 467) Customer or policyholder.

Insurer (p. 467) The insurance company that issues the policy.

Interest (p. 259) Principal × Rate × Time.

Interest-bearing note (p. 279) Maturity value of note is greater than amount borrowed since interest is added on.

Interest-only mortgage (p. 366) Type of mortgage where in early years only interest payment is required.

Inventory turnover (p. 438) Ratio that indicates how quickly inventory turns:

$$\frac{\text{Cost of goods sold}}{\text{Average inventory at cost}}$$

Invoice (p. 171) Document recording purchase and sales transactions.

Just-in-time (JIT) inventory system (p. 435) System that eliminates inventories. Suppliers provide materials daily as manufacturing company needs them.

Kilo- (Appendix D) Prefix indicating 1,000 times basic metric unit.

Last-in, first-out (LIFO) method (p. 433) This method assumes the last inventory brought into the store will be the first sold. Ending inventory is made up of the oldest goods purchased.

Least common denominator (LCD) (p. 40) Smallest nonzero whole number into which all denominators will divide evenly. *Example:*

$$\frac{2}{3} \text{ and } \frac{1}{4} \quad \text{LCD} = 12$$

Level premium term (p. 468) Insurance premium that is fixed, say, for 50 years.

Liabilities (p. 385) Amount business owes to creditors.

Liability insurance (p. 476) Insurance for bodily injury to others and damage to someone else's property.

Like fractions (p. 40) Proper fractions with the same denominators.

Like terms (p. 116) Terms that are made up with the same variable:

$$A + 2A + 3A = 6A$$

Limited payment life (20-payment life) (p. 469) Premiums are for 20 years (a fixed period) and provide paid-up insurance for the full face value of the policy.

Line graphs (p. 516) Graphical presentation that involves a time element. Shows trends, failures, backlogs, and the like.

Line of credit (p. 283) Provides immediate financing up to an approved limit.

Liquid assets (p. 384) Cash or other assets that can be converted quickly into cash.

List price (p. 172) Suggested retail price paid by customers.

Liter (Appendix D) Basic unit of measure in metric, for volume.

Loan amortization table (p. 346) Table used to calculate monthly payments.

Long-term liabilities (p. 385) Debts or obligations that company does not have to pay within 1 year.

Lowest terms (p. 37) Expressing a fraction when no number divides evenly into the numerator and denominator except the number 1. *Example:*

$$\frac{5}{10} \to \frac{1}{2}$$

Maker (p. 279) One who writes the note.

Margin (p. 204) Difference between cost of bringing goods into store and selling price of goods

Markdowns (p. 204) Reductions from original selling price caused by seasonal changes, special promotions, and so on.

Markup (p. 204) Amount retailers add to cost of goods to cover operating expenses and make a profit.

Markup percent calculation (p. 205) Markup percent on cost × Cost = Dollar markup; or Markup percent on selling price × Selling price = Dollar markup.

Maturity date (p. 259, 279) Date the principal and interest are due.

Maturity value (MV) (p. 259, 279) Principal plus interest (if interest is charged). Represents amount due on the due date.

Maturity value of note (p. 279) Amount of cash paid on the due date. If interest-bearing maturity, value is greater than amount borrowed.

Mean (p. 512) Statistical term that is found by:

$$\frac{\text{Sum of all figures}}{\text{Number of figures}}$$

Measure of dispersion (p. 520) Number that describes how the numbers of a set of data are spread out or dispersed.

Median (p. 512) Statistical term that represents the central point or midpoint of a series of numbers.

Merchandise inventory (p. 385) Cost of goods for resale.

Meter (Appendix D) Basic unit of length in metric system. A meter is a little longer than a yard.

Metric system (Appendix D) A decimal system of weights and measures. The basic units are meters, grams, and liters.

Mill (p. 457) $\frac{1}{10}$ of a cent or $\frac{1}{1,000}$ of a dollar.

In decimal, it is .001. *In application:*

$$\frac{\text{Property}}{\text{tax due}} = \frac{\text{Mills} \times .001 \times}{\text{Assessed valuation}}$$

Milli- (Appendix D) Prefix indicating .001 of basic metric unit.

Minuend (p. 9) In a subtraction problem, the larger number from which another is subtracted. *Example:*

$$50 - 40 = 10$$

Mixed decimal (p. 69) Combination of a whole number and decimal, such as 59.8, 810.85.

Mixed number (p. 36) Sum of a whole number greater than zero and a proper fraction:

$$2\frac{1}{4}, 3\frac{3}{9}$$

Mode (p. 513) Value that occurs most often in a series of numbers.

Modified Accelerated Cost Recovery System (MACRS) (p. 418) Part of Tax Reform Act of 1986 that revised depreciation schedules of ACRS. Tax Bill of 1989 updates MACRS.

Monthly (p. 236) Some employers pay employees monthly.

Mortgage (p. 367) Cost of home less down payment.

Mortgage note payable (p. 385) Debt owed on a building that is a long-term liability; often the building is the collateral.

Multiplicand (p. 13) The first or top number being multiplied in a multiplication problem. *Example:*

Product	=	Multiplicand	×	Multiplier
40	=	20	×	2

Multiplier (p. 13) The second or bottom number doing the multiplication in a problem. *Example:*

Product	=	Multiplicand	×	Multiplier
40	=	20	×	2

Mutual fund (p. 498) Investors buy shares in the fund's portfolio (group of stocks and/or bonds).

Net asset value (NAV) (p. 498) The dollar value of one mutual fund share; calculated by subtracting current liabilities from current market value of fund's investments and dividing this by number of shares outstanding.

Net income (p. 392) Gross profit less operating expenses.

Net pay (p. 237) See **Net wages.**

Net price (p. 172) List price less amount of trade discount. The net price is before any cash discount.

Net price equivalent rate (p. 176) When multiplied times the list price, this rate or factor produces the actual cost to the buyer. Rate is found by taking the complement of each term in the discount and multiplying them together (do not round off).

Net proceeds (p. 280) Maturity value less bank discount.

Net profit (net income) (p. 204) Gross profit − Operating expenses.

Net purchases (p. 392) Purchases − Purchase discounts − Purchase returns and allowances.

Net sales (p. 391) Gross sales − Sales discounts − Sales returns and allowances.

Net wages (p. 242) Gross pay less deductions.

Net worth (p. 384) Assets less liabilities.

No-fault insurance (p. 479) Involves bodily injury. Damage (before a certain level) that is paid by an insurance company no matter who is to blame.

Nominal rate (p. 301) Stated rate.

Nonforfeiture values (p. 471) When a life insurance policy is terminated (except term), it represents (1) the available cash value, (2) additional extended term, or (3) additional paid-up insurance.

Noninterest-bearing note (p. 280) Note where the maturity value will be equal to the amount of money borrowed since no additional interest is charged.

Nonsufficient funds (NSF) (p. 97) Drawer's account lacked sufficient funds to pay written amount of check.

Normal distribution (p. 521) Data is spread symmetrically about the mean.

Numerator (p. 35) Number of a common fraction above the division line (bar). *Example:*

$$\frac{8}{9}, \text{ in which 8 is the numerator}$$

Omnibus Budget Reconciliation Act of 1989 (p. 420) An update of MACRS. Unless business use of equipment is greater than 50%, straight-line depreciation is required.

Open-end credit (p. 351) Set payment period. Also, additional credit amounts can be added up to a set limit. It is a revolving charge account.

Operating expenses (overhead) (p. 392) Regular expenses of doing business. These are not costs.

Ordinary annuities (p. 317) Annuity that is paid (or received) at end of the time period.

Ordinary dating (p. 182) Cash discount is available within the discount period. Full amount due by end of credit period if discount is missed.

Ordinary interest (p. 261) Calculating simple interest using 360 days per year in time.

Ordinary life insurance (p. 414) See **Straight life insurance.**

Outstanding balance (p. 351) Amount left to be paid on a loan.

Outstanding checks (p. 97) Checks written but not yet processed by the bank before bank statement preparation.

Overdraft (p. 95) Occurs when company or person wrote a check without enough money in the bank to pay for it (NFS check).

Overhead expenses (p. 439) Operating expenses *not* directly associated with a specific department or product.

Override (p. 237) Commission that managers receive due to sales by people that they supervise.

Overtime (p. 237) Time-and-a-half pay for more than 40 hours of work.

Owner's equity (p. 384) See **Capital.**

Paid-up insurance (p. 469) A certain level of insurance can continue, although the premiums are terminated. This results from the nonforfeiture value (except term). Result is a reduced paid-up policy until death.

Partial products (p. 13) Numbers between multiplier and product.

Partial quotient (p. 14) Occurs when divisor doesn't divide evenly into the dividend.

Partnership (p. 384) Business with two or more owners.

Payee (p. 90, 279) One who is named to receive the amount of the check.

Payroll register (p. 240) Multicolumn form to record payroll data.

Percent (p. 144) Stands for hundredths. *Example:*

$$4\% \text{ is 4 parts of one hundred, or } \frac{4}{100}$$

Percentage method (p. 242) A method to calculate withholdings. Opposite of wage bracket method.

Percent decrease (p. 149) Calculated by decrease in price over original amount.

Percent increase (p. 149) Calculated by increase in price over original amount.

Percent markup on cost (p. 205) Dollar markup divided by the cost; thus, markup is a percent of the cost.

Percent markup on selling price (p. 210) Dollar markup divided by the selling price; thus, markup is a percent of the selling price.

Periodic inventory system (p. 430) Physical count of inventory taken at end of a time period. Inventory records are not continually updated.

Periods (p. 297) Number of years times the number of times compounded per year (see **Conversion period**).

Perishables (p. 217) Goods or services with a limited life.

Perpetual inventory system (p. 430) Inventory records are continually updated; opposite of periodic.

Personal property (p. 456) Items of possession, like cars, home, furnishings, jewelry, and so on. These are taxed by the property tax (don't forget real property is also taxed).

Piecework (p. 238) Compensation based on the number of items produced or completed.

Place value (p. 3) The digit value that results from its position in a number.

Plant and equipment (p. 385) Assets that will last longer than 1 year.

Point of sale (p. 100) Terminal that accepts cards (like those used at ATMs) to purchase items at retail outlets. No cash is physically exchanged.

Points (p. 368) Percentage(s) of mortgage that represents an additional cost of borrowing. It is a one-time payment made at closing.

Policy (p. 467) Written insurance contract.

Policyholder (p. 467) The insured.

Portion (p. 144) Amount, part, or portion that results from multiplying the base times the rate. Not expressed as a percent; it is expressed as a number.

Preferred stock (p. 386) Type of stock that has a preference regarding a corporation's profits and assets.

Premium (p. 467) Periodic payments that one makes for various kinds of insurance protection.

Prepaid expenses (p. 385) Items a company buys that have not been used are shown as assets.

Prepaid rent (p. 385) Rent paid in advance.

Present value (PV) (p. 296) How much money will have to be deposited today (or at some date) to reach a specific amount of maturity (in the future).

Present value of annuity (p. 323) Amount of money needed today to receive a specified stream (annuity) of money in the future.

Price-earnings (PE) ratio (p. 492) Closing price per share of stock divided by earnings per share.

Price relative (p. 518) The quotient of the current price divided by some previous year's price—the base year—multiplied by 100.

Prime number (p. 41) Whole number greater than 1 that is only divisible by itself and 1. *Examples:* 2, 3, 5.

Principal (p. 259) Amount of money that is originally borrowed, loaned, or deposited.

Proceeds (p. 280) Maturity value less the bank charge.

Product (p. 13) Answer of a multiplication process, such as:

$$\text{Product} = \text{Multiplicand} \times \text{Multiplier}$$
$$50 = 5 \times 10$$

Promissory note (p. 279) Written unconditional promise to pay a certain sum (with or without interest) at a fixed time in the future.

Proper fractions (p. 35) Fractions with a value less than 1; numerator is smaller than denominator, such as $\frac{5}{9}$.

Property damage (p. 476) Auto insurance covering damages that are caused to the property of others.

Property tax (p. 457) Tax that raises revenue for school districts, cities, counties, and the like.

Property tax due (p. 457) Tax rate $\times$ Assessed valuation

Proximo (prox) (p. 184) Same as end of month.

Purchase discounts (p. 391) Savings received by buyer for paying for merchandise before a certain date.

Purchase returns and allowances (p. 391) Cost of merchandise returned to store due to damage, defects, and so on. An *allowance* is a cost reduction that results when buyer keeps or buys damaged goods.

Pure decimal (p. 69) Has no whole number(s) to the left of the decimal point, such as .45.

Quick assets (p. 396) Current assets − Inventory − Prepaid expenses.

Quick ratio (p. 396) (Current assets − Inventory − Prepaid expenses) ÷ Current liabilities.

Quotient (p. 14) The answer of a division problem.

Range (p. 520) Difference between the highest and lowest values in a group of values or set of data.

Rate (p. 144) Percent that is multiplied times the base that indicates what part of the base we are trying to compare to. Rate is not a whole number.

Rate of interest (p. 297) Percent of interest that is used to compute the interest charge on a loan for a specific time.

Ratio analysis (p. 395) Relationship of one number to another.

Real property (p. 456) Land, buildings, and so on, which are taxed by the property tax.

Rebate (p. 349) Finance charge that a customer receives for paying off a loan early.

Rebate fraction (p. 349) Sum of digits based on number of months to go divided by sum of digits based on total number of months of loan.

Receipt of goods (ROG) (p. 183) Used in calculating the cash discount period; begins the day that the goods are received.

Reciprocal of a fraction (p. 48) The interchanging of the numerator and the denominator. Inverted number is the reciprocal. *Example:*

$$\frac{6}{7} \rightarrow \frac{7}{6}$$

Reduced paid-up insurance (p. 470) Insurance that uses cash value to buy protection, face amount is less than original policy, and policy continues for life.

Remainder (p. 14) Leftover amount in division.

Repeating decimals (p. 67) Decimal numbers that repeat themselves continuously and thus do not end.

Residual value (p. 413) Estimated value of a plant asset after depreciation is taken (or end of useful life).

Restrictive endorsement (p. 91) Check must be deposited to the payee's account. This restricts one from cashing it.

Retail method (p. 437) Method to estimate cost of ending inventory. The cost ratio times ending inventory at retail equals the ending cost of inventory.

Retained earnings (p. 386) Amount of earnings that is kept in the business.

Return on equity (p. 396) Net income divided by stockholders' equity.

Revenues (p. 391) Total earned sales (cash or credit) less any sales discounts, returns, or allowances.

Reverse mortgage (p. 367) Federal Housing Administration makes it possible for older homeowners to live in their homes and get cash or monthly income.

Revolving charge account (p. 351) Charges for a customer are allowed up to a specified maximum, a minimum monthly payment is required, and interest is charged on balance outstanding.

ROG (p. 183) Receipt of goods; cash discount period begins when goods are received, not ordered.

Rounding decimals (p. 67) Reducing the number of decimals to an indicated position, such as 59.59 → 59.6 to the nearest tenth.

Rounding whole numbers all the way (p. 5) Process to estimate actual answer. When rounding all the way, only one nonzero digit is left. Rounding all the way gives the least degree of accuracy. *Example:* 1,251 to 1,000; 2,995 to 3,000.

Rule of 78 (p. 347) Method to compute rebates on consumer finance loans. How much of finance charge are you entitled to? Formula or table lookup may be used.

Safekeeping (p. 100) Bank procedure whereby a bank does not return checks. Canceled checks are photocopied.

Salaries payable (p. 385) Obligations that a company must pay within 1 year for salaries earned but unpaid.

Sales (not trade) discounts (p. 391) Reductions in selling price of goods due to early customer payment.

Sales returns and allowances (p. 391) Reductions in price or reductions in revenue due to goods returned because of product defects, errors, and so on. When the buyer keeps the damaged goods, an allowance results.

Sales tax (p. 454) Tax levied on consumers for certain sales of merchandise or services by states, counties, or various local governments.

Salvage value (p. 413) Cost less accumulated depreciation.

Selling price (p. 219) Cost plus markup equals selling price.

Semiannually (p. 236) Twice a year.

Semimonthly (p. 236) Some employees are paid twice a month.

Series discount (p. 176) See **chain discount.**

Short-rate table (p. 473) Fire insurance rate table used when insured cancels the policy.

Short-term policy (p. 472) Fire insurance policy for less than 1 year.

Signature card (p. 90) Information card signed by person opening a checking account.

Simple discount note (p. 283) A note in which bank deducts interest in advance.

Simple interest (p. 259) Interest is only calculated on the principal. In $I = P \times R \times T$, the interest plus original principal equals the maturity value of an interest-bearing note.

Simple interest formula (p. 262)

Interest = Principal × Rate × Time

$$\text{Principal} = \frac{\text{Interest}}{\text{Rate} \times \text{Time}}$$

$$\text{Rate} = \frac{\text{Interest}}{\text{Principal} \times \text{Time}}$$

$$\text{Time} = \frac{\text{Interest}}{\text{Principal} \times \text{Rate}}$$

Single equivalent discount rate (p. 177) Rate or factor as a single discount that calculates the amount of the trade discount by multiplying the rate times the list price. This single equivalent discount replaces a series of chain discounts. The single equivalent rate is (1 − Net price equivalent rate).

Single trade discount (p. 174) Company gives only one trade discount.

Sinking fund (p. 326) An annuity in which the stream of deposits with appropriate interest will equal a specified amount in the future.

Sliding scale commissions (p. 239) Different commission. Rates depend on different levels of sales.

Sole proprietorship (p. 384) A business owned by one person.

Specific identification method (p. 431) This method calculates the cost of ending inventory by identifying each item remaining to invoice price.

Standard deviation (p. 520) Measures the spread of data around the mean.

State unemployment tax (SUTA) (p. 244) Tax paid by employer. Rate varies depending on amount of unemployment the company experiences.

Stockbrokers (p. 492) People who with their representatives do the trading on the floor of the stock exchange.

Stockholder (p. 492) One who owns stock in a company.

Stockholders' equity (p. 384) Assets less liabilities.

Stocks (p. 492) Ownership shares in the company sold to buyers, who receive stock certificates.

Stock yield percent (p. 493) Dividend per share divided by the closing price per share.

Straight commission (p. 239) Wages calculated as a percent of the value of goods sold.

Straight life insurance (whole or ordinary) (p. 469) Protection (full value of policy) results from continual payment of premiums by insured. Until death or retirement, nonforfeiture values exist for straight life.

Straight-line method (p. 414) Method of depreciation that spreads an equal amount of depreciation each year over the life of the assets.

Straight-line rate (rate of depreciation) (p. 44) One divided by number of years of expected life.

Subtrahend (p. 9) In a subtraction problem smaller number that is being subtracted from another. *Example:* 30 in

150 − 30 = 120

Sum (p. 8) Total in the adding process.

Tax rate (p. 456) $\dfrac{\text{Budget needed}}{\text{Total assessed value}}$

Term life insurance (p. 468) Inexpensive life insurance that provides protection for a specific period of time. No nonforfeiture values exist for term.

Term policy (p. 468) Period of time that the policy is in effect.

Terms of the sale (p. 179) Criteria on invoice showing when cash discounts are available, such as rate and time period.

Time (p. 260) Expressed as years or fractional years, used to calculate the simple interest.

Trade discount (p. 171) Reduction off original selling price (list price) not related to early payment.

Trade discount amount (p. 171) List price less net price.

Trade discount rate (p. 171) Trade discount amount given in percent.

Trade-in (scrap) (p. 413) Estimated value of a plant asset after depreciation is taken (or end of useful life).

Treasury bill (p. 281) Loan to the federal government for 91 days (13 weeks), 182 days (26 weeks), or 1 year.

Trend analysis (p. 394) Analyzing each number as a percentage of a base year.

Truth in Lending Act (p. 343) Federal law that requires sellers to inform buyers, in writing, of (1) the finance charge and (2) the annual percentage rate. The law doesn't dictate what can be charged.

Twenty-payment life (p. 469) Provides permanent protection and cash value, but insured pays premiums for first 20 years.

Twenty-year endowment (p. 469) Most expensive life insurance policy. It is a combination of term insurance and cash value.

Unemployment tax (p. 244) Tax paid by the employer that is used to aid unemployed persons.

Units-of-production method (p. 415) Depreciation method that estimates amount of depreciation based on usage.

Universal life (p. 470) Whole life insurance plan with flexible premium and death benefits. This life plan has limited guarantees.

Unknown (p. 116) The variable we are solving for.

Unlike fractions (p. 40) Proper fractions with different denominators.

Useful life (p. 413) Estimated number of years the plant asset is used.

U.S. Rule (p. 264) Method that allows the borrower to receive proper interest credits when paying off a loan in more than one payment before the maturity date.

U.S. Treasury bill (p. 281) A note issued by federal government to investors.

Value of an annuity (p. 317) Sum of series of payments and interest (think of this as the maturity value of compounding).

Variable commission scale (p. 239) Company pays different commission rates for different levels of net sales.

Variable cost (p. 220) Costs that do change in response to change in volume of sales.

Variable rate (p. 367) Home mortgage rate is not fixed over its lifetime.

Variables (p. 116) Letters or symbols that represent unknowns.

Vertical analysis (p. 387) Method of analyzing financial reports where each total is compared to one total. *Example:* Cash is a percent of total assets.

W-4 (p. 241) See **Employee's Withholding Allowance Certificate.**

Wage bracket method (In Handbook) Tables used in Circular E to compute FIT withholdings.

Weekly (p. 236) Some employers pay employees weekly.

Weighted-average method (p. 432) Calculates the cost of ending inventory by applying an average unit cost to items remaining in inventory for that period of time.

Weighted mean (p. 512) Used to find an average when values appear more than once.

Whole life insurance (p. 470) See **Straight life insurance.**

Whole number (p. 2) Number that is 0 or larger and doesn't contain a decimal or fraction, such as 10, 55, 92.

Withholding (p. 242) Amount of deduction from one's paycheck.

Workers' compensation (p. 244) Business insurance covering sickness or accidental injuries to employees that result from on-the-job activities.

Classroom Notes

Metric System

John Sullivan: Angie, I drove into the gas station last night to fill the tank up. Did I get upset! The pumps were not in gallons but in liters. This country (U.S.) going to metric is sure making it confusing.

Angie Smith: Don't get upset. Let me first explain the key units of measure in metric, and then I'll show you a convenient table I keep in my purse to convert metric to U.S. (also called customary system), and U.S. to metric. Let's go on.

The metric system is really a decimal system in which each unit of measure is exactly 10 times as large as the previous unit. In a moment, we will see how this aids in conversions. First, look at the middle column (Units) of this to see the basic units of measure:

U.S.	Thousands	Hundreds	Tens	Units	Tenths	Hundredths	Thousandths
Metric	Kilo- 1,000	Hecto- 100	Deka- 10	Gram Meter Liter 1	Deci- .1	Centi- .01	Milli- .001

- Weight: Gram (think of it as $\frac{1}{30}$ of an ounce).
- Length: Meter (think of it for now as a little more than a yard).
- Volume: Liter (a little more than a quart).

To aid you in looking at this, think of a decimeter, a centimeter, or a millimeter as being "shorter" (smaller) than a meter, whereas a dekameter, hectometer, and kilometer are "larger" than a meter. For example:

1 centimeter $= \frac{1}{100}$ of a meter; or 100 centimeters equals 1 meter.

1 millimeter $= \frac{1}{1,000}$ meter; or 1,000 millimeters equals 1 meter.

1 hectometer $= 100$ meters.

1 kilometer $= 1,000$ meters.

Remember we could have used the same setup for grams or liters. Note the summary here.

Length	Volume	Mass
1 meter:	1 liter:	1 gram:
= 10 decimeters	= 10 deciliters	= 10 decigrams
= 100 centimeters	= 100 centiliters	= 100 centigrams
= 1,000 millimeters	= 1,000 milliliters	= 1,000 milligrams
= .1 dekameter	= .1 dekaliter	= .1 dekagram
= .01 hectometer	= .01 hectoliter	= .01 hectogram
= .001 kilometer	= .001 kiloliter	= .001 kilogram

Practice these conversions and check solutions.

1 PRACTICE QUIZ

Convert the following:

1. 7.2 meters to centimeters
2. .89 meter to millimeters
3. 64 centimeters to meters
4. 350 grams to kilograms
5. 7.4 liters to centiliters
6. 2,500 milligrams to grams

✓ **Solutions**

1. 7.2 meters $= 7.2 \times 100 = 720$ centimeters (remember, 1 meter = 100 centimeters)
2. .89 meters $= .89 \times 1,000 = 890$ millimeters (remember, 1 meter = 1,000 millimeters)
3. 64 centimeters $= 64/100 = .64$ meters (remember, 1 meter = 100 centimeters)
4. 350 grams $= \dfrac{350}{1,000} = .35$ kilograms (remember 1 kilogram = 1,000 grams)
5. 7.4 liters $= 7.4 \times 100 = 740$ centiliters (remember, 1 liter = 100 centiliters)
6. 2,500 milligrams $= \dfrac{2,500}{1,000} = 2.5$ grams (remember, 1 gram = 1,000 milligrams

Angie: Look at the table of conversions and I'll show you how easy it is. Note how we can convert liters to gallons. Using the conversion from meters to U.S. (liters to gallons), we see that you multiply numbers of liters by .26, or 37.95 × .26 = 9.84 gallons.

Common conversion factors for English/metric					
A. To convert from U.S. to	**Metric**	**Multiply by**	**B. To convert from metric to**	**U.S.**	**Multiply by**
Length:			*Length:*		
Inches (in)	Meters (m)	.025	Meters (m)	Inches (in)	39.37
Feet (ft)	Meters (m)	.31	Meters (m)	Feet (ft)	3.28
Yards (yd)	Meters (m)	.91	Meters (m)	Yards (yd)	1.1
Miles	Kilometers (km)	1.6	Kilometers (km)	Miles	.62
Weight:			*Weight:*		
Ounces (oz)	Grams (g)	28	Grams (g)	Ounces (oz)	.035
Pounds (lb)	Grams (g)	454	Grams (g)	Pounds (lb)	.0022
Pounds (lb)	Kilograms (kg)	.45	Kilograms (kg)	Pounds (lb)	2.2
Volume or capacity:			*Volume or capacity:*		
Pints	Liters (L)	.47	Liters (L)	Pints	2.1
Quarts	Liters (L)	.95	Liters (L)	Quarts	1.06
Gallons (gal)	Liters (L)	3.8	Liters (L)	Gallons	.26

John: How would I convert 6 miles to kilometers?

Angie: Take the number of miles times 1.6, thus 6 miles × 1.6 = 9.6 kilometers.

John: If I weigh 120 pounds, what is my weight in kilograms?

Angie: 120 times .45 (use the conversion table) equals 54 kilograms.

John: OK. Last night, when I bought 16.6 liters of gas, I really bought 4.3 gallons (16.6 liters times .26).

2	PRACTICE QUIZ

Convert the following:

1.   10 meters to yards
2.   110 quarts to liters
3.   78 kilometers to miles
4.   52 yards to meters
5.   82 meters to inches
6.   292 miles to kilometers

✓ **Solutions**

1.   10 meters × 1.1 = 11 yards
2.   110 quarts × .95 = 104.5 liters
3.   78 kilometers × .62 = 48.36 miles
4.   52 yards × .91 = 47.32 meters
5.   82 meters × 39.37 = 3,228.34 inches
6.   292 miles × 1.6 = 467.20 kilometers

Name _____   Date _____

Appendix D: Problems

DRILL PROBLEMS

Convert:

1. 65 centimeters to meters

2. 7.85 meters to centimeters

3. 44 centiliters to liters

4. 1,500 grams to kilograms

5. 842 millimeters to meters

6. 9.4 kilograms to grams

7. .854 kilograms to grams

8. 5.9 meters to millimeters

9. 8.91 kilograms to grams

10. 2.3 meters to millimeters

Convert (round off to nearest tenth):

11. 50.9 kilograms to pounds

12. 8.9 pounds to grams

13. 395 kilometers to miles

14. 33 yards to meters

15. 13.9 pounds to grams

16. 594 miles to kilometers

17. 4.9 feet to meters

18. 9.9 feet to meters

19. 100 yards to meters

20. 40.9 kilograms to pounds

21. 895 miles to kilometers

22. 1,000 grams to pounds

23. 79.1 meters to yards

24. 12 liters to quarts

25. 2.92 meters to feet

26. 5 liters to gallons

27. 8.7 meters to feet

28. 8 gallons to liters

29. 1,600 grams to pounds

30. 310 meters to yards

WORD PROBLEMS

31. **Given:**   A metric ton is 39.4 bushels of corn. Calculate number of bushels purchased from metric tons to bushels of corn.
    Problem: Soviets bought 450,000 metric tons of U.S. corn, valued at $58 million, for delivery after September 30.

Index

Accelerated cost recovery, 418
Accelerated depreciation, 418
Accounts payable, 385
Accounts receivable, 385
Accumulated depreciation, 413
Acid test ratio, 396
Addend, 8
Addition
  checking, 8
  of decimals, 71
  of fractions, 40
  of whole numbers, 8
Adjustable rate, 366
Adjusted balance, 96
Algebra equations, 116
Amortization schedule, 371
Amortization table, 347
Amount
  of an annuity, 317
  financed, 342
  of markdown, 204
  of markup, 205
  of simple interest, 259
  of trade discount, 171
Analysis
  horizontal, 388
  ratio, 395
  vertical, 387
Annual percentage rate, 343
  table, 343
Annual percentage yield, 301
Annuities
  amount of, 317
  certain, 318
  contingent, 318
  due, 318
  ordinary, 317
  present value of, 323
  sinking funds, 326
Application of percents, 144
Arithmetic
  calculations, 8
  mean, 512
Assessed value, 456
Assets
  acid-test, 396
  current, 413
  plant and equipment, 385
Asset turnover, 396
Automatic teller machine
  (ATM), 89
Automobile insurance, 476
Average daily balance, 352
Average inventory, 458
Averages
  mean, 512
  median, 512
  mode, 513
  weighted mean, 512

Balance sheet, 384
Bank discount, 280, 282
  maturity value, 280
  proceeds, 280
Banker's rule, 260
Bank reconciliation, 96
Bank statement, 95
Bar graph, 515
Base, 144
Beneficiary, 467
Biweekly, 236
Blank endorsement, 91
Blueprint, 6
Bodily injury liability, 467
Bond discount, 496
Bond premium, 496
Bonds
  cost of, 495
  reading, 495
  yields, 496
Book value, 413
Borrowing, 9
Breakeven point, 219
Broker commission, 494
Brokers, 492
Business insurance, 470
Business ratios, 395

Calculating due dates, 181
Calendar year, 181
Cancellation
  of fractions, 47
  of insurance policy, 478
Capital, 384
Cash advance, 309
Cash discounts, 179
Cash dividend, 493
Cash value (of life insurance), 469
Catalog list price, 176
Chain discounts, 176
Charge accounts, 350
Check, 89
  endorsement, 89
  register, 89
  stub, 89
Checking accounts, 89
Circle graph, 517
Closing costs, 368
Coinsurance clause, 474
Collision insurance, 474
Commissions
  broker, 494
  differential pay, 238
  drawing accounts, 239
  and salary, 238
  straight, 239
  variable, 239
Common denominator, 40
Common divisor, 40

Common stock, 386
Comparative balance sheet, 387
Comparative income statement, 387
Compensation
  insurance, 468
  payroll, 244
Complement of discount, 174
Compounding, 299
Compound interest
  amount, 299
  present value, 296
  tables, 300
Comprehensive coverage, 477
Compulsory insurance, 476
Constants, 116
Consumer groups, 343
Contingent liability, 282
Contribution margin, 219
Conversion of markup
    percent, 213
Conversions of fractions, 37
Conversions of percents, 139
Cost, 204
  markup based on, 204
Cost of goods sold, 389
Credit line, 284
Credit memo, 97
Credit period, 179
Cumulative preferred stock, 492
Current
  assets, 384
  liabilities, 396
  ratio, 396
  yield, 493

Daily balance, 352
Daily compounding, 299
Dating
  end-of-month, 184
  receipt-of-goods, 183
Days in a month, 181
Debit card, 89
Debit memo, 97
Decimal fraction, 67
  conversions with, 67
  rounding of, 67
Decimal numbers, 65
Decimal point, 2, 67
Decimal system, 2
Decision-making process, 2
Declining-balance method, 417
Deductible, 477
Deductions, 343
Deferred payment, 343
Denominator
  of a fraction, 35
  least common, 40
Deposit, in transit, 97
Deposit slip, 90

Depreciation, 413
 declining-balance, 417
 schedule, 417
 straight-line, 414
Difference, 9
Differential pay schedule, 238
Digits, 3
Discount period, 180, 283
Discounting interest-bearing
  notes, 180, 283
Discounting note, 283
Discounts
 bank, 282
 bond, 496
 cash, 179
 chain, 179
 complement of, 174
 markdown, 204
 series, 176
 single equivalent rate, 177
 trade, 179
Dissecting and solving a
  word problem, 6
Distribution of
  overhead, 439
Dividends
 in arrears, 492
 in division, 14
 on stock, 495
Division
 checking, 15
 of decimals, 73
 of fractions, 48
 long, 15
 short, 16
 shortcuts, 16
 of whole numbers, 14
Divisor, 14
Dollar markdown, 216
Dollar markup, 205
Down payment, 342
Draft, 89
Draw, 239
Drawee, 90
Drawer, 90
Driver classifications, 476
Due date
 for cash discount, 179
 for a note, 180

Earnings
 gross, 237
 net, 237
 per share, 493
Effective rate, 281, 301
Electronic deposits, 98
Electronic funds transfer, 95
Employee's withholding allowance
  certificate, 241
End of credit period, 180
End-of-month (EOM), 184
Endorsement, 91
Endowment life insurance, 469

Equations, 116
 basic, 116
 word problems, 121
Equity, 385
Equivalent fractions, 38
Escrow, 368
Estimated useful life, 413
Estimating, 5
Exact days-in-a-year calendar, 181
 exact interest, 260
 ordinary interest, 261
Excise tax, 455
Expenses, operating, 392
Expression, 121
Extending term life insurance, 470

Face value
 of an insurance policy, 467
 of a note, 280
Fair Credit and Charge Card Disclosure
  Act of 1988, 351
Fair Labor Standards Act, 237
Federal Income Tax Withholding
  (FIT), 242
Federal Insurance Contribution Act
  (FICA), 241
Federal Unemployment Tax Act
  (FUTA), 244
Federal tax, 242
FICA (Medicare and Social Security),
  241
Finance charge (interest)
 for installment, 343
 for open-end credits, 352
Financial ratios, 395
Financial statements
 balance sheet, 384
 income statement, 389
 ratios, 395
Fire insurance
 building, 472
 cancellation, 472
 coinsurance clause, 474
 content, 472
 premium, 472
 short-term rates, 473
First-in, first-out method, FIFO, 433
FIT; see Federal Income Tax Withholding
Fixed assets; see Plant and
  equipment, 385
Fixed cost, 219
Fixed rate mortgage, 367
FOB destination, 173
FOB shipping point, 173
Foreign currency, 73
Formula, 116
Fractional equivalent, 38
Fractions
 adding, 40
 cancelling, 47
 converting to higher terms, 38
 converting to lower terms, 37
 decimal, 67

Fractions—Cont.
 dividing, 48
 equivalent, 38
 improper, 35
 least common denominator, 40
 like, 40
 mixed numbers, 36
 multiplication, 47
 proper, 35
 raising, 38
 reducing, 37
 subtracting, 43
 types of, 35
 unlike, 40
Freight, 173
Frequency distribution, 515
Full endorsement, 91
FUTA; see Federal Unemployment
  Tax Act, 244
Future value, 299
 annuities, 317

Graduated commissions, 367
Graduated payment, 367
Graphs
 bar, 515
 circle, 517
 line, 516
Greatest common divisor, 37
Gross commissions, 237
Gross pay, 204
Gross profit, 392
Gross profit method, 437
Gross sales, 391

Higher terms, 38
Home equity, 366
Horizontal analysis, 388
How to dissect and solve a word
  problem, 6
How to read The Wall Street Journal; see
  insert in text

Improper fractions, 35
Incentives, 238
Income, 389
Income statement, 389
Indemnity, 474
Index numbers, 577
Individual Retirement Account, 316
Installments
 APR, 343
 Truth in Lending Act, 343
Insurance
 business, 470
 cancellation of, 478
 collision, 477
 comprehensive, 477
 endowment, 469
 extended term, 470
 fire, 472
 life, 468
 limited pay life, 468

Insurance—*Cont.*
  no-fault, 479
  nonforfeiture, 470
  policy, 468
  reduced paid-up, 468
  term, 468
Insured, 467
Insurer, 467
Interest
  add-on, 259
  compound, 296
  effective, 281
  exact, 260
  on installments, 347
  ordinary, 261
  simple, 259
  simple versus discount, 280
Interest-bearing notes, 279
Inventory
  average, 458
  FIFO, 433
  LIFO, 433
  periodic, 430
  perpetual, 430
  specific indentification, 431
  turnover, 438
Invoice, 171
IRA, 316

Just-in-time, 435

Knowns, 116

Last-in, first-out method,
    LIFO, 433
Least common denominator, 40
Level premium, 468
Liabilities
  bodily injury, 476
  current, 396
  long term, 385
  property damage, 476
Life insurance
  beneficiary, 467
  cash value, 469
  endowment, 469
  extended term, 470
  limited pay, 468
  nonforfeiture options, 476
  paid-up, 469
  policy, 468
  premiums, 467
  straight life, 469
  surrender values, 469
  term, 469
Like fractions, 40
Limited pay life, 469
Line graph, 516
Lines of credit, 283
Liquid assets, 384
List price, 172
Liter, Appendix D
Loan amortization table, 346
Loan type, 367

Long-term liabilities, 385
Lowest terms, 37

MACRS; *see* Modified Accelerated Cost
    Recover System (MACRS), 418
Maker, 279
Margin, 204
Markdowns, 204
Markup
  on cost, 205
    equivalent, 213
  on retail (selling price), 210
Maturity value
  of an annuity, 317
  of compound interest, 298
  of discounted notes, 279
  of simple interest, 259
Mean, 512
Measure of dispersion, 520
Median, 512
Medicare, 241
Merchandise inventory, 385
Meter, Appendix D
Metric
  basic units, Appendix D
  prefixes, Appendix D
Mills, 457
Minuend, 9
Mixed decimal, 69
Mixed number, 36
Modified Accelerated Cost Recovery
    System (MACRS), 418
Monthly payment
    calculation, 367
Mode, 513
Mortgage, 367
Mortgage note payable, 385
Mortgage types, 367
Motor vehicle insurance
  compulsory, 476
  optional, 476
Multiplicand, 13
Multiplication
  of decimals, 72
  of fractions, 47
  of whole numbers, 13
  shortcuts, 14
Multiplier, 13
Mutual fund, 498

Net asset value, 498
Net earnings, 240
Net income, 392
Net pay, 237
Net price, 172
Net price equivalent rate, 176
Net proceeds, 280
Net purchases, 392
Net sales, 391
No-fault insurance, 479
Nominal interest rate, 301
Nonforfeiture options, 471
Nonsufficient funds, 97
Normal distribution, 521

Notes
  discounted, 280
  interest-bearing, 280
  noninterest-bearing, 280
  payable, 385
  promissory, 279
Numerator, 35

Omnibus Budget Reconciliation Act
    of 1989, 420
Open-end credit, 351
Operating expenses, 392
Ordinary annuity, 317
Ordinary dating method, 182
Ordinary interest, 261
Ordinary life insurance, 414
Outstanding balance
  installments, 351
  mortgages, 367
Outstanding checks, 97
Overdrafts, 95
Overhead, 439
Override, 237
Overtime, 237
Owner's equity, 384

Paid-up insurance, 469
Partial payments, 186
Partial product, 13
Partial quotient, 14
Partnership, 384
Payee, 90, 279
Payment due dates, 181
Payroll
  commissions, 238
  deductions, 241
  overtime, 237
  register, 240
Percentage, 144; *see also* Portion
Percentage method, 342
Percent decrease, 149
Percent increase, 149
Percent markup on
  cost, 205
  selling price, 210
Percents
  converted to decimals, 139
  converted to fractions, 142
  defined, 138
  rounding, 140
Periodic, 430
Periods, 297
Perishables, 217
Perpetual, 430
Personal property, 456
Piecework, 238
Place value, 3
Plant and equipment, 385
Points, 368
Policyholder, 467
Portion, 144
Preferred stock, 386
Premium, auto, 476
Prepaid expenses, 385

Present value
   of an annuity, 323
   at compound interest, 296
Price
   list, 172
   net, 172
   selling, 204
Price earnings ratio, 492
Price, relative, 518
Prime number in calculating
     LCD, 41
Principal, 259
Proceeds, 280
Product, 14
Profit, 389
Promissory note, 279
Proper fraction, 35
Property damage
     liability, 476
Property tax, 457
Proximo, 184
Purchases, 391
Purchases discounts, 391
Purchases returns, 391
Pure decimal, 69

Quick assets, 396
Quick ratio, 396;
    see also Acid-test ratio, 396
Quotient, 14

Range, 520
Rate
   APR, 343
   bank discount, 280
   compounding, 297
   effective, 301
   nominal, 301
   percent, 144
   per period, 299
   with portion, 144
   property tax, 457
   trade discount, 174
Ratios
   of financial reports, 395
   summary table, 395
Real property, 456
Rebate, 349
Rebate fraction, 349
Receipt-of-goods, 183
Reciprocal, 48
Reconciliation, 96
Reduced paid-up
     insurance, 470
Reducing fractions, 37
Remainder, 14
Repeating decimals, 67
Residual value, 413
Restrictive endorsement, 91
Retailing, 205
Retail method, 437
Retained earnings, 386
Return on equity, 396
Revenues, 391

Reverse mortgage, 367
Revolving charge account, 351
Rounding off
   all the way, 5
   calculations, 5
   decimals, 67
   whole numbers, 4
Rule of 78, 347

Safekeeping, 100
Salary, 240
Sales
   discounts, 391
   markup on, 210
   net, 389
   returns, 391
   tax, 454
   terms, 179
Salvage value, 413
Scrap value, 413
Selling price, 219
Semiannually, 236
Semimonthly, 236
Series discounts, 176
Service charge, 95
Short-rate table, 473
Signature card, 90
Simple discount note, 280
Simple interest, 259
Single equivalent discount
     rate, 177
Single trade discount, 174
Sinking fund, 326
Sliding-scale, 239
Social Security, 241
Sole proprietorship, 384
Solving a word problem, 6, 121
Special endorsement, 91
Specific identification
     method, 431
Standard deviation, 520
State income tax, 240
Statement, bank, 95
State unemployment, 244
Statistics
   averages, 511
   graphs, 514
Step approach to finding largest
     common divisor, 37
Stockbroker, 492
Stock dividends, 495
Stockholders, 492
Stockholders' equity, 384
Stock yield, 493
Straight commission, 239
Straight life insurance, 469
Straight-line method, 414
Straight-line rate, 414
Straight piece rate, 239
Subtraction
   of decimals, 72
   of fractions, 43
   of whole numbers, 9
Subtrahend, 9

Sum, 8
Surrender values, 469

Taxable earnings column, 241
Taxes
   FICA (Social Security and
     Medicare), 241
   income, 242
   sales, 241
   unemployment, 244
Term
   compound interest, 299
   of annuity, 317
   of insurance policy, 468
   of sale, 179
Term life insurance, 468
Time, exact, 260
Trade discount, 171
Trade-in value, 413
Treasury bill, 281
Trend analysis, 394
True interest rate, 301
Truth in Lending
   Act, 343
Turnover, inventory, 438
Twenty-payment life, 469
Twenty-year endowment, 469
Types of fractions, 35
Types of mortgages, 367

U.S. Rule, 264
Unemployment taxes, 244
Units-of-production method, 415
Universal life, 470
Unknowns, 116
Unlike fractions, 40
Useful life, 413

Value, assessed, 456
Variable commission scale, 239
Variable cost, 219
Variable rate mortgage, 367
Variables, 116
Vertical analysis, 387

Wage bracket method; *see* The Business
     Math Handbook
Wage bracket table; *see* The Business
     Math Handbook
Wage computations, 241
Weighted-average
     method, 432
Weighted mean, 51
Whole life insurance, 470
Whole numbers, 2
   numeric, 3
   reading, 3
   writing, 3
Withholding, 242

Yield
   bond, 496
   stock, 493

Classroom Notes

Classroom Notes

Classroom Notes

Classroom Notes

Classroom Notes

Classroom Notes

Classroom Notes